The Younger Pitt

John Ehrman, F.B.A, F.S.A., F.R.Hist.S., was born in 1920 and educated at Charterhouse and Trinity College, Cambridge. After the war, in which he served in the Royal Navy, he returned to Cambridge as a Fellow of his old College, Trinity. He was the Lees Knowles Lecturer, Cambridge, 1957-8, and James Ford Special Lecturer, Oxford, 1976–7.

By the same author

The Younger Pitt published in four volumes

The Younger Pitt: The Years of Acclaim
The Younger Pitt: The Reluctant Transition
The Younger Pitt: The Consuming Struggle, vol III and vol IV

THE
YOUNGER PITT

THE CONSUMING STRUGGLE
Vol. IV

JOHN EHRMAN

CONSTABLE • LONDON

This digital edition printed 2004 by
Constable & Robinson Ltd
3 The Lanchesters
162 Fulham Palace Road
London W6 9ER

First published in Great Britain 1996
by Constable and Company Limited

This paperback edition first published 1986
Reprinted 1996
ISBN 1 84529 143 3

A CIP catalogue record for this book
is available from the British Library

To Susan

AS AT THE START
SO WITH MY LOVE
AT THE END

Due to constraints of binding a large volume, *The Consuming Struggle* is printed and bound in two volumes.

The contents, acknowledgements, source references and the index have been printed in both volumes and should be used in reference to both volumes.

Volume III includes pages 1–492
Volume IV includes pages 493–855

Contents

Contents

PART FIVE

Illustrations

Illustrations

Introduction

In Pitt's last nine years, from 1797 to January 1806, the cumulation of events was on a different scale from anything he had known. A sudden financial crisis struck and was met. Unrest and disaffection rumbled and flared, even affecting the home fleets at a dangerous moment. The problems of Ireland erupted in the rising of 1798. Preparations for invasion were set on foot in France, rising towards a peak from the start of the Napoleonic War. Three Allied Coalitions collapsed in succession, the third after high hopes. And Pitt himself resigned without warning in 1801, introducing a pattern of political uncertainty which, despite his return three years later, lasted to his death.

The final months of all in the story soon passed into national legend: the Army of Invasion poised in the camp of Boulogne with the landing barges massed below; Nelson dying in the hour of victory amid the thunder of Trafalgar; Napoleon at Austerlitz watching the rout of the two most imposing European Empires, Britain's two allies, and the Emperors themselves retreating from the field. Such scenes had an epic quality. But the preceding years had their own share of drama; and in perspective they were highly significant, for some of the developments had formative effects well beyond the immediate concerns. The fears of invasion, vivid at either end of the period and seldom far away meanwhile, did much to forward a surge of patriotic sentiment which remained a historic memory – it was to these years that the country looked back almost a century and a half later. And there were other consequences for the medium and indeed the long term. The financial alarm brought about a suspension of the convertibility of the pound which continued as a restriction for over twenty years, prompting the start of a public debate on monetary and banking policy whose influence was felt for a further century at least. Wartime needs also led Pitt by stages to change the basis of wartime taxation with the first clearly entitled direct income tax. The Irish rebellion led to the Union. In the war itself, Bonaparte's expedition to Egypt in 1798 raised questions for the British position in India which had mounting implications, stretching from south-east Europe to Arabia and central Asia, for the transition of a colonial into a genuinely imperial Power. And the political transactions in the five years following Pitt's sudden stepping down did much to mould the identities and conceptions of party emerging over the next two decades. It proved a notable period for the nation, at home and overseas. For Pitt himself it was mostly one of consuming pressure, not the less so for recurring visions of success, and in its later years of an adjustment to a personal situation which he had not encountered before.

For in 1801 it was indeed a long time – seventeen years – since Pitt had been anything other than First Minister, in an Administration of which he was soon the acknowledged focus and with Parliamentary majorities that after a decade changed from normally comfortable to normally commanding. His resignation exposed him to the unaccustomed experience of being out of office, and possibly disposable by others as one piece on the board. He dealt with that unattractive prospect in his own way. Nonetheless when he reassumed his old post he found himself hampered by the conditions which had changed in the interval since he had chosen to retire. His thoughts and conduct in those years accordingly present an interest of their own; and, it may be argued, particularly in the interval itself. For if Pitt by temperament and inclination was above all a man for government, it was in the unfamiliar freedom from the daily constrictions of power that he then formulated his aims, and acted in what proved in fact to be an exchange of one set of limits for another. The course of his path, the effort to reconcile a high and visible pursuit of 'character' with the reasons and inducements in favour of his return, comes as close perhaps as any passage in other phases of his life towards yielding an insight into his nature and his conception of himself. He died less than two years into his second Ministry, at a moment of disaster and the lowest point in his career. But the news stunned and awed supporters and opponents alike. His colleagues resigned, unwilling to face an imminent Parliamentary challenge without him; and Fox himself was heard to say that it seemed as if something was missing from the world.

I have tried throughout these volumes to show Pitt as a man moving among men on a busy stage. Their assumptions and attitudes were a frame for his own; and given the state of his papers theirs have often had to do duty for his. I must record my acknowledgments to owners and custodians for leave to consult their collections. Her Majesty The Queen gave gracious permission for me to inspect and cite a document acquired for the Royal Archives. I am very grateful also to the Duke of Buccleuch and Queensberry, the Marquess of Normanby, Earl Bathurst, the Earl of Harewood (and Dr W.J. Connor), the Earl of Harrowby (and Mrs Jane Waley), Viscountess Eccles, Viscount Sidmouth, Lord Kenyon, the Administrative Trustees of the Chevening Estate, Mr Giles Adams, Mrs Mark and Mr Nicholas Bence-Jones, Mr N.J. Llewellen Palmer, the late Mr W.H. Saumarez Smith, Mr K.J.M. Maddox Wright, and the owner of the Loan 72 papers at the British Library. The Spencer papers which I earlier failed to see at Althorp are now in the possession of the British Library. I wish to make similar acknowledgments to the authorities of that library (particularly to Mr Michael Borrie and Dr Frances Harris), of the Bodleian Library (and particularly Mrs Penelope Sturgis), the Cambridge University Library, the County Archives or Record Offices of Devon, Hampshire and Suffolk (Ipswich) and the Centre for Kentish Studies, Coutts and Company, the House of Lords Record Office, the John Rylands Library of the University of Manchester, the National Library of Scotland, the National Maritime Museum Greenwich (particularly Dr Roger Knight), the National Trust, Nottingham University Library, Pembroke College Cambridge, the Public Record Office, the Scottish Record Office, the Sir John Soane Museum, the William L. Clements Library of Michigan University, Duke University North Carolina, and the Huntington Library and Art Gallery California. I must also record my thanks for permission to read unpublished theses by I.S. Asquith, R.A. Cooper, C.J. Fedorak, G.B.A. Fremont, S.R. Cope, Michael Duffy, Clive Emsley, A.D. Harvey, Austin Vernon Mitchell, P.K. O'Brien, Christopher Oprey, Norman Frank Richards, W.A.L. Seaman, T. Naff, James Walvin, and the late J.R. Western.

Changed circumstances have led me to lean more heavily on research assistance than was the case in the two earlier volumes. I have been particularly fortunate in finding a series of meticulous medievalists, whose training proved very well adapted (though not confined) to examining the massed volumes of Foreign Office papers. First and foremost has been Dr Anthony Smith, to whose skilled labours over several years I would like to pay grateful tribute; and I would also thank warmly Drs Richard Brent (not a medievalist), Simon Payling, and Colm McNamee. Mrs Rosemary Bigwood continued assiduously to search papers in Scotland. Mr Douglas Matthews kindly agreed to undertake the index.

It is a pleasure once more to acknowledge help received, from those who have answered questions, provided information, or read parts of the book. I would like to thank Miss Myrtle Baird, Mr Giles Barber, Professor Daniel Baugh, Mr E.M.G. Belfield, Lord Blake (and Mr D.L. Jones of the House of Lords Library), Mr T.G.J. Brightmore, Mr Adrian Burchall, Professor Ian Christie, Professor J.C.D. Clark, Miss P.M. Clark, Dr J.E. Cookson, Dr J.G. Denholm, Miss Rosemary Dunhill, Professor Michael Durey, my daughter-in-law Mrs Edwina Ehrman, Dr C.J. Fedorak, Dr G.B.A. Fremont, Mr John Fuggles, Professor Norman Gash, Dr A.D. Harvey, Dr Peter Jupp, Mr J.B. Lewis, Dr Piers Mackesy, Mr Charles Maisey, Dr Peter Mathias, Professor P.J. Marshall, Dr Jennifer Mori, Professor Patrick O'Brien, Dr Richard Olney, Captain C.H. Owen, Dr D.B. Robinson, Dr Nicholas Rodger, Professor H.G. Roseveare, Dr John Rule, Viscount Sandon, the late Sir Robert Somerville, Mrs Elizabeth Sparrow, the late Miss Dorothy Stroud, Mr Richard Walker, Mr S.G.P. Ward, Dr Roger Wells, Mr and Mrs David Wilkinson, Dr Philip Williamson, Dr W.H. Zawadzki.

Illustrations have been reproduced by gracious permission of Her Majesty The Queen (fig. 7) and kind permission of the Trustees of the National Portrait Gallery (frontispiece, figs. 2a, 2b, 5c, 8, 9b, 12, 15a, 17a, 18b), the Trustees of the British Museum (figs. 1, 10, 13b), the Governing Body of Christ Church, Oxford (fig. 3b), the Trustees of Sir John Soane's Museum (fig. 4), the Master and Fellows of Trinity College, Cambridge (fig. 5a), Lord Braybrooke and English Heritage (fig. 5b), the Trustees of the National Maritime Museum (fig. 15b), the Bishop of Lincoln (fig. 17b), the Earl of Harrowby (fig. 18a).

I would add two special words of gratitude at the close. First to Jennifer Martin, whose contribution extended far beyond the call of duty, typing impeccably and promptly large quantities of almost indecipherable manuscript for this volume, as she did for part of its predecessor, and enlisting the aid of her daughter-in-law Christine Martin at moments when the stream threatened to over flow. And finally to my publisher Ben Glazebrook, who has never shown the slightest hint of an impatience which he must have felt over the years, and whose forebearance, personal kindness and ccare for the volumes I can only salute.

July 1995   J.E.

This reprint contains some corrections, mainly in the footnotes.

August 1996   J.E.

This digital edition is published in two volumes, this introduction, the contents and illustrations, sources and index to both appearing respectively in III and IV.

September 2004   J.E.

Part Four

CHAPTER XV

Resignation

I

On 3 February 1801 Pitt asked the Speaker, Addington, to dine with him at between five and six o'clock. The guest however was delayed by business, the Minister ate alone, and Addington arrived at half past seven. At nine o'clock Pitt was reminded that his private secretary, whom he had told to be available in the evening, was still waiting. He said he would not be long. But it was ten or half past before the official was summoned, and in Addington's presence given a letter to be copied; and when that was done it was taken to the Queen's – Buckingham – House. The length of the talk between the two men was not at all surprising. For it was in effect between an outgoing and an incoming Minister; the document contained Pitt's 'immediate' resignation.[1]

This account, by Pretyman, stated that the day's course of events, with what had gone before, showed that 'the decision' of immediate resignation 'was only just formed' and neither it nor the letter itself known to any

1. B.L. Add. Ms 45107; Pretyman's draft account, based on letters and notes in 1801–2 (see Ashbourne, *Pitt: Some Chapters of his Life and Times*, 309n1; Holland Rose, II, 442–4) for the unpublished part of his Life of Pitt (see I, xi), ch. 24, f. 16. There is another copy of the chapter, varying in places, in Add. Ms 45108; and others again for the volume, in varying states, are in the Pretyman Mss at Ipswich and at Pembroke College, Cambridge.

As will appear below, I attach importance to the Bishop's version of the event: it is indeed one of the rare instances in which his biography is useful. It seems likely however that his ascription of the date, to 4 February, is wrong. Pitt dated his letter the 3rd on the document sent to the King (and published in *Letters from His Late Majesty to the Late Lord Kenyon on the Coronation Oath . . .; and Letters of the Rt. Hon. William Pitt to His Late Majesty, with His Majesty's Answers Previous to the Dissolution of the Ministry in 1801* [ed. by Dr Henry Phillpotts] (1827), 40–2), of which there is a copy in his own papers in P.R.O. 30/8/101. Moreover the King seems to have written a 'note' to Addington on the 4th about arrangements (see *L.C.G. III*, III, no. 2341 on p. 485). Addington's own letter to the King, obviously after his conversation with Pitt and itself dated the 4th (op. cit., on p. 484), may strengthen the attribution, since it would presumably have been written as soon as possible the following morning.

The private secretary was John Carthew, who held a Junior Clerkship at the Treasury; a post he was able himself to resign a few weeks later, on receiving the more lucrative appointment of Collector of Customs for Jamaica. He told George Rose that Pitt called him in at 10 o'clock (*Rose*, I, 286); Pretyman says 10.30. See I, 577n1 for a customary time of dinner which, quite apart from politicians' exigencies, was gradually moving later in the day as the decades went by.

one else. On 2 February Pitt had told his colleagues of a correspondence with the King in the past two days. But 'the impression which he left upon their minds was that he did not propose to resign', and when he wrote the letter of the 3rd, which he did 'after weighing the arguments for and against' before Addington came, it was 'without however absolutely resolving to send it'.[1] One cannot certify where the Bishop got his information: it could have been in part from the secretary Carthew, who seems to have written a narrative, or in general from Addington,[2] who was then still on amicable though not particularly close terms. But it probably came mainly from Pitt, for Pretyman arrived in town on receiving a letter from the Minister of the 6th, and talked to his old friend on several occasions over the next two to three weeks.[3] He was confident later that he wrote with knowledge, and he was prepared for one of his rare personal accounts to be published – as he later expected – while some of those most closely concerned were still alive.[4] His record of Pitt's day may well be considered correct. Its emphasis, on the solitary nature of the final resolve, pointed the extent of the personal element in a culminating act.

The issue on which that was taken had surfaced within the past week. But it had been maturing over some months, and debated, exploited and postponed over the past two years. Ever since the idea of a union with Ireland had been raised in 1798, the prospect had revived of crowning the series of reliefs for Irish Roman Catholics by enabling them to sit in Parliament (now prospectively unified) and hold higher offices in their own land.[5] The link between the two concepts, of Union and Emancipation,[6] in fact became progressively stronger; for when the former failed in effect at the first attempt, the latter, ruled out shortly beforehand, was called in aid of success. The Cabinet's guidance in the matter to the Lord Lieutenant, towards the end of 1799, had not amounted to a categorical assurance: rather it was an expression of the 'sentiments' of all those present.[7] But by the time that the bills for the Union passed in the summer of 1800, a sense of obligation had built up; and the argument accepted earlier, that positive 'engagements' should be

---

1. B.L. Add. Ms 45107, ff. 16, 18. This last phrase may also have carried a tendentious implication. Within a few months of the resignation, Pretyman and some of Pitt's other friends had turned violently against Addington, and were impugning his conduct.

2. N 1 above.

3. Holland Rose, II, 422–3; Pretyman to Mrs Pretyman, nd but 10 February, 25 February 1801; Mrs Pretyman to Pretyman, nd but endorsed 8 February 1801, same to her sister Harriot, 15 February 1801 (all in Pretyman Ms 435/45). Rose mentioned Carthew's 'Narrative', held apparently by the Bishop, eighteen months later (to Pretyman, 10 August 1802; Pretyman Ms 435/44).

4. See I, xi. The volumes to 1793 were published in 1811, and the rest were designed to follow shortly.

5. See for what follows Ch. VI, sections III and IV above, particularly pp. 175–7, 189–92; for the previous disastrous handling of that prospect, II, Ch. XI, section IV.

6. For this term as used see p. 177, n1 above.

7. P. 191; and see 192 above.

The Palace of Westminster

Henry Addington, Viscount Sidmouth, *by Beechey*

avoided 'until the business [of Union] shall be completed',[1] might be held to imply the need to consider the complementary measure when the main object had been achieved. Such indeed proved to be the case. There had apparently been some discussions in the summer of 1800 – certainly in August –, though if so they were said to have been 'preliminary' and sparsely attended. But in September, '*now that the Measure was carried . . .* It was thought necessary that an early decision should be made by the Cabinet upon the language to be used to the Catholics'. The Castle in Dublin, anxious to pursue the hopes raised in the campaign, was bringing pressure to bear; and in response Pitt called a meeting on 'the great question' for the end of the month.[2]

Put off for a day by the more urgent business of Portugal and Egypt,[3] the discussion on 1 October proved inconclusive. Grenville – earlier a convert – seems to have been the strongest advocate for the cause, the Lord Chancellor Loughborough its strongest opponent. Pitt himself pointed out the likely difficulties – probably from 'the Law', certainly from the Church of England, certainly again from the King. In the recollection of one participant, indeed, he spoke '*against it*'.[4] Nonetheless he was impressed, as before, by the merits of the case, and 'undertook' to speak to the King 'the moment He [George III] returned' from Weymouth.[5] Matters were left there. But other preoccupations took over: the threatening developments in Europe, the effects of the second failed corn harvest at home. There was perhaps little time, there was certainly little energy to spare for Ireland in the next few weeks, when moreover the Minister suffered and was recovering from a particularly worrying relapse

1. P. 191 above.

2. Camden's account, written probably between August 1803 and May 1804; Camden Ms U840 0127, Maidstone. This important document is printed with a commentary by Richard Willis in 'Pitt's Resignation in 1801 . . .', in *Bulletin of the Institute of Historical Research*, Vol. XLIV, No. 110, 239–57, and reference hereafter will be made to the article. See also Pitt to Loughborough, 25 September 1800 (Stanhope, III, 268), and for discussion in August, George III to Addington, 7 February 1801 (Pellew, *Life of Sidmouth*, I, 298, where a passage is wrongly italicised). For the term the Castle see p. 158, n1 above. Castlereagh, the Irish Secretary, came to London for the meeting (Windham's diary for 1 October 1800; B.L. Add. Ms 37924).

The phrase 'great question' was used in point of fact to distinguish Emancipation from two others which accompanied it: tithe reform in Ireland, and financial assistance for Irish Catholic clergy and Dissenting Ministers, likewise discussed in 1798 (pp. 177–8 above).

3. Windham's diary for 30 September, 1 October 1800 (B.L. Add. Ms 37924). See pp. 407–9 above.

4. Liverpool's recollection in the following February (*Glenbervie*, I, 157). He referred there to a meeting on 9 October, for which there seems to be no other evidence; but in March 1801 the same account was circulating, 'with a confidence which almost amounts to an assertion', of a meeting on the 10th (*Correspondence of Charlotte Grenville, Lady Williams Wynn . . .*, ed. Rachel Leighton (1920), 64). She was Grenville's sister. For Grenville's own earlier conversion see p. 175 above.

Four months later, Pitt asserted his continuing belief in the power of obstruction from interests well represented in the Lords (see *Memoirs and Correspondence of Castlereagh*, IV, 39).

5. Willis, op. cit., 250. Cf. p. 385 above for the King at Weymouth.

in health.[1] The recovery continued; but so did the pressures. Pitt did not follow up his 'undertaking'; he did not move at all; and it was not until the end of the year that the question was propelled finally from the wings.

The interval was crucial in one respect at least which could itself have been decisive. It thrust into a narrow margin of time and narrow circles of advice a conflict of views which, given ampler thought, might perhaps have been digested sufficiently to forestall or avoid the confrontation that emerged. This is not to say that the views would have been reconciled, or indeed wider consultation have necessarily proved helpful. But a formula might – perhaps – have been found that allowed some adjustment, or some reasonable pretext for a process of retreat. As it was, an available range of judgment was excluded, and the burden of restraint cast the more heavily on the Minister and the King, the two men centrally concerned.

In the King's case the delay proved serious not least because he *had* in fact already been alerted; and the ensuing silence only fed his suspicions. For when Pitt summoned the Cabinet in September he took care to request the Lord Chancellor's attendance;[2] and the Lord Chancellor, down at Weymouth with the monarch, took care to pass on the news. How much difference this was to make one cannot readily tell. As time went by, it was held to have been a great deal. The disclosure was certainly all of a piece with Loughborough's past – 'Even the warm admirers (if there be any such) of his Lordship's political career will scarcely ascribe to him any very ardent zeal on the abstract merits of the question.'[3] He had, it seems, already expressed doubts on its wisdom which were 'put in circulation' to counter arguments from Castlereagh in Ireland, before the Cabinet meeting and indeed before he himself saw the King. He was said later in fact to have shown his paper to George III during his visit.[4] But that document itself was not necessarily an unbiassed impersonal exercise; it had its own history, traceable to the last occasion on which the issue had been thrust to the fore. Every one could recall the King's views then, in the Fitzwilliam affair of 1795. To override the Test Act of 1678 and admit Catholics into a Parliament would be to effect 'a total change in the principles of government',

1. See p. 82 above; and for the preoccupations, Ch. VIII section IV, Ch. X section I.

2. Pitt to Loughborough, 25 September 1800 (Stanhope, III, 268).

3. So Stanhope (op. cit., 264), with unusual asperity. And for a contemporary verdict cf. Camden, in Willis, op. cit., 250. See also p. 192, n2 above.

Pitt's options of course were then open; no sudden *pressure* on the King need follow if Loughborough was indiscreet.

4. Willis, op. cit., 250. The result may well have been an early version of a later paper by Loughborough which is printed in Pellew, op. cit., I, 500–12. Camden is explicit that it was in circulation before the visit to Weymouth. I have not found a copy to confirm such a date; there is one of Castlereagh's dated September 1800 in B.L. Add. Ms 35919, and see *Memorials and Correspondence of Castlereagh*, IV, 392–400.

There may in fact have been three papers on either side, on the three questions mentioned in p. 497, n2 above (*Glenbervie*, I, 185).

'overturning the fabric of the Glorious Revolution'.[1] His very title of King, the succession of his House, lay in its protection of the Protestant Reformed Religion. He was Supreme Governor of the Church of England as by law established, and to subvert the Establishment of Church and State would be to break his Coronation Oath. The matter of the oath indeed weighed heavily on him; and it was Loughborough, alert as ever, who seems at that time to have vibrated that chord. For, despite a denial later, he had then given an opinion in the King's sense, which differed significantly from that of another luminary, Lord Chief Justice Kenyon, who himself had checked his answers with the Attorney General.[2] Their verdict indeed emphatically did not support the royal fears. But that fact apparently had made no difference in 1795. As would become apparent in due course, George III had not changed his mind when Kenyon advised that Parliament could pass any bill 'up to the extent of the most unreasonable requisition that can be made', and that it was the King alone – not the two Houses which together with him formed the King in Parliament – who was 'under the promissory Oath'. Nor – the opinion had continued – did that oath 'preclude' him from reaching a judgment on its application in a given case. Its phrasing was 'couched in general terms', and while Fitzwilliam's proposal was 'certainly . . . inconsistent' with the relevant Test Act, it did not appear to break any clause in the Glorious Revolution's own Bill of Rights.[3] This must have been – as Loughborough was later to pretend of his own advice[4] – unpalatable doctrine. But, after an interval of six years, it proved not to have affected the King's profound belief that 'the subject is beyond the decision of any Cabinet of Ministers'.[5]

1. See II, 432. This was the second Test Act, 30 Car. II, c2, 'disabling Papists from sitting in either House of Parliament'. Since then of course the Irish Parliament had become juridically independent (I, 196), on the self-same basis.

2. For Loughborough's denial – which included a claim to have given advice exactly on the lines of Kenyon's (see below), see *Rose*, I, 299–301, for 13 February 1801; for a comment on it, John Lord Campbell, *The Lives of the Lord Chancellors . . .*, VI (1847), 297–8. The opinion, of 10 March 1795, is published in *L.C.G. III*, II, no. 1215; as, at no. 1219, is a letter from the King to the Archbishop of Canterbury.

Loughborough does not appear in a kinder light from the fact that, while he could not have foreseen Fitzwilliam's behaviour on arrival in Ireland in 1795 (for which II, 420–38), he had urged the appointment in full knowledge – shared by others – of the latter's sympathies.

3. *Letters* [in 1795] *from his Late Majesty to Lord Kenyon . . . with his Lordship's Answers*, 2–26 and particularly Kenyon's final letter at 21–6. Its central argument was 'that the Supream Power of a State cannot limit itself'. The Attorney General was Sir John Scott, who as Lord Eldon became Loughborough's successor in due course. His opinion (signed 'J.S.'), that 'a judgment . . ., *being constitutionally advised*' should 'determine' the issue, was published by the Hon. George T. Kenyon in *The Life of Lloyd, First Lord Kenyon* (1873), 320. All the mss (which were not all calendared in the H.M.C. *Report* of his forebear's papers) are in the possession of the 6th Lord Kenyon.

A stimulating brief commentary on the place of the oath in the relationship between King and Parliament may be found in Richard Pares's *King George III and the Politicians*, 140n3.

4. N2 above, and particularly *Rose*, I, 301.

5. Expressed on 6 February 1795 (II, 432), a month before the correspondence had opened.

That categorical statement had not of course aimed at a form of return to divine right. In George III's eyes it declared rather, with a typically literal interpretation, the defence of a balance from which the Crown's function – unique in this aspect – could not be removed. Further sharp if passing warnings within the next four years showed no shift in sentiment: 'No further indulgences must be granted to Roman Catholics' in Ireland; 'I should become an enemy to [Union] if I thought a change of the situation of the Roman Catholics would attend the Measure'.[1] It was all too clear that he was bound to be a 'consecrated obstruction'.[2] The question was, how should he be handled now? For reasoned argument was not the sole consideration here. Emotion – deep emotion – was involved, within a system of cruel physical tension;[3] and neither the Cabinet collectively nor, it would seem, any member individually had mentioned the case for Emancipation as a project since rejecting Fitzwilliam's intemperate approach.[4] It was the more telling that the case against had not gone by default. There had been a suspicion in 1798, when the King was stirring, that 'somebody about him' was 'agitating his Mind and inflaming his Prejudices' on a topic on which he found it hard to 'think calmly'.[5] Had they known of the Lord Chancellor's recent action, his colleagues would have been highly disturbed. For while he could no longer be said to be *reponsible* for George III's obduracy, in so far as he ever had been, he had stirred the passion always lurking in this matter of 'decided dislike'.[6] In point of fact Loughborough may well not have nursed any systematic far-sighted intent; and he certainly could not forecast the future, as his surprise was later to show. His manoeuvre, at a time when the King was

1. To Pitt, nd but probably May 1798 (and see p. 171 above); George III's docket on Portland to George III, 30 January 1799 (*L.C.G. III*, III, n2 to no. 1913).

2. As Bagehot called him, in the heyday of Victorian liberalism (*The English Constitution* (1867), 68).

3. See I, 647–8 for the effect of porphyria, the most likely source of George III's afflictions.

4. No Minute had been recorded of the meeting in November 1799 (see p. 192, n2 above), and Camden, who as a former Lord Lieutenant was closely concerned, did not believe that Portland, as Home Secretary, had ever 'mentioned the result' to the King, who 'had never been spoken to with openness & decision at this time on this subject by any of His Ministers' (Willis, op. cit., 249, and see p. 176 and n2 above). There is no evidence to suggest any official approach subsequently, and indeed such a move before the passage of the Union in the summer of 1800 would have been odd.

5. Dundas's view, as given to Pitt (see p. 175, n3 above). He had not been sure who it might be; and perhaps it was not then Loughborough, or Loughborough alone.

6. Willis, op. cit., 250. He may not however have been the only Minister to do so. By Loughborough's account at any rate, for what it is worth, the Lord Privy Seal Westmorland – who, though a former Lord Lieutenant of Ireland, had attended few if any of the meetings on the subject in the summer (Willis, op. cit., 250), but was closely in touch with the Court as a former Master of the Horse (see II, 423) – showed the King a letter from the Irish Lord Chancellor Clare, a forceful champion of Union without Emancipation (see pp. 176–7 above), which 'very much disturbed his Majesty' (*Rose*, I, 301). Even so, Loughborough took care to ascribe this event to October 1800. Camden suggests – indeed seems to state – that Clare first knew of the Government's *decision* only towards the end of January 1801 (Willis, op. cit., 251–2).

clearly unhappy with his Government in its conduct of the war,[1] was an instinctive reaction, the use of a sensitive nose detecting an interesting scent. He was out to bolster his standing in the closet, with some pleasure doubtless at Pitt's expense. Observing the royal response as he must have done, he was the better able to guard his flank.

Parliament met on 11 November 1800 after the summer recess. The Act of Union was due to come into force on 1 January 1801. When nothing more was heard from London on the Catholic question, the Castle in Dublin began to fret once more.[2] Ministers, always apt to be less accessible during the session for all but immediate business,[3] were beleaguered even more than usual. But Castlereagh left for London again in December, and his paper and Loughborough's were 'recirculated' in the Christmas recess.[4] By then it was indeed inescapably necessary to attend to the problem. The King's Speech had to be written for the opening session of the first Parliament of 'the United Kingdom', and something must either be said or omitted; in the former case, perhaps with some statement of intent, while Opposition itself in the latter might well bring the matter forward.[5] A meeting took place accordingly early in January, which soon resolved, at Pitt's instance, that in 'a Measure of such delicacy and importance ... the absolute decision' should be taken, after reflection, in a few days' time.[6] It was however generally agreed that, whatever had been said in November 1799,[7]

1. See Ch. XII, sections I, III above.

2. Cornwallis to Portland, 1 December; same to Major-General Ross, 14 December 1800 (*Correspondence of Cornwallis*, III, 306–7, 311). See p. 194 above for the date for the Act to take effect.

3. Cf. I, 514–15.

4. Willis, op. cit., 250; Loughborough having shown his to the King – once more, and now perhaps formally – on the 13th (Pellew, op. cit., I, 500, where the text is given).

5. As indeed the Lord Lieutenant warned from Dublin (Cornwallis to Portland, 1 December 1800; *Correspondence of Cornwallis*, III, 306). See likewise Portland to Pitt, 24 January 1801 (P.R.O. 30/8/168), and specifically on the need to frame the Speech, Pitt in retrospect to Chatham, 5 February 1801 (Ashbourne, *Pitt*, 310). Cf. p. 190 above.

6. So Camden; I do not know the date of this meeting early in the month; it may have been on the 4th or 5th (*Correspondence of Lady Williams Wynn*, 64) or perhaps the 11th after Pitt had had a long talk on the subject with Grenville and Dundas (Pitt to Canning, 10 January 1801; Canning Ms 30). If the latter, Liverpool and Chatham were the only absentees (Windham's diary, B.L. Add. Ms 37924). The sequence of events that follows relies again mainly – though not solely – on Camden's account of the Cabinet's proceedings over the rest of January, the most detailed that exists; see Willis, op. cit., 250–4. The dates there can be determined by reference to the day on which Parliament was intended to be opened, which serves as his marker.

In placing weight on Camden's account, it must of course be borne in mind, as has been pointed out (by Charles John Fedorak in 'Catholic Emancipation and the Resignation of William Pitt in 1801', *Albion*, Vol. 24, No. 1, 51), that he was one of Pitt's most loyal friends. I do not think myself that this invalidates his statement of events, and his attitude moreover was not uncritical of Pitt throughout.

7. Pp. 191–2 above.

it should be viewed as a 'new' question and 'one' that was 'now to be determined'. That process opened, introducing a fraught week, on the 25th.

The flavour of the meeting that day may be given best in Camden's words.

We were summoned to Lord Grenville's office[1] and with the exception of Lord Chatham then at Horsham with his Regt. and Lord Liverpool who was ill, all the Cabinet attended, but the [Lord] Chancellor was absent. It was observed by Mr. Pitt that the Question pressed, that the Chancellor knew of the Cabinet, that his opinion was known, that it was not likely to be changed and that we might and ought to proceed without him. Lord Grenville held the same opinion and conceived the Chancellor to be absent from design.[2] Lord Spencer and I combated these Observations by saying, however fixed the Chancellors Opinion might be and however determined our own, It was not respectful to him and his Office and it did not give us fair Ground to state, when the Determination of the Cabinet was known, that such determination took place in the absence of so important a Character and one who was known to be [word missing] to that Measure, which would probably be carried. Mr. Pitt upon these observations promised to see the Chancellor and to summon another Cabinet for the next Day, but he observed that as we were met, It was desirable to learn the opinions of Individuals and he proceeded as We sat round the Room to collect those Opinions. It was at this time supposed we should meet the next day but even under that supposition, it is hardly credible that opinions should be given upon so momentous a Subject, with so little previous discussion or Explanation. No arguments were used by those who were for or against this Question in favor of the Opinion they had formed at this time and scarcely any Qualification was given on either side in delivering such opinion except by myself, who said that from everything I had heard of the Kings Opinion being so decided, from the suspicion I entertained of the Church from my knowledge that strong Prejudices were entertained by the Law, I thought Mr. Pitt should proceed with the utmost caution, that confident in his taking the previous measures of softening the King's Mind and preparing those of others, I gave my voice for attempting the Measure at this Period and therefore on that Day, Mr. Pitt Ld. Grenville Mr. Dundas Ld. Spencer Mr. Wyndham [*sic*] and (with modifications) myself, did in the sort of Manner I have described give our Opinions.[3]

1. In Downing Street (see I, 575; and also op. cit., 309).
2. According to a note of a conversation three weeks later, Liverpool ascribed this remark to Pitt (*Glenbervie*, I, 169).
3. Willis, op. cit., 251–2. Two words noted there as illegible have been supplied from the original in Camden Ms U840 O127.
Portland had conveyed his 'apprehensions of the consquences of countenancing that measure' on the eve of the meeting (to Pitt, 24 January 1801; P.R.O. 30/8/168). Cf. p. 190 above for him in 1799.

On breaking up, Camden and Spencer urged that another meeting should take place the next day with Loughborough present. Pitt however thought it had been agreed that he should see Loughborough and discover his wishes; the Lord Chancellor did not so wish; and no such meeting was held.[1]

Matters then began to get out of hand. Pitt 'certainly imagined our Determination to be made', and at dinner that evening at Camden's where Castlereagh and Clare – also over from Ireland – were of the company, he told the former and bade him tell the latter. This Castlereagh did the next day, the 26th, the Irish Lord Chancellor predictably receiving the news 'with infinite concern'.[2] By some channel or other – Loughborough, Westmorland or Clare or some or all of them could easily have supplied it – the information then reached the King; and on the 28th a bombshell fell. At the Levee that morning, George III marched up to Dundas and said 'in a loud voice and agitated Manner, "What is the Question which you are all about to force upon me? what is this Catholic Emancipation which *this young Lord, this Irish Secretary* has brought over, that you are going to throw at my Head? I will tell you, that I shall look on every Man as my personal Enemy, who proposes that Question to me, and added, I hope *All* my Friends will not desert me." ' Dundas, astonished, did his best to turn the conversation, and when that proved impossible, to draw the King aside. But on George III repeating his last remark he did his best to parry it, and hurried off as soon as possible to Pitt.[3]

The Minister in turn, who was about to go to Court himself, summoned a Cabinet at once instead.[4] The episode was indeed very serious. The Levee was said to be particularly crowded, since Parliament was due to be opened the next day. The King's remarks had been heard by a number of people, and above all the ominous words that any one proposing a measure would be treated as a personal enemy. Pitt of all men had good cause to remember that phrase: it had heralded his own summons to office in 1783, and sustained him in the ensuing struggle for power.[5] At the

1. Pitt's impression is indeed upheld by Windham (diary for 25 January 1801; B.L. Add. Ms 37924).

2. Cf. p. 500, n6 above.

3. This, again, is Camden's version (Willis, op. cit., 252–3). Whether he was there or not it is impossible to tell. He adds that the King's behaviour to other Ministers present was not marked by 'any extraordinary Expression or Manner', although Pitt referred to such language being held at the Levee 'to more than one of his Ministers' (to Chatham, 5 February 1801; Ashbourne, op. cit., 310). Wilberforce records very much the same remarks in his diary for the day (*Life of Wilberforce*, III, 7). Sylvester Douglas (recently made Glenbervie) has a less vivid account, which he notes that he heard from Dundas at the Levee itself 'five minutes afterwards' (*Glenbervie*, I, 147). For the latter's account towards the end of the year of an earlier, calmer though premonitory conversation – probably in the summer of 1799 – see *Memoirs of the Life of . . . Sir James Mackintosh*, ed. by his son James Mackintosh, I (1835), 170–1.

4. Willis, op. cit., 253.

5. See I, Ch. VI and particularly 127.

Cabinet, which according to one account some days later was fully attended, every one gave (in most cases repeated) his opinion on the measure itself. Pitt by now – compared with his stance in October – had 'entirely gone over' to Emancipation; Loughborough, Westmorland and Liverpool, specifically mentioned, were against, Liverpool – as at the earlier time – treating an 'attempt . . . lightly' as 'absurd'.[1] That however was certainly not Pitt's opinion; by another account at the time, he 'declared that He must go out if it was not carried'.[2] Meanwhile there was an immediate problem to be settled. Parliament was to be opened the next day, there was a Speech to be read, and whatever it contained the ensuing debate on the Address might easily introduce the question. Ministers decided that the opening must be postponed, and that Pitt should 'put on Paper the Heads of the plan intended to have been submitted to the King and should after communicating it to the Cabinet wait on his Majesty with it'.[3]

The next day, the 29th, was a curious one. Pitt had agreed to prepare the paper for his colleagues, in conjunction with Grenville, 'by the morrow'. But in the event they were not called together,[4] and the political world was left to wonder at the hurried postponement of the opening of Parliament. There was naturally much speculation in the next few days, until the King went down on 2 February and read a speech which contained one innocuous paragraph on the Union.[5] By then the rest of the Cabinet's intended procedure had been overtaken.

For on 29 January George III began to act on his own initiative. He let it be known in various directions how his mind stood – to Loughborough of

1. Liverpool on 9 February (*Glenbervie*, I, 158). His recollection of an occasion only a few months before was probably accurate.

2. Windham's diary for 28 January 1801 (B.L. Add. Ms 37924).

3. Camden's account; Willis, op. cit., 253. When Pitt advised the King of the desirability of postponing the Speech (6 pm, 28 January 1801; *L.C.G. III*, III, no. 2330), which he proposed should be for four days, he gave as the reason the slow progress made so far in swearing in Members. This scarcely sounds convincing, even if his reason for specifying four days (because 30 January would be the anniversary of the execution of Charles I, when all public offices were shut, and that would be followed by a weekend) was, usefully, more so. The impression of uncertainty may be reinforced by the fact that for the first time in recollection the Speech from the Throne was not read in the Cockpit (for which see I, 575) on the eve of the session, but to a more select company at 10 Downing Street. According to one newspaper which may have been well informed, the change arose from Ministers' judgment of an 'indecorum' in anticipating the contents by the more familiar procedure (see Aspinall, op. cit., 476n1; and *The Times* of 30 January 1801 for the Cabinet's timetable on the 28th).

Cf. for the postponement p. 502 above.

4. Willis, op. cit., 253. According to *The Times*, most members of the Cabinet on the 28th, which broke up at 6 pm (see n3 above), met again at Portland's from 9 until midnight. If this was so, there might not have been much time to prepare the heads of a paper.

Loughborough said a little later that Grenville had declined to do this on his own, as was at first suggested by Pitt himself (*Rose*, I, 303).

5. *P.H.*, XXXV, col. 866.

course, and to the Archbishop of Canterbury, for both of whom a chance occasion offered, and through the Archbishop indirectly perhaps to a member of the Government, Auckland.[1] More important, he wrote to Addington, whom he knew to be opposed to Emancipation, asking him to 'open Mr. Pitt's eyes on the danger of his ever speaking to me on a subject on which I can scarcely keep my temper'.[2] The consequent comings and goings are obscure. But the Speaker moved between Downing Street and Buckingham House perhaps twice or three times in the next two days.[3] He saw Pitt at once, on the 29th, and the King on the evening of the 30th; when by one account he stayed for four hours.[4] Some kind of an 'opening' for peace offered, on which, according to himself, he wrote to George III in hopeful terms, and he was then asked to report in person on the evening of the 31st or alternatively on the next day.[5] He went along at the earlier time. By then Pitt for his part had written the letter to the King, in the light of what he had heard from Addington, which he had owed since the 29th.[6]

1. *L.C.G. III*, III, nos. 2329, 2336 for the first two; and see also *Glenbervie*, I, 394–5 for the reason why a letter from the King to the Primate of Ireland at the same time (op. cit., no. 2333) was not sent. The occasion – perhaps an auxiliary to the impasse that was shortly to develop (see Camden's opinion; Willis, op. cit., 255) – was a vacancy arising for an Irish Parliamentary seat to which one of the Castle officials long known to favour Emancipation (cf. p. 176 above) aspired. The King was out to block him.

The exact position hitherto of Auckland, who was appointed Joint Postmaster General by Pitt in 1798 after a period of coolness (p. 74 above), remains as uncertain to posterity as he himself would have wished. Suspected of already trying to influence, or gratify, George III through the Archbishop Dr Moore (see II, 65), who was his brother-in-law – and conceivably also kept in touch by his old ally Loughborough (see I, 116n3, II, 176) –, he now showed, by a letter to Pitt of 31 January which alluded to Addington, that he knew what was going on (P.R.O. 30/58/4; printed in *L.C.G. III*, III, 480n2). According to a story of Liverpool's, he also wrote a letter to Moore designed for the King, which the latter interpreted as such (*Glenbervie*, I, 168–9 for 14 February 1801). In any case he had had a good chance to see how the wind lay at the Levee, where moreover he and Clare were said to be recipients of the King's reiterated thoughts following the outburst to Dundas (Willis, op. cit., 253).

2. Pellew, op. cit., I, 285–6; also printed in part in Ziegler, *Addington*, 92–3. There is a version with some considerable differences at Windsor (*L.C.G. III*, III, no. 2331), perhaps a draft. It does not contain the significant phrase about the King's temper, which presumably exploded into the letter he finally sent.

3. Camden states that 'From Thursday to the Saturday evening [ie 29–31 January], There were frequent Messages, *all* carried by Mr. Addington between the King and Mr. Pitt' (Willis, op. cit., 254). This impression of incessant contact may be overdone.

4. For this last see *Rose*, I, 268, 309. Rose elsewhere mentions two visits to the King on the evening of the 30th (op. cit., 303). Otherwise, see Addington's account to Glenbervie on 4 November 1801 (*Glenbervie*, I, 227), and same to George III, 30 January 1801 (*L.C.G. III*, III, no. 2234).

5. Willis, op. cit., 254; Pellew, op. cit., I, 287. Windham noted on the 30th, 'Saw Mr. P & found, that all was changed, from the time of the Cabinet on Wednesdy. [the 28th] & that He conceived He must give way' (cf. p. 504 above); which presumably referred to the 'opening'.

6. See ibid.

How far and in what detail the Minister had been in touch with colleagues in the interval, it is hard to tell. Loughborough claimed a fortnight later that on the 30th Pitt sent him the draft of a political Test for Irish Catholics and Dissenters; and the 'idea' of the letter to the King was discussed with Grenville, as the Cabinet had wished.[1] But that may well have been the sum of it, and the phrasing would seem to have been the Minister's own: he sent his copy of the letter to his cousin the next day, 1 February, and proposed to show it on return to Castlereagh 'and one or two of our colleagues'.[2] Whatever his remaining uncertainties, he had not much hope of the outcome after despatching it to the Queen's House.[3]

The main argument was presented – and this was probably wise by now – succinctly.[4] Emancipation, Pitt wrote, in his view 'would be attended with no danger' to the Established Church or the Protestant interest in Britain or Ireland. Circumstances had changed greatly since the period in which 'the laws of exclusion' had been passed; political dangers from Catholics had been 'gradually declining'[5] and 'amongst the higher orders particularly, have ceased to prevail'. The proportion of Catholics in Parliamentary seats and public offices would not constitute a threat in the new larger unity. And a Test by oath, which would be introduced, would contain strong safeguards, including a disclaimer of politically 'obnoxious tenets' which would include an acknowledgment that that would not be overriden by a priest's Absolution if it was ever broken. The Catholic clergy themselves moreover might be brought into closer attachment to Government by Emancipation, and more easily superintended and controlled, particularly if they were given some financial provision by the state.[6] In general, 'the higher orders of the Catholics' and 'a large class' of Irish subjects might be the more readily conciliated to the Union itself.

Pitt then moved to what was now the central issue. He acknowledged with 'inexpressible regret' such a difference over a matter on which 'he

1. Pitt to Grenville, 1 February 1801 (*H.M.C., Dropmore*, VI, 434). For the Cabinet, see p. 504 above; for Loughborough, *Rose*, I, 303.

2. Pitt to Grenville, 1 February 1801 (*H.M.C., Dropmore*, VI, 434); Grenville to Pitt, sd (Holland Rose, *Pitt and Napoleon*, 271). Dundas 'assured' the King some days later that he did not know of Pitt's first letter until after it had gone (George III to Addington, 13 February 1801, *L.C.G. III*, III, no. 2357 on p. 499; and cf. pp. 495–6 above), and Windham, the other convinced supporter in Cabinet, saw it only on 1 February (diary, B.L. Add. Ms 37924).

3. See his letter to Grenville on 1 February (n2 above).

4. *Letters from the Right Honourable William Pitt to the Late King, with His Majesty's Answers, Previous to the Dissolution of the Ministry in 1801* (in the same compilation as the *Letters . . . to the Late Lord Kenyon* for which see p. 495, n1 above). This document of 31 January is at pp. 29–36, and was reprinted in Stanhope, III, Appendix, xxiii–xxviii. Pitt's copy is in P.R.O. 30/8/101.

5. George III might have found this a curious description, taken in itself, of events in Ireland in recent years.

6. As Dissenting ministers might be also (cf. p. 177 above).

finds himself obliged to add, that this [his own] opinion is unalterably fixed in his mind'. He hoped that the King would 'maturely . . . weigh' the views he had submitted; and – clearly without much expectation of a change of mind – went on to state the immediate possibilities he saw open to himself.

> In the interval which your Majesty may wish for consideration, he will not, on his part, importune your Majesty with any unnecessary reference to the subject; and will feel it his duty to abstain, himself, from all agitation of this subject in Parliament, and to prevent it, as far as depends on him, on the part of others. If, on the result of such consideration, your Majesty's objections to the measure proposed should not be removed, or sufficiently diminished to admit of its being brought forward with your Majesty's full concurrence, and with the whole weight of Government, it must be personally Mr. Pitt's first wish to be released from a situation, which he is conscious, that, under such circumstances, he could not continue to fill but with the greatest disadvantage.
>
> At the same time, after the gracious intimation, which has been recently conveyed to him, of your Majesty's sentiments on this point, he will be acquitted of presumption in adding, that if the chief difficulties of the present crisis should not then be surmounted, or very materially diminished, and if your Majesty should continue to think, that his humble exertions could, in any degree, contribute to conducting them to a favourable issue, there is no personal difficulty to which he will not rather submit, than withdraw himself at such a moment from your Majesty's service. He would even, in such case, continue for such a short further interval as might be necessary, to oppose the agitation or discussion of the Question, as far as he can consistently with the line, to which he feels uniformly bound to adhere, of reserving to himself a full latitude on the principle itself, and objecting only to the time, and to the temper and circumstances of the moment. But he must entreat that, on this supposition, it may be distinctly understood, that he can remain in office no longer than till the issue (which he trusts on every account will be a speedy one) of the crisis now depending, shall admit of your Majesty's more easily forming a new arrangement . . .

He ended on a significant note.

> He has only to entreat your Majesty's pardon for troubling you on one other point, and taking the liberty of most respectfully, but explicitly, submitting to your Majesty the indispensable necessity of effectually discountenancing in the whole of the interval, all attempts to make use of your Majesty's name, or to influence the opinion of any individual or descriptions of men, on any part of this subject.

The letter received a prompt reply.[1] George III wrote the next day. After expressing his 'cordial affection' and 'high opinion of [Pitt's] talents and integrity', he fastened on his own 'religious obligation' under the Coronation Oath. The 'fundamental maxims' of the Constitution required that, given an established Church, 'those who hold employments in the State must be members of it'. He was therefore 'prevented from discussing any proposition tending to destroy this ground . . . and much more so that now mentioned . . ., which is no less than the compleat overthrow of the whole fabrick'. If Pitt would assure him that he would 'stave off the only question whereon I fear from his letter we can never agree', he for his part would 'certainly abstain from talking on this subject, which is the one nearest my heart'. He could 'not help it, if others pretend to guess at my opinions, which I have never disguised'; but if those who differed from him 'will keep this subject at rest, I will, on my part, most correctly on my part, be silent also'. It would be a 'restraint' laid on him only from 'affection' for Pitt, 'but further I cannot go'. He still hoped however that the Minister's sense of duty would prevent him from retiring 'to the end of my life'. By the time that he dated this letter, the King had asked Addington to form a Government in the eventuality which he clearly foresaw.[2]

All was not quite over yet. While the outside world buzzed with rumour,[3] the exact situation was still a guarded secret, shared fully only between George III, Addington and Pitt. And Pitt himself seems still to have had some misapprehensions or qualms. He appears to have been in a curious – fundamentally an untenable – position: prepared on 28 January to contemplate going, on the 30th to think of giving way, on the 31st to write in a sense which virtually ruled that out of court.[4] If howevever Pretyman is to be believed, he again gave his colleagues the impression on 2 February that 'he did not propose to resign'.[5] He cannot however have had much hope by then, and on further reflection he hardened once more. After weighing the whole case by himself, he wrote his final answer to the King on the 3rd.[6] He fastened on one point: 'the import of one

<hr/>

1. 1 February 1801; *Letters from . . . Pitt . . . with his Majesty's Answers*, 37–9. Reprinted in Stanhope, III, Appendix, xxviii–xxx. The original is in P.R.O. 30/8/104. George Rose, to whom Pitt showed the correspondence on 5 February (*Rose*, I, 287), misdated this letter to the 2nd (op. cit., 289).

2. Addington's subsequent account to his friend Charles Abbot (for whom see p. 477 above), in *Colchester*, I, 222.

3. London newspapers convey the atmosphere.

4. See pp. 504, 505, n5 above for the first two occasions. The immediate evidence, from Windham, carries conviction.

5. P. 496 above. Who were the 'colleagues' mentioned it is hard to say. There is no record of a Cabinet meeting on that day, when the King opened Parliament and Pitt was reported to be indisposed (perhaps diplomatically) with gout (*The Morning Post* and *The Morning Chronicle* of 4 February 1801); as indeed he was said to have remained, in Downing Street, for the next few days (*The Sun* of 6 February; and see Windham to Pitt, 5 February 1801 (Dacres Adams Mss formerly P.R.O. 30/58/4), and *Colchester*, I, 222).

6. *Letters from Pitt*, 40–2; reprinted in Stanhope, III, Appendix, xxx–i. See p. 506, n4 above. Pitt's copy is in P.R.O. 30/8/101.

passage in your Majesty's note which hardly leaves him room to hope, that your Majesty thinks those steps can be taken for effectually discountenancing all attempts to make use of your Majesty's name, or to influence opinions on this subject'. These nevertheless were 'indispensably necessary during any interval in which he might remain in office'. He had therefore to 'consider the moment as now arrived when . . . it must be his first wish to be released, as soon as possible, from his present situation'; and he trusted that the King would form a new arrangement without the need for 'any long delay'.

His wish was granted, as of course he knew it would be.[1] The King informed his outgoing Minister on 5 February that he would 'attempt' 'without unnecessary delay . . . to make the most creditable arrangement, and such as Mr. Pitt will think most to the advantage of my service'.[2] By then Addington had accepted the post of First Lord of the Treasury, and on the 10th he announced the King's 'intention' to appoint him to an office under the Crown and resigned accordingly as Speaker of the House of Commons.[3]

II

Why exactly, it has been asked from that day to this, did Pitt resign? The occasion has remained one of the 'special mysteries' of the age.[4] After all, while he ended by stating that his view on Emancipation was 'unalterably fixed', that had not been the case a few months earlier, when he was impressed by the difficulties and Liverpool even thought that he was 'against' an attempt.[5] So far in fact had he been from pursuing the matter,

1. Many years later, Addington was said to have remarked that the 'dismissal' from the King took Pitt 'quite by surprise' (*The Croker Papers* . . ., ed. Louis J. Jennings, II (1884), 339–40, referring to a conversation in 1839). If applied strictly to the royal letter of 1 February, this hardly seems likely; cf. p. 508 above. But he may have been talking more generally.

2. *Letters from Pitt*, 43–4, reprinted in Stanhope, III, Appendix, xxxi–ii (Rose again misdates this letter to the 4th (*Rose*, I, 290)); Addington to George III, 4 or 5 February 1801 (the former in *L.C.G. III*, III, no. 2341, the latter in Pellew, op. cit., I, 292–4).

3. *P.R., 3rd ser.*, XIV, 117; after Addington had told 'all his friends' in the House the day before (Pellew, op. cit., I, 312).

4. Pares, *King George III and the Politicians*, 1. The degree of mystery has not been reduced by the fact that, from his own testimony, Addington destroyed a 'mass' of Pitt's letters to him (Pellew, op. cit., I, 461). Pellew himself told Pitt's biographer Lord Stanhope that he was sure these related 'chiefly, if not entirely, to the circumstances of their private lives' (27 November 1861; Stanhope Ms U1590 C405/1). Another cleric however, Dean Milman, who had also known Addington long and well, stated that the latter had 'selected . . . every paper and document' relating to a later transaction with Pitt (for which see pp. 586–90 below) 'unfavourable to Mr. Pitt' (to Sir George Cornewall Lewis, 7 January 1858, in the latter's *Essays on the Administrations of Great Britain from 1783 to 1830* (1864), 277). One cannot be sure that a 'selection' may not also have applied to 1801.

5. P. 497 and n4 above. Chatham, who was in his military command in southern England for much of the time, wrote in February that when he saw his brother in town 'he did not seem, in the least to have made up his mind' (to Camden, 2 February 1801; Camden Ms U840 C102/6, Maidstone). But when was that exactly? From Pitt's own language (5 February; see Ashbourne, *Pitt*, 309–10), it is hard to tell.

in an increasingly hectic period, that it lay dormant or latent until exploded by the King's pre-emptive strike. Nor did every one in the Cabinet, even in January, see it as a question of pressing priority; and almost all were astonished that a result of such magnitude should have issued from such a cause. Why then did Pitt himself take so determined a stand? And why had he not prepared the ground better, with his colleagues and with the King?

The reason for delay in the autumn of 1800, when the Union had been passed, is not hard to find. It lay in essence in the unhappy combination of threats, domestic and foreign, leading to a 'crisis',[1] with the collapse of Pitt's health in September–October and its uncertain state over the rest of the year. He did not find the energy and thus the time to face more than the immediate challenges; and that underlined a tendency to which in any case he was always prone. For even by the broad standards of persons in high office – seldom given to narrowing options far in advance – and with an exception by and large in matters of finance, Pitt was apt to wait until late in the day to tackle the practicalities of a policy. He relied on his powers of assimilation to master a subject when it came to the fore;[2] and this was certainly the case in this instance, when the subject was an awkward one. As George III observed, the Minister was 'apt to put off laborious or disagreeable business to the last, but then, when forced to it, got through it with extraordinary rapidity'. It was pertinent that the King should have made his remark – in a context not bearing on the explosive issue – at this particular moment.[3] For Pitt's caution, or suspension of judgment, at the end of the summer in 1800 would not necessarily have affected his final stance in January 1801.

We must move, however, from the Minister's circumstances and an aspect of his temperament to his mind. Why should he have resolved at or by that later date that a measure must be *shortly* introduced? The Government was under no immediate or in fact categorical obligation. That had been specifically avoided in the guidance to Cornwallis of November 1799, and the Ministry could have postponed the question, no doubt hinting where required at future progress. Pitt was brought to the point by the unwavering repetition of the case, impelled by the Rebellion and first emanating from the Castle in 1798, that Union was essential for harmony, and since 1799 that Union itself could not be achieved, or if achieved, then attain its object, without the prospect of Emancipation. Cornwallis and Castlereagh's insistence and the latter's reiterated advocacy from December 1800, strongly reinforced by the convert Grenville and the unwavering conviction of Dundas, all in accord with his own milder preference,[4] persuaded him that

1. Pitt's word now (p. 507 above).

2. Cf. I, 325.

3. See p. 105 above. He is reported as doing so at the Levee on 28 January 1801 (*Glenbervie*, I, 149). As someone addicted to regularity himself, he added that 'this sort of irregular mixture of delay and hurry was the chief cause of his [Pitt's] ill health'.

4. For which cf. in 1792–3, II, 221–2; in 1795, op. cit., 436; in 1798, pp. 175 and n4, 177–80. For Grenville's and Dundas's thoughts see pp. 175–6, 497, 502 above.

the case held good. It was a pragmatic decision, on secular grounds, strengthened – though for his own part not decisively – by the sense of a recent obligation to the Catholics;[1] and after his troubles with Ireland over some fifteen years he was heartened by what he saw as a ray of hope. The pros and cons had been rehearsed while the Union was in draft and then in the balance. Now it was established, and if the structure was to stand complete it needed its coping stone.

If the outcome therefore was not inescapable – if the Government was not irrevocably pledged – the attractions, now placed in a new context, were nonetheless greater than ever before. The circumstances had changed, in the vital respect of Union, from those of Fitzwilliam's day, even if the conclusion, ironically, was that for which he had been dismissed. Pitt moreover may well have wished to grasp the opportunity before it was seized by others – perhaps Fitzwilliam himself – whose proposals could not be so closely controlled and might have to be amended or even opposed.[2] Such a thought may have contributed to the way he moved. Certainly he did so in haste rather than with ordered speed.

For the Minister's course was not well prepared: he showed no real sign at the outset of attempting to buttress himself before he reached the King. He knew of course that he could scarcely hope to mobilise a range of influential opinion; to seek a 'previous concert with the leading men of every order in the State', as George III himself had in fact laid down in 1795 when he ruled out a decision on this subject by the Cabinet alone.[3] That would have been all too likely to backfire; when he had taken advice from experts in recent years, he had experienced the old sharp divisions once more.[4] But within the Cabinet itself there is no indication that he tried seriously to persuade waverers, or to convert or isolate dissenters. Loughborough and Westmorland, probably Liverpool, would doubtless not have budged, though Westmorland, as an old favoured friend and colleague who had concurred in the resolution of 1799, might perhaps have been asked at least to keep quiet at Court. Portland however, initially well disposed in principle, was allowed to drift into mild opposition; and while Camden, from an opposite starting point, ended in qualified but open support,[5] Pitt gave him remarkably sparse attention at the critical time. Nor did he attempt to influence Chatham, absent though the latter might

1. See p. 496 above. But also 501–2.
2. Cf. p. 501 above.
3. To Pitt, 9 February 1795 (Stanhope, II, Appendix, xxv). According to Camden however, the Minister had undertaken in the summer of 1800 to 'sound considerable Persons in the Country' (Willis, op. cit., 250). That never happened; and by the turn of the year he was unlikely to have had the time or inclination to favour such a course.
4. Pp. 176–7, 182 above.
5. Willis, op. cit., 253 for Camden; and also 257, where Camden described himself later as a 'loose' supporter of the measure. Portland was not counted in favour at the meeting of 25 January (op. cit., 251), and according to Stanhope (III, 273) was now 'inclining, though gently, against the Catholics'.

be.[1] His handling moreover of a crucial meeting disturbed two of his eventual supporters: he collected votes summarily, without discussion – a 'hardly credible' procedure on 'so momentous a Subject' – and clearly did not want to call another, but to go straight ahead.[2] He did not in fact pay much heed, throughout, on a Ministerial question to be 'brought forward . . . with the full weight of Government', to any of his colleagues except Grenville and, rather less in this instance, Dundas. He could claim a majority in Cabinet when he approached the King – six to five, but one of course was enough. No dissent was formally recorded, and in any case strict collective responsibility was not an obligatory – rather indeed, an uncertain and limited – concept.[3] But the position, in his own words, was really that 'as far as our discussions went, the opinion of what would be a majority of the whole Cabinet seemed to be in favour'.[4] He had a buttress of a kind, visible enough for him to emerge. Nonetheless it hardly gave solid assurance, in this particular instance, in tackling George III.

When Pitt moved to that stage, however, he gave the impression that he was in unyielding mood. Having failed to talk to the King earlier with intent[5] – for which he might perhaps be given the benefit of pressures and mischance – or to write to him in the recess as soon as his colleagues requested, and acting now against the ominous background of the royal outburst, his letter of 31 January could be taken almost as an ultimatum rather than a genuine attempt to conciliate or persuade. It may have been a 'most masterly Exposition of the Question itself'.[6] But what, as the King read on, was he being offered beyond that? An 'interval' in which he should 'weigh' his Minister's advice 'maturely', during which Pitt would not 'importune' him further in private or public and would try to ensure

---

1. Chatham did not have 'a word' from Pitt until the latter wrote on 5 February after resigning (Chatham to Camden, 2 February 1801, Camden Ms U840 C102/6; Pitt to Chatham, 5 February 1801, in Ashbourne, op. cit., 309–10). But the brothers did not think alike about the question (implicit in Chatham to Camden on the 2nd and to Pitt on 6 February, in P.R.O. 30/8/122; more explicit in Addington to Chatham on the 9th, in P.R.O. 30/70/4, and George III to same on the 18th, in *L.C.G. III*, III, no. 2365).

2. Willis, op. cit., 252; see p. 502 above.

3. The distinction between issues recognised as involving Government and those that were not – the latter including as notable examples Parliamentary reform and the treatment of the slave trade – is exemplified in I, 224–5, 392, 394. For collective responsibility cf. op. cit., 180–2, 628–32. Another instance of 'one is enough' may be found in II, 553. The recording of dissent on a Minute, an apparently new and certainly highly unusual practice, did not apply here since there was no Minute – not surprisingly, since normally that was taken in order to be shown to the monarch; and the Minister most given to it, Grenville (see II, 555, and also p. 58 above), was in any case one of the majority in this case.

4. To Chatham, 5 February 1801 (Ashbourne, op. cit., 310). And cf. Loughborough's statement (correct enough here) in *Rose*, I, 304.

5. I put it like this because the King claimed not to have been told Pitt's views as he had heard Grenville's and Dundas's in conversation in the past, and similarly those of Grenville again and Spencer early in January (see *L.C.G. III*, III, no. 2346; Pellew, op. cit., I, 285).

6. In Camden's view (Willis, op. cit., 254).

that others kept quiet while the monarch for his part, as an 'indispensable necessity', 'effectually' discountenanced any use of his own name and refrained from influencing any one else. There might be a 'short' extension if required, since he had intimated his hope that Pitt would not go during 'the present crisis'.[1] This was the language of limited truce, phrased in demanding terms. For the rest, it was of resignation as soon as possible if the Minister's 'unalterable' decision was not met.

Such peremptory statements conveyed a sense of resolve which was sustained in Pitt's own reflections. He seems almost certainly to have wavered at times; but only to return to his opening position, which from George III's point of vantage might be seen as one of threat. The fact that the monarch did not react at once more fiercely than he did – for his tone was one of regret rather than anger – may be ascribed to several possible causes. But one could well have been that, whatever the tone, the threat did not represent a challenge of ultimate authority on the issue itself. For, after all, the conclusion was not one of conflict but rather of retirement. Pitt was not attempting to attack the royal prerogative on such a subject; the letter pointed indeed the other way. If he was saying in effect that the King must take his opinion or leave it, he guessed or recognised what 'the . . . answer . . . must be'.[2] When he saw Addington after the Speaker's first visit to the Queen's House, he said at once 'I know the King's business. It is to desire you to form a new Administration'.[3]

The Minister in fact knew well enough that on this question it was he who would have to give some ground, in conditions in which both men would not find it easy to move. George III claimed that he himself could have 'averted' the clash given proper warning; Pitt may have hesitated even very late in the day. But the former was presumably thinking in terms of some form of Ministerial retreat that could have been unobtrusive, and if the latter was brought to consider an extended interval he set the limits of manoeuvre by insisting that it be short.[4] His sense of 'hurry'[5] was now persistent. And in fact it may have been heightened by an issue generically distinct from the specified question itself. For that had recently taken colour from an event on which a challenge *could* be discerned. George III's

---

1. Camden stated (ibid) that the Minister meant by that phrase 'the Continuance of the War'. It seems to me that he meant the 'present' combination of alarming troubles at home and those from the Northern confederacy plus the outcome of the measures preparing for the latter (Ch. XII, section IV above).

2. To Grenville, 1 February 1801 (*H.M.C., Dropmore*, VI, 434).

3. Addington's account as reported some nine months later (*Glenbervie*, I, 277–8).

4. George III to Addington, 7 February 1801 (Pellew, op. cit., I, 298); and cf. same to Dundas, sd (*L.C.G. III*, III, no. 2346). According to Liverpool, who was caustically sceptical throughout and may not have represented Pitt correctly on every point, the word 'short' was important in discouraging the hope of an 'opening' (*Glenbervie*, I, 169; and for 'opening' see p. 505 above). The Minister's decision here however seems to have been supported immediately afterwards by Dundas (see Dundas to Pitt, Sunday morning 8 o'clock [1 February]; Dacres Adams Mss, formerly P.R.O. 30/58/4).

5. P. 510, n3 above.

distinctly qualified response to the demand for restraint, after his remarks at the Levee, was given particular prominence in Pitt's final reply.[1] This might have been a pretext on the Minister's part to confirm escape from an intolerable position. On the other hand, it could have focused on a factor which ensured that the position *was* intolerable to him: on one reason in particular among those which soon would be sought for an acceptable answer to the 'mystery' of his going.[2]

For Pitt's behaviour appeared so bewildering that some hidden cause was widely adduced. Relief of Irish Catholics could surely not explain in itself his sudden departure at such a time. 'The current crisis' was real, abroad and at home. This issue seemed to have come out of the blue. What was he of all men doing, after the responsibilities of seventeen years? The political public was at a loss; and it was not alone. So too were men, Parliamentarians and officials, normally in touch with what was going on; so were some at least in the outer ring of Cabinet; so indeed were some of those centrally concerned.

There was less agreement as to what the cause might be. George III thought at first, or professed to think, that the Minister had simply been led astray on the principle – '(though it appears most extraordinary)' – by a combination of Camden, Castlereagh and Canning.[3] Politicians – Tapers and Tadpoles and some of their seniors – sought glimpses of a politician's motive. Pitt was lured into a trap by Grenville and Dundas, both of whom knew that they had lost the royal favour and could leave more easily if they were in his company after provoking him to stand on impossible ground.[4] Or it might be Addington who had played false, claiming to have tried to prevent Pitt's going but, as the sole

1. Pp. 508–9 above.

2. See p. 509 above.

3. To Addington, 13 February 1801 (*L.C.G. III*, III, no. 2357 on p. 499). This was a curious trio to cite. Castlereagh of course was a convinced and urgent proponent of Emancipation. But Camden, as we have seen (pp. 502, 511, n5 above), was only moderately in favour, and in any case, as might have been expected from their normal roles, seems to have followed Pitt rather than have led. Nor, by his own account, was he kept fully informed. Canning's influence could certainly still count, and was generally assumed to be strong; but in point of fact it had weakened over the past year from absence through marriage (see p. 96 above), and there is no sign of it in this instance in a normally revealing correspondence. The King may have thought on such lines in his initial surprise. Later however he concluded that the Catholic question was not the real reason for the resignation, and said that he had told Pitt so. He 'believed' rather that 'Pitt had determined to withdraw himself' and that the issue was 'a pretext' (account of a conversation with Glenbervie, 19 August 1801; *Glenbervie*, I, 389).

4. The reports and surmises of that capable, unattractive place-hunter Glenbervie give perhaps as good an indication as any other of what was being bruited, though he tends to turn hints into assertions. See him here for conversations with Thomas Pelham in October 1801 in respect of Dundas (*Glenbervie*, I, 263) and with Addington in November relating to both men (op. cit., 277).

go-between, really working for himself.[1] Or again, it was Pitt himself who had deliberately set the field. He was tired of Grenville, or of Windham and perhaps Spencer, and was disposing of them by this means, intending to come back unencumbered at some point.[2] The suspicion of an intended return was indeed quick to form: Fox from his retreat was naturally predisposed to think the whole affair a 'juggle', but the thought occurred also to others who were equally in the dark.[3] If however they were right, what lay behind such a problematic manoeuvre – or alternatively the readiness to accept a lure? There was still a reason, or a mixture of reasons, to be found.

Three main possibilities were canvassed, as they have been canvassed by historians since. The first was the state of Pitt's health, and conceivably of his mind. The old rumours of madness – Chatham's legacy – revived, and there were also hints that he had burned out: that the powers 'which had become mature so early' were now 'quite gone'. Such an impression indeed was said to have been held by Dundas in the previous autumn, citing an instance affecting the terms of an appointment.[4] That had been the period of Pitt's temporary collapse, and there were signs of continuing debility. Both Addington and the doctor Farquhar began to drop hints, and Pitt himself seemed to show unusual emotion when it came to the point of resignation itself. On his first audience of the King since his final letter he was said to have wept in the closet, and was certainly seen to be exceptionally agitated as he emerged.[5] He was undoubtedly in poor shape; attacked by gout again at the beginning of February, and observed to be 'much shaken – gouty and nervous' – at the end of the month.[6] Pretyman wrote in his account that one of 'several collateral circumstances, which contributed' to a decision itself taken specifically on the

1. George Rose chose to suspect this almost at once (*Rose*, I, 292–3).
2. 'an idea . . . in circulation' in February in respect of Windham and Spencer (*Glenbervie*, I, 159); one in Pelham's mind in October and Liverpool's in December in respect of Grenville (op. cit., 263, 294).
3. *Memoirs and Correspondence of Fox*, III, 320, 325; *Glenbervie*, I, 159, 163; *Malmesbury*, IV, 3–4 (all in February).
4. *Glenbervie*, I, 174, on Dundas in 'October or November last', when 'He . . . seemed to think that Pitt's mind was probably worn out, and might any day become extinct'. Others, with lesser qualifictions to do so, let it be known that they had 'unquestionable authority' or 'positive proof' that 'he has been . . . mad' (the now politically inactive Lord Guilford (formerly George North), and the veteran independent MP Sir William Pulteney; op. cit., 175, 180). Rose attributed the illness at that time 'almost if not entirely' to 'the State of his Mind' (Pretyman Ms 435/44); some months later, Addington ascribed Pitt's decision in part to 'the state of his health of body and mind' (Pellew, op. cit., I, 320 for August); while Farquhar (for whom see p. 79 above) apparently remarked earlier that there were 'circumstances about Pitt's health known only to Mr. Addington and himself' (*Glenbervie*, I, 174).
5. This was Liverpool's account, at the time. He compared Pitt's agitation with that of Chatham on resigning in 1761 (*Glenbervie*, I, 169). The Minister was also said, whether truthfully or not, to burst into tears when talking of 'the present explosion' to 'his intimates' (op. cit., 167).
6. P. 508, n5 above; *Malmesbury*, IV, 17.

Catholic question, was declining health, a hope for recovery in private, and his 'Feeling therefore release from Office to be of great importance to himself in this respect'.[1]

At the same time Pretyman coupled with this 'circumstance' a second which he termed 'the principal', and which 'had great weight' with Pitt: 'an idea that another person would be more likely to be able to make peace with the French Government than himself'. This was itself conditioned by two assumptions: his conviction that 'immediate Peace was of the utmost importance to the Country', and that he had 'good reason to expect that he should be consulted by the new Ministers', to whom he hoped to give 'some assistance'.[2] One experienced observer, looking back, took the matter farther: Liverpool was sure that Pitt went because he found it 'impracticable for that Ministry to make peace', but equally because 'he found it impracticable to make war'.[3]

The third possible reason advanced was separate from the others. It was, as Canning was reported to have put it, that 'if on this particular occasion a stand was not made, Pitt would retain only a nominal power, while the real one would pass into the hands of those who influenced the King's mind and opinion out of sight'. He went in fact 'not on the Catholic Question simply as a measure in which he was opposed, but from the manner in which he had been opposed', which if accepted would have left him 'as a Minister . . . on a footing totally different from what he had ever before been in the Cabinet'.[4] Others concurred in effect from within the Cabinet itself. Camden noted that Emancipation 'was not so much the actual as the ostensible reason for . . . Retirement from Office', an event which arose from 'collateral Circumstances' that came to a head at the King's Levee, 'making the Disagreement so public'. And Dundas, while observing that the reason given for resignation was the real one, placed that in context by stating simply – as reported – that 'The King was prepared to oppose us on the popery question'.[5]

---

1. Draft account for his Life of Pitt in B.L. Add. Ms 45108, bundle F, f. 21. Cf. p. 495, n1 above.

2. Loc. cit., ff. 20–1. The first 'idea' seems to have been encouraged by the familiar declarations in France that peace would never be concluded with him in person.

3. Conversation with Glenbervie, 7 December 1801 (*Glenbervie*, I, 294–5). Bearing in mind the paucity of his attendance in Cabinet after the summer and of his communication – and now sympathy – with Pitt himself (cf. pp. 285, n2, 292, n6, 457, 502, 504 above), it seems fair to call him an observer.

The same possibility had struck the experienced Malmesbury at the time as having perhaps 'some degree of truth' (*Malmesbury*, IV, 39). Others later repeated it; eg Bland Burges in his notes for a sketch of Pitt (see I, 322), Bland Burges Mss, Box 73–4, Bodleian Library.

4. Conversations with Malmesbury, 8 February 1801, 20 October 1802 (*Malmesbury*, IV, 75). Canning acknowledged that he had been 'one of those who strongly advised Pitt *not* to yield' (op. cit., 4). As he was apt to do, and particularly now that he was less in contact, he may have overestimated his influence; cf. p. 514, n3 above.

5. Willis, op. cit., 257; Dundas in conversation in 'the summer' of 1801 (recorded in November by Sir James Macpherson's son from his father; *Memoirs of the Life of . . . Sir James Macpherson*, I, 170).

These various explanations need not of course be seen as mutually exclusive or distinct. They may perhaps be taken rather as framing a perspective which ended at the point of the act. That is not to say that the point itself was set ineluctably in advance: when we look at the course of events in the final phase we can see the intervention of the unexpected. As Pitt himself acknowledged, he 'did not foresee the extent of the consequences to which within this week the question had led'.[1] But of course that miscalculation had its roots in a set of past developments. In appraising his own role, the state of his health must clearly be assessed, with some care. One can hardly expect to judge accurately now. But taking the scene as a whole – the whole range of Pitt's activities – in the autumn and winter of 1800, one may perhaps argue that this factor, while significant, did not become a determinant. In all probability Pitt was suffering something like a breakdown when he went to stay with Addington early in that October.[2] If so, it seems to have been brief and, so far as his mind went, evanescent. The main alarms referred specifically to that period,[3] and while the effects were visible they did not govern a conduct of diverse policies which in their totality do not show a lessening of control. That said, Pitt was undoubtedly conscious of his weakness and tiredness; he was operating at the edge of capacity, and would be very glad of some rest. His health sealed a failure to approach George III, at an appropriate stage, which events and his habits made likely in any case; and it was a contributory element in his final decision, to the extent at least that it would gain him a respite which he welcomed rather than feared.

Where there was most visibly a loss of control by the end of 1800 it was in 'making war';[4] contrasting indeed with Pitt's energies in other spheres: in the plans for finance, the containment of disaffection, above all perhaps his continued imposition of a middle course in the fight against dearth – which he viewed as the most critical of his problems – with his successful rejection of pressures from either wing.[5] The persistent indecision in the sphere of strategy through much of the year, the failure to impinge on largely frustrating events, more intimately the rising differences between Grenville and Dundas, affected the tone of the Ministry as well as the spirits of the Minister himself. He was fretted and depressed by the disunity which he did not know how to remove. And as the cement of the inner group crumbled, one has the strong impression that uneasiness grew in the Cabinet's outer ranks. Liverpool was withdrawn not only by age and illness; Camden uneasy at the unaccustomed need to pronounce on strategy; Windham on the contrary even more irritated by the amount of information still being withheld; Loughborough of course absorbing

1. To Chatham, 5 February 1801 (Ashbourne, op. cit., 310). And cf. p. 509, n1 above.
2. See p. 82 above; and 515 and n4 above for the possible breakdown witnessed by Addington himself at Woodley.
3. Pp. 82–3 above.
4. P. 516 above.
5. Cf. Ch. X, section 1 *passim*.

the atmosphere at Court; Chatham, it would seem, in some sympathy with Dundas's views.[1] Portland and Spencer, who had been the most suspicious on joining,[2] were now in fact perhaps the most steadily engaged; Westmorland the most insensitive to any changes of mood. Pitt's forceful handling of two important occasions in these months – the critical meetings on Egypt and on Emancipation[3] – reflected the need to dominate colleagues who were more divided than ever before.

At the same time, as those occasions showed, he could still so dominate. His primacy was not in doubt, within the structural limits of the age. Rather, it was taken for granted, and despite the recent vacillations and weakness he was still held broadly – one might almost indeed now say traditionally – in great respect. The idea of his pre-eminence was so long accepted; the familiar impression remained so lofty; the skills, Parliamentary, financial, administrative, were still flexibly deployed. The ball remained in his court. If he was looking for a pretext to go, that would undoubtedly be from his own choice.

In the circumstances, it was natural for others to suspect such an inclination, and to attribute it primarily to the war. The charge in fact was levied publicly, of all people by Auckland, whose manoeuvres in recent weeks, increasingly suspected despite not inadequate concealment, had led Pitt in the upshot to sever relations. He did so in a chilling response to a long letter of uncalled-for advice. In return he was told, in the course of a Lords' debate, that it was 'not in human nature . . . that generals, inured to great actions, and born to achieve them, can, without motives of good and superior import, get into their post-chaise and quit their army in the time of action'. A 'mystery' therefore remained.[4] The accusation was of course denied. Pitt claimed that 'he had lived to very little purpose for the last seventeen years, if it was necessary for him to say, that he had not quitted his situation in order to shrink from its difficulties'.[5] In point of fact however one might view his position in a rather different perspective. For the setting of the war itself was altered from that which had lately been wearing him down; he was now looking at it in a changing light. As has been seen, he of all the Cabinet had no intention now of continuing

---

1. These impressions are drawn from uneven evidence; that for Liverpool (eg p. 285, n2 above on his treatment over the London flour bill) and for Windham being the most explicit. There were rumours of unhappiness in the Cabinet in London newspapers and general correspondence in the course of 1800. Dundas's view of its 'state' at the end of the summer will be recalled from p. 387 above.

2. See II, 404–7.

3. Pp. 409–10, 502 above.

4. 20 March 1801 (*P.R., 3rd ser.*, XIV, 516). See p. 505, n1 above for the manoeuvres. The letters, highly characteristic on both sides, are printed in *A.C.*, IV, 122–6, and there is an expostulatory postscript from Auckland of 7 February in Dacres Adams Mss, formerly P.R.O. 30/58/4. Pitt said in conversation that his conduct had been 'very scandalous' (Pretyman to Mrs Pretyman, 25 February 1801, Pretyman Ms 435/45); and see *Rose*, I, 294–5, 365–6, 400.

5. Commons' debate, 25 March 1801 (*P.R., 3rd ser.*, XIV, 614).

hostilities any longer than he could help; he had been reluctant earlier to envisage a campaign beyond the extreme limit of 1801, and at the start of the year he was looking to one shorter than that.[1] His eagerness for action in Egypt, and also in the Baltic where other considerations operated in any case, drew strength accordingly from the need for early victories from which to talk the more effectively to France. The discussions with the French envoy Otto had failed despite his anxiety to explore them; the negotiation projected in company with Austria had disappeared with her fall. Now we must, and could, proceed on a different basis, and we wanted some successes to make Bonaparte lower his tone.[2] The events of 1800 closed a chapter, in personal experience as well as strategy itself. Whatever lay ahead, those oppressive failures related to the past.

Any impulse towards escape from wartime desperation had thus changed its context. Pitt's eyes were set more firmly than ever on peace. Pretyman's stress on this factor as 'the principal' of 'collateral circumstances' accorded with the developments shaping the Minister's mood. And the Bishop's rider also applied.[3] For as things turned out, Pitt could plead a solution which might absolve him from the charge of desertion as well as leading to his desired result. He was looking in fact to the confidential arrangement which had been conceived under the same assumption – 'that another person would be more likely to make peace with the French government than himself' – but had then been dropped, in 1797.[4] The abortive precedent would indeed have borne a close resemblance to the reality now; for, then as now, he had good reason 'to expect that he should be consulted by the new Ministers' and that 'his long experience might enable him to afford some assistance'. If he were to resign – and 'nothing would have induced him', according to Pretyman, if there was any danger of Opposition coming in – he and the King and Addington himself knew what had been proposed before.[5]

1. Cf. pp. 387–8 above; and for the rest of this paragraph, in its linked contexts, Ch. XII, sections III–V above.

2. It is reasonable, I think, to interpret a letter to Canning in this sense (10 January 1801; Canning Ms 30). But see Mackesy, op. cit., 200n37, in disagreement here with Willis, op. cit., 240n4.

3. See p. 516 above. At the same time, such is the need for careful definition in making a comprehensive assessment, one should note that Addington towards the end of his life, taking a strict view, denied that Pitt's 'real object' was to see peace made (in a conversation at the age of 82; *The Croker Papers*, II, 339–40).

4. See pp. 46–8 above – including the heavy hint that Pitt might return when he wished.

5. B.L. Add. Ms 45108, ff. 20–1.
According to Addington himself, the King said to Pitt in his presence a little later that in appointing him he was sure that this was what Pitt 'would . . . have recommended' (Addington's daughter's notes on her father's conversation, quoted in Pellew, op. cit., I, 331–2n). Cf. also Pitt to Chatham, 5 February 1801 (Ashbourne, op. cit., 312). That could well have been so; and in fact the outgoing Minister may well have moved a stage beyond. There is an undated list of possible posts, in and outside Cabinet, which although a later hand has ascribed it to a later occasion (1804, which in point of fact is impossible), seems to me likely to apply to the point at which Pitt urged Addington to come in (Dacres Adams

But none of these circumstances, 'collateral' though they might prove, furnished the *occasion* of Pitt's going. If they framed the perspective, that had still to be shaped by the point.[1] Dundas observed later that historians would doubtless consider the reason given as 'a mere pretext'; and they would be able to find 'very plausible arguments' for another cause.[2] And yet the occasion itself provided in truth the determining motive. The Minister himself pointed to it with an emphasis which should be given full weight. The King's language at the Levee

> was so strong and unqualified on this subject as to show even then (what has since been more fully confirmed) that his mind was made up to go to any extremity rather than consent to the measure in question. Intimations to the same effect reached me from other quarters, and some in a way which left me in no doubt of the industry already used on the question, or of the imprudent degree to which the King's name was committed on a question not yet even regularly submitted to him. Under these circumstances, with the opinion I had formed and after all that had passed, I had no option . . .[3]

Two linked questions in fact were involved: the King's pronouncements, in what amounted to public, on the political consequences in a matter admittedly affecting the royal prerogative; and the legitimacy of opinions and influence coming from persons either not carrying responsibility or conveying their individual views in advance of an opinion formed collectively in Cabinet. It was on this combination that Pitt fastened as personally intolerable, under his reading of the balance as it stood. His own background of course played its part. He had an inherited suspicion of the Court,[4] he had never stood close to it, and indeed had been the more determined to proclaim his independence after his original controversial appointment stemming from the King's war with Fox.[5] Where therefore

---

Mss, formerly P.R.O. 30/58/8, f. 96). The fact that the name of the First Lord of the Treasury is (uniquely in such notes) left blank, and that those of Grenville and Dundas are included (ie before they insisted, as they did shortly afterwards (p. 524 below) on resigning with Pitt), supports such a conclusion. It would also suit the supposition that Pitt at that time was tired of some of his colleagues (p. 515 above): Grenville is to be Lord Privy Seal, Hawkesbury becoming Foreign Secretary; Windham, Chief Justice in Eyre; Loughborough (naturally) to be replaced, by Eldon; Camden left in doubt; Liverpool to disappear; even Dundas to be taken at his word, expressed from time to time, and left in charge of India alone.

    1. See p. 510 above.

    2. *Memoirs of Sir James Mackintosh*, 170. He was illustrating his contention that, 'from his experience in affairs, he had been taught to have very little faith in historians'.

    3. To Chatham, 5 February 1801 (Ashbourne, op. cit., 310).

    4. Eg I, 65.

    5. Op. cit., 113–37.

the monarch saw an assault on his constitutional duty – on a role which no one else could assume in this instance – the Minister saw an assault on the valid process of constitutional advice. The ground, it might be held, in point of fact was not as well marked out as the protagonists declared.[1] Their views took their place in a perennial debate on the interpretation of law and convention which usually lacks an irrefutable answer to the problems from which the differences arise. The Lord Chancellor for instance, in his particular role, could argue a duty to the sovereign as well as to his colleagues; the King took his stand on a prerogative which his chief Minister was not challenging here in itself; the Minister, on precedents and practice proclaiming the territory of Ministerial competence. This last contained its grey areas. But he himself was clear that the bounds were being invaded illegitimately in this case.

As so often, again, constitutional stances derived their force from working relationships. When Cornwallis in Dublin heard from Castlereagh that Pitt favoured Emancipation, he observed that 'if Mr. Pitt is firm he will meet with no difficulty'.[2] That he could so conclude so easily, and be wrong, showed a misreading not only of relative strengths on the question itself but also of George III's feelings in general now about Pitt, and Grenville and Dundas. For all three, and particularly the first and the last, had been falling increasingly from grace. The King had never liked Grenville; he very seldom liked Grenvilles, and the Foreign Secretary's obduracy and 'cold and dry' manner certainly did not appeal.[3] This was a failure of personality: the two men were not often in conflict on foreign policy. Even so, the King sometimes had his reservations, and these had recently been growing as Grenville moved more firmly towards the prospect of talks on peace. The case was otherwise with Dundas. George III may not have been attracted by the Scotchman's rather coarse personality; but it was on matters of policy in this case that angry differences arose. The Secretary for War had no easy hand to play, dealing with affairs of the army which always lay close to the Hanoverian heart; and some clashes over appointments[4] and anxieties over the auxiliary forces preceded the monarch's disapproval of the conduct of strategy itself. It was ironical that Dundas came to share that last sentiment from his own point of vantage. But he was responsible for implementing the plans; the results did not commend themselves; and the King, increasingly recalcitrant throughout the campaign of 1800, showed himself particularly strongly opposed to the expedition for Egypt. The fact that his opinion had to be taken more frequently as the Cabinet had to be more

---

1. Cf. I, 180–3, Ch. XIX, section IV.

2. To Castlereagh, 14 January 1801 (*Correspondence of Cornwallis*, III, 331). Dundas too had once remarked, though under different circumstances – probably in 1798 (see p. 175, n3 above) – that 'sooner or later he [the King] must make up his mind', on the Irish Catholic question, to what he described as 'the plainest of all political truths' (to Pitt, nd; P.R.O. 30/8/157). But, he continued, that would mean careful as well as firm handling.

3. Camden's account (Willis, op. cit., 256).

4. Eg p. 319, n5 above.

frequently consulted,[1] and that he was then obliged reluctantly still to accede, brought his underlying uneasiness and the consequent friction to the surface. By the summer he was thoroughly dissatisfied with a situation he could not affect; and the simmering resentment, vented largely on Dundas, naturally bore quite as largely on Pitt.

Unfortunately, in this last instance it met with no discernible result. On the contrary, the King was conscious, as he had been for some time, of a growing inattention on the Minister's part. The long relationship, never personally intimate, had been handled by and large with skill and mutual forbearance from the early years,[2] beyond the Regency crisis, and into the rising tests of war. More lately however, as Pitt himself confessed, 'other Business and want of Health often made him postpone both written and personal communication with the King'.[3] Catholic Emancipation was not the only subject concerned. He had in fact become careless, neglecting to show the monarch even the 'outward marks of respect' of presenting himself with proper frequency at Levees. 'He has regularly been 6 weeks in London', a colleague lamented, without putting in an appearance at a function which office holders were expected to attend and could be followed by a conversation in the closet.[4] Not surprisingly, the atmosphere cooled; the King sought other company from the Cabinet, and when Windham was summoned to Weymouth for a spell in August 1800 there was some speculation that he was being tested as a possible alternative. His 'odd, absent, and unacquiescent manner' did not prove encouraging,[5] and the possibility was indeed remote. When it came to the point, George III might not find it simple to dispose of Pitt – Pitt after all disposed of himself in the event, and in any case the King could still see real benefits from the services to which he had become accustomed: from the celebrated Parliamentary talents, the massive reputation at home and abroad. Such considerations may well have tempered his response to his Minister's first letter in 1801. Nonetheless he had been growing impatient, to an extent that seems indeed to have been recognised, producing some mingled concern and impatience among Ministers in return. Over the past three years, Canning is said to have remarked, 'so many concessions . . . had been made [to the monarch] that Pitt had been obliged to make his stand' in the Catholic dispute.[6] The language from that source was often high-flown: it is hard to tell precisely what the concessions were

1. Cf. p. 457 above.
2. Cf. in particular I, 635–43.
3. To Camden (Willis, op. cit., 255).
4. See op. cit., 256; and cf. I, 181.
5. So at least Thomas Pelham, who was often well informed, told Malmesbury some months later, referring to the King's dissatisfaction 'for a long time' with Pitt's and 'particularly' Grenville's '"authoritative" manners towards him'. Malmesbury himself was said to have been in mind for Foreign Secretary (*Malmesbury*, IV, 22–3).
6. Op. cit., 4. Cf. p. 516 above. He added that 'many important measures had been overruled'. One wonders what he had in mind.

other than in some matters of patronage – always a sign of standing in an area where the monarch could stage a show of strength.[1] Nevertheless the feeling was real: Dundas himself spoke of the King's 'aversion' to Pitt.[2] Each party, if brought to the point, could see the other as a threat to be contained.

And Pitt was not the man, when the issue touched a chord, to wait to fight another day. Surviving as long as he had, he was very often accused of an inordinate love of office. He most certainly enjoyed power – he certainly thought of himself as born to achieve it,[3] and took good care to retain it in his own haughty way. But the same pride could operate, occasionally and suddenly, in an opposite direction: it had done so fleetingly in the affair of Ochakov, and it did so now.[4] After the delays and lack of concentration, and the tactical errors which heightened the odds against his success, he had committed himself and now could not see a withdrawal on acceptable terms. Compromise would be a synonym for retreat, and he preferred to go out on a high note. Such a conception of himself ran deep; it had done so from the start, and in essence it would not fail to the end.

But still, men would very soon be asking, exactly how much might that mean? For, it would soon be evident, the drama was not yet played out. There was more confusion to come, compounding what already existed; and the mystery attached to his resignation did not disappear with the immediate event.

III

In arranging to go as soon as possible, Pitt had proposed that this should be as soon as he had introduced his budget – an appropriate final need and intention –, which he would do on 18 February.[5] Meanwhile Addington set to work to form a Ministry, in which he was able to count on his predecessor's support. Pitt indeed was at great pains to make it clear that, while he had sought Emancipation as a measure of Government, he looked on his resignation as applying to himself alone.[6] He counselled adherence to the incoming Ministry – membership if

1. Cf. I, 641–2. And see Lord Holland's *Memoirs of the Whig Party*, I, 92.
2. According to the memoirs of Lady Anne Barnard (née Lindsay), who was often in his company; quoted by Mackesy, op. cit., 198.
3. And cf. p. 455 above.
4. See II, 30–1 for Ochakov. Bland Burges pointed an apparently paradoxical conclusion in retrospect for 1801. It was Pitt's 'Extraordinary adherence to power and place' that explained 'the true cause of his resign.' (Bland Burges Mss, Box 73–4).
5. Rose to Pretyman, 6 February 1801; Pretyman Ms 435/44.
6. P. 507 above. There may indeed have been 'matter . . . of consideration How those who even had not agreed to it should act' when he resigned (Camden, in Willis, op. cit., 257) interesting allusion to an idea of collective responsibility; but this, if briefly entertained, was most unlikely in this case, particularly given his own attitude, to be seriously held.

invited, loyalty in any case. But, as he knew in at least a few instances, some others were resolved to leave as well. The five colleagues who had sided with him on the vote in Cabinet – Grenville, Dundas, Windham, Spencer, Camden – tendered their resignations; Dundas, in any case long tired of his post, apparently feeling particularly strongly a debt of honour after the guidance given to Cornwallis in November 1799, and all agreeing that the recent circumstances gave them no choice.[1] Among others who opted to go once arrangements had been made for their successors were Cornwallis and Castlereagh – naturally – in Ireland, and four men who felt a personal loyalty to the Minister: George Rose, Charles Long, Canning, and Canning's friend Granville Leveson Gower. These last went without Pitt's approval and indeed against his wish.[2] But there was no concerted move in general,[3] and he did all he could to ease the path for his successor – the incumbent he expected to advise – at a critical time.

Everything therefore was set for a smooth transition; and indeed Addinton himself, for all his improbabilities, would have seemed to the outgoing Minister to bring several advantages over and above his presumed dependence. He was not cumbered like some of the more likely choices with an awkward record on Irish Catholic relief. He was not implicated in the Cabinet's damaging quarrels over strategy and the question of peace. And – a salvaging point for a politician – he had been chosen as much by his predecessor as by the King. At this curious moment therefore he went far towards suiting them both; and in fact their relations were now on a conspicuously cordial plane. The Minister gave the monarch his full due for acting from conscience – as did also the colleagues who resigned – while George III went out of his way to reciprocate at Court. When Pitt appeared at the Levee on 11 February, for the first time since the correspondence, the King was profuse in his praises – 'you have acted throughout this business like *yourself*, and *more* I cannot say'; 'I don't care who hears me – . . . I cannot say too much of your conduct' – and on receiving the report of the final piece of Parliamentary business which the outgoing Chancellor had stayed to

1. Dundas remarked that if he had abandoned his 'pledge', he could not have walked the streets as a gentleman (Matheson, op. cit., 300). For the resigners' agreed view see Willis, op. cit., 257.

2. He 'wished most anxiously all his private and personal friends to remain in office' (Rose's diary for 5 February; *Rose*, I, 291), and see for him and the others op. cit., 296–8, 308, 366–9; Long to Pitt, 4 February 1801 (Dacres Adams Mss, formerly P.R.O. 30/58/4) and see also *L.C.G. III*, III, no 2339n5; Canning to Rev. William Leigh, 7 February (Canning Ms 15), same to Rev. John Sneyd, 14 February (Bagot, op. cit., I, 180), Pitt to Canning, 15 February 1801 (Canning Ms 30). For Cornwallis see his *Correspondence*, III, 337; for Castlereagh his *Memoirs and Correspondence*, IV, 49–50.

3. One other young man resigned, in his case from the Board of Control for India to which he had been recently appointed. This was Buckingham's heir and Grenville's nephew Temple.

conduct, he wrote a letter that was highly unusual, and worthy of note.[1]

> My Dear Pitt, as You are closing much to my Sorrow Your Political Career, I cannot help expressing the joy I feel that the Ways and Means for the present Year have this Day been agreed in the Committee without any Debate and apparently to the Satisfaction of the House
>
> George R

These few lines in point of fact were remarkable in three respects. The style of address was unique, in Pitt's experience and that of any Minister since the young King's callow days with Bute had ended over thirty years before. At the same time, the opening phrase showed firmly George III's view of what had occurred.[2] He did not expect to see Pitt in office again. He had won, and he was profoundly and genuinely grateful that he had been allowed to do so without a bitter struggle on this most personal of issues. And thirdly, the letter, showing the familiar grasp of the forms and content of business, was written on the eve, indeed in the dawning stage, of an unforeseen and alarming event.

Since 13 February the King had not been well, and on the 17th he was rather hurried in his manner.[3] On the 18th itself, when he wrote to Pitt, he seemed to be quite in order; but the next evening his behaviour was odd, though he then took a Privy Council calmly and afterwards talked for two hours to one of the prospective Ministers. But that was the last such occasion for a time. On the 20th and 21st the symptoms of the earlier attack, in 1788, showed ever more clearly, and on the 22nd it had to be recognised that the King was in the grip of his past affliction. No one could tell how long that might last. But as things stood Pitt and his colleagues would remain in office, for they had not been able to return their Seals and take formal leave, while Addington and some of his future colleagues had been sworn in at the Council but had not kissed hands. The crisis mounted, superimposed on the wider domestic and foreign crisis. On the night of the 22nd the King was delirious; and while his condition thereafter fluctuated bafflingly, he was hidden from view, with distressing reports, over the rest of the month.

1. The account of the Levee of 11 February, written by Pretyman, is printed in Ashbourne, op. cit., 315–16; the King's letter, of the 18th, often quoted since, in Stanhope, III, Appendix, xxxii–iii. I have quoted it in its expressive original style from P.R.O. 30/8/104.

The King was alluding to the fact that the Minister's budget motions passed unanimously; the first time, according to Rose (to Pretyman, 6 February 1801; Pretyman Ms 435/44) that this had happened in seventeen years.

2. As Bagehot was the first to observe when the document was published, in his review of Stanhope's final two volumes on their appearance (*The Collected Works of Walter Bagehot*, ed. Norman St John Stevas, XIV (1986), 255–6).

3. For the rest of this paragraph see Ida Macalpine & Richard Hunter, *George III and the Mad-Business* (1969), 111–20. And cf. I, 644 for October 1788.

Confusion and uncertainty were inevitable. In one vital respect they were held at bay; they were not allowed to disrupt the immediate conduct of the war. Problems might naturally arise: some diplomats for instance who had received news of Grenville's departure were starting to send despatches to his successor.[1] But the business had to be sustained; the King's Government must go on; and fortunately fleets and armies were largely in hibernation. Matters were dealt with sensibly, producing some unusual constitutional arrangements. Each Cabinet seems to have met on its own – Addington's at a dinner on 17 February and apparently at a meeting on the 22nd, Pitt's on the 22nd and perhaps the 25th[2] – but elements of both were joined together on three occasions at any rate, Pitt and Dundas, according to the Addingtonian record, 'attending' twice to give information and minuted once on the same footing as the rest.[3] Two substantial decisions were in fact taken, or confirmed, in this brief period. The Channel fleet, now in readiness, was ordered to sail for the Baltic; and the Portuguese were told, finally and categorically, that they could expect no further British reinforcement, and if they judged it necessary were therefore free to make peace.[4]

Urgent continuity, as might have been expected, was thus preserved. But the situation could scarcely be allowed to drag on. Indeed it must be resolved if the King did not recover fully within the next few weeks, for the Government would then be unable to meet some of its statutory charges for which the royal assent was required. The Treasury experts, Pitt and Rose, reckoned after a time that unless George III was shown to be *'quite well'* before 12 March a Regent must thereafter be in position, for that purpose specifically and of course for the royal sanction to all relevant business.[5] This was only a cloud on the horizon in the second half of

1. Eg in the important cases of Austria and Prussia; see P.R.O., F.O. 7/62, 64/60.

2. Pellew, op. cit., I, 347; Aspinall, 'The Cabinet Council, 1783–1835', 149; Windham's diary for 22 February (B.L. Add. Ms 37924).

3. Aspinall, loc. cit., 149 and n3. Referring to one of these occasions, at which 'two Prime Ministers' as well as other duplicates were present, he called it 'surely the most extraordinary Cabinet meeting ever held'.

The Addingtonian meetings produced Minutes, prospectively for the King's eye as required by the nature of the subjects (cf. I, 629), which are printed from the papers of Grenville's nominated successor, in *L.C.G. III*, III, no. 2371n2. None is dated there, but on the first occasion, on 22 February, Dundas's presence was required in particular since 'he only', as the relevant Secretary of State (cf. p. 367 above), could sign the instructions for the fleet for which see immediately below. Grenville was invited to attend, as Pitt had been (Hawkesbury to Grenville, 22 February 1801; B.L. Add. Ms 69067), but did not do so.

4. Cf. p. 391 above. The advice to Portugal was indeed to seek terms; if however she did not, and was invaded, Parliament would be asked to approve a subsidy of £300,000 and a loan to be negotiated in the City if possible for £500,000, for which she had been asking.

5. *Rose*, I, 327, for 5 March. The date turned on the latest day in the Parliamentary calendar to which an examination of the physicians, by the Privy Council or representatives of the House of Commons, could be deferred. A bill would have to become law by the 23rd of the month. See also on 'the money business' *Colchester*, I, 246.

February. But the whole question was brought more swiftly into focus by the prospective Regent himself.

For the Prince of Wales of course now emerged on the scene. When the King's incapacity was acknowledged, he requested Addington to call on him at once, and Pitt on the following day.[1] The former stalled however, and it was the latter who then went to Carlton House. The meeting was not likely to be easy, and the Minister seems to have ensured that it was not: he was said to have been 'more stiff and less accommodating than he should have been'.[2] The former Regency crisis, the Prince's debts, not least Ministers' politeness to his wife – Pitt himself took care to call at her house at Blackheath from time to time[3] – lay between two men who were poles apart by nature and one of whom was awkward and shy. Pitt made it clear, when asked, that he was still *'de facto* in the situation of Minister', and, speaking as such, that the Prince should not consult with Opposition. Summoned again three days later, he followed this by saying that if he had to introduce a Regency bill it would be closely on the lines of that passed in 1789. The Prince in point of fact knew by then that his old claim of Right[4] would no longer be accepted by responsible figures – Portland, Spencer, Loughborough – once its supporters but now long ensconced in Government. There was therefore likely to be no alternative to Parliamentary sanction, and he appeared accordingly if reluctantly to acquiesce.[5] How he would have acted in the event it is impossible to say. He managed to talk several times to Addington; he saw much of Moira, whom indeed he named to Pitt as an adviser; and there were, as was to be expected, 'great flockings of minor politicians to Carlton House'. There was in fact a flurry of Cabinet making, which reached the stage of lists. But all in that quarter was in flux;[6] all must wait on events.

It is not impossible indeed that Pitt himself might have been called on to stay if a Regency had been required. In the mass of surmise – of rumour, notes and memoranda – one proposal, approved it seems by the Prince, recommended such a course on the basis that Emancipation would not be raised again during such a period, whatever might conceivably follow in a new reign. In that case, with the issue disposed of, the King on a presumed recovery would surely wish to turn again to the superior abilities of his former Ministry.[7] Whether or not Pitt himself

1. *The Correspondence of George Prince of Wales, 1770–1812*, ed. A. Aspinall, IV (1967), nos. 1590–1.

2. This was Pelham's account (*Malmesbury*, IV, 17).

3. Perforce joining in the parlour games which she enjoyed (see eg Lady Minto's account of an evening in August 1799 (*Life and Letters of Sir Gilbert Elliot*, III, 61)). Blackheath of course lay not inconveniently on the road to Holwood; see eg *A.C.*, IV, 88.

4. See I, 653–4.

5. *Rose*, I, 311, 317, 325–6.

6. See Aspinall in *Correspondence of Prince of Wales*, op. cit., 182–5 for a useful synopsis.

7. The paper, undated and written in a copper-plate hand with the words 'Apd, GP' in the Prince's hand at the head, is now in the Royal Archives at Windsor (RA 3/77). It may be taken as referring to this time, though precisely at what point it does not disclose; and

knew anything of such a plan, one cannot say without fresh evidence; one may perhaps judge that he did not. He seems never to have given any sign of doing so; there seems to be no record of contact beyond the two meetings mentioned – and in fact the Prince then told Addington that he might '*look to him*';[1] – and though the idea seems to have been heard of on 'good authority',[2] its circulation would appear to have been limited and brief. If the possibility *was* disclosed to him, or mentioned, or hinted, it could have been a factor bearing on his subsequent behaviour. But in all the circumstances, the document might be thought to have been a 'position paper', to be held in reserve against possible need.

However that might be, and while Carlton House continued to buzz with projects, the Minister for his part made a further seemingly unexpected move. On 2 March George III's illness reached a point of crisis which appeared to threaten his life, but in fact proved to be the turning point towards a recovery as swift as that in 1789.[3] Pitt was almost certainly already uneasy about the effect produced by his resignation. A report that now reached him from Buckingham House seems to have brought him to the point. For he was told in the next few days by one of the attendants that the monarch, reviving and taking an interest once more, asked 'how much' he had been 'affected, "for he must know to what causes all my illness has been owing." '[4] The Minister, 'struck extremely with this relation', responded at once. He asked for a message to be given to the King that, whether in or out of office, he would not himself 'bring forward' the Catholic question again, and would try to defer it if 'agitated' by others, in the course of the present reign; and the pledge was repeated in his name some months later by George Rose.[5]

seems to be genuine, though the source and later provenance are unknown. I am most grateful to Miss P.M. Clark and to Professor I.R. Christie for the opportunity to see the document after it came to light. Its interest is perhaps greatest as a possible pointer to the Prince's subsequent political judgment in a similar situation.

1. Abbot's account of Addington's conversation at the time (*Colchester*, I, 249).
2. See *Glenbervie*, I, 180, for 24 February.
3. Cf. I, 662.
4. This is the phrase as given by Charles Abbot, who was seeing a great deal of Addington, was a prospective junior member of his Ministry, and had the story from him (*Colchester*, I, 255). The remark had been made to the younger Willis, the son and assistant of the 'mad-house' clerical doctor of 1788–9 (see I, 652–3) who was called in again now, much to the King's distress. Malmesbury (IV, 30) gives a more dramatic and much quoted version, it would seem on lesser authority.
5. See Pretyman to Rose, 14, 18 August 1801 (*Rose*, I, 426–7). The attendant concerned, the elder Willis, gave the message, and wrote to Pitt that the King exclaimed, 'Now my mind will be at ease' (Stanhope, III, 304–5, from a letter in Dacres Adams Mss, formerly P.R.O. 30/58/4, nd but from internal evidence 6 March). The Bishop was not happy; he thought that a statement of such importance should be repeated with complete precision through a more reliable channel, and Rose did this, in terms prepared beforehand, when he saw George III at Weymouth in August (the text is given in *Rose*, I, 360, in the form of a letter; but the original ms, in B.L. Add. Ms 42772, is inscribed 'Substance of what I shall say to the King', and see also Rose to Pretyman, 16 August, 9 September 1801; Pretyman Ms 435/44). For the message via Willis see also Ashbourne, op. cit., 318n1.

Sir Walter Farquhar. *Engraved W. Sharp after Raeburn*

Lady Hester Stanhope, by family tradition *Unknown*

Walmer Castle

Pitt as Colonel of Volunteers. *Acquatint by Joseph Stadler*

Several people knew of the promise: according to Pretyman they included Addington, and Malmesbury heard of it within forty-eight hours from Pelham, who seems to have had the news from the Duke of York, to whom the King himself had spoken.[1] But it was certainly not bruited abroad, and Pitt, notably, did not tell Grenville, who was then at Dropmore.[2] In so far as it *was* known or rumoured, it caused further surprise. After all that had happened, after Pitt and four Cabinet colleagues had summarily resigned, he had, it seemed equally summarily, abandoned the declared cause. Why did he do it? The question has often been repeated since. The King himself said later that he was surprised by the extent of the concession, and also by Pitt's own comment on it when the two men met again. He was indeed then taken aback, after what he had been told, by a remark from the Minister that he had acted as he did 'for private reasons of his own'; a statement which George III naturally found disappointing and was also obscure. Exactly when that occurred is not certain.[3] If it was soon after the message had been conveyed, it may have been simply an instance

1. Pretyman to Rose, 14 August 1801 (Stanhope, III, 304); *Malmesbury*, IV, 31–2, for 7 March.

2. Grenville 'confirmed' to Fox three years later, when their relations had grown warm, 'the extraordinary fact of Pitt never having told him of his offer to continue without Catholic Emancipation, in the year 1801' (Fox to Grey, 19 April 1804; *Memorials and Correspondence of Charles James Fox*, ed. Lord John Russell, IV, (1854), 45, and see also 20). The statement is plain enough; and certainly Grenville's cousin and associate Lord Carysfort did not learn of the presumed pledge until the summer or autumn of 1803 (see *H.M.C., Dropmore*, VII, 193) – though one must remember that he had been absent as Minister in Berlin at the time (cf. p. 393, n2 above). Grenville's firm conviction of the need for Irish Catholic representation in Parliament – much firmer now than Pitt's – may well have been the cause of his not being informed explicitly of an event of which he must have heard rumours; one that was mentioned at once by the King himself, and known to enough people of secondary importance – the Willises, Rose, Pretyman – to prevent it being fully concealed.

3. The evidence is itself obscure. Pelham recounted the story later, in September 1809, when he was told it by the King (see *L.C.G. III*, III, xix, n1). But *when* had the King heard Pitt say this? According to Pelham, it was when the two men 'met again' after the assurance was given. It might therefore have been within a matter of weeks, when Pitt finally took his leave. But equally it might not have been until three years later, when we know that the subject was discussed between them, possibly for the first time, in (or soon after) May 1804. George III told Rose the story in August of that year, quoting Pitt's remark as something 'lately told him', the remark itself being, in Rose's italics, that 'he [Pitt] had *now private reasons* for not reviving the subject'; and when Rose expressed surprise, the King 'said he was sure he had not mistaken Mr. Pitt' (*Rose*, II, 157). He told the same story the next month, this time to Glenbervie (*Glenbervie*, I, 389), using the words 'lately' and 'upon the late occasions', though the account does not mention the word 'now' in Pitt's remark, itself given rather differently – 'Pitt declared to him that not only from regard to his Majesty but also for private reasons of his own, he was resolved never to stir the question'. It may be therefore that the matter was not raised, or that Pitt did not then make this particular remark, at an earlier point, and that when he did so it related to his circumstances, which had changed, by or at the later time.

of the social awkwardness to which Pitt could be prone; on the other hand, he was usually disposed to be watchful of the King. Later explanations have varied, once more, of the message itself. The hostile case was put perhaps most cogently by the great historian Lecky: the move perfectly suited Pitt's interests, enabling him to escape any continuing commitment to the Irish Catholics and to preserve his own political future intact.[1] Prosecuting counsel might possibly seek further aid in some circumstantial speculation. If Pitt knew that he might have been summoned in a Regency, but with a veto on Emancipation,[2] that could have eased his way towards a pledge to the King, extended though it was to a reign. And he might indeed have wondered how long the reign itself would last, after this second frightening collapse.

There could also be a less hypothetical submission to insert into such a case. For Pitt had in fact already been considering whether he should not change his mind. On 24 February he admitted that 'what had happened to the King in some sort shook his determination', formed when or after he resigned, 'never to come into office without full permission to propose' Emancipation once more. He also confessed that he had formed his view on the measure at the turn of the year from only a 'few people',[3] and agreed apparently that the final decision in Cabinet had been 'hasty'.[4] Altogether therefore he was being led into tentative second thoughts; a fact which could have told when he pledged himself in this fresh direction.

The story of Pitt's retirement is full of loose ends, and motives are seldom unmixed. The whole 'intricate affair' indeed, to borrow from a curiously apposite description of a different affair, 'still remains enveloped in all that kind of mystery which ever accompanies events produced more from a concurrence of awkward circumstances, than from fixed design'.[5] In this particular instance, an exclusively hostile explanation can appear coherent in its own terms. At the same time there is consequential evidence that demands attention, and another version of events may be

---

1. *A History of England in the Eighteenth Century*, VIII (1890), 523–5.

2. But see pp. 527–8 above for my reservations here.

3. A practice of which he was accused at the time (cf. p. 192, n3 above for procedure in, probably, 1799) in the case of Ireland, and has been quite recently in comments on the handling of his Irish Propositions in 1785 (see David R. Schweitzer, in *Parliamentary History*, vol. 3, 129–45).

4. Pretyman to Mrs Pretyman, 25 February 1801, reporting a long conversation the night before (Pretyman Ms 435/45). The quotations are of the Bishop's rather than perhaps Pitt's own words. An extract from the letter printed in *English Historical Documents*, XI, 164–5 wrongly attributes it to Rose writing to Mrs Rose; see also Ashbourne, op. cit., 316. Cf. pp. 172–3, 192, n3, 502 above for the Minister's chief sources of advice earlier and for the relevant occasion in Cabinet.

How long and how deeply Pitt had been troubled by the effect on the King it is hard to say. He was reported on the 26th to 'feel it a great deal' though 'too haughty to confess it' (*Malmesbury*, IV, 20, with no authority stated); but Pretyman himself found him 'in higher Spirits' in general at that point than 'he had scarcely ever' seen him.

5. Thomas Paine, *Rights of Man* (1791), 39. He was writing about the people's march on Versailles from Paris in 1789.

suggested, differently proportioned and rather more complex, which takes closer account of an associated final, brief development. For if it was a fact that by his concession Pitt had guarded his future, what was there to stop him from following up his growing hesitation and seeking reinstatement at once? Was it not indeed his patriotic duty to do so? He knew that there was widespread anger as well as bewilderment at his resignation; that it was seen in fact by many as shameful, as deserting his King and country at such a time.[1] And he was left in no doubt of the pressures for his return; Canning, Rose and Pretyman bore down on him, and so now did some of his former colleagues. Dundas, intensely scornful of Addington's capacity, was 'caballing' as the weeks went by; Camden may have joined him; even Loughborough, with reasons of his own, sought to raise the option.[2] Perhaps most telling, strong remonstrances came from the rather unlikely quarter of Portland, who, having not resigned and indeed agreed to continue as Home Secretary, was best placed to act as a bridge and give effective advice. He was clear that Pitt should go back. The Minister had been wrong to resign in the first place, and support for his successor from the back benches was 'idle. Pitt and Office cannot be separated'.[3] Even the Duke of York weighed in, through the active channel of Tom Pelham.[4] Such intimations could not but have an effect. And there was a further consideration, for Addington himself made it clear that his attitude to Emancipation was pragmatic. He told prospective colleagues that he wished to avoid 'the *abstract question*'; 'it was enough . . . that *now* was *not* the time'.[5] In such circumstances, therefore, Pitt had gone quite as far as was needed in giving his promise. On every public ground, it could be argued, he would be right to offer to resume the reins.

1. According to Pretyman, he half acknowledged this in the conversation recorded in p. 530, n4 above. Mrs Pretyman for her part was so worried by the prospect of the Minister being actually attacked in the streets on the 'pretence' of his conduct over Emancipation, at a time already of marked disaffection caused by the price and dearth of bread, that she begged her husband not to go out with him in his carriage (nd, but endorsed 8 February 1801; Pretyman Ms 435/45).

Pitt was also being blamed for the Cabinet's laxity in not having 'prepared the way in the Closet for the measure' in the first instance and coped better with these whom '*they knew to exist in their very bosom*' (presumably Loughborough at least) who were about the King (Malmesbury to Minto, 10 February 1801; NLS Ms 11109. I owe this information to Dr David Wilkinson).

2. For Dundas see *L.C.G. III*, III, no. 2346, n1 on p. 488, Ashbourne, op. cit., 322–3, *Colchester*, I, 258; for Loughborough, *Rose*, II, 334 (and for his reasons, p. 553, n3 below); for Canning, Ashbourne, op. cit., 319–21, *Malmesbury*, IV, 34–7; for Rose and Pretyman, working in tandem, *Rose*, I, 317, 329, Pretyman to Mrs Pretyman as in p. 530, n4 above, two letters from Rose to Pretyman of 28 February 1801 in Pretyman Ms 435/44. Grenville, by contrast, held aloof at Dropmore. Spencer was upset by the effect on the King of Pitt's resignation (*Malmesbury*, IV, 20), but I do not know if he expressed an opinion on a possible return.

3. *Malmesbury*, IV, 43–4.

4. Op. cit., 37–8.

5. *Colchester*, I, 240–1, for 18, 20 February. The quotations, with the emphases, are Abbot's.

But that did not happen. He wavered at first. While others were canvassing an amended Ministry, to include elements from both Cabinets,[1] he allowed an approach to Addington to see if that unfortunate man would agree to stand down. Portland was the medium. Hardly surprisingly, the suggestion was rebuffed. After being urged to come in by both the King and Pitt, having given up the safe and lucrative Speakership, and formed his Ministry, and tasted importance, Addington was in no mood to be dismissed. If others were prepared to speak to the monarch, that was their affair.[2] And when Pitt was informed of this reaction, he withdrew at once into himself. He was naturally sensitive to the dilemma, and indeed uncertain what Addington could be offered in lieu.[3] As it was, the rejoinder seems finally to have dictated how he himself should act.

Nor was this surprising. For, by now encumbered with embarrassments, as he himself observed,[4] the episode pointed Pitt towards a decision which in fact he may have preferred. His options had become mutually exclusive. On one side lay genuine immediate sympathy for the King and probably some sense of guilt now adequately purged, together with a call to duty impelled by affairs both abroad and at home. It was clear to all that a new, obscure Minister was a poor refuge in the current storms; it was also clear to most that the King should be preserved in possession of his faculties if a Government flavoured with Opposition, in whatever degree, was to be kept out. For even if Pitt was aware – which may be thought distinctly doubtful – that the Prince might turn to him, he could scarcely count on that when ostensible signs from Carlton House pointed the other way. In any case, whatever George III's drawbacks as Ministers might see them, he was far preferable to a Regent as unpredictable as his heir. Disinterested and interested reasons combined to argue a formidable case. On the other side however, to go back would be seen as a surrender to the forces against which he had resigned. It could also be seen as an ultimate, shabby betrayal of the Irish Catholics;[5] it would remove any prospect of desirable private rest; and it might, in his view, reduce the chances of successful peace talks, to be conducted otherwise with his guidance but by another hand. The difficulties were genuine. But with Addington's answer his course seemed clear. He had done his best to ease the King's mind, which would also offer an additional opening at some point for his own return: he would now leave it to others (like Addington

---

1. Dundas's list is printed in Feiling, *The Second Tory Party*, 399–400. It shows himself freed at last from his former post as Secretary of State, and possibly retained at the India Board with a seat in Cabinet.

2. *Colchester*, I, 258–9.

3. Ibid; *Rose*, I, 329. And see Dundas to Thomas Pelham, 11 March 1801 (B.L. Add. Ms 33107).

4. Pelham's account of a conversation with him on 9 March (*Malmesbury*, IV, 38–9).

5. For perhaps a greater sensitivity on Pitt's part now to this aspect of the question see *Malmesbury*, IV, 38. Cf. p. 511 above.

in a contrary sense) to pave the way for such a step. He would not press – he would not stoop to press – for office. If he was to accept it, Addington must withdraw voluntarily and the King in turn show that he willingly approved. This, at the end, was a settled conviction. By these and maybe other signs, he must be made to feel that he was called by the country itself.[1]

Such an attitude may be seen as high-minded or less than high-minded depending on one's starting point: as a final evasion, on lines already suggested at his resignation by critics, or on the contrary as embodying the 'Character' by which Pitt always set such store. It certainly struck a central chord; it satisfied his conception of himself, and after the hesitations, the weighing of choices and contradictory impulses, it may have come as a relief from the continual compromises of power.[2] He reverted swiftly to his earlier stance. Addington should stay undisturbed. When he was told on 9 March that George III would like to see him the next day, before any other politician, he declined to go until his successor had been received.[3] It was not until the 14th that he had his own audience, and delivered the Seals which he had been given on 19 December 1783.

1. See his interesting conversation with Pelham, riding in from Wimbledon to Downing Street on 9 March. His 'principal' difficulty was now 'how Addington would feel it' (ibid).

Rose told Loughborough, when the latter was sounding the possibility of a return (p. 531 and n2 above), that in his 'clear conviction' Pitt could not 'again be the King's Minister till called upon by the country to come forward' (*Rose*, I, 335). He must have known Pitt's mind, and Pitt, when told, agreed 'most heartily'.

2. Cf. II, 31, 41; and for his subsequent invocations of 'Character' see p. 565 below.

3. *Rose*, I, 339–40.

CHAPTER XVI

Domestic Interlude

I

On 15 March 1801 Pitt became 'a Free Man' for the second time in his career.[1] He moved to a small furnished house in Park Place, at the western upper end of St James's Street, taking over the remainder of a one-year lease from a retiring Under Secretary at the Foreign Office, Edward Fisher. This was his base in town for the next twelve months or so, and the rent is unlikely to have been high. He moved thereafter, perhaps in April 1802 though not in regular occupancy before October, to a small house, 14 York Place in the northern end of Baker Street, for which he paid an annual rent of £210. These successive sums were an addition to his expenses which he had long been spared.[2] Small as they were, they could not be brushed aside, for the first consequence of resignation was the urgent need to look to his finances.

These had seldom engaged his attention until the past year. When his private secretaries had remonstrated, as Pretyman and then Joseph Smith did at intervals, he would agree that he should mend his ways; but he never did so for long.[3] By the summer of 1800, however, things had come to a pass that seriously alarmed those who were watching the process. George Rose, brought in despairingly by Smith, found such 'A History of Debts and Distresses as actually sickened me'. To his horror, there appeared to be an immediate danger of bailiffs in Downing Street: of 'an Execution or something as bad' for £600 and an 'unpleasant expose' of another £400, and this after Pitt's 'diamonds' had been sold – alas, less

---

1. Cf. I, 105.

2. He had paid no rent or 'coals and candles' in Downing Street. For the move to Park Place see Stanhope, III, 313. One may identify its location – for there was another street of that name, recently built near the Marylebone Road on the line of what is now Baker Street – from a reference to Pitt being a 'neighbour' of Spencer's at Spencer House (in St James's Place); see Thomas Grenville to Lord Grenville, 24 February 1802 (*H.M.C., Dropmore*, VII, 80). The house, said to have been no. 12, has disappeared; as a modest terraced building on short lease it would not have attracted a high rent. Fisher left London in February 1801 for Lisbon, where he became Secretary to the Legation under Frere (for whom see p. 391, n4 above).

The house in York Place is now marked by a plaque. The rent appears in lists of expenses assembled by Joseph Smith (Saumarez Smith Mss).

3. See Ch. III, section II above.

534

rewardingly than his great-grandfather's famous Indian stone – to meet pressing claims for a further £680. Such minor sums showed the small extent of his immediate resources. But of course 'The Evil' went much deeper, '& a Cure should be attempted without delay'.[1] Others had said the same before; but the possibility of attention this time looked rather greater, for Pitt himself appeared at last to be worried. Rose indeed attributed the strain which produced his collapse in October partly to his private affairs.[2] The immediate hope was disappointed, by that event and the continuing load of public business. But his retirement from office meant that the situation must be faced.

The anxious little group gathered round. So far as could be seen in the previous summer, the debts then amounted to some £46,000, of which it was reckoned in October that some £12,000 was in tradesmen's bills. Somehow or other by March 1801 all but £500 worth of these last were paid.[3] But the calculations at that time soon proved, once more, to be highly optimistic;[4] and what was to be done about the bulk of the obligations, amassed over so many years? The only capital asset of any note was Holwood, which however was also a 'Sink of Expense'.[5] It should therefore really be sold to help meet the deficit and effect retrenchment. Pitt's much loved personal retreat in that case would disappear. But the sacrifice would still fall far short of the demands; something more must be found, to clear up the past and shield him against the future. Four possibilities could be envisaged: a vote from Parliament to pay off the debts; a gift of money from the King, as in the case of North in 1777; a private subscription among his friends; the bestowal of some place for life. The difficulty would be to persuade him to accept any of these ideas.[6]

They were not in fact new: all had been put forward while the Minister was still in power, and the only one he would then consider, and that very

1. Rose to Pretyman, 21 July, 18 October 1801 (Pretyman Ms 435/44; the first printed in précis in Holland Rose, II, 475). Some at least of the figures on which he worked may be found in B.L. Add. Ms 42772, ff. 231–61.

The diamonds were set in gold boxes which Pitt had received as presents from foreign rulers.

2. Rose to Pretyman, 18 October 1801 (n1 above).

3. Figures to the nearest thousand and in the third instance hundred pounds. Rose to Pretyman, 21 July 1801 (n1 above); Pretyman to Rose, 24 July 1801 (B.L. Add. Ms 42773); bills categorised in detail in lists for 10 October 1800 and 25 March 1801 in Saumarez Smith Mss (aj, ak, am). See also some evidence in P.R.O. 30/8/218, and cf. a summary of demands to the latter date with a slightly lesser total in B.L. Add. Ms 42772, f. 229.

4. Cf. p. 76 above.

5. This can indeed be verified from the relative domestic expenses of London and Holwood detailed in P.R.O. 30/8/219 part 6. Taking the most recent year, 25 June 1799–25 June 1800, the former are given as £7,365 and the latter as £10,663. Cf. or rather contrast for the eighties I, 598–9.

6. Rose to Joseph Smith, 13 July 1801 (Saumarez Smith Mss); same to Pretyman, 21 July 1801 (Pretyman Ms 435/44).

doubtfully, was the last. Given his personal disdain for such expedients,[1] it would doubtless attract sarcastic comment; but it seemed perhaps less objectionable than the first, which he 'peremptorily declined', or the second which would give or appear to give the King a hold over him as it had done with North, or the third which he argued would appear to entitle the subscribers to his favour.[2] He had dismissed for that reason many years ago a proposal for a gift of £100,000 from the City, when he was far less in debt than he had become since;[3] and while his relationship to his friends and the King in 1801 was different from that in 1800, embarrassments might still arise if he should ever hold a post again. On the other hand, as Pretyman argued, the embarrassment would be immediate if he agreed to accept a sinecure from Addington.[4] When George III offered a very generous gift of £30,000, and was politely refused, there seemed to be no prospect of affording relief in the face of compelling need.[5]

Rose and the Bishop did not give up. On the contrary, since Pitt was not moving, they took matters into their own hands. With Camden's assistance they pressed the case for a select private subscription, meeting at first with no success from the proposed recipient – in fact a greater initial disinclination even than in the case of the offer from the King.[6] Confronted however finally by the inescapable – some of the remaining creditors, by now found to be still numerous, had become 'extremely importunate' – Pitt at length agreed provided that he knew and approved the names involved. Early in August therefore Pretyman told him that six of those most concerned – he himself, Rose, Camden, Tom Steele, Charles Long, and Carrington (Bob Smith) – would see that 'he would suffer no inconvenience or embarrassment'. Thus brought to the point, Pitt consented – one may wonder if he remembered his own alleged joke when Fox had been similarly aided – and summarily 'ended the

---

1. The only sinecure he had accepted, as Lord Warden of the Cinque Ports, came with the King's express command that it was not to be declined; see I, 602, II, 189–90, and for Pitt's attitude in general I, 602–3.

2. Rose to Pretyman, 21 July 1801 (p. 535, n1 above).

3. In 1788; see I, 603n1.

4. Holland Rose, II, 476.

5. The King had asked twice on his recovery in March if Pitt was going to be in financial straits (*Rose*, I, 333, 338). The offer was made to Rose probably in June or early July, with the stipulation that it was to be managed so that the recipient did not suspect its origin. This proved impossible, and while Pitt was and remained genuinely grateful he declined at once (see Rose to Pretyman, 12, 13 July 1801, Pretyman Ms 435/44).

6. Rose to Pretyman, 12, 21, 31 July 1801 (loc. cit.); Camden to Rose, Most Secret 23 July, Rose to Camden draft 26 July, Camden to Rose 28 July 1801 (B.L. Add. Ms 42772); Pretyman to Rose, 24, 26 July 1801 (B.L. Add. Ms 42773). See also Pretyman to Mrs Pretyman, two letters nd (Pretyman Ms 435/45). Some of this correspondence is printed in *Rose*, I, 404–23.

conversation'.[1] The participants 'advanced' their contributions, almost certainly with his knowledge and on his insistence, with a claim on the beneficiary's estate;[2] and without immediately disclosing details to him they approached some others, raising in the end at least £11,700. Five of the original six paid £1,000 apiece and Long £700 in two instalments, with further sums coming from Bathurst, Dundas, the Dukes of Gordon and Buccleuch, Robert Dundas (Chief Baron of the Exchequer in Scotland), Wilberforce and Joe Smith, and also apparently from the Duke of Montagu and 'Mr Hamilton'. Of the wider group, only the Chief Baron and Hamilton appear to have claimed their money after Pitt's death.[3]

So Pitt was saved from 'unpleasantness'. More debt remained, including to his bank. He had long surrendered to Coutts his salary as First Lord of the Treasury, and when the payments, as usual in arrears from the Department, had been completed – which they were in August 1802[4] – neither that nor his revenue as Chancellor of the Exchequer was available any longer to offset what he owed in that quarter. There still remained the income from the Cinque Ports, as yet unattached and the salary worth some £3,000 net, and he talked of 'selling' that in part or of insuring his life and assigning the policy against his borrowings.[5] It was the old sad story,

1. The Bishop's account indeed gives a glimpse of relationships and attitudes on such a subject. 'I instantly said, "Then I believe, Sir, we need not trouble you further; you and J. Smith can engage for the thing being done." Thus ended the conversation' (to Rose, 7 August 1801; Stanhope, III, 346–7).
When a subscription for Fox had been made some years before, without his own knowledge, a question had been raised how he would take it. 'Why, said Pitt [according to the story], why I suppose he will take it quarterly, or perhaps it may be half-yearly' (op. cit., 346).

2. I put it like this because Pitt's will, made on his deathbed, directed that a sum of £12,000 plus interest from October 1801 be paid to (ie divided between) Long, Steele, Carrington, Pretyman, Camden, and Joseph Smith (facsimile in Pretyman Ms 108/45); and a letter from Camden to Rose of 23 July 1801 (p. 536, n6 above) makes it clear that this was indeed a loan, which as such could be charged on his estate.

3. There are minor differences in two accounts here. The most complete list was compiled later by Rose and is given in Stanhope, op. cit., III, 348. The Duke of Montagu and Mr Hamilton (whom I cannot identify further) figure in a letter from Charles Long, who was a channel for some of the contributions, specifying them as claimants (to Chatham, 9 June 1806; Saumarez Smith Mss). His amounts too differ occasionally from Rose's, and he seems to make it clear that one of £200 which Rose uncertainly ascribes to Pepper Arden – by then Lord Alvanley (for whom see I, 107–8, 127–8) – came as a further instalment from Long himself. For Bathurst see I, 592, p. 87 above; for the Duke of Gordon, I, 583. Some of the contributors from Scotland may doubtless have been canvassed by Henry Dundas.

Perhaps not surprisingly in view of the gravity of the case, and after his efforts, Rose was disgusted with the paucity of some of the contributions, above all from Carrington and also from Camden (to Pretyman, 21 July 1801; Pretyman Ms 435/44). Pretyman, from the first group, sought to be repaid after Pitt's death; see Steele to Chatham, 27 June 1806 (Saumarez Smith Mss) and Mrs Tomline's memorandum nd but 1828 (Pretyman Ms 562:1828).

4. Coutts's Ledger 161 (Coutts's Bank). And cf. p. 75 above.

5. See Rose to Pretyman, 12 July 1801 (Pretyman Ms 435/44); Pretyman to Mrs Pretyman, two letters nd but almost certainly July, and 1 August 1801 (Pretyman Ms 435/45); same to Rose, 7 August 1801 (Stanhope, III, 347–8).

even 'if', as Pretyman put it, 'he resolves to do something'.[1] But something was done at any rate to reduce his current overdraft at the bank over the next three years, with the aid of payments raised probably on the life insurance of which he had talked.[2] Moreover, Holwood was sold. The price did not reach his initial expectations. He brought up the idea, apparently for the first time, in July 1801, citing a figure however – probably £20–24,000 – which Rose found optimistic; but he was not keen to proceed for a year, either with that or with a sale of some of his Cinque Ports' income,[3] and in the event the property was put up for auction in October 1802. It went for £15,000 to a Mr George Pocock who took possession six months later.[4] It is hard to tell if anything more was done to raise funds, by disposals on which to raise fresh loans. Once the pressure was removed, in fact, the distasteful subject seems to have been dropped. It is perhaps symptomatic of the situation, following the carthartic experience of 1801, that no further systematic record of Pitt's household expenses survives in the files.[5]

Nonetheless, some running economies were made. Pitt had professed himself ready to manage on a much lower income, and although the prospect seemed highly unlikely to those who knew the facts best – 'Conceive . . . Mr Pitt living upon £1,000 a year'; the attempt would only run him 'still further into debt'[6] – he did succeed in shedding some of his costs. Even before Holwood was sold, his household servants there had been reduced to one footman, one groom with a boy, a cook and one housemaid with a charwoman occasionally; he had parted with his carriage horses, and when in London jobbed by the week or month in 'a common chaise'.[7]

1. Pretyman to Rose as in p. 537, n5 above.

2. Coutts's Ledgers 143, 152, 161, 203–4. In March 1802 he received a sum from a Company 'on Minet & Co' – the well known insurance house – and this continued, at £300 a year, on the same security thereafter. An estimate by Pitt of expenses and income in January 1802 survives in Stanhope Ms U1590 S5 C44.

3. Rose to Pretyman, 12 July 1801 (Pretyman Ms 435/44); same to Joseph Smith, 13 July 1801 (Saumarez Smith Mss); Pretyman to Mrs Pretyman, nd and 1 August 1801 (Pretyman Ms 435/45). The figure for Holwood may in fact have been suggested by Smith, and Pitt himself soon revised it downwards.

4. See Lord Cranworth (then living at Holwood, by then in a different house near the old site) to Stanhope, 5 September 1860 (Stanhope Ms U1590 S5 60/6); 'Minutes as to Sale of Holwood' (loc. cit., S5 C44). The last part of the payment was made, with interest for delay, in June 1803. Stanhope (III, 349) calls Pocock 'Sir George'; in the Minutes he is Mr. Perhaps he was the man who sat silently for Bridgwater in the Commons for some twenty-three years, finally achieving a baronetcy in 1821?

5. P.R.O. 30/8/202–3, 218 contain the last such lists surviving in point of date.

6. Rose to Pretyman, 12 July 1801 (Pretyman Ms 435/44); Pretyman to Mrs Pretyman, nd (loc. cit., 435/45).

7. Rose to Pretyman, 23 August 1802 (loc. cit., 435/44); and see also Pitt to Canning, nd but endorsed August 1801 (Canning Ms 30). One newspaper spotted the common chaise in the summer of 1801 (*The Morning Post*, 1 July). There were seven servants on the books at Holwood in 1800 (P.R.O. 30/8/202). Taking the tax on their wages as a basis, this was therefore a return to the situation in his early days in office (see I, 599).

Such savings were of course made possible by the change of circumstance which made them desirable. There was no further need to maintain an establishment in the 'vast awkward House' in Downing Street,[1] or even one at Holwood equal to the incessant movements of colleagues and friends. 'London incidentals', including 'London stables'; official dinners – no small burden when they occurred, to judge by bills of fare; even the quota of Court dresses required not least for continual wear in the Commons, could now also presumably be curtailed.[2] And with Downing Street vacated there must have been less room for books: a matter of by no means marginal significance, for such purchases cost him not insignificant sums.

Pitt does not seem to have added greatly to his library in the later eighties and early nineties.[3] But in the last few years of the century his purchases appear to have taken a spurt, and – perhaps the Grenville brothers were talking to him – he began to have some of his books well bound.[4] The booksellers Thomas Payne and Walter had occasionally repaired or provided some bindings before; but in 1799 the latter executed rather more, and in 1801 Pitt employed the well known Staggemeier for a folio Horace and a Virgil (to be added to the well thumbed quartos and duodecimos of his youth), as well as two sets of plates to voyages and substantial sets of classical French authors. He had tools cut to impress his crest, and some of the volumes survive.[5] The direction of his purchases was also changing to some extent. Of course, as earlier, some current pamphlets and volumes found their way onto his shelves,[6] and he had probably bought some at any rate of the works on agriculture in pursuit of his farming at Holwood. The latter's numbers may have increased as he turned his attention to Walmer; and European, particularly French, titles – historical, legal, literary, including the works of Voltaire in seventy volumes – and military manuals (English and some French) figure prominently in the booksellers' bills and in the list at his death. Again, our knowledge comes largely from the efforts to clear up his debts in the spring of 1801, when books accounted for some £714 out of the grand total at that time of £11,482. Thereafter, as in other areas, the curtain descends once more. We have only a glimpse, not unrevealing, of his

1. See I, 84. Eighteen to nineteen servants (including a private clerk, Robert Betty) were on the books there in 1800 (P.R.O. 30/8/202).

2. Cf. for dress on the Treasury bench I, 40. Items (h) and (l) in a bundle of bills in the Saumarez Smith Mss indicate examples, as do bills of fare in P.R.O. 30/8/219 part 6 for dinners in Downing Street. An estimate in January 1802 of expenses for Walmer, in Pitt's hand (Stanhope Ms U1590 S5 C44), shows a marked drop for living expenses.

3. This paragraph is based largely on the Saumarez Smith Mss, accounts and bills, bundles C(i), I, s, t, aj; also on Pretyman Ms 562:21 and P.R.O. 30/8/215–17.

4. See II, 419. The three brothers were at work in the years at the turn of the century on the plan which resulted in the publication at their expense of a celebrated edition of Homer – one copy of which went to Pitt (Thomas Grenville to Pitt, 20 July 1801; Dacres Adams Mss, formerly P.R.O. 30/58/4).

5. See I, 14n2.
6. Eg pp. 248, n1, 275, n3 above.

reading and the extent to which that developed as later preoccupations were added to the interest in English history, mathematics and above all the classics which predominated at the start and endured throughout.[1]

II

There was therefore scope for savings to set against the loss of income, alienated in any case as some of that had been for almost a decade. Much however would turn on the openings for spending at Pitt's remaining country house. Would his circumstances be seriously bettered when his domestic interests were concentrated there?

Although he sat conspicuously loose to possessions, Pitt must have been affected by the sale of Holwood. His improvements had given him many happy days, and he had unfulfilled ambitions.[2] Fortunately for his spirits, Walmer remained, and he had long shown his liking for it: the place had indeed become something of a retreat in the summer recess. Now it could serve as a base when he was not required or did not wish to be in London. At first there was not much change. Holwood was not put on the market until 1802, and in 1801 itself he was held intermittently in the capital by the demands of the turn-over as agreed with Addington. It was common gossip, though true only in part, that he was consulted by the new Ministry, and he was even seen entering the Treasury, reputedly to give directions to 'the principal Clerks'.[3] He was also spotted killing time sometimes in the unaccustomed role of 'a *Bond-street lounger*', though he had earlier refused the flood of dinner invitations with which he was immediately assailed.[4] He stayed within easy reach for much of the time, going to Holwood and paying visits, including one late in the year to Cambridge where he stayed in the Master's Lodge at Trinity, returning via the Pretymans in the Bishop's palace at Buckden where invited guests were astonished, as so often were those who did not know him, by his range of memory and speed of apprehension, but above all his friendliness and wit.[5] Walmer did not see more of him than usual that year. But from 1802 he settled for longer spells from the spring to the autumn.

1. Cf. I, 576 and n3.
2. Cf. I, 590–4, pp. 85–8 above.
3. Eg *Malmesbury*, IV, 47, 53; *Glenbervie*, I, 220–1, 251, 262, 268. Newspapers naturally took up the strain. The quotation on the Treasury comes from *The Morning Post* of 23 June 1801.
4. Loc. cit., 10 June 1801, and cf. William Wellesley-Pole to his brother Marquess Wellesley on Pitt 'lounging about the streets in the morning, generally by himself' (Iris Butler, *The Eldest Brother* (1973), 262). For the dinner invitations see *Life of Wilberforce*, III, 8.
5. Mrs Pretyman gave a gratified account of her guest at Buckden (memorandum of 17 December 1801; Pretyman Ms 435/29). He certainly made a memorable impression there on the Master of Trinity, Dr Mansel, whom he had missed at Cambridge: 'The Power of Language cannot express what he is'. It was on this occasion too that, in a conversation on the classics, it seemed to the listeners 'as if he had been doing nothing at all in his life but studying Greek and Latin' (see I, 15).

'Air and exercise' were what he had always enjoyed there.[1] That remained the case, though the exercise was diminished at first. Pitt had two relapses in health in 1802, and despite an interval during which he enjoyed riding and shooting and sailing, he was clearly weakened in the late summer; when Canning took his family to stay for some weeks in the Castle's cottage, his own barouche had to take his host for outings in place of a horse. Recovery however, as so often, appeared to be swift: Pitt was soon able to attend a Hunt dinner and to be taken sailing again, his friends resumed their visits, and the parties drove around the coast when they were not inspecting his works at home.[2] For improvements were in hand. The Castle's surroundings were bleak – exposed to the Channel winds, with no garden to speak of; nor in fact did the Lord Warden own any land lying beyond the moat itself. Pitt arranged to rent some forty acres in three parcels, through which at some point he made a path to the beach and a sea walk; and in 1802 planting began. One hundred and thirty-four fruit trees – predominantly nectarines, peaches, pears, plums, and cherries – were bought, with five vines, and by 1805 'Forest trees, shrubs &c. in the different Plantations' shielded and shaded the property to the tune of over £550.[3] Some of the changes were effected with the aid of his niece Hester Stanhope, who went to live with her uncle in August 1803. She helped find specimens, and may once in his absence – so she recalled dramatically many years later – have drafted in soldiers from Dover to level and replant an area which she knew he was hoping to change.[4] The Castle itself, on the other hand, does not seem to have attracted comparable attention, though it may have been given some fresh comforts after the tenures of largely absentee Lords Warden in possession of a small if improved Tudor fort. In the winter of 1804–5 Pitt considered some

---

Cf. I, 107. His conversation with intimates, as always (op. cit., 107–8, 587–9), was uninhibitedly lighthearted. His nephew Mahon, who with his friends saw a good deal of him in these years, recalled it as 'very lively and cheerful' with 'a vast fund' of anecdotes and mimicry, which 'he preferred . . . to that of a graver character' (Stanhope, IV, 85).

1. To Edward Eliot, 13 September [1793]; Stanhope Ms U1590 S5 O7. And cf. II, 292. The Marquess Curzon of Kedleston, *The Personal History of Walmer Castle and Its Lords Warden* (1927), 44, gives a further example of country pursuits.

2. Pitt to Addington, 7 June, same to Dundas, 5 September 1802 (see Curzon, op. cit., 70–2); same to Windham, 8 June (Holland Rose, II, 473); Canning's diary, 31 July–3 August, 13 September–11 October 1802 (Canning Ms 29d); Canning to Grenville, 3 October 1802 (B.L. Add. Ms 69038). The days at sea were reported from time to time in the newspapers, and are mentioned in correspondence.

3. List in Pretyman Ms 562:3. For the leases see Curzon, op. cit., 122–4, 157; they appear to have cost Pitt £30 a year in 1802 (Stanhope Ms U1590 S5 C44). The efforts were worth while. By the late 1820s the Castle was described as having 'a beautiful pleasure ground & quite sheltered by plantations' (*The Journal of Mrs. Arbuthnot 1820–1832*, ed. Francis Bamford and the Duke of Wellington, II (1950), 294).

4. *Memoirs of the Lady Hester Stanhope in Conversations with her Physician . . .*, II (1845), 66–7. For another example in the same cause see Stanhope's *Miscellanies, Second Series* (1872), 76.

plans for enlargement;[1] but they were too expensive, and if an alternative was put in hand it did not affect his own quarters. He occupied a gloomy, rather cramped upstairs study, with no view and an adjacent 'slip' of a bedroom.[2] His normal architectural inclinations seem to have been intermittent and perforce restrained.

Greater opportunities offered with farming, also long a lively interest. He expanded earlier modest operations in 1802, a bumper year at last for corn.[3] The results were a regular object of inspection by visitors, and of study and inquiry by himself: he had a country gentleman's collection of agricultural works and was held by a neighbouring recognised expert to be the best gentleman farmer he had come across;[4] and as at Holwood 'the farm' formed an important element of the economy as well as of his pleasures. Whether the operations were successful, or to what extent, it is impossible to tell. Pitt was thought to have spent an average of just under £2,000 a year on farming at Holwood in 1799–1800; but he reckoned at the beginning of 1802 to show a profit on sales there of – as far as I can see – some £1,700.[5] Comparable figures for Walmer in succeeding years have not survived in the same manner. It would be pleasant to think that his recreation also yielded some helpful return.

Residence at Walmer also gave Pitt satisfaction in a different way. As he put it, he liked to be there 'not merely for the sake of my farm, but for the duties which . . . belong to my official situation'.[6] For in 1803 there opened the prime period of Bonaparte's prolonged threat of invasion, and the Lord Warden was Constable of Dover Castle and Admiral of the Cinque Ports. This particular incumbent was obviously going to meet his

1. Lady Hester Stanhope to William Dacres Adams [Pitt's private secretary from 1804], 23 January [1805]; same to Pitt, 24 January (Dacres Adams Mss, formerly P.R.O. 30/58/9). She mentioned 'improvements' which included 'buildings' in February (to William Jackson; see The Duchess of Cleveland, *The Life and Letters of Lady Hester Stanhope* (1914), 67). But what these were I do not know.

2. See Curzon, op. cit., 138–44; Stephen Pritchard, *Deal and Its Neighbourhood* (1864), 344.

3. There is no mention of 'Farm' in the accounts for Walmer of 1799–1801, unlike those for Holwood (P.R.O. 30/8/201–2); nor indeed in earlier years in the same series, where Walmer scarcely figures in any respect. But Pitt was selling hay and other produce there on a small scale in 1800 (Saumarez Smith Mss). In 1802 however he entered on 'a beautiful new farm' (to Dundas, 5 September; Stanhope, III, 391), with an enthusiasm which soon led one newspaper to speculate that he had decided to 'devote himself wholly to agriculture' (*The Morning Chronicle*, 2 October 1802).

4. See Pretyman Ms 562:21 for the books and cf. p. 538 above for the economy. The expert was the great naval administrator Admiral Middleton, long retired into Kent (*Life of Wilberforce*, III, 71–2 for the autumn of 1802).

5. P.R.O. 30/8/201–2; Stanhope Ms U1590 S5 C44. He himself was optimistic later, having 'no doubt' that when he had made up his farm account at Walmer for the Christmas quarter of 1802 it would show a 'satisfactory surplus' (to Lord Carrington, 18 January 1803; Bodleian Mss Film 1121).

6. To Pretyman, 28 June 1803; quoted in Curzon, op. cit., 101.

responsibilities, and he did so with the keenest interest. He at once raised his new local Corps of Volunteers,[1] of two (later three) battalions, with Hawkesbury – who was MP for Rye – as Colonel-in-Chief, and Carrington and his own Stanhope step-nephew Lord Mahon, appointed respectively Governor of Deal and Lieutenant of Dover Castle, in the two subordinate commands. They were kept up to the mark as far as possible; but the main thrust came from himself, for Pitt entered with gusto on the activities which he claimed his position required. It was probably at this point that he acquired most of his manuals on tactics and arms,[2] and he spent much time, in sight on clear days of the cliffs of Calais –

The coast of France – the coast of France how near![3] –

inspecting defences and exercising the troops. He was said soon to be 'already an excellent soldier';[4] he certainly plunged into the military art. Hester Stanhope reported that he 'absolutely goes through the fatigue of *a drill sergeant*', with 'parade after parade, at fifteen or twenty miles distant from each other'; 'hard riding' which she herself, an accomplished horsewoman, found as much as she could manage.[5] His activities were grist to the print sellers, and excited some ridicule from those who were sceptical of the prospect of a landing; among whom indeed was the commander of the district, Major General John Moore. Busily engaged in developing his system of training light infantry which would bear fruit in the Peninsular War, he was not impressed by part-time forces – much as Pitt himself indeed was said to have joked about the conscript militia;[6] and when the Volunteer Colonel asked where he and his men would be stationed on marching 'to aid you' 'on the very first alarm', the General pointed to a nearby hill where they could 'make a most formidable appearance to the enemy, while I with the soldiers shall be fighting on the beach'. Pitt is said to have been amused by the retort.[7] He played his part to the full, often wearing his

1. Cf. pp. 122–5 above. He also became Colonel of a battalion of Volunteers raised by Trinity House of which he was still Master (p. 84 above), to help defend the lower reaches of the Thames.

2. P. 539 above.

3. Wordsworth, 'Poems Dedicated to National Independence and Liberty', Sonnet XI, *Poems in Two Volumes* (composed September 1802; published 1807).

4. Lord Mulgrave (see p. 90 above) to Major-General Edmund Phipps (Curzon, op. cit., 106). And cf. other military opinions in October 1803 (*Diary of Farington*, VI, ed. Kenneth Garlick and Angus Macintyre (1979), 2151). The competent General Sir David Dundas found the Cinque Port Volunteers fit to act with regular troops (Glover, *Peninsular Preparation*, 236).

5. To Francis Jackson, 19 November 1803 (Cleveland, op. cit., 54). The impression gains strength from some of Pitt's letters to Carrington in 1803–4 (see Bodleian Mss Film 1121).

6. See p. 38, n3 above.

7. John Carrick Moore, *The Life of Lieutenant General Sir John Moore KB*, II (1834), 8; *The Creevey Papers . . .*, ed. Sir Herbert Maxwell, I (1903), 29 for the General's scepticism of invasion.

regimental Colonel's uniform when at Walmer, and applying himself to the detail of his 'Camp Equipage' – a bear's skin for warmth and two square leather trunks, which could be strapped to a horse, containing pewter eating utensils.[1] His concern naturally extended beyond the manoeuvres and drills. He was involved in the arrangements for 'driving the country' – the removal of horses and transport in an invasion – and when the threat persisted he greatly encouraged the construction of an inner line of defence, in the form of the Royal Military Canal still visible across the Romney marshes, and later the development of the Martello gun towers which in due course stretched along the Kent and Sussex coasts.[2] Characteristically, given the opening, he turned a sinecure into a working post.

These activities also affected his social life. They brought him into regular contact with the local officers – 'vulgar sea-captains and ignorant militia colonels' as his niece characteristically remembered them. Higher up the official ladders, he saw a good deal of Moore, and caught a glimpse of Nelson when the Admiral was stationed for a time in the Downs to harass the French preparations on the opposite coast.[3] He also saw more than he would have done otherwise of the local people, among whom he became increasingly interested in the fishermen through the activities of the Deal luggers, which were now armed. On one occasion they sailed in formation past the Castle to salute, and Pitt and his party then embarked to proceed down the line, returning the cheers 'with no less enthusiasm'.[4] These years of threat gave tangible local expression to his love of country. He was clearly exhilarated to find himself in the front line.

III

The arrival of Hester Stanhope brought a vivid new element into Pitt's bachelor life. She came to live at Walmer after a long spell at Burton Pynsent with her grandmother Chatham, followed by a tour on the continent after the old lady died in 1803. Any such domestic prospect had filled him at first with dismay: he was said to have exclaimed that under no circumstances could he offer her a home. But when it came to the point he met the need. For Hester was in fact literally homeless; she had left her father and stepmother – the successor to Pitt's elder sister Hester – in

---

1. To Carrington, 6 April 1804 (Bodleian Mss Film 1121).

2. See II, 261 for driving the country; Peter Bloomfield, *Kent and the Napoleonic Wars* (1987), 30–2, and P.A.L. Vine, *The Royal Military Canal* (1972), chs. 1–3 for Pitt's involvement in that project in particular.

3. *Memoirs of the Lady Hester Stanhope*, II, 68; *Diary of Sir John Moore*, II, 110; Carola Oman, *Nelson* (1947), 424, 480; Curzon, op. cit., 66–8. Nelson greatly admired Pitt in the abstract, but was not particularly keen to visit a retired Minister who had never done anything by way of patronage for him or his relations. He went once to pay his respects at Walmer, where however he learned that 'Billy' was sleeping late; but he may have visited again after Pitt had boarded his ship, where he found the Admiral seasick and bored.

4. Pritchard, *History of Deal and Its Neighbourhood*, 225; and see op. cit., 228, which drew on memories of Pitt's regard for the boatmen.

1800, as did the other children earlier or later in one way or another.[1] And in the event the coming turned out to be a blessing, for the niece was captivated by her uncle and the uncle became deeply fond of his niece. Handsome, spirited, emotional, Hester 'proved', in her own nephew's happy phrase, 'to be . . . a light in his dwelling',[2] brightening years which were soon to grow ever more dispiriting and bleak. Not every one looked on her with such favour. She already showed the budding qualities which would flower so extravagantly in the exile at Djoun: the fearlessness and power to impress, the indiscretions, the arrogance, the addiction – compulsion – to make believe. Her tongue was too sharp, and she was too sure of her impulses for her own good. But if Pitt sometimes mildly disapproved he was endlessly tolerant, delighted by her youth and deeply grateful for her devotion. Her presence did not alter his habits; those continued much as before. But it gave to his capacity for affection a freshening colour in the time that remained.

Hester however was not the only young Stanhope to claim his concern. Family life at Chevening, where his brother-in-law 'the Citizen Earl' held sway, had grown increasingly forbidding. For Stanhope, an epitome in public affairs of the high-minded, scientific Man of Reason, had proved a sad failure in his domestic life. That had not always been so. He seemed affectionate, if eccentric, when the daughters of his brief happy first marriage were young; but by the mid nineties there were growing strains and by 1800 the two younger girls, Griselda and Lucy, had found husbands – the latter at barely sixteen. In 1800 too Hester left home and did not go back; and she was followed shortly by her eldest half-brother Philip, Lord Mahon, who, still a minor, escaped through her connivance to a German university. He in turn was followed two years later by his brothers, Charles and James. By 1803 therefore all the third Earl's children had left.[3]

Pitt became involved in the effects of these goings on. His early friendship with Stanhope, born of close ties and their collaboration in the campaign for Parliamentary reform, had long been replaced by mutual public disapproval as the two men went their separate ways.[4] The private disruptions deepened the chill, particularly perhaps when Pitt unhesitatingly deployed his patronage and influence. In the absence of help from their father the married girls needed places for their husbands, which were found – Controller General in the Customs in the case of Lucy's Mr Taylor. Mahon's Lieutenancy of

1. See I, 68.
2. Stanhope, IV, 87.
3. See Aubrey Newman, *The Stanhopes of Chevening* (1969), ch. 8.
In Lucy's case, though perhaps not Griselda's, her early marriage was due in part at least to a wish to escape from 'an unnatural father' (to Pitt, nd; Stanhope Ms U1590 C30).
The Earl's second wife was Louisa Grenville, the daughter of Pitt's maternal uncle James; thus extending the cross-fertilisation between the three stocks. The young Mahon for his part married one of Carrington's daughters.
4. See I, 68–70, 107, 140, 219n2, 227–8, 242n2, 264, 483, 630 followed by op. cit., 230n2, 267–8 for a relationship which was beginning to change before the course of the French Revolution and then the onset of war drove 'the Democrat' and the Minister into opposite camps.

Dover Castle was worth £700 a year, and two other sinecures brought him altogether a further annual £1,000. And when the two younger brothers took commissions in the army – James after briefly trying the navy – their benefactor kept a watchful eye on their prospects.[1] His protection was not confined to such forms. Griselda was lent the cottage at Walmer for a time while still unmarried, as a respite from home; he gave his enthusiastic blessing to her rather rash choice of husband, as he had done to Lucy's; and they continued to seek his advice on their affairs. His concern indeed could generate its own awkwardness if something went wrong, as it did when Taylor managed at one point to provoke his censure. Relations became distinctly cool, and there was a scene in the end; for Lucy seems to have shared something of Hester's spirit, and there is a glimpse of Pitt's anger and his niece's defiance at a chance encounter, when he gave her a 'Complete Cut' 'looking steadfastly at Me the other day in Parliament Street without deigning to Answer my Salutations'. She did not take that lying down, objecting strongly to being treated with 'pride and Contempt' and demanding an explanation.[2] In general however it was a very different story. Philip, while still under age, had Pitt's support in resisting a proposal from Stanhope to break the entail on the Chevening estate, and continued to seek counsel on financial matters, which was given sagely from an all too full experience. The three brothers could count when required on hospitality, advice and affection, and in fact on being treated as kin in a very real sense.[3]

These formed his closest family attachments. The incidence of business largely kept him from regular visits to his mother in her last few years; nor did his allergy to correspondence decrease with time, or with more leisure when that came. But though a plan to go down to Somerset in January 1802 was thwarted by the weather and a bad cold, and one for July by the state of public affairs, he managed to go over at least twice from a stay in Bath in the last two months of the year. Old Lady Chatham died with little warning a few months later, in April 1803, and was buried in Westminster Abbey in the vault that held her husband and their eldest daughter. She had become a marginal though still respected memory in Pitt's life, a reminder of the passage of years which was now introducing young figures across the private, as in the public, spectrum.[4]

1. Newman, op. cit., 189–90, 224–5, and for Mahon's appointment at Dover Castle see p. 543 above.

2. What happened thereafter I do not know. See Lady Lucy Taylor to Pitt, nd (but probably 1805), Stanhope Ms U1590 S5 C30; she addressed him on this occasion as 'Dear Mr Pitt'. For Griselda at the cottage see Lady Griselda Stanhope to Pitt, nd but in 1796 (loc. cit. S5 C29); and in general Sir Tresham Lever Bt, *The House of Pitt* . . . (1947), 304–6.

3. They were in point of fact Pitt's first cousins three times removed, through the marriage of their great-grandfather the first Earl to one of Pitt's great-aunts (see I, 68).

4. See Catherine Stapleton to George Rose, 11 February 1801, thanking him for the first personal information received at Burton Pynsent on Pitt's resignation (*Rose*, I, 363); Pitt to Hester Countess of Chatham, 5 January 1802 (P.R.O. 30/8/12); same to Canning, 14 July 1801 (Canning Ms 30), confirming *The Morning Post* of 30 June; Stanhope, III, 405, 423; Rose's conversation with Pitt, 8 April 1803 (*Rose*, II, 30), and cf. my II, 547 in 1795, when Pitt paid tribute indirectly to his mother.

That latter process indeed cast up one figure who would form a curious link with the future. Pitt had been brought into the lives, more or less distantly, of several children of his early friends – as godfather for instance to the young Duke of Rutland, as one of a group of possible protectors of Wellesley's offspring while their father was in India[1] – and these relationships included, as a ward, a young man who would become one of Queen Victoria's Prime Ministers. For in 1795 the young Lord Haddo in Scotland, orphaned at the age of eleven by his mother's death, and anxious – in a sense not unlike the Stanhope children – to be freed from an unsuitable grandfather, sought Dundas's advice and then took the step, available under Scots law, of nominating him and Pitt, with some others, as his guardians or curators. The two colleagues proved their worth. They insisted in due course that the boy should proceed, as he wished, from school to Cambridge; and after he succeeded in 1801 as fourth Earl of Abderdeen he kept in touch with both his protectors, announcing to Pitt for instance from a tour of Greece his conversion – which was lasting – to Philhellenism, and regarding them as his 'only friends' in his hopes of a political life.[2] So, as a new century opened, the 'school-boy' of the early 1780s[3] found horizons reaching to a rising generation for elements of which he was a focus and would remain a yardstick into a transforming age.

IV

The improvement in health which Pitt hoped might come from less strain proved tantalisingly intermittent. On leaving office, already unwell,[4] he suffered a bad attack. But he then settled down and though apparently tired in the autumn of 1801 he emerged the next year, after his usual winter colds and some passing trouble in the spring, to enjoy an encouraging spell of several rejuvenating months. This however did not prevent an attack in September which, if brief, was very severe.[5] He himself ascribed it to over-tiredness from shooting, and a change of weather. But that was in order to play down any reports that might reach his mother, and was clearly inadequate to account for the old symptoms – stomach pains, vomiting and faintness, failure of the bowels, inability to take food – whose strength on this occasion alarmed his doctor and

---

1. For the latter see Iris Butler, *The Eldest Brother*, 181.

2. The boy's letter informing the Minister of his nomination as a guardian is in P.R.O. 30/8/107, as is one from Patras in November 1803 stating that he had embraced Philhellenism. There are a few letters to him from Pitt in B.L. Add. Ms 43227, and his thoughts on Pitt's death are set down in a memorandum in Add. Ms 43337. See also Muriel E. Chamberlain, *Lord Aberdeen . . .* (1983), 21–2 for the guardianship.

3. Cf. I, 128.

4. See p. 82 above.

5. See p. 541 above.

himself.[1] The speed of recovery surprised Farquhar.[2] But he was seriously worried, and persuaded his patient to go later to Bath for the waters, which Pitt did in the second half of October, lodging in Pulteney Street until he left on Christmas Eve.[3] He professed at once to find that they did him good, and one visitor indeed was favourably impressed by his condition.[4] In February 1803 however he had a fresh attack of 'bile' – the word he generally used – followed by gout.[5] Again it soon passed, and though in May he looked worn, by his own standards he had another good summer on the whole. Increased political activity from the autumn may have brought on renewed attacks; but it is hard to say exactly when, and at the turn of the year he was thought by his friends to look better than he had done since 1797.[6] Nonetheless by the spring of 1804 Hester Stanhope was ill at ease. He was eating only 'a crust of bread' at supper, and had a constant cough which he would not attend to while he pursued his military duties. She may, naturally, have been over-anxious. But she had seen some worrying ups and downs.[7] Taken all in all, the variations in a period of comparative rest did not augur particularly well if that should be removed.

One aspect of the question moreover began again to disturb Pitt's friends. For some time after his resignation he seems to have cut down on his drinking. No cellar accounts have survived for these years; the veil descends there, as for domestic details generally. But silence from others may be eloquent, and after his bout of illness in 1802 he was ready by and large to be moderate. He confined himself at Bath to two 'very small'

---

1. Pitt to Catherine Stapleton, 17 September 1802 (Stanhope, III, 393); same to Farquhar, 13 September – 'the symptoms are such that I do not at all know how to proceed' (Stanhope, *Miscellanies, Second Series*, 65); Farquhar to ?, 24 September 1802 (Stanhope, III, 392–3), and see his retrospective account edited by Rosebery in *The Monthly Review* for December 1900, at 49–50.

2. Same to Rose, 10 October, and see again on 15 October – 'wonderfully recovered' – and same to Pitt, 21 October 1802 (P.R.O. 30/8/134).

3. See Stanhope, III, 400–28.

4. Pitt to Rose, 7 November 1802 (op. cit., 405); Rose to Pretyman, 21 November, 3 December 1802 (Pretyman MS 435/44), and see also Camden to Pretyman, 22 November 1802 (Stanhope Ms U1590 S5 01/12).

5. Pitt to Farquhar, 9 February 1803 (Stanhope, *Miscellanies, Second Series*, 66–7); Farquhar's account, in *The Monthly Review*, December 1900, 50.

6. Rose to Pretyman, 14 May, 30 June 1803 (Pretyman Ms 435/44); Hester Stanhope to Jackson, October 1803, 14 January 1804 (Stanhope, *Miscellanies, Second Series*, 69, 72); and see also Huskisson to Viscount Melville [Henry Dundas], 15 December 1803 on his 'vigorous Health, bodily Strength, and light cheerful Spirits' (S.R.O., GD 51/1).
In his later account, however, Farquhar dated 'a renewal of the former unpleasant symptoms' to 'some months' after the attack of bile in February 1803 (*The Monthly Review*, December 1900, 50).

7. To Farquhar, 15 April 1804 (copy in Stanhope Ms U1590 C419/8, published in part in Stanhope's *Miscellanies, Second Series*, 73–4). 'Nobody', she added, 'is so like an angel when he is extremely ill, and few persons less tractable when a little ill'. It will be remembered, when she talked of 'extremely ill', that she had been with Pitt probably for some eight months (p. 544 above). Cf. for the cough p. 80 above.

glasses of madeira at dinner and '*less* than a Pint of Port' afterwards.[1] Nonetheless he was becoming tired of restraint; calling on Camden in his way there from Walmer, he had consumed almost three bottles of port in all at dinner and supper.[2] Old habits returned, and in the spring of 1804 he was said to have been drinking 'a good deal too much wine at dinner' and 'considerable quantities' of wine and water at night.[3] Again, it was not a good sign at a point when public pressures were mounting once more.

What *was* wrong with Pitt? We may ask the question at this point, for the symptoms were now all too familiar and they were not going materially to change. They persisted, once his childhood passed, from his twenties – a decade mostly of good health – when he had to retire into Solomon's Porch to be sick during a Commons' debate, through the stiffness, the acute stomach pains and the failure to retain nourishment which became more evident in his later thirties, to the extremities of a condition which in his forties would lead to his death.[4] Drink had accentuated the damage, as it would continue to do. But the basic damage was accentuating the effects of an intake which though heavy was not fatally so.[5] He may well have incurred renal disease, though less probably final renal failure to judge from what the physicians found at the end.[6] The underlying cause, or causes, one may think, lay more likely elsewhere; and the fact that the exposure to illness was not banished by reduced tension suggests further-more that it, or the combination, was not purely psychosomatic. Farquhar was accused retrospectively of culpable ignorance[7] – a charge of course always readily levied against fashionable medical men – and indeed his diagnosis does not take one very far. Pitt 'wanted Constitutional Stamina'; 'The Mind was constantly acting upon a weak frame of body'; too much wine 'operated unquestionably to weaken the Powers of the Stomach'; gout 'in addition' must be given its weight.[8] Certain things might be

1. Rose to Pretyman, 21 November 1802; and see also same to same, 3 December (Pretyman Ms 435/44). Port, one must repeat (see I, 586), was a lighter drink than it later became. Cf. p. 82 above for 1798.

2. Rose to Pretyman, 21 November 1802 (Pretyman Ms 435/44).

3. Hester Stanhope to Farquhar, 15 April 1804 (Stanhope Ms U1590 C419/8; a passage omitted in the printed version, for which see p. 548, n7 above). She qualified this however by saying that he was reported lately to have been 'very moderate'.

4. Cf. I, 9, 29, and also 106, 594; II, 461–2; pp. 79–83 above.

5. Cf. I, 585–6.

6. On one occasion, in May 1803, the diarist Thomas Creevey noted that Pitt looked yellow (*The Creevey Papers*, ed. Sir Herbert Maxwell (1903), I, 14–15). I have not come across other such references, and while cirrhosis of the liver can of course be responsible for such an appearance he does not seem to have shown accompanying symptoms, then or later, and there are a number of causes which might have accounted temporarily for it.

7. 'Sir Walter Farquhar's ignorance' figured among the causes of Pitt's death in Bland Burges's notes for a sketch of the Minister (Bland Burges Mss, Box 73–4, Bodleian Library).

8. *The Monthly Review*, December 1900, 56.

hazarded on such observations by way of preliminary comment. One may question if the want of stamina was as generalised as Farquhar implied; Pitt's powers of speedy recovery constantly astonished his friends and doctors alike, and in 1803–4 he could ride his niece, in her youthful prime, almost into the ground.[1] In many respects he was tough physically, as he was mentally; for one may suggest further that while his state of health most certainly responded to his sense of pressure, that did not necessarily mean – and Farquhar may not have intended it to mean – that he was governed by hypochondria. The recesses of the psyche are convoluted; but he does not appear to have struck others in that light. Rather he seems to have had a high tolerance of pain, to judge from an early example; to have borne its later onslaughts as far as possible with 'good humour'; and otherwise indeed to have paid little attention to himself.[2] Farquhar moreover may have tended to telescope the process of decline from the perspective of the final period. Pitt's friends, anxious as they were, convey a rather different impression until quite late in the day: one of sporadic setbacks rather than of sporadic intervals – and the doctor naturally saw more of his patient in bad times than in good.

However that may be, Farquhar's reading of the case assembled, rather than proportioned, its elements. He could not point methodically from symptom to cause. Nor was that at all surprising or to be condemned in the current possibilities of knowledge. Perhaps the strongest area of medical study in England in this period was that of gout, and he allowed amply for the disease – the diffused gout which had plagued the Elder Pitt. Later opinion has done likewise: in our own terms for hyperuricaemia, in a form of irregular gout occurring particularly in 'a lean subject, with a greater tendency to gastro-intestinal disturbance, particularly pylorospasm'.[3] Research in recent years however has raised certain doubts about the exact behaviour of irregular gout; and there is no record of Pitt showing typical signs of the culminating phase of deforming arthritis with tophi (urate deposits). An associated possibility, or aggravation, may however be mentioned. On some occasions at least in the later nineties he was prescribed laudanum, contained in 'Powders' and 'Draughts' as a sudorific;[4] and if sometimes in these particular years, no

1. See p. 543 above for the last; and cf. 548, n2.
2. See I, 594 for the first point; *The Monthly Review*, loc. cit., 49 for the second; Hester Stanhope to Farquhar, 15 April 1804 (Stanhope, *Miscellanies, Second Series*, 74) as an example of the third. See also Mulgrave to Pitt, 25 April 1804 (P.R.O. 30/8/162), sending a bottle of vinegar before a debate 'As I am persuaded that you will not take proper precautions for yourself'.
3. R. Guest Gornall, 'The Prime Minister's Health, William Pitt the Younger'; *The Practitioner*, vol. 179, 607–12. *OED* defines the pylorus as 'The opening from the stomach to the duodenum'. I am much indebted to the late Dr Guest Gornall's article, and to a long and careful investigation of Pitt's recorded symptoms by Mr T.G.J. Brightmore FRCS, for my own amateur's remarks.
4. Bills from S. Chilver, February 1797 – December 1800; Saumarez Smith Mss, bundle of bills, ai.

doubt sometimes in others as well. There would have been nothing unusual in this: opium was widely taken in moderation throughout the century both medically and for pleasure – it could be bought across the counter – and it could have been confined here to an intermittent need. But if the instances were regular, as one may suspect, it might well have had some contributory effect. Farquhar's mounting concern concentrated more specifically on the spasms themselves; and here too he has been followed, for different reasons, by some medical opinion, fastening on possible cancer of the bowel – an explanation consonant with Pitt's later condition whether or not it can be prolonged to cover the more occasional upsets of earlier years. A further suggestion has been made in the same area, complementing that of gout: a recurring gastrointestinal lesion, an inherent generic weakness, which was exacerbated by the successive attacks occurring largely, though not only, in times of stress.[1] This, if a layman might comment, would seem to be of distinct interest. But a confident solution is now doubtless unattainable, as it was to Farquhar from the nature of his evidence. The visible process itself on the other hand was uncomfortably suggestive. After some three years' respite from office, and allowing for improvement after a steepening decline, Pitt's health was still uncertain, and in the early months of 1804 it continued to give cause for concern.

1. This is Dr Guest Gornall's opinion (ibid).

CHAPTER XVII

The Pursuit of 'Character'

I

The House of Commons began to take in an altered political scene when, on 16 March 1801, Pitt walked to a seat 'on the right hand side of the chair, in the third row from the floor'.[1] The disappearance of the famous figure from the Treasury bench struck forcibly home.[2] For so many years he had been a fact of national life. Half a generation had passed since he appeared, equally suddenly, on the centre of the stage; there were undergraduates in their first year at university – the young Aberdeen was one – who had scarcely been born when Pitt became First Lord of the Treasury.[3] The sense of bewilderment and lack of guidance among Ministerial supporters was momentarily acute.[4] Nonetheless the necessary adjustments, by and large, were soon made. Politicians, like others, abhor a vacuum; after the shock, the transition proved smooth; and the example in Parliament was echoed out of doors. Looking back in the summer, it could seem surprising 'how little sensation [Pitt's] going has made in the country, . . . no address, no subscriptions, no stir of any kind'.[5]

There were several reasons for this passivity. The first was supplied by Pitt himself. It was his intention from the start to give 'the fullest Support to the Formation and to the Measures of any Administration composed of Persons acting on the same General Principles as I had done'.[6] There

1. *Colchester*, I, 260. Dundas, Canning and Castlereagh were soon sitting there with him (*Glenbervie*, I, 205, for 25 March). According to *The Times* of 17 March he sat four or five rows behind the Treasury bench, which might have been possible following the enlargement to meet the consequences of the Union with Ireland (see p. 194 above). Cf. I, 39 for the political implications of seating customs when Pitt had first entered the House.

2. By one account in fact, such new Ministers as were on the Treasury bench when Pitt walked in 'made way and offered him his place' (*The Morning Post*, 17 March 1801). It would have been instinctive reaction.

3. See p. 547 above. To be precise, Aberdeen had been born in January 1784, a month after Pitt's appointment. He succeeded to his Earldom in August 1801.

4. See eg the picture of the House drawn on 9 February, when the prospect dawned, by a future Speaker (*Colchester*, I, 230–1).

5. William Wellesley-Pole to Marquess Wellesley, 3 July 1801 (Iris Butler, *The Eldest Brother*, 263).

6. Pitt to Canning, 16 April 1801 (Canning Ms 30), recalling their first conversation on the subject in February.

seemed no reason to doubt such immediate continuity in the new Cabinet. Four of its members remained from his own, and in the same offices: Portland as Home Secretary, Chatham as Lord President of the Council, Westmorland as Lord Privy Seal, Liverpool at the Committee, or Board, of Trade.[1] Of the four entrants other than Addington himself as First Lord of the Treasury and Chancellor of the Exchequer, the Foreign Secretary was Hawkesbury, favoured politically and personally by Pitt; the Secretary for War and the Colonies was Lord Hobart, once Westmorland's capable Chief Secretary in Ireland and more recently Governor of Madras, who sought Pitt's blessing in advance; the First Lord of the Admiralty was St Vincent, politically less sympathetic but who likewise consulted the outgoing Minister, and moreover made it clear to his colleagues that he would follow a tradition of sailors in that office by confining his advice to naval affairs; and the Lord Chancellor was Lord Eldon, who as Sir John Scott had been Pitt's respected Attorney General over a period of some six years.[2] This last appointment moreover removed the most likely potential source of trouble at Court, for Addington took care at once to see that Loughborough was replaced, and the unregretted figure disappeared, leaving in the process a fresh footnote to constitutional history.[3] All in all therefore, Pitt could proclaim his approval, as did others among his departing colleagues. He discouraged any signs of division; his own support was unequivocal; and he took occasion, in the few debates in which he intervened, to declare it in the months remaining before the summer recess.[4] This contribution to stability

1. The last, more strictly speaking for inclusion in the Cabinet, as Chancellor of the Duchy of Lancaster.

There was soon a reshuffle, to accommodate Thomas Pelham (see p. 173 and n1 above), wanted by Addington at the outset but hesitant to accept. In July he became Home Secretary, Portland becoming Lord President and Chatham moving to the post of Master General of the Ordnance (for whose claim to a position in Cabinet see II, 261n1) vacant since the resignation of Cornwallis (p. 524 above).

2. Having moved in 1799, with a Barony, to the Lord Justiceship of the Common Pleas, which he continued briefly to hold with the Lord Chancellorship. For Hawkesbury's earlier relationship with Pitt – slightly soured by the affair of the London corn bill (p. 285, n2) – see p. 91, above. Hobart's effectiveness is glimpsed in II, 221–2; in 1799 he had married Eleanor Eden, which would not have conduced to a warm personal view of Pitt. St Vincent's politics are noted op. cit., 357; for a comment on the conduct of naval First Lords in Cabinet see Pares, *King George III and the Politicians*, 20 and n5, and also I, 634. For consultations with Pitt, see Charles John Fedorak, 'The Addington Ministry and the Interaction of Foreign Policy and Domestic Politics, 1800–1804'; Ph.D. thesis, University of London, 1990, 43–5.

3. He seems to have continued to turn up at Cabinet meetings after Eldon had received the Great Seal, until asked to stop (the evidence is assessed in Aspinall, *The Cabinet Council 1783–1853*, 149–50). If this was so, it marked a decisive end to any inherited doubts.

Loughborough appears to have been greatly taken aback when Pitt first resigned (see George III to Addington, 5 February 1801, Pellew, op. cit., I, 294; *Colchester*, I, 223, diary for sd). Addington was quite clear that he must go (see op. cit., 227–8).

4. *P.R., 3rd ser.*, XIV, 610–12, XV (1801), 82, 113, 116, 393–5. In these and other discussions he was speaking usually when obliged to defend past policies of his own. Parliament rose early in July.

was received broadly with relief. And other steadying factors by then were also carrying their own weight.

For of course the traditional element was present in the complex sustaining any Government; just as it had been when Pitt himself had begun with a less auspicious prospect. The new Ministry was spared embarrassment, and perhaps threat of defections, by his endorsement of its policies; it also enjoyed to the full the fruits of approbation by the Crown. This indeed was apparent at once. The King owed Addington a debt, he set out to honour it, and with the greater satisfaction as he contemplated '*his own Chancellor of the Exchequer*'.[1] Given such backing from both quarters, Addington had every chance to settle in. As George III remarked in the spring, drawing him and Pitt aside at a Levee, 'If we three do but keep together, all will go well'.[2]

Addington himself furthermore soon became accepted, sometimes with a certain relief, by many who now found themselves among his regular Parliamentary troops. His advent was far from popular in higher society – a doctor's son, without connexions or the compensation of discernible talents, despised by the families accustomed to one another's company at the top. The office of First Lord of the Treasury – acknowledged, despite its circumscriptions, as something special – had admittedly not been filled in such a way before.[3] Pitt himself, a penniless younger son, had been a surprising choice, but he had a political heritage and an identifiable social place. By the same token, as well as the personal contrast felt by the late Minister's surviving colleagues, there was no enthusiasm in some quarters of the Cabinet itself. That however was not entirely the case within the House of Commons. If Addington was greeted with astonishment as Minister, he had been respected and well liked as Speaker: competent, fair, on easy terms with backbenchers and particularly the country gentlemen. He had had little chance in his career to

1. George III to Addington, 15 March 1801 (Stanhope, III, 321); phrased with the usual attention to form, Pitt having just returned the Seal of that particular office (p. 533 above).

2. Pellew, op. cit., I, 331no, citing notes by Addington's daughter of conversations with her father.

3. And indeed the same contempt had been shown in a lesser instance, when Addington had been first elected Speaker on Pitt's influence in 1789 (see *Life and Letters of Sir Gilbert Elliot*, I, 320). It was overdone. Dr Anthony Addington came from a family which had moved in modest but unmistakable ascent from yeomen to gentlemen in the seventeenth century. His grandfather had been to New College Oxford, his mother was directly descended from the Washingtons of Sulgrave (thus sharing an ancestry with George Washington), and he himself had been sent to Winchester followed by Trinity College Oxford. It was unusual in point of fact with such a background for him to have become a medical practitioner, a profession standing in such distinctly low social esteem (see ch. I by Dorothy Warren in E.M.G. Belfield, *The Annals of the Addington Family* (1959)). Almost inevitably however his son was familiarly known as 'the Doctor' in political circles.

Dundas underlined the social distinction between 'the first Minister of the country' and others when he lamented the 'degradation' of that particular office being filled by 'a person of the description of Mr. Addington' without other justifying pretensions (to Pitt, 7 February 1801; Holland Rose, II, 441).

make a mark in debate, and it soon became clear that he would not do so now – Pitt indeed, commenting on his successor's prospects, agreed that one could not be confident there.[1] But the lack of brilliance was not wholly uncongenial to many worthy foot soldiers in the House; Addington's 'mediocrity . . . suited their mediocrity', and 'an empty and pompous manner' adopted defensively with 'the choice few' vanished largely or entirely in a less demanding clime. With the country gentlemen he was 'easy, frank, jovial, loved Port wine as well as the most resolute fox-hunter': a not unwelcome change to many after the distant frigidity of Pitt.[2] He could draw on a fund of mild goodwill as he emerged to do his duty by church and state. And he was soon assisted further by a sudden crop of good news from overseas.

This began in fact to reach London only a few weeks after he took office. In mid April it was learned that the Tsar had been assassinated on 24 March; an event privately forwarded from London and openly greeted with delight.[3] Within the next forty eight hours a despatch was published from Nelson announcing that the fleet which had sailed in February, in hostile response to the Armed Neutrality, had engaged and defeated the Danes. A month later news of a complementary success was received from another region: the Danish and Swedish islands in the Caribbean had been taken as part of the same response.[4] And by then the other earlier source of acute anxiety had been removed. After the vexatious delays, Abercromby had effected his landing in Egypt on 8 March. Nine weeks later, Pitt walked into a committee of the Commons at work on its papers bearing the report, of which he had just been told, of a victory near Alexandria.[5] It proved to be the indispensable prelude to the occupation of the country, a consummation marred only by the death in action, learned in mid May, of the General himself.[6] After the dismal showing in

1. Pretyman's account of a conversation on 25 February 1801 (Pretyman Ms 434/45). And cf. *Glenbervie*, I, 174.

2. Dean Milman's description half a century later, given in the course of a defence of Addington (Cornewall Lewis, *Essays on the Administrations of Great Britain*, 272. Lord Holland, in less friendly fashion, had earlier written much the same (*Memoirs of the Whig Party*, II, 212–13). Later in his career, while at the Home Office, Addington himself wrote that he wished to be remembered as 'the country gentlemen's secretary of state' (*H of P*, III, 46 & n35).

3. The news came on 13 April. Cf. p. 470 above for British complicity or instigation.

4. See pp. 399, 411 above. The captured islands were St Thomas and St Croix (Danish) and St Bartholomew (Swedish) in the Leewards. Their surrender moreover was accompanied by that of the Dutch St Martin, all in a fortnight in March, and followed by the evacuation of the neighbouring Dutch St Eustatius and Saba. Nelson's despatch on the battle of Copenhagen on 2 April was published in *The London Gazette* of the 13th.

5. *Colchester*, I, 266, for 3 May. Cf. p. 411 above for the landing.

6. A loss which was particularly bitter for Dundas, one of Abercromby's closest friends and acutely aware of the risks inherent in the expedition. Pitt for his part had a regard for the veteran commander whom he had been obliged to remove from Ireland (pp. 163–5 above); one of the relics preserved at Walmer, indeed, is an engraving of the General believed to have been hung there in the Minister's day.

1800 these were very welcome grounds for relief, particularly since the campaign in Egypt showed the first clear victory in what was essentially a European context by a British army on its own against the French. The Tower guns could be fired more than once, and street windows lit – the last occasions on which to celebrate battles won in the Revolutionary War.[1] There was at last indeed something real to cheer. Bonaparte's main thrust to the East was checked, and thus, it seemed, any complementary action there with Russia; and the immediate position in northern Europe was entirely changed. The lesser Baltic Powers could be taken temporarily at least out of the reckoning; while Russia's own position might be wide open once more. Whatever her relations with London now, she was unlikely to move so swiftly in favour of Paris; Paul's removal, as Bonaparte admitted, had thrown French plans into disarray. The serious pressures on Britain were eased, alike for Asia and for maritime warfare, and the threat of invasion itself was reduced and perhaps postponed.[2]

The run of good news furthermore was received at a particularly opportune time. It could now prove a significant aid to peace. For the new Cabinet had in fact already decided to embark on an approach to that end: on 19 March, five days after Pitt left office, Addington submitted its first Minute to the King, advising unanimously that such a step should be taken without delay.[3] George III, still barely recovered from his illness and in any case in no real position to object, gave his 'full' approval. The summary improvement in the bargaining position therefore came at a useful point.

This turn of events by land and sea could be seen as redounding to the credit of the late Administration as well as fortifying the prospects of its successor. It cheered Pitt at a juncture when already he could feel that his resignation had not been in vain. The new Ministry was acting precisely as he wanted, and the cavils he himself might have encountered at Windsor could now be discounted, as he and Addington must have known. If a negotiation followed, he could not be held in France to be an obstacle to its progress, while he nonetheless remained available to give his advice.[4] And that moreover might be accomplished without a risk of obstruction from his own former Foreign Secretary, for Grenville had declined to take a part in the immediate proceedings after his retirement

---

1. The victory also had a longer term effect, in the decision, some three years later, to provide Government money for a building in which the British Museum could house 'the Egyptian Antiquities' brought home. It was one reached the more readily by Pitt 'as a just Memorial of our Military Glory acquired in that Expedition' (Speaker Abbot's words after seeing the Minister; diary for 28, 29 June 1804, P.R.O. 30/9/33) – a not untypical attitude on his part to the place of the arts in the nation's life: cf. p. 85, n3 above.

2. See pp. 397, 411 above.

3. *L.C.G. III*, III, no. 2373. It may be noted that it was Addington himself, not the Foreign Secretary as in normal usage, who wrote enclosing the Minute on this occasion.

4. Cf. p. 516 above.

and could perhaps be held at arms' length.[1] Pitt was thus freed from the most prominent of the constraints to which he had been progressively more exposed: in this respect it might indeed appear that 'Out of office, ... he had at last a government he could depend upon'.[2] There was in fact a period of quiescence in which the conjunction of constitutional factors was remarkably favourable to the Administration. The weight of the Crown's influence, always limited directly but indirectly extensive and cogent,[3] was accompanied by open support from the most formidable source of possible disapproval, and a suspension of disbelief, pending the outcome of peace talks, on the part of his partners in resignation and, in this area, even of Opposition itself.[4]

The outcome, however, would be the test. It emerged in October. A *Gazette Extraordinary* was published on the 2nd with the text of Preliminary Articles of Peace signed in London on the 1st by Hawkesbury and, as the French negotiator, Otto.[5] The terms were not of course necessarily final; that awaited the Definitive Treaty. But they were valid until then; they pointed to the conclusive settlement, and were followed by an immediate cessation of arms. They stipulated the retention by Britain of Ceylon (formerly Dutch) and Trinidad (formerly Spanish), the return of all other British conquests to their pre-war owners, the establishment of a free port at the Cape of Good Hope – Dutch once more –, the evacuation of Elba by the British and of the Neapolitan territories, the Papal States, and Egypt by the French, the restoration of Malta to the Knights under the guarantee of a third Power, and the integrity (qualified by a secret article) of Portugal and Turkey and their possessions.[6]

1. See p. 524, 526, n3 above for Grenville in the period of the Ministerial interregnum. According to one subsequent report, Pitt reached the point a month or so later of advising Hawkesbury, who (likewise on his advice) had sent papers concerning fresh conversations with Russia to his predecessor, that he might as well throw the resulting comments into the fire (*Glenbervie*, I, quoting Liverpool, 295).

2. R.G. Thorne in *H of P*, IV, 817.

3. A background to this statement may be found in I, Ch. II sections II and III, and 635–43.

4. Grenville, for instance, was said to have observed in September that there had been no measure of Government of which he did not approve; Canning was brought by Pitt in August at least to consider the possibility of joining the Ministry; Tierney from Opposition started talking inconclusively to Addington at the beginning of October with an eye to an accession of himself and some others (*Glenbervie*, I, 268–9, diary for 24 October 1801, quoting Addington on Grenville's remark 'six weeks ago'; Hinde, *George Canning*, 101; A.D. Harvey, 'The Grenville Party, 1801–1826' (Ph.D. thesis, University of London, 1972, 33).

5. For the French text see *Consolidated Treaties*, ed. Parry, 56 (1969), 213–16.

6. The secret article recognised that Portugal's frontiers with Spain in Europe and with the French territory of Guiana in America were nonetheless subject to the terms of a recent treaty with France at Badajoz in June. See *L.C.G. III*, III, nos. 2534–5. The full French text of the treaty may be found in *Consolidated Treaty Series*, 56, as in n5 above; the English text, omitting the secret article, in *inter alia P.H.*, XXXVI, cols. 25–8. For Otto see pp. 384–6 above.

The settlement came as a complete surprise – it had been an exception-ally well kept secret – to every one beyond the King and Cabinet and Pitt himself.[1] To some it was highly unwelcome; and to none more than the colleagues who had retired with him, who were left in a state of outrage where they were not simply dismayed. Their feelings, whether justified or not, may be understood by a comparison of the terms with the ideas 'settled at the Cabinet' in the previous autumn.[2] The Foreign Secretary had then urged as a 'sine qua non' the retention of the Cape of Good Hope, Ceylon, and Cochin in southern India. For the rest, any territories in India returned to France or Holland should be held by them purely as commercial factories; all other British conquests should be negotiable, balanced against advantages to be obtained from a Continental peace, particularly in a settlement of the Low Countries (details being suggested) which would 'rescue' that region from its current 'dependence on France'; the pre-war positions of The Two Sicilies and Portugal should be restored; and the French should leave Egypt. The paper had been sent to Addington soon after the change of Ministry, and returned in April.[3] But despite the help since afforded by Nelson and Abercromby, the contents seemed to its author, as to others, to have been largely neglected or aban-doned in the ensuing talks. No provision was made in the preliminary treaty for the future of the Low Countries, the original *casus belli* and of vital interest. The Cape, the staging post for what had become our Eastern empire, was thrown away. Malta, with its relevance to the Near East as well as southern Europe, was given up. Our overseas conquests, both Eastern and Western, were apparently jettisoned except for Trinidad. In Europe, apart from the southern half of Italy, the French stayed where they were.

All this, according to former Ministers taking such a starting point, was bad enough. It was equally disturbing that much of the detail of the terms seemed still to be left for the final treaty. And what about trade, on which nothing was said? Would the Eden treaty of 1786 come into force again, together with the pre-war arrangements reached in some other parts of Europe?[4] All those who had left the Cabinet with Pitt were profoundly shaken, as he soon learned. The treaty, Grenville told him, was 'most mis-erably defective', 'an act of weakness and humiliation'. 'It seems to me', Spencer wrote, 'that we give up every thing we have taken from France without her making a single concession to us'. Camden, though not counting on much in advance, had at least 'expected our Honor to be maintained' with the safety of our possessions in the East and West Indies

---

1. Addington wrote to some at least of the other former Cabinet Ministers on 1 October, informing them that a treaty had been signed but without giving details.

2. See p. 388, n2 and Ch. XII, section III above.

3. Pellew, op. cit., I, 257–60; Addington to Grenville, 24 April 1801 (B.L. Add. Ms 59306), with the copy of the paper which had been Pitt's. The argument lying behind the claim for India had first been rehearsed in 1787; see I, 441–2.

4. For which see I, Ch. XVI.

and the retention of the Cape. Perhaps the most telling remark of all came from Dundas; 'The only consolation I have is that My time of Life gives me some chance to escape being a witness to the calamitous consequences'.[1]

This broadly unanimous conclusion did not spring in each case from an identical premiss. Windham indeed, whose public expressions soon became the most extreme, condemned the very principle of a settlement, explicitly before he knew the terms. 'The Country', he told Addington, had 'received its death blow' from the act of agreement itself; he remained unalterably opposed, it seemed, to recognition of a republican France.[2] The rest had been prepared in varying degrees to accept the prospect of talks; from Dundas, seeing no strictly strategic need but reluctantly acquiescent, to Grenville and Spencer, acknowledging the force of serious though perhaps not conclusive pressures, to Camden who sought peace even on 'a narrow' though still balanced 'Compass' of expectations.[3] But such shades of emphasis did not disrupt their consensus now on the result. That was clear enough. The immediate difficulty for them was to decide how to act.

For this must take into account their attitudes to Pitt: their feelings for his position and, particularly in some cases, for himself. He at once made it clear, to them and to some other close adherents, that he supported the treaty in full. He did not pretend that 'in *every* Point' the terms were 'exactly what I would have wished', and he singled out the return of the Cape for regret. Nevertheless, taken all in all, the outcome was 'highly creditable', 'very advantageous and on the whole satisfactory';[4] and this was obviously going to be his public stance. What then were his late colleagues to do? Apart probably from Windham, none was anxious to proclaim his complete disagreement. Neither Grenville nor Spencer wished

1. Grenville to Pitt, 6 October 1801 (*H.M.C., Dropmore*, VII, 50–1), and see also 2 October (Dacres Adams Mss, formerly P.R.O. 30/58/4); Spencer to same, 3 October 1801; Dundas to same, 6 October 1801 (both Dacres Adams Mss); Camden to Spencer, 9 October 1801 (B.L. Add. Ms temporary Althorp G42), disclosing that he had told Pitt he was 'unwilling and unhappy', and cf. same to Grenville, sd (B.L. Add. Ms 69067).
  See further Grenville to Spencer, 6, 9 October 1801 (B.L. Add. Ms, temp. Althorp G42), Spencer to Camden, 14 October 1801 (loc. cit.). The longest and perhaps most deeply considered rejection of the terms is to be found in a private memorandum by Dundas for his, and posterity's, use, 14 October 1801, in S.R.O., Melville Mss, GD 51/i, ff. 556–61; cf. for his earlier thoughts p. 421, n2 above.

2. Windham to Addington, 1 October 1801 (*The Windham Papers*, II, 172–3). Cf. pp. 222–3 above. One wonders how he would have responded if a Ministry with Pitt at its head had concluded any treaty other than one that insisted specifically on the restoration of the Bourbons.

3. Camden to Spencer, as in n1 above. Dundas, Grenville and Spencer likewise alluded in their letters specifically to their attitudes to a negotiation.

4. Eg, beyond the former Cabinet Ministers, to Long, 1 October 1801, and Mulgrave nd (Stanhope, III, 351–2), to Canning, 1 October 1801 (Canning Ms 30), to Bathurst, 2 October 1801 (B.L. Loan Ms 57, vol. 2). To Bathurst a little later he expressed a deeper anxiety about the Cape (18 October 1801; *H.M.C., Bathurst*, 26).

to damage any chance of overturning Addington's Government in favour, as they hoped, of Pitt's own return. To Spencer, he was 'and always must be the Man to whom the Country must look for its Salvation', and Grenville equally acknowledged the importance of the public 'holding high Pitt's character and reputation'. It was therefore to be hoped that he would not speak now in a way that would deal 'so great a blow to both'; in that case, Grenville felt, those who differed from him would have publicly to state their own views.[1] This however was farther than all of them would go. Camden confessed that while he did not understand or approve of Pitt's position, he could not take 'a very hostile line'. He had been accustomed always to trust the great man's judgment, he was governed by the need to 'keep up Mr Pitt's Consequence & Character', and in the last resort by their 'old & intimate acquaintance'. He could not 'make a Breach'.[2] And neither could Dundas: he too could not 'appear in open conflict with Mr Pitt'. The background in his case was rather different: there were the memories of differences over strategy, and strong reservations about the familiar eagerness for peace.

> But with all his faults there are a thousand honourable and amiable qualities in him, and it is impossible for me to separate myself in affection from him. My mind is perfectly prepared to abandon every Publick Pursuit; but I could never bring myself to appear in any Situation adverse to him.[3]

Much had happened in the past two years to dent the long-standing confidence. The personal loyalty and protective devotion survived.

Some of the former colleagues commented among themselves on reasons and factors of temperament lying, as they saw them, behind Pitt's decision. Grenville did not elaborate on his shock at having been misled by 'the impressions resulting from an intimacy of near twenty years'. But Spencer pointed to a common experience of 'how open [Pitt] is to be influenced by plausible Opinions' from men whose abilities did not qualify them to 'lead a Mind like his'; and 'once pledged' it was not easy to 'extricate one's self'.[4]

1. Spencer draft to Dundas, looking back from 13 November 1801 (B.L. Add. Ms temp. Althorp G44); Grenville to Pitt, 2, 6 October (Dacres Adams Mss, formerly P.R.O. 30/58/4; *H.M.C., Dropmore*, VII, 50–1), same to Camden, 13 October 1801 (Camden Ms U840 C112/4).

2. Camden to Spencer, 9 October 1801 (B.L. Add. Ms temp. Althorp G42). According to Lady Spencer, who was staying with Camden in the country at the time and found him 'in the deepest despondency', his first reaction had been to tell Pitt that he was 'likely to desert him on the extraordinary support he Pitt seemed to say he intended to give' to the treaty (to Spencer, nd but received 11 October; B.L. Add. Ms temp. Althorp G293).

3. Dundas to Spencer, 17 November 1801 (B.L. Add. Ms temp, Althorp G221).

4. Grenville's faulty expectation of Pitt's reaction to the treaty is clear from this phrase on 2 October after he learned the truth (p. 559, n1 above. Spencer's comment was made on the 13th (to Dundas, see p. 456, n6 above). Cf. I, 322 for a similar, retrospective verdict on his career throughout.

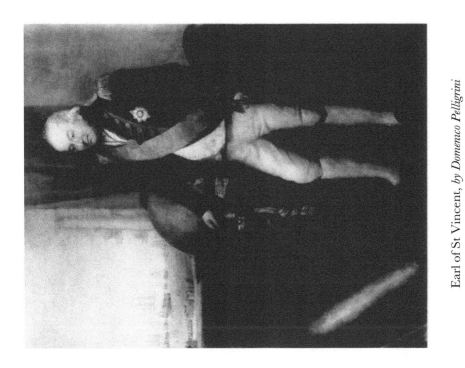

Earl of St Vincent, *by Domenico Pelligrini*

Lord Hawkesbury, *by Lawrence*

King George III, *by Peter Edward Stroehling*

This kind of criticism would certainly spring to mind here; Dundas for his part drew attention to a deeper vein. He had guessed in the months following resignation, as he saw Pitt 'loitering about London', that he was 'lending his name' to a process that had now ended badly; partly from the feeling, which Dundas indeed had shared, that the new Ministry should not be denied strength while working for its 'great and leading measure'. But he also pointed to that disposition which he himself had often had to check, 'to seize at the object immediately in contemplation': a stimulus no doubt in prosecuting wartime operations, but dangerous in aiming for a peace for which there was 'no Sacrifice at times He was not ready to make'.[1]

There was much in fact in this latter contention, which Spencer's might be taken rather to complement. For if Pitt lent himself unduly to persuasion over these terms, it was because he felt his own strong inducements to do so. It is hard to tell how far he had been in detailed touch with the progress of the talks. Addington must of course have been very glad of such backing; but he was also anxious to show himself in charge of his Ministry, and one cannot tell exactly when and why he consulted the oracle, or what the oracle replied.[2] Whatever the extent of personal involvement, however, Pitt was prepared to go to great lengths for a settlement. According to a later story, he sat up with Addington to discuss the finances 'some few nights' before the talks ended, and declared that 'the war could not be carried on, and that peace must be made'.[3] This account, at second hand from a good source, may have suffered in passage, and seems likely in any case to be an approximation. Pitt's high concern for the finances did not extend to the point where he thought that

---

1. Dundas to Spencer, 17 November 1801 (p. 560, n3 above) – partially explaining the 'lounging' noted by others (p. 540 above). For the whole passage, including the well known phrase 'He is either in a Garrett or a Cellar', see Feiling, op. cit., 165–6.

2. Addington's natural anxiety to be his own man is disclosed in *Colchester*, I, 223. *He* sent the Cabinet's first Minute to the King (p. 556, n3 above), and *he* announced the news of the Preliminaries to the retired Ministers (p. 558, n1 above). According to one report, the King wished to encourage recognition of his superiority in the Cabinet (*Glenbervie*, I, 220 for 14 April 1801, quoting Huskisson).

On the question of Pitt's involvement in the peace talks, primary evidence is hard to come by. Fedorak, 'The Addington Ministry', 70 alludes to his contact with the Ministry 'throughout the spring and summer' on the handling of Russia after Paul's death. But he does not enlarge on its extent in that respect, or in the talks with France. Addington's first biographer mentioned the '*impossibility*' of the Minister's being able to consult his predecessor in every instance (Pellew, op. cit., I, 333), and Holland Rose (II, 468) states that Pitt 'at some points criticised the conditions of the Preliminaries'. Much of course would have been done by word of mouth; but one must remember that Pitt was much at Walmer during these months, and while Addington was reported as saying that he had see him 'a great deal . . . during the summer' (*Glenbervie*, I, 268, for 24 October) the fact that Hawkesbury sent Pitt a report of 150 pages on the terms on 28 September (Fedorak, loc. cit., 101–2) might even suggest (though by no means conclusively) a lack of recent regular contact in the final, fluctuating run-up.

3. Lord Holland's *Memoirs of the Whig Party*, I, 184–5. He was 'assured' of this by 'Lord Liverpool (then Lord Hawkesbury)', who would have had it from Addington. Hawkesbury succeeded to the Earldom in 1808.

war could not be sustained.[1] But allowing for that strong qualification, it was undoubtedly a central element in a range of factors all pointing him in the same way. The decision itself to negotiate, indeed, could hardly have been formed so quickly without his prior influence: a First Lord of the Treasury and a Foreign Secretary who had been respectively Speaker of the Commons and Master of the Mint could surely not have otherwise taken such a step in the Cabinet's very first Minute.[2] Pitt was impelled not only by a resolve that the subsequent efforts should not be weakened: he was also under a strong commitment to endorse them if he possibly could.[3]

When the time came to give his verdict in detail, he did not hedge. On the contrary, he went farther than some, already worried, thought he need have done. The tone may well have been coloured by an aspect of his disposition on which one of his friends indeed warned him: 'when you take a part to which from any circumstance it is suspected you are not naturally inclined, you are apt to go beyond what the Occasion requires; and in order to speak with zeal, to speak without discretion'.[4] There was wise observation in this: Pitt was quick to outface a challenge. But the 'circumstance' here needed qualification, for in this instance he was fully prepared to argue a genuine if unappealing case. He did so on two main propositions.[5] First, the war on the Continent was over. We lacked any surviving ally with whom to act there effectively, and some former and some existing partners had signed treaties for themselves. Our influence was correspondingly limited, both to shield them and to guard our own interests in Europe. We held a weak hand, and had played it to the best of our ability, as the agreements showed[6] considering that our own bargaining points in the region were confined to the Mediterranean – to Egypt and the islands of Minorca and Malta. The outcome in those three instances was tolerable. Egypt's security was restored by its acknowledged return to Turkish dominion; Minorca would always go in war, as history suggested, to the strongest maritime Power, and was of no great use in peace (a weak argument, one might say, since resources for repossession

1. Eg pp. 267, 282, 334 above; and in fact he alluded to this explicitly when he came to defend the treaty in debate (see *P.R., 3rd ser.*, XVI (1802), 108). The distinction however was not one likely to have been drawn too fine by a political world well aware of his anxiety. Thus as early as March he was said to be telling Addington that the state of the finances required peace (*Malmesbury*, IV, 53; 'I always', the diplomat added, 'perceived these to supersede in Pitt's mind every other consideration').

2. P. 556 above. Hawkesbury had been placed at the Mint in 1799.

3. He was indeed so anxious to declare his 'great satisfaction' with the results that he did so as soon as Parliament reassembled on 29 October, while acknowledging that it was not the correct occasion, with a special intervention in the debate on the Address (*P.R., 3rd ser.*, XVI, 17).

4. Bathurst to Pitt, 16 October [1801] (P.R.O. 30/8/112).

5. Speech in the Commons, 3 November 1801 (*P.R. 3rd series*, XVI, 99–112).

6. He made the point, in talking of Portugal, that the Ministry had managed to stop Bonaparte taking a further significant bite at the cherry, particularly in Brazil, after the treaty of Badajoz whose terms were now openly recognised (op. cit., 102; cf. p. 557, n6 above).

would thereby be needed); and while a 'more definitive arrangement' for Malta could undoubtedly have been wished, the island's strategic significance should now be taken in conjunction with that of the Ionian Islands, forming a new republic and, like Malta itself, removed in practice from French hands.[1] We must recognise moreover that if we had pressed to keep the base we would ourselves have been pressed for 'more than equivalent' concessions elsewhere, which would have fallen on more important regions overseas. For given our current impotence in Europe, our negotiating interests lay overwhelmingly in the East and West Indies; and while, again, he regretted the loss of the Cape of Good Hope – though now a free port – he gained satisfaction from the retention of Ceylon and Trinidad. Ceylon was, 'of all the places upon the face of the globe, the one which will add most to the security of our East-Indian possessions';[2] Trinidad, well placed to threaten Spain in South America and providing the best available transatlantic naval station – preferable in his view to St Lucia, Guadeloupe or Martinique –, was 'the most valuable' of our conquests in the Caribbean. In the circumstances, our best aim throughout was to protect our 'ancient possessions', rather than try to keep acquisitions which 'we did not materially want'. '. . . they would only give us a little more wealth; but a little more wealth would be badly purchased by a little more war'.

These judgments on the terms were conditioned by Pitt's view of 'the general complexion of peace'. The arrangements did not fully answer all his wishes; but they had been agreed by Ministers as those best suited to give reasonable chance of a lasting settlement, by 'a rule of prudence, which ought never to be deviated from, not unnecessarily to mortify the feelings or pride of an enemy'.[3] 'Security was our object', and moderation was now the means. Events had obliged us to drop the alternative, on which we had placed our hopes, of replacing revolutionary aggression by enabling the return of a 'venerable system' deriving from a monarchy which, despite its defects, had been built on 'regular foundations'. We had therefore to adapt to changed circumstances; 'for he did not know a more fatal error, than to look only at one object, and obstinately to pursue it, when the hope of accomplishing it no longer remained.'[4] Obviously

1. In 1799. 'The Seven Islands', as he called them, were now lying under Russian and Turkish protection.

2. In passing, he made the point that the retention of Cochin in southern India (see II, 562, 628, 647), which had also been called for, was much less important now that Tipu had been destroyed (p. 438 above) and it was no longer 'a frontier post'.

3. An observation greeted with an obviously ironical 'hear, hear' from some Members (*P.R., 3rd ser.*, XVI, 102). Later in his speech, perhaps stung by this, he observed that while he had refused to negotiate with Bonaparte at the close of 1799, he had pointed explicitly to circumstances, such as those which had arisen since, in which he 'might wish' to do so (cf. p. 343 above).

4. 'Object' meant here, as the context showed, a subsidiary object, not the main end. See pp. 227–8 above for Pitt's latest position on the monarchy in the course of the war, summed up again on this occasion (*P.R., 3rd ser.*, XVI, 109–10).

however it took both sides to achieve a lasting peace, and we had perforce to weigh the odds on Bonaparte's future conduct. Would he rest content with France's gains, after balancing them against her losses – in men, in trade and capital, in 'habits of industry' –,[1] and restore her to the orbit of policies which other Powers could accommodate? Pitt was inclined to think there was a good chance; and he later confirmed that he had been genuine in this.[2] On the kind of balance he was accustomed to draw – on the reasoned assumptions by which he moved – he applied his answer to a confessedly open case. But if he should be proved wrong the sequel was plain. While we ought to be scrupulous in honouring the agreements and avoiding grounds for irritation,[3] 'This . . . was not to be done by paying abject court to France'. If we could not rest on our hopes for peace, we must depend for security 'only upon ourselves'. We had therefore to remain cautious, and while he himself was disposed to look towards 'every thing that was good' he was bound to act, in providing for our continued safety, 'as if he feared otherwise'.

The argument was carefully articulated, as was certainly required to meet a narrow scrutiny; and Pitt was sincere in his defence of a measure which he thought '*necessary*' on the grounds he gave.[4] At the same time, his concern went farther. It was not bounded by the measure itself. For he had in fact formed a resolution which was intended to govern his relationship with the Ministry in every respect. He regarded himself as 'pledged' to Addington's support not only in this instance but throughout; a pledge which, according to one surprised account, 'he considered as solemnly binding, not redeemable by any lapse of time, nor ever to be cancelled without the *express consent* of Mr. Addington'.[5] However these words, which were reported as Canning's, are to be taken, they certainly conveyed a sense of engagement by which Pitt felt bound in honour. Whether he would be prepared 'a toute outrance to abide by every measure' of Addington's remained to be seen: one intimate to whom he likewise 'completely opened' his mind 'upon future conduct' was left with the suspicion that it was 'almost too romantic to realize'.[6] But he was determined at any rate to stand on 'Character'; the same character, paradoxically, that his friends feared must be lost by the course he chose. He later acknowledged

---

1. By this phrase, as Pitt pursued the converse theme of British resources, he seems to have meant that forced expropriations and heavy impositions could not match the benefits and rewards of a constitutional framework for a healthy economy (cf. p. 419 and n2 above).

2. To Malmesbury in April 1802 (*Malmesbury*, IV, 64). Cf. p. 337 above in 1799.

3. Pitt later contended in some detail that although the terms had been 'rather hastily drawn up' they were so framed as not 'very likely to occasion disputes' (*Malmesbury*, IV, 67–8).

4. Op. cit., 65. And see also 77.

5. Malmesbury's version, at second hand, in October 1802 (op. cit., 75).

6. Countess Spencer to Spencer, received 11 October 1801 (B.L. Add. Ms. temp. Althorp G293); Camden to same, 9 October 1801 (loc. cit., temp. Althorp G42). Malmesbury reported Canning's expressions as denoting a 'strict and solemn engagement' (IV, 76).

his resolve: he did not deny ambition, but it was for '*character*, not office'; and that indeed was what he sought ever since he had decided to resign.[1] The pursuit of course was older than that, amid the complexities of Ministerial life, and in what may have seemed to him a simpler setting he was now making it the regulator of his conduct.[2] Public life however is seldom simple for those exposed to prominence. One set of complexities replaces another. And as Pitt's ideal continued to sustain, so it came increasingly to disturb his course.

II

Pitt's support for the Preliminaries, which so deeply shocked many of his friends and late colleagues, proved to have done him less harm with opinion at large. The prospect of peace was now popular enough for the terms, where regretted, to be largely shrugged off. Signs of impatience with the war, perceptible in 1795, rather more visible in 1797, and in 1800 a preoccupation of Ministers,[3] had not diminished since. On the contrary they had risen, Copenhagen and Egypt notwithstanding, after the simultaneous collapse of the Alliance and, still more, of the corn harvest again.[4] The signing of the treaty was hailed for the most part with profound relief. Mail coaches were garlanded, windows lit as for a victory, and the emissary bringing the French ratification was greeted – it was said to his alarm – by a mob which unhorsed his carriage and drew him through the London streets. There seemed, one doubter admitted, to be 'real enthusiasm and frantic joy', among labourers, farmers and manufacturers alike;[5] and in the instant euphoria a favourable gloss was widely put on the terms. William Cobbett, pursuing life as a journalist after recently returning from America, reported a 'universal' condemnation of them soon rising among 'merchants, planters, and gentlemen'.[6]

1. Op. cit., 78; the italics and quotation marks were attributed by Malmesbury once more to Canning in their conversation, some three weeks after the latter had talked to Pitt. And cf. pp. 528–33, 552–3 above.

2. *Malmesbury*, op. cit., 76.

3. Cf. II, 601–3; pp. 39–40 above for 1797; 334–6 for Pitt on the eve of 1800, 339, 386–8 for Dundas at either end of that year, 381–3 for Grenville in the final stage of the Second Coalition.

4. See p. 277 above.

5. Granville Leveson Gower to Canning, 17 October 1801 (see Mackesy, *War Without Victory*, 212–13). The mob itself was rumoured to have been incited by that archetypcally suspect figure, a radical saddler.

6. To Windham, 7 October 1801, citing a 'change' from a few days before (*The Windham Papers*, II, 173–4). Arriving from America in 1800, and hoping for literary patronage from Government, he had been favoured in particular by Windham, and his views may now have been affected by financial difficulties in conducting his short-lived newspaper *The Porcupine* (Ministerialist under Pitt), which in the following month led to negotiations with Windham and the Grenville brothers and their associates that ended in their taking shares to help found *Cobbett's* famous *Weekly Political Register*.

But three per cent Consols, which initially rose seven points, stayed high; and the settlement, significantly, gained approval from distinguished men in a position to judge. Famous figures from the armed forces, Cornwallis, Nelson, St Vincent – the last of course a Minister – spoke in support in the Lords, and both Houses in fact had little difficulty in accepting the result. The regular Opposition itself could hardly cavil at peace, and while Grenville's hostility was such that he forced the peers to divide, he gathered only ten votes, and Windham did not venture to call a division in the Commons.[1]

Pitt's regrets were therefore caused by private rather than public considerations. He was naturally saddened by the damage to old ties. Lady Spencer, who 'stumbled' on him shortly after the terms were announced, thought that he appeared 'very ill and . . . much broken', and when she hinted her disapproval 'he seemed to fix his eyes upon me with a look of peculiar & melancholy anxiety'.[2] It was a distressing time, for himself and for others who themselves were taking divergent ways. The resulting 'disagreements', one of them forecast, 'promise an unpleasant winter amongst the old friends and connexions'.[3] But immediately at least this was scarcely the case, and early in 1802 the tensions in fact seemed to be somewhat relaxed. In February Spencer felt able to pay a call on Pitt in Park Place; his 'neighbour' returned it with 'unusual promptitude', and the next day dropped in on Thomas Grenville for 'a very familiar, easy, and friendly discussion of all the late events'.[4]

Those developments related in point of fact to French behaviour since the Preliminaries had been signed. The Ministry, and Addington in particular, at work on his budget, wanted the Definitive treaty quickly out of the way. They assumed indeed that this would be so; but their expectations proved wrong. Six more months passed before the final settlement was signed at Amiens, and in those months Bonaparte raised varied alarms. He sent a strong fleet with a force to San Domingo in December, to crush a revolt under Toussaint l'Ouverture;[5] a move which could be taken as ominously placed, and was shadowed at sea in due course. Public anxiety grew with the news a month later – of which Ministers were already aware – that he had acquired the Spanish colony of Louisiana, of commercial and strategic importance and, when combined with the terms of Badajoz and a modifying sequel, forming an uncomfortable

---

1. The figures in the Lords, including the tellers, were 114 to 10 (*P.R., 3rd ser.*, XVI, 70). For St Vincent's acceptance of office see p. 553 above.

2. To Spencer, nd but received 11 October (B.L. Add. Ms temp. Althorp G293). When the Commons debate came on some three weeks later, he was anxious to speak quite early before he was 'exhausted by fatigue' (*P.R., 3rd ser.*, XVI, 99). But cf. pp. 547–8 above for the fluctuations in health.

3. Camden to Bathurst, 2 November 1801 (*H.M.C., Bathurst*, 29).

4. Thomas Grenville to Grenville, 24 February 1802 (*H.M.C., Dropmore*, VII, 80). And see his letter of the 20th (ibid). Cf. p. 534, n2 above.

5. For whom see p. 144 above.

accession of transatlantic strength.[1] Such developments were the more unwelcome given the current emphasis on the safety of overseas possessions.[2] And by the same token there was some anxiety for India, since in the absence so far of specific confirmation by the French of earlier treaties, the advantages to Britain of the Convention with France of 1787 could be held to be at risk. So too, as at the time of the Preliminaries, could those of the Eden treaty, on which continuing silence in Paris disturbed British merchants and manufacturers.[3] Furthermore there appeared to be causes for apprehension from the Continent itself. The Preliminaries had barely been signed when the French secured the remodelling of the Batavian republic in the Low Countries. A domestic *coup d'état* was soon effected in Switzerland, the third in nineteen months, in their continuing thrust towards control. The strategically vital canton of the Valais, overlooking the passes into Italy, was directly occupied at the same time. And over the turn of the year a further worrying development took place to the south, when Bonaparte recast the constitution of the Cisalpine republic which he himself had set up, and assumed the post of President. Internal changes in that region in point of fact were in many ways needed, and proved not unpopular. But the rearrangement, with his own involvement, ran contrary to guarantees in the treaty of Lunéville; and these summary, and in Switzerland devious activities showed the familiar signs of that restless aggression which Pitt for his part was hoping would have died away.[4] By both their actions and their silences the French were engendering rising unease.

It was thus 'to declaim against the insolence and ambition of Bonaparte' that Pitt paid his visits to Spencer and to Grenville in February 1802.[5] He did so against the background of the disturbingly lengthy negotiation. He does not seem to have been consulted this time as he had been in the previous spring and summer, and shortly before the treaty was signed he was noticeably disturbed. Nor was he much pleased by the result. Canning at least was convinced of that, and while he supported the Ministry in the ensuing debate he did so briefly and his enthusiasm appears to have been restrained. The terms were not always as adverse in fact as was sometimes proclaimed: compromises were reached on one outstanding problem remaining from the Preliminaries, the arrangements of payment for exchanges of prisoners of war, and in principle on an indemnity to the Prince of Orange for his losses to the French. The main target

1. Cf. pp. 557, n6, 562, n6 above. Bonaparte in point of fact ended by refusing to ratify the treaty of Badajoz, and managed to extract a few minor advantages in a treaty of Madrid signed in late September.
2. Eg in Pitt's recent speech on the Preliminaries, p. 563 above.
3. See I, 441–2 for the Convention of 1787; pp. 558–9 above for the initial silence on the treaty of 1786, and worries on the part of former Ministers at the lack of such detail in the Preliminaries.
4. Cf. p. 564 above. See p. 390 for Lunéville.
5. *H.M.C., Dropmore*, VII, 80.

for condemnation in England was the provision for Malta, already suspect in its initial terms under the Preliminaries. The restoration of the island to the Knights had then been accepted, if reluctantly, as likely to be under the mantle of a garrison provided by Russia. But that was now replaced in prospect by a small force from The Two Sicilies, the other Power with claim to an interest: an obviously ineffectual guarantee of neutrality, particularly, in the critics' view, when the constitution of the Order was to be amended to include a 'democratic' *langue*, which would presumably extend French influence. The Knights' sources of revenue furthermore would remain frozen in France and in territories controlled by her, and a veto was placed on a resumption of their trade with the Barbary States.[1] Nor was a wider surety, in the form of agreement to these terms by Austria, Russia, Spain and Prussia, a credible safeguard when the British garrison was due by the arrangements to leave within three months.

Ministers were themselves unhappy in private about the issue of the island. In public they could present an argument which, strictly speaking, it was hard to controvert. For the new Tsar Alexander I, in contrast to Paul, had intimated that he did not wish to provide the garrison, and no Power other than The Two Sicilies could be found to fit the legal and practical need. The trouble was that neither France nor Britain, given Russia's abstention, was likely to admit any substantial alternative Power sympathetic to the other. A weak garrison from Naples suited France, and Britain was in no position to find something from another source. But this, here as elsewhere in the treaty, was the real crux. The Preliminaries had been accepted in the hope that peace would be given a fair chance; now Bonaparte's behaviour was lowering that prospect in English eyes, and the Government was blamed for not bringing the public concern firmly into the talks. In point of fact again, this would not have been simple on any formal basis. There was no point on which to make a legally supportive stand. The guarantees for stability in Europe were contained in a treaty of France with Austria. The cessions of territory in the Americas comprised in one case a transfer between allies, and in the other was recognised (to all purposes)[2] by a provision in the Preliminaries. The lack of specific reference to earlier treaties moreover could be argued either way in the law of nations.[3] The situation was unsatisfactory, but not conducive to specific challenge. It was as much the circumstances as the settlement itself that left the Ministry exposed.

1. The stipulations for Malta were contained in article 10 of the Treaty of Amiens, for the French texts of which see *Consolidated Treaties*, 56, 291–304 and the English text, *inter alia* *P.H.*, XXXVI, cols. 557–64. For the position of The Two Sicilies see p. 208, n1 above; for the debates on and relating to the treaty, *P.R.*, *3rd ser.*, XVIII (1802), 127–32, 145–83, 191–219, 284–91, 304–13, 319–449. Pitt's interventions – the second concerning form only – were made on 3 and 6 May, in the discussions prior to the main debate.

2. P. 557, n6 above.

3. As indeed it was in the debate on the treaty in disagreement between the Lord Chief Justice and the Lord Chancellor (see *P.R.*, *3rd ser.*, XVIII, 358–61).

This was not the whole story. Hawkesbury was not making a great impression as Foreign Secretary.[1] Addington (whether or not with Pitt's advice) had checked or overruled him at times in the talks on the Preliminaries, and the Foreign Office might have handled the second round more effectively now. That in turn was partly due to the inadequacy of the negotiator on the spot, the respected but disappointing figure of Cornwallis, who was outfaced by his opposite number Louis Bonaparte and often misjudged the odds.[2] More perhaps therefore might have been gained, or salvaged. But settled as he was in his judgment for peace, Addington was not in any case prepared to risk an option for war.

Whether Pitt, with Dundas and Grenville beside him, would have acted differently, one cannot say. But his doubts of Addington in these months were not confined to the negotiation. An incident in February suggested a relationship which by its nature was vulnerable to strain. In a Commons' debate early in the month tribute was paid to the Minister's rectitude in financial matters, to be contrasted with a disgraceful irresponsibility on the part of his predecessor, who among other derelictions was said to have withheld action on some budgetary expenses which were thus passed on. Steele, a member of the Government following Pitt's earlier request, helped to rebut the last charge in some detail, and Addington himself was content to dismiss it in a few words. No one in the House seems to have expected more.[3] But Pitt, down at Walmer, took umbrage, and a correspondence ensued, agitated and hurt on Addington's side and severe on his own. The matter was trivial. But it disclosed some interesting facets: Pitt's readiness to take offence on a question affecting his conduct, based here on a newspaper report picked upon by Canning, and Addington's alarm and surprise at his treatment by the lifelong arbiter of his career. The affair was soon ostensibly cleared up.[4] But it left an impression. It showed the extreme importance still attached by the one man to the other's goodwill, and it may have contributed to the sudden warming in relations between Pitt and the Grenvilles' circle. In March he paid a visit

1. Fedorak, loc. cit., ch. 3 *passim.*

2. Pitt is said to have observed earlier that the veteran Field Marshal had always wished to conduct a diplomatic mission, but had now found a singularly unpromising one (Countess Spencer to Spencer, 11 October [1801]; B.L. Add. Ms temp. Althorp G293).

3. See *P.R., 3rd ser.,* XVI, 479. The debate is not included in *P.H.,* XXXVI. Steele had remained in his office of joint Paymaster General. The accusation came from Tierney on the Opposition benches, whose relationship with Addington was not unfriendly.

4. The main correspondence, containing letters of 9 to 17 February 1802 by Pitt, Steele and Addington, is to be found in the Dacres Adams Mss, formerly P.R.O. 30/58/4, and the Sidmouth Mss at the Devon R.O., 152M/C1802 OZ 188. Some are printed in Stanhope, III, 369–70. Canning's part emerges from his diary for 8–9 February ('Wrote to Pitt (at Walmer) about last night's debate'; Canning Ms 29d) and the letter itself of the 9th (loc. cit. Ms 30).
According to one account however – from a partial source – there was widespread indignation in society at Addington, and some at Steele for not defending Pitt more vigorously (Countess Spencer to Spencer, nd, received 11 February 1802; B.L. Add. Ms, temp. Althorp G293). For Steele in earlier days see I, 107, 109n1, 127, 131.

to Dropmore, and dined thereafter, with others, at Spencer House for 'a little confidential conversation' at any rate, '. . . before he shall have again involved himself in new pledges to the measures of the present Administration.'.[1]

His support however was maintained in Parliament until the session ended in June. As well as approving the terms of the Definitive peace treaty, Pitt spoke in approval of the budget, on which he had been consulted at any rate in outline and which Addington managed well.[2] Equally to the point, he did not speak when Canning brought a motion, hostile in intent to Addington, calling for papers on the cultivation of land in Trinidad.[3] The subject, so the mover thought, was chosen adroitly; for he was now chafing at his constraint in deference to Pitt's wishes[4] and emerging more fully as a gadfly of Government. The aim, itself perfectly genuine on behalf of a cause he had always held strongly, was to forward the abolition of the slave trade by confining the sale of Crown lands in this new British possession to buyers who did not import fresh negro labour. Strictly speaking, that was not necessarily anti-Ministerial. Conveniently however, it could make trouble between Addington and Pitt, for Addington had been a gradualist in earlier debates on the trade, and a progressively more conservative one, and ought to be embarrassed on a question of policy which Pitt ought to feel obliged to support.[5] Canning indeed made no bones about this; 'Though I must not goad and pelt the Doctor, as I could wish, I am enabled just to put a thistle under his tail, and Pitt must aid and abet me'. The prospect was 'delightful', and he went to work with

---

1. Spencer to Grenville, 15 March 1802; and for the visit, Grenville to Pitt 3 March, Pitt to Grenville 4 March, Thomas Grenville to Grenville 15 March 1802 (*H.M.C., Dropmore*, VII, 85, 86, 91–2), Grenville to Buckingham, 12 March 1802 (Buckingham, III, 200), same to Thomas Grenville, 12, 14 March 1802 (B.L. Add. Ms 41852).

One other small matter seems also to have irritated Pitt at this time. A commission had been set up, to investigate the use of labour on West Indian plantations (see p. 435 above) for which he reckoned himself responsible but Addington claimed the merit (Rose to Pretyman, 26 February 1802; Pretyman Ms 435/44). He seems in effect to have been more dissatisfied with the Ministry's 'general want of dignity & . . . littleness of character' (in Grenville's description) than with its policies at this stage (Grenville to Thomas Grenville, 14 March 1802; B.L. Add. Ms 41852).

2. *P.R., 3rd ser.*, XVIII, 452–5. Consultation with Pitt was later affirmed by the then joint Secretary of the Treasury, Nicholas Vansittart (Pellew, op. cit., II, 61). In point of fact however it may not have extended to detail (Pretyman to Mrs Pretyman, after talking to Pitt, nd but probably March 1802; Pretyman Ms 435/45), and the provisions, while agreeable to the former Chancellor, were distinctly Addington's own.

3. For a step bearing on this question a few years earlier see p. 430 above.

4. His jokes and remarks in society at Addington's expense had long been well known, and some of the squibs –
      Pitt is to Addington
      As London is to Paddington
is the enduring example – were beginning to gain circulation. For a list of those attributed to him see Cornewall Lewis, *Administrations of Great Britain*, 249n1.

5. For Addington's position on the slave trade by the middle nineties, *H of P*, III, 40.

zest.[1] But he miscalculated. Pitt, made aware in February – a good month for the purpose – showed signs at first of co-operation. But he was soon 'cooling' and imposing delays; and when the motion was finally brought in May he was able to stay silent, for Addington dished Canning by stating that there was no intention of making grants of land in Trinidad – orders had indeed been sent out to that effect; that the question should not be taken on its own, since a commission had in fact been appointed to inspect labour practices there in relation to those in the other British islands; and finally that he hoped for a Commons' committee after the summer recess which would review once more the whole case for gradual abolition of the trade.[2] The proposer was rueful. 'The Dr. bitched it,' he had to admit, '. . . and promised me more than I wanted without a contest'.[3] Pitt does not seem to have had occasion to intervene on any other issue before the recess.

There was some consolation, however, for opponents of Addington despite this disappointment. For on 28 May Pitt's birthday, which Dundas in earlier years had marked with a private dinner, was celebrated on a greater scale at Merchant Taylors' Hall in the City, thanks largely to Canning's efforts exploiting an idea from elsewhere.[4] Pitt was not there in person: his presence in fact was not intended, for the dinner was designed by its impresario as a political demonstration.[5] Members of the Government were invited, though Addington (and Chatham) did not come and Hawkesbury appears to have felt awkward enough to retire for his meal to a private room. The Hall was crowded, with well over nine hundred people, the flower of society according to Canning himself. In the midst of the proceedings a song was sung by Charles Dignum, the tenor from Drury Lane, with words supposedly by a certain Claude Sprott. One verse, and one line above all, has withstood the years.

> And oh! if again the rude whirlwind should rise,
> The dawnings of peace should fresh darkness deform,

1. To Hookham Frere, 7 March 1802 (see Ziegler, op. cit., 151–2); Canning's diary and correspondence with Pitt, February–May 1802 (Canning Mss 29d, 30). For 'the Doctor' see p. 554, n3 above.

2. *P.R., 3rd ser.*, XVIII, 554–63. Cf. however p. 570, n1 above for Pitt's temporary irritation with Addington over the credit for the commission. The affair, with its political connotations, is treated at length by P.C. Lipscomb in 'Party Politics 1801–1802: George Canning and the Trinidad Question' (*H.J.*, XII, no. 3, 442–66; cf. p. 429, n4 above).

3. To the Rev. William Leigh; quoted by Wendy Hinde, *Canning*, 108.

4. It was suggested to him, as a sign of proper regard for Pitt (Fox's friends celebrated his birthday annually in this fashion), by the MP Sir Henry Mildmay, and on Canning's suggestion relayed to the City, where it was taken up (see Hinde, op. cit., 108). See eg p. 128, n2 above for Dundas's dinners.

5. Canning himself was careful not to let Pitt know, in case of a veto. An invitation however did reach him, from Spencer who had agreed to take the chair. At first indeed it looked as if that might be accepted; but Pitt then declined, for fear in fact of 'Topics being started' which could lead to 'great Awkwardness and Indelicacy' (to Spencer, 24 May 1802, and see also 26, 28 May; B.L. Add. Ms temp. Althorp G48).

The regrets of the good and the fears of the wise
Shall turn to the Pilot that weathered the Storm.

When this had been called for again amid vociferous enthusiasm, Spencer rose to propose a toast to the Pilot. It was heady stuff, at least to some, and the real author was able to report that the accounts of the evening had moved Pitt himself.[1]

In the months that followed there was indeed no lack of pressures on the figure soldiering and farming at Walmer, to separate him from Addington and give some firm indication of intent. Some of those most closely attached to him seized on such chances as came their way: Rose and Pretyman and Canning in particular watched assiduously for comforting signs. These at first did not seem to amount to much. The Bishop noted in July that Pitt now thought Addington a man of 'consuming vanity and of very slender abilities'; Canning too found him 'evidently dissatisfied with A & the general tone of the Govt.'; and in August Rose reported a comment that 'the Doctor, – an Appellation he is familiar with' was 'a stupider Fellow than he [had] thought him'. Such remarks were gratifying. But they did not presage action. Pitt indeed stated that he would 'do nothing' himself. Might he however now let others make his feelings known?[2] Canning in July thought this probable; and it was on developments from other quarters, which might lead back to the main target in due course, that livelier hopes came thus perforce to rest.

1. Canning to Leigh, 1 June 1802 (Hinde, op. cit., 109); and see Pitt to Spencer, 31 May 1802 (B.L. Add. Ms temp. Althorp G48). For Chatham's absence, 'though in Town & specially invited', see Rose to Pretyman, 29 May 1802 (Pretyman Ms 435/44). According to Rose, the enthusiasm easily exceeded anything he had witnessed in 1784 or on the King's recovery – presumably in 1789. Some reservations however on the tone of the occasion are noted in Hinde, op. cit., 109.
Canning's own copy of his first version has the more provocative lines,
    'While we turn to thy hopeless retirement our eyes,
    We shall long for the Pilot that weathered the Storm'.
2. Notes by Pretyman in July (Holland Rose, II, 477); Canning's diary for 19 July (Canning Ms 29d); Rose to Pretyman, 10 August 1802 (Pretyman Ms 435/44). See also Grenville to Thomas Grenville, 31 August 1802, reporting Canning's impressions (B.L. Add. Ms 41852). Something of the old amiability however endured. When Addington proposed a visit to Walmer from a stay in Eastbourne in August the response was cordial, and when it had to be put off Pitt offered to sail down the coast to him (see Pellew, op. cit., II, 73–6).
He knew the 'appellation' of 'the Doctor' well enough. His godson the Duke of Rutland remembered many years later his coming into a meal 'rubbing his hands with delight at having escaped home to his company' from listening to 'the doctor travelling with his own horses for the last hour and a half, and we thought he would never arrive at the end of the stage'. The Duke could not recall the date of this story – he thought it was 1802, but from his own description it could have been 1804–5 (see *The Croker Papers . . .*, ed. Louis J. Jennings, III (1884), 183). But at all events Pitt confessed to laughing at a speech by Sheridan in a debate of December 1802 quoting the well known lines on Dr Fell (*Malmesbury*, IV, 146).

They were not themselves easy to interpret. Such clues as emerged from Opposition were in fact disappointing; for depressed and largely ineffectual since the virtual retirement of Fox, it was fraying at the edges in the changing conditions. This was perhaps hardly surprising: a 'Party' whose identity had rested so largely on Pitt's existence was likely to be affected by his disappearance,[1] and – since Fox still declined to fill an active role, and both great rivals were thus absent – the lesser men were confronted by an unfamiliar scene. Personal relations did not help. Tierney disliked Sheridan, as Sheridan disliked him and Charles Grey; Fox distrusted Sheridan, and Tierney was disenchanted with Fox. On the other hand Tierney had long been friendly with Addington, and pre-ferred the thought of joining him[2] to that of co-operating in some way with the Grenvilles, which might moreover point at some stage to Pitt's return. He hoped to carry others with him, in some cases perhaps into office: Moira and Erskine and if possible Grey, while the veteran Thurlow and the youthful Duke of Bedford might bring their own kinds of weight from the Lords. Moira in turn would convey a sense of approval by the Prince of Wales, as indeed would Sheridan, who was also from his own point of vantage considering his relations with the Government. Such possibilities could hardly encourage canvassers of movements to weaken the Ministry, even though by the spring the prospect of its reinforcement had declined. For the Prince was not pleased with Addington, who failed effectively to prosecute a long-standing claim to his military promotion, Moira stood out for too great a reward, Grey was always uncertain and in the end withdrew, and the Duke of Bedford died. Nor had Addington himself been entirely happy to contemplate an accession which could bring its own problems, including probably – though Fox himself was not involved – some suspicious queries from the King. In the event Tierney and Sheridan, in their different ways, remained in touch with the Ministry; but 'the Party' as an entity continued in its own style of broad if temperate opposition, distinct, one may argue, in form and essence from its most credible but still unlikely allies.

These clearly were by now 'the Grenvilles' or 'Grenvillites', as they were often loosely called: the three brothers, with Spencer and Windham and some relations, dependants and adherents, extending to a separate friendly connexion centred on Fitzwilliam and a small number of inde-pendently minded peers and MPs.[3] Their relative cohesion in confronting the Ministry over foreign affairs had by now indeed led to their being described as 'the New Opposition'. But this was misleading in some respects, as a key to their own character and in comparison with that of

---

1. For 'the Party' in its earlier form, of which the Foxite Whigs claimed to be the true heirs, see II, 53–6; for Fox's announcement of withdrawal from the Commons' pro-ceedings, p. 42 above.

2. Cf. indeed p. 557, n4 above.

3. Affiliations and numbers are examined in Harvey, 'The Grenville Party 1801–1826', and in James J. Sack, *The Grenvillites 1801–29* . . . (1979), chs. I–III.

'the Old Opposition'.[1] For attitudes varied even within the family. The eldest brother Buckingham was more anxious to attack over a wider front, and the second, Thomas, more readily attracted to Whigs across the floor,[2] than was the youngest, Lord Grenville himself. And while their influence was sometimes, and importantly, at odds with his public primacy, he was always the accepted Parliamentary focus for the group, and at this period held the orthodox disapproving view of party, which indeed he never wholly shed. Nor was his main object at this time favoured by Fox or Tierney or Sheridan or Grey, for it was to see Pitt restored to his former office. The tactics would be governed to some extent by circumstance. But Grenville was for long clear about their limits: 'I am far enough', he declared at the start, 'from any idea of putting myself at the head or at the tail of what is called opposition', and he lamented his position later as it slipped into something different.[3] The group itself, moreover, while visibly a group,[4] was not as strictly disciplined or indeed organised as was sometimes supposed, and at this stage was not closely in touch with others. In spirit it remained for some time closer to a traditional connexion than to a third party; and its historical significance lies indeed in its transition from the one to the other, suiting it thereafter to fill a leading role which lasted for a further twenty years.[5]

The situation in the summer of 1802 did not therefore look unpromising for the Government. It held a general election in July, the first for a United Kingdom, in which, allowing for the sizeable Irish element and suspending judgment on the relations between the 'New' and 'Old' Oppositions, there was 'little or nothing', in Addington's words, to mark a real change from the results of the last such occasion in 1796.[6] At Westminster itself the 'Old Opposition' was unsure of the ground, the Grenvillites were wary of junction, and Pitt remained apparently not prepared to take a hand. Events, however, then moved once more in a way that unsettled him afresh. For from August to October a whole series of disturbing, indeed menacing signs could be seen on the Continent. The remodelling of the Batavian constitution[7]

---

1. The terms, probably coined by London newspapers, came to be used by them as a convenient shorthand.

2. Recalling old ties; cf. II, 32n5, 189n2.

3. Grenville to Sir John Newport, an old and intimate friend, 12 November 1801 (Eng. Ms d 80, Bodleian Library). Cf. his remark in the Lords on 3 November that he was not 'a professed oppositionist' (*P.R.*, *3rd ser.*, XVI, 63), and his dislike of 'a peevish harassing opposition on the details of business' in February 1803 (Buckingham, III, 250). For later similar expressions see Harvey, loc. cit., 80, 301–2.

4. Some at least of its leading members were observed as early as November 1801 to be sitting together near the Bar of the Commons, on the bench occupied by Burke after he broke with Fox (Harvey, loc. cit., 29).

5. There is some degree of difference (though not, it seems to me, a sharp one) between the authorities here – Harvey, Sack, and Jupp in *Lord Grenville* – in their assessments of the Grenvillites at this stage and thus of timing in the emergence of a new party. I incline towards Jupp's view (op. cit., 315–19 and n51).

6. *H of P*, I, 160–6. See II, 622–3 for 1796.

7. P. 567 above.

had included a pledge to reduce the size of the French forces in Holland; but that did not take place, and Bonaparte was now refusing to withdraw them from Flushing or Utrecht. At much the same time he crowned a rearrangement in Piedmont by annexing it directly to France, as he did also the island of Elba and then the duchy of Parma. Finally, and more important to feeling in Britain, he intervened directly in Swiss affairs with an Act of Mediation early in October.[1] These developments followed and accompanied demands in London, to restrain the activities of French émigrés, exile French princes, and curb the tone and language of the press. The combination roused the Government to object – 'the Doctor', wrote Camden, 'is extremely warlike'[2] – and to state British interest in 'certain' European states; eliciting a statement in return that, given the cantons' unsettlements, France 'could not do' without Switzerland being properly secure. This short space of time, which had been meant to improve relations with an exchange of Ambassadors, marked instead, and openly, a turning point for the worse.

It also stirred Pitt to take political soundings. In July, returning from a visit to Cambridge for the general election, he had told Grenville he 'much wished' to come to Dropmore for 'a couple of days', and they seem to have agreed to see each other again if the latter visited the Kent or Sussex coast.[3] That seems to have been postponed, and in September Pitt suffered the serious blow to his health.[4] In mid October however Grenville stayed some days at Walmer, where he found in long conversations that matters appeared to have moved. Pitt had not been in touch with Ministers since July, until Castlereagh had come down in the past week to bring him up to date. But from what had been happening in Europe, and this personal report, he now thought that war was likely. Much would turn on what might develop in Switzerland, and the subsequent reaction from Austria and Russia. If they remained passive, our own freedom of action was removed.[5] But if war came, he did not believe that the Government had the necessary talents or reputation in the country. In such case therefore, 'if he saw his Services desired by the King & the public' he ought not allow the state of his health, 'however bad', to stand in the way.

> But he said with the same openness, what I cannot deny, that the having formed that determination in his own mind was of itself a strong reason against his taking any steps which should appear to have a tendency to accelerate (much more to force) such a change in the direction

---

1. Cf. ibid above for earlier events. The exact sequence of annexations now was Elba in August, Piedmont in September, Parma (with Placentia) in October on the death of the Grand Duke.
2. To Bathurst, 24 October 1802 (B.L. Loan Ms 57, vol. 2).
3. Pitt to Grenville, 12 July, 3 October 1802 (*H.M.C., Dropmore*, VII, 99–100, 111–12).
4. P. 547 above.
5. See Fedorak, loc. cit., 184 for two memoranda written by Castlereagh at Walmer, the second, for Pitt, preserved in Cambridge University Library Ms 6958/2919.

of affairs; as his hope of acting with advantage if he resumed the Government must be founded on its being manifest that the thing was not of his seeking, but that he undertook so difficult a task only in compliance with the wishes of the public and in Obedience to the command of the King, *if His Majesty should think it useful to His services to lay these commands upon him.*[1]

'Here then we are', Grenville commented, 'in a situation perfectly new'. In point of fact the novelty was not complete. Pitt's mind was still focused on a deep desire not to appear to be making trouble; to behave in such a way that if he departed from his pledge to Addington it would be in response to a public demand which was shared or accepted by the King. In a sense therefore changing events were serving to reinforce an old determination. This indeed had been made clear recently to Canning, on his own prolonged visit before Grenville arrived: it was at this point that Pitt defined his ambition as being for '*character*, not office'.[2] But of course whether or not his 'romantic' intention could be sustained,[3] the assent to a return was notable in itself; and the question then arose for the 'New Opposition' how that might come about. Might Addington be persuaded to retire of his own accord? But probably that could be effected only by Pitt. Might the King decide to remove his Minister? That presented formidable difficulties. The only other means of achieving the object would therefore be by persuasion, through Parliamentary pressure; and it was for that course that the Grenvilles and Canning, in loose conjunction, resolved to plan.[4]

III

The immediate effects of this increased momentum were not helpful to any one concerned: to the Grenvilles, to Canning, to Pitt's other well-wishers, or to Pitt himself. The first two overplayed their hands, and the last was not prepared to make any commitments. At the beginning of November Grenville indeed warned his brothers not to count their chickens by expecting something 'much more nearly brought into the shape of a proposition, than this matter is, or' – he added cautiously – 'probably ever will be'. '. . . we are moving too fast,' he commented as he watched

---

1. 'A point', Grenville added, 'of which he as well as myself seems to entertain no little doubt'; Grenville to Thomas Grenville, from Walmer, 19 October 1802 (B.L. Add. Ms 41852). He wrote in similar strain to Buckingham, again from Walmer, the next day (Buckingham, III, 211–13).

2. See p. 565 above, and 541 for Canning's stay in the Castle's cottage at Walmer.

3. Cf. Camden over eighteen months earlier (p. 564 above).

4. The possibilities, as notified by Canning, were listed by Malmesbury in October (*Malmesbury*, IV, 80–2). The latter was not himself then a Grenvillite, but was being called on for information about the Court which he gained through the Duke of York.

the first results of his report; and he was right.[1] Buckingham – a liability as so often – at once set to work to construct a Cabinet, from which Addington and Hawkesbury would be specifically excluded. With agreement from brother Thomas and probably from Spencer, he moreover induced Grenville to accept this demand: a misjudgment which at once placed the latter in difficulties. For Grenville had in fact discussed with Pitt the same question of a future arrangement, but one which included Addington and Hawkesbury in a combination of present and past Ministers.[2] He was therefore now obliged to follow up by confessing that he had found more problems from his associates than he had then expected, and that 'any such compromise' would 'totally' destroy the group's 'means of being any use'.[3] The reversal was awkward for him, and ill timed. It could be represented as a design to 'storm the closet', the ultimate triumph of that exercise of party which Grenville himself was at pains to condemn.[4] And it came furthermore at a point when Pitt had learned that the Ministry was at last disillusioned with Bonaparte and prepared more openly to face a break. If this proved to be so, it was likely that, despite his misgivings, he would feel bound to support such efforts.[5] In that event Addington could carry on for the time being, and the Grenvilles' house of cards would fall to the ground.

Canning too made a mistake. He was now closely enough in touch with the brothers to be told their ideas, if still with some reservations, and indeed to sound Pitt on their behalf over the future of the Catholic question – producing the uncommunicative response that 'we should feel . . . a sincere desire to find, if possible, such a solution as might be satisfactory to his Majesty, and at the same time not inconsistent with the maintenance of our public characters'.[6] His independent exertions, however, were not always welcome. Shortly before Parliament was to meet in November he hatched a

1. Grenville to Buckingham, November 1802 (Buckingham, III, 214; between the 1st and the 8th). A 'congress' was intended, to take place at Stowe, a prospect of which he disapproved (to Thomas Grenville, 2 November 1802; B.L. Add. Ms 41852).

2. Buckingham to Grenville, 1 November 1802 (*H.M.C., Dropmore*, VII, 117–22). He also disliked any idea of including Dundas; and trusted, naturally, that 'Surely, surely' Thomas would be found a place. His letter, and a milder one from Thomas himself (op. cit., 115–17), reveal the nature of their brother's tentative discussion with Pitt on possible arrangements.

3. Grenville to Pitt, 8 November 1802 (op. cit., 123–4), after the 'congress' (n1 above) which he attended in the event. Spencer was also there, but Windham was not, through ill health. See also *Malmesbury*, IV, 91. Jupp, op. cit., 319–20 sums up the exchange.

4. Cf. p. 574 above; and I, 635 for the suspicion attached to storming the closet. Grenville had indeed at first thought it 'ridiculous' for the 'congress at Stowe' to review 'what sort of Government the King or Pitt or both should make' (to Thomas Grenville, 2 November 1802; B.L. Add. Ms 41852). When he attended, however, his brothers soon 'fully' convinced him that they were right (Thomas Grenville to Spencer, 10 November 1802; B.L. Add. Ms temp. Althorp G46).

5. Grenville to Thomas Grenville, 25 October 1802 (B.L. Add. Ms 41852).

6. Grenville to Thomas Grenville, 2 November 1802 (B.L. Add. Ms 41852); 'Paper given to Mr. Canning', 8 November 1802, in Pitt's hand and Grenville's files (*H.M.C., Dropmore*, VII, 123).

plot with some of his intimates, and then with Malmesbury, to give notice of a motion for an Address to the throne if the Ministry was not 'strengthened' within a fortnight. The threat was to be heightened privately by an unsigned letter to Addington, warning of an undisclosed list of supporters; and the plan was to be kept secret, particularly from Pitt, by now established in Bath to take the waters before the session opened. Not surprisingly, it miscarried. Pitt soon learned of it, and Canning hurried down to see him only to receive a veto on anything of the kind. Malmesbury, likewise in Bath and revealed as involved, was similarly told, pleasantly but firmly, to stop.[1]

These episodes, coming from both quarters, helped strengthen an anxiety not to be rushed which Pitt showed more strongly the more strongly he was pushed. He was pleased in any case with the improvement in the country's finances since the peace – 'a revenue equal to all Europe . . ., and a commerce as great as that of all Europe' –, a justification he could plead for his judgment on peace in his own final stage;[2] and he confirmed his immediate stance in fact only two days before he saw Canning. On 15 November he wrote to Grenville that any idea of his returning to Government was 'out of the question, unless in the event of war having taken place, or at least being inevitable'. If that were to come about, he might be called 'in such a way' that he would not be at liberty to decline; 'though', he added, 'your decision [clearly referring to the vetoes on Cabinet membership] would add the greatest possible discouragement to the attempt'. Otherwise he saw 'nothing to be gained by the public, and much to be lost to my own credit and character by listening to the idea'.[3] This recalcitrance was soon extended, though as it turned out abortively, to contact with the Ministry itself. According to Rose, who was staying

---

Cf. pp. 560, 570 above for Grenville's own position in relation to Pitt's pledge of March 1801 – which does not seem to have affected significantly a continuing desire for the latter's return. Some suspicions, incidentally, remained in some quarters that Pitt in fact intended to raise the Catholic question again if he returned to office; Lord Redesdale for one, the former John Mitford (see II, 82, 429–30) and now Lord Chief Justice of Ireland, held them in the summer of 1803 (to Pitt, 16 May 1803; Holland Rose, II, 486, and see also by inference in a further letter of the 22nd in Dacres Adams Mss, formerly P.R.O. 30/58/4).

1. Canning's diary, 19, 21, 25–6 October 1802 (Canning Ms 29d); Canning to Grenville, 30 October–19 November 1802 (B.L. Add. Ms 69038); Grenville to Thomas Grenville, 2 November 1802 (B.L. Add. Ms 41852); *Malmesbury*, IV, 83–117, 142 – a good account of a stupid business to which he rather foolishly lent himself after being sounded in general on York (p. 576, n4 above); *Rose*, I, 484–92, similar to the 'Notes' he sent to Pretyman (Pretyman Ms 435/44). This particular cat seems to have been let out of the bag by Mulgrave (*Malmesbury*, IV, 107–8, 166), writing after Pitt had already complained of 'some of my Friends . . . running much faster in their Ideas than I can keep pace with' (15 November 1802; Normanby Mss box J, 387). See p. 548 above for Pitt's visit to Bath.

2. Malmesbury's account a month later, on 13 December, of 'a sort of panegyric on the state of the country'. Pitt added 'laughingly' and 'a *debt* as large as that of all Europe' (*Malmesbury*, IV, 146–7). Cf. p. 420 above for his confidence in the finances if given a breathing space from war.

3. *H.M.C., Dropmore*, VII, 126–7. Since he was answering a letter which, giving him 'great pain', was Grenville's of the 8th (see p. 577, n3 above), the nature of the 'decision' and 'discouragement' is clear.

assiduously at hand for as long as he could, Pitt decided 'to have no Responsibility whatever . . . on the Subject of foreign Politicks', and definitely not to go to London – he had earlier been doubtful – for the forthcoming opening of the session. He also thought of writing to Addington and Hawkesbury 'in a Style' that would 'prevent all further Attempts to draw him into confidential Communications'; and while in the event he did not go so far, thinking it 'too formal', he told the Foreign Secretary, who sent him some despatches to read, that he did not know enough to comment and would be remaining in Bath for a while.[1]

This abstention from commitment, though varying in tone, lasted through the winter. Pitt stayed put in Bath until Christmas Eve, while assorted friends, sometimes competing, sought to gain his ear. Camden, Carrington and Bathurst, Rose, Malmesbury, Mulgrave, Pretyman and Canning saw or wrote to him in November. From another direction, Addington's brother Hiley talked to him early in that month, and Castlereagh late in December. When his departure finally seemed certain, Addington himself wrote requesting a meeting on return.[2] It was not in point of fact a favourable moment, for a variety of incidents had upset Pitt in recent weeks. The most substantial concerned the Minister's budget for the forthcoming year, in which he proposed to make an unprecedentedly large issue of short-term unfunded Exchequer bills: a reversal, in his predecessor's view, of the principle of funding Government borrowing and more recently of trying to meet 'extraordinary' expenses within the year, objects moreover with which he claimed Addington had specifically concurred. This proved indeed to be a serious cause of grievance, for it touched Pitt in what was always his most sensitive point.[3] He was also annoyed by offensive remarks in *The Times*, a Ministerialist journal which was known to have close contacts with Hiley Addington; and by the conferment of a peerage

---

It was in this period – on the 21st – that he made his remark quoted in I, 153, in answer to a comment that public opinion could not declare itself 'quite alone and unaided'; "Yes, often in a way not only unknown, but in a manner as if it had no concerted beginning" (*Malmesbury*, IV, 112–13, giving the whole double quotation marks).

1. Rose to Pretyman, 21 November 1802 (Pretyman Ms 435/44); Rose's diary for 22 November (*Rose*, I, 494–5).

2. Addington to Pitt, 12 November 1802 (Dacres Adams Mss, formerly P.R.O. 30/58/4); Pitt to Addington, 30 December 1802 (Pellew, op. cit., II, 108); *Rose*, I, 514–15.

3. See *Rose*, I, 512–14, 517–18. Pitt also complained of a remark in Addington's budget speech which he thought reflected on his own management of naval expenses (Pellew, op. cit., II, 102n); of alterations to the arrangements of the second Sinking Fund (for which see I, 268); and of 'gross errors', as Rose put it, 'arising from the most childish *ignorance*' in the presentation of the figures. See also the draft, nd, of an indignant message for the press from Rose, castigating Addington's financial ignorance (Dacres Adams Mss, formerly P.R.O. 30/58/8). The issue of the Exchequer bills – a 'gradual' one, to be made on the security of the Vote for 1803 – was for £5 million, with a further £6 million authorised for the next year. Pitt argued persistently that this contravened the leading efforts of his own Administration, in both peace and war (and cf. I, 258–69, II, 517–19); Addington held that the enlarged issues were justified by an increase in trade which needed correspondingly to be sustained (and cf. pp. 10–12 above for practice under Pitt since 1797).

on Dundas, arranged in fact in August but of which he had heard nothing from the recipient himself.[1] He was therefore in no friendly mood, as he showed in his reply, alluding to 'many' matters which caused him 'regret and anxiety', and disclosing that he was breaking his journey with Rose and then with Malmesbury and finally Grenville.[2] Nevertheless he felt obliged to accept the invitation, and the meeting duly took place on 5 January 1803.

Despite this prelude, the two men in the event got on better than perhaps either had expected. Indeed they met again twice in the next three weeks.[3] Pitt seems to have lectured Addington on finance. But he was prepared to wait and see if the errors would be admitted, and meanwhile discussed foreign affairs amicably enough – as he had done recently with Castlereagh[4] – and found his doubts somewhat eased. The greatest point of interest however, to the Minister and his anxious critics alike, yielded nothing definite. Addington put out a feeler, apparently at the last minute, on the possibility of Pitt acting with him; but the response, according to Pitt's account, was that the King's wishes would have to be learned first. The tone of the talks was civil. There was doubtless some amiable chat overnight. But it was elusive; the intentions remained opaque.[5]

Richard Pares, in *King George III and the Politicians*, 129n2, noted that 'In 1801–2 it was very hard to rouse [Pitt] against Addington's mistakes in foreign policy, but he immediately pricked up his ears when he thought he saw Addington making mistakes on finance'. The contrast may be somewhat overdrawn, but the emphasis, at this point, is valid. Not long afterwards, Grenville · observed that Pitt's 'dislike of the whole system of the present government, and *particularly of the finance measures* of the present session, is open and undisguised, avowed to all his friends' (to Buckingham, 15 February 1803; Buckingham, III, 251). He continued indeed to pursue his complaints through Steele in the Treasury (eg Steele to Pitt, 5, 11 February 1803; Stanhope Ms U1590 S5 06/54); and see *Rose*, II, 35 for his thoughts as late as April.

1. *The Times* accused him on 2 December of skulking in retirement when he should be openly supporting the Ministry, and renewed the attack on the 14th (see *Rose*, I, 509, 511, 518). For Pitt's reaction to Dundas's peerage see op. cit., 516–17.

2. Pitt to Addington, 30 December 1802 (Pellew, op. cit., II, 108). The reply was indeed written from Dropmore. See *Rose*, I, 514–18 for the conversations at the first stop, and *Malmesbury*, IV, 152–7 for those at the second. The journey ended moreover in company with Canning for part of the last stage (op. cit., 158).

3. The first meeting took place at the White Lodge in Richmond Park, which George III had offered to Addington in 1801 and in fact refurnished for him. There was a further brief one in Downing Street, and longer talks at the White Lodge again on 17–18 January, when Pitt dined and slept.

4. See p. 579 above for Castlereagh's call at Bath.

5. According to Rose a month later, Pitt said that Addington mentioned the possibility of co-operation in an embarrassed manner as they were returning to London together (he put it on the 17th) and had driven as far as Hyde Park before raising the subject (diary for 21 February 1803; *Rose*, II (1860), 27–8).

Impressions of the talks themselves varied with the point of view: cf. Addington to Hiley Addington, 8 January (Sidmouth Ms 152M/C1803 OZ F1/1), Hawkesbury to Liverpool, 9 January (B.L. Loan Ms 72, vol. 55), Canning to Malmesbury, 10 January (*Malmesbury*, IV,

Their very opacity nonetheless gave rise to trouble in due course. Canning recorded from a conversation with Pitt at the time that there was 'Something like discreet hint at the shadow of an offer – but so faint that it is good for nothing. Not even (as I hope)', he added, 'for A. to quote which I much dreaded'.[1] His hope was premature. Three months later Addington told a confidant that 'in January intimation came to him on the part of Mr. Pitt, that Mr. Pitt was less disinclined to return to power', and he accordingly informed Steele, Spencer Perceval, Long and 'others of Mr. Pitt's friends' that he for his part would be 'no obstacle to so desirable an end'. He affirmed much the same indeed directly to Pitt. Information had come from 'a most respectable channel' that the latter might 'conquer his personal unwillingness' and return to 'an official situation' provided the King and Cabinet agreed; and 'some expressions' to the same effect had 'dropped' from Pitt himself at the close of their talks.[2] This gives a definite impression, at a time when memories were actively in dispute.[3] Pitt did not accept it, and from the nature of the case there is no supporting evidence either way. Something may have fallen, relayed or direct, which allowed the Minister to harbour expectations; for Pitt, beset in London on all sides as he knew he would be, may well have used shades of language according to whom he talked. He was in contact once more with Government and Addington himself as he had not been effectively for several months, and also with friends less committed to outright opposition – as Canning complained – than some of those whom he had lately seen.[4] Such exposures may have somewhat shaken recent impressions. Canning for one certainly thought so: Pitt was 'Still determined to do right [ie oppose the Ministry] – but . . . not *so* determined as a week ago'; his answer to Addington's feeler was 'general, as *he* says, safe from misunderstanding. I hope so'; 'he promises & vows to take a Line fair to the Country & to himself but I am not so confident as I was'.[5] The difficulties arising

164), Canning's diary for 17 [?18] January (Canning Ms 29d) and his letter to his wife in Marshall, *The Rise of George Canning*, 233–6; Pitt to Rose, 11, 28 January and Rose's diary for 20–1 February 1803 (*Rose*, II, 5–9, 18–28).

1. Diary for 17 [?] January 1803; Canning Ms 29d.

2. Conversation with Abbot on 19 April 1803 (*Colchester*, I, 413); Addington to Pitt, 18 April 1803 (Pellew, op. cit., II, 125). The channel is said to have been 'the Right Hon. John Sullivan' (ibid, and see also 117) – an obscure intermediary, one might have thought. He was presumably the MP who had been made Under Secretary for War and the Colonies to his brother-in-law Robert Hobart (for whom see p. 553 above) and became a Privy Councillor in 1805.

The word 'power' in Abbot's report is almost certainly recorded inaccurately; 'an official situation', in Addington's own phrase, is much more credible in the light of the current situation and of subsequent events. As the latter would show, he was not thinking in January of ceding his own place; in fact he later affirmed that in the next few weeks he consulted some of his colleagues on a plan for Pitt's return in which he himself (Addington) retained his position (to Pitt, 21 April 1803; Pellew, op. cit., II, 129).

3. To be discussed on pp. 589–91 below.

4. *Malmesbury*, IV, 150, 168, 172.

5. Diary for 17[?], 20 January 1803 (Canning Ms 29d). And see 26 January.

from his position – from the pledge to a successor of whom he now had doubts – were mounting inexorably and pressing at too great a speed.

His reaction was swift. After his opening talks with Addington he seemed prepared to attend Parliament following the Christmas recess. But after their close he went down to Walmer, and stayed there for two and a half months.[1] Both sides were surprised and aggrieved by his absence: the Grenvilles because they had hoped for closer contact and his vivifying influence in the debates, Addington because he wanted to pursue the lead which he thought had been tentatively supplied.[2] Meanwhile the tone of Anglo–French relations deteriorated still farther. Bonaparte's resentment of the London newspapers was a continual irritant, while British uneasiness was fuelled by growing effects from the hardening of trade restrictions. In such an atmosphere there were plenty of occasions for worry, in Europe and beyond. Hawkesbury had opened an approach to Russia in the autumn for a fresh defensive alliance which as yet showed little sign of fulfilment; and now anxiety for the Continent deepened as Austria consented under pressure to a realignment of German territories, virtually obliterating the small free cities and petty principalities, which dealt a mortal blow to her domination of the Diet and favoured Prussia above herself. A more acute source of acrimony arose farther afield. At the end of January a report – the Sebastiani report – was published in Paris from an officer sent officially to Egypt, which decried the effectiveness of the British force there and claimed that the occupation could be ended by an expedition of six thousand men from France. This aroused a storm in London, and the temperature rose farther in late February following an angry scene between Bonaparte and the British Ambassador Whitworth. The French were still not out of Holland;[3] they were indeed being reinforced; and early in March a naval force left Brest bound, as it transpired, for Indian waters. At that same time Parliament was asked for and voted further supplies to increase the forces; the militia was embodied; and fresh military dispositions were made for Britain and Ireland and India itself.

These were reasons enough for Addington to wish to bind Pitt more securely. For Ministers were coming under greater strain as they seemed unable to stem the tide. In point of fact their despatches to Paris were taking a progressively firmer line, and Bonaparte himself was out to seize

1. Leaving finally on 9 April. On Parliament see Grenville to Buckingham, 10 January 1803 (Buckingham, III, 242) – an attitude unchanged from the turn of the year (same to Thomas Grenville, 3 January 1803, reporting on Pitt at Dropmore (see p. 580 and n2 above), B.L. Add. Ms 41852).

2. Eg on the one side same to Buckingham, 15 February, 12 March 1803 (Buckingham, III, 251, 262–3); on the other, *Colchester*, I, 414 – 'But Mr. Pitt stayed at Walmer during February and March'. The disappointment was the greater because at first he hinted at and then announced his intention to return in mid February (Pitt to Carrington, 18 January 1803, Bodleian Library Mss Film 1121; Grenville to Pitt, 30 January 1803, *H.M.C.*, *Dropmore*, VII, 141, and see also Pitt to Rose, 16 February 1803, *Rose*, II, 9), and then put off an appearance until, he hoped, after Easter (same to same, 2 March 1803, op. cit., 10).

3. Cf. pp. 574–5 above; and 206 for Whitworth.

advantages and show his power rather than precipitate a war at this point.[1] But the Cabinet's deliberations had few visible results, and if the public at large did not yet anticipate a final break there was a growing feeling of frustration, and eyes were focusing more sharply on the silent absentee. The Government still did not have to worry unduly about opposition in Parliament. The Grenvilles were resigned for the time being to a limited campaign; they were not popular, did not command either sufficient or consistent strength, and while waiting for Pitt to declare himself had not made serious approaches elsewhere.[2] In the 'Old Opposition' Fox remained neutral, if unbenevolently, while peace lasted, and other elements varied in their often indecisive responses. Tierney was still disposed – in fact now more strongly – to favour Addington; Grey, who was not, disliked the thought of assisting the Grenvilles, and at one remove Pitt; and the Carlton House politicians, centred on Moira, Sheridan and Erskine, and pursuing a distinctive course when the Prince's finances were concerned, were likewise not particularly anxious to embarrass the Ministry in other respects.[3] While Addington remained open to reinforcements from among these assorted interests, he therefore feared neither them[4] nor the 'New Opposition', if such it could be termed. But Pitt was another matter; and driven by hope from the recent talks and rising alarm from the trend of events, the Minister decided in March to make a more specific approach.

IV

He did so through Dundas, now created Viscount Melville.[5] The channel was one on which he must have congratulated himself. Dundas's initial

1. Pitt for his part indeed wondered, though far from confidently, if he might not be merely 'bullying' (to Chatham, 2 March 1803; copy in P.R.O. 30/8/101).

2. For a limited campaign see Grenville to Buckingham, 30 January 1803 (Buckingham, III, 248), Thomas Grenville to Grenville, 25 January, 1, 20 February (*H.M.C., Dropmore*, VII, 138–9, 141, 146); for unpopularity cf. p. 202 and n2 above. Indications of strength in differing circumstances in the summers of 1802 and 1803 are given on pp. 574, 606 below.

3. The Prince's further need of financial rescue at this time was a prime factor in his attitude towards the various sectors of the Parliamentary world.

4. As had been suggested in fact in January when opportunity arose to make a pair of appointments outside the Cabinet, from which Tierney, the clearest prospect, did not benefit.

5. In I, 132 I referred inexcusably to *Pitt's* creation of Dundas as a peer.

Melville was apparently going down to Walmer on a visit in any case, and Addington in point of fact may have tried to seek pointers earlier through Chatham. Certainly there was an unusually constant flow of letters from the elder to the younger brother between late February and late March 1803. But while these elicited Pitt's views on Malta, on Bonaparte's conduct, and – at greater and indignant length – on what he saw as the failure to prepare financially on proper lines for a possibly lengthy war, they failed to draw him on his intentions. I have not found the letters themselves; but Pitt's replies – including one answering a question from Chatham through Camden on the prospect of his coming to town – are in Dacres Adams Mss, formerly P.R.O. 30/58/4, for 24, 27, 28 February, 2, 8, 25 March 1803, all except for the letter of 8 March printed in Stanhope, IV, 3–10, 17–18, 25–6. The last drew attention to his attitude as already learned by then by Melville.

scorn of the Administration had been largely assuaged by its survival,[1] a *modus vivendi* for management in Scotland, and consultation on Indian affairs.[2] His acceptance of the task now might seem to augur well for its prospect as well as for his own future. Whatever the reservations over past divergences, he looked back with pride to past achievements[3] and wished profoundly to see Pitt once more in office; and his influence, coming from the most loyal and confidential of the old inner circle, might surely be expected to carry considerable weight. This however proved to be optimistic; recent circumstances had left a mark, as other voices were heard in Dundas's long absence – a factor always to be reckoned with – and the acceptance of a peerage raised Pitt's suspicion that some unannounced arrangement was on the cards.[4] Such impediments might well have been removed when the two met on 20 March, if the message itself had been at all congenial. But whatever Addington may have intended, that turned out not to be the case.

One cannot be sure in point of fact how far Melville was able to say all that was wished. In conversations ranging widely over two days, the critical issue seems scarcely to have been explained. From Pitt's account as reported afterwards, his visitor 'began cautiously to open his proposals. But he saw it would not do, and stopped abruptly'; and from Melville's own, which was seen by Pitt at the time, 'there was no room for any discussion' of the detailed offer.[5] The leading proposition was certainly quite remarkably inept. Addington and Pitt should be Secretaries of State in a Ministry in which the First Lord of the Treasury should be Chatham.[6] Given the relative positions of the two brothers over the past twenty years, and Chatham's alignment in 1801,[7] such an arrangement was unlikely to be welcome. But in any case the central point, that Pitt would not come back as First Lord of the Treasury himself, ruled out any possible alternative at once. '"Really"', he said to Wilberforce later – 'with a sly severity, and it was almost the only sharp thing I ever heard him say of any friend' – "I had not the curiosity to ask what I was to be."'[8]

1. Which he had not expected at the start; see *L.C.G. III*, III, no. 2346n1 on p. 488 (cf. p. 531 above). See pp. 579–80 above for the peerage.

2. Where he had been succeeded in 1801 by Viscount Lewisham (soon to succeed as Earl of Dartmouth), who gave way to Castlereagh in July 1802.

3. Cf. pp. 421, 558–9 above.

4. Canning, it may be noted, had suspected this long before (diary of 4 June 1802; Canning Ms 29d).

5. Wilberforce's account of a conversation with Pitt, nd but from the context probably soon after the event (R.I. and Samuel Wilberforce, *Life of Wilberforce*, III, 219); Melville to Addington, 22 March 1803 (Pellew, op. cit., II, 115). Abbot stated (*Colchester*, I, 414) that Pitt 'dictated' the letter. But he seems to have limited himself to deleting some phrases which he thought 'too flattering' to Addington (*Rose*, II, 31).

6. Ibid.

7. See p. 512 n1 above.

8. *Life of Wilberforce*, III, 219. Pitt's words were given there in inverted commas.

Melville's account to Addington makes this sound quite possible; for while he 'did not conceal from him' [Pitt] – a revealing phrase – 'the idea you mentioned, of his returning to

The response was taken on grounds of both principle and personal choice. This was the occasion on which Pitt expressed his belief, 'pointedly and decidedly', in

> the absolute necessity there is, in the conduct of the affairs of this country, that there should be an avowed and real Minister possessing the chief weight in the council, and the principal place in the confidence of the King. In that respect there can be no rivalry or division of Power. That Power must rest with the Person generally called first Minister; and that Minister ought . . . to be the Person at the head of the Finances.[1]

The maxim, matured from long experience, stood independent of the immediate context. But that itself was equally discouraging to Addington's plea. For Pitt reiterated his desire to remain in a private station, supporting Government as at the start if it could prove competent. He did not disguise his concern at 'many things' in its handling of foreign affairs and financially at home; if the former situation were not so critical he doubted if he could have kept silent on the latter. He had decided however, for the present at any rate, to take no part in Parliament, and stay at Walmer. And as to office, 'nothing could induce him to come forward except an urgent sense of public duty, and a distinct knowledge that his services . . . are wished and thought essential both in *the highest quarter*, and by all those with whom . . . he might have to act confidentially'. He thus seemed to be confirming his position of the autumn, which he reinforced by arguing that current exchanges with France, so important as the situation worsened, should not be prejudiced by any return of himself. That was an immediate point, to which – shades of February 1801 – he appeared to attach importance.[2] But it was obvious in any case that he could not be recruited except at the head of affairs.

---

a share of the government with a person of rank and consideration at the head of it perfectly agreeable to him, and even specified the person you had named . . . there was no room for any discussion on that part of the subject, for he stated at once, without reserve or affectation, his feelings with regard to any proposition founded on such a basis' (Pellew, op. cit., II, 115). A subsequent memorandum by Grenville, recounting Pitt's description of the occasion, would seem to confirm the point (dated 1803; Buckingham, III, 284). Rose's account, from a conversation with Pitt on 8 April, specifies that Addington had hoped 'Mr. Pitt would . . . be satisfied with naming the First Lord of the Treasury, and filling the office of Secretary of State' (*Rose*, II, 31), and Grenville noted that there was mention later of the Exchequer as a potential alternative (Buckingham, III, 282). But of course Pitt was unlikely to have followed his immediate veto of the plan with a question as to his own prospective position. Cf. also *Malmesbury*, IV, 177, and for Canning's account Marshall, *The Rise of George Canning*, 233.

1. Melville to Addington, 22 March 1803 (Pellew, op. cit., II, 116). I have altered the orthography of the document as I quoted it in I, 281 to give the flavour of the original in Sidmouth Ms 152M/C1803 OZ 326, which I had not then consulted.

2. Cf. p. 516 above. The original ms of the letter is printed in Pellew, op. cit., II, 114–16; copies exist in Melville's papers (B.L. Add. Ms 41002) and in Pitt's (Dacres Adams

In the next fortnight, however, such a prospect was thrust to the fore. Relations with France were now at a highly critical stage. The Government had decided by the turn of the year, in parallel with Pitt's own strong opinion, to postpone the withdrawal of troops from conquests due for return, and in addition above all from Malta.[1] This last question assumed a growing prominence in the worsening atmosphere: a 'perfidy' denounced by Bonaparte in response to British accusations of infringements elsewhere. On 13 March he unleashed a furious outburst on Whitworth, before a large audience, accusing Britain of being determined on war. Talks however continued, with Hawkesbury seeking fresh conditions to meet British views of recent developments. Malta should be garrisoned by Britain for ten years, after which the island would be handed over to the Maltese themselves; a proposal altered later to a cession to Britain of the neighbouring island of Lampedusa by its unfortunate sovereign, The Two Sicilies, in return for British recognition of the French creations of the kingdom of Etruria[2] and the Cisalpine (now named Italian) and Ligurian republics. France for her part should provide compensation for Sardinia's losses, withdraw her troops from Holland as proclaimed earlier, and from occupation of Switzerland. These were distinctly sterner demands, reflecting the growing complaints and indeed, as it proved, a decisive change of attitude. For, despite a continuing failure to bring Russia into a closer relationship, but conscious of a noticeable fall in commercial activity and a sharper public sense of resentment and gloom, the Government resolved by the end of March to set a limit to further talks with Bonaparte, and by mid April to bring him swiftly to the point.[3] The pace therefore was quickening fast, war seemed suddenly to be closer, and with that prospect, and what it meant for the Ministry, Pitt's presence was the more strongly desired.

Addington indeed was now prepared, after the failure of his compromise, to cede his place to his predecessor outright. It cannot have been a pleasant step to take. He was not anxious to retreat, let alone to be humiliated.[4] He

---

Mss, formerly P.R.O. 30/58/4). See further Pitt to Rose, 2 March 1803 (B.L. Add. Ms 42772) for his determination not to raise his grievances about finance immediately in public at this critical time; a week earlier he had threatened that he might intervene if further forthcoming measures and the budget itself looked unsatisfactory (to Chatham, 24 February 1803; P.R.O. 30/8/101).

1. Fedorak, loc. cit., 187–91. Pitt's own attitude by the end of 1802 emerges from *Malmesbury*, IV, 156; and cf. p. 558 above.

2. Cf. p. 782 below.

3. See Fedorak, loc, cit., 192–7, 204–7; and cf. p. 582 above for Russia. The proposal for Lampedusa was put forward after that for Malta, made on 4 March, was clearly not going to be accepted. Hawkesbury informed Whitworth on 30 March and 13 April of the Government's successive decisions on the limit to talks. The public seems to have awoken early in March to the possible imminence of war.

4. Or as Macaulay unfairly and inimitably put it, 'He was, indeed, under a delusion much resembling that of Abou Hassan in the Arabian tale. His brain was turned by his short and unreal Caliphate' (Essay on Pitt, 1859 in *The Miscellaneous Writings* . . . (with the misprint 'Abon') (1860), 359).

liked being First Minister and was not dissatisfied with his performance; and furthermore he was not already in immediate danger of supersession. He could still look to the King's favour and adequate Parliamentary majorities, and while there were signs of dissatisfaction in the Cabinet his colleagues were unlikely as yet to rebel.[1] If he stuck it out, he might carry on. But there could also have been less happy thoughts: an apprehension perhaps of the hazards of war, for which he was inexperienced, that could lead to mounting public disgust; a sense of alarm, from the evidence of the earlier occasion on which Pitt had taken umbrage,[2] of the prospect that his lifelong superior might now decide to take the field; and a suspicion at any rate that some of his Cabinet would not be sorry for a direct change.[3] On the other hand he could reflect that his sacrifice would be recognised as preserving the complexion of Government, bringing the desired strength to bear without surrendering to any section of his opponents. Whatever the outcome, a fresh intermediary moreover was available in welcome form. For Charles Long, one of Pitt's circle with whom he had earlier been in touch, was at Walmer after Melville left, had then borne a message suggesting a meeting, and was permitted to talk to the Minister on return. Never an advocate of a rupture – suspect indeed to Canning, and not very partial to Rose – his moderating influence might be brought into play. He was accordingly authorised by Addington to enlarge on a fresh approach, which he did by letter on 3 April and possibly a further visit on the 5th.[4]

The Minister now professed real anxiety to see Pitt come forward as quickly as possible. The talks with France should present no obstacle, for one way or another the issue was likely to be clear very soon.[5] An arrangement based on Pitt at the Treasury, and providing for respective interests, should not be out of reach; he named the persons with the greatest surviving claims on himself, and others whom he hoped would not be wholly dismissed. He was prepared to see Canning in some post, despite some personal resentment, and also Rose. His only objection was to an immediate admittance of the Grenvillites, though they might perhaps come in later.

---

1. His favour with the King, resting still above all on the Catholic question, had been stressed three months earlier by an observer at Court (see *Malmesbury*, IV, 140); his strength in Parliament now, and indeed a surviving popularity in the country, was noted later by Cornwallis (*Correspondence of Cornwallis*, III, 506–7). The degree of approval within the Cabinet was more dubious, as suggested below; but events nonetheless would shortly reveal support under pressure.

2. See p. 569 above.

3. There is evidence of this last in Melville to Long, 28 March 1803 (B.L. Add. Ms 40102); Long to Pitt, 3 April 1803 (Dacres Adams Mss, formerly P.R.O. 30/58/4, partly printed in Stanhope, IV, 28–30); Malmesbury's diary January–March 1803, for the opinion of Pelham, admittedly an initially reluctant member of Cabinet (*Malmesbury*, IV, 188, 197–8, 213, 232, 284; and see p. 553, n1 above for Pelham's reluctance).

4. Long to Pitt, 3 April 1803 as in n3 above; his movements are given in Buckingham, III, 284 and *Malmesbury*, IV, 177–8, 183. See p. 581 above for Addington's earlier statement to him and others; *Malmesbury*, IV, 168 for Canning's suspicion of him – together with Ryder, Steele and Camden – in January (cf. p. 581 above).

5. Cf. p. 586 above.

Long added his own gloss to these statements. He knew that Hawkesbury and Castlereagh were convinced of the need for Pitt to take over, though the former held views – attributable he thought in part to Addington – on 'what Ministers had a right to expect from you and your friends', and was also opposed to the return in any capacity of his predecessor at the Foreign Office, whose policies he thought 'very ill suited to the circumstances of the present times'. Similar sentiments, favourable to Pitt and unfavourable to Grenville, were being echoed in the City, and Long himself questioned the wisdom of bringing in the latter at once. He hoped that the proposed meeting, for which he offered his own house at Bromley, could be held very soon; and it duly took place there a week later, on the 10th.[1]

It did not go as the friends of an accommodation would have wished. For at some point Pitt disclosed the conditions on which alone he would agree to act. He could come in only in answer to the King's expressed wish, and with authority to submit for George III's consideration an arrangement which could include, subject to the royal concurrence and that of the first of the parties concerned, *'those who were in the former as those who are in his present* Government'.[2] Addington was told that he himself could be given an office for which there was no exact, if any, precedent: a Speakership of the Lords distinct from the Lord Chancellorship, with financial provision and naturally a peerage. The categorical statement of intent – the first he had heard, whatever his earlier surmises – must have come as a shock. He needed time to reflect, and two days later gave a provisional reply. He was very willing, as Pitt knew, to leave his post, and he did not want the experimental Speakership. He was going to consult his colleagues, who were

---

1. Long to Pitt, 3 April 1803 as in p. 587, n3 above. He also cited the Lord Chancellor, Eldon, with Hawkesbury and Castlereagh, but at second hand. He knew furthermore that Melville, like himself, was against Grenville's immediate return (copy of Melville to Long, 28 March 1803; B.L. Add. Ms 40102).

For the house at Bromley see p. 89 above. According to Abbot (*Colchester*, I, 415), Addington left on the 11th. Pitt stayed on, since he was required in any case to be in London some days later, following the death of his mother which occurred at Burton Pynsent on the 3rd (see p. 546 above). She was to be interred in the Abbey by the side of Chatham, and the funeral took place on the 16th.

2. Pitt to Addington, 15 April 1803 (Pellew, op. cit., II, 122–4). Pitt sent a copy to Grenville on the 17th (with the same italics) which is printed in *H.M.C., Dropmore*, VII, 159–61, and see 157. There was no disagreement subsequently that these two central points had been made. Stanhope (IV, 32–3) mentions a third: Pitt's earlier proviso that no arrangement should take place until the talks with France were over, and the question of peace or war was decided (cf. pp. 586–7 above). Rose may conceivably have stiffened his resolve over this at the last minute (Rose to Pitt, 9 April 1803; copy in B.L. Add. Ms 42772). But whether or not that was so – and the letter may not have reached him in time – the stipulation, if made, might have reflected continuing suspicion of an appeasing accommodation with France (see Buckingham, III, 284 for Pitt's possible impression from Long on 29 March) from which Pitt could then dissociate himself if it looked like sanctioning a potential or increasingly shameful peace.

meeting the next day, on the wider issues, and suggested a further conversation after that.[1] This however evoked a discouraging response. Pitt could see no point in a further talk, for he had nothing to add.[2] Meanwhile, on 13 April, the Cabinet met. The result might have been guessed. Ministers would warmly welcome a 'union of those who had concurred in opinion respecting the leading measures of government'; but they could not advise the admission of 'some of those' whose 'declared opinions' were otherwise. Addington communicated this on the 14th.[3] On the same day he had a reply.[4]

> My dear Sir,
>   I need only acknowledge the receipt of your
> letter, and am yours sincerely,
> W Pitt

That appeared to be conclusive. There was however more to come. For Pitt decided to put on paper his version of what had occurred. On 15 April he sent Addington a long letter which opened an increasingly stiff correspondence revealing, among other things, the kind of misconceptions and differences in emphasis always liable to arise from unrecorded private talks.[5] Both parties harked back to January. The Minister was accused of relaying to his colleagues Pitt's remarks at that time as 'a specific and positive proposition', which they had not been. The fact was rather that it was he, Addington, who had made all the running, while Pitt had made it clear,

---

1. Addington to Pitt, 12 April 1803 (Pellew, op. cit., II, 119–20, with a copy in *H.M.C., Dropmore*, VII, 158). *Colchester*, I, 414 records his reluctance, if he stayed in any post and had to take a peerage, to do so in this way rather than with 'a regular office and duties' and a provision that could not be challenged.

2. 13 April 1803 (Pellew, op. cit., II, 121, with a copy in *H.M.C., Dropmore*, VII, 158–9). There is a draft in P.R.O. 30/8/102).

3. Addington to Pitt, 14 April 1803 (Pellew, op. cit., II, 121–2, with a copy in *H.M.C., Dropmore*, VII, 159). His own copy has against the words 'some of those' 'viz. Lord Grenville and Mr Windham'. According to Canning the opposition in Cabinet included Hawkesbury (see Marshall, *Rise of Canning*, 243; and also op. cit., 233–7 for a long account to his wife, after seeing Pitt, of events from Melville's visit in March onwards).

4. Pellew, op. cit., II, 122.

5. For what follows see Pitt to Addington, 15, 21, 22, 24 April 1803 (Pellew, op. cit., II, 122–4, 127–8 (with the first also in *H.M.C., Dropmore*, VII, 159–61 and the second in P.R.O. 30/8/102)); Addington to Pitt, 18, 21, 24 April 1803 (Pellew, op. cit., 124–7, 129, with Dacres Adams Mss, formerly P.R.O. 30/54/4, in addition for the last. Sidmouth Mss 152M/C1803 OZ 201–4 contain some of the letters from both parties throughout). According to the report of an account or accounts said to have been assembled on Pitt's behalf, he regarded the information in Addington's letter of the 14th as equivalent to a 'Minute of Cabinet', which would be the only record if he did not provide his own (*Malmesbury*, IV, 180–1).

Pitt's state of mind is also revealed in the progressively chillier subscriptions to his letters, which Addington duly copied. The old 'yours affectionately' of many years had lasted until January 1803. It was replaced on 13 April by 'yours sincerely', and that sank after the 15th to 'your faithful and obedient servant'.

in giving him an indication of his own ideas, that the only ground on which he would return to office would be 'some direct previous intimation of his Majesty's wish to that effect, together with full authority to form, *for his Majesty's consideration*, a plan of arrangement in any manner I thought best'. Having done that, he had no intention of pressing 'any point' – rather, he would judge if he could proceed; and he had said further that he would not make 'a distinct proposal' to former colleagues until such authority was available. Meanwhile he had wished Addington to understand that he could give only an 'outline' of his ideas, to enable the Minister to decide how far they might be recommended to the King; and that they included his own intention to bring in some of those past colleagues, provided they consented, to whom the Cabinet's reservations now applied.

Such a missive obviously demanded a riposte. Addington built his case on a significantly different impression. Agreeing that Pitt had not 'origin-ated' a 'proposition', he gave his own account of January, from which the rest flowed. Their talks then had appeared to justify his belief that his pre-decessor might return to 'an official situation'[1] if given to understand that it was the wish of the King and of 'his Majesty's confidential servants'.[2] He had hoped to learn more following the meeting, and then tried per-force through intermediaries, receiving in due course an agreement to a further talk and also verbal information, from Melville, that Pitt 'had no wish for any material change, but such as might be necessary ... respect-ing myself'. There was no objection on that score – he himself did not want 'any official situation whatever'.[3] But when Pitt on 10 April placed his ideas on the footing now confirmed in his letter, the members of the Cabinet had been told and gave advice as the King's servants. The exchanges ended indeed by returning to the start. Pitt stressed that he had thought he was being sounded then on a return to form 'a new plan of arrangement' in his 'former situation' – 'certainly' not to provide 'an accession of strength to the present government'; Addington that he had then had in mind 'precisely' what he suggested through Melville, on which he had in fact consulted Eldon, Hawkesbury, Castlereagh and Spencer Perceval before Parliament met.[4]

By this stage therefore disagreement was virtually complete, and Pitt called for his letters – to which he added Melville's from Walmer – to be shown to the King. Addington concurred, and presented them by the end of the month. George III's reaction was variously reported. He refused to read the package, or even to take notice of it, and was said to have remarked a day or two later that it was 'a foolish business from one end to

1. Cf. p. 581 and n2 above.
2. Cf. Melville on 22 March, on p. 585 above; '. . . both in the *highest quarter*, and by all those with whom . . . he might have to act confidentially'.
3. According however to Rose's account of his conversation with Pitt on 8 April, the latter had been told a few days earlier by Long that Addington still intended to remain in the Cabinet as a Secretary of State (*Rose*, II, 32).
4. And cf. p. 583, n5 above.

the other, which was begun ill, conducted ill, and terminated ill'. This reflected on both participants. He was also said however to have observed that Pitt was 'putting the Crown in commission'; 'he carried his plan of *removals* so extremely far and high that it might reach *him*'.[1]

V

From the King's point of vantage his final comment, as reported, was a not unnatural one. For Pitt's conditions could indeed appear dangerously close to storming the closet. He was disclaiming any such intention, as most politicians would do and he was entitled by his earlier career;[2] and he meant what he said, in his own sense. He had been forcibly reminded two years before of the monarch's latent strength, albeit on an exceptional issue; he was genuinely anxious to spare George III excitement and worry as far as he could;[3] and at the end of the day he had placed the royal consent in a position which was central to his own. If the King jibbed at an immediate introduction of Grenville, Pitt would not try to force it; he would doubtless decline to do anything more. The pressure would then lessen. Nonetheless there would still be pressure, indirect and not necessarily of his seeking, in a context in which George III had been specifically solicited to extend an invitation which would deprive him of a favoured Minister and the latter's influence over the change. The terms were high: authority to submit a list for a new Government 'in any manner' Pitt 'thought best'.[4] It was a far cry from the junction of like interests which Addington had envisaged, and had claims to expect.

For the Minister felt that he had reason to be surprised. To some of his critics his conduct had been disingenuous: even if he may have had some 'real misconceptions . . . there was also a wilful error, and a great appearance of cunning'.[5] He may indeed have pushed his interpretation of Pitt's inconclusive remarks to the limit. If the latter gave the impression to Melville that 'he had no wish for any material change' apart from that

1. See *Malmesbury*, IV, 187, 185. The first of these accounts was Pelham's, who reported the words; the last expression was attributed to Malmesbury – who was unsympathetic of course to Addington – to the way in which the Minister might have 'told his story'.
   Canning claimed some days later that the King's opinion had softened, and hinted that this was due to the Duke of York (to Pitt, 3 May 1803; Dacres Adams Mss, formerly P.R.O. 30/58/4).
2. Cf. I, 45–7, 135–6, and particularly 635–43.
3. See eg his emphatic remarks to Malmesbury in November 1802 (*Malmesbury*, IV, 116–17); also *Rose*, II, 23.
4. P. 590 above. There are notes, nd in Pitt's hand in P.R.O. 30/8/197, of posts (senior and junior) and names. I find them hard to date, and Melville appears as Dundas. But they might relate to this time.
5. Malmesbury's own verdict (*Malmesbury*, IV, 185). Some others, long suspicious and having older ties with Pitt, would have been less disposed to accept a qualification.

affecting Addington, such a remark from a prospective successor had still to be more precisely tested; and some of Addington's own versions stretched the limit itself. Would Pitt, given latitude, really have confined his expectations, as was alleged, to 'one friend' in the Cabinet, or to two less senior Ministerial posts for Ryder and Long?[1] In point of fact he had covered the ground more widely to one of Addington's messengers at least, mentioning Hobart and Pelham unfavourably, Canning and Rose for possible office, and speculating at large on the Departmental boards.[2] There were other thoughts moreover which may have remained discreetly concealed: Hawkesbury to leave the Foreign Office, Liverpool – old and ill – the Duchy of Lancaster, Hobart and Pelham to be retired (not merely moved), Addington himself to be retained if necessary as a Secretary of State with a peerage if he would not take the proposed Speakership of the Lords.[3] Furthermore, and more significantly, Pitt had very recently raised Grenville's name.[4] There were qualifications to be made to this aspect of the Minister's case.

Nevertheless he could genuinely think that he had cause to make it. If the evidence was by no means hard, it had seemed for some time to point one way. The issue of course focused on the question of the Grenvillites, and Addington must have been aware that Pitt had been holding aloof from them since January, and indeed from the small circle of his own most intractable friends. These last had in fact become distinctly worried. Rose went to Walmer only twice in two months, and his correspondence was limited to answering some queries on finance, with a warning to be careful in any remarks in public. Canning, already disturbed by Pitt's visits to Addington, was dismayed and almost incredulous when his subsequent approaches to his friend were checked and then effectively stopped. As Malmesbury noted in the middle of March, those whom Pitt 'considered as the more immediate followers of his political fortune' found his behaviour 'an unfair mystery'; and Malmesbury himself, a more judicious witness, believed that he was 'meditating some plan' probably on his

---

1. *Colchester*, I, 414 for the first allegation, attributed to Addington directly, *Malmesbury*, IV, 183 for the second, summing up '*Addington's and his friends*' account', and see op. cit., 177 for a variant. The opening idea seems to have been that Pelham would make way for Pitt at the Home Office – the first Cabinet office for which Pitt himself had ever been considered, in 1782 (see I, 83) – and that St Vincent, who was unhappy at the Admiralty (p. 553 above), might be succeeded by Melville or perhaps Spencer.

2. See Long to Pitt, 3 April 1803 (Stanhope, IV, 28–9); the references there to his conversation with Addington clearly follow his talk with Pitt a few days before (p. 587 above). According to an account of the whole affair said to emanate from Pitt, Addington himself had 'courted details of every sort . . . and disposed of places, without reserve' in the talks in January (*Malmesbury*, IV, 179).

3. *Rose*, II, 33–5, for conversation with Pitt on 8 April. See p. 553, n1 above for the Chancellorship of the Duchy of Lancaster as an office valid for a Cabinet place. Pitt was also becoming worried by St Vincent's conduct of the Admiralty, and, though not mentioned there, the First Lord was probably destined for summary retirement.

4. Long to Pitt, 3 April 1803, as in n2 above.

own.[1] As for Grenville, Pitt had thought earlier that his language would make it 'quite impossible' for them to manoeuvre together, and they had not seen each other since the turn of the year.[2] They did so at length at the end of March. When that happened, however, the occasion gave every sign of justifying Addington's complaint.

It certainly came at a critical moment. For as Long left Walmer on 30 March, having given Addington's message, he saw Grenville's carriage arrive.[3] As soon indeed as he had heard of Melville's earlier visit, Grenville had decided to follow it up.[4] By the time he reached the Castle, the quickening pace of events enabled him to report, in the military metaphors he now chose to use, that 'The garrison has proposed to capitulate'. 'Our commander in chief' however had not decided 'what time he shall allow them'[5] – a somewhat extravagant impression of resolve. The cousins reviewed the scene abroad and at home. They agreed on the line to be taken with France, and Pitt then inquired if the Grenvillites were likely to 'assist' him if he were asked to come in. After a natural caveat on the state of affairs at the time, Grenville made three conditions. He and his associates must be free to state to the King their continuing support for the Irish Catholics' relief if and whenever the question was raised in Parliament. They would not disavow their public disapproval of the past policies of possible colleagues. And – earnestly urged – it must be made clear that they were joining 'a new government' formed by Pitt, not negotiating through him a share of power with the current Ministry. This meant that he should not seek to settle arrangements when he met Addington, whom Grenville did not trust; rather, he 'should state the absolute necessity of his [Pitt's] first receiving the King's commands'. 'After some discussion, Mr. Pitt seemed satisfied as to the propriety of this line', and Grenville left him 'fully determined to adhere to it'. Some contingencies were also discussed: George III's likely reaction to the thought of Grenville's return, which would earlier have been unfavourable but Grenville himself was now inclined to think might have been eased;[6] and also the possibility of a more extensive arrangement, to include Moira and Grey and perhaps Tierney (but not Fox, who was said to be prepared to stand aside) – a speculation which Pitt deprecated, though he was

1. *Rose*, II, 5–30, with a few other letters in B.L. Add. Ms 42772; *Malmesbury*, IV, 167–70, 172, 174–6, 231–2 for a good view of Canning (and see p. 581 above for the latter's doubts in January), with his own opinion in 176.

2. See *Rose*, I, 503 for Pitt on Grenville at the end of November 1802; Buckingham, III, 267 for Grenville on Pitt as late as 22 March 1803.

3. This was Addington's account on 19 April (*Colchester*, I, 415). Grenville confirms his arrival on the day that Long left (Buckingham, III, 284). For the message carried by Long see p. 587 above.

4. To Buckingham, 29 March 1803 (op. cit., 269–70). From Pitt's letter to him of the 23rd (*H.M.C., Dropmore*, VII, 150) it seems clear to me that Grenville proposed himself.

5. To Thomas Grenville, 1 April 1803, written from Walmer (B.L. Add. Ms 41852).

6. Cf. p. 521 above. If however a difficulty clearly remained, he, and Spencer, would not accept an 'intrusion' which would then be 'adverse to all our principles'.

struck by the merits of seeking as wide a Parliamentary consensus as possible in placing before the country the 'exceedingly strong measures' he thought he might have to bring in. Finally, Grenville returned to his group's objection to Addington and Hawkesbury. He would not insist on their exclusion from the Cabinet; but they should not hold 'efficient offices', a conclusion to which, he found, Pitt appeared already disposed.[1]

Grenville however does not seem to have been particularly hopeful of success. Despite the fact of Pitt's question, and apparent concurrence with much of what he heard, 'almost all those' who would shortly 'surround' him wished to confine an arrangement to his 'party' and Addington's, and that would be the likely result.[2] He may well have been right about the majority of Pitt's friends;[3] and in any case he was already depressed. For if Addington felt that he had cause for grievance, so too did his leading critic. The Grenvilles were tired of waiting for Pitt to make up his mind and show that he had done so; of hearing views in sympathy with their own on foreign affairs and the Ministry's weaknesses, only to find them modified or action postponed within a matter of weeks. At the end of January, Grenville himself had written in despair to the man who 'alone' could 'save his country' but was 'still waiting, and deliberating upon personal delicacies'. That had not appeared to make much impression,[4] and it was not surprising that he took the latest conversation with a pinch of salt.

In point of fact moreover Pitt's feelings may still have been ambivalent. The outcome of any talks he might hold with the group could not be taken for granted. He could do without the prospect of further embarrassment over the Catholic question, and an insistence at the moment of junction on Addington's past misdeeds. On the other hand the past beckoned; and if that held memories of aggravations when he had been in search of peace,[5] he felt the strength that his cousin could bring now that war was on the cards. He had already told Long to raise the question of the Grenvillites with Addington;[6] and whatever the

---

1. Grenville's main account of the conversation was given in a 'narrative', dated simply 1803, which was shown to Buckingham (Buckingham, III, 289–90). Pitt's reaction to the ideas of a wider arrangement, however, is described in Grenville's letter of 1 April to his brother Thomas (as in 593, n5 above). Cf. p. 577 above for the attitude to Addington and Hawkesbury.

2. 'Narrative', in Buckingham, III, 289.

3. In February, Canning, admittedly extreme, thought that 'all' the 'old friends' except Rose were also 'Addington's', pointing specifically to Ryder, Long, Steele and Camden (*Malmesbury*, IV, 168, 172, and see also 150; cf. p. 581 above).

4. Grenville to Pitt, 30 January 1803 (*H.M.C., Dropmore*, 140); Pitt to Grenville, 3 February 1803 (op. cit., 141–2). The Grenvillite Minto (see pp. 239, 573 above), who had been connected with the group since the treaty of Amiens, had earlier conclued that 'Pitt is an eel, and no man can tell what part he will take' (*Life and Letters of Sir Gilbert Elliot*, III, 266).

5. Cf. eg pp. 55, 57–8, 382 above for the divergencies over the searches for peace with Rose, I, 511 for late in 1802 (then instancing Spencer as well).

6. Long to Pitt, 3 April 1803 (p. 592 and n2 above).

balance of his views may have been, his mind was made up to explore in the course of the week after Grenville left.

It is important to be clear on what Pitt was about to demand. He would not necessarily refuse to take office without Grenville, and Spencer. The account of his last recorded conversation before meeting Addington is specific that 'nothing' was 'decided' on that. The issue at hand was separate, but it was one on which, in distinction, he was 'resolute' by then: that he must be 'allowed to communicate as freely as possible with them, and to act on their advice'.[1] His immediate object in fact was freedom of action, as an integral part of the King's invitation itself; and it was here in fact, one may think, that Grenville's urgings dovetailed with his own mounting sentiments. For while Pitt's insistence on a prior royal summons was of course far from new, the argument now – stressing a mistrust of negotiation with and through Addington – may have been highly significant, particularly coming at the moment it did.

The chronology indeed should be borne in mind. Pitt's marked and apparently sudden change of emphasis on 10 April and in his subsequent letters can perhaps be best explained on a combination of grounds. One must remember in the first place that he often came to a decision very late in the day;[2] and this was the first time that he had been strictly obliged to do so in this case. Nonetheless he had of course given his position in principle much thought: 'he had revolved the great question of his *coming forward* again and again in his mind'.[3] And his review – his survey of the relationship of his personal to the public interest – impressed many of those who heard it even when they did not agree. One of the former junior Ministers, calling at Walmer a few days before Pitt left, felt the old veneration. 'Every thing that drops from Him', he wrote,

> is so marked by superior Virtue & superior Sense that it is impossible not to love & admire in Him something different even from all other Men. Neither Ambition or Interest will lead him to do any thing which, with the most severe Judge, could lessen those feelings for Him, & tho' it is not very unlikely He may soon come into power again, the resumption of it, should it take place, will be upon terms & in a manner, not less creditable to his Character, than his retreat.[4]

---

1. *Rose*, II, 33, 36, diary for 8 April. 'Act on their advice' is ambiguous. I have taken it as meaning 'after having heard their advice'; the alternative would run counter to his very freedom of action.

2. Cf. p. 510 above.

3. Malmesbury's account of a conversation on 29 December 1802 (*Malmesbury*, IV, 154).

4. Huskisson to Mrs Huskisson, 5 April 1803 (B.L. Add. Ms 38737). It need not be inferred from this that he was the recipient of a secret. While he was no longer in office or indeed in Parliament, he knew something at least of what was going on – Pitt was said to have expected him to bring a further letter from Long (Grenville's 'Narrative'; Buckingham, III, 285) –, and the prospect of the meeting with Addington, and rumours of Pitt's return to office, were in the air.

Others, watching the same processes of thought, were similarly struck, in earlier months and at the time of the acerbic correspondence itself.[1] His 'provident thinking mind' surveyed this sensitive issue in the balanced, comprehensive way it had surveyed so much else.[2]

At the same time he was not a disembodied spirit. There was also a temperament to take into account. For Pitt had been astonished in the past fortnight by a proposal that struck at the centre of his vision of himself. One might indeed say that he had been outraged by Melville's message – Wilberforce was certainly surprised by an impression of resentment he had never encountered before.[3] But then neither had Pitt ever encountered such an experience: it was quite unfamiliar – in fact quite unknown. He was not used to being treated as a piece on the board to be placed as others decided: he filled the position around which the board was arranged. 'This young man', Dundas had noted long ago, 'does not choose to suffer it to be doubtfull who is the effectual Minister'. At the very start, in 1782, he had announced that 'he never would accept of a subordinate situation'.[4] That had referred to a post outside the Cabinet, in a prospect of the very first offer he might receive. The term could long since have been taken as applying to all places but that at the top.

The insult, for so it was taken, was not eased by the fact that it came from Addington. For the awkwardness inherent in the relationship between a predecessor and successor was enhanced in this case by the circumstances of the transfer and, more lastingly, of a lifetime. Pitt had been fond of Addington, in a literally patronising kind of way; and if the patronage proved quite gratifying when the beneficiary proved to be a good Speaker, it remained marked enough for him to be taken for granted, at least for a good many years. The episode in 1797 pointed to that. Thereafter the quality and balance of the friendship had tilted less steeply: Pitt allowed Addington more into his confidence and showed him that he had a place in the scheme of things, while Addington (and he alone apart from Farquhar) had been privy to Pitt's lowest moment – to the breakdown, or something approaching it, in 1800. His company moreover, if not lively, was not uncongenial. He had a good memory from which to swap quotations, and a young family with which Pitt could indulge his fondness for children.[5] It is hard to assess Addington's own view of what nonetheless remained an uneven relationship: two observers

1. See *Malmesbury*, IV, 154–7; *Life of Wilberforce*, IV, 95. Wilberforce, it is true, had heard only Pitt's version at the time.
2. The phrase was Malmesbury's (IV, 94). For some idea of the surveys themselves see op. cit., 154–7 for late December 1802, *Rose*, II, 18–27 for February 1803.
3. P. 584 above.
4. See I, 133, 80.
5. See pp. 89–90 above in general, including for Addington's place as a confidant in the Emily Eden affair and in the duel with Tierney; 46–8 for the thought of putting him in the Treasury in 1797; 82 for 1800; 90 and B.L. Add. Ms 62112 for Repton's reminiscences of quotations and playing with the children at Woodley.

at any rate thought that he was less devoted than he appeared.[1] That would not have been astonishing, and since 1801 his sense of consequence had naturally grown. Genuine friendship and respect may have accommodated some hidden resentment; but Pitt was not likely to have gauged such a combination, and a rather careless personal regard, diminished by the political differences, seems to have survived into 1803.[2] If he shared jokes at the Doctor's expense, he was not unkindly.[3] Suspected slights, however, were not taken so lightly,[4] and the offer through Melville not lightly at all. It stung to the quick in its affront to 'the Pride and Dignity' of his 'Character',[5] and the tone of the reaction could have suggested the extent.

An emotional surge – progressively visible in a deepening chill – may therefore have added its flavour to a proclivity from which Addington indeed had once benefited. For when Pitt took a stand on a question that might reflect on his personal integrity, he was likely to state and defend it without compromise. So it had been on the Preliminaries of peace in 1801.[6] So it was now, and the impact would have been formidable when he announced his conditions, whatever his manner,[7] and more so when he entered on the subsequent dispute. Appearing in the aftermath of Melville, Grenville benefited from a mood of disgust. But if that heightened the tone, the issue of course lay in the content of what Pitt said. Given the apparent turn-round after the impression of recent months, even recent days, was that determined, or seriously affected, by his cousin's belated visit?

Most of those concerned by the result suspected that it was. Addington, grasping at his earlier indications, professed himself certain, and others, in and out of office, seem to have felt the same.[8] They could point to Pitt's tendency to be swayed, as they saw it, by the advice closest to hand, which Hawkesbury had feared on the eve of the January talks.[9] That had been largely withdrawn in the interval, until this intervention at almost the last minute by the most considerable source of danger of all. How else

1. See p. 90, n4 above. And Canning's rising stream of verses (see p. 570 and n4 above) can hardly have helped.
2. See p. 572 above for a lowered opinion of Addington's capacity; *Malmesbury*, IV, 113, 127–8, 130 for a survival of qualified personal cordiality.
3. Cf. p. 572, n2 above.
4. P. 569 above.
5. Melville's descriptive phrases, in a different context to Pitt himself (16 June 1803; Dacres Adams Mss, formerly P.R.O. 30/58/4).
6. P. 562 above.
7. He himself represented the conversation as amicable (*Rose*, II, 37–8).
8. For Addington see Pellew, op. cit., II, 120n, and also 118. John Mitford, now Lord Redesdale, and Malmesbury reached a similar conclusion (*Colchester*, I, 417; *Malmesbury*, IV, 187), as almost certainly did the leading members of Cabinet, and Melville and Long out of office.
9. To Liverpool, 9 January 1803 (B.L. Loan Ms 72, vol. 55). And cf. Grenville from an opposite point of view almost a year before (to Thomas Grenville, 25 February 1802; B.L. Add. Ms 41852).

therefore to account for the seeming reversal of attitude? And in point of fact, whatever Grenville's own doubts of the prospect,[1] the suspicions were probably germane, if not in the way perhaps that all their authors supposed.

For if Grenville had an effect its central import was not to reverse an immediate attitude so much as to supply a link in an argument whose main intent was clear but which had still to be detailed and put in place. His representations confirmed rather than inverted an aim which Pitt had long held in view. As the latter had repeated often in the past year, and particularly in the past six months, he would not take office – the chief office – except in response to a call from the country. That might come of course in one or more of several forms: from the effect of votes in the Commons, from public petitions and addresses, from a wish – an invitation – expressed by the monarch as head of state. In the circumstances of 1802 attention had focused on the last, and it was a cardinal point from which in essence Pitt did not budge. Grenville's impact lay precisely here. His emphasis, a fortnight before the meeting with Addington, on the vital need to establish this procedure, to avoid detailed preliminary bargaining with a Minister in whom he had little faith, returned Pitt, in so far as he needed it, to his own central belief. Such an approach would rescue the former Minister from further consequences of misinterpreted remarks; and also from immediate debate among others on what he might be empowered to do. This in fact accounted for Pitt's displeasure when he learned of the Cabinet's collective advice *before* Addington talked to the King. Subsequent conversations were not ruled out: Pitt indeed had told Melville that if he formed a Ministry it must be on 'a distinct knowledge' that it was thought essential 'both in *the highest quarter*, and by all those with whom . . . he might have to act confidentially'; and he apparently advised Addington himself in the course of their meeting to 'take full time to consult his colleagues at leisure'.[2] But the consultation, like any move that he for his part was 'enabled' to make, was conditional on the monarch's 'previous authority';[3] he was not prepared to accept what he chose to term 'a Minute of Cabinet' in advance.[4] Addington might be forgiven for thinking that the distinction in practice could be unreal: after all, as was pointed out, 'the usual way' of forming a Ministry was 'with *carte blanche* from the King' combined with terms to be reached with persons on the ground.[5] But the

---

1. P. 594 above.

2. See p. 585 above for the statement, made by Pitt (and – 584, n5 – checked by him) to Melville; *Rose*, II, 38 for a conversation on 11 April (given in Rose's words) in which Pitt described the meeting with Addington.

3. Pitt to Addington, 15 April 1803 (see p. 588 and n2 above).

4. Cf. p. 589, n5 above.

5. Buckingham to Grenville, 1 November 1802 (*H.M.C., Dropmore*, VII, 118). He could certainly cite an example, though hardly a normal one, from his own experience in 1783 (see I, 123–7).

case in this instance had a special feature. If Cincinnatus was to be called from his plough, it must not be through any prior manoeuvre.

The answer indeed, as not seldom in Pitt's eyes, could be argued to serve both tactics and principles – the kind of claim that particularly infuriates opponents. For he was in search not only of a way to preserve a wide freedom of action; his position in these years out of office had been followed at some length because to him it presented basically a moral problem. His deepest desire was to maintain, and show that he was maintaining, his 'Character': the note was sounded as strongly in April 1803 as in March 1801. That needs no fresh emphasis, and the assertion was not fraudulent. The difficulties lay in its application to a scene which he himself had largely set.

Those complications had not been felt in the first year, and not seriously in the first eighteen months – for Pitt's grievances early in 1802 scarcely raised critical questions of choice.[1] One must bear in mind moreover that, amid his mounting doubts and periodical objections, he was by no means in total disagreement thereafter with the Government's stance over peace or war. When indeed he was kept well informed, his apprehensions were apt to diminish even if they were not removed;[2] his censures bore rather on the Ministry's inadequate use, in his view, of the cards it held. The resulting differences could be sharp; but they had their limits, within the limited opportunities available in an essentially unfavourable state of affairs. Thus Pitt would have wished Ministers to make it clear sooner than they did that British forces would not be withdrawn from their conquests while Bonaparte was straining the provisions of the peace. But he had shared the hopes for some time that this would not be necessary, and his discontent was markedly reduced once the decision was taken. He would have liked to see more urgent efforts to restore links in Europe. But he was content to drop hopes of effective objection over the testing issue of Switzerland when other Powers were clearly not going to respond.[3] He was not happy with the Government's timing and tactics; he thought that Addington and Hawkesbury were often inept and had no clear pattern in view. His own approach would have been to take a stand on certain definite issues: the line would be drawn at any French effort to grasp 'maritime power'. By this he meant an attempt to take outright possession of Holland or its colonies, or Portugal, or above all British 'establishments and power' in India.[4] Beyond that however he was exercised, like Ministers, on how best *'to bear and to forbear'*.[5] He, like they,

1. See pp. 569–71 above.

2. Pp. 579–80 above for Castlereagh's visit and the meeting with Addington over the turn of 1802–3, and *Malmesbury*, IV, 154–5 on the former's effect.

3. Cf. p. 575 above.

4. Malmesbury's account of a conversation on 29 December 1802 (*Malmesbury*, IV, 156). In fastening on 'maritime power', Pitt specifically made a distinction, as things stood, with intervention in other Continental affairs.

5. Op. cit., 157. This passage, though, unlike its predecessor, not in double quotation marks, reads as if intended to convey Pitt's own words.

would have liked to stay at peace while our revenues were being replenished; if at all possible, for four or five years.[1] His misgivings focused on wrong turnings, as he saw them, from the highroad of diplomatic and strategic deterrence and domestic financial encouragement necessary to achieve that end. If and when war came, the dilemma of the past few years would of course be largely removed; and increasingly he referred his own moment of decision to or near to that point.[2]

It was against such a background – not one of consistently clear or rising disapproval – that the more personal pressures played their part in inducing Pitt to stay aloof. The process was not straightforward. There can be little doubt that his immediate views were affected by his company, particularly in the autumn and early winter months of 1802–3: he himself recognised the dangers by returning to Walmer as soon as he could. Again however one may also recognise the limits to the effects. The Grenvillites, and Canning separately, stoked the fire in February 1802; but the embers soon died down. Rose and to a lesser extent Malmesbury, followed by Grenville and Canning, helped fan them in November and December; but after his talks with Addington and exposure to wider circles in London in January 1803, Pitt took care to distance himself successfully once more. No one indeed, from whatever quarter, could predict results. The Grenvilles were aware that they could not count on having his ear. Canning, losing ground for some time through absence, lost more by rashness and importunity. Neither Malmesbury nor Rose – two sources from whom we gain much of our information – was really in a position to carry significant weight: the former, though respected for his foreign experience, had never stood close to Pitt, while the latter, devoted as he was and indispensable for his knowledge of political and financial statistics, knew to his sorrow that his master now found him something of an irritant and a bore.[3] Others, in occasional contact, could not rely on more than an attentive hearing. In the last resort Pitt remained elusive, guided by his own reasoning and instincts and his demands on himself.

There was thus ample reason for confusion, which those demands

---

1. Ibid, and see also 110. And cf. op. cit., 146–7 (p. 578 above).
2. Eg pp. 575, 578 above, and *Malmesbury*, IV, 109.
3. Cf. for Malmesbury in the past I, 521, 622n1; II, 178 & n5, 296, 405 & n6, 648; Chs. XV, XVII *passim*. Rose was always ready furthermore to turn his experience at the Treasury to public use. Both his *Brief Examination into the Increase of the Revenue, Commerce, and Manufactures . . . since the Peace in 1783* and its sequence *from 1792 to 1799* – see p. 415 above – went through several editions, and in the latter case contained a panegyric on Pitt in 1806. But, often as he had been accustomed to see and advise Pitt – summoned indeed as he was at once when his master resigned (see pp. 523, n5, 524, n2 above) – it was normally for professional purposes (in this last instance to let it be known in Parliament that the Minister wished his successor to have general support). He was not in the inner circle, and indeed lamented more than once his hero's 'neglect' and 'unkindness' stemming from the later nineties (to Pretyman, 30 July 1800, 6 February, 28 May 1801; Pretyman Ms 435/44). From some of his expressions, it seems clear that this referred to personal treatment as well as disappointed hopes of preferment.

increased. For Pitt had good cause to be pulled more than one way. He must have felt frustrated as he watched the signs of Addington's short-comings; there was at least one point at which he appeared eager to be summoned soon.[1] On the other hand he was far from certain if he could then stand the pace. Although he made use of his health to avoid embarrassments, and sometimes privately admitted the fact, he also gen-uinely feared the physical effects of office.[2] He could manage in semi-retirement – he was highly active in his soldiering.[3] But Downing Street and the full burden of the Commons would impose sterner tests. These conflicting thoughts were imposed on the wider uncertainties; and placed as he was, Pitt in any case made some mistakes. Drawing his impressions largely from what he could read and hear, his information was erratic and there were times when he was distinctly out of touch. His contact with official sources, at least after the first six months, was less regular than was widely supposed; and like others in similar case, he was sensitive to the overtones of observations bearing on his past. He took more notice of published comments now than he had done in office, particularly when he suspected a Ministerial hand at work.[4] Nor in point of fact was he congen-itally suited to his situation. He had proved a tough and skilful politician, despite a certain lasting 'Inexperience of men and the world'.[5] But he had done so, almost at once, from a position of power. The compromises and adjustments came from an eminence; perspectives were different else-where, and he was not well fitted, and scarcely prepared, to adapt. He would have cordially endorsed the view that the Pitts, relying on recogni-tion of their talents, were not quite like other party leaders; that in certain aspects he and his father in fact formed a special case.[6] By upbringing and experience he was indeed 'fitted peculiarly for one life and one situation, and' until now they had been 'those which he followed and held'.[7]

This mixture of attitudes, uncertain at one level, assured and tenacious at another, was however given specific shape by a particular event. Pitt's 'pledge' to Addington at the outset first governed and then haunted his conduct. Its effect indeed was shaken almost, though not quite, to destruc-tion only in the spring of 1803. Precisely what Pitt had said we cannot tell; by Canning's account it had put him in Addington's hands to an extra-ordinary extent for not only the immediate but the indefinite future – a promise 'solemnly binding, not redeemable by any lapse of time, nor ever

---

1. In mid to late November 1792 (see *Rose*, I, 488, 492, 503).

2. The mixture, and conflict, can be gauged from eg *Malmesbury*, IV, 112, 135; *Rose*, I, 492, 495, II, 10–11, 22–3; *H.M.C., Dropmore*, VII, 142 (and note also 130); Pellew, op. cit., II, 115. See also p. 508, n5 above.

3. See p. 543 above for his stamina there.

4. Eg p. 579 above, for a period in which there was at least one other, minor, instance. A fiercer and understandable reaction was provoked the next year (pp. 621–2 below).

5. Bland Burges's phrase; I, 588.

6. Cf. Pares, *King George III and the Politicians*, 79, 77.

7. I, 138.

to be cancelled without the *express consent* of Mr. Addington'.[1] To what extent Addington himself relied on it, again we cannot tell: he seems honourably to have kept his counsel throughout. But there is evidence that to Pitt it remained of high importance. The purport was suspected or, more narrowly, known in some political circles even if the exact wording may not have been vouchsafed. Camden hinted at something unusual in the autumn of 1801; Canning was more specific a year later; Malmesbury, convinced that Pitt was *'fettered*, or at least at liberty *on parole'*, heard directly in the winter that he could not regard himself as *'uncommitted'* in the steps he might take; Grenville at much the same time rebuked his cousin, more generally, for still 'deliberating upon personal delicacies, which a *very strict* conscience would perhaps not allow to influence even a vote upon a turnpike bill'.[2] Pitt's publicly proclaimed resolve to support his successor's Ministry was given a special meaning by his private commitment to the successor himself.

Under this added impetus, his conception of his conduct appeared to his friends excessively 'romantic'.[3] He came to appreciate the point; but he did not thereby dismiss the dilemma: rather, 'he did not know very well how to separate himself from himself'[4]. The initial pledge, given at a moment of exceptional inner tension when 'Character' lay in the centre of his view, had become an awkward ingredient of a set of circumstances in which that character had to be sustained amid changing public demands. For while Pitt's particular constraint was so prominent a factor in moulding his responses to developments, it could not be taken in isolation from the rest. He had a national duty to consider, and he was now facing a growing need to place his private pledge in the balance with that duty's competing claims. Should he show active support for Government in a rising crisis; or seek to bring desirable pressure to bear by criticism or even attack? As things stood, he was subject to conflicting accusations of allowing irresponsible silence to weaken Ministers in the eyes of the people, and from other quarters of protecting them unduly from their deserts. He gave the matter plenty of thought, for both public and personal reasons. But he held fast, through varying moods, to the arguments against a premature step. Restraint – inaction – indeed seemed to provide the wisest answer; on every count, the pressures should be allowed to mount of their own accord. He must not be suspected of working for office; his image and his role should be preserved; this was his duty as well as his wish; he felt himself reaching out towards the country. Here must lie

1. P. 564 above.
2. See ibid, n6 for Camden and Canning; *Malmesbury*, IV, 136, 155 for Malmesbury in December 1802; *H.M.C., Dropmore*, VII, 140 for Grenville at the end of January 1803.
3. Camden to Countess Spencer, 9 October 1801 (p. 564 above).
4. Malmesbury's account of conversation of 21 December 1802; *Malmesbury*, IV, 115. The words, not in double quotation marks, sound nevertheless like Pitt's own. Canning had said in October that Pitt felt he had gone too far in the first instance and pledged himself too deeply (op. cit., 75–6).

his justification. And for a moment it may have seemed in fact that the dilemma might be resolved. Addington's offer in April 1803 – the *voluntary* proposal to make way[1] – might enable the pledge in effect to be redeemed, while a consequent invitation from the throne with a grant of freedom of action, if hardly a sign to Ministers of continuing assured support, would announce to the public the nature of the return. The moment passed, and further uncertainies lay ahead. But, if not decisively, it marked a turning point. For if Pitt's responses to events were not finally settled, and his relations with the Parliamentary connexions remained obscure, he had declared a position, and his relationship to Addington shifted to a new plane. A different scene moreover opened for any moves he might now make. For on 2 May Whitworth in Paris called for his passports; he left on the 12th, and on 18 May Britain declared war.

1. See p. 587 above.

CHAPTER XVIII

Return to Office

I

As the last days of peace ticked away while the Government awaited Whitworth's return, politicians began to gather pending the end of the Easter recess. Pitt had gone back to Walmer after a round of conversations and visits following his stay with Long. But he was in London in mid May, settled in the small house at the northern end of Baker Street of which he had seen little in the past year.[1] A few days later the Foxite Thomas Creevey watched him on his way to Westminster in his 'forlorn, shattered equipage', and later stood near him behind the throne in the opening Lords' debate. He thought his countenance 'no longer red, but yellow', 'much changed and fallen, and every now and then he gives a hollow cough'; and sensed a general feeling indeed that 'the fellow' *was done*.[2] The physical signs were noted likewise when Pitt spoke in the Commons on the 23rd, in a debate on the failure of the exchanges with France. While his voice had not lost 'any of its depth and harmony, his lungs seemed to labour in those prodigious sentences which he thundered forth without effort', and he showed 'strong marks of bad health'.[3] His powers of mind nevertheless were perceptibly intact. The speech, in support of war, produced an astonishing effect. This was aided by the circumstances: Pitt rose on a dramatic occasion, five days after notice of hostilities was given, and in a House in which 150 Members were new from the election of the previous year and many of those who were present would not have heard him before.[4] The excitement was evident as he walked in, and when he rose to his feet in due course it was to a 'violent' cry of 'Mr. Pitt! Mr. Pitt!'. Cheered before he opened, and at frequent intervals, he sat down to vociferous bursts of applause.[5] And that was not

1. See p. 534 and n2 above for York Place.
2. Diary for 21 May 1803 (*The Creevey Papers* . . ., ed. Sir Herbert Maxwell, I (1903), 14–15). Cf. p. 549, n6 above for the yellow look.
3. J.W. Ward to the Rev. E. Copleston, 30 May 1803 (Stanhope, IV, 50). Cf. however p. 548 above for his remarkable capacity for swift recuperation, if now from a progressively enfeebled state.
4. See *H of P*, I, 281; and p. 574 above for the election. One of the Members first returned then was Creevey.
5. Ward's account; Stanhope, IV, 48–50.

surprising, for by all accounts the listeners had heard one of his greatest orations: according to Fox indeed 'the best he ever made in that style'.[1] From the same side of the floor, Creevey was aghast: 'its effect was dreadful', for 'the great fiend' 'in the elevation of his tone of mind and composition, in the infinite energy of his style, the miraculous perspicuity and fluency of his periods, outdid (as it was thought) all former performances of his'.[2] Shortly after its close the House adjourned, until on the following day it heard perhaps the greatest oration that Fox in his turn ever made.[3]

According to tradition, the published accounts did little justice to this, almost certainly the finest of Pitt's war speeches.[4] By mistake, the doors of the gallery were shut for a time and reporters – essential for all their inadequacies[5] – could not get in. The triumph however was followed by a sequel which somewhat dimmed the auspicious lustre and brought the Parliamentary temperature down to a more normal level. In endorsing the declaration of war Pitt upheld the Ministry's action, and he was not in general disposed at this period to attack.[6] But neither was he prepared any longer to provide automatic support; it was noted that the speech, 'strong' for war, was 'silent as to Ministers', and that was naturally taken, after his long absence, as 'negative censure'.[7] The impression soon deepened, but with ambiguous effect. A rich Lancashire Member and militia Colonel, Peter Patten, who might be classed as independent, had been thinking

1. *Memorials of . . . Fox*, III, 223. The ranks of Tuscany indeed could not forbear to give their due. Sheridan paid 'just tribute to the Scoundrel's talents' (*The Letters of Richard Brinsley Sheridan*, ed. Cecil Price, II (1966), 196), and Grey thought the speech unfortunately 'one of the most magnificent pieces of declamation that ever was heard' (*L.C.G. III*, IV, no. 2745n2). Cf. from another quarter *Malmesbury*, IV, 256.

2. Diary for 24 May 1803 (*The Creevey Papers*, I, 15). Another listener, in this case in the gallery, was Pitt's future, and last, private secretary, William Dacres Adams. Turning to his neighbour, he quoted the lines from Pope's Homer describing the reappearance of Achilles in the field (Stanhope, IV, 51). The impression 'out of doors' is powerfully conveyed in *Memoirs of the Life of Sir Samuel Romilly . . .*, ed. by His Sons, II (1840), 105.

3. He himself at the time thought it his best. According to an observer, he remarked in its course that Pitt's was one 'which, if Demosthenes had been present, he must have admired, and might have envied' (*Memoirs and Correspondence of Francis Horner, M.P.*, ed. Leonard Horner, I (1843), 221).

4. Ie 'in that style' (see Fox above). Stanhope (op. cit., 45), reared in the Pittite ethos, placed the speech with those on the North–Fox coalition in February 1783 (see I, 113) and the slave trade in April 1792 (op. cit., 400–1).
The report in *P.R.*, 4th ser., III (1804), 330–40 was adopted in *P.H.*, XXXVI, cols. 1387–98. Notes for the speech in Pitt's hand, nd but endorsed in another 'May 23, 1803', are in P.R.O. 30/8/195.

5. Cf. I, 53 for the early 1780s, and p. 478 above.

6. Some hopeful would-be intermediaries indeed thought it not impossible that he was prepared to come into office on the lines that Addington had finally proposed. A scheme was hatched late in May, by the ever busy Dean of Christ Church, Cyril Jackson, which was to involve the Duke of York and Portland as the channels. It was in fact relayed to Addington himself. Not surprisingly, nothing more was heard (*Malmesbury*, IV, 255–6, 259; *Colchester*, I, 422–4).

7. Malmesbury's diary for 24 May (*Malmesbury*, IV, 256) – he does not himself relate it to the absence –, and cf. Canning's impression on the same day (Hinde, op. cit., 117).

since early in April of bringing a motion for an inquiry into the state of the nation. Delaying in the rumoured hope of a change of Ministers, he then put himself in Canning's hands, and replaced his initial idea by a series of censures on Government for its handling of the negotiations with France. After further postponements for tactical reasons he introduced that motion on 3 June. Pitt was in a quandary, apparently unsure whether to support or to oppose.[1] But in the end he decided to escape by an alternative motion of his own, to pass to the orders of the day – in other words to the next business.[2] This evasive tactic did not suit any of the other interested parties. The Grenvilles wished to support Patten; the Ministry wished to face the challenge; Fox wished on this occasion to go with the Grenvilles; his associates, who were at cross purposes with them at the time, decided to abstain and leave them in the lurch. Pitt was thus connected with no other force. He mustered 58 votes against 335, and on hearing the result walked out of the Chamber.[3]

It was an unexpected debacle. Canning deserted his friend for the first time in his life, as indeed he was obliged to do by his own role, and stayed to act as a teller for Patten in the subsequent debate.[4] Pitt's speech on this occasion was thought puzzling and feeble, in contrast with that of only eleven days before. And the episode revealed the limits to his influence when acting on his own from a stance which seemed irrelevant to all the leading figures apart from himself. He admitted his mistake: 'it was perhaps not good *generalship*', and he knew he would be blamed. He had wished to avoid any impression of personal bad feeling, preserve silence on the past, and do nothing to upset the King, while making it clear to the public that he had '*no* connexion *whatever*' with Ministers, and – so his conversation was described – 'was at liberty to remove them if he pleased'.[5] This somewhat abstruse message was not picked up, and the

1. Thus Hawkesbury thought that he was going to support the Ministry (to Liverpool, 30 May 1803 and 'Sunday' (endorsed 1803 and in fact 5 June), B.L. Loan Ms 72, vol. 55); Addington, that he had been inclined at first to support the censure (Pellew, op. cit., II, 138).

2. According to Canning, he had earlier intended to move to adjourn, and if Ministers then brought counter resolutions 'to go away' (conversation with Malmesbury on 1 June; *Malmesbury*, IV, 260).

3. See *P.R., 4th ser.*, III, 525–7 and 534 for the list of the minority on Pitt's motion. The figures for the division given here include the tellers. *H of P*, IV, under Patten and Pitt, gives succinct accounts and a range of references; Pellew, op. cit., II, 136–42, one from Addington's point of view; *Memorials of Fox*, III, 223 sums up Fox's own. He too in fact left the Chamber. In a debate in the Lords the day before, Melville (with whom Pitt had been in touch) lost a motion to adjourn by 18 to 106, on a motion of censure similar to Patten's which was brought by Fitzwilliam.

4. In which the figures including tellers were 36 to 277. In the Lords on 2 June they had been 14 to 96 on two of Fitzwilliam's resolutions; a third was defeated on the 6th by 17 to 86 and the rest did not go to a division.

5. See Malmesbury for 8 June (*Malmesbury*, IV, 263–4, and also 260). The account does not give double quotation marks, and one might compare the last phrase with Richard Pares's conclusion (*King George III and the Politicians*, 127n1) that Pitt, 'who did not believe

episode did him no immediate good. It heartened Ministers, who had shown visible alarm and did not soon forget 'the trial' in their relief at the outcome. It heightened Addington's animosity, already aroused, more than Pitt himself might have wished. It may have visibly increased some suspicions – he was again looking very ill – that he was in decline. And the King made his own feelings clear: he received Addington's report of the vote with 'much pleasure', as a proof that Parliament meant to support the executive and 'not faction'.[1]

The failure may indeed have deepened a feeling which had been abroad since April; that, notwithstanding his recent impressive performance, Pitt would not in fact be quickly summoned back. Most of those concerned at the time of the recent talk with Addington – including Melville – had deplored the line he took, and thought that the chance of his return had been indefinitely delayed.[2] The size of his defeat now, which at once became a talking point, seemed to confirm the judgment; and he himself settled into a role familiar to a politician in his position. He would not oppose 'idly' or depart from 'a general line of support'; but he *would* speak, most decidedly,

---

that the House of Commons ought to drive Ministers out of office' – and indeed see his statement to that effect to Grenville (26 May 1803; *H.M.C., Dropmore*, VII, 169) and his remarks in the debate itself (*P.R., 4th ser.*, III, 525–6) – was hoping to frighten them out of it and to show (or one might say, remind) the King that he himself was ready to come in.

Possibly however the phrase as given owed something to a letter which Pitt may have received recently from Melville. Written on 27 May from Scotland, it told him that 'You have it in your power at this moment to overturn what you conceive to be a feeble and incompetent Government' – and begged him to refrain (S.R.O., Melville Mss, GD 51/1/63).

1. George III to Addington, 4 June 1803 (*L.C.G. III*, IV, no. 2752). The 'trial' was recalled some five months later, in typically ungraceful style, by the Lord Privy Seal, Westmorland (p. 553 above), who was then reported as saying that his old friend and political benefactor (see I, 17, II, 221, 411, 423) 'was to have swallowed us up at once, but he made the trial, and Mr. Addington appeared a greater man than he' (Carysfort to Grenville, 30 October 1803; *H.M.C., Dropmore*, VII, 194); and see also for his attitude at this point Pretyman to Rose, 7 November 1803; B.L. Add. Ms 42773. But then he had observed when Pitt resigned that the Minister was a man of talents but the King was 'the only thing of real consequence' (*L.C.G. III*, III, n1 on p. 488). Addington's feelings about the speech, expressed later, were undisguisedly hostile (note in Sidmouth Ms 152M/c1803/Z10). Hawkesbury, who was seen to be highly 'agitated' when Pitt rose (see *Diary of Farington*, VI, ed. Kenneth Garlick and Angus Macintyre (1979), 2048), found it 'most unaccountable', wondered if Pitt's mind was not 'completely unhing'd', and commented that he looked 'dreadfully' (to Liverpool, 'Sunday' [5 June 1803]; B.L. Loan Ms 72, vol. 55). For the prospective effect on public opinion cf. the similar views from the very different quarters of Liverpool (to Hawkesbury, 7 June 1803; loc. cit., vol. 49) and Thomas Grenville (to Buckingham, sd; Buckingham, III, 304).

2. *Colchester*, I, 416–17 for disapproval, and see copies of Melville to Long, 28 March, same to Pitt, 14, 16 April 1803 (B.L. Add. Ms 40102), 16 June 1803 (Dacres Adams Mss, formerly P.R.O. 30/58/4); *Malmesbury*, IV, 187 for the feeling by the end of April on the prospect of Pitt's return. Redesdale (see p. 597, n8 above), who was among those who had then disapproved of his conduct, reckoned however in May that he would probably be 'compelled' to come into office (to Pitt, 2 May 1803; Dacres Adams Mss formerly P.R.O. 30/58/4); and cf. p. 606, n5 above for possible influence from Melville himself.

on '*weak or pernicious half measures*', financial or otherwise.[1] This traditional disclaimer of faction was genuine. The resumption of war – the advent of the Napoleonic War – was not unpopular when it came; it was in fact widely viewed as unavoidable, and Pitt in the Commons endorsed the recognition of the need for unity.[2] Nor indeed had he ever linked such a moment with one for an increase in pressure on his part; he had pointed to it rather as the most likely occasion for a call which he had not actively sought.[3] After the meeting with Addington he had returned to his former position. He professed to see (and doubtless genuinely saw) no reason for 'ill-humour' from the collapse of the exchange – a dismissal which can hardly have mollified Addington himself – and was said to have remarked that he intended to support Government if and when war came.[4] In these early months moreover he was attaching high importance to his military duties. His conviction that Bonaparte would revive the plans for invasion which had perforce been dropped in 1801, and that they would focus on the Kentish coast, made him the more determined to play his part there.[5] He attended Parliament as necessary over the rest of the session, prolonged to the middle of August; but his thoughts and sometimes he in person also ranged to Walmer, and his political course into the summer was much as he had foretold. He intervened, and indeed twice divided the House, in a debate on a partial remodelling of his own measures for the income tax, and Addington gave way on one feature of what in fact would prove a most successful reform.[6] He also kept a keen and indeed increasingly impatient eye on developments in defence, making suggestions in confidence – from the arming of fishing luggers, on which he took his own steps with his favourites at Deal, to comments on the plans for augmenting the land forces and improving coastal obstructions, on which his advice was sometimes sought – but giving broad public support to Ministerial measures requiring consent before the House rose.[7] Whatever his feelings in private, such conduct could be broadly seen as 'manly

1. Conversation on 8 June 1803 (*Malmesbury*, IV, 264).

2. On 27 May, in the debate on Russian mediation (*P.R., 4th ser.*, III, 470, 473).

3. Cf. pp. 575–6 above.

4. *Colchester*, I, 418, citing information from Addington via Steele. And cf. *Malmesbury*, IV, 185.

5. See pp. 542–4 above.

6. The debate, on 13 and 14 July, was on the Property Duty bill (*P.R., 4th ser.*, III, 739–50). Speaker Abbot noted that on the 13th 'language in a tone of great asperity, passed from Mr. Pitt towards Mr. Addington' (*Colchester*, I, 432), and Hawkesbury that Pitt was 'particularly tenacious & even out of humour' (to Liverpool, 16 July 1803; B.L. Loan Ms 72, vol. 55). The reform itself, a significant one, is considered on pp. 678–81 below.

7. In debates on 20 and 23 June and 18, 20, 22 July (*P.R., 4th ser.*, III, 616, 644–52, 770–5, 793–9, 825–9, 835). The measures and their background are discussed on pp. 706–7 below. See p. 544 above for the Deal fishermen.

There are some letters from Pitt to the Ministers concerned in the spring and summer – to Hobart (B.L. Add. Ms 40862), Pelham (B.L. Add. Ms 33111–12), and Charles Yorke who until August was Secretary at War (B.L. Add. Ms 45040–1) – particularly on the Volunteers. The Government seems also to have passed on some items of intelligence on France, as late as October (see P.R.O. 30/8/335).

and becoming'; though scarcely by the Grenvilles.[1] But the Grenvillites themselves, apart from Windham, scarcely matched their private with Parliamentary hostility, and other elements in opposition likewise kept a generally low profile and in some cases gave approving signs or hints. When the long recess began and politicians scattered, confined now to letters and country visits, the Ministry could be seen to have made a politically success-ful transition from peace.

Much of course might arise before Parliament met again, which it did in the event late in November. If Pitt's expectations were correct the French would try to land, and the menacing assemblies of camps and barges along the Channel coast kept forces deployed throughout the summer months. His own activities were a microcosm of what was happening, often less intensively, elsewhere. The British camps of regular troops grew in their turn, gentlemen drilled their Volunteers and militia, fortifications and obstructions were strengthened or put in hand. The preparations seen in the final months of the earlier war were repeated on a larger scale; and defence kept the authorities busy not only in England but also in Ireland, for a brief rising in Dublin – Emmet's rising –, though easily put down, gave a cautionary shock. Beyond these visible preoccupations, a strategy was developed conforming to the Ministry's view of the facts. In this early stage it was strictly economic and maritime. Shortly after hostil-ities opened, and not surprisingly after earlier threats,[2] the French moved into northern Germany, invading Hanover and gaining control of entry to the Weser and the Elbe. A blockade was mounted accordingly to deny seaborne trade, as was one on Le Havre for access from the Atlantic. A watch had already been set, on St Vincent's system,[3] over the naval bases of Brest, Lorient and Rochefort, and Nelson was despatched to the Mediterranean with an equivalent to St Vincent's own former brief, to observe Spanish movements on both sides of the Straits, watch Toulon and the north Italian ports, cover Malta and as far as possible protect Sicily and Naples. Farther afield, Wellesley in India was ordered to retake Cochin and some of the Dutch East Indies, and the small force in the West Indies, earlier strengthened at sea,[4] to do likewise with St Lucia, Tobago and if possible Martinique, aims extended when the planters of Dutch Guiana called for a British return. These enterprises were largely success-ful, St Lucia and Tobago being taken in June – as by a separate venture were the islands of St Pierre and Miquelon off Newfoundland – while entries to Guiana were secured by the end of September at Demerara, Essequibo and Berbice, with Surinam following in May 1804.

1. Cf. Malmesbury (IV, 277) with Thomas Grenville (Buckingham, III, 311). For 'manli-ness' in the context of the Constitution see I, 48.
2. See p. 393 above.
3. See p. 326 above.
4. And see p. 566 above; and II, 562 and p. 562, n3 above for Cochin.

No one could quarrel with these plans, and achievements. The Caribbean conquests, cheaply gained, were particularly popular with mercantile interests,[1] and with all those who favoured a war with commercial motives to a close involvement in Europe. A more open question remained; were the Ministry's efforts, diplomatic and administrative, strong enough to sustain designs for operations in Europe itself? Pitt urged more than once at the start that offensive possibilities should be borne in mind, and Addington sympathised; and while nothing, as it seemed, could be done on the Continent for the present, such a future was certainly taken into account. The system of blockade and overseas conquests was not in fact necessarily to be confined to the strategy favoured earlier by Dundas;[2] the search continued for a European ally, directed primarily to Russia with hopes subsequently of Austria, and even of Prussia whose stated protection of northern German territory had now been rudely challenged and upset.[3] The Ministry was embarked on the system bequeathed by its predecessor, and time would be needed to judge the outcome. And the same applied to an appraisal of its handling of manpower, arms and finance. There might be opportunities for Parliamentary critics if results were slow or seemed inadequate. Meanwhile it was hard for them to focus their sights.

That of course did not prevent them from thinking about the prospects, and in one case at any rate along lines that would soon produce an effect. The process came from within the 'Old Opposition' rather than the 'New'. The elements of the once cohesive Whig party were no more united than they had been for at least the past year. One prominent figure had in fact effectively departed, for Tierney at last achieved his hopes of office; at the end of May 1803 he became Treasurer of the Navy, way being made by Addington's brother-in-law Charles Bragge.[4] Erskine, who likewise had long made his own tacit peace with Government, sat on the fence uncomfortably in the spring and summer debates; and Sheridan too, who approved of the war and was personally on good terms with Addington, preferred his Ministry to a return by Pitt and may have also had an eye on a post, though in his case the situation was complicated by his involvement in the Prince of Wales's affairs, on which the Prince himself was once more dissatisfied with Government. The position at Carlton House was indeed confused, as the heir apparent, roused by the war, enlarged his political concern. Nor could that be ignored, for a mounting enthusiasm for the throne, particularly under threat of invasion, rubbed off, in a sense paradoxically here, on the reversionary

---

1. See Christopher D. Hall, *British Strategy in the Napoleonic War 1803–15* (1992), 109, for some particular reasons.

2. Pitt on 6 and 23 June, Addington on the 6th (*P.R., 4th ser.*, III, 548–9, 644–7, where Pitt alluded to Marlborough's campaigns). Cf. pp. 353–5, 367–8 above for Dundas in the later stages of the Revolutionary War.

3. For this last see p. 609 above.

4. Cf. pp. 557, n4, 573 above.

interest borne more actively in mind by politicians since the King's disability in 1801. Fox was surprised by his impression of the Prince's strength in Parliament later in the year. In the spring and early summer, however, it was difficult to tell how the Prince himself would settle. At first he pursued ideas of support for the Ministry, and there were some 'famous dinners' to that end; but by the summer he seemed to have shifted towards the Grenvillites. And this suited Fox, and Grey; for while they were not in full agreement – Grey was not as hostile to the war as Fox, distrusted the Grenvilles, and was sceptical indeed of all the options he foresaw – both were guided primarily by a fear of Pitt's return. Unless Addington therefore was to be favoured in preference – and Fox was now increasingly disinclined to that course – a strengthened Opposition with the Whigs at the core might best limit the effects of such an untoward event or even, given Pitt's apparent indecision, perhaps forestall it. Pitt might have to be kept in play, or he might be left to his own devices; the choice was not resolved. But Fox was back in the fray, there might be a congenial link with the Grenvilles through Fitzwilliam, by now wholly reconciled after their long separation; and though he recognised in June that there was nothing to be done for the time being, he was resolved not to raise any obstacles to a possible future 'coalition' with 'any persons who are capable of acting in *real* opposition' – something which Pitt had shown that he was '*not*'.[1]

At the same time it had to be admitted that the odds against such a development were high; as Fox noted, there was a great distaste among his own associates for 'anything like a junction with the Pitts or Grenvilles'.[2] Nor do the Grenvilles themselves appear to have been inclined to a close connexion; it seems unlikely indeed that they had moved tentatively even as far as Fox. They continued to grumble about the Government's inadequacy and some aspects of its measures. But there was no systematic opposition: indeed they gave broad public assent; and some contacts were maintained with individual Ministers, though Windham finally went too far for Addington himself[3] – and for that matter for Thomas Grenville – in attacks in August on the plans for manpower. There was no attempt to strengthen links with some of the more extreme elements on the fringes of their own connexion, and as the brothers collogued between Dropmore and Stowe in the summer recess they could see little chance of making much impression on an 'idle and popular system of *laisser faire*'.[4]

1. To Dennis O'Bryen (the veteran Foxite pamphleteer and journalist), 26 June 1803 (*Memorials and Correspondence of Fox*, IV (1857), 9). For even more tentative thoughts before war was declared, including a mention of Fitzwilliam, see Fox to Grey, 12 March 1803 (op. cit., III, 398–9); for Fitzwilliam's own relations with Fox, my II, 226–7, 417–18.

2. To Lord Holland, 6 June 1803 (*Memorials and Correspondence of Fox*, III, 222–3). And see same to Grey on Pitt, 19 October 1803 (op. cit., 430).

3. Cf. p. 589 and n3 above.

4. Thomas Grenville to Grenville, 6 September 1803 (*H.M.C., Dropmore*, VII, 110); he was talking of the state of affairs in Parliament. And see Canning's opinion that Addington could 'hobble on and outlast the Country' (to Frere, 25 August 1803; quoted in Fedorak, loc. cit., 285).

Nonetheless by the time the new session opened in the autumn the critics could hope to find some grist for their mills. Foreign policy lay beyond serious attack: Parliament still hardly expected to debate an absence of commitments by convention or treaty. The Ministry in point of fact was engaged in a wide range of efforts; some to preserve existing but passive alliances (with Portugal and the Ottoman Empire), some, as mentioned, to revive the driving forces for a fresh Coalition, others to ensure benevolent neutralities (with Denmark and Sweden, The Two Sicilies, the United States), others (with the Batavian Republic and Spain) to delay likely renewed enmities or mitigate the effects. The results or indications naturally were mixed: revealing the familiar obstacles in the cases of Russia, Austria and Prussia, reasonably hopeful with the two Northern Powers, indeterminate in the Mediterranean, abortive with Holland but usefully time-consuming with Spain, negligible with Portugal, fluctuating with the United States.[1] The conduct of strategy also as yet escaped adverse attention. Neither sins of omission or commission could be brought to book: a lack of operations against the Continent could scarcely be condemned, and while the only alternative to such a commitment – renewed involvement with subversion inside France – was set actively on foot in due course, that was only from the autumn, to end once more in failure the next year.[2] Criticism was however able now to fasten on important aspects of administration, for growing disputes were surfacing in both the naval and the military spheres. The former would occupy Pitt himself some months later, to the accompaniment of a rising storm. The latter, which would also play a major part in the course he set himself, began to impinge as experience of the problems attending a rapid expansion of forces, above all of the auxiliary forces, could be digested by the reassembled legislators returning as part-time colonels and captains from their 'countries' once more. They brought a weight of irritation, not felt strongly before, from which the Oppositions, Old and New, might benefit, if not yet systematically at least on certain issues contributing to a mood.

The possible prospect of some shift in atmosphere – it could not be put higher than that – may in fact have encouraged less passive aspirations among the anti-Ministerialist groups. They could scarcely look for significant accessions or perhaps even sympathy from the bulk of the country gentlemen on whose support Addington particularly liked to rely.[3] Any hopes of his discomfiture must rest rather on their own 'factional' exertions; and if those were to be at all effective they should be more effectively linked. Amid all his difficulties, Fox was still, it seemed, the keenest for the chase. He remained circumscribed by his followers in

1. See Fedorak, loc. cit., ch. Seven.
2. Cf. for earlier p. 471 above.
3. See pp. 554–5 above.

the first few weeks of the session; in mid December indeed he was complaining that virtually none of his friends backed him in the House, and that when he was absent they sniped at his 'allies upon the bench next the bar'.[1] Nevertheless he had shown clear signs of the direction in which he would like to move. He had hoped to raise the question of Ireland afresh, including that of the Catholics, in the light of Emmet's rising and partly as a bait to the Grenvilles; and while the idea proved unpopular with his party at this stage, and with his advisers in Ireland itself, information on possible tactics passed between the two Opposition wings. At the end of November likewise he decided to support Windham if the latter attacked the Ministry over some of its military arrangements. That occasion duly came, on 9 December; Windham's associates had been forewarned; and the debate in fact marked the first time that Fox and the Grenvillites part-nered one another in this way.[2] Shortly afterwards he met the two younger Grenville brothers, at the house of their brother-in-law Lord Fortescue in Grosvenor Square; and his language in general began to reveal the path he might wish to pursue. It was at this point that he dared to allude to the group as 'allies', and he was prepared to consider bestowing the prime accolade on the Grenvilles and Windham themselves: 'You know I always thought among all their faults, that they had one good quality, viz., that of being capable of becoming good party men'.[3]

None of this meant that Fox could look to a rapid outcome. The debate of the 9th was the kind of specific occasion which could perhaps be pre-dicted; but it was far from presaging systematic contact, let alone a junc-tion. Whoever suggested the meeting moreover, it seems to have been concerned largely with the subject of tactics on Ireland, and the Grenvilles for their part had still given no hint of an interest in a regular connexion –

1. To Grey, 17 December 1803 (*Memorials of Fox*, III, 444). For his deepening anxieties over the party, and the Prince of Wales again, from August onwards, see op. cit., 424–46. Cf. p. 574, n4 above for the description of the Grenvillites.

2. On Ireland see Fox's letters to Grey and to Richard Fitzpatrick in *Memorials of Fox*, III, 435, 441–2, 231; same to Thomas Grenville, 20 December 1803 (B.L. Add. Ms 41852); Thomas Grenville to Grenville, 21 December 1803 (*H.M.C., Dropmore*, VII, 201). Windham told Fox of his intention, which the latter had guessed, to attack the Ministry on the Army Estimates, when the two men met in the street some days beforehand, and the likelihood of support was passed on at once to the Grenvilles (Fox to Grey, 27 November, same to Fitzpatrick, 30 November 1803, *Memorials of Fox*, III, 433, 438–40; Thomas Grenville to Grenville, 30 November 1803, *H.M.C., Dropmore*, VII, 197. See also Harvey, loc. cit., 74–6). In view of the divisions within the party's ranks however, its leader was anxious that his speech should be seen as arising from 'an accidental [rather] than an apparently concerted occasion' (to Fitzpatrick, 2 December 1803; *Memorials of Fox*, III, 439). For Emmet's rising see p. 609 above.

3. Fox to Grey, 17 December 1803 (*Memorials of Fox*, III, 443); he picked them out here from the rest of 'the new opposition'. The fact of the meeting is disclosed in Thomas Grenville to Grenville, 21 December 1803 (*H.M.C., Dropmore*, VII, 201); the identity of the house, op. cit., 104. I would agree with Jupp (*Lord Grenville*, 327) that, from the tone of Fox's language to Grey on the 17th, the talk probably took place by that date. Fortescue was married to Hester Grenville.

indeed they had recently suspected Fox of veering towards the Ministry, without apparently having considered attracting him themselves.[1] The obstacles in any case remained serious: opposing views on the new war, the history of the past decade, Lord Grenville's sense of caution on the dangers of such a step. For beyond the memories of political enmity there lay the dissonant concepts of political conduct. The Old Opposition – or specifically Fox and his followers – took pride in acting as a self-proclaimed party: that form of alignment which in principle was still distinct in Parliamentary life. Members of the New Opposition, loosely grouped, still liked to explain themselves otherwise, and Grenville in person condemned the thought of setting out to undermine the executive.[2] He was moreover delicately balanced, as was Fox but from a different position, between opportunities and hazards which it would be imprudent to ignore. There was now widespread acceptance of the view that at some point the French would try to invade; if not immediately – though that might still be so – in the course of the coming year. The need for a different Government, as he in particular saw it, became the more pressing, and might now command rather stronger support from the doubts coming to light. On the other hand, Addington might make serious efforts, for the same reason, to strengthen his ranks: Tierney might be an earnest of selective additions from men starved of the loaves and fishes, and broadly supportive of the Napoleonic where they had opposed the Revolutionary War. The connexion must be held together; but an exclusive junction with Fox could hold unforeseeable risks. And in such circumstances there was a course to which the Grenvilles could readily turn: an answer in essence already proposed, which should now be set more firmly in place. A more amply inclusive arrangement had convincing merits. In the last week of December Windham seems to have visited the brothers, the two younger at Dropmore and then Buckingham at Stowe. On the last day of the year Lord Grenville sent a letter to Pitt, urging talks between them in the Christmas recess with a view to 'an understanding between the considerable persons in the country, forgetting past differences, and uniting to rescue us' from the dangers that lay ahead.[3]

---

1 Their suspicion was aroused when Addington showed signs in November, as they and Fox himself believed, of a readiness to contemplate the chances for talks on a renewed peace. Since Fox had gone into decided opposition only when war was declared, and was driven moreover in the Grenvilles' eyes by his dread of a return by Pitt, they watched him closely for a rapprochement with Government which however they do not seem to have thought of trying to prevent. See Thomas Grenville to Buckingham, 25 November 1803 (Buckingham, III, 333–4).

2. Cf. p. 574 above.

3. 31 December 1803 (*H.M.C., Dropmore*, VII, 203–4, from Grenville's copy. The original is in the Dacres Adams Mss, formerly P.R.O. 30/58/4). He went on to stress that 'The success of such an experiment depends entirely on the advantages which the present moment affords for it'. The sequence of probable conversations can be deduced op. cit., 201–3.

See pp. 593–4 above for Grenville's suggestion to Pitt in March of a 'comprehensive' Ministry, with qualifications, if Addington retired from his post.

II

Pitt thus lay, in a freshly changing context, once more in the forefront of politicians' thoughts. The Grenvilles turned to him again, their past frustrations the greater from their desire: 'It is the first wish of my heart', Grenville himself wrote now, 'that our lines may entirely agree'.[1] Fox, who remained sure, as in the autumn, that 'nothing' would 'induce Pitt to make the *saut perilleux*, and jump into opposition', protested against the fact that nonetheless he had 'always to be considered in our deliberations'.[2] Addington, keeping on terms with elements among the Whigs in order to weaken the party, was the happier to do so since it also helped him to 'set Mr. Pitt . . . at defiance'.[3] The shadow fell, as it had done unevenly, lengthening or shrinking, for almost three years, on the different areas of the Parliamentary scene.

Grenville soon had an answer to his letter, from Walmer. Pitt would be glad to meet without loss of time and hoped to be in London in the next few days.[4] The visit however was likely to be brief; his attention was clearly focused on his military duties; and these indeed were inescapable, for the political manoeuvre discussed at Dropmore coincided with a prospect, earlier than expected, of the very crisis it sought to anticipate. Despite the time of year, the invasion so long debated might in fact be at hand.[5] Signs, discernible for some months, were multiplying now. The Brest fleet and the Texel squadron were victualling once more, large troop reinforcements were said to be marching to the northern coast, late in December Bonaparte inspected the gunboats and barges still gathering at Boulogne. The wind set fair from France at the close of the month. Final defensive measures were accordingly in train. The Bank of England's bullion would be moved to Worcester and its books to the Tower, the Stock Exchange would close, Cornwallis was to command the regular army of reserve, the King on his own insistence would take station at Dartford or Chelmsford to cover a southern or an eastern landing. Pitt's return was delayed. But he arrived at York Place on 8 January, for a short stay in a welcome bout of

1. To Pitt, 31 December 1803; as in p. 614, n3 above. A fortnight earlier Fox had suspected that the Grenvilles were 'very much out of humour' with Pitt (see *Memorials of Fox*, III, 444). That was in proportion to their persistent eagerness for his leadership.

2. Fox to Grey, 27 November 1803 (op. cit., 435), and cf. 19 October (430).

3. Pretyman's phrase, to Rose, 7 November 1803 (B.L. Add. Ms 42773). When the Bishop had recently told Westmorland, who was again treating Pitt lightly in conversation, that he and others would soon have to choose between the latter and Addington, the Lord Privy Seal 'seemed not to be very comfortable' and began to hedge (ibid).

4. Pitt to Grenville, 4 January 1803 (*H.M.C., Dropmore*, VII, 204–5).

5. Pitt for his own part was sure that the French meant business, but inclined to think that the undertaking might be delayed until the spring (to Alexander Hope, 18 January 1804; S.R.O., Hope of Luffness Mss, GD 364/1, bundle 1137).

bad weather; and on the 10th and 11th and, briefly, the 12th the two men talked there.[1]

The outcome put paid to Grenville's initial hopes. Pitt would not take part in an arrangement for concerted systematic opposition, or in communications beforehand. He made it plain that he condemned some of the Ministry's measures and intentions. He agreed that a comprehensive Administration was the desirable end. But he could not approve of working with the Foxites, and furthermore he did not agree that the object sought could best be attained by the means proposed.[2] He set down his reasons a few weeks later, after his verdict had led Grenville to go his own way. They may be given here as the most cogent statement of his case as applied to the moment – and one which would prove of some prophetic interest for a future that would not be long delayed.[3]

Pitt thought that Grenville's 'system' would

not be productive of any increased credit to yourselves, or any advantage to the public. The immediate effect of an active opposition will be to harass a Government confessedly not very strong nor vigorous in itself, and in a situation of the country the most critical, with the constant distraction of Parliamentary warfare. Such a line, though conducted by the first talents and abilities, will, I am confident, not be supported by any strength of numbers in Parliament, nor by public opinion. It will therefore have very little chance of accomplishing its object of changing the Administration, and certainly none of doing so in time to afford the country the benefit of abler counsels to meet the difficulties of the present crisis. Those very difficulties it will in the mean while certainly aggravate; and even if, sooner or later, it should make a change necessary, I am afraid that instead of leading to the establishment of a comprehensive Administration (such as you describe) it will tend to render the attainment of that object more difficult if not impossible. Whatever unfavourable impression may at any time have existed in the highest quarter towards any of the parties engaged in such a system, will, of course, be strengthened and confirmed; and the natural consequence will be a determination, even in case of a change being found necessary, to put, if possible a negative on them, in forming a new Government. In the event of such being the state of things, I cannot help foreseeing great mischief to the public,

---

1. Pitt to Grenville, 8 January 1804 (*H.M.C., Dropmore*, VII, 206). There were three conversations, one on each day (Grenville to [Buckingham], 11 January, same to Thomas Grenville, 13 January 1804; B.L. Add. Ms 41852. It is clear from the contents of the first letter that it was addressed to the Marquess). See also Thomas Grenville to Buckingham, 13 January 1804 (*H.M.C., Dropmore*, VII, 206).

2. Grenville's letter of 11 January (n1 above).

3. Pitt to Grenville, 4 February 1804 (*H.M.C., Dropmore*, VII, 212–14). The omissions relate to the actual course which Grenville had taken meanwhile (see below).

and the source of great uneasiness and embarrassment personally to myself; as nothing is more probable than that a call might then be made upon me which I should feel it impossible to decline, and that I should have no means either of forming that comprehensive Government which I agree with you in thinking most desirable, or of obtaining the assistance of those with whom, from public and private feelings, it has been the greatest happiness to me to act during almost the whole of my political life. . . . I need hardly add that the line which I must take . . . will be simply that of giving my opinion fairly on the measures and conduct of Government in important points, and suggesting whatever may appear to my own mind most essential to the public safety, abstaining at the same time from all attempts to embarrass the Government by any system of opposition. . . .

Grenville was deeply depressed even before the conversations ended. 'All hope of such a decided and open pact' would have to be dropped.[1] In point of fact that did not rule out a meeting of minds on some occasions; Pitt went on in his letter to mention a forthcoming debate on a new Ministerial Volunteer bill, and the general issue of the land forces, on which he would be glad to have a further talk.[2] It was possible, as Buckingham indeed forecast, that he would 'gradually heat himself' in Parliament even if he left the Grenvillites to make the running in systematic opposition.[3] In such circumstances, perhaps the group might have waited on events which could yet be moving their way. But under this latest discouragement they were in no mood to do so;[4] on the contrary, the opposition so strongly required should now be brought to its highest strength. Communications to that end were opened at once. Grenville had already seen Windham, and agreed that debating activity should be stepped up. Brother Thomas and Spencer went to Stowe to confer while he himself stayed to take soundings in London. Thomas got in touch with Lord Carlisle, an experienced Portland Whig but now linked with the Grenvilles and boasting some influence of his own, and was then set, as the family's natural channel, to approach Fox. The two men went for a morning ride on 26 January, on 'half way'

1. To Buckingham, 11 January 1804 (B.L. Add. Ms 41852).
2. To Grenville, 4 February 1804 (*H.M.C., Dropmore*, VII, 214).
3. To Grenville, nd but 14 January 1804 (op. cit., 208). He commented that in such case Pitt would be in a position to involve himself in successful developments at a time of his own choosing: a 'game' however which would damage his reputation, and in practice could not be sustained.
Pretyman, who had been trying to keep in touch with Grenville for some time through Carysfort (see p. 529, n2 above, and *H.M.C., Dropmore*, VII, 192–5), and had just seen Pitt, likewise thought that the latter would find himself in the event taking a stronger line than he intended or 'even allowed to be probable' (to Carysfort, for Grenville, 13 January 1804; op. cit., 209–10).
4. Grenville to Buckingham, 30 January 1804 (Buckingham, III, 342), describing Pitt's 'views of middle lines, and managements and delicacies *ou l'on se perd*'.

ground.[1] The offer of a joint systematic opposition was made, to bring down the Ministry and replace it with one on 'the broadest possible basis', the first step being an assault on the pending Volunteer bill. Fox was told of the likelihood of some accessions centred on Carlisle; he already knew of Fitzwilliam's goodwill; and gathered that contact with Pitt was ended, though of course that elusive figure might complicate matters in the event of Addington's fall by presenting himself as a loosely associated but essentially independent choice. All this was music to the listener's ears. It appeared to confirm his recent suspicion that the Grenvilles were out of humour with Pitt, and that there was no imminent risk of a take-over from that quarter.[2] And he was not at all perturbed by the thought of a move which, as in the early eighties, would appear to many to damage the very concept of party. On the contrary, he had long justified such unions by the prospect of bringing the righteous towards their goal; 'As a Party man, he thought it a good thing for his party to come into office, were it only for a month'; and the means were perfectly acceptable – *'he loved coalitions'*.[3] He welcomed the proposal at once. But of course he must consult others, which would take some days.

So must the Grenvilles themselves. In their case it was not too difficult. Once the plunge was taken, the 'New Opposition' as a whole was prepared to go a long way. Past differences were to be put aside in the service of national defence, and of Ireland; some division of labour might be reached, Windham leading on the first question and Fox on the second; and Windham from the start was ready to pronounce the dangerous word Coalition. Some qualms remained: Minto, a supporter since the treaty of Amiens, would have preferred a loose connexion only, and Grenville himself, forward as he was in his efforts, was nonetheless anxious to limit 'communication' to the two questions from which the proposal had sprung.[4] But differences were not allowed to become obstacles; the target must not be missed; there was a general eagerness to move ahead and start to reap results. Fox's path was not so simple, as he soon discovered. Grey

---

1. Same to same, 11, 15 January 1804 (B.L. Add. Ms 41852); Thomas Grenville to same, 13 January 1804 (*H.M.C., Dropmore*, VII, 206–7); Buckingham to Grenville, nd but 14 January (op. cit., 207); Thomas Grenville to Grenville, 25, 26 January 1804 (op. cit., 210–11); Fox to Fitzpatrick, 27 January 1804 (*Memorials of Fox*, IV, 15–19); same to Grey, 29 January 1804 (op. cit., III, 449–52).

2. If Fox was reporting correctly, Thomas may have gone too far in his version of the Grenvilles' position. For Fox's earlier suspicion of their annoyance with Pitt see p. 615, n1 above.

3. See II, 180, for the later possibility in June 1792.

4. *Life and Letters of Sir Gilbert Elliot*, III, 303–4; Grenville to Pitt, 31 January 1804 (*H.M.C., Dropmore*, VII, 212). See in general Harvey, 'The Grenville Party', 78–9 (though I place a rather different interpretation on Windham's sentiments – see the letters to his election agent Thomas Amyot of 1 and 5 January 1804 in *The Windham Papers*, II, 227–9), Sack, *The Grenvillites*, 75, 77, Jupp, *Lord Grenville*, 328–30. Cf. p. 593 above for Grenville's earlier insistence to Pitt on the need for a statement of continuing disapproval of the Ministry's past in any arrangement that might be formed with Addington and others.

agreed to the objects specified, but even then reluctantly and in hopes that a general co-operation need not be actively pursued. Other old companions were even more chary, and the Carlton House politicians – Moira, Erskine, Sheridan – joined the Dukes of Norfolk and Northumberland to remonstrate and oppose.[1] Enough support or acquiescence however might be enlisted to try the experiment. A month after Grenville had approached Pitt he wrote to inform him of the approach to Fox, before the consequence was 'openly declared in Parliament' when the proper occasion arose.[2] Despite continuing doubts and disputes in the Old Opposition, it was clear in February that this could follow, and early in March 1804 the effects began to be felt.

Both the major coalitions in the past two decades had quite lengthy spans of life, and lengthier repercussions. The union of the Northites and Foxites in 1782, the accession of the Portland Whigs to Pitt's Ministry in 1794, created new relationships many of which endured as times changed. Each had its effects, some lasting, on the shape of political development; and so, as it proved, did the arrangement of January 1804. Indeed that coalescence could be seen later to have filled a highly significant role in a long-term development of cardinal importance, for its success and failure in the shorter term gave a distinctive form to the issue which finally opened the course of transition from one constitutional epoch to another. The line can be traced back; from Catholic Emancipation in 1829 – itself providing a preparatory context for the Great Reform Bill of 1832 –, which emerged from the 'great question' of Irish Catholic Parliamentary relief[3] as that was championed for some twenty years, with varying degrees but broad unity of purpose, by the assorted heirs of the Ministry of All the Talents headed by Grenville and Fox in 1806–7 and swiftly falling on a proposal that raised suspected echoes of that cause. The Irish question in fact, one of the two initial ingredients of their junction, would lead to their disappearance from office as it had led to Pitt's. And here a separate line might be said to intersect. For the junction itself, in the shape it took, owed its existence to the state of affairs which had evolved in the past three years from that last signal event.

This indeed was clear. Despite Pitt's support of Addington for a time, which preserved a period of calm, his departure had admitted conditions easily tending to fragmentation. The fact could be observed increasingly from the autumn of 1801: 'Parties . . . so strangely chequered and confused'; 'the confusion of . . . parties greater than ever'; ''tis difficult to say who are *with* or who *against*'; 'the strange confusion of parties and

1. Harvey, loc. cit., 81–2.
2. 31 January 1804 (*H.M.C., Dropmore*, VII, 211–12).
3. Fox to Fitzpatrick, 30 November 1803 (*Memorials of Fox*, III, 438). He wrote 'the great question of Ireland'; from the context he was referring to such relief.

opinions'.[1] Such an impression persisted through the Ministry's continued successes when divisions were called in a debate; and it was not
confined to counting the principal connexions as consistently reliable
entities. In 1803 Fox, using his favourite term, perceived three or four 'distinct parties': the Foxites, the Grenvillites, the Pittites depending on
whether they acted on their own (as in the case of Patten's motion) or with
others, and the Ministerial benches.[2] But these main distinctions were by
no means absolute: they could be blurred on a given occasion; the larger
connexions, as always, were composed of smaller and potentially shifting
groups (Canning at one point described the Grenvillites as 'the Grenvilles
and Windhams', 'Ld. Fitzwills', 'Straglers', and 'Us and P's friends');[3] and
the 'Foxites' were no longer all strictly Foxites – witness Sheridan or
Tierney – in the former Opposition sense. In these circumstances every
one was affected; for to the ordinary Parliamentarian as well as the leader
an accustomed framework had been summarily removed. '. . . to whom or
to what can we pledge ourselves', ran one letter signed 'MP' in a London
newspaper. 'I remember when a man was asked whether he was . . . a
Pittite or a Foxite? There was some sense in that; we knew what we were
about; but now that the main armies are broke down into independent
corps, and each has its own discipline, we know not how to handle our
votes, shoulder our consciences, or where to look for the word of
command'.[4] An apparently homogeneous pattern was reverting in
extreme form to its components, and the process was underlined as Pitt's
own true position seemed ever more in doubt. He might still be lumbered,
in the general view, with the 'Catholic millstone'. He might have damaged
his chances of being summoned to office on his own terms, and sunk to
that extent in the Parliamentary stakes.[5] But that last impression could
quickly be revised. He remained an unknown quantity in prospect.
Viewed indeed from any part of the House, the scene still looked like
Hamlet without the prince – literally so in the increasingly frequent,
rumour-laden spells of absence at Walmer. Nor was that sense diminished
with the advent of a combination which might hold a promise of reducing
the choices; for politicians as a whole had still to assess their relationship
with him. One Grenvillite summed up, probably in retrospect, his impression of the 'general assessment' at this time: 'contempt mixed with pity for
Mr. A., dislike and respect for Ld. G., admiration and distrust of Mr. F.[,]

1. Quotations for November 1801, December 1802, January and June 1803 respectively,
in *H of P*, I, 348–9.
2. To Holland, 6 June 1803 (*Memorials of Fox*, III, 222).
3. To Hookham Frere, 9 June 1803 (see Sack, *The Grenvillites*, 69).
4. *The Morning Chronicle*, 19 November 1801 – an early point in these years, one might
have thought, for such a sharp impression. As often under change, the memory of a recent
past was somewhat simplified; even more so that of the immediately preceding years, for
which the writer depicted a choice of 'Tory or . . . Whig'.
5. Hobart to Auckland, 30 January [1804] (*A.C.*, IV, 190) for the first; p. 607 above for
the second.

and for Mr. P., veneration confidence and desire'.[1] The strength of the combined Opposition, in numbers and reputation, would be affected by – might even turn on – his conduct in the coming months.

Pitt could not bring great numbers from his own reliable friends in the Commons. A probable minimum might be gauged from the most unpromising occasion, the debate on Patten's motion. The 58 votes he then secured represented something like a core of personal support, with some others perhaps to be added from absentees – and Canning normally to be included –; to be compared with Fox's account of 69 Foxites and 36 Grenvillites present. His direct contribution on such lines was proportionately much more significant in the Lords; in the debate on Patten's motion it garnered 18 votes there compared with the Grenvillites' 14 and the Foxites' 10.[2] But of course this was only a small part of the story. The core in the Commons could expand into wider support depending on the issue; and even if that was denied in the vote as the Ministerial ranks hung together, his interventions could exert mounting influence outside the division lobbies themselves.

At the end of January 1804 it was still impossible to forecast exactly how Pitt would behave. He was said to be 'extremely bitter' against the Ministry;[3] but his rejection of Grenville's approach made it clear that he would not be tied down. In point of fact however he was ready to move, in his own way. He would seem to have been growing distinctly alarmed at the Admiralty's conduct of its administrative affairs; and his experience of a novel personal commitment to military duties had strengthened his earlier conviction that the Government would lack grasp in a dangerous war. As a serving colonel he was no longer so diffident of his ideas on military affairs, at least on the ground.[4] And there may have been a further more intimate ingredient in a combination of pressures driving him towards action in what would become a decisive stage.

For Pitt may well have felt an added incentive to administer the rod from a personal resentment roused at times already, but now to a fresh height. The occasion had arisen in the late summer of 1803, and been sustained since, by the appearance of a pamphlet that included a strong attack on his conduct in the recent exchanges with Addington which could have been made only with connivance from 'a confidential man'.

1. The reading was that of Charles Williams Wynn, who was married to the Grenvilles' sister Charlotte (quoted in Harvey, loc. cit., 82).

2. See p. 606 and n3 above; Fox to Holland, 6 June 1803 (*Memorials of Fox*, III, 222). Names of those thought to have voted with Pitt on his alternative motion to Patten's are given and discussed by Aspinall in *L.C.G. III*, IV, n1 on p. 103; as are those for the subsequent minority on the original motion in op. cit., n2.

The figure of 58 may be set against the calculation of 'the Party attached to Mr. Pitt' in very different circumstances in May 1788; thought to number 52, of whom 'not above twenty' would survive in an election if he were no longer Minister (I, 619, but see also ibid, n3).

3. See *Colchester*, I, 477; and for some examples from the autumn *Rose*, II, 54–60.

4. Cf. II, 489.

The tone throughout, and some evidence that the Treasury liked the publication, led to the inference that it was approved officially and that Addington himself was involved. Pitt took instant and deep offence, and a response was prepared under his supervision after consulting Rose and Long. The 'pamphlet war' – for more followed – naturally excited interest; each of the two main pieces went through several editions. It continued into January 1804, and meanwhile Pitt refused to communicate privately with individual Ministers on 'any political subject'. As had been the case indeed at an earlier point, and was much more so now, he proved acutely sensitive to personal charges thought to be inspired by his successor. In point of fact that particular suspicion was almost certainly misplaced here; Addington always categorically denied any knowledge of the business, and the culprits are more likely to have been his brother Hiley and brother-in-law Charles Bragge.[1] The affair caused bad blood. Pitt's resentment of Addington himself may have eased after a time; but it had been kindled against the Ministry in general, and the fuel could not but be added to a smouldering fire.[2]

1. Stanhope (IV, 88–95) and Ziegler (*Addington*, 195–7) amplify Pellew (*Life of Lord Sidmouth*, I, 145–7) on the affair. The attack was launched in August or early September 1803, in *A Few Cursory Remarks upon the State of Parties, during the Administration of the Right Honourable Henry Addington. By a Near Observer* [Thomas Richard Bentley] (1803). The rejoinder under Pitt's supervision, written by Thomas Courtenay, a young clerk in the Stationery Office whose father was Bishop of Exeter, appeared as *A Plain Answer to the Misrepresentations and Calumnies contained in the Cursory Remarks of a Near Observer. By A More Accurate Observer* (1803), and there were at least three other commentaries before the end of the year, though these were not directed by Pitt himself. The *Plain Answer* evoked *A Plain Reply to a Plain Answer; being a more fair State of the Question between the Late and the Present Ministers* (1804) which came anonymously from the pen of a Dr Bissit, as well as two other specimens of *Reply*, both apparently by Bentley. Finally one may notice *The View of the Relative Situations of Mr. Pitt and Mr. Addington previous to and on the Night of Mr. Patten's Motion* (1804) – a sideblow on one aspect of the case – which was known to be by Robert Ward, the MP who later became Plumer Ward. Not written in collusion with Pitt, or indeed shown to him, but eliciting a letter of gratitude in January 1804, it sparked off *A Letter to Robert Ward Esq. MP, occasioned by a Pamphlet, intituled, A View of the Relative Situations . . .* (1804). The publications can be found in the B.L. *Catalogue of Printed Books*, under Pitt and Sidmouth.

The quotation is from Wilberforce (Stanhope, IV, 89), and Pitt's refusal to continue corresponding privately on political questions was given in a letter to Castlereagh (op. cit., 90–1). Charles Long claimed to know that one of the joint Secretaries of the Treasury, Vansittart, sent copies of the offending pamphlet to 'several persons' (op. cit., 89). *Rose*, II, 51–4, 61–4 shows Pitt's anger and determination that charges should be answered, though letters from the former to Pretyman expressed dismay that the latter's 'military Avocations' held up publication of the *Plain Answer* for over two months (Pretyman Ms 435/44).

2. See eg Canning's impression on 9 January 1804 of his hostility to the Cabinet – 'No shabby tenderness, except for Cast.[lereagh]' (quoted in Marshall, op. cit., 259); and Grenville's on the 30th, 'The most decided hatred and contempt' (to Buckingham, Buckingham, III, 342). Both men of course were eager to find hopeful signs, and Pitt's persistent uncertainties were not to be dismissed ('Saw Pitt – all bad again ratio sublopsa'; Canning's diary, 10 January 1804, Canning Ms 29). But the force of their expressions is not to be dismissed.

It was against such a background that Pitt summoned his *fidus achates* Pretyman and disclosed his views before Parliament resumed after the short recess. The Bishop relayed them, doubtless with his own familiar predilections but in a broadly convincing account.[1]

His opinions and feelings, both upon public and private grounds, are such that it cannot, I think, be long before he fully expresses them; but this probably will not take place till it is called forth by some new occurrence, I mean some objectionable measure or palpable omission on the part of Ministers, and they will soon furnish such an opportunity. In that case Mr. Pitt might not confine himself to the point in question, but might take a retrospective view, so far at least as to afford him a ground for declaring his conviction of the incompetency of Ministers, and the danger in which this country is placed by their negligence and want of talents. . . . Mr. Pitt cannot bear the idea of a teasing, harassing opposition; but, as far as I can judge, he is ready to stand forward whenever there shall be an opportunity of exposing the incapacity of Ministers, in any important degree or upon any material point.

And so it proved. The die was not yet finally cast. In the first half of February Pitt still felt qualms about 'anything like Hostility'. But they were overcome now without much ado and he determined to come out 'pretty strongly' on questions of defence.[2] By way perhaps of preface and to repeat his repudiation of systematic attack, he is said to have let it be known that he had no ground of complaint against Addington and felt no personal hostility.[3] He may have reckoned or hoped, after the battle of the

---

Some months later the faithful Rose noted that Pitt was being 'a little led, as in former instances, by resentment against political opponents' (diary for 10 May 1804; *Rose*, II, 130). This was clearly one of the instances.

1. To Carysfort, 13 January 1804 (*H.M.C., Dropmore*, VII, 210). The Bishop's point of view must be remembered: an intense desire from the start to see Addington removed, and a corresponding inclination to build on every hopeful utterance, as he saw it, from Pitt (eg pp. 572, 615, n3 above). He was moreover anxious to salvage something from an apparently doomed chance of general co-operation with the Grenvilles. But allowing for all that, his report seems to ring true in the circumstances at this point.

One must call Pretyman 'Tomline' from now on. He had been given licence in November to change his name on inheriting a property in Lincolnshire.

2. Rose to Tomline, 11 February 1804 (Holland Rose, II, 496–7). In conversation with Malmesbury on the 19th, Pitt reiterated his intention 'in all simple and plain questions, . . . to support Government; but when Government omitted any thing he thought the state of the country required to be done, or did it weakly or inefficiently . . ., he then should deliver his sentiments clearly and distinctly, but not even then in a spirit of opposition' unless and until Government would 'not adopt what he thought necessary' (*Malmesbury*, IV, 289). See also Lady Melville in London, after talking to Pitt, to Melville in Scotland, 22 February 1804 (S.R.O., Melville Mss, GD 51/1).

3. *Colchester*, I, 482, diary for 23 February 1804, after talking to Addington among others, and referring to 'recent' communications received indirectly from Pitt, one said to have been through Chatham and the other through Steele.

pamphlets, that this would clear one area of dispute. He now waited for the opportunity which would 'furnish' itself.

It was not long delayed. The Government intended to introduce a bill to consolidate the growing series of Acts regulating the Volunteers, which, particularly under the pressure of speed in a subject of inherent complexity, had thrown up a growing list of contested interpretations;[1] and on 8 February the Home Secretary, Charles Yorke,[2] duly brought it before the House. He was anxious to keep the business strictly to the necessary detail. But that was a forlorn hope with Windham and Fox alike resolved to march onto wider ground, and in the event the debates ranged more freely, in all on eleven days in a period of some seven weeks. Pitt missed the first discussion.[3] But he was there for the second on 27 February, and spoke in eight of the next nine – on every occasion in fact except the last, for the third reading of the bill on 22 March.[4]

His opening was ominous. He rejected Government's attempt to confine the range of inquiry; an explicit departure from his position before Christmas, when he had opposed such a stance by Windham.[5] He then set out on his own line, which in point of fact was at variance with those of Windham himself and Fox. Unlike theirs, his tone remained ostensibly dispassionate; and the guiding principle was very much his own – an emphasis on the merits of the Volunteer system which they did not share. He was not joining with the Oppositions.[6] But that did not reduce the effect, for here was a further critical view and the critical element was soon apparent. As Canning claimed to detect,

1. In particular, fresh sets of regulations had redefined allowances of pay, and with them services, as recently as June and August 1803.

2. See p. 608, n7 above; succeeding Portland.

3. To Rose's distress (to Tomline, 8 February 1804; Pretyman Ms 435/44). Pitt had come up from Walmer by the 6th (same to same, 6 February 1804; loc. cit.), but the motion was postponed and he seems to have returned (see Lord Lowther to Mulgrave, 11 February 1804; Normanby Mss, Box VII, bundle 13).

4. The debates may be followed in *P.R.* (*Stockdale* series), I (1804), 385–424 with 425, 490–527, 533–79, 605–25, 651–63, op. cit., II (1804), 17–24, 26–33, 43–54, 152–84, 186–203, 224–45. The reports there scarcely differ from those in the new compilation, *Cobbett's Parliamentary Debates* (henceforth *P.D.*), which from 1803 was printed by T.C. Hansard. Since vol. I of this latter series, starting on 22 November 1783 after the summer recess, settled down in pagination only on 29 February 1804 (see its 'Directions to the Reader', iv), I have used *P.R.* (*Stockdale*) in general for the period until *P.D.*, II begins early in April after the Easter recess.

5. *P.R.* (*Stockdale*), I, 507–8. Cf. op. cit., 165 for 9 December 1803, the occasion of Windham's attack on the Government (p. 613 above).

6. He continued for that matter throughout the next two and a half months to sit where he had sat hitherto; 'under the gallery', with Yorke and Tierney for instance 'below' him and Fox 'opposite' (eg *P.R.* (*Stockdale*), I, 510, 541, 562, op. cit., II, 1420). One may perhaps draw attention again (cf. pp. 619–20 above) to the looseness of the current state of the House bearing in mind the reduction in recent decades of the flexibility in seating arrangements for leading figures (I, 39).

with delight, 'There was a studious abstinence from all hostility – but this abstinence was so constantly *announced*, that it became itself hostile'.[1] The burden of the policy itself was familiar. It had been stated before.[2] Volunteers supplied the means 'upon which', with the regular army, 'we must . . . ground our reliance for ultimate security'.[3] They were more effective, and desirable, than the militia, as a force to help repel the enemy, and also – an unspoken advantage in this instance – to help subdue any unrest should he land. They could certainly however be made more efficient; and it was thus upon this expansion and improvement that the main effort should fall. Pitt had never thought much of the ancient primary source of defence, and his preference for the voluntary system was undoubtedly stimulated by his beloved levies on the Kentish coast.[4] It was also set in context and gained in strength from the Government's persistent attempts to reach a more 'scientific' provision of military manpower;[5] for if his emphasis was a personal one, he was not alone in seeking a comprehensive 'permanent system' which the earlier war had failed to supply. Windham and, with less experience, Fox had equally been deploying their ideas, and in point of fact all alternatives or corrections now derived from Ministerial schemes in the short-lived peace and the hostilities since. Pitt's answer on this larger theme had itself been evolving,[6] and would shortly be delivered. Meanwhile he concentrated on the means to give greater scope to his favourite component.

He had plenty to say. There should be a proper weighting of the Volunteers' dispositions: certain coasts needed larger numbers than others and than most of the inland counties. Training must be improved, requiring longer periods to which payments for service could be applied; current subsidies were inadequate to sustain a desirable 'permanent duty' of up to three weeks at a time, for which a sum of £2–300,000 should suffice. Field officers from regular regiments should be attached to Volunteers' battalions for better discipline and instruction, and commanding officers of the battalions themselves should be given greater powers to enforce the regulations if men failed to turn up or wished to cut their time short. The rules governing Volunteers' exemptions from the ballot, and the provisions for payment while on duty, which had become increasingly confused in

1. To Mrs Canning, 28 February 1804 (Marshall, op. cit., 260).
2. Eg *P.R.*, *4th ser.*, III, 773, 793; *P.R.* (*Stockdale*), I, 165, 271–2.
3. *P.R.* (*Stockdale*), I, 508.
4. Eg p. 38, n3 above for the militia; and see II, 328–9, 401–2, 451, 486–7, and p. 294 above. The contrast between the two arms of defence could be exaggerated. If militia were sometimes thought unreliable in times of domestic unrest, particularly security, so too were the more highly favoured Volunteers, particularly from the larger towns. This had been seen in the worst years of the recent dearth (p. 295 above) and it may indeed have been one of the reasons why the extent of Pitt's enthusiasm was thought, as it was by many, to be extreme.
5. The word was Yorke's (see Western, *The English Militia in the Eighteenth Century*, 237).
6. He had in fact been working on it from at least the previous November (to Mulgrave, 9 November 1803; Normanby Mss, Box VII, bundle 13).

successive enactments, must be cleared up.[1] Earlier practices, earlier modes of thought, must not be allowed to stand in the way, for 'Comparisons between this and the last war were absolutely idle. The whole of the preparations of France for invasion [in the] last war were hardly equal to an advanced guard of one of its numerous ports at present'.[2]

The outcome of Pitt's effort was seriously disappointing in his eyes. One of his strongest demands, for the attachment of regular officers, was as strongly opposed – largely, it would seem, through persistent mistrust of closer links, in a form which might bestow undue authority, between the standing army and the auxiliary forces responsible to the Lords Lieutenant and the Home Office.[3] Much detail remained muddled or obscure. He gained some ground on pay for 'permanent' spells of duty, though not, he complained, enough; and commanding officers were empowered to arrest in cases of misbehaviour at musketry drill. Otherwise he found that an originally 'flimsy' bill still fell far short of 'fair expectations'.[4] If he did not oppose the completed measure directly – absent as he seems to have been at the final reading – he was clearly left in no friendly mood.[5]

In the second half of March Pitt therefore felt more dissatisfied than he had done a month before.[6] He had said in private that he would not pronounce the Government unfit until it had shown itself determined to reject his suggestions.[7] This was now broadly the case; and the atmosphere moreover had recently worsened from a separate occasion. Early in the month he had decided to call for papers relating to the state of the navy, to enable him in due course to demand an inquiry,[8] and in the

1. Cf. p. 624, n1 above.
2. Debate of 9 March 1804 (*P.R. (Stockdale)*, II, 31).
3. Cf. pp. 123–5 above.
4. Debate of 19 March, near the end of the Committee stage (op. cit., 176–7, but cf. the account in *P.D.*, I, col. 945), and see *Malmesbury*, IV, 289 for his description in February of the bill as introduced. The objections to the field officers, proposed as adjutants to battalions, can be followed throughout the discussions. Commanding officers needed their increased power; for one sidelight on discipline and feeling in a Volunteer battalion see J.E. Cookson, 'The rise and fall of the Sutton Volunteers, 1803–4', in *Historical Research*, Volume 64, Number 153, 46–53.
5. See p. 624 above for the third reading. Nor, despite a misunderstanding in the course of the debate on the 19th, repeated in the Speaker's diary (*P.R. (Stockdale)*, II, 176–8; *Colchester*, I 489), did he vote for a motion to recommit the bill at that point. On the contrary, while calling for further amendments, he opposed that course (see also Pitt to Alexander Hope, 13 April 1804, S.R.O., Hope of Luffness Mss, GD 364/1, bundle 1137; Canning's diary for 18, 19 April 1804, Canning Ms 29d).

The bill in point of fact did not become law until 5 June (44 Geo. III, c54). It was held up by amendments in the Lords which caused further discussion in the Commons of the Houses' respective rights as well as of the contents themselves.
6. Eg his remarks on 28 March, in *P.R. (Stockdale)*, II, 332, 335–6.
7. See Canning to Granville Leveson Gower, 9 February 1804 (P.R.O. 30/29/8(3)). And cf. p. 623 and n2 above.
8. *P.R. (Stockdale)*, II, 85–94. The papers were lists of warships in commission on 31 December 1793, 30 September 1801 and 31 December 1803, with their services at each date; of contracts for gun vessels in 1793, 1797 and 1803, with costs and times specified; of

debate that followed on the 15th he went much farther than any one had heard him in public before. Declaring that the navy's condition was defective in many respects in guidance and materiel, he castigated Ministers – 'contrasting the terrible activity of the enemy with the alarming supineness of our government' – and the Admiralty above all. He was not – or not yet – calling for a vote of censure on St Vincent.[1] But he left no doubt of his own view that 'between his lordship as a commander on the sea, and his lordship as First Lord of the Admiralty, there is a very wide difference'. The case perforce rested at this early stage. It could not immediately be taken farther, for his motion was defeated by 203 to 132.[2]

Just before he rose to speak on the state of the navy, Pitt gave notice that he would be returning to the question of the land forces; and he repeated his intention before the House rose for the short Easter recess.[3] The passage of the Volunteer Consolidation bill by no means exhausted his intention of speaking his mind: on the contrary, he was about to expand his field of view. He accordingly announced on 18 April, through Charles Long (pleading Pitt's own temporary indisposition), that he had a motion to introduce in the following week.[4] When he did so, it was in some quite complicated circumstances, marking the latest stage in a long series of Governmental measures. The Ministry's efforts to expand the land forces had in fact been under way by then for over two years: from the month indeed in which it signed the Definitive treaty of peace. At that point, in March 1802, it began to draft new Militia bills for England and Scotland which were placed before Parliament in April and became law in June, whereby among other things a Supplementary force was added to the 'old' militia, of half the latter's size, as had been done on a rather larger scale in 1796.[5] The aggregate target was 70,000 men; the 'old' militia was embodied when war threatened in March 1803; the supplementary followed two months later when hostilities opened; and by the end of the year they had

---

ships built in the royal dockyards in 1793 and 1801; and likewise in private yards. If some of these were refused, he wished to move nonetheless for an Address to the King for the production of the first.

1. For whom see p. 592, n1 above.

2. Including tellers. The debate is in *P.R.* (*Stockdale*), II, 85–148; the report of Pitt's speech at the close looks patchy there and in *P.D.*, I, cols. 922–7 from which I have taken the quotation. Speaker Abbot noted the result in terms of votes for Pitt with Fox and the Grenvilles against Addington with 'the Prince of Wales's friends' (*Colchester*, I, 488).

3. See his remarks on 15 and 28 March (*P.R.* (*Stockdale*), II, 85, 332–3), and Canning's diary for 19–25 March 1804 (Canning Ms 29d). Pitt intended to pursue his naval inquiry as well, after the Admiralty published some papers following that debate (Lord Lowther to Mulgrave, 5 April 1804; Normanby Mss, Box VII, bundle 13). Other events however took priority.

4. *P.D.*, II, col. 143*, in the debate on the Army of Reserve Suspension bill, for which see below. Parliament had returned from the recess on 5 April. The interval was due to the fact that Pitt wished to wait until Members from Scotland and Ireland, thought to be sympathetic to his cause, had arrived (see Lowther to Mulgrave, 5 April 1804; as in n3 above).

5. 42 Geo. III, cs 90, 91. Cf. II, 642 for 1796; and see pp. 124, 244 above.

together reached the intended strength. In 1803 also the Ministry added to the regulations for the Volunteers which it consolidated in February 1804, in the form contested in detail by Pitt. Before that process was concluded,[1] two further steps were taken to strengthen the militia, one to augment the numbers in Ireland, the other to confirm acceptance of an offer by several regiments there to extend their service to Great Britain.[2] Besides these various provisions, however, a scheme had been adopted in the summer of 1803 by Additional Forces Acts[3] for what became known as an Army of Reserve, distinct from the other two main auxiliary arms. Conscripted by ballot, as in the case of the militia, the recruits could volunteer for overseas service in addition, on the lines introduced for the militia in 1798–9.[4] The target in this case was a force of 50,000 men (34,000 from England, 6,000 from Scotland, 10,000 from Ireland), and by the end of the year it was reckoned that some 34,000 'effectives' had been secured. In the spring of 1804 this grew to some 37,000 and the total on paper was a good deal higher – over 45,000 before death, unfitness and above all desertions were subtracted.[5] The Government, concluding that the practicable limit had been reached, then decided that recruitment should cease, and accordingly introduced a bill in April for Suspension.[6] Meanwhile it brought in the motions affecting the Irish militia. It was thus in a flurry of legislative movement that Pitt again intervened.

He had hoped indeed to delay the process, by his own declared but as yet untitled motion. That ploy however failed, other complications followed, and when he came to speak, on 25 April, it was in the opening debate on the suspension of the Acts for the Army of Reserve.[7] Two days beforehand however he was able to give an extensive survey of his views, thanks to a motion on the defence of the country brought with prior agreement – but a markedly different line of approach – by Fox.[8] In a single week therefore in the second half of April he trained his guns afresh on the state of the land forces, and now in a way that brought matters to a head.

That process must be followed within its context of a political struggle. For Pitt was now quite clearly intent on forcing the Ministry to resign. By

---

1. See p. 626, n4 above.
2. See *P.D.*, II, cols. 31–3, 40, 70; 9, 11 April 1804.
3. 43 Geo. III, cs 82 (for England), 83 (Scotland), 85 (Ireland).
4. Pp. 124–5 above.
5. *P.R.* (*Stockdale*), II, 633; *P.D.*, II, cols. lxv–vi. Numbers to the nearest thousand. The examination of the figures for 'effectives' by the Hon. J.W. Fortescue in *The County Lieutenancies and the Army* (1909), 73 is set in proportion by Glover, *Peninsular Preparation*, 230.
6. *P.D.*, II, col. 265 and see also 308–9.
7. See op. cit., cols. 143*, 174, 178, 265; Pitt to Yorke, Private, 30 April 1804 (B.L. Add. Ms 45041).
8. Op. cit., cols. 182–249, and particularly 205–24. Pitt had indeed been hoping for some such opportunity of 'speaking at large' since the end of March (Canning's diary for 30 March–1 April; Canning Ms 29d).

the end of March he was 'strongly confirmed . . . in the full conviction that every week for which its existence may be protracted will be attended with increased danger to the country'.[1] The final judgment turned on its record stretching back into the period of peace. How well justified therefore were his castigations? We may take the naval administration first, since it provided the opening instance of overt, unconcealed assault.[2] Had the Admiralty in point of fact done as badly as he claimed?

Certainly the First Lord himself had become a liability to the Government. At the start St Vincent could be seen as a 'shield and backbone' for a Cabinet unsure of its strength;[3] a naval hero in whom the public might properly place its trust. Three years later he was the member perhaps most susceptible to criticism; a weak spot in the political defences which his attacker was now out to undermine. Pitt indeed has been widely accused of using the Admiral's disputed credibility simply as a pretext to start the campaign for his own return to office.[4] His motives in point of fact are more likely to have been mixed. For if the state of naval affairs seemed to offer an opening for political advantage, that was because they furnished seemingly ample grounds. There was no denying that relations throughout the system on shore were worse than could easily be recalled. The Admiralty was scarcely – in one vital instance, not at all – on informal speaking terms with the Navy Board Commissioners; the dockyard authorities, at different levels, were wary and apprehensive; merchant shipbuilders and timber contractors resentful and disturbed. A pattern of arrangements always conducive to hierarchical strains, but, with all its familiar imperfections, yielding proven results,[5] was being put to the question by a process in which it seemed that the balance could be seriously upset.

St Vincent had brought to Whitehall the qualities for which he had been known, and feared, as a great Commander-in-Chief, with formidable standards of excellence, whether evoked or imposed. He also carried to the highest pitch the sea officer's habitual opinion of the organisation ashore. He had no use for officials; when they failed to meet his demands they felt the lash of his pen, and he came to the Admiralty convinced that the civil branch of the navy was 'rotten to the very core'. Only 'a radical sweep in the dockyards' could 'cure the enormous evils and corruptions in them';[6] and the dockyards did not stand alone. He grasped at the advent

---

1. To Melville, 29 March 1804 (*Secret Correspondence connected with Mr. Pitt's Return to Office In 1804 . . .*, ed. Lord Mahon [5th Earl Stanhope] (1852), 13); henceforward *Secret Correspondence.*

2. See p. 627 above.

3. Eg the anecdote, from personal memory, of Jedediah Stephens Tucker (St Vincent's private secretary) in his *Memoirs of Admiral the Right Hon*. *The Earl of St Vincent . . .*, II (1844), 127. And cf. Pitt himself on 15 March 1804 (*P.R. (Stockdale)*, II, 14).

4. An early promulgator of this charge was old Lord Liverpool, by then thoroughly disenchanted with Pitt (to Lord Hervey, 26 December 1804, quoted in Fedorak, loc. cit., 294).

5. See pp. 463–4 above.

6. Tucker, op. cit., II, 123.

of peace for an onslaught that would produce massive reforms, to be supported by a Ministry which otherwise was to leave him free for his task.

The end was admirable, and far from surprising: there was indeed ample room for reforms. The vital point of course lay in the choice of means; how far might a frontal onslaught succeed within a possibly brief length of time? St Vincent was later criticised by no less an authority than Middleton – his successor, as Lord Barham – for plunging into such a course before the peace could be judged secure; for if his judgment proved wrong, his method was 'madness and imbecility in the extreme'.[1] Here perhaps was one reformer dwelling rather typically on another; but the charge was a fair one, for though St Vincent had acknowledged that he could not embark on his sweep until there was peace,[2] he sustained it with equal ferocity after war had been declared. Some significant beneficial effects were gained overall for the medium and longer terms.[3] The investigations were placed at the start (despite the Cabinet's doubts) in the hands of a full-blown statutory Commission of Naval Enquiry, whose labours led directly in due course to the creation by the Ministry's successor of a different Commission, for Revising and Digesting the Civil Affairs of the Navy, which itself yielded useful results.[4] Fresh impetus was given to the dockyard engineering works already being undertaken by Samuel Bentham, operating from the post established earlier for him in independence of the Navy Board.[5] Changes in the recruitment and training of apprentices paved the way for the foundation of a school of naval architecture. A new dockyard post of timber master produced improvements in quality and financial savings, after a time. There was a general shake-up which undoubtedly accelerated a process that bore fruits in due course. It has to be said, however, that these benefits were bought dearly in the immediate term; the Commission for Revising achieved improvements in its turn largely by a more moderate approach. Difficulties which Bentham had faced earlier in his unusual position were heightened by St Vincent's more insistent support; the arrangements for apprentices were based on assessments which were partly incorrect, and the numbers of entries in fact fell over the first three years; the timber masters caused such disruption that by 1804 relations with contractors were virtually broken off. Other innovations proved damaging too, but without the comfort of posthumous advantage. A rapid reduction of the dockyard establishments in search of savings, and an upper age limit for recruitment of 28 (soon raised to 35), saw the disappearance of sizeable numbers of older men who could still do skilled or useful work, and discouraged

1. *Letters and Papers of Lord Barham . . .*, ed. Sir John Knox Laughton, III (1911), 69. For Middleton see p. 462 above.
2. Tucker, op. cit., II, 123.
3. In what follows I have drawn largely on Roger Morriss, 'St Vincent and Reform, 1801–04', in *The Mariner's Mirror*, Vol. 69, No. 3, 268–90.
4. The initial Act was 43 Geo. III, c16; amended and extended by c45 Geo. III, c45.
5. P. 464 above.

recruitment – since qualification for long service payments and pensions was affected – to yards already short of men in 1801. These last regulations were in fact altered and then abolished after St Vincent left, when those for the timber masters had also to be reviewed. And the same applied to shipbuilding itself, where the First Lord's strong dislike of contractors and preference for the royal yards led to an unsuccessful programme for remodelling the latter's shipwrights' organisation, and a sacrifice of fuller production at a time when, as Pitt asserted, there were empty merchant slips and docks along the Thames.[1] The reduction in orders, designed to foster an improvement in performance, ended again by damaging the navy's relations with its sources of supply.

Such methods were the opposite in essence to Pitt's. He too could be high-handed, and attack abuses, and he could point to his share of reforms; but if that last had quite often fallen short of expectations, the successes had lain within a framework of policy working with, not against, the grain.[2] Greater attention to earlier practical improvements, which St Vincent scarcely recognised as such, greater political sensitivity, less 'want of foresight and due consideration' in reaching for desirable aims,[3] could well have gained more ground in an undertaking that was bound to be opposed. St Vincent might claim that nothing less than full achievement was necessary, and that moderation would fail – he might indeed have instanced the fate of Middleton's proposals over ten years before.[4] But that did not remove – rather, it placed a premium on – the need for well digested information and thought, and there were serious reasons for questioning his assumptions, with their controversial results. Pitt may have been worried about the First Lord as early as the first half of 1803. When he moved to his general attack on the Ministry in March 1804 Addington himself later judged it to have been because he 'could not endure the conduct of Lord St Vincent and the Admiralty'.[5]

Pitt's own assumptions and answers could themselves be questioned. The belief in the imminence of danger, which he stressed[6] and for which he had earlier been thought alarmist in some quarters, was now very largely

1. This policy however was not alone responsible. Disarmament in 1802–3 – a nominal cut of some 50 per cent in the financial provision for the navy, from some £13,800,000 to some £6,700,000 – had an effect which a subsequent increase in 1803–4 could not wholly reverse.

2. Cf. I, 319–23.

3. The words were those of the Commissioners for Revising, in their Third Report published in 1806, applied to the changes made in dockyard apprenticeship, imposed six days after the Admiralty received an outline of a scheme.

4. See I, 314–17.

5. This was reported of a conversation some forty years later, in 1846; *Letters and Papers of Admiral of the Fleet Sir Thomas Byam Martin . . .*, ed. Sir Richard Vesey Hamilton, III (1903), 195. See p. 592, n3 above on Pitt in 1803.

6. Eg on 10 March, in one of the debates on the Volunteer bill, he was reported as saying that a landing might take place 'in the course of a few weeks at farthest', and again that 'the crisis was at a certainty approaching' (*P.R. (Stockdale)*, II, 29, 32).

accepted; but he may have underrated the enemy's difficulties, and among them the effect of the Admiralty's dispositions which in its view might well deter and if not would upset or destroy an attempt. His own tactical solution was dubious; resting disproportionately on his favoured gunboats, it received short shrift from some respectable professional opinion.[1] He had always been interested in the navy,[2] and he could call on the experience of higher direction in war. But the depth of his involvement with the Cinque Ports may have been affecting his perspectives, and it is hard to tell if or how far he took advice. The same applies to some of the figures he produced in Parliament. As so often, statistical comparisons demanded careful expert scrutiny, and there was an amateurish flavour to some of his charges and claims. He followed criticisms made by the Navy Board which had become public property,[3] and he had old contacts on whom perhaps he called. But evidence seems to be lacking; even Rose appears not to have been brought in, Middleton had not been consulted and did not know who was, and Pitt's surviving papers show only scattered signs of preparation.[4] In point of fact, though he claimed to have been told in advance that Government would produce two of the lists he sought, he can scarcely have expected to achieve more,[5] or indeed a significant victory – the usual Ministerial majorities were unlikely to be overturned at the first attempt –, and he may accordingly have reckoned on serving notice of a further threat for which there would be opportunity to mature a fuller case.[6]

1. Delivered with effect by Sir Edward Pellew, fresh from sea, in the Commons' debate of 15 March (*P.R. (Stockdale)*, II, 104–5). Nelson however, with his experience of the waters concerned (p. 544 above), seems to have placed some faith in 'brigs or schooners and . . . gun or mortar boats', forming a flotilla which could be highly effective in 'a calm' (memorandum of April 1804; *Correspondence of Prince of Wales*, IV, no. 1845).

2. Eg for background I, 20–1, 313.

3. Informed newspaper attacks on St Vincent had swelled from January.

4. See Roger Morriss, *The Royal Dockyards during the Revolutionary and Napoleonic Wars* (1983), 198 for Middleton. There are two lists in Pitt's papers in P.R.O. 30/8/257, ff. 27–28v, which could relate to his motion, one undated and one of 10 February 1804. Both are in a hand which looks like that of the recent Secretary of the Admiralty, Evan Nepean – long one of the group of officials in various posts for whom Pitt felt respect (see I, 179, 324, p. 119 above) – who had become increasingly dissatisfied with St Vincent and in January was appointed Chief Secretary of Ireland. It would be interesting if this attribution is correct, for the undated paper contains a distinctly critical comment on the Admiralty for selling gun vessels since October 1801 which could have been repaired at reasonable expense.

It might also be conjectured that Melville, who as a former Treasurer of the Navy had kept a possibly not disinterested eye on the process of reform since the beginning of 1803, might have talked to Pitt. But they did not meet often, and this is only conjecture.

5. *P.R. (Stockdale)*, II, 141 for his expectation. Fox however thought that the Government would have done better to offer to release more lists, which would have stopped the Old Opposition (full of St Vincent's past friends; see II, p. 357 above) from dividing against him, and forced Pitt rather to call for a vote of censure that would have been lost (to Lauderdale, 15 March 1804; *Memorials of Fox*, IV, 25).

6. His performance in the debate itself was not greatly admired. Canning thought the opening speech 'unimpressive' and Fox called it 'vile', though both rated the winding-

The situation was rather different for the campaign of which he had warned on the military issues, and which followed a month later.[1] Some of the arguments had already been aired in the debates on the Volunteers, and Pitt was clear on his lines of approach.[2] He did not claim that the Ministry had failed to provide adequate aggregate strength; he acknowledged that there were plenty of men in all for the immediate needs of defence.[3] This indeed could scarcely be disputed; in the spring of 1804 the regulars and militia amounted to some 184,000, the Army of Reserve effectively to some 37,000, and the registered Volunteers to some 462,000 – figures which may be compared with those in the last active years of the previous war.[4] His case was that the proportions were wrong, revealing serious causes and producing dangerous effects. At the centre of the imbalance lay his usual whipping-boy, the militia. It should not have been enlarged to such an extent, and should now be reduced in England to a strength of 48,000 while the Army of Reserve – already taking some of the militia's available balloted manpower – was expanded to one of 64,000 men.[5] The latter was more likely to help supplement the regular troops, out of the mass of conscripts, with volunteers for unrestricted service in a war of much greater dimensions than those of its predecessors, when such aid was sought from within the militia itself.[6] The haphazard use of some of the Irish militia for a force disposable in 'special urgency' could scarcely be called adequate and did not reflect 'well-considered views'. But the Army of Reserve in its turn was not being raised on a sound basis, as in fact the bill for a suspension of recruitment showed.[7] He thoroughly approved the principle of this type of selective conscription for a limited period;[8] for levying 'an armed peasantry', as it was often called, in a form 'suitable to a commercial country', which would skirt familiar problems of entanglement between the militia and the standing army while supplying more effective support. But if it was to be satisfactorily achieved, the methods of recruitment must be changed. At

---

up more highly (Canning's diary for 15 March, Canning Ms 29d; *Memorials of Fox*, III, 456). And cf. *Life of Wilberforce*, III, 150, and Fedorak, loc. cit., 294 citing Lord Hardwicke to his brother Charles Yorke.

1. See pp. 627–8 above.
2. Again however there is little if anything in his papers. Undated notes in his hand in P.R.O. 30/8/240, f. 110v, attributed later to 1805, could possibly relate to this time.
3. Speech of 28 March 1804 (*P.R.* (*Stockdale*), II, 332–3).
4. Cf. *P.D.*, II, cols. 203, 211 with op. cit., cols. lxii–lxvi. See p. 628 above for the Army of Reserve, and 459 for 1799–1800.
5. Speech of 25 April 1804 (*P.D.*, II, cols. 272–3); Pitt drew attention to the effect on the militia of the ballot for the Army of Reserve on 27 February and again on 16 April (*P.R.* (*Stockdale*), I, 515; *P.D.*, II, col. 133*). He later (*P.D.*, II, col. 485) corrected the figure of 48,000 for English militia to 40,000, with 8,000 from Scotland.
6. Cf. pp. 627–8 above.
7. P. 628 above.
8. He had indeed already made this abundantly clear, in February (*P.R.*, (*Stockdale*), I, 515) and again on 23 April (*P.D.*, II, col. 222).

present the dissatisfaction was such that the scheme was being halted while still short of a target inadequate in itself. Quotas, placed at present on counties and administered by their Lords Lieutenant, should fall, within that framework, on parishes; and the men should be attached specifically to 'the corresponding [regular] regiment', which they might be expected to see as an obvious choice.[1] Improvements of this nature, to administration and morale and efficiency, would lessen the existing marked disproportion between balloted men and substitutes (no fewer indeed, by Government's own account, than 34,300 of the latter to 2,607 or 2,807 of the former)[2] which again was a striking indication of failure in the system as it stood. Greater financial inducements should be produced to this end, and greater responsibility given to commanding officers in applying resources. Such alterations, accompanied by others which he had sought for the Volunteer battalions, could quickly provide 'a defensive force' which under better training and discipline could even become 'as good and efficient as your regular force'.

There was weight in these charges. They were not trumped up. The system for military manpower remained incoherent in many important respects. The Militia Act of 1802 'made permanent a number of expedients that had been found useful in the 1790s',[3] but it did little more; the improvements for the Volunteers had been modest; and recruitment for the Army of Reserve was revealing the extent of the practical flaws. Pitt would prove his intention of tackling the inadequacies as soon as he had the chance. Remedies, however, were not easy to find or effect. There were indeed keys to be found; but their discovery took longer than any one, including himself, envisaged in 1804, and meanwhile defenders of the Ministry, at the time and later, might point in response to flaws in his attack.

For there were undoubted weaknesses. In the first place, the Ministry could argue that whatever the shortcomings of its programme it had produced forces of a size, as he in fact acknowledged, adequate to a pressing need, and the Volunteers in particular had been encouraged to grow as never before. Nor were the limitations on the latter's role necessarily disastrous; no other leading politician shared Pitt's view of their value to anything like the same extent – many not at all[4] –, and the most experienced soldier of the period commended the practice of raising the men, in such critical circumstances, at the expense if necessary of training and

---

1. He had favoured an idea on similar lines earlier (*P.R., 4th ser.*, III, 825).

2. See the figures (taken here to the nearest hundred) in *P.D.*, II, cols. lxv–lxvi. Balloted men were given as 2,273 and substitutes as 23,086 in England; as 286 and 4,715 respectively in Scotland; as 48 and 6,528, plus 200 'recruited', in Ireland.

Substitutes were written into the Militia Act of 1757, with provisions elaborated by subsequent legislation including the Act of 1802 (for which see p. 627 and n5 above); and accounted for a substantial proportion of that force. The precedent was followed in the analogous balloting system for the Army of Reserve.

3. Western, *The English Militia in the Eighteenth Century*, 240.

4. Including his nearest allies on this range of questions, Windham and the Grenvilles.

materiel. Pitt, it could be suggested, was lacking in the very sense of proportion for which he was calling; he wished 'to make the volunteers more
of soldiers than their constitution can possibly admit'.[1] Nor was the policy
for the Army of Reserve as defective as he made out: Melville for one
thought it 'a most undoubted and unexceptionable Recourse for the
recruiting of the [regular] Army' – indeed he thought it 'madness' to
attack it at this point; and he continued to defend the provisions later, after
Pitt had died.[2] The results in point of fact stood some at least of the tests.
Recruits were used to form second battalions where needed for existing
regiments: an arrangement, facilitating training and the maintenance of
the first battalions at strength, that would prove a mainstay in the
Peninsular War, and in due course a precursor of the celebrated Cardwell
system. The county quotas moreover did not, as was sometimes feared,
seriously diminish recruitment for the regulars, and the latter's numbers
contined to grow to a strength which was higher in December 1803 than
when peace was signed provisionally in October 1801.[3] Nor again, the
argument could go, had Pitt been roused earlier by these policies; he had
remained silent or broadly supportive for two years on programmes he
condemned in the third. And indeed they could not be unfamiliar to him,
for in many respects they looked back to his own. The Army of Reserve
drew on his abortive plan of 1796 for balloted quotas for the regular
infantry.[4] The Militia Act and the Volunteers Consolidated Act included
regulations dating from his time. Yet he was now engaging in a sudden
outright assault, and in terms which could be called disgracefully severe.

For it was the tone as much as the content of the speeches in April that
struck home. From the tenor of reports it was indeed scathing. Pitt was now
going to the limit in attack, as he had done initially in the Government's
defence.[5] Ministers could not do right even when they borrowed ideas from
others. 'No one measure can they claim as their own; no one measure have
they improved and perfected; very many have they weakened by their
delays, and destroyed by their incongruities'. The spirit of the nation must
be 'separated from the tardiness, languor, and imbecility of ministers in
every thing of which they have assumed the direction'. They had provided
for an expansion of the militia; but had postponed its embodiment in
peacetime in a period when action would have been prudent and deter-
rent. And, even 'drawing a veil over their conduct' at that time, 'What

1. Cornwallis to Major-General Ross, 18 December 1803 (*Correspondence of Cornwallis*,
III, 509). Pitt himself indeed admitted only a few months later that 'very many' of the
Volunteer battalions were not up to the mark (10 March 1804; *P.R. (Stockdale)*, II, 30). That
was the reason for his proposals for improvements to the bill for their regulation.

2. Melville to Pitt, 16 April 1804 (Dacres Adams Mss, formerly P.R.O. 30/58/5); same
to Castlereagh, 16 July 1807 (*Memoirs and Correspondence of Castlereagh*, VIII (1851), 80).

3. As indeed was rightly claimed by Addington's brother Hiley (Glover, *Peninsular
Preparation*, 231, 238).

4. Which itself followed his Quota Act for the navy of 1795; see II, 642, 497.

5. Cf. p. 562 above.

measures have they ever adopted that have not been thwarted by some other of their measures?' They were 'incapable of acting upon any thing like system, of adopting or executing any well-digested or energetic plan for . . . defence'.[1] Example was piled on example, giving such passages cumulative strength. Pitt spoke professedly with 'much consideration and reluctance'; but that was of course the more damning, and the indictment was virtually complete. It was 'enforced' with 'grave vehement declamation . . . and some touches of that bitter, freezing sarcasm, which everybody agrees is his most original talent, and appears indeed most natural to him'.[2] Altogether it must have been a withering onslaught to endure.

Pitt's specific charges against the conduct of defence were distinctly uneven in quality. Some may have been misconceived, some were exaggerated, some much to the point. Collectively they were not trivial, and in raising them he could show factual cause. The spur came from his belief in a prospect markedly different from any in the previous war: of a struggle potentially much greater in scale and, at any moment, in fierceness, demanding an overdue reappraisal of all the means at Government's command. He was passionately convinced of this – the impact of his year at Walmer should not be underrated – and if he was unfair in some detail to Addington he was intent on being fair to the country. The threads of the past two years indeed were being drawn together in an atmosphere of crisis; for Pitt's conviction of the danger was now matched acutely by one of the Ministry's lack of grasp. He saw a failure both to discriminate and to apply: to distinguish where innovations were necessary and to bring those attempted to best effect. On the one hand there was an inability to shake sufficiently clear of earlier arrangements for the land forces, largely his own in a lesser conflict,[3] and then to handle the improvements proposed; on the other, to control St Vincent's experiments in an area of proven achievement where methods that had sustained operational success should be modified, not undermined. And this failure in defence, as he saw it, focused an impression of general incompetence – partly urged on him by others, and exacerbated lately by personal resentment[4] – which had long been maturing and should no longer be gainsaid. Pitt could recall his feelings at different times on the handling of finance and diplomacy, of administrative and legislative business; on a 'stupidity' in Addington himself for which he felt growing contempt.[5] Such a verdict may be tested

---

1. Debate of 23 April 1804 (quotations from *P.D.*, II, cols. 209–10, 212–13).

2. Francis Horner to his father, 24 April 1804; quoted in Stanhope, IV, 158. He also stressed the amount of detail.

3. Cf. p. 635 above.

4. See pp. 576–600, 621–2 above.

5. See p. 572 above. In December 1803, Huskisson found that the Minister was 'completely an Object of Contempt' to Pitt (to Melville, 15 December 1803; S.R.O., Melville Mss, GD 51/1) as well as the 'Loathing' arising at that time from the effects of the

to some extent by his own experience when faced with the situation he would shortly inherit. It can also be assessed in the light of the Ministry's behaviour as his attacks took root.

III

That did not take long. The effect indeed turned out to be virtually instantaneous. The main speeches in April formed in fact a coup de grâce as much as a mounting assault. For by the time they were delivered as the public sign of his complete opposition, Pitt was well advanced more privately in the preparations to unseat the Ministry, and make his own position clear. This last however still demanded skilful balance; there were definitions to be drawn. From late in March, certainly from Easter,[1] a current appeared to be setting his way; nonetheless he had to navigate eddies that might yet divert or upset his course.

One such indeed was already visible. For the politics of these weeks developed in the shadow of a sadly familiar but unpredictable event. In February 1804 George III was struck by his malady once more. The attack was serious and, as in 1801 if less instantly, it was something with which Pitt would have to reckon. If the King did not recover, at least fully for some time, there would be a new state of affairs, at a point when the fight against the Ministry should be under way and in fact rising to a peak. If conversely he could resume his functions, the illness remained a factor to be borne in mind in any dealings that might arise between the two men. In the event the worst was over soon, and by mid March George III was on the mend, though he appeared weaker than before and distinctly vulnerable for the next two months.[2] Meanwhile however the prospect arose – and lingered uneasily thereafter – that a Regency might have to be introduced.

Pitt was very soon obliged to consider his own case in such a circumstance. He had declined to join the Grenvilles and Fox in regular opposition to a Government which nonetheless he meant to criticise on

---

pamphlet war (see pp. 621–2 and n1 above): a marked change from the same reporter's earlier impressions in the spring (p. 595 above).

The contempt, familiar from private conversations and expressed now in the Commons, also reflected on the First Minister when it was applied to the Ministry as a whole; see eg Pitt's speech on 2 March on the Volunteer Consolidation bill, which consisted largely of a lesson in drafting and procedure (*P.R.* (*Stockdale*), II, 613–25).

1. See p. 627 and n4 above.

2. The King was out of sorts on 25 January, improved quickly, but relapsed in the second week of February, when the crisis of the attack came and went. By the end of that month he was said to be much better, and the recovery continued throughout March. He was not free of doctors however even by the summer, his Ministers continued to advise him to take care, and it was July before he lost the intermittent but all too familiar symptoms of hurry and irritability that marked the illness. See Macalpine and Hunter, *George III and the Mad-Business*, ch. 7.

measures he disliked or wished to see improved. He held no brief for Addington and hoped that under pressure the Minister would resign. Moreover in February he thought he had cause to believe that the King's opinion had altered 'with respect to Persons and particularly myself', and also that 'a large proportion of the Cabinet' felt 'strongly' the need for a change.[1] This background was certainly not unfavourable to a constitutional judgment which in any case was soundly based. For Pitt maintained the stance he had taken in 1789 and 1801. He disapproved of any arrangement that could detract from the King's normal scope for choice on a recovery, or would 'anticipate his decision' at this stage if recovery was incomplete. Such doctrine did not derive merely from his personal feeling for the monarch; it embodied 'a Sense of what is right in itself'.[2] It was a setting compatible with the warning – then assuming normality – which he had lately given Grenville,[3] and with his approach, on the same assumption, to developments in the next two months.

Those mounted swiftly from the latter part of March. By its close Pitt could confirm that he was in growing demand. The approach of a more likely invasion season combined with the first sign of his open discontent naturally roused interest in his prospects, and the various alternative sources of authority, current and potential, became anxious to find out how he stood. The heir to the throne, the Regent in waiting, was now on the alert, but undecided as to his best course. His attitude to Addington was ambivalent. The Ministry had earned some credit for helping to secure fresh Parliamentary aid for his shattered finances; but also some resentment in the course of a recent open quarrel with his father following the persistent failure of his pleas to be granted military promotion and

---

1. Pitt to Melville, 21 February 1804 (S.R.O., Melville Mss, GD 51/1). His 'authentic' information on the King derived from the tone of George III's remarks before the attack, presumably within the Court.

2. Ibid. There was of course much discussion in various quarters of what might have to be done if George III's incapacity continued for long. The Ministry suspected that Carlton House and also the Foxites were contemplating the establishment of a Regency with a council which would favour Opposition. Pitt's judgment however was extracted from him by Melville, then up in Scotland, who argued that it was cruel to confront the King any further with his constitutional responsibilities, that the repeated attacks must leave an impression of uncertainty both at home and with potential allies, and that this introduced a new factor in setting terms for a Regency which should be established soon and, he hinted, be for life (to Pitt, 19 and see also 25 February 1804; John Rylands Eng. Ms 907). Pitt for his part in conversation with others deprecated hasty action, though a Regency must come if George III did not recover soon, and thought that in such an event it was bound to be on the same lines as those settled in 1789 (*Malmesbury*, IV, 291 for 19 February; Alexander Hope (son of the Lord Advocate of Scotland, Charles Hope, who was Melville's brother-in-law and confidant), diary for 22, 27 February, 5 March [mistakenly entered as February] 1804, S.R.O., Hope of Luffness Mss, GD 364/1, bundle 1154). When motion to adjourn the Commons, to force a Ministerial communication about the state of the King's health, was brought by a private member on 27 February, he spoke against it (*P.R.* (*Stockdale*), II, 478–81).

3. Pp. 616–17 above.

a regional command. The conflicting effects could be seen in the attitudes and actions of the politicians around him as the Prince brought these personal preoccupations into his view of public affairs. He had not turned his back on the Ministry: Sheridan and Erskine could still hope for office, and his principal associates protested against Fox's junction with the Grenvilles and voted against Pitt's motion on the navy on 15 March.[1] At the same time he was said to have invited Pitt's views, unsuccessfully, during the King's illness, and more to the point he put out a feeler following the debate itself. This was done through Moira, whom he was supposed to favour as his Minister under a Regency, and Moira had advised him in such case to seek 'a union of all talent' which should include Melville and Pitt. There was the difficulty of course that Pitt could not be fitted easily into 'a subordinate situation'; as Moira put it, 'he never can be subordinate in any Cabinet', and his own business therefore in any such arrangement would be 'to moderate between Mr. Pitt and Mr. Fox'.[2] The problems indeed were easy to forecast, and they were confirmed by an instant response. Pitt did not see how, 'under any circumstances', he could join 'any government without being at the head of it'.[3] He had long concluded that 'the head of the Finances' should be the First Minister, and as was duly explained to Moira that post was 'appropriate' for himself.[4] Given the Prince's temperament moreover, little reliance could be placed on his ideas, or for that matter on the likelihood that Moira would in fact be favoured if the time came.[5] The tentative sounding could be

1. Cf. pp. 573, 610–11, 619 above. For a résumé of the Prince's position in the past year see Aspinall's introductions to the year 1803 and 1804 in *Correspondence of Prince of Wales*, IV, 341–52, 474–5, as well as the letters themselves and his textual notes; for Sheridan and Erskine, and the protest at the coalition, p. 619 above; for the vote on 15 March, p. 632.

2. Charles Hope to Melville, 22 March 1804 (*Secret Correspondence*, 9). Moira, a capable General as well as the Prince's wisest confidant (see II, 322–3 for the former), was currently commanding in Scotland and had just returned from London to his post. Cf. II, 182 for George III's comment on a not dissimilar proposal some twelve years before.

3. To Melville, who had forwarded the information, 29 March 1804 (*Secret Correspondence*, 12).

A point arises here however of whose significance I am not quite certain. On 19 February Malmesbury reported Pitt as saying that 'it was right and a duty to contribute towards forming a new Administration by any means in his power', and '*a paramount one, and superior to every thing with him*' if the King himself should call for his services. In that specific case 'he should be ready to offer them, unconditionally, to take any part His Majesty commanded, or seemed desirous he should take' (*Malmesbury*, IV, 290). This referred therefore to an approach from the King, not from a Regent. Whether his expressions on 29 March – 'any circumstances', 'any part' – would relate to such a call under a Regency, I really find it impossible to say. As one reads the relevant part of the letter it might suggest not.

4. Melville to Pitt, 6 April 1804 (*Secret Correspondence*, 22). Cf. pp. 584–5 above for his earlier identical explanation for Addington.

5. Pitt was distinctly sceptical about the Prince's statements to Moira, which he did not believe were confined to him alone (to Melville, 29 March 1804, *Secret Correspondence*, 11–12).

marked.[1] But there was no sequel; events decreed otherwise; and even as the message was received from the reversionary interest, a testing signal came from a more immediate source.

For on 20 March Pitt was handed a note in the Commons from the Lord Chancellor, proposing a conversation; and the two men met on the 24th, probably for 'a tête-à-tête dinner'.[2] Eldon's purpose was apparently to see whether Addington could remain in the Cabinet if he stepped down, and on hearing that this was 'inadmissable' he said that the Minister's colleagues would not give him up.[3] While the opening was almost certainly his own, he could hardly however have concealed the hope that Pitt would 'take the government',[4] and Pitt himself a fortnight later was prepared to name those who shared the Lord Chancellor's view. Castlereagh, Yorke, Hobart, Chatham, above all Portland would, he thought, follow if Eldon led; and Hawkesbury probably felt likewise, if less strongly or openly. Unless Addington went of his own accord, it was hard to see how they could give effect to their wishes as things stood.[5] Nonetheless this list embraced six or seven of the eleven men concerned, and of the rest – when Addington was subtracted – Liverpool was now virtually a passenger, St Vincent was unhappy, and only Westmorland was then left.[6] The Cabinet clearly lacked confidence, before his own campaign had got under way. In such a state it might indeed be ready to crumble when pressure was applied. That prospect could not of course be taken for granted. But it must be thought promising so far as it went.

Looking simply at the record, such a sense of disillusionment in the Cabinet may seem excessive. The Government might point to some serviceable stewardship, at home and abroad. Addington's handling of finance was patchy, but it gained Pitt's approval at some points as it did

---

1. And may be noted for comparison with the Prince's position at one point in 1801 (pp. 527 and n7–28 above).

2. Horace Twiss, *The Private and Public Life of Lord Chancellor Eldon* . . ., I (1844), 438; Alexander Hope's diary for 25 March (S.R.O., Hope of Luffness Mss, GD 364/1, bundle 1154); *Colchester*, I, 529, recording a conversation with Addington in October 1804.

3. This is Hope's report – which also confirms the date – after talking to Pitt the next day. Pitt had told him earlier, on the 17th, that he could not sit in Cabinet with Addington (S.R.O., Hope of Luffness Mss, GD 364/1, bundle 1154).

4. Ibid.

5. Pitt to Melville, 11 April 1804 (*Secret Correspondence*, 28). He thought the Lord Chancellor 'the person . . . most likely to give effect to his opinion', but as yet only if Addington himself seemed prepared to go. He also thought that Portland had remained for so long only out of regard for the King and in the hope of influencing him when the time came (for another possible reason initially see p. 470 above). Cf. p. 588 and n1 above for an earlier estimate of favourable names. Alexander Hope, who was well informed, stated in February that 'a large part' or 'most' of the Cabinet wished for Pitt's return (diary, 22, 25 February 1804; S.R.O., Hope of Luffness, GD 364/1, bundle 1154).

Hobart was perhaps the most doubtful of the names given. The King thought later that he had been the only Cabinet minister who was prepared in the end to continue with Addington (see *Glenbervie*, I, 389).

6. See pp. 607, n1, 615, n3 above for the last.

his anger at others, and in both cases the Minister had not shrunk from taking initiatives of his own.[1] The naval reforms, about which he had felt uneasy,[2] certainly caused continuous disruption while only problematically fostering results for the medium term. The programme for the land forces, in the midst of old obstacles and of its own shortcomings, could be termed more immediately productive while falling short of its difficult aims. The conduct of foreign policy, less persistently visible, was by no means as supine as critics held; if there appeared to be little drive and nothing concrete to show, the conditions were uncertain and the problems remained stubborn as often before.[3] Pitt himself could have testified that his wartime alliances had responded only to acute stimulus, and this was largely lacking from France in the eyes of Europe during the transitory peace and the opening stage at least of a war declared by Britain. As it was, the object was not neglected in London when – if only when – the scene began to change; though ground was not won, it was not lost by default, and later efforts did not spring unheralded from untended soil. Meanwhile some of the enemy's colonies were mopped up. Where there were achievements they were not spectacular. But neither were the failures, and a balance could be struck that showed some degree of mild success.[4]

But such an enumeration by particulars is seldom a full clue to a Government's standing. And the trouble in Addington's Ministry lay inescapably with himself. Of course it was a hard act to follow Pitt, and in circumstances where he owed his predecessor a debt. But in any case he had failed in the circles that mattered to make a clear impression of his own. It was not that he was void of ability, as his enemies declared; but no one could deny that it was commonplace, and better suited to a secondary place. Nor was it the case that – like North for instance near the end – he left Departments to their own devices, within the currently predisposing framework of their own powers and rights.[5] He was not a cypher.[6] But that was little consolation – a poor combination in fact – when he himself made mistakes in the detail of business and his talents were judged inadequate to the 'controul of Public affairs': not sufficient to inspire admiration from his colleagues, or provide a bulwark when they themselves fell short. One cannot reject a verdict so widely held by those in a position to reach it; as with Shelburne in his day, for very different reasons, knowledgeable contemporaries had made up their

1. To be discussed on pp. 678–80 below.
2. P. 630 above.
3. This will be discussed further in Ch. XIX below.
4. Cf. C.D. Hall, 'Addington at war: unspectacular but not unsuccessful', *Historical Research*, Vol. LXI, No. 146, 306–15. One can hardly say that the outbreak of war was itself a failure to be laid mainly at the Ministry's door; it was probably unavoidable.
5. Cf. I, 183, 304. The Admiralty under St Vincent was of course something of an exception, as in Pitt's early days the Department had been under Howe (op. cit., 315).
6. See p. 561, n2 above.

minds.[1] As Canning proved, the Doctor was an easy subject of derision.[2] He may have had sound sense, 'temperance and conciliation', but there was no detectable flair, his management of patronage lacked confidence, and in particular he was 'not well fitted for the warfare of St. Stephen's'.[3] His awkwardness in debate, always a liability, told the more as the temperature rose; he could not dominate the exchanges, he lacked a cutting edge, and equally – indeed above all – the desirable killer instinct. More surprisingly, after his experience as Speaker, he could be inept in his grasp of procedure – a necessary aspect of command of the House in which Pitt was seldom at fault. And above all, in the current prospect he suffered from one particular disadvantage. He could never shake off his sense of subservience to Pitt himself. Whenever his predecessor stirred, Addington was assailed by doubt. This was not a reassuring fact for the bulk of the Cabinet in March 1804.

One may look also at the other side of the equation. The inclination towards Pitt would have drawn on the disinclination for Addington. But it has also to be accounted for in its own right. It had been present earlier, in various degrees. Now however it had grown, in the face of his prospective threat and the signs and assumptions of his public standing which his emergence underlined. One must be cautious in such situations of too confident a statement about public opinion – whatever definition of the public may be applicable at the time.[4] Addington may well have still been popular in the country at his own level of acceptance, and not less so from the coalition of the Grenvilles with Fox; a union of opposites which attracted its measure of doubt and indeed scorn.[5] Pitt for his part had his varied detractors: of his performance in the previous war, his refusal conversely to come forward since, of different aspects of his domestic policies, of the principle and manner of his resignation. A spectrum cannot be uniform. But an image can be domi-

---

1. Cf. I, 86. The phrase quoted came from the Duke of Montrose after Addington had fallen (to Pitt; 26 December 1804, P.R.O. 30/8/160); at much the same time Charles Long, a sensible judge, was more scathing, citing among other things undue reliance on the judgment of others (to Pitt, 6 December 1804; Dacres Adams Mss, formerly P.R.O. 30/58/5). The King himself, indebted as he was to Addington and indeed remaining fond of him, later made it clear, with little sentiment, that he had found him not up to the job – 'not equal to the government of the country' (as reported by Rose of a conversation on 30 September 1804; *Rose*, II, 156); 'there was one thing wanting in him as a Minister, and ... to be plain, it was talents' (in conversation with Glenbervie on 15 August 1804, recorded on the 19th; *Glenbervie*, I, 390). George III said in fact that at the end he told Addington this to his face.

2. P. 570, n4 above.

3. The phrases are those of Wilberforce (*Life of Wilberforce*, III, 153, 148). Fedorak, loc. cit., ch. Nine, is interesting on patronage and management.

4. Cf. here eg I, 145 with II, 107.

5. See eg *Correspondence of Cornwallis*, III, 510–11; Pellew, op. cit., II, 275–6. Fox indeed was reported, after he died but on good authority, to have 'often' said that he thought Addington's Ministry 'the most popular one' of the reign and that at this time he still had 'the general voice of the country in his favour' (see Pellew, op. cit., II, 274n).

nant, and it was one of which politicians were conscious here even if their arrangements might not respond. Beyond the Cabinet, Moira drew the lesson in advising the Prince of Wales that his 'only chance of governing the country without Mr. Pitt, with any degree of comfort, was at least to satisfy the public that the refusal came from Mr. Pitt'.[1] Absence in itself of course can make the heart grow fonder; and in this instance there was something more. For whatever his own aggrieved associates felt at first, and aggrieved Addingtonians later, Pitt's behaviour since his departure in 1801 seems to have made a clear impression 'out of doors'. It was one consistent with the old reputation for 'manliness' and responsibility; of a prolonged refusal to undermine his successor for his own advantage or sanction others in their designs and manoeuvres to press his claim.[2] The character thus displayed could hope the better to weather attacks when he at last intervened; it was hard to accuse him of scheming when he had abstained for three years. He may indeed have regained some lost moral ground in this significant interval. For when he returned to the office he had quitted amid such controversy, it was with some at least of the quality of legend that would gather round him in his final phase.[3]

Surveying the state of the forces, and encouraged by what he heard respecting himself, Pitt was becoming optimistic towards the end of March. He even thought then that he would receive 'an Offer' in the coming Easter recess, and a little later that the Ministry might simply draw quietly to its close.[4] And if that did not happen – if Addington persisted – matters would soon be put to a major trial of strength. He would then be acting with the allied Oppositions, and was taking steps to muster absent forces from Ireland and Scotland not a few of whom would buttress his own strength.[5]

This last aspect cannot be ignored. For Pitt's partnership with the Grenvilles and Fox was not, as indeed he would remind them, a comprehensive junction. The different elements – factions, as critics could call

1. Charles Hope to Melville, 22 March 1804 (*Secret Correspondence*, 8–9); and see likewise the Earl of Darnley's panegyric on Pitt to the Prince of Wales on the 13th (*Correspondence of Prince of Wales*, IV, 523). Cf. also pp. 620–1 above for a retrospective dispassionate Grenvillite assessment.

2. The first fact was noted and given weight by Richard Pares, *King George III and the Politicians*, 78 and n3.

3. The contribution of the interval is indeed suggested interestingly by Darnley (n1 above) and from another point of view by Pitt's supporter Lord Lowther in a letter to Mulgrave of 22 February [1804, though misdated 1803], in Normanby Mss, Box VII, bundle 13.

4. Canning's diary for the week of 24 March 1804 (Canning Ms 29d); Pitt to Mulgrave, 13 April 1804 (Normanby Mss, Box J, J/388).

5. To Melville, 29 March 1804 (*Secret Correspondence*, 13, 15–16). Detailed calculations were sent in reply on 4 and 5 April (John Rylands Eng. Ms 907). Cf. p. 627, n4 above.

them – exchanged information and concerted their plans. There was much coming and going in particular on the timing and content of Fox's motion of 23 April on defence.[1] The alliance worked in practice for its main purpose: the troops were gathered, the programme was agreed. But Pitt and his partners were not particularly close. The preparations for 23 April for instance revealed marked irritation with shifting tactical demands, and there were continuing doubts and reservations while the campaign was under way. The materials were in fact too disparate for sus-picions to be laid aside. Many of the Grenvillites and Foxites themselves remained wary of one another, though their leaders became less so as the weeks passed; Fox and Thomas Grenville laboured hard, and Lord Grenville too played his part – by mid April Fox found him 'a very direct man'.[2] But that growing mutual tolerance, assisted by the similar feelings for Irish Catholic relief, was increasingly encouraged, in different degrees, by their growing doubts about their ally. They knew well enough the strong desirability of acting with him: Fox once complained of the difficulty of framing a motion that would 'not in some view be objection-able to Pitt'.[3] But they became impatient of his vacillations over the timing and shape of the attacks; 'this eternal uncertainty', Thomas Grenville called it, which 'worried and disconcerted' Fox, while Fox himself complained that 'Pitt . . . does not know always his own mind'.[4] In mid April, as the climax was expected to draw near, he was distinctly depressed: 'as to any arrangement with Pitt, I feel the difficulties (amount-ing nearly to an impossibility) more and more every day'.[5]

The vacillations which caused these complaints were in point of fact genuine enough. They showed a familiar tendency to hesitation at a certain level, as well as reasonable reservations on the drift of some of Opposition's own tactical ideas.[6] But the reaction they occasioned in both of its wings did not arise merely from annoyance. It also reflected serious unease. The Grenvilles had not felt the same about Pitt since the talks in January. Lord Grenville himself made the best of the situation; although their 'lines' diverged more than he had expected, these were at any rate now 'less different' than they had been since the Preliminary

---

1. For which see p. 628 above. On the ups and downs of this see eg Pitt to Melville, 11 April 1804 (*Secret Correspondence*, 30); Canning's diary, 10, 12 April 1804 (Canning Ms 29d); Thomas Grenville to Grenville, 31 March 1804 (*H.M.C., Dropmore*, VII, 217–18); and above all Fox to Grey, 2, 13, 17 April 1804 [the first printed incorrectly 2 August] (*Memorials of Fox*, III, 459, IV, 41–2). The word faction was bruited, naturally enough, by those who dis-approved.

2. To Grey, 17 April 1804 (*Memorials of Fox*, IV, 42).

3. To Robert Adair, March 1804 (op. cit., 32).

4. Thomas Grenville to Grenville, 31 March 1804 (*H.M.C., Dropmore*, 217). For another, though less knowledgeable Grenvillite view, in mid April and without reference to Fox, see *Life and Letters of Elliot*, III, 316.

5. To Grey, 19 April 1804 (*Memorials of Fox*, IV, 45).

6. Cf. p. 456 above for the first. Canning's diary for these months (Canning Ms 29d) gives some impression of the second.

peace treaty was signed.[1] That did not remove his or his brothers' acute disappointment; they deeply deplored Pitt's refusal to depart from 'middle lines', thought him 'disgraced' by the stance he had adopted, and resented his consequent freedom to take a part with them at any time he chose.[2] While they still wished for his return to office, they could not recover the enthusiasm that had survived earlier checks. And Fox for his part was ready at heart to suspect the worst. He stressed to his friends the importance of the association. But he made it clear – and he meant what he said – that it had a dual object: first and foremost to get rid of Addington, but also to place a restraint on Pitt if or when he succeeded to the post.[3] He was sure at the start that his old antagonist had not changed his spots, and their co-operation did not weaken his belief. Pitt remained 'a mean, low-minded dog'; 'a sad stick'; he could not 'act like a man'; there had always to be an '*If*' in forecasting his moves. It was 'impossible not to suspect . . . his ways of proceeding', for in essence he could not 'give up his hopes' of 'the Court! the Court!'[4] As Fox indeed contemplated once more that old source of evil, his doubts of its old saviour[5] became the more sombre even as the partners worked for joint success.

Such misgivings in point of fact were again inapposite when applied to the immediate campaign. Pitt was certainly wary of the coalition at the start. They would not 'persuade or gain him over'; his style of attack would not be theirs, but would depend on '*opinion* unconnected with party'; he acknowledged a respect for 'many' members of the existing Government.[6] The distance however narrowed progressively, as in fact it was likely to do. Once he had decided to castigate the Ministry, on a limited but vital front, Pitt was not going to pull his punches or stand aloof, the less so as he became increasingly convinced of Addington's ineptitude from the inadequate responses to his successive proposals on

---

1. To Bathurst, 13 January 1804 (Bathurst Mss; B.L. Loan Ms 57, vol. 2).

2. Grenville to Buckingham, 30 January (see p. 617, n4 above); Thomas Grenville to Grenville, 13 January (*H.M.C., Dropmore*, VII, 207); Buckingham to same, nd but 14 January 1804 (op. cit., 208). Pitt on the other hand asserted a month later that while the leading Grenvillites 'were not satisfied, yet they were in a good humour with him' (conversation of 19 February with Malmesbury; *Malmesbury*, IV, 289).

3. To Grey, 28 March (*Memorials of Fox*, III, 458); to Richard Fitzpatrick, 28 January, 24, 25 February (op. cit., IV, 22–3); to Earl of Lauderdale, 30 March, 9 April 1804 (op. cit., 35–6, 39–40). At a meeting of his friends in March Fox was reported as saying, perhaps with both parts of his object in mind, that Pitt's return to office would not be the misfortune that Sheridan for example, who was present, thought (Alexander Hope's diary for 24 March 1804; Hope of Luffness Mss, GD 364/1, bundle 1154).

4. To Grey, March, 28 March, 13, 17, 29 April 1804 (*Memorials of Fox*, III, 455, 458, 464; IV, 41, 45). I have quoted from March only. Comparable comments could be cited from the weeks before co-operation.

5. Cf. I, 134, 137.

6. For the first two reported remarks see his conversation with Malmesbury on 19 February (*Malmesbury*, IV, 290); for the third, Alexander Hope's diary for the 22nd (Hope of Luffness Mss, GD 364/1, bundle 1154).

defence.[1] He needed the advantages which the Grenvillites and Fox would supply: the numbers they would bring into the lobby in which his own were insufficient,[2] and the skills, allied to his own, in the preceding debates. The two contributions were not necessarily indistinguishable – he had himself observed of the Treasury bench that '*out-debated . . .* they will be, . . . *outvoted . . .* they will not be' – but of course the combination would provide the likeliest means of forcing Ministers to give up.[3] The planned assaults, if they had to take place,[4] would therefore be carried through by the combined associates. Beyond that, however, Fox's doubts were of greater significance; for they revealed the diversities of approach, potentially dissonant if too starkly suspected, to the prospect, unknowable in detail, that would follow a victorious campaign.

The uncertainties of course were rooted in the various partners' conception of the partnership. Fox's in essence was the simplest. He viewed it in the terms of 'party' which he had proclaimed for so long and for which an alliance offered the only real hope of exercise in office. That was the supreme good, the end to which coalition was the means;[5] a concept not shared or at least admitted by the Grenvilles, particularly by their leader.[6] The qualification however is necessary at this point, for Grenville had in fact reached an intermediate stage; still hostile to the principle of comprehensive opposition to the executive, and thus sensitive to charges of faction, but affected in practice increasingly, and perhaps more than he appreciated, by the influence of regular close co-operation, not least under Fox's charm.[7] Pitt had indeed forecast the consequence of their 'compact'; whatever Grenville might have thought at the start, it was 'delusive' to suppose that he and his associates would not be bound, if successful, to Fox.[8] It was not a position that he for his part proposed to share if he was called on to form a Government himself.

Pitt had in fact stated his position at the outset. It was on record in his letter to Grenville of 4 February; the junction would have an all too fore-seeable effect on the King's opinion and thus on its authors' prospects in

1. Cf. Buckingham's forecast as early as 14 January (p. 617 above), and see p. 629 for Pitt's increasing anger and his feeling, as the debates wore on, that the Government was a dangerous liability.

2. For one example see Thomas Grenville to Grenville, 31 March 1804 (*H.M.C., Dropmore*, VII, 217). Cf. p. 621 above.

3. Conversation on 19 February (*Malmesbury*, IV, 290). He did not however entirely rule out the alternative, though he then thought it improbable, that they would go from a consciousness of their inadequacy 'under the pressure of the times'.

4. But see p. 643 above for Pitt's opinion by the beginning of April, as compared with that of mid February in n3 above.

5. Cf. p. 618 above.

6. See p. 574 above.

7. Of the brothers, and probably the inner group as a whole, Thomas stood closest to Fox. But Lord Grenville too, at first sight surprisingly but perhaps less so when his chill was exposed to the warmth, seems to have begun to yield quite quickly to it. See Jupp, op. cit., 333.

8. Conversation with Malmesbury of 19 February 1804 (*Malmesbury*, IV, 289).

any arrangement.[1] This was written before George III's illness. But that event reinforced Pitt's judgment: options should be kept open, in this instance until the future was clear; the monarch's constitutional powers should not be prejudiced; and if his health recovered and he called for Pitt's services it would be a *'paramount'* duty to provide them, one indeed *'superior to every thing'* else.[2] This last feeling of 'delicacy' began to carry rather less weight as he grew more determined to dislodge the Ministry; in March he allowed that there could be cases when 'considerations of public safety' decreed a limit.[3] But the one consideration did not extinguish the other. At the end of that month he re-emphasised the importance, 'and still more from his last illness', of the monarch's exercise of his 'free option' in wishing to exclude from his Cabinet persons 'against whom he has long entertained . . . strong and natural objections'. The consequence followed, particularly in the circumstances. If the King could not be persuaded and 'sincerely convinced', Pitt would not 'force . . . upon him' someone he had refused to accept.[4]

This conclusion may have owed something to Pitt's feeling for a man whose physical state he found sincerely distressing; and perhaps to a recognition of the King's popularity in the stern years since the first attack.[5] But in essence it was an attempt to apply normal constitutional doctrine, as he had done in 1801, once more in abnormal conditions – even more abnormal in fact than on the past two similar occasions, for on the first, in 1788–9, he had himself been and remained Minister, and on the second, when he had submitted to the royal prerogative, a successor was soon found of whom both George III and he approved. This time he might have to advise from a more anomalous position, and on a potentially controversial change. For while he was committed to guarding the King's constitutional right, Pitt was also prepared to say what his own advice would be. It was in fact scarcely a secret, and in the next few weeks its emphasis was made known. He had moved in the past twelve months as far in his ideas of a successor to the Ministry as he had in his relations with the Ministry itself. In March 1803 he had demurred when Grenville raised the prospect of an extended Government which might include Moira and Grey and perhaps Tierney, though not, it was agreed, Fox.[6] By January 1804 however the scene was changing, and while he deplored the way chosen by Grenville he was ready to accept the desirability of a

1. Pp. 616–17 above.
2. See p. 638, n2 above for his letter to Melville of 21 February on the question of a Regency, and p. 639, n3 for the remarks on his role if summoned in the event of the King's recovery.
3. Lowther to Mulgrave, 26 March 1804 (Normanby Mss, Box VII, bundle 13); Pitt to Melville, 29 March 1804 (*Secret Correspondence*, 12–13).
4. Same to same as in n3 above. And see also Lady Melville to Melville, 6 March, reporting from a conversation with Pitt that he would not 'press' on the King anyone 'who could be disagreeable to him' (S.R.O., Melville Castle Mss, GD 51/1).
5. See I, 644, 661; pp. 610–11 above.
6. See pp. 593–4 above.

'comprehensive Administration': a Ministry of 'talent' as it was being called, which he soon made clear could enlist from all quarters, though Addington and St Vincent specifically would be barred from the Cabinet.[1] There was little doubt thereafter that if the time came he would propose an arrangement on such lines, and early in March he sent a word of such assurance to Fox – 'not quite a Message – but a *communication*' – at the same time cautioning that

> He would *not* say he would do all in his power to prevail upon the K. to make a *large* Govt. – because he was not prepared to make it a *sine quâ non* – the only proof he can give of his sincerity.

This was received on the face of it 'perfectly well';[2] and the prime connotation of 'large' was now indeed evident enough. Later in the month Pitt named 'the friends of both Mr. Fox and Lord Grenville' as the element which the King might wish to exclude; and on 11 April he disclosed that he had explained the situation 'through pretty certain' channels to the former and directly to the latter, if despite his intention he was obliged to form a 'narrow' Government.[3] A week later he took matters a step farther. On the 18th he asked Grenville to call, and told him, according to the latter's report, that if called on to form a Ministry,

> although [he] does not pledge himself not to form an exclusive government, yet . . . his earnest endeavour will be for his own sake, as well as that of the King and the country, to induce his Majesty to authorize him to converse with Fox and me, on the means of forming an united government.[4]

A similar message was conveyed to Fox, as before through a second party who in this case was Canning's friend and associate Leveson Gower. It was greeted privately with marked reserve.[5] Nevertheless, a few days before the partners' assault was due to reach its peak of effort, Pitt had made his intention explicit and his position clear.

1. Pitt to Grenville, 4 February 1804 (p. 616 above). Cf. Moira on 'a union of all talent' (p. 639). For the confirmation that Addington would be excluded see p. 640; for the inclusion of 'the most capable persons of the present Government' but the exclusion of him and also St Vincent, Pitt to Melville, 29 March 1804 (*Secret Correspondence*, 14–15).
2. The bearer of the communication was Canning (diary for 7, 9 March 1804; Canning Ms 29d). See also loc. cit., 2, 24 March, for Pitt's settlement on 'a large Govt.'.
3. Pitt to Melville, who was proffering advice from the north, on 29 March, 11 April; Melville to Pitt, 3 April 1804 (*Secret Correspondence*, 14, 20, 27).
4. Grenville to Buckingham, 29 April 1804 (Buckingham, III, 348–9).
5. See Fox to Grey, 18, 19 April 1804 (*Memorials of Fox*, IV, 42, 44–5). He heard more, at first hand from Grenville, the next day. His response to the news was to comment that Pitt was 'not a man capable of acting fairly, and on a footing of equality with his equals', and he cited (as he had done earlier; op. cit., III, 452, IV, 22) Pitt's silence over his pledge to the King on Irish Catholic relief in March 1801. See pp. 528–9 and n2 above.

The final statement to Fox, more precise it would seem than the previous communications,[1] was not made gratuitously. Pitt had received a message indirectly from Addington two days before. It had in fact originated earlier, probably in the first days of April, but awaited his return from Walmer where he had gone for the Easter recess and stayed on for a further ten days. When he came back, on the 16th, it was with the impression that, despite earlier hopes, the Minister would not go quietly but on the contrary would fight on. So at any rate Addington was saying to others, and would continue to say.[2] The reality however was more fluid; his mind was not firmly made up, and he was anxious to take a sounding of how matters lay in the other camp. If, so it was reported, he could be assured that Pitt was not 'connected' with Grenville and Fox, he 'was inclined to resign his situation'.[3] The purport in fact was the same as it had been in April 1803,[4] made more acute now by the Parliamentary warfare and above all the need to add Fox to the reckoning. Transmitted through Castlereagh and thence Camden – from a familiar Ministerial link to one of Pitt's more sympathetic friends[5] – the signal however fell on deaf ears; the response indeed was a distinct rebuff. In a tacit reminder of the acrimonious epilogue to the previous approach, Pitt stated that he would explain his ideas to the King in person or, if in the circumstances this was not thought desirable, he could do so to the Lord Chancellor – accepted of course as the keeper of the King's conscience in Cabinet, but of whose own recent approach Addington had not in fact known at the time.[6] Pitt indeed was anxious to grasp such an opportunity, for he had wished to write a letter to the monarch ever since Eldon had made contact but was unable to do so from what he had learned of the vulnerable state of George III's health. He now seized a chance which Addington continued to provide; for further communications followed

1. See Fox to Grey, 19 April 1804 (*Memorials of Fox*, IV, 44).

2. Pitt to Melville, 11 April 1804 (*Secret Correspondence*, 28–9); and cf. *Colchester*, I, 497 and Pellew, II, 277 for a fortnight later. See p. 643 above for Pitt's recent hope. He was probably resting his opinion in mid April on a statement by Addington to Tom Steele, which Steele passed to Camden and Camden (without mentioning Steele's name) to Pitt down at Walmer. The incident is recorded in a detailed undated memorandum on the events of the next three weeks by Bathurst (*H.M.C., Bathurst* (1923), 34–41), which in view of his old friendship with Camden and Pitt, shown markedly at this time (op. cit., 32–4, 41–2), may very well have been based at least in great part on an account from Pitt himself.

3. Op. cit., 34.

4. Cf. pp. 587–8 above.

5. *H.M.C., Bathurst*, 34. Cf. eg pp. 575, 579 above for the first; 594 and n3 for the second, and also Thomas Grenville to Grenville, 13 February 1804 (*H.M.C., Dropmore*, VII, 214).

6. *H.M.C., Bathurst*, 34–5. See p. 640 above. Addington learned of that conversation indeed only in the next week or two, and expressed his anger at a Cabinet meeting around the turn of April and May. Eldon's conduct was subjected to much debate in the next century, by Pellew, Brougham, Campbell in his *Lives of the Chancellors*, and Stanhope among others.

swiftly on the letter of the 16th. Pitt was first asked to try to postpone for a few days Fox's motion on defence and his own intervention on the Army of Reserve, so as to allow time for the King to respond;[1] and was then informed that an answer must await the result of that motion when it came, but that in any case Addington then intended to resign, on the assumption (even though still unconfirmed) that Pitt was not bound to Grenville and Fox.[2] The exact timing of these last successive communications is not clear. But they certainly suggested a despairing mood. Anything might happen soon; and it was against such a background that Pitt had talked to his cousin again.

While the latest messages however hinted that the end might be near, in other respects they can scarcely have been welcomed. Both, if in different measure, could compromise Pitt's freedom of manoeuvre – his access to the monarch and, in the second case, the tenor of his prospective advice. With Fox's motion set for 23 April, he accordingly wrote his own letter for the King and sent it to Eldon on the 22nd.[3] It informed George III, or confirmed, that Pitt would shortly be declaring his opinion of the Ministry 'and particularly ... of the person now holding the chief place in it'. A more adequate Government was needed for the defence of the country and to gain co-operation in Europe. He had his views on its nature. But whatever those might be, he was determined 'to avoid committing himself to any engagements the effect of which would be likely to occasion, in any contingency, a sentiment of dissatisfaction or uneasiness in your Majesty's mind'.[4]

The postponements of the debates meanwhile were achieved; if in Pitt's own case not wholly in response to Addington's plea.[5] Fox consented, though his suspicion was naturally aroused.[6] But if the Minister hoped to split the partnership or embarrass Pitt in his dealings with the King, he had tried in vain. The position had been mapped out for some time; Pitt's restriction of scope was one he himself had set; these messages

1. Pitt to Melville, 29 March, 11 April 1804 (*Secret Correspondence*, 13–14, 29). This was doubtless a genuine reason, particularly at the start. It was also doubtless complemented, particularly later, by a wish to fend off Pitt's threatened direct unsolicited approach to George III. See pp. 643–4 above for the prospective debates.

2. *H.M.C., Bathurst*, 35.

3. Pitt to Eldon, 22 April 1804 (Twiss, *Life of Eldon*, I, 439–40). He asked for it to be put in the King's hands before the debate if possible.

4. Pitt to George III, 21 April 1804; Stanhope, IV, Appendix, i–iii. A copy in his hand of the final version is in Dacres Adams Mss, formerly P.R.O. 30/58/5. He altered the original wording slightly on learning that the Lord Chancellor did not intend to deliver the letter before the debate the next day (see Stanhope, IV, 154–6).

5. Due to speak on 18 April on the Army of Reserve, he arranged through Long (on the plea of gout; see p. 627 above) to do so on the 20th, when he expected a larger attendance. On that day however he was 'surprised' to find that the Government had not finalised some extra clauses in the bill, and that it accordingly wished to put off the second reading to the 25th (see *H.M.C., Dropmore*, VII, 218–19; *P.D.*, II, cols. 143*, 174).

6. Fox to Grey, 17, 18 April 1804 (*Memorials of Fox*, IV, 41–3). See p. 645 above for his suspicion.

forwarded moves in directions for which they had not been intended; and while a brief delay for Fox's motion was accepted in case word came from the monarch, 'the oppositions' agreed at once that otherwise the attacks would go ahead.[1]

The preparations indeed were by now almost complete. Government's majorities in the Commons had been adequate but not brilliant since the vote on Pitt's naval motion, which despite his initial disappointment was thought by others to have produced a 'shake'.[2] The surviving division lists for various stages in the passage of the Volunteer and Irish Militia bills showed some stabilisation; but mostly in thinnish Houses and on matters not at all of the first concern. On 16 April, however, the third reading of the Augmentation bill for Irish militia brought a majority of only 21 on a vote of 235; and since that subject, in one expert's view, was not such as particularly to favour Opposition, the outcome would have impressed Pitt the more strongly with the conviction that it would reinforce Addington's alarm.[3] But it was not only, or even mainly, in the Commons that the Ministry had growing cause for unease. Under Grenville's skilled leadership the fight was being waged with great effect in the Lords.[4] From late in March the peers subjected the Volunteer Consolidation bill in particular to continual pressure; on the 23rd, 26th and 27th, on 5, 6, 9, 11, 12, 18 and 19 April. The Ministers found themselves unable to carry a leading measure in the upper House without delay and significant amendment – an unusual phenomenon – and the normal majorities were under evident strain. After an initially good figure of 30 on 5 April, they slipped to 20 or less – once to 9 – by the 18th; and the position worsened steadily over the next few days. On 19 April Government actually suffered a defeat by one vote in a skirmish over the war in India, and on that same day the opposition peers mustered 49 votes, their highest yet, on the Irish Militia Offer bill. That was repeated (proxies being included) on the 24th, and in a vote, following immediately, on the third reading of the Augmentation bill the number

1. Grenville to Buckingham, 18 April (Buckingham, III, 349); Fox to Grey, sd (*Memorials*, IV, 42). The phrase was Minto's (*Life and Letters of Elliot*, III, 315).

2. See p. 632 above, for a majority of 71 in a division of 331. Canning's diary of 16, 17 March 1804 (Canning Ms 29d) reveals Pitt's first response, quickly followed by greater satisfaction; for some other opinions see *Memorials of Fox*, IV, 24–5, *Glenbervie*, I, 372, Lowther to Mulgrave, 26 March 1804 in Normanby Mss, Box VII, bundle 13.

3. *P.R. (Stockdale)*, II, 499; Pitt to Melville, 17 April 1804 (*Secret Correspondence*, 31). For the bill see p. 628 above. George Rose had judged it to be 'a weak Question', and was sorry in fact that Pitt had decided to attend (to Tomline, 15 April 1804; Pretyman Ms 435/44). The majorities recorded for the period 19 March to 13 April were 117 in a main division of 239, 70 in one of 178, 57 in 131, 58 in 142 (*P.R. (Stockdale)*, II, 182, 410, 445, 481). There is a detailed assessment of the minority for the naval debate of 15 March, with some possibly later attribution of allegiances, in Pitt's papers, P.R.O. 30/8/197, ff. 242–5. Closer analysis of the lists might cast light for general purposes on the significance for voting patterns of the business discussed on the particular occasion.

4. For the significance of what follows see the account by McCahill in *Order and Equipoise*, 85–8; and subsequently in greater detail in 'The House of Lords and the Collapse of Henry Addington's Administration', *Parliamentary History*, Volume 6, Part I, 69–94.

rose farther, to 61 or 62. All these divisions were lost to majorities respectively of 28, 42 and 32.[1] But it was more significant that an energetic canvass for attendance or proxies should have been so successful, that Grenvillite estimates proved remarkably accurate, and that signs of disintegration – the bishops were starting to hang back[2] – were increasing among the Ministry's supporters. A sterner test indeed was looming, for a plan had been laid to move for a debate on the state of the nation, to be introduced by the Marquess of Stafford, the son of the former Lord Gower who had been Ambassador in Paris at the start of the Revolution.[3] Already however one Grenvillite peer reckoned that 'the game was up';[4] and in the event Stafford's motion was not required. The Lords by this point in fact had done their share of the work; Addington indeed said later that it was they who enabled Pitt 'to overthrow the Government'. He claimed further that it was Pitt's own 'ascendancy' in the House which brought about such a situation, from the many creations he had made in his time.[5] This was probably not the case directly; a contemporary calculation suggested that such men were divided equally on the issues.[6] The influence was in part more subtle and in a sense more widespread. It was the fact that the former Minister was in serious opposition rather than a personal debt that induced some of the peers involved to 'risk temporary opposition' themselves.[7] The result was a portent from a powerful quarter which Members in the lower House could not ignore.[8] If Addington must meet his fate in the Commons, he was already badly weakened in another place.

Meanwhile the troops were gathering in the Commons themselves, not least as 'the *Levies* from Scotland and Ireland' were steadily coming to

---

1. See for the Volunteer and Irish Militia bills from 23 March to 24 April *P.R.* (*Stockdale*), II, 246–50, 266–93, 301–5, 357–61, 365–9, 377–9, 386–7, 411–12, *P.D.*, II, cols. 5–7, 11–20, 26–31, 67–8, 105–7, 141–2*, 145–65, 166–71, 251–6. For the question of the final figure on the 24th see McCahill, op. cit., 85n1.

2. Cf. pp. 485–7 above.

3. Pitt to Melville, 18 April 1804 (*Secret Correspondence*, 33); it might have been for this prospect that Pitt compiled his own list of peers in April, giving totals of 50 for himself, 22 against and 25 unmarked (P.R.O. 30/8/234, ff. 299–300v). It may however have referred to one of the other debates or been an unspecific estimate; he was now 'amazingly keen' and scrutinising 'the lists of the two Houses' (Minto on 27 April; *Life and Letters of Elliot*, III, 321). For Gower see I, 563, II, 201.

4. Minto on 25 April (*Life and Letters of Elliot*, III, 320).

5. Pellew, op. cit., II, 274n8. Thomas Grenville, from an opposite point of vantage, likewise claimed – with some exaggeration – that the Lords 'frightened the wretched Doctor from his seat'. One contemporary analysis gave Pitt perhaps 33 supporters at this point in the upper House, compared with 13–14 for Grenville, 10–18 for Fox, and perhaps 17 for the Prince of Wales (McCahill, *Parliamentary History*, Vol. 6, 68, 75–6). For Pitt and the peerage in past years see I, 624–5; pp. 489–92 above.

6. The calculation was Spencer's, citing 64 men (32 against 32) out of the relevant total of 87 (which Pellew (n5 above) gave as 80).

7. McCahill, op. cit., 87–8; Turberville, *The House of Lords in the Age of Reform*, 134. By 29 April there were rumours that the opponents in the Lords would rise to 93 (*Colchester*, I, 499).

8. See Sack, 'The House of Lords and Parliamentary Patronage in Great Britain, 1802–32'. Cf. I, 143, and p. 488 above for influence in the Commons.

hand.[1] The effect of the exertions was underlined by the Ministry's ineptitude in rallying its own forces – a damaging blow to morale in weeks in
which that was coming under strain.[2] When the two great trials of strength
took place at last, on 23 and 25 April, the combined effects of oratory and
numbers were visible to all. Fox's motion on defence drew a fuller House
than had been known in recent divisions, and on a vote of 460 (excluding
the tellers) the Government's majority was 52. Two days later the bill for
suspending recruitment to the Army of Reserve passed by 37 on a vote of
443.[3] These were damning figures in divisions of that size. Although
Ministers were reported as thinking that they might still be able to whip up
a further ten to fifteen laggards, and Fox indeed apparently said more than
once later that they could have carried on, Addington himself anticipated
a further loss of support and concluded that the problems would now be
very great.[4] He saw the King on the 26th, probably with the Lord
Chancellor, to represent the difficulties and tender his resignation if that
was wished. It was not; George III was angry and unwilling to agree. But
on the 27th the Lord Chancellor had an audience at which he delivered the
letter which Pitt had sent him on the 22nd, but which, pending developments, he himself had kept meanwhile.[5] Conversations took place in the
next two days, between Eldon and the King and among Ministers, and on
the 29th Addington told his colleagues that he had made up his mind to go.
On the evening of 30 April he brought in his budget for the year, as he had
already given notice, and as Pitt had done in his case after his resignation;
and then asked the agreement of the House – as the Lords had just been
asked, on the eve of Stafford's motion – to postpone discussion of various
business already announced.[6] That morning the Lord Chancellor had
called by command on Pitt in York Place, to tell him that the King wished
to see in writing his ideas for a new Administration.[7]

IV

So at the end of April Pitt stood on the threshold of office. There seemed
little likelihood that he would not enter, for he had resolved to accept

1. Lowther to Melville, 5 April (Normanby Mss, Box VII, bundle 13); Pitt to same, 29
March, 11 April 1804 (*Secret Correspondence*, 16, 27).
2. See Fedorak, loc. cit., 311–13. Ashbourne, *Pitt and his Times*, 327–8 gives an example of
a canvassing letter from Pitt.
3. *P.D.*, II, cols. 249–51, 319–20.
4. *Colchester*, I, 499 for Ministers, and op. cit., 500 for Addington's own expectation of a
further fall to 22 on any subsequent division; Pellew, op. cit., II, 274n for Fox's remark,
which his nephew Holland once told Addington that he had 'often' made (cf. p. 642, n5
above).
5. P. 649 and n6 above.
6. *P.D.*, II, cols. 358, 336. See p. 652 above for Stafford's motion; p. 523 for the fortuitous
comparison of the introduction of the budget with Pitt's case.
7. There are some variations in the accounts of this sequence of events. Bathurst's
memorandum (*H.M.C., Bathurst*, 35), which like Abbot's and Malmesbury's diaries

whether under a 'large' or an 'exclusive' arrangement.[1] He was however pledged, and determined, to press for the former, and by the best account he made this clear to Eldon, stating that while he was willing at this point again to communicate through the Lord Chancellor it was on condition that if the King rejected his advice he must be granted an audience, for it was 'from his [the monarch's] mouth alone that he could receive a final refusal'.[2]

On 2 May he accordingly set out in a letter to Eldon his arguments for 'a comprehensive system'.[3] They fell under three heads. First, there were the great domestic advantages to be gained from uniting 'as large a proportion as possible of the weight of talents and connexions, drawn without exception from parties of all descriptions'. This was widely desired, for the former differences over the French Revolution were 'to all practical purpose, superseded' by Bonaparte's conduct; and the moment was highly favourable, before any disappointments in perhaps a long war and heavy burdens on 'all classes of persons' had their likely effects. Secondly, a firm and stable Administration, 'not thwarted or embarrassed by any powerful opposition either in Parliament or the country', would offer the best and perhaps the only means of achieving a fresh combination on the Continent. And thirdly, a comprehensive Government should remove anxiety over a revival of the question of Irish Catholic relief; for while Pitt's 'own conduct' on this was 'fixed', as the King knew, 'under all circumstances', he foresaw that the subject could cause 'great inconvenience and embarrassment' if the country was divided by 'powerful parties'. On such grounds therefore he asked permission, for the King's 'personal

---

(*Colchester*, I, 498; *Malmesbury*, IV, 296) settles the date of Addington's visit to the King as the 26th, does not, unlike them, mention his accompaniment by the Lord Chancellor. The latter's account of George III's reaction, apparently given to Portland from whom Malmesbury had it '*quite warm*', moreover differed to some extent from Addington's own, which sounded more strongly favourable to himself (*Malmesbury*, IV, 296). Bathurst is evidence for Pitt's letter of the 22nd being handed to the King by Eldon on the 27th, and for further conversations on the two following days (*H.M.C., Bathurst*, 36); Malmesbury (IV, 297) states that Ministers deliberated at the same time. Pellew (op. cit., II, 277) dates Addington's statement to the Cabinet to the 29th, the day on which Pitt acknowledged a letter from Eldon informing him that the King had read his letter of the 22nd (Twiss, op. cit., I, 441). Bathurst (op. cit., 36) and Stanhope later (IV, 162) ascribe Eldon's call at York Place to the morning of the 30th.

    1. P. 648 above.

    2. Bathurst's memorandum, op. cit., 36. See p. 649, n2 above for my view that in essence this was Pitt's own account.

    3. The main letter, 'to be laid before the King', is published in Stanhope, IV, Appendix, iv–viii; a covering note to Eldon, in Twiss, op. cit., I, 442–3. In the former Pitt referred to the procedure as being 'in conformity to what passed between us yesterday'. Unless Bathurst's memorandum was inaccurate, this means either that the two men met again on 1 May, or that an important letter was begun then and completed the next day. Since Pitt apologised for its length and the delay, and sent it at 1.45 p.m., the latter explanation seems the more likely. Rose (II, 115) however stated in his diary that the letter was sent to Eldon on the 3rd.

repose and comfort', to talk to Grenville and Fox to learn how far it might be practicable to submit details of a possible arrangement which might include others as well, 'some' coming from the present Ministry.

The approach was not well received, and least of all the part on which Pitt had laid particular personal weight. On the contrary, George III showed his hostility, and the burden of his reply fell very largely on the old unfortunate subject. He had been pleased by the earlier 'assurances' that Pitt was not committed to any political engagement.[1] That impression however may since have been weakened;[2] at all events there was no mistaking the altered tone. Receiving the unwelcome communication on the 3rd, the King replied on the 5th.[3] After lamenting that his former Minister had taken a rooted dislike to the man who had rescued his King and country in 1801, when 'the most ill-digested and dangerous proposition was brought forward by the enemies of the established Church', he returned with passion to the Test Act and his Coronation Oath. As for Fox, he was astonished that there could be any thought 'for one moment' of bringing his name forward. If Pitt persisted, he for his own part could not accept his services; he would turn to men who were not 'seekers of improvements' which could only tend to destroy 'that noble fabric' which was the envy of foreign lands. In a covering note addressed to '*his* excellent Chancellor' – an emphasis reminiscent of a letter to Addington three years before – he doubted if after this Pitt would opt for an interview: he would probably instead 'prepare another essay, containing many empty words and little information'.[4]

But Pitt did so opt. He replied the next day with a direct letter, by the Lord Chancellor who called in the morning, persisting in a request to be seen and heard. After making the briefest possible reference to Catholic relief, he insisted that an audience was necessary if he was to retain any hope that his services could be employed.[5] This did the trick.[6] Eldon was summoned to Buckingham House early in the afternoon to tell Pitt to come there on the following morning, and this the former Minister did,

---

1. See Pitt to Eldon, 29 April 1804 (Twiss, op. cit., I, 441); *H.M.C., Bathurst*, 36.
2. There is a hint that this may have been so from Addington, now ready to depart but whose role if any in these few days is hard to specify. On 1 May he saw George III and walked with him in the garden (presumably of Buckingham House) for an hour and a half. The next day he gave his friend Abbot to understand that Pitt was 'supposed to be much more committed with the rest of the Opposition than has yet appeared' (*Colchester*, I, 502–3). He did not see the King again, by his own account, until the 4th (and then, by another account, stayed two and a half hours; Bathurst, op. cit., 37), when he was shown or apprised of the contents of Pitt's letter of the 2nd, the King having 'settled his written answer' on the 3rd (*Colchester*, I, 504).
3. Geoge III for Pitt, 5 April 1804 (Stanhope, IV, Appendix, viii–x).
4. Same to Eldon, sd (Twiss, op. cit., I, 443).
5. Pitt to George III, 6 May 1804 (Stanhope, IV, x–xii). There are copies in P.R.O. 30/8/104, Dacres Adams Mss formerly P.R.O. 30/58/5, and Pretyman Ms 435/45.
6. Stanhope (IV, 167) states that Eldon had made 'renewed representations' to the same end. He probably did; but with no great pleasure, as Pitt by now was himself indeed aware (see p. 656, n3 below).

on 7 May, after asking the King's physicians (five in all) to be available before he had his audience.[1] He had by then seen a calculation of potentially hostile forces in the Commons, drawn up by two experts, Long and Rose, in case he did not have his way with George III.

	English	Irish	Total
The Prince	29	12	41
Mr. Fox	70	9	79
Lord Grenville	22	1	23
Mr. Addington			
(including persons who would oppose from former disappointment, &c.)	60	8	68
Doubtful persons, of whom we have some knowledge, 58; suppose only half of these against			29
			240

leaving 70 Irish members, and many English ones, quite uncertain.

If thirty of these ('a sanguine estimate') were added, there could thus be 270 Members opposed to a 'narrow' Ministry at the start.[2] He had also offended Eldon by hoping, as he ate his breakfast when the Lord Chancellor called to accompany him, that the latter had said nothing which might prejudice the King against any proposition he might make. As a result, Eldon refused to be present when Pitt saw the doctors.[3] He questioned them 'for some time', and asked in the end if they were willing to certify in writing that George III was recovered sufficiently to be able fully to discharge his duties. Having obtained their signatures to a statement which he drew up, he then went into the King, with whom he talked for almost three hours.[4]

It was a curious interview. Pitt, like others, had of course heard all kinds of reports about the King, and moreover had seen very little of

1. Bathurst, op. cit., 38.

2. *Rose*, II, 118–19. For detailed analysis see *H of P*, I, 169–72.

3. Twiss, op. cit., I, 447–8. Pitt's question was perhaps hardly surprising, for on the 3rd Eldon had informed him that while of course he would act as the channel to and from the King he did so out of duty, and for his part thought it most unfortunate that the proposals had been put at this time. If the King asked him for his opinion, therefore, he would have to state it (nd, but endorsed by Pitt, 'Delivered Personally After stating the same Sentiments verbally, Thursday May 3rd 1804 (Secret)'; P.R.O. 30/8/132). He wrote much the same to Rose (see *Rose*, II, 115–16) when the latter, rather presumptuously, sought to enlist him in Pitt's support.

4. *H.M.C., Bathurst*, 38. Malmesbury's diary of 9 May (*Malmesbury*, IV, 303–4) relays an account by Lord St Helens (the former diplomat, who was a Lord of the Bedchamber). The doctors' paper is in P.R.O. 30/8/228.

him for over three years.[1] He did not know what to expect. But what he found proved a surprise. George III was calm and collected, in possession of his most gracious manner and indeed of the situation. When Pitt congratulated him on looking better than on his recovery from his last illness, he replied that 'that was not to be wondered at as he was then on the point of *parting* with an old friend, and he was now about to *regain* one'.[2] This courteous and astute rejoinder – assuming at the start that Pitt would be coming in – set the tone for the long talk that followed, in which the recent invalid appears to have displayed a striking example of his kingcraft.[3] It was small wonder that Pitt on emerging told Eldon that the monarch 'had never so baffled him in any conversation he had had with him in his life'.[4] Where suggestions were made which did not please, he 'digressed a good deal', returning 'exactly at the parts from which he went off'. He agreed that a broad Administration was desirable, though he did not always like the sound of the members proposed; Grenville and probably Melville – whom he seems to have felt had recently betrayed him and his Government[5] – were accepted only reluctantly as candidates for office. But in general there were few difficulties over Grenville's leading associates, though the King would prefer Spencer in a post other than the Admiralty and Windham without a 'situation of business'. Fox's friends were apparently not discussed at this stage; but Pitt had the impression that some need not be excluded from office, or perhaps even from the Cabinet. There would however be no place in Cabinet for Fox himself. After a particularly long digression the King flatly refused to accept him, and despite Pitt's urging 'with all the reasons he could find, and with the utmost earnestness', he did not budge. He did not object to Fox being given a post abroad.[6] But he would not contemplate the prospect of office for the man whom he saw as the most dangerous of politicians:

1. St Helens said not 'anything' (p. 656, n4 above); but that was not correct if rare and slight contacts, mostly at Court, are taken into account (see occasional mentions in newspapers, and Stanhope, IV, 169).

2. Rose's account, diary for 7 May (*Rose*, II, 121–2). The same appears in *H.M.C., Bathurst*, 40.

3. One may recall Dr Johnson's impression many years before, 'Sir, his manners are those of as fine a gentleman as we may suppose Lewis the Fourteenth or Charles the Second'. A lesser but more experienced observer, worried by royal coldness on one occasion, remarked that the King was 'supposed to possess a very considerable share of that art which James I, I believe, used to call by the coarse but forcible term of kingcraft' (*Glenbervie*, I, 356).

4. This was Eldon's account, in a letter undated but probably written later, in 1810 or 1811 (Twiss, op. cit., I, 449). Pitt said further that 'he never saw the King, when he would more willingly have taken his opinion about the most important of all subjects, peace or war'.

5. See *Rose*, II, 123 with n1, for Melville. But the reason given there – that Melville, returning to London in April, had voted against the Ministry in the Lords – cannot be checked from the surviving lists of the minorities, where his name does not occur.

6. Op. cit., II, 122–4.

whom indeed he had expelled from the Privy Council with his own hand.[1]

By one account, Pitt 'agreed' at the audience 'to form a Government on these terms'.[2] It was a consequence implicit in his position, particularly over the past three months; but in any case he was far from being cast down at the close. In a list of Cabinet posts which he had made for his own eye probably within the last fortnight, he had included Fox as a Secretary of State with Melville and Fitzwilliam, and Spencer at the Admiralty.[3] The first must now be struck out, and Spencer probably shifted; nonetheless the King had come a long way from the course that might have been envisaged two days before. He had accepted Grenville. He sounded ready to accept others whom his new Minister might recommend. And in Pitt's own view there might even be a 'fair opening' for the great outcast himself in the not too distant future. For since he could be offered a post abroad, there happened to be one which in the circumstances might attract him: the embassy at St Petersburg, currently in the hands of an incumbent who was something of a stopgap and moreover wished to leave. After all, Fox had been a Russophil in his time, some of his sympathy had survived intervening disappointments, his interest had recently revived; and he would be placed at a point of high significance for the conduct of the war.[4] If he would go, it could improve the chances of his being admitted to the Cabinet after an interval; and even if the offer was declined, Pitt did not place great odds against the possibility that he himself, when once in regular touch, could 'gradually reconcile the King's mind'.[5] When the

1. When George III alluded to this last decision, Pitt was said to have reminded him that he for his part had not favoured it, since it would give Fox too much prominence. The story came from Farquhar, not necessarily a reliable source (*Malmesbury*, IV, 303). Cf. pp. 116–17 and n1 above.

2. The wording comes from Canning's diary for 7 May (Canning Ms 29d), and he had seen Pitt immediately after the latter's return (*Rose*, II, 124).

3. Windham, it may be noted, was not destined even then for a prominent place of 'business'; he was to be Chancellor of the Duchy of Lancaster. The list, undated, is reproduced as the frontispiece to Stanhope, IV. Its details are given on p. 670 below in comparison with the eventual results. Notes in Pitt's hand, nd but almost certainly at this time and relating to both senior and junior posts, may be found in P.R.O. 30/8/197, ff. 32–3v.

4. The Ambassador was Rear-Admiral Sir John Borlase Warren; an agreeable and adequately successful sailor who was appointed in 1802, succeeding Lord St Helens (Alleyne Fitzherbert), who himself had succeeded Whitworth in 1801 almost a year after the latter left in disagreeable circumstances (see p. 000 above). Fox's most dramatic effort on Russia's behalf had been in the very different circumstances of the Ochakov affair (see II, 22–3 and section IV); and a residual sympathy from early days weathered the subsequent final partition of Poland and his party's final loss of confidence in Catherine II. More lately, he had pressed the Ministry to pursue the hope of Russian mediation on the eve of war in 1803 (p. 605 above).

5. *Rose*, II, 124. And cf. Leveson Gower to Canning, 1 June 1805: 'He flattered us at the Time, I remember, with the Hope that by an habitual Intercourse with the King, he should acquire influence sufficient to persuade H.M. to agree to the formation of the broad administration he had originally recommended' (*Letters of Lord Granville Leveson Gower*, II (1916), 90).

prospect of activity arose, the old optimism was not dead. On the morning of 8 May, following the audience, Pitt was 'in the highest spirits possible'.[1]

His hopes however, as it proved, had already been overtaken. For much had happened on the previous evening. As soon as Pitt left the King he made contact with Grenville and Fox, calling on the former and sending Leveson Gower to the latter to tell him what had passed.[2] Grenville's reaction was scarcely promising; but that scarcely seems to have made an impression,[3] for Fox himself had yet to give his response, and Pitt seems to have thought – indeed to have been confident – that 'so fair an opening presented itself' for him that he would not refuse.[4] The news of the King's veto had apparently leaked in the course of the same afternoon of the 7th, and Pitt therefore despatched a note asking Fox to meet him the next day.[5] He was not indeed alone in his expectations at that point, for the recipient himself was 'perfectly reasonable'. Fox must always of course have counted on trouble from George III – he certainly did so on the eve of Pitt's audience[6] – and he at once offered to stand aside 'if his friends could be taken care of'. Grey and Lauderdale, he hoped, could be included in the Cabinet, some 'Peerages & provisions &c.' found for others; and this may indeed have been 'undertaken' by Leveson Gower for Pitt, who would do likewise 'for the King'. It was not surprising that, as Canning recorded, so helpful a message was greeted with delight. But it soon fell to him to bring Pitt, at a peak of optimism, the news that the prospect was dead.[7]

This was not Fox's doing. He acted as he said he would. He went to a meeting called by the Prince of Wales at Carlton House the same evening, and spoke to that effect. His offer however was rejected decisively; his associates would not come in without him, and the feeling was such as to end any prospect of the conversation with Pitt.[8] The outcome also shifted

---

1. *Rose*, II, 125.

2. Op. cit., 124; *H.M.C., Bathurst*, 39; Grenville to Pitt, 7 May 1804 (*H.M.C., Dropmore*, VII, 220). Canning, who with Leveson Gower saw Pitt on his return from the Queen's House, records that his companion 'carried the intelligence' to Fox, and he himself to Grenville (diary for 7 May; Canning Ms 29d) – presumably in the latter case before Pitt did so himself. Leveson Gower seems to have been admitted to a certain amount of Pitt's confidence in recent months (*Letters of Leveson Gower*, I, 457).

3. Grenville to Pitt, 7 May 1804, as in n2 above.

4. The words are those of Rose, who discussed the prospect with Pitt and Tomline and applied the judgment to them all (diary for 8 May; *Rose*, II, 125). Did the financial inducement of a major embassy also enter their minds?

5. *H.M.C., Bathurst*, 39. The meeting was to be at Lord Stafford's (cf. p. 652 above). These developments followed one another quickly. Pitt returned to York Place at half past three (Canning's diary for 7 May 1804, Canning Ms 29d); he sent his message to Fox at about five.

6. This is clear from a letter to Thomas Grenville (nd but endorsed 6 May 1804; B.L. Add. Ms 41856). And cf. p. 645 above.

7. Canning's diary, opposite entries for 7, 8 May (Canning Ms 29d). He of course gathered his information about Fox on the 7th from Leveson Gower.

8. Which could have marked the only occasion since 1782, if tradition is to be believed, on which the two men would have talked in private alone; see I, 100.

the emphasis finally to Grenville, himself accepted by George III and, it might be thought, in a more sensitive position in relation to Pitt. But the Grenvillites likewise were adamant. At a conference, again on the same evening, leading members decided that they could not join a Ministry from which Fox was barred.[1] Some at least already had an inkling in fact that he might respond generously to a ban; for even before Pitt's audience he had disclaimed any engagement binding enough to influence his partners against accepting an offer which might be worthy of their notice.[2] They were greatly moved by this magnanimity – it obviously lay behind Grenville's immediate attitude to Pitt's news[3] – and the influence acted in a direction which Fox had thus not invoked and may well indeed not have wished. They felt deeply reluctant to seem to be abandoning their ally;[4] and, as Grenville himself explained it, such a prohibition when applied to a broad Ministry affirmed not merely a personal but a principle of 'exclusion'. They could not take part in a Government formed on such 'a system', which must then apply to all the subsequent arrangements. This was their decided opinion.[5] Unless therefore something further occurred, it spelt the end of the design so laboriously built up.

The destruction of his hopes came to Pitt as a shock, after he had raised them so high. He had persuaded himself that he stood a chance – a good chance – of squaring the circle, and the disappointment was clearly severe. In retrospect his optimism can seem to have been slenderly based, though possibly the anticipated conversation with Fox might at least have gained useful time.[6] But he had no doubt now that he had reached the end of that road. He had no intention of bringing further pressure to bear on George III; against the background of the recent illness and of his own views, he saw no justification for any attempt to storm the closet, and after what had passed within Opposition he was not going to do any such thing. In his own eyes indeed he had gone farther than he promised, in the strength of his attempts to achieve a comprehensive

---

1. All reliable accounts agree about the meetings, both of them on the evening of 7 May. The Grenvillites' was held at Camelford House, which Grenville and his wife had used for some years as their base in London. The Prince appears to have said in conversation that Fox attended that conference as well as his own at Carlton House; but there is no other evidence, and it seems most unlikely (Harvey, loc. cit., 89).

2. Fox to Thomas Grenville, for Grenville, nd but endorsed 6 May 1804 (see p. 659, n6 above); answered by Thomas Grenville at half past midnight on the '6th' (*Memorials of Fox*, IV, 53).

3. See for one indication *Malmesbury*, IV, 322.

4. Though not all in equal degree. Minto for one (who had not been present at the meeting) was far from happy afterwards (see Harvey, loc. cit., 91).

5. Grenville to Pitt, 8 May 1804 (copy in *H.M.C., Dropmore*, VII, 222–3. The original is in P.R.O. 30/8/140).

6. Rose, who for his part was more shocked than he had ever been in the course of his political life, was strongly disposed to think that the personal meeting might have 'set matters right' (*Rose*, II, 126).

Administration.[1] He was in fact furious with Grenville as well as with Fox's party, though naturally not Fox himself; so much so that Rose, watching his anger, was worried that it was influencing him too much.[2] Eldon recalled him saying, 'with some indignation, he would teach that proud man, that, in the service and with the confidence of the King, he could do without him'.[3] Reasoning and temperament must indeed have been pointing him the same way. He had foreseen the problem likely to arise from Grenville's junction with Fox: the effect on the King, and on Grenville himself, drawn deeper than he supposed into a binding alliance.[4] He had done all he could, as he saw it, despite doubts among his friends and followers[5] and in ways which he did not always welcome, to underwrite the efforts for a comprehensive Ministry; and in an audience of almost three hours had gained the inclusion of the Grenvillites themselves, men who had worked with him in the past and were his natural colleagues for the future.[6] And now it was Grenville who had thrown away the prospect of anything but a 'narrow' alternative, and on an argument, as Pitt told him, that negated his own past membership of a Government which had come to accept 'exclusion' as a principle in the case of Fox.[7] The country wanted a broad Ministry at this time of danger. The King was a central element of constitutional stability, more than ever at such a point. Where, it might be asked, was Grenville's doctrine leading him, in this new alliance with an old foe who lived by a theory of party which he himself had denied?[8]

The case was a strong one. It was also one that would not take cognizance of the reasons which had led Grenville reluctantly by stages towards this point: the puzzlement and anger, shared with his late colleagues, at the initial championship of the terms for peace, the complications of conscience, extravagant as he and others found them, in relation to Addington, the consequent hesitation to topple the Minister or, until recently, undermine the Ministry. If Pitt was not going to move decisively – if he was not going to move at all – how could anything effective be done except by looking elsewhere? And when he had been finally driven to act, how indeed should his course be interpreted? Might he not be making use, as Fox more predictably was disposed to believe, of the efforts of the joint Opposition so as to gain office on his own terms?[9] One observer, experienced but unsympathetic, saw a more intimate influence also

1. *H.M.C., Bathurst*, 40.
2. *Rose*, II, 127 and n1. See also Canning's account, in *Malmesbury*, IV, 321, of his 'great *anger*' with Grenville and 'great *pleasure*' at Fox's conduct.
3. Twiss, op. cit., I, 449.
4. Cf. p. 646 above.
5. This point was made shortly afterwards by Castlereagh (to Wellesley in India, 18 May 1804; Stanhope, IV, 184).
6. Cf. p. 617 above.
7. See *H.M.C., Bathurst*, 40.
8. Cf. pp. 574, 614 above.
9. See pp. 617, 645 above.

at work: a long-standing desire on Grenville's part, and now an opportunity, to liberate himself from a long partnership in which he had been subordinate and moreover uneasy in the later years.[1] That may not have been impossible. But in any case, secure as so often in the virtue of his conduct, Grenville could see cause enough to justify his sense of dis-illusionment and steer him along a 'clear line'.[2]

Meanwhile he was far from convinced that nothing more could be tried. He wanted Pitt to send on his letter of explanation to the King, and press again for Fox.[3] He met with a flat refusal, as did some of Pitt's own followers considering a meeting to urge the same aim.[4] It did not take place. Grenville was told to write to George III direct if he wished.[5] And on the 9th Pitt requested a further audience, and offered to form a Government on a more restricted basis.[6] This was agreed, and Addington was instructed to deliver up his Seals the next morning. By noon on 10 May Pitt was First Minister once more.[7]

1. Malmesbury, never enthusiastic about his former Secretary of State, claimed to have perceived 'for many years' that '*emancipation from Pitt*, strange as it may seem,' had been 'the ruling wish in Lord Grenville's mind' (*Malmesbury*, IV, 302).

2. Eg, comparing his position with Pitt's in the autumn of 1802, 'It is a great satisfaction to us to recollect that *our line is clear*' (to Buckingham, 20 October 1802; Buckingham, III, 212); and cf. same to Thomas Grenville, 24 January 1803 (B.L. Add. Ms 41852).

3. To Pitt, 8 May 1804 (*H.M.C., Dropmore*, VII, 221), enclosing the letter in p. 660, n5 above.

4. *H.M.C., Bathurst*, 40. By this account, Pitt said in fact that any one who attended could not be regarded as his friend.

5. Ibid.

6. He found George III less composed than before: 'there was a hurry of spirits and an excessive love of talking' (to Eldon, 9 May 1804; Twiss, op. cit., I, 445) which must have reinforced his judgment that further disturbance could have been dangerous – and would surely have strengthened some others (eg p. 638, n2 above) in their earlier opinion that a Regency for life should be established while the King was out of action.

7. Malmesbury states that Pitt kissed hands in the afternoon (*Malmesbury*, IV, 305). Bathurst, who gives 11 a.m., an hour after Addington called (*H.M.C., Bathurst*, 40), is I think to be preferred.

Part Five

CHAPTER XIX

An Impaired Ministry

I

The formation of a new Government, or a major accession such as that of the Portland Whigs to Pitt in 1794, normally involved arrangements of the kind that made him 'bilious'.[1] The connexions concerned would seek their dues in posts and perquisites – the 'pasture' from which the flocks must be fed[2] – and the bargaining could be close and protracted before all was complete in the Departments and at Court. If he had had to accommodate Grenvillites, and Foxites, and perhaps Carlton House, as well as elements of the late Administration, the bilious attacks might have been severe indeed. That would have been the price to pay for a Ministry of all the talents. But no such prospect was in sight now, and the problem was very different. It was not a question of trying to contain an exceptional range of demands and obligations; rather of how to fill the places from a depressingly narrow choice.

For in this respect Pitt's situation at the start of his second Ministry was not unlike that at the start of his first. In May 1804 as in December 1783 the material to hand out of office was distinctly weak.[3] His own former colleagues or close followers not associated with Grenville could scarcely boast convincing candidates for high posts. Melville in fact was the sole exception; somewhat tarnished in his old friend's eyes by his unheralded peerage at the end of 1802, but still with special claims to attention and thought to be anxious for the Admiralty. Otherwise it was a thin field, as the occupants themselves were painfully aware: Camden indeed was the only such figure with Cabinet experience, and he had then, and still, carried little public weight.[4] There remained the late Ministry, collectively

---

1. See I, 234. I there applied his reference to the whole business of patronage. But while that might be permissible, the remark in point of fact was directed specifically to 'arrangements' of the sort under mention here. And cf. Camden now: '. . . you have told me that nothing makes you so bilious as Arrangements' (to Pitt, 21 December 1804; P.R.O. 30/8/119). For 1794 see II, 402–19.

2. Eg 'there was not pasture enough for all'; the verdict of Sir William Scott, Eldon's eldest brother [for whom see I, 147n1, 276], on the failure of Addington's overtures to Pitt in the spring of 1803.

3. Cf. for 1783 I, 129–31.

4. See pp. 583, 632, n4 and above for Melville, and also *Rose*, II, 130; p. 669 below for Camden.

excoriated in Pitt's own recent attack. However, he had allowed for some inclusion in principle, before the final assault,[1] and some accession now could be argued on various grounds. Castlereagh was known to have remained sympathetic and had indeed been a link with Addington, used by the latter at times to explain his position and pass on wartime news. Portland had deplored Pitt's going in 1801 and long wished for his return. Eldon's relationship as Lord Chancellor with the King gave him a special standing. Chatham could be deemed still to have a, somewhat trying, family claim. Even Hawkesbury, a stronger case for objection, might perhaps qualify by his early ties and possibly the advantage of preserving the remnants of Liverpool's countenance.[2] And there was a further point. Some proof of reciprocity in meeting the need to carry on the King's Government might help limit active opposition from the Addingtonians recently spread behind the Treasury Bench.

For that distinction, between the personal and the official, had now to be borne seriously in mind. Addington had succeeded in attracting his own measure of support as well as of criticism in the past three years, and the country gentlemen and others who liked him for himself, and gave credit to his policies and thought him ill-used, might well now amount to a following – at any rate a sympathetic group. Their numbers in the Commons were put, by two experienced if perhaps over-anxious judges, at some 68: a figure to be compared with Pitt's minimum of 58 on a bad occasion a year before.[3] Such a connexion, even if loose and untested, would not necessarily be coterminous with 'the party of the Crown', that extended body of placemen whose core would help sustain any Administration of which the sovereign approved.[4] The Addingtonians had thus to be brought into the Parliamentary reckoning, as an element distinct from the body of which they had hitherto been taken as a part.

Pitt was therefore left to rely very largely, at the worst reckoning, on George III's support. His immediate dependence in any event was of course obvious to all. As he himself acknowledged, if he was to show that he could do without Grenville it must be in a very real sense 'with the confidence of the King'.[5] Recalling his stance a year before, it was a

---

1. P. 639, n3 above.

2. Pp. 575, 640, 649 above for Castlereagh; 531, 640 for Portland; 649–50, 656, n3 for Eldon; II, 464, p. 512, n1 above for the qualifications to Chatham; 91 above for Pitt's personal support of Hawkesbury in the later nineties; pp. 292, n6, 457, 513, n4, 629, n4 for the decline in Liverpool's always guarded approval.

3. For which see p. 606 above. The estimate was that of George Rose and Charles Long in combination on 5 or 6 May (*Rose*, II, 118–19; p. 605 above). Fox put the number rather lower; and Addington personally was much weaker proportionately in the Lords. The two experts however compiled their figures, covering the various possible forces of opposition in the Commons, in the hope that they would help Pitt to bring pressure on George III on 7 May to accept the need under all permutations for Grenville and Fox and their associates to join a broad Government.

4. Cf. I, 40–3 (and particularly 42, lines 28–30); p. 554 above.

5. P. 661 above.

singular outcome, as indeed the process that produced it had been for Grenville himself. The prospect for the new Ministry was certainly clouded. It faced an unknown degree of opposition from two linked connexions, with two possible auxiliaries in the shape of Carlton House and the late Minister's friends. On a sombre assessment these might together muster some 211 votes, with a further 29 'doubtful' and at least 30 'quite uncertain', bringing a possible total of 270 'at the first onset'.[1] That was an uncomfortable figure, if all those concerned were resolved to be awkward. And it might in fact turn out to be too low, in the light, or murk, of another possibility. For who could say that the King had entirely recovered, and would not collapse again quite soon – and if so perhaps finally, by death or in practical terms? Pitt was worried when he saw George III for the second time, on 9 May, after the heartening evidence of only two days before. Noting the familiar signs of excitability he inferred that 'exertion of all sorts' must be kept within limits; and later in the month he became more alarmed. The King's 'imagination', he then heard, was 'heated and disordered'.[2] Others of course gathered much the same, and the effect might presumably be felt among the 'doubtful' and 'uncertain', and indeed the less deeply committed adherents of the connexions themselves. Some observers had wondered if such a consideration had not influenced the Grenvilles when they decided to remain with Fox.[3] It was, more certainly, something that politicians would weigh now with more time to reflect.

When all this had been said, however, Pitt did not despair of the future from his circumscribed state. He naturally wished to put a good face on it; but his sanguine temperament, and early experience, could be brought to bear on a situation which might not be altogether dark. Even before he first saw the King he thought that if necessary he could form a lasting Government without the Grenvilles, and when the need arose he was ready to defend his case. For a start, he was not convinced by the calculation of numbers: he found it unduly pessimistic; and even if he was placed in a minority, perhaps on one of the defence bills he would introduce, he reckoned that he could survive the rest of the session without great embarrassment until the long recess. Having done so, he could take steps: 'in the summer he should undoubtedly be able to strengthen the Administration in one way or another'; and he stated this so decisively that further discussion was closed.[4] In his forecast of the short term he

1. Cf. p. 656 above.

2. Pitt to Eldon, 9, 26 May 1804 (Stanhope, IV, 175; Twiss, op. cit., I, 453); for the meeting see p. 662, n6 above. See further eg *Rose*, II, 146–8, *Colchester*, I, 516, *Malmesbury*, IV, 318, *Life and Letters of Elliot*, III, 342.

3. Eg Malmesbury, on 7 and again 30 May (*Malmesbury*, IV, 302, 322); and see also *Life of Wilberforce*, III, 161.

4. Rose's accounts of conversations on 5 or 6, 8, 10 May 1804, and reflections (*Rose*, II, 119, 127–8, 130–1); it must be remembered that by now he was liable to irritate Pitt (p. 600 and n3 above). For his own part he thought that Melville had persuaded his recovered friend that the estimate of forces showed 'despondency'. Analysis in recent years (Sack, *The Grenvillites*, 79) has however broadly confirmed the figures given for the Grenvillites.

may have had several considerations in mind. For if his situation was awkward, his opponents had problems too. In their different ways they would all be angry, and wish to make their anger felt; but they would tend to be divided – the Addingtonians would emerge from a background markedly different from the rest – and for the moment they might not dare collectively to go too far. In the desire for a change of Government the widespread call had been for Pitt himself, latterly at the head of a comprehensive Ministry; and the personal sentiment survived in varying degrees when that last hope was foiled. Nor, conversely, were the leaders of the connexions well placed in person to exert a wide appeal. Addington lacked the prestige and charisma which his successor could offer; the Grenville clan was unpopular; and Fox remained as instinctively suspect to many as before. Pitt had undoubtedly caused dismay by accepting the King's commission so readily: even within his own circle some disapproved in principle, and most of his associates were uneasy about the outlook ahead.[1] But there was also a countervailing sentiment on which he could expect to draw. Many, in Parliament and beyond, would have been unhappy if he 'took the Cabinet by storm'.[2] He had been highly criticised at his resignation for deserting the King; when both King and country were now in crisis, that charge could easily be made again. Forcing the closet at such a point would have been widely seen as repulsive, 'desertion' of his recent partners as a lesser evil; and the choice in the circumstances, if disappointing, as nonetheless the best.[3] Moreover, Pitt might calculate, George III for his part would not wish to withdraw his support. He depended on his new Minister, at least initially, as the Minister depended on him. In the light therefore of such considerations, the political prospects seen as a whole might be taken as less daunting than they appeared at first sight.

There was one more sombre feature, however, of which Pitt was well aware. The past three years out of office had been relatively kind to his health; nevertheless it had not improved basically, it remained distinctly suspect, and the sudden relapses could be frightening when they occurred. There had been occasions when he had made diplomatic use of these facts.[4] But they could certainly not be dismissed, and the position was not encouraging now. His state in the spring gave some cause for worry: his appetite had gone, a racking cough persisted; and he was about to shoulder the burden once more, with no political elbow room. A heavy

---

1. Grenvillites in fact, grasping at all straws, formed the impression that virtually none of his friends approved; see Spencer and Minto to their wives, the first on 10, 17 May (B.L. Add. Ms temp Althorp G294), the second on 11 May 1804 (*Life and Letters of Elliot*, III, 394). But in point of fact some did so (*Rose*, II, 131); and apprehension of a weak Ministry seems to me to have been the central feature in many cases of the doubts.

2. Redesdale (formerly John Mitford, see p. 597, n8 above) to Speaker Abbot, 5 May 1804 (*Colchester*, I, 510).

3. Eg *Life of Wilberforce*, III, 160–1.

4. Pp. 508, n5, perhaps 627 and n4 above.

task lay ahead in the Commons, and it would fall at once almost wholly on himself. The experience of his youth would be largely repeated; but he was far from feeling youthful. When he remarked, on leaving the King, that he would teach Grenville a lesson, he added 'though he thought his health such that it might cost him his life'.[1]

The pattern of the Ministry was broadly predictable. Not surprisingly, an effort to recruit Moira, in the Carlton House group, failed to neutralise the Prince of Wales; and there was no escaping from the available area of choice.[2] Pitt managed to provide five members for the Cabinet, apart from himself, from his own resources. Melville, as expected, went to the Admiralty. Camden became Secretary of State for War and the Colonies. Lord Harrowby – an old friend as Dudley Ryder – moved into the Foreign Office. Mulgrave was made Chancellor of the Duchy of Lancaster; and the Duke of Montrose found himself President of the Board of Trade. Melville excepted, these were not politically resounding appointments, and in two cases they introduced little effective strength. Camden in fact was most reluctant, not unreasonably, to occupy his important post. He knew his limitations – he had been similarly unwilling to face the hazards of Ireland in 1795 – and it took pressure from his old mentor to induce him to accept.[3] Harrowby, though a second choice for his post – the first had been Moira[4] – was of higher calibre than his colleague, with respectable qualifications for his notable advance. He had indeed long been seen as a rising man, who might expect to profit further from the long friendship with Pitt – one of the companions in the early days at Wimbledon and Goostrees, his second in the duel with Tierney. A series of secondary posts had shown him to be business-like and well informed: a brief spell as an Under Secretary in the Foreign Office itself at the end of the eighties, then Vice President of the Board of Trade for over ten years and simultaneously Joint Paymaster General for nine, with a short time as Treasurer

1. Twiss, op. cit., I, 449. Cf. I, 131 for his position as sole Cabinet Minister in the Commons – one that continued in his first Ministry for five and a half years – with pp. 671–2 below. See p. 548 above for Hester Stanhope's uneasiness in April.

2. See *Rose*, II, 123, 128–9.

3. For his views on the role of a Secretary of State and his own insufficiency see a letter to Pitt, nd but almost certainly at this point, in Camden Ms U840 C209/3. The appointment was indeed greeted with general astonishment. There is a possibility however that it was intended as a temporary measure until an opening occurred for his return to Ireland: he certainly figured as Lord Lieutenant in a list by Pitt, nd but clearly relating to this period, of Cabinet and other Ministerial appointments (Dacres Adams Mss, formerly P.R.O. 30/58/8), and meanwhile, according to a recently influential Member for an Irish seat, he was to have 'the management of the Irish Members' at Westminster (William Wickham to Abbot, 24 May 1804; *Colchester*, I, 516–17). Whether Camden was aware of this forecast, I do not know.

See II, 439 for 1795, and p. 560 above for his deep feeling, indeed his sense of duty, towards Pitt.

4. Dacres Adams Mss, formerly P.R.O. 30/58/8.

of the Navy thereafter until Pitt's resignation, continuing in accordance with the latter's wishes under Addington though only for some months. These were valid recommendations. There were also drawbacks: a manner – rather buttoned up and sharp; '*missey*' one observer called it – which many people found unattractive, but which derived largely from the more serious handicap of constitutional ill health, dating from childhood in blinding headaches and indeed forcing his retirement from office in the autumn of 1801. In 1803 he had moved away altogether from Addington. 'At the top of the second-rate men' – so he was memorialised some forty years later – he was perhaps unlikely, as Pitt's third Foreign Secretary, to carry the weight of his predecessor Grenville, but was certainly superior to the first, Carmarthen, the aggrieved Duke of Leeds.[1]

These were Pitt's major appointments from his own quarter. Mulgrave and Montrose occupied lesser posts. Of slighter note in the political world, the former had proved intelligent and clear headed in his sphere. One of a set of competent brothers, a man of varied interests – achieving a notable collection of Old Master paintings, and befriending Haydon and Wilkie – he was above all a capable soldier who had shown a grasp in two important missions, and a talented debater on military affairs. He earned the respect of Grenville, as he did later of Wellington, and Pitt was accustomed to call on him at times for military advice.[2] As Chancellor of the Duchy – that convenient home for a range of purposes – he now brought an affectionate loyalty which had grown in the wartime years, and a prospect of useful aid at the middle level.[3] Montrose's inclusion pointed to other inducements. A friend, or perhaps in this instance a friendly acquaintance, possibly from Cambridge days, he had graced a junior Lordship at the Treasury for six years, been Joint Paymaster General with Ryder for nine, and known his new Department briefly as Vice President, in fact preceding Ryder there. He had also held a senior appointment at Court for five years as Master of the Horse, making way for Westmorland when the latter was found a place after leaving Ireland as Lord Lieutenant. While not devoid of parts – he was a ready and self-confident speaker, and does not seem to have been inept in his posts – he now met, at an awkward point, a further call of convenience. A peer of some note in Scotland, though without Parliamentary patronage and at times on prickly terms with Melville, and a devoted adherent of the King, he

1. *DNB*; *GEC*, VI; it was Glenbervie who described him as 'missey', and Grenville who judged him to have been at the top of the second-rate men. See also I, 108, 310; II, 465n2; p. 127 above. For Leeds's disappearance see II, 26.

2. *DNB*, *GEC*, IX. The missions were those of 1793 to Toulon and 1799 to Austrian headquarters; see II, 316–17, pp. 240–1 above.

3. He was indeed thought of at first for higher things, even an alternative choice to Moira – equally a soldier – as a Secretary of State in Pitt's undated list in p.669n.4 above.

brought that advantage and some 'acres' to Ministerial 'abilities' which were more pronounced elsewhere.[1]

This last indeed was quite as much to be seen in the recruits from the late Cabinet as among those now introduced. Pitt found himself obliged by his own scarcity to include more of the former than he would have wished, and furthermore in their former posts. Eldon continued as Lord Chancellor, Westmorland as Lord Privy Seal, Portland as Lord President of the Council, Chatham as Master General of the Ordnance, Castlereagh as President of the Board of Control. There was in fact only one change of office within the group. Hawkesbury, having proved perhaps surprisingly stiff in the face of Pitt's earlier political demands, and widely seen as unimpressive in his post, was moved, to his disappointment, from the Foreign to the Home Office.[2] Of course it would be unrealistic to divide the new Cabinet into two contrasting parts. Some at least of those now taken from Addington had once been urged by Pitt himself to support him, and in the past year most had been hoping in some degree or other for his own return.[3] But there was a distinction; and certainly their numbers would have been lower if the Grenvilles, let alone Fox, had joined. As it was, the balance in appointments was not uneven. Pitt brought with him five of the twelve members; more important, they provided two of the three Secretaries of State, and likewise the occupants of the two most important posts in running the war with himself.[4] In some

---

1. See I, 635 & n2 for the phrase of acres as applied to Pitt's first Ministry; *DNB* and *GEC*, IX for Montrose, and also his letter to Pitt of 14 May 1804 – and others of 21 and 24 November – (P.R.O. 30/8/160, Dacres Adams Mss formerly P.R.O. 30/58/5) for relations with Dundas. He had been at Trinity when Pitt was first at Pembroke although away in practice (see I, 12–13) for much of the time. Consenting at the Minister's plea to open a Great Office for Westmorland (see II, 421, 423), he can count as a 'political' Master of the Horse (McCahill, *Order and Equipoise*, 163n3). While he may be called a 'dignified' rather than 'effective' member of Cabinet by type, he seems to have been a sensible and not unaccomplished grandee.

The Duke became Joint Postmaster General at the same time (outside the Cabinet), displacing Auckland from the office he had secured from Pitt in 1798 and preserved under Addington in 1801. Although that assiduous man of affairs need not indeed have been surprised at his removal now after his conduct at that latter time (p. 518 above), he made a last effort to protect his finances, writing to the Minister, and also to George III in a letter which however only excited disgust (see *L.C.G. III*, IV, no. 2857). Pitt acted rather typically: he did not bother to answer Auckland, and obtained a pension for Lady Auckland (Stanhope, IV, 230–2). So far as he was concerned, the episode extinguished the final flicker of a long, at one point embarrassed, and increasingly unsatisfactory relationship.

2. Not all these men had held their recent posts unchanged throughout Addington's Ministry: Chatham had started as Lord President of the Council and Portland as Home Secretary. For Hawkesbury in the abortive exchanges between Pitt and Addington in May 1803 see p. 588 above. His performance at the Foreign Office, alluded to on p. 569, is assessed on pp. 693 below.

3. Cf. pp. 552–3, 638, 640 above.

4. As Rose remarked, Camden's appointment to the War Department was 'of mighty little consequence, as all that business will be done by [Pitt] himself' (to Tomline, 12 May 1804; Pretyman Ms T435/44).

respects moreover one might perhaps have expected less risk of strain than in a broader Ministry; the most potentially disruptive of issues, relief of the Irish Catholics, was unlikely to arise, and the size of the Cabinet was less unhandy than the alternative would almost certainly have been.[1] Nor was it indeed bereft of ability: Eldon was a powerful legal luminary, Castlereagh – though a poor speaker[2] – would grow into a notable Secretary for War and a great Foreign Secretary, Hawkesbury, already an efficient leader in the Lords,[3] was a future Prime Minister for an exceptionally long span, Melville could point to impressive experience in a prominent career. In many respects the available material did not suffer unduly by comparison, even if a 'Combined Administration' would, or should, have contained more obvious strength.

Pitt's 'Sketch . . . at the beginning of May'[4]		Cabinet as formed
'Mr Pitt	Treasury	Pitt
Lord Melville ⎫		Camden
Mr Fox ⎬	Secretaries of State	Harrowby
Ld Fitzwilliam ⎭		Hawkesbury
Ld Spencer	Admiralty	Melville
Ld Grenville	Ld President	Portland
D of Portland	Privy Seal	Westmorland
Lord Eldon	Ld Chancellor	Eldon
Ld Chatham	M. General of Ordnance	Chatham
Mr Windham	Chancellor of Duchy	Mulgrave
Ld Castlereagh	Board of Controll	Castlereagh
Ld Camden	Lord Steward	[see n4]
Ld Harrowby	Committee of Trade	Montrose
Mr Grey	Secy at War	[see n4 below]
Mr Canning	Secy to Ireland'	,,

The missing names were all too clear. Nonetheless, as a later Prime Minister observed, Pitt's second Cabinet contained two future heads of

1. See pp. 528–9, 619 above for the first, 320, n1, 454 below for the second.
2. See pp. 666–7 above for the implication for Pitt at this point.
3. Where he had been sent for that purpose, summoned by writ in his father's second title, in November 1803.
4. Stanhope, IV, frontispiece, for the 'sketch'. Cf. Pitt's 'nearly certain' list on 12 May (to Bathurst; B.L. Loan Ms 57, vol. 2; omitted from the letter as printed in *H.M.C., Bathurst*, 41–2). One may note the size of the Cabinet as considered in the former document: fifteen members – a figure itself not reached in the event until 1818 and paralleled thereafter on occasions in the twenties and early thirties – as compared with twelve in the Ministry as subsequently formed. Like other First Lords of the Treasury before and after him, Pitt disliked the idea of a large body; it would have been forced on him here in order to accommodate all the interests concerned. The process in fact would have involved some novel constitutional additions. There was a precedent for including the Secretary at War (see II, 411–12, 414) – designed here to meet the need for Grey (p. 659 above); but none for the

Government – and the Ministry as a whole a further two.[1] Some of the absent qualities moreover related above all to oratorical powers; a possible gauge but not a guarantee of executive weight. While the overall impression was disappointing, the greatest weakness at the start might indeed have been thought to lie in general in the Parliamentary sphere.

That fact was reflected in the process of filling all the places; for while this did not take unacceptably long – the Cabinet itself was completed within a week – the inherent difficulties were remarked almost at once.[2] They applied as fully to the junior as to the higher posts; some of Pitt's approaches there met with failure, and some with noticeably tardy success. A bid for tolerance from Carlton House had no more effect at this level than it had at Moira's, when Tierney at once refused an offer to remain Treasurer of the Navy.[3] Another cast in the same direction failed when the young Lord Henry Petty, a son of Lansdowne's and marked down in a list at this time, would not part from Fox.[4] Less predictably, old friends did not always respond as might have been hoped. Euston, who had advised against any alternative to a comprehensive Government, would not take office for that reason as Paymaster General or Master of the Mint. Bathurst likewise declined the latter post, though from genuine diffidence, before being persuaded to accept by a personal plea. Canning himself, held in mind for the Cabinet under a broad Ministry, refused at first to consider any post and left town to be out of the way, before yielding, like Camden and Bathurst, to a feeling of guilt. Personal jealousies played their part in this case, as of course so often in forming

---

Secretary to the Lord Lieutenant for Ireland – a device to find room for Canning when in London; while the Lord Steward, one of the Great Officers of State falling under the Court, was surprising indeed, an arrangement presumably intended to kill two birds by inserting another reliable Pittite into both places. The President of the Board of Control for India had already been included, for the first time, in 1801 – clearly to secure Castlereagh – and the office was retained thereafter in successive Cabinets until it was itself abolished in 1858.

One may note also in the same list, in terms of persons, that Grenville was not meant to go to the Foreign Office (cf. pp. 515, 587–8, 593 above); or Windham to an 'efficient' Department, even before Pitt heard the King's views (p. 657 above); or Westmorland to stay as Lord Privy Seal – which he did not only in the new Ministry but in every successor thereafter, with one brief exception, for a further twenty-one years. It may be seen in addition that under a broad Ministry Pitt might have had four Cabinet colleagues with him in the Commons, rather than the one – Castlereagh – whom he gained in the event.

1. Rosebery, *Pitt*, 247. Portland and Hawkesbury, Spencer Perceval and Canning respectively.

2. Eg *Malmesbury*, IV, 305 for 10 May. Perhaps the difficulties encouraged Pitt all the more to leave almost all of the survivors of the late Cabinet in their former posts. The rest of the arrangements, in the Departments and, more protractedly, at Court, were completed by the last week in the month.

3. For Moira see p. 669 above; for Tierney earlier, pp. 593, 610 and at this point *Rose*, II, 135.

4. See Stanhope, IV, 190; *H of P*, IV, 784. It might not have seemed a very hopeful prospect given Lansdowne's (Shelburne's) relations with Pitt (I, 88, II, 228, 390n6); but three seats in the Commons under his patronage could be at stake.

Administrations; the favoured disciple of earlier years found it hard to see Hawkesbury and Castlereagh confirmed at a level in which he would be on the fringe. But that was not the sole cause of trouble. Canning's consistent and vehement championship of a Pittite-Grenvillite Ministry, which in the past few months had brought him closer to Grenville himself, forced him to disapprove of what Pitt had done, and while he was induced to become Treasurer of the Navy he did so from loyalty alone.[1] His feelings were compounded moreover by the knowledge that two of his intimates took other paths. Granville Leveson Gower, once attached to Pitt likewise by 'political idolatry', and employed recently as the channel to Fox, was prepared, perhaps again partly for personal reasons – he was flirting half seriously with Hester Stanhope – to continue in support, but would not accept office; while another close friend, Lord Morpeth, also approached, would not go so far, and after almost a decade as a Pittite turned increasingly to Opposition.[2] Some others in broadly the younger generation felt much the same.[3] If a web of old ties had been loosened in the course of 1801, wider and, as it proved, deeper strains were experienced in May 1804.

Among his disappointments, Pitt might have felt this cooling or loss of promising younger men as keenly as that of more important persons. For they were the seed corn: the kind of adherents in whom he could take a hopeful interest, and find perhaps his keenest satisfaction. A leaven of youthful lieutenants and followers looking to his personal example, liberally minded, and some with the added advantage of inherited political connexions – these were congenial spirits, who could supply a distinctive flavour to the more widespread influence he might hope to exert and bequeath. It was a type with which he felt at home, among the various elements in his Parliamentary spectrum; pointing to the future, forming a hopeful object of patronage amid the rest. And now it was troubled and

1. For Euston (I, 17, 107, 150) see his letters to Pitt of 5 May and nd but 1804 (P.R.O. 30/8/133); for Bathurst, *H.M.C., Bathurst*, 41–2 and P.R.O. 30/8/112. Canning's feelings may be followed in Canning Mss 29d and 30, and P.R.O. 30/8/120.

2. Leveson Gower moreover represented more than himself, high though he stood in Canning's affections. As Stafford's son he had gained for his friend the social and political favour of a great family connexion. Morpeth for his part stemmed from one of the Old Whig clans, his father Carlisle, once a Northite in the Coalition with Fox and an active opponent of Pitt in the eighties, having moved with Portland in the following decade. Pitt now in fact sought his support, and gained it, without acceptance of office; the son however had links with the Devonshire House set which led him, as recent politics allowed, to harbour more kindly political views of Fox. For both Leveson Gower and Morpeth see *H of P*, IV, with pp. 658, n5–59 and n2 above additionally for the former, who in March 1804 had been able to claim that he was on 'intimate and confidential Terms' with Pitt (*Correspondence*, I, 456–7).

3. Eg J.W. Ward [the future first Earl of Dudley], who had 'admired Pitt's astonishing talents almost to enthusiasm' (though he had actually *seen* something of them only when his hero was out of office, having himself entered Parliament only in 1803 – cf. p. 604 and n3 above) but now deplored a preference, as he saw it, for 'office to real glory'. He soon joined Brooks's, and began to act with Opposition (*H of P*, V, 478).

becoming divided as it had not been significantly hitherto. A certain strand was weakened in the pattern of attitudes which had together made up the fabric of his support; rather, if more narrowly by the nature of the case, as the Dissenting interest had been weakened more than a decade before.[1] And this emerging and sometimes sharp sense of division could not be limited to such men alone; it was likely to affect a range of opinion, in and out of doors, hitherto sympathetic and still largely regretful, which in the event hardened and became firmly set. Such a response was not clearly predominant: Pitt was largely given the benefit of doubts and acknowledged to be doing his best, in a situation in which his presence was widely sought. Nor did the effects seem at once pre-ordained. As had been seen in the past few years, politics could take its twists and turns, and his current line of action did not necessarily dictate his future: he intended indeed to recruit co-operation in the summer,[2] and who could yet tell from which parts of the House that might come? But, immediately at least, important dividing lines had been marked out and others sketched; and in the event the combination of decisions at this point proved to have a lasting effect.

For Pitt's acceptance of the King's refusal of Fox for the Cabinet, and his construction of a Government including 'so singular a gang',[3] left an impression which, by its finality as matters turned out, would not be effaced. It would in fact endure in what remained of his life, and help shape a subsequent verdict. The occasion indeed was of distinct importance in the process of assigning a retrospective label to a career which hitherto had not been so open to such treatment. There had arguably been room in his conduct and policies over the past two decades to pin on them a broad designation of party whose own revival had not yet taken place. Signs of such a generalised emergence in usage, bequeathed in particular by the subterranean relics of Toryism, were certainly apparent, and becoming more articulate from the 1790s.[4] But if there was a trend it was colloquial and uneven, and more common in a public than a Parliamentary connotation; and a distinction can be drawn between the two. The term Tory, as a definite ascription in the latter setting, would have seemed quite inapposite at the time. Politicians of differing descriptions had shared or been divided irregularly in their attitudes to many of the most prominent questions of recent years: on Parliamentary reform (where Fox himself was lukewarm), on the repeal of the Toleration Acts, the successive measures against discontent and subversion, possible measures of Irish Catholic relief. One has only to recall who agreed with

1. See II, Ch. III, section II.
2. P 667 above.
3. J.W. Ward again (*Letters to Ivy from the First Earl of Dudley*, ed. Samuel Henry Romilly (1905), 23, for 18 May 1804). And cf. from a more important and different quarter, reflecting on the disappointment at that time, Viscount Lowther to Camden, 30 January 1805 (Camden Ms U840 C244/3).
4. This is picked up, again briefly, on pp. 837–8 below.

whom when, and the contexts in which they moved, to see why later nomenclature was not then applied; that was done, with growing confidence, in the decades after Pitt's death. But while such issues would be called on in the nineteenth century to define a fundamental development, in the contemporary Parliamentary context it was not so much they themselves as the way in which he formed his second Ministry, associating him at a critical moment with Eldon and Hawkesbury (Liverpool) and Castlereagh, the ogres of ensuing Whig and Liberal tradition, that would cast him as a Tory. Other major questions could then be brought into play to assess the aims and assumptions of his wartime 'Tory Ministries'. But it was the question of his relationship with the royal prerogative, particularly in the area of Ministerial appointments, revived from the case of 1783 to be concentrated on the manner and effects of his return in 1804 after an interval which seemed likely at moments to produce a very different answer – it was this great matter of traditional central concern that provided one of the keys to the development in terminology and groupings which marked the early decades of the nineteenth century.

II

And now it was time to pick up the threads. The incoming Minister had to reacquaint himself with the diplomatic despatches, to work with the benefit of official knowledge on the problems of naval and military strength, to review and forward the provision for a war which, like 'All modern Wars', was seen from London as centring on 'a Contention of Purse'.[1] This last task, of immediate importance at such a stage in the Parliamentary session, was already conditioned in point of fact to a considerable extent. Addington had taken care, like Pitt in 1801, to introduce his budget before he resigned;[2] and there were sufficient reasons for Pitt now to continue broadly on the lines laid down. Any major departure, if desired, would have to be taken swiftly, indeed hurriedly; and the new political balance might pose dangers if a challenge were then to emerge. This could happen if taxes were raised sharply above what was already proposed; and while trouble otherwise might seem unlikely – for the House respected his mastery of figures, and was seldom roused dangerously by budgetary detail[3] – the comfort, internal as well as external, of a new uneasy Administration should be protected as far as possible at the start. Nor indeed was there an unavoidable obligation to do anything drastic at once. Pitt had called for a change of Government in order to achieve 'exceedingly strong measures', and confront 'great and heavy

1. See II, 412.
2. Pp. 523, 653 above.
3. Cf. I, 279.

burdens' as the war went on.[1] But despite an attack on some of its aspects he had largely approved the first wartime budget, and where he had not it had largely been revised;[2] and he scarcely had time at this point to relate Addington's estimate for existing requirements to a provision for others which he himself might find desirable but had not yet reviewed.

The financial situation indeed was not unhealthy after a year of limited war.[3] The renewal of hostilities had naturally demanded fresh supplies, and a second budget for the year followed in June 1803. Its predecessor, introduced six months before, had been much reduced from that for 1802, the anticipated first full year of peace but still heavily burdened with expenses in the run-down from the late war. The estimates for the armed forces themselves had dropped accordingly to £14,957,000 from £26,685,000, out of totals for expenditure of £22,826,000 and £41,169,000 respectively.[4] That process was reversed, in the new circumstances, to a figure for the armed forces of £23,055,000 out of a total of £33,701,000; itself some 10 per cent below the average level of estimates in the last three years of the Revolutionary War.[5] The demand must be met as usual from higher taxes together with bills of credit and loans, and Addington followed Pitt's principle in the later nineties of seeking as large a proportion from taxation as he thought that Parliament would bear. He legislated in the first place for an increase of £3 million to be found in the traditional form from consumption[6] – a not inconsiderable demand, since in 1802 he had already raised an extra £4 million to help service repayment of accumulated debts. The fresh addition was to come from customs and excise duties, which were now allotted in intention to a new class of 'War Taxes'. But that same category included further revenue to be found, less traditionally in form, elsewhere: from a 'Property Tax', expected to produce £4½ million for the rest of the financial year, a sum which would account for just under 8 per cent of the total supplies.[7]

1. P. 594 above for March 1803; 654 for May 1804. The context, as phrased for the latter remark in particular, was clearly in large part financial.

2. Detail is given on pp. 679–80 below.

3. Cf. pp. 609–10 above.

4. Figures to the nearest thousand pounds throughout. See Cooper, 'British Government Finance, 1793–1807', 396–9, which amplifies and refines the statement as presented in *P.R.*, *3rd ser.*, XVII, 413–14, and *4th ser.*, I, 328–9. For second budgets in the later nineties see II, 517; on this occasion there was certainly no choice.

The Estimates for the separate forces were not so constructed as to cover other budgetary items relating to additional expenditure incurred largely on the same behalf in the past, above all through the servicing of funded and unfunded debt.

5. Cooper, loc. cit., 400–2, which is to be preferred for detail to the statement in *P.R.*, *4th ser.*, III, 568. The average for 1799–1801 takes account of a comparison of two budgets in 1799; the figures for the three years on that basis are £37,015,000 and £37,587,000 respectively.

6. See I, 248, II, 521.

7. Estimated at £33,990,000 with which to meet the expenditure given above.

An understanding of the budgetary presentation in June 1803 is complicated by the fact that in 1802 Addington had consolidated the stamp duties and assessed taxes with the

In the winter of 1803–4 receipts from customs and excise were said to be coming in well.[1] But the Property Tax could not be gathered continuously in that way; and the figure estimated for it moreover could hardly be more than a broad prognosis. Nor was this surprising. For in its purpose new Property Tax was old Income Tax writ large;[2] and experience of Pitt's forerunners, so highly suspect in 1799 and 1800, could not but leave doubts of the prospective success of collection. If however the major disadvantage could be significantly reduced, such a type of direct levy might account for a larger share of the supplies than the immediate projected percentage might suggest.[3] The Treasury had learned some lessons from the initial administrative mistakes, and the political hostility, if still deep, might at any rate prove less obtrusive at a point when Napoleon excited an even deeper feeling.[4] A measure therefore was introduced which sought to improve on Pitt's model, reducing the latter's rate of levy from 10 to 5 per cent at the higher levels but offsetting the effect by one innovation harking back in fact to the now defunct Land Tax, that once central element of direct taxation itself introduced by war, which persisted through the eighteenth century until the Income Tax was developed at the close. The arrangement proposed was for 'taxation' – assessment and collection – 'at the source', ensuring that a person receiving income from property would do so with his proportion for payment already deducted.[5] This would not affect every one subject to a levy – a fact to be borne in mind in judging some of the claims made later for its importance –, since a probable majority of those concerned were self-employed (many farmers, small

---

customs and excise duties: a useful move which took Pitt's peacetime remodelling of the revenue a step farther. When however he designated these last two duties as 'War' rather than 'Permanent' taxes (for which see I, 240), it meant that they could not be shown in the budget under the latter heading, while the fact that their produce was paid into an extended Consolidated Fund (for which initially see I, 270–2) confined the sum *shown* under War Taxes to the produce expected from the so-called Property Tax. Although the total revenue expected from customs and excise was estimated at £8 million this did not in fact appear at all, directly, in the budget statement itself, though it was listed indirectly in the Ways and Means (see for the consolidation A. Farnsworth, *Addington Author of the Modern Income Tax* (1951), 37, 50, and for the budget statement Cooper, loc. cit., 282, 400–1).

1. Nicholas Vansittart [see p. 570, n2 above] to Addington, 9 January [1804]; quoted by Cooper, loc. cit., 288–9.

2. Though the latter title, visible in conjunction with that of Property at an earlier stage, disappeared in the Act itself (43 Geo. III, c122); see Farnsworth, op. cit., 57–61. The measure was in fact broadly known as the Property Act during its lifetime and thereafter until Peel secured his Act for the Income Tax in 1842 (for which see p. 263 above).

It was a coincidence that the property tax of 1990 bore the same name; the general designation of poll tax was in fact accurate.

3. Cf. pp. 265, and for Pitt's tax in general 259–68 above.

4. As Addington recognised in a 'memoir of finance' written in June 1803 (Sidmouth Ms 152M/C1803/OT29).

5. Farnsworth (op. cit., 42–7) lays particularly stress on the Minister's consultation of the early Land Tax statues. The relevant provisions here were sections VI and XIII in W & M, c1 of 1692. Cf., for Pitt, p. 106 above.

entrepreneurs in trades and manufactures) who continued to pay their taxes in the same manner as before.[1] Nonetheless the design had two important advantages. It did much to reduce the evasion allowed by Pitt's care for the basic objection to his tax, which he himself well understood: a concern for the privacy of information on wealth which Government had felt obliged to invade. But at the same time the new method tended itself to underwrite that privacy, since it could at least be claimed that 'publicity of Income' was 'precluded' by the lack of need for a detailed return.[2] The last consideration was not in fact true in every respect, for Addington, intent on increasing the yield of his tax by assessment at source in all of its schedules, arranged for income from the Funds – from Government stocks – to be reported separately, thus disclosing its origin. This was indeed an aspect of the measure that was opposed by Pitt, who would have preferred inclusion as before in one comprehensive statement; but the Minister carried the day, though only when the Commons in this instance set the threshold of tax higher than he would have wished.[3]

Pitt's objections however were not confined to that point, and the Treasury in point of fact may have been the less disposed to yield it because he was contesting others at the same time. His attack indeed embraced not only the production of a separate schedule for the Funds but their inclusion in the method of collection at source itself. If that was to be done it would involve a breach of the contract made by Government with fund holders in raising a Loan; for since the interest was always to be disbursed 'without any deduction whatever' in advance, that stipulation would be 'violated' if part was withheld for tax when the dividends were paid to the Bank of England. The argument, aimed at the need to retain the confidence of the creditor, particularly at the start of a new war, was mounted vigorously enough for the proposal to be dropped.[4] And the same fate met a further clause at which he likewise protested: to exclude exemptions and abatements for unearned income in the form of dividends and interest, though such relief was to be allowed for income earned by 'personal industry'. 'It was a fundamental principle that a tax on income should be equal and general' in type, and this differentiation moreover could bear on the ways in which capital might be deployed – not by any means only in large amounts –, thereby discriminating against enterprise and also against support of the stocks. The need for confidence was thus again invoked to reinforce a

1. See O'Brien, 'Government Revenue, 1793–1815', 416–17.

2. Cf. Addington's speech of 5 July (*P.R.*, *4th ser.*, III, 710) with a later memorandum in his papers, attributed to 1806 or 1807 though catalogued under 1802 (Sidmouth Ms 152M/C1802/OT14).

3. See Pitt's speech of 13 July in *The Times*, 14 July 1803 (with which cf. *P.H.*, XXXVI, cols. 1664–7), in the absence of a proper report in *P.R.*, *4th ser.*, III, 740–1; Addington's budget speech of 30 April 1804 (*P.D.*, II, 347).

4. *The Times*, 14 July 1803, for Pitt's speech. In the ensuing Act, however, provision was made for stockholders to pay their tax direct to the Bank once the dividend was received (43 Geo. III, c122, section LXX), and following Pitt's death the original proposal was reintroduced and passed (46 Geo. III, c65, section CIV *et seq.*).

matter of principle; and although the Ministry could claim that its provision was still lessening a burden on the rewards of labour and Addington indeed achieved an easy majority here in the debate, he was not prepared to make an issue of the question if that might delay the measure as a whole, and reliefs were accordingly applied across the board.[1] The episode reflected the Minister's continuing apprehension of Pitt, despite the recent outcome in the affair of Patten's motion;[2] and the concession struck – he himself thought by about a quarter – at the yield intended from the tax. Even so, the initial target proved not inaccurate, and the result in the end was on the right side. Against the estimate of £4,500,000, a sum probably of £4,6–800,000 was received in due course, though slowly and erratically, for the period from June 1803 to April 1804.[3]

Encouraged perhaps, despite the lags, by returns that began to grow as he prepared his next budget, Addington repeated these provisions for the Property Tax in 1804. Had he been sure of continuing safely in office he might have proposed some amendments, including perhaps a renewed attempt to levy income from the Funds at source.[4] As it was, he left matters where they stood; increased his other 'War Taxes' of customs and excise by £1 million; and sought a Loan of £10 million as in the previous year. The estimates for the armed forces, after twelve months of war, were placed – belatedly in Pitt's view[5] – at some £34,900,000, with total expenditure at £38,700,000: a figure to be countered by supplies of £41,200,000 – an almost exact return on both sides of the ledger to the budget of 1802, but with a halving of the Loan set then and reliance on a surplus from 1803 expected to be gained by a higher yield from the consolidation of taxes.[6] Pitt therefore inherited a forecast of adequate resources

---

1. For Pitt see *The Times*, 14 July 1803. The majority was 150–50. Addington's attitude was noted by Speaker Abbot on that day (*Colchester*, I, 432).

2. See p. 606 above.

3. For Addington's estimate of the effect of the amendments see *P.D.*, II, cols. 347–8. Only some £363,000 was actually paid in for the tax by 5 April 1804 (see Cooper, loc. cit., 404), but under the method of deduction at source it was then known pretty well what would be coming. Nevertheless the final amount received for the period was given variously over the next three years, not surprisingly in view of the late introduction of the first wartime budget, the business of assessment and collection under new legislation, and the consequent allocation of arrears between two financial years. Figures ranged from £4,800,000 in a report based on still incomplete returns in the spring of 1804, to one of £4,600,000 by Pitt in February 1805, to £4,692,000 and £4,761,000 both in 1806 (see Farnsworth, op. cit., 91–2). The report of the Royal Commission on Income Tax in 1919 put the sum at £4,900,000 (Mitchell & Deane, op. cit., ch. XIV, table 16). All these are net; gross figures for 1803 were given in the Finance Accounts published in the Parliamentary Sessional Papers of 1868–9 (see Mitchell & Deane, op. cit., ch. XIV, table 3).

4. Farnsworth, op. cit., 97, citing a memorandum in Addington's papers of 21 April 1804, and cf. p. 679 and see n4 above. See pp. 638–40 above for the political situation in the second half of the month.

5. Cf. pp. 635–6 above; and see *Rose*, II, 13–14.

6. Cooper, loc. cit., 403–4, 396 respectively. See loc. cit., 285, and see p. 677, n7 above for the consolidation of 1802.

for a year of greater if still limited effort. He contented himself with tidying up some residual awkwardnesses: clearing off civil list debt and providing for future revenue, ironing out some impracticalities in the consolidation of stamp duties and increasing the yield, and securing a higher Vote of Credit (£3.3 as against £2.5 million) designed largely to meet past deficiencies some affecting estimates in the budget itself.[1]

The Property Tax proved increasingly remunerative over the rest of its life. After a continued slowish spell in 1805–6, with some £4.6 million collected in the latter year, its produce reached £10.2 million in 1808, £12.4 million in 1810, and £14.5 million in the year of Waterloo. The levy's proportion of the aggregate gross yield from taxation also rose, from perhaps some 9 per cent in 1806 to around 20 per cent in 1815.[2] Useful from the start, by the end of the Napoleonic War it was rivalling the customs duties as a contribution to a source of supply, from taxes as a whole, which was meeting at least 65 per cent of gross expenditure.[3] Of comparable significance for a more distant future, its regulations offered a model for Peel's measure in the forties, itself recognised as a basis for its successors into our own time.

Given this posterity we should consider a little further the connexion between Pitt's and Addington's measures. Was the latter so profound a transformation of the former as to make its protagonist – as has been argued – the real 'author of the modern income tax'?[4] That of course is to assume that the man responsible for the design was in fact Addington himself. Pitt, initially neutral, had by then come to hold a low view of his successor's financial capacity: when his anger was first roused at the turn of 1802–3, and he lectured the Minister on the error of his ways, he gained the impression that – seemingly unlike the Secretary of the Treasury, Vansittart – Addington understood so little that he could not take in the points.[5] Preparation of the new tax was of course bound to

1. Cooper, loc. cit., 294–5; *P.D.*, II, cols. 921–2, 937–9, 960–4.
2. Mitchell & Deane, op. cit., ch. XIV, table 3 – with n(a) – where the aggregates for 1806 and 1815 are given as £51.1 and £73.9 million after deducting from 'total gross income' some £2.9 and £4 million respectively for revenues from the Post Office and the Lottery. But cf. O'Brien, 'Government Revenue, 1793–1815', 9, table 4, which gives a slightly lower figure for 1806 and one of £69.7 million for 1815 with an addition of £6.2 million of 'other revenue'. Figures of collection can themselves be difficult: sources close to the time in the annual House of Commons' *Accounts and Papers* gave a gross collection for the Property Tax in 1806 of £6.2 million and in 1815 of £15 million (see O'Brien, loc. cit., 422, table 10).
Revenue continued to come in from the tax after 1816, the final £0.2 million in 1820 (Mitchell & Deane, op. cit., ch. XIV, table 3). But that was a run-down from sums due.
3. Cf. op. cit., ch. XIV, tables 3, 4, giving gross expenditure in 1815 as £112.9 million, with O'Brien, loc. cit., 532, table 38 for a figure of £107.8 million.
4. See the title of Farnsworth's book, p. 677, n7 above. He points for support to expressions from Gladstone (op. cit., 131) and the Royal Commission of 1919 on the Income Tax (132–3).
5. *Rose*, II, 23, and cf. op. cit., I, 517–18.

involve the experts: Vansittart himself certainly consulted one outside source, a well known writer on the income tax, Henry Beeke, who was already concentrating on the subject of collection; and material from officials, within the tax system and the Treasury, was doubtless to hand as it had been for Pitt.[1] Normal processes would be followed. The Treasury Secretary however later declared that Addington set out in person to 'remodel' the earlier tax 'entirely'; and the Minister for his part took pride in stressing that his scheme was not merely an older one 'revived'. He looked on it as a true variant, a true 'property and income tax', whose detail – always critical in financial measures – was treated in a newly effective way.[2] He took time to study precedents and analogies, and certainly gave the scheme the impetus required. If he has been reasonably blamed as a Chancellor for technical shortcomings, some evident only after his fall, he might be allowed a due proportion of the credit in an instance of success.

The question remains how far this single main innovation changed the nature of the tax itself. There are caveats to be offered to the more extreme claims. A good deal of the effects of improvement may be allowed to administrative experience at large; and the numerical limits to those principally affected by the method should be borne in mind.[3] Taxation at source proved fallible in its early days, as collection of the Income Tax had done before its operations had been brought to a close. Time was needed in both cases. Nevertheless, from the stance of someone looking to the past in 1803, there was also need for an initiative if the yield was to match the intention and vindicate the earlier political risk. Addington took the step. Beyond that, Pitt had already put the principles in place, and in a comprehensive and enduring combination. There was now the precedent of a direct levy on income, earned and unearned; of one single tax which included the assessments and abatements in a series of 'cases' or schedules;[4] of rates which were progressive, graduated along the scale. These were firm foundations, laid – as Addington could hardly

1. Beeke to Vansittart, 6 April 1804 (B.L. Add. Ms 31229); and see *DNB*. Appointed regius professor of modern history at Oxford in 1801, he had earlier published a work on Pitt's tax which earned praise from McCulloch in due course. Vansittart consulted him on financial questions in general, and he has indeed been said (*DNB*) to have suggested the idea of an income tax to Pitt. Perhaps he did, though there is no sign of it in Pitt's papers – not that that is conclusive; but in any case, as Stanhope pointed out (III, 164–5), others – 'speculative financiers and writers of pamphlets' – had done the same. The official processes in 1803 could probably repay closer study. For material provided by Tax Commissioners in 1799–1800 cf. pp. 266–7 above.

2. Cf. p. 678 and n2 above for title; Sidmouth Ms 152M/C1803/OT29 for Addington's claim.

3. See pp. 678–9 above.

4. Farnsworth (op. cit., ch. 4) lays stress on Addington's 'schedules' of 1803, which in point of fact comprised an amended version of Pitt's 'classes' of 1799. The difference lay rather in the assessment at source for each class of schedule distinct from the rest, which Addington contrasted with Pitt's 'general assessment' of aggregate income after report.

have done – in the face of great reluctance and, as it emerged, limited consent. They encompassed and made conceivable the base on which the frame of further method could be built. As Addington stated, his design 'hinged' on 'the same principles' as Pitt's; as Pitt himself would show, Addington's mode of assessment and collection had come to stay.[1] The two contributions were not on a par. The first was fundamental, the second an improvement. Together they provided continuity in a concept that accommodated future needs by advances which proved containable within the concept itself.

Such a benign perspective, assigning complementary roles, might not have gratified either party at the time. Addington was anxious to stake his claim as a financier, while Pitt now placed little faith in his successor's grasp. Although indeed he was said to have been given the gist of the budget's contents in advance, and approved the purport of the new tax – the Grenvilles believed at first that he would support both throughout –, he was ready enough to show his feelings when he had studied all the small print.[2] The impact was felt in Addington's withdrawal of some of his pro-posals in order to forestall a fight.[3] But trouble was not in fact to be avoided later, for not all Ministerialists were prepared to turn the cheek after the recent differences between the two men. The pamphlet war which began in the later summer centred on Pitt's political demands in the spring;[4] but it included allegations and claims over the respective financial performances, not least on income tax – a fact which fostered Pittite suspicions of Vansittart's involvement in the opening move. It was understandable that the subject of finance – the one that first turned Pitt's rising doubts into hostility[5] – should have become embroiled in the more dramatic contentions over acceptance of office. On a longer view, the points of disagreement over the Property Tax itself do not bulk so large in a process which would prove as potent in tapping sources of cash as the foundation of the Bank of England in King William's war had proved for access to public credit.

1. Op cit., 59 for Addington and cf., in friendlier terms, *P.R., 3rd ser.*, XVII, 416; pp. 686–7 below for Pitt.

2. P. 677 above. He received 'a general account from . . . a Cursory View' of the supplies three days in advance, from Steele presumably by permission (Pitt to Rose, 12 June 1803, B.L. Add. Ms 42722; and cf. *Colchester*, I, 427), and approved 'the Principle' of the taxes including 'the Income Tax' – though he thought the forecast of their produce 'in some Instances . . . very questionable'. His 'object' would therefore be 'to endeavour to smooth as much as possible all Difficulties of Detail'. When he failed to do so a month later in the debate on the bill for the Property Tax, and was criticised for his attitude, he countered with the argument that he had informed Addington of his reasons as soon as he was shown the measure itself, again in advance, and had thus had the chance to study detail at the proper stage (see *P.R., 4th ser.*, III, 741–2). For Grenvillite opinion at the start see Thomas Grenville to Grenville, 16 June 1803 (*H.M.C., Dropmore*, VII, 170–1), same to Spencer, 14, 18 June 1803 (B.L. Add. Ms temp. Althorp G51).

3. Cf. pp. 679–80 above.
4. See pp. 621–2, 583–91, above.
5. See p. 579, n3 above.

In introducing his first wartime budget Addington had repeated a truism: however much was raised within the year it could not hope to meet expenditure, and 'a very considerable amount' of money would remain to be raised by loans. The level of naval and military activity had enabled him so far to moderate the extent; but he could hardly expect – though he showed a sign of doing so – that such a state of affairs might persist.[1] The Loan for 1802 had been set at £23 million, none had been included in the first budget for 1803, one for £10 million in the second, and that figure was repeated for 1804. Pitt let it stand as announced, and stock was issued in the 3 per cents.[2] At the same time he took steps to satisfy an old obligation to subscribers in an earlier loan: the Loyalty Loan of 1796, whose scrip had soon sunk to a discount but was due to be repaid at par or converted into different stock. This last would place a charge on the Consolidated Fund of about £1.5 million, which would have to be met by further taxation; though in the event that was delayed, in a settlement of conversion, to the following year. Otherwise his borrowing was to be by means of Exchequer bills against the enlarged Vote of Credit intended to meet the past deficiencies and provide some £1.3 million of additional cover.[3]

In the event some £19.1 million of these bills was issued in 1804; not as large a figure as in 1801–2 or 1805–6, but one that would have seemed dangerously high in the first half of the previous war. Together indeed with other short-term bills and debentures, a total of £26.7 million of unfunded Government paper was placed on the market in the course of that year.[4] The process continued to fuel the wider dispute over the enlarged circulation of paper money which was developing significantly in this decade; and perhaps with sharper focus from the history of this particular Chancellor of the Exchequer. After all, he had set his face long ago against an accumulation of floating debt, and had castigated Addington only twenty months earlier for authorising an unusually large tranche of Exchequer bills. Rose himself sounded a note of reluctance in conforming to the issue now.[5] Two considerations however may be borne

---

1. Cf. his speeches of 13 June 1803 and 30 April 1804 (*P.R.*, *4th ser.*, III, 575, 577; *P.D.*, II, col. 356); and see pp. 609–10 above for strategic conditions in 1803. Pitt himself of course had underestimated the rising cost of the Revolutionary War, at least for some years. He had however learned his lesson by the later nineties, and was far from underrating Napoleon now.

2. For which see II, 522–3. Cf. p. 269 above.

3. See II, 639–41 for the Loyalty Loan and its aftermath, and *P.D.*, II, cols, 258–60, 971–6, *Colchester*, I, 524–5, *P.D.*, III (1805), cols. 549–50 for Pitt's approach and eventual settlement by conversion from 5 per cent to, once again, a 3 per cent stock; p. 681 above for the Vote of Credit and past deficiencies.

4. O'Brien, loc. cit., 494–5, tables 15, 16; and cf. p. 272 above. The largest element apart from Exchequer bills was £4 million in Navy bills.

5. See pp. 272–5 above for the growth of public discussion on monetary and banking practice and theory; Rose to Pitt, 21 June [1804] (P.R.O. 30/8/173) for Pitt's complaint of Addington's issue.

in mind. Pitt's wrath at the end of 1802 was aroused largely because his successor was taking this line in a period – if uncertain – of peace; for the two men had agreed that the supreme priority in peacetime lay in funding, to reduce the National Debt. It was war that imposed a recourse to further 'extraordinary' supplies. And in those circumstances – the second point – the intellectual climate was in a state of change. For experience from the last conflict could now be held to allow a more flexible approach; a larger element of unfunded debt was admitted, at least by the managers, to greater respectability. The crisis of 1797 proved a turning point in the treatment of the money supply, and if some Exchequer bills 'ought not', as Pitt argued, 'to be considered as currency',[1] borrowing by Government reflected an opinion now evident equally within the Bank of England, that wartime finance need not be conducted so strictly under the former constraints. An expanded economy – as Addington had claimed indeed in his own peacetime defence – could absorb a proportionately greater amount of short-term obligations; and the premium on Exchequer and Navy bills that persisted largely between 1798 and 1804, surviving variations in circumstances including a downturn in the foreign rate of exchange, certainly showed a revival in their popularity.[2] Increasingly large issues during the Napoleonic War marked the extents to which Government was prepared to go; as discounts, succeeding premiums, suggested the shifts to which it could be put. But skills were not wanting in managing the operations, interest rates did not rise beyond those of the later 1790s, and in the time remaining to him Pitt continued on a path which was followed by later Chancellors until 1815.[3]

The growing use of unfunded instruments did not mean an abandonment of funded debt. Neither Addington nor Pitt wished to issue more in new bills than they redeemed in old;[4] and beyond that lay the wartime annual budgetary loans which, if low in 1804 from an optimistic forecast of expenditure, maintained a policy confirmed the year before. Addington in fact had then revived the 1 per cent Sinking Fund to redeem new debt, which he had abolished in the brief full year of peace.[5] But a sharper test came for Pitt himself in his budget of February 1805. For by then the situation was changing. Spending on the armed forces had exceeded the estimate of April 1804, and the new allocations amounted to some £39,550,000. A further £9½ million was tabled to meet inherited

1. Speech of 27 November 1800 (*P.R., 3rd ser.*, XIII, 301). He was referring to those of longer date.

2. O'Brien, loc. cit., 507, table 21, 528, table 34. In March 1806 Huskisson, recently retired as joint Secretary of the Treasury, told the new Chancellor Lord Henry Petty that Exchequer bills had proved popular with the market in recent years (cited loc. cit., 148). See p. 579, n3 above for Addington's defence against Pitt.

3. O'Brien, loc. cit., 495, table 16, 505, table 20.

4. Mitchell & Deane, op. cit., ch. XIV, table 6.

5. Cf. I, 268, where the penultimate line of para. 2 should read 'almost unaltered'. See p. 680 above for his forecast of expenditure, made in 1804.

deficiencies (once more) and past obligations, plus – a fresh element in the calculations – possible payments to the tune of £5 million to potential allies. This made a total of some £49,100,000, for which ways and means were estimated to produce a surplus of some £302,000. But that figure was reached by allowing for a Loan of £20 million; twice the size of that for the previous year.[1] The sum – scarcely surprising when expenditure was higher and revenue lower than expected, and Pitt was hoping to support a more active war – involved funding on the usual lines, which meant higher taxation to service the interest. So too did a change in procedure, replacing the normal Vote of Credit by including a contingency sum for the army within its own Vote – which itself would be met by funding and thus avoid a greater issue of Exchequer bills.[2]

The familiar combination of means – of taxation and loans – therefore held good, and the taxes themselves were of the familiar kind. The load was widely distributed: postal charges were to rise, as were taxes on salt and on horses, those on legacies were extended, the rate of Property Tax was increased. Unusually however for Pitt's fiscal proposals – the Income Tax had been a great exception to what was by then virtually a rule – some recalcitrance was shown in the Commons: the higher tax on farm horses (about 60 per cent) was rejected in a thin House, and that on salt for export had to be modified. The resulting loss of revenue, put at £405,000, was made good by a string of heterogeneous increases, hurriedly advanced since time did not permit of 'a distinct plan'.[3] The episode was not particularly important. But it furnished a commentary: on the Minister's recourse to a wide range of sources thinly spread in a long-favoured pattern; and on the political circumstances early in 1805, which could allow a rebuff, if less serious, of a kind recalling youthful setbacks twenty years before.[4]

Embarking on the finance of his second major war, Pitt kept in place the design inherited from his own past.[5] The budget of 1805 repeated in essence those spanning the turn of the century, when the treatment of funded and unfunded debt, of direct and indirect taxation, had assumed the shape and broadly the proportions it would thenceforward retain.

1. See Cooper, loc. cit., 405–6, and also 305–8. The deficiencies on revenue as given in the budget of 1804 included £2,800,000 on the Consolidated Fund and an amount, hard to state precisely from budgetary accounting practice in 1803 and a continuing slow pace of collection in the first two years, which had still not been received in Property Tax. The obligations were the £1½ million on the Voluntary Contribution (see pp. 107–8 above) and £1 million to the East India Company. Foreign affairs and strategy are discussed in section III below and Ch XX, section I.

2. Cooper, loc. cit., 310, citing Huskisson's memorandum of 8 March 1806 (p. 685, n2 above). Votes of Credit were reintroduced following Pitt's death.

3. Loc. cit., 309–10, 314–15. The quotation is from Pitt (speech of 22 March 1805; *P.D.*, IV (1805), col. 86). His defeat on the horse duty was by 76 to 73 (*P.D.*, III, col. 863).

4. Cf. I, 248–56, II, 521 for the earlier pattern; I, 251–4 for the rebuffs. The political scene early in 1805 is sketched in Ch. XX, section II.

5. For what follows cf. Ch. IX and in particular pp. 275–6 above.

The Sinking Fund continue to fill its role of supporting confidence by substituting terminable annuities for undated debt. Short-term bills could be employed more effectively to anticipate revenue, given the more sophisticated attitude to the money supply that emerged from the crisis of 1797. The Income Tax had come to stay as a wartime measure after its initial traumatic reception, and now in a form, as he tacitly acknowledged by continuing its recent method of collection, that would prove much better adapted to the task. The capacity of taxation to help meet costs within the year beyond the servicing of funded borrowing had thereby, potentially at least, been notably advanced. The management of debt – the operations on the market – had gained from experience; Pitt indeed was able to secure better terms for his larger Loan in 1805 than those of the year before, and over a long period the Treasury's tactics developed to meet demands on an ever rising scale.[1] The change of Chancellor was signalled by some useful tidying up, and then by provision for prospective allies. But not by a change of direction; no major innovation was introduced. Pitt himself would doubtless have faced growing pressures, political and personal, which did not encourage further initiatives or perhaps an expenditure of energy on business which was not compelling. But in any case that last was not called for here; the requirement was rather to monitor the performance of a system whose shape was already set. For the guiding lines had been laid earlier. They had not altered in the interval of the past three years. And they would in fact be followed intrinsically by other Chancellors over a further decade.

III

When the returning Minister took stock of foreign affairs he had one specific direction in which to move. As soon as war was declared – indeed during its approach – British policy returned to the aim of the previous conflict: the establishment of Continental partnerships, whether bilaterally or, in the case of the relevant most important Powers, by a single Alliance into which others might be drawn. The core of any such combination would be, as before, Russia and Austria and Prussia; and there was also a legacy here of a preferred approach. In the British view the best basis for any such treaty would be an agreed plan on the territorial future: the likeliest change of common action in war would be gained by a common approach to the peace. This, and perhaps only this, might counter operational disruptions while a campaign was under way; so indeed it had been thought in London earlier, in 1798, before the proposal

---

1. Cooper, loc. cit., 308–9 for the terms of the Loans of 1804 and '05. The same verdict on the decisive imprint of earlier years on this whole area of business may be inferred from a well qualified judge; when William Newmarch in 1855 published his tables on the loans from 1793 to 1816, he did so in a work *On the Loans Raised by Mr. Pitt during the First French War.*

died on the road to the Second Coalition.[1] But whether or not it could be achieved now, there must in any case be a system of alliances if – in the constant British phrase – 'Europe was to be saved'.

The assumption, and its implication that Britain should take some part directly in the Allied designs, reflected Pitt's own acceptance of such a strategy when that had been queried in the previous war.[2] His conviction was the stronger now from his reading of Napoleon himself. 'I see various and opposite qualities – all the great and all the little passions unfavourable to public tranquillity – united in the breast of one man, unhappily, whose personal caprice can scarce fluctuate for an hour without affecting the destiny of Europe'.[3] This new dimension, already perceivable towards the end of the recent conflict, was confirmed in his view in the interval of peace, and the slower processes of maritime pressures were a correspondingly poor second best on their own which could leave the Continent subject indefinitely to such dangerous dictation. The earlier strategic verdict was vividly reinforced; as indeed had been shown by his successors in office when war broke out again.

For Addington and Hawkesbury had themselves embarked on the search for allies, and given it a particular form. They had been reluctant at first in peacetime to appear to be pre-empting events: indeed they were then accused of 'dreading alliances' and hoping to hold aloof.[4] As that began to prove difficult, however, their attitude changed. The Swiss crisis in the late summer of 1802 led them to sound Austrian and Russian reactions, and though these were disappointing the Ministry in October proposed a defensive treaty to Russia, a move which was then reported to Pitt and approved.[5] The opening was declined. Nonetheless the climate seemed not wholly discouraging, particularly to a Foreign Secretary who professed himself always alert to 'Changes . . . of men' as well as of 'opinions'. The former indeed might be viewed in the next eighteen months as symptomatic to some extent of the latter; first from the appearance of a new Chancellor in St Petersburg in the form of Count Alexander Vorontsov, the brother of Count Simon the long-resident Anglophil Ambassador in London,[6] and then, more significantly,

1. Pp. 134–5, 137, 201–2, 209, above.

2. See Chs. XI, section IV, pp. 366–8, 377–8 above for Dundas's growing dissent.

3. Undated memorandum (Stanhope, IV, 225). It was apparently among the documents that now constitute the Dacres Adams Mss, formerly in the P.R.O.; but I have failed to find it. The paper however apparently bore a watermark of 1803, and the contents, on prospects for Europe, would seem to point to that year or perhaps 1804.

4. *Malmesbury*, IV, 74 for 11 May 1802. The critic was their colleague Pelham, on awkward terms with them from the start (see pp. 553, n1 above).

5. Cf. Castlereagh's visit earlier to Walmer (p. 575 above). See Fedorak, loc. cit., 181–6, and for the rest of this paragraph 213–16, 221–2; G.B. Fremont, 'Britain's Role in the Formation of the Third Coalition against France 1803–1805' (D. Phil. thesis, Oxford, 1991), 32, 36, 59, 79; and cf. p. 599 above.

6. Though the personal effect was in fact exaggerated. Count Alexander was concerned as much to appear amicable as to forward a change of policy, and in any case

from his replacement by the Polish Prince Adam Czartoryski, a leading intimate of the new Tsar Alexander, a close associate in his programme for reforms, and now placed effectively in charge of foreign affairs. For the Tsar himself, embarked on a course very different from that set by Paul, disappointed by the failure of efforts for mediation which persisted with France after war had been declared, and angered by the invasion of Hanover,[1] was showing some signs in 1803 of sympathy with Britain; and this perhaps might be deepened by Czartoryski himself, who was thought to be at least considering a closer connexion.

Russia was indeed viewed from early in the process as the most promising target for British efforts, despite the stormy relations towards the close of the last war. Some solid reasons could be adduced. In the first place, there might be some hope of building on a certain similarity of approach. For discussion of a design for Europe, as advocated in London, was likely to be music to the ears of a Tsar who – in one sense here resembling his predecessor – wished to figure as the arbiter of a settlement reflecting the fact of Russia's power, and in his own case directly inspired by his ideals. Such a setting therefore might provide an inducement to be attached to others. But it was in those others that a British Government stood to reap one particular advantage, for Russia's interests lay partly in regions – south-east Europe, the Near East – which were now also of interest to Britain itself, and the two Powers had a cause in common from their keen suspicions of encroachment by France. If that threat appeared to gain ground – and given Bonaparte's earlier vision it seemed likely enough – there was thus a focus of concern to encourage a connexion of ampler range.

There was of course a reverse side to this coin. The very fact that the two Powers' interests were now meeting directly – for Britain more directly than with Austria or Prussia – meant that they were liable to diverge and in some aspects at least to clash. Ochakov had pointed the lesson already,[2] and there was one example currently to hand. The two Governments were linked uneasily over the fate of Malta, for one of them the *casus belli* with France and of significance too for the other with a claim that was acknowledged but not given effect. The latent problem seemed to have been eased at one point by a message from St Petersburg that the British could remain freely in possession.[3] But this was sent as a statement of intention, which was not guaranteed in any form; and while later in the year the Russians supported a continuing British presence, that was

---

retired from ill health at the beginning of 1804, while Simon unfortunately thought very little of Hawkesbury's talents: 'absolutely incapable of transacting common business', 'an actual imbecility . . . as a man of business', in contrast to his admitted adequacy in Parliament; Rose's report in August 1803 (*Rose*, II, 46). See also *Malmesbury*, IV, 68.

1. See pp. 555, 658, 609 above.
2. II, Ch. 1, particularly 28–9.
3. In January 1803; see Fedorak, loc. cit., 191–2, and a similar impression was gained two months later. Cf. pp. 154, 208, n1, 364, 397 and n1, 395 above.

clearly not meant to be taken as abandoning their ultimate concern. There was room for dispute here, in a situation with potential effects for good or for ill. Russia, and perhaps Britain, might yet profit from her access to the central Mediterranean, which could facilitate Allied pressure, as well as her own influence, on southern Europe; Britain would exploit the tenure of a base supporting a presence in the eastern basin. The heightened shift in perspective in London in the later course of the Revolutionary War was firmly established when the Napoleonic War began.[1] Henceforward talks with St Petersburg would be affected by the fact.

Meanwhile however the Russians had still not ruled out the alternative attraction of France: an unknown quantity, arousing as elsewhere in Europe resentment competing with caution, but also offering more specific inducements than Britain, which must be coolly weighed. In July 1803 the British again proposed a treaty, but now for an offensive alliance including Austria, and the prospect of a subsidy was specifically held out. While however this was received politely, there was not an acceptance even of preliminary talks. The Russians saw no reason at that point to be other than extremely wary. They were waiting, quite openly, to see what would happen if the French invaded England. They also wished to be sure before anything else of Austria's military intentions and terms.[2]

That remained the position over the rest of the year, and it was of the kind that the British reckoned they had experienced from European capitals all too often.[3] Nor could they pretend to themselves that Austria might apply the spur. Relations between London and Vienna were on an even keel: in fact Starhemberg, the Ambassador who had endured many tiring passages with Pitt and Grenville, greatly preferred Addington and Hawkesbury – less egotistical and obstinate, perhaps the wisest Ministers indeed to govern England for a long time.[4] There had been no pressing reason in the past two years for Britain to be stern with Austria, and Addington approved a successful appeal to postpone repayment of

1. See pp. 395–7 above.

2. Fedorak, loc. cit., 216–18. The subsidy would be based on the rate of that given in the Second Coalition.

3. In November 1803 Czartoryski did move so far however as to suggest joint diplomatic action against France; and this has been held (see Sherwig, *Guineas and Gunpowder*, 146) to have met with less interest in London than might have been expected. In point of fact there may have been some misunderstanding here, either between Czartoryski and Warren, the Ambassador in St Petersburg [see p. 658, n4 above] or between Simon Vorontsov and Hawkesbury in London. Both Governments preferred a comprehensive or at any rate a wider alliance to a bilateral one; but imprecise language or degree of emphasis, perhaps on the British part, might have caused confusion. The evidence seems to be incomplete; see Fedorak, loc. cit., 222–3.

4. Opinions given from October 1803 down to the beginning of May 1804 (see Fedorak, loc. cit., 241). He was of course quick to congratulate Pitt in due course on his accession to office, as was his duty, adding for good measure that 'There is nothing he does not expect from [his] genius and talents and he begins to hope that the affairs [presumably of Europe] will now take a more favourable turn' (19 May 1804; P.R.O. 30/8/180).

advances from the last wartime British loan. This had eased a running sore to some extent; and in any case the familiar predilection for an alliance with the Emperor held good at the outbreak of war. His geographical position provided a strategic key to effective Allied operations; his army still enjoyed a high reputation, and was thought to have largely recovered once again from defeat; the 'old system' of diplomacy remained 'natural' provided military considerations allowed.[1] In July 1803 Vienna therefore was coupled with St Petersburg in a simultaneous approach; and when the expected demand for financial aid was received it was met sympathetically – indeed a secret Convention was proposed in London, though the figure was drastically reduced.[2] But these were early negotiating counters, and were recognised as such; for both parties knew that the immediate point of any such agreement would be to strengthen the Austrians' influence on Russia. They themselves might fear French designs, in Italy and Switzerland and within the German Diet. But they had twice been forced to sue for peace in the past six years; their resources, if resilient, were still weakened; and even those who were prepared to contemplate a further war – and their views were contested within the Court – were deeply concerned not to risk too much too soon. If the Russians' first reaction to a British offer was to await news from Vienna, it appeared to Vienna that the ball lay in Russia's court.

Expectations of wider success turned on the outcome in those two quarters. For the third main possibility offered the least immediate hope. Prussia had good reason not to be dissatisfied with French patronage of her aspirations to greater influence in Germany at Austria's expense. On the other hand the occupation of Hanover could not be to her taste, and Hawkesbury decided to sound the prospects at least when her former partners were approached. The offer of a subsidy was included in a proposal for an offensive alliance. But, as he half expected, the envoy in Berlin thought it not worth while to deliver such a message; he confined himself to one for a defensive alliance, and nothing material followed over the rest of the year.[3] For the rest the Ministry tried to hold the ring, with deterrents, suggestions or propositions as the case might be. The Dutch were warned against hostile activity at the risk of war. The Spaniards, in receipt of a French subsidy and posing a threat to Portugal, were given to understand that they would be viewed as neutral so long as their neighbour was left alone and their ports were kept fully open to British shipping. The Portuguese for their part were enjoined to stay neutral, which seemed indeed the best that could be expected from a government already

---

1. Cf. II, 271, 296, 558 (for Pitt, allowing for the difference in circumstances, in 1795); pp. 210, 321–2 above. And see Duffy, 'The Austrian Alliance', 495–6 and above all 452–60.

2. Fedorak, loc. cit., 219. The opening Austrian figure was £2 million; the British, £3–400,000.

3. Fremont, loc. cit., 135–41. The potential subsidy was set at £750,000, a third being paid on a declaration of war, a third when the French had been driven out of Hanover, and the rest when they had retired across the Rhine. The envoy was Francis Jackson.

obliged to pay an annual tribute to France and unimpressed now by a suggestion from London that its fleet, with the Prince Regent, should set sail for the safety of Brazil.[1] Similar advice to preserve a benevolent neutrality was given along the southern arc: to The Two Sicilies by a special mission, and equally to the Turks. In the far north there was a somewhat different emphasis, in seeking to safeguard trade and naval supplies. The Danes and the Swedes were actively wooed, in circumstances now tending to encourage a cautiously amicable response. The former indeed, chastened it was hoped by their experience of Nelson[2] and alarmed by the French occupation of Hanover – that warning bell sounding across northern capitals –, were visited by a special mission urging friendly non-belligerence at least or if possible a defensive alliance. And Sweden likewise was offered proofs of greater cordiality: assurances of a settlement of certain claims from the previous war and the prospect of talks, long sought in Stockholm, on improved terms for trade. Beyond Europe itself, one hope bearing on wider waters had to be abandoned. France's acquisition of Louisiana, of strategic significance for Britain and holding uneasy implications for the United States,[3] had quickly tilted a balance of sentiment in Washington that was normally uncertain. Encouraged indeed by a shared apprehension, Addington contemplated seizing New Orleans in the event of war and – an unusual conception – transferring it by agreement to American control. The moment however passed; the Americans secured Louisiana themselves, by purchase in the spring of 1803; and when war came only weeks later Bonaparte had ensured that Britain had not gained a transatlantic ally.

Pitt therefore took over in a situation which had been given a definite focus. The outgoing Ministry, it could indeed be argued, had done as much in Europe as it reasonably could. In conditions not highly conducive to visible diplomatic success, achievement was likely to be limited to holding variable ground and preparing the way where opportunity might offer for subsequent results.[4] Addington and Hawkesbury had avoided quarrels with neutrals, taken initiatives, and settled on their main line of effort. By and large they had shown safe judgment; the record, when scanned, seemed unexceptionable. At the same time, the circumstances that limited policy were not such as to make great demands. Choices and skills are tested harder when opportunity opens up. Nor indeed were the circumstances alone responsible for an impression that was uninspiring. For the fact was that the Ministry managed, as in other matters, to look tame and rather second rate. This may have been unfair

1. An abortive precedent in fact for Canning's celebrated and successful pressure six years later.
2. P. 555 above. And cf. 394 above.
3. Pp. 144–5 above, 566.
4. Cf. p. 641 above.

in essentials. But essentials are not everything in diplomatic usage, and the feeling here máy have been encouraged by a tendency on Hawkesbury's own part to appear inept, sometimes in quite minor but telling ways. The Russian Ambassador may well have been too harsh; the Austrian, on favourable ground, too complimentary. But the Foreign Secretary does appear at least at times to have been maladroit; and Addington for his part did not escape blame.[1] George III himself, an experienced judge of departmental competence, seems to have had no doubts: he was reported to find Hawkesbury 'the worst man of business possible' – a deficiency not eased by 'a vacant kind of grin'.[2] The emphasis, as in Vorontsov's case, fell precisely on *business*: a knowledge of practice and forms, and an ability to avoid obscurities and slips. Capacity in the higher function of judgment on policy was less a matter of remark, and Hawkesbury's Parliamentary performance was widely acknowledged; but the future Prime Minister's spell at the Foreign Office was never viewed as a notable phase in his long career. Altogether, the change of Government in 1804 brought a change of atmosphere in this, as other, areas; from a sense of mildness and humdrum punctuated by embarrassment to one of greater sternness and purpose with Pitt clearly in charge. It was perhaps symptomatic of a mood that Addington, referring in his final budget speech to a war lasting possibly three years, should have talked of an expenditure which might permit a reduction in the national debt when he was already prepared to embark on subsidies for three potential allies.[3]

The contrast in Pitt's ensuing budget of February 1805, with a provision of £5 million for such purposes, was thus easy to note.[4] One may also note that he had not had occasion to bring a sum before Parliament meanwhile, and that this figure was itself still perforce prospective. The interplay of impression – valid in itself – and substance was indeed encapsulated here, the former bringing a sharper urgency to bear on a process which responded only in part. For while things certainly began to move in 1804, they did not reach a point at which financial arrangements could be settled or treaties of alliance signed. Pitt could take some comfort on arrival from one sign of possible specific accord. In the winter of 1803–4 the British had continued to suggest a comprehensive partnership

---

1. Cf. pp. 569, 641–2 above, and Fedorak, loc. cit., 213–14 for Addington. See too p. 690, n3 above.

2. *L.C.G. III*, IV, no. 2793n1 (Robert Ward's report, on evidence unknown, in December 1804); *Rose*, II, 157 in September 1804 (a direct account), but Rose was hostile in general to Hawkesbury. The Foreign Secretary had moved by then to the Home Office, but the King was talking equally of the past and for his views earlier see *Malmesbury*, IV, 63. Cf. for balanced retrospective verdicts on Hawkesbury at this time *H of P*, IV, 303, and Norman Gash, *Lord Liverpool*, 49–50.

3. *P.D.*, II, cols. 356–7; pp. 690–1 and ns 2, 3 above. His statement, naturally containing the proviso of 'an unforeseen occasion', suggests either a distinctly sceptical view of the level of activity in Europe in the coming year or an equally distinct reluctance to trouble his audience with a policy liable to become controversial.

4. See p. 686 above.

to Russia, with no more success than before.[1] But this did not exclude a rising desire in St Petersburg for co-operation in the eastern Mediterranean and a common attitude towards Turkey's European territories, provoked by growing signs of French interest in and around the coasts of Dalmatia and Greece. Such suggestions had indeed been made with varying degrees of strength by either party in the past eighteen months,[2] against a background of fragmentation in the southern Balkans themselves. The main lines of overlapping but not wholly coinciding interests were clear: both Powers were opposed to a spread of French influence in the region, let alone French action, and both therefore professed to be in favour of preserving the Ottoman Empire intact. Local difficulties however had obtruded; for while Russia subscribed to the latter policy it was only as an immediate means of enforcing the former, and Britain was not anxious to see an increase in Russia's influence on the Porte. Their policies accordingly could diverge on the ground, and in fact had been doing so, occasioning squabbles that had to be kept within bounds in a wider cause. There was the question – a high one for Russia – of the claim to protect the Orthodox Church and the Sultan's Slav and Greek subjects. And there were the complicating enticements of the powerful Albanian Ali Pasha on the Adriatic coast, ingeniously exploiting his three possible suitors – French, Russians and British – in his endless quest to expand at the cost of Constantinople. These problems now fell on a situation in and around the Ionian Sea which had altered significantly since a Russo-Turkish force had expelled the French from Corfu in 1799.[3] The independent republic of the Seven Islands, established thereafter[4] under limited and recognised Turkish protection but sustained in practice by a continuing Russian presence, had collapsed in 1801 when the latter was withdrawn with the change of regime at home, some of the islands going their own way – Zante in fact, with a touching faith in the Royal Navy, hoisting the British flag. That interlude however did not last long. In 1802 a Russian force returned and the republic was reinstated with a new constitution drawn up largely under the aegis of the Enlightened new Tsar. The islands in fact had become virtually a protectorate, to Turkey's dismay and Britain's unease;[5] and in this strained atmosphere rising complaints from the Russian and British Residents in Corfu became an increasingly awkward fact of life for their superiors.[6] If France was

1. See p. 690 above. In December 1803 and February 1804 Hawkesbury repeated his proposals. Historians have made conflicting claims on behalf of Russia and Britain for credit in first proposing an alliance, covering the period from late 1802 to early 1804. Both Fedorak, loc. cit., 222–3 and Fremont, loc. cit., 78–9 come down emphatically in Britain's favour, giving Addington's Ministry its due.
2. See Fremont, loc. cit., 39–49.
3. See p. 396 above.
4. P. 563 above.
5. Cf. p. 396 above.
6. Fremont, loc. cit., 47–54. The British consul was promoted to Resident in July 1803, keeping pace with Russia's representative.

providing the opportunity for an understanding between London and St Petersburg, the two Powers' own differences were cumbering the way.

But now it seemed that the issue was really being forced. French vessels around the coasts, French agents ashore, brought the issue to a point. In March 1804 the two Governments confirmed that each would oppose partition of the Ottoman Empire, Russia established consulates in key areas of Greece, and prepared a sizeable force for Corfu for which Britain was asked to reserve troops in Malta if an addition was required.[1] This request was certainly a sign of the times. To think of admitting foreign troops to such a sphere of influence showed an unusual sense of need in St Petersburg; and it was one that might do something to satisfy Britain's growing sense of concern. Five years earlier the Foreign Secretary, perhaps only half jokingly, had toyed with the idea of acquiring Corfu for ourselves:[2] compliance with this invitation might now farther a watch on Russians as well as French designs. It was not surprising in all the circumstances that Czartoryski did not want an agreement by treaty in this case,[3] and there was no hint that a result would lead to anything beyond itself. Nevertheless, within its limits the move presented an opening through which it might be possible to probe the chances of success on a more extensive diplomatic front.

The timing could not but be welcome to an incoming Minister. And in the summer there were other favourable developments. The crowned heads of Europe, amid their internecine jealousies, did not take kindly to mistreatment of their order, and Tsar Alexander was a prominent upholder of that faith. Reasons of state were reinforced by a personal championship of the Kings of Sardinia and The Two Sicilies, the one deprived of a suitable indemnity for his mainland dispossession in the previous war,[4] the other powerless following a return of French troops, in breach of a bilateral treaty, so as to keep a watchful eye on the British from the foot of Italy. In May 1804 the principle of legitimacy itself suffered a direct assault, when Bonaparte proclaimed himself Emperor of the French with a hereditary succession. This profound insult, following the shock of the execution of the Bourbon Duc d'Enghien in March,[5] led Russia to suspend diplomatic relations. The threads, it might seem, were being drawn together in the face of geographical and moral threat; and

1. See *Select Despatches . . . relating to the formation of the Third Coalition against France 1804–5*, ed. John Holland Rose (1904), vi–ix; hereafter *Third Coalition*.

2. P. 202, n5 above.

3. *Third Coalition*, ix. He agreed to consider the notion, suggested by the British Ambassador, of a treaty of one or two articles, but that was clearly just to be polite. His insistence was on secrecy; the Russians were still not anxious to over-expose themselves to any quarter.

4. See pp. 320, 322 above: a double blow in the Tsar's eyes because of Austria's behaviour at the time.

5. The notorious sequel, following on his kidnap from foreign territory, to the discovery of a fresh plot (the Cadoudal plot) to assassinate Bonaparte and effect an armed coup, in which British funding was involved (see pp. 469–70 above).

indeed on the eve of the declaration from Paris Czartoryski was talking of an Anglo-Russian operation to expel the French from Neapolitan terri-tory.[1] In the next few months the two complementary propositions – British in Corfu, Russians and British in southern Italy – were examined in greater detail as closer discussions took place.

These proved both hopeful and cautionary. Pitt and Harrowby were quick to take up some elements of the Russians' request of March.[2] Britain could certainly offer diplomatic co-operation in handling the Porte. The respective Ambassadors in Constantinople and agents in the provinces should work with their counterparts to stiffen the Turks, and if necessary to reassure the latter – who might need saving in spite of them-selves – that any occupation of 'important Posts' would be temporary, purely for denial to the French. We would of course also be supportive at sea: Nelson would be ordered to detach a squadron to cruise in neigh-bouring waters. As so often, the constraints lay mainly in the immediate capacity for military help. We would try – as in fact we had done unsuc-cessfully in the late war – to raise Albanians for British service; and we accepted the pressing desirability to provide our own troops, to the tune of some 10–15,000 men. Some of those could undoubtedly come from the garrisons of Gibraltar and Malta; but more would then have to be sent from home, under a continuing threat of invasion, and the Russians must appreciate that time was needed to re-order dispositions, prepare the for-mations and find the shipping. It must also be recognised, were there to be landings in Italy, that little could be expected from the Neapolitan forces, since the King and his Ministers would almost certainly have to take refuge in Sicily if the French moved on Naples itself.[3]

These warning passages, naturally enough, were not accepted with much pleasure; the Russians foresaw a delay of two to three months before a British force would be properly available for southern Italy. They also pro-fessed not to understand the reference to temporary possession of Turkish posts.[4] Their disgruntlement must have been the greater from another

1. Warren to Hawkesbury, no. 32, 12 May 1804 (*Third Coalition*, 10), received 5 June (P.R.O., F.O. 65/55). There had been a hint of this earlier, on 27 April (*Third Coalition*, 4). It will be recalled that Pitt returned to office on 10 May.
This Russian suggestion may indeed have been encouraged by one from Warren in March, stressing the advantages to both Powers of expelling the French from the extreme south of Italy (see Piers Mackesy, *The War in the Mediterranean 1803–1810* (1957), 52). Czartoryski's response however contained a note of caution, in case the British, wishing to jockey Russia into an alliance and in particular to safeguard their own use of the base at Naples (cf. p. 205 above), tried to force the pace.

2. P. 695 above.

3. Harrowby to Simon Vorontsov, no. 2, 26 June 1804 (F.O. 65/55). The comment that Turkey 'must be saved in spite of itself' repeated 'the forcible Expression' of the Russians' own 'Sentiments'. Warren told Czartoryski however that the existing Mediterranean gar-risons could make a timely contribution (to Harrowby, no. 58, 24 July 1804; *Third Coalition*, 25).

4. Ibid. The word given there is 'ports', but I have read 'posts' in Harrowby's no. 2 to Vorontsov, above.

communication sent in the same despatch, which reached St Petersburg at the same time. For Pitt was now prepared to put figures to the earlier mention of financial aid to allies, and the result was not at all to the Russians' liking. They must be clear that there would be an overall limit, and moreover that the sums required approval by Parliament, which would need to be satisfied by terms ensuring that a force 'would actually be collected and put into action against France'.[1] The total available would be £5 million, and of this Austria would need £2 or £2½ million; Prussia, if responsive, perhaps £800,000 to £1 million; and other, smaller states – notably Sweden, particularly if Prussia could not be gained – £4–500,000. This left £1 million 'at least' for Russia herself. Advances of payment might perhaps be made, on earlier precedents, to assist preparations, if necessary before final terms were agreed; but in such case merely to allow time for the latter to be properly worked out. And we would be content for the Russian Government, in view of its closer knowledge of the Continental scene, to handle negotiations with the other Powers concerned, keeping in touch throughout with our envoys in the capitals and subject of course to our approbation. The aim would be a single treaty of alliance covering the terms particular to each.

This procedural proposal – a not impractical one in the circumstances[2] – might in fact prove attractive. The sums themselves however were unlikely to be accepted on the spot – 'nugatory' in fact was the immediate reaction[3] –, and the relegation of his country to the leavings from others was hardly flattering to the Tsar. The view ahead was far from settled. But both sides were staking out their positions; and while the prospects would be decided less by themselves than by Napoleon, there was now at least a readiness to explore the ground.

That indeed could soon be seen. In London it was given effect by a change of Ambassador to St Petersburg. Warren had been wanting to come home for some time; but Pitt in any case had decided to recall him, and if Fox had been available that would have underlined the importance now assigned to the post.[4] As things stood, a fresh atmosphere was shown by a lesser but interesting appointment, that of Granville Leveson Gower, young but intelligent and not inexperienced, and known above all to have enjoyed Pitt's confidence: clearly a personal choice.[5] And from St

---

1. Harrowby to Vorontsov, 26 June 1804 (*Third Coalition*, 14–19). The ms copy in F.O. 65/55 is numbered 1 and will be referred to as such, distinguishing it from no. 2 as numbered in that file (p. 696, n3 above).

2. Cf. p. 687 above.

3. Warren to Harrowby, after talking to Czartoryski, no. 58, 24 July (*Third Coalition*, 24–5).

4. See p. 658 above and *Rose*, II, 140–1 for Warren.

5. Cf. pp. 59n3, 674 and n2 above for his social and political background; 59 for his experience in Malmesbury's mission to Paris in 1796. His personal attractions were undoubted – and were taken to heart too seriously by Hester Stanhope (p. 674 above); he himself moved through life coolly enough. There is no suggestion that Pitt was sending him off by way of separation; but Leveson Gower's refusal of a post in the new Ministry (ibid) certainly opened the way to one abroad.

Petersburg there came an equally suggestive move, in the form of a blue-print from the Tsar for the basis of a future system for Europe. Such a line of approach suited the British,[1] though not necessarily with such far-reaching aims. Its appearance now proved significant, offering a setting in which Pitt could develop his own thoughts, and also a focus for a mission to London sent to discuss the immediate prospects.

These indications of more purposeful contact, emerging as the summer wore on, were more fully visible in the autumn. Leveson Gower was named in July, but it was October before he left, arriving in St Petersburg at the end of the month. The Russian special envoy for his part was ready to leave by mid September, reaching London finally in mid November. Even more than the new British Ambassador, he was a personal choice. Count Nicholas Novosiltsov was one of the Tsar's group of advisers on reform, an expert on agricultural questions – which indeed were rumoured at first to be the reason for his visit[2] – and entirely dependent on his master, whose first real essay in diplomacy, with Czartoryski's guidance, this may in fact have been. Certainly the paper bore proof of Alexander's propensity for large concepts. A peace settlement should see the establishment of institutions in the spirit of constitutional self-determination and founded on human 'sacred rights'; a continuing league of Great Powers, headed by Russia and Britain, to guarantee European peace; and a code of law for the guidance of all European states which would include a demand on their forces to unite against a transgressor. Forward looking indeed, and in the second proposal prophetic in spirit of 1814. Meanwhile much might usefully be done by way of territorial rearrangements when peace arrived. Here Czartoryski came into his own, largely shaping the Tsar's official document and providing a memorandum for Novosiltsov's guidance which drew on an earlier survey of the Foreign Minister's own thoughts on a system of Russian policy.[3] His pattern derived from a combination of long-term factors: a predilection for partnership with Britain, that model of constitutionalism and an essential source of trade with Russia – which however must take closer account of Russia's own commercial interests; a keen dislike of Prussia, as a restless element in Germany and a likely threat to Russia as an enemy to possible Polish independence under the aegis of the Tsar; and a belief in Russia's special interests in south-east Europe – her need for safe

1. Cf. pp. 687–8 above.

2. Czartoryski however wrote directly to Pitt recommending Novosiltsov to the Minister's full confidence (10/22 September 1804; Dacres Adams Mss, formerly P.R.O. 30/58/5); and see also Warren to Pitt on the same day (loc. cit.).

3. The latter's text is published in Patricia M. Grinsted, 'Czartoryski's System for Russian Foreign 1803, A Memorandum', in *California Slavic Studies*, V, 19–91. For the Tsar's instructions and Czartoryski's 'notes' to Novosiltsov, and the English translation in *Memoirs of Prince Adam Czartoryski and his Correspondence with Alexander I*, ed. Adam Gielgud, II (1888), 41–51, see W.H. Zawadzki's biography of the statesman, *A Man of Honour . . .* (1993), 107 and n65.

commercial access to southern waters and her responsibility to protect the Christian subjects of the Turkish empire. These premisses produced their consequences in a situation revolving around France. The French themselves must be contained within their just historical limits, though their future form of government was not to be dictated; their neighbours must be supplied with stronger defences; and their own forms of authority should be placed on more secure foundations, some constitutionally monarchical – in Sardinia and the Dutch Netherlands – and perhaps federal in Germany. The recurrent problem of Poland might be solved by its enlargement into a Great Poland, with the Tsar perhaps as king, which would absorb Prussian territory; Prussia herself being compensated in western Germany, while Austria might preserve the balance by expanding into Bavaria and Swabia. The Ottoman Empire should be preserved, unless it might be federated by agreement, the Tsar being recognised as Protector of the Slavs in the East. And Britain of course would receive its rewards, most obviously overseas, and hopefully in return would mitigate the claims of its maritime code.

The British Government meanwhile was preparing to answer the most recent Russian questions, and ask some of their own. By the time that Novosiltsov arrived, his instructions crossed those issued to Leveson Gower in October. These had been very full, and much space was devoted to Italy and south-east Europe.[1] In the British view, an attempt to expel the French from Neapolitan territory was unrealistic – indeed 'the height of rashness' – without help from Austria. But modest blocking operations might well prevent them from obliging the King to leave the mainland, and some 1,500 to 2,000 troops could be sent for that purpose to augment a small Russian force from Corfu, Malta in turn being reinforced, probably by 5–6,000 men, in a few months' time. Meanwhile the Russians should explain more precisely their intentions over Turkey. It was accepted that they were anxious to fill an active role in improving the lot of their co-religionist Greeks; but how exactly, and to what extent, given their declared opposition to any partition of the Ottoman Empire? The Tsar was in danger of being placed in 'an embarrassing position'; and so were we, more particularly since misunderstandings were arising between the respective local representatives. These problems needed sorting out. Beyond them, the new Ambassador – recognised in private as having wide discretion[2] – must take an active part in farthering Russia's efforts for the general system of alliance, to include Austria at any rate and possibly Sweden as well.

The arrival of Novosiltsov quickly raised Pitt's hopes. The Minister was

---

1. They were contained in a series numbered as despatches from Harrowby, nos. 1–7, all dated 10 October (P.R.O., F.O. 65/66; published – except for no. 7 on the seizure of a vessel in the Mediterranean by a British warship, and for much of no. 3 on complications in Albania and the Morea – in *Third Coalition*, 41–50).

2. Hawkesbury to Harrowby, 5 October 1804 (referring to 'Lord Granville'); Harrowby Mss, vol. XII, Sandon Hall.

soon convinced that 'the principles' on which the two Powers could build were 'so completely our own' that we need not hesitate to contract a 'provisional engagement' in advance of a treaty. The aim of confining France to her '*ancient* limits', but not forcing an explicit Bourbon restoration, was 'very satisfactory'.[1] Talks could proceed; and on that basis they did so over the next two months. During that time therefore the balance of attention shifted heavily to London: Leveson Gower in St Petersburg could scarcely expect to make much progress directly on the main question, and in point of fact he heard nothing on it from his Government until the early spring of 1805. He naturally found this frustrating.[2] As it happened, however, circumstances were largely to blame. Mischance struck early in December 1804, forcing Harrowby out of action from a serious accident, and when it became clear that he could not carry on a successor had to be found. Pitt was recognised to be very much in control of business, and the appointment of Mulgrave[3] in due course ensured a replacement who could be expected to work easily under his direction. But this had to wait until the turn of the year, for the extent of the damage to Harrowby remained uncertain for a while, and in addition to losing his Foreign Secretary the Minister was also engaged, under pressing difficulties, in political manoeuvre.[4] The provisions for a treaty and, no less importantly, the Tsar's blueprint for Europe needed careful study and a comprehensive response. It was January before Pitt could address himself to final composition.[5] When the result was complete it marked the opening of a new stage.

The prospects with Russia at this point looked not unhopeful; and Pitt was always ready to hope. 'His schemes, large and deep. His hopes sanguine',

1. Pitt to Harrowby, 20 November 1804 (loc. cit.).

2. A batch of despatches, on specific problems, reached him on 22 November 1804, and a further similar series, of early November, on 5 February 1805. The results of Novosiltsov's mission were drafted to him on 21 January 1805, arriving in St Petersburg on 6 March. In January he complained of his lack of information (despatches from London nos. 10–15, and from St Petersburg no. 8, for 1804 (F.O. 65/56), nos. 1–3 and unnumbered, and nos. 3, 4, 7 respectively for 1805 (F.O. 65/57)). See also Leveson Gower to Harrowby, 9 January 1804 [misdated for 1805]; Harrowby Mss, vol. X.

3. For whom see pp. 90, 240–1 above.

4. Followed on pp. 717–25 below. Mulgrave in point of fact was being consulted on the Russian negotiation (among other business) in mid December (to Pitt, 15 December 1804; Dacres Adams Mss, formerly P.R.O. 30/58/5). He received the offer of the Foreign Secretaryship on the 31st, accepting the next day (Normanby Mss, Box J; the reply being misdated 1804). Where despatches had to be signed in the brief interval, Camden seems to have acted – the other Secretary of State, Hawkesbury, would scarcely have done (cf. p. 693 above).

Harrowby had found himself, as often (p. 670 above), in poor health before the serious accident of a fall on the head (to Pitt, from Bath, 18 November 1804; P.R.O. 30/8/142).

5. Cf. Simon Vorontsov to Czartoryski, 9/21 January 1805 (*Memoirs of . . . Czartoryski*, II, 70).

Wilberforce recorded of a conversation at the start of the year.[1] By the end of 1804 moreover there seemed to have been some movement in both Vienna and Berlin. To British eyes the former might have looked minimal: the Austrians showed no sign of abandoning the shelter of neutrality; rather in fact some worrying signs of subservience to France. They refused to condemn the execution of d'Enghien, or – disgusting the Tsar in particular – the transformation of Bonaparte into his Imperial style. Such rebuffs were borne, if impatiently, in London for the sake of keeping a potential ally in play, and Pitt, while preparing to wield the stick by ostensible hints of a move towards Prussia, was ready to provide the carrot of financial aid – £200,000 a month in the first three months of an Allied campaign.[2] By then the British envoy, confessing to pessimism, could only suggest co-operation with the Tsar to force on the Emperor a decisive change of Ministers; and his advice was accepted in the autumn.[3] In point of fact however the situation was soon to prove somewhat better than it might have appeared. There had never been much doubt in Vienna that war with France would come at some point. The differences between the 'peace' and 'war' parties focused on the diplomatic tactics best suited to prepare for the event. Procrastination and caution had won so far, and were still ostensibly in the ascendant. But Austrian troop movements in the border lands with Italy suggested a hardening of attitude; the tone of their Ministers' conversations with diplomats began to change; and secret talks with Russia, maintained though not steadily pursued through the year, suddenly quickened, despite familiar mutual suspicions over south-east Europe, to yield a secret treaty of defensive alliance in November against France. The fact was closely guarded: the British were not officially informed.[4] But it became known confidentially from St Petersburg; and while there was no question yet of seeing one leg of a tripod offensive Coalition in place, a triangular conference was mounted in the Russian capital at which a British financial contribution was discussed.

Berlin, curiously enough, was seen in London in a rather more hopeful light than Vienna, at least for most of the year. The British envoy, Francis Jackson, was more sympathetic to his Court than was his counterpart Arthur Paget; and while there was little on which to build, for Frederick William II barely contested French activities in Germany and readily

---

1. *Life of Wilberforce*, III, 210, for 8 January 1805.

2. Harrowby to Arthur Paget [Minister in Vienna], no. 3, Most Secret and Confidential, 24 July 1804 (F.O. 7/70).

3. Paget to Hawkesbury, no. 6, 9 April 1804 (loc. cit.); Harrowby to Paget, no. 8, 11 September 1804 with Most Secret and Confidential and Separate despatches enclosed (F.O. 7/71); Leveson Gower to Harrowby, no. 7, Secret and Confidential, 24 November 1804 (F.O. 65/56).

4. It was indeed only in August that the British envoy was told of the existence, but not the trend or detail of talks that had been long if fluctuatingly under way. See *Consolidated Treaty Series*, 58 (1969), 15–32 for the French and Russian texts.

accepted Bonaparte's new title, any signs of change tended to be greeted as harbingers of more to come. Comfort was gained from the fact that Prussia signed a defensive agreement with Russia on northern Germany in May 1804, following the latter's pressure; and the appointment of Baron Hardenberg, held to be sympathetic, to the post of foreign affairs was welcomed by British Ministers as a straw in the wind. But in point of fact such assessments were largely mistaken: Prussia was far from wishing to risk a relationship with France which had earlier proved rewarding. Pitt however did what he could, offering the prospect of financial aid on a declaration of hostilities, and pressing Russia to join with Britain to bring further weight to bear.[1] In the autumn indeed Czartoryski was once more at work. But to no avail; indeed the reverse, for the Prussians, so far from being emboldened by these signs that the two Powers might be closing ranks, moved towards France with talks in which the future of Hanover itself was discussed. That however was not known in London. At the end of 1804 Pitt did not discount the chances of finding a third ally, and perhaps within the comprehensive Alliance on which he had set his heart.[2]

The hope of such a combination drew its greater urgency from the threat of the peril still visible across the Channel. Napoleon's troops and barges were gathered thickly from Ostend and Dunkirk to Calais and Boulogne.[3] An alliance with Continental armies, even if these were distant, might therefore not only be the key to outright victory: it was also desirable as a menace or counter to the mass of force otherwise available for invasion. A European Coalition could play its part in the defence of the island as well as that of continental Europe: a valuable, perhaps in some circumstances essential complement to the seapower through which Britain could assist the war by land. The exercise of that power, in all its forms, was of course the Government's continuous preoccupation; and even by the later stage of a peace which was clearly becoming only an interrupted struggle it was served with stern and if necessary ruthless purpose. That had already been seen in the matter of Malta. In the autumn of 1804 it was seen further in the matter of Spain.

Anglo-Spanish relations, bound to be uneasy from the start of the war, had been strained progressively through the year. Addington's Ministry had qualified its acceptance of a necessarily unbenevolent neutrality with warnings that no naval armament could be allowed.[4] Since the French

---

1. See Harrowby to Jackson, no. 1, Most Secret and Confidential, 24 July 1804 (F.O. 64/65). The sum mentioned – £250,000 with talks on a package to follow – was to be communicated only if it could not be withheld while other figures (see p. 701 above) were under discussion with other Powers. The offer was repeated in the autumn (same to same, no. 12, 4 November 1804; F.O. 64/66).

2. 'Prussia much better'; Canning's diary for 21 November 1804, after a visit to Pitt (Canning Ms 29d).

3. Cf. pp. 542, 608 above.

4. Given in January and February 1804. Cf. p. 691 above.

had insisted, in a secret Convention of October 1803, that their warships calling in Ferrol and Cadiz could be repaired in the yards and French seamen travel freely to and fro, trouble could obviously arise between London and Madrid, even without the normal disputes over the conduct of neutral trade. Early in September the offlying British squadron reported that Spanish warships in Ferrol were fitting out for sea, that a reinforcement was expected from Cadiz, and operations seemed likely to be mounted in conjunction with the French. As one possible sign of Napoleon's intentions for the Channel this was serious news. An explanation was demanded of the Spaniards, they were told that their warships could not leave port meanwhile, and the British Minister was instructed to leave if no acceptable answer was received.[1]

Meanwhile a more drastic step was taken. A group of Spanish frigates carrying bullion from America was known to be on its way home, and on 18 September the Cabinet met to approve the despatch of orders to intercept and detain them, with the object of holding the treasure pending a satisfactory outcome in Madrid.[2] Things however did not go as planned. The British force – one of four frigates, equal in numbers though somewhat superior in strength to the Spaniards – met the incoming ships on 5 October; but it was too small to ensure immediate surrender, and an engagement followed in which one of the Spanish vessels blew up before the rest struck their flags. There was heavy loss of Spanish life – which heightened later criticism of the affair in England – and on 12 December 1804 Spain declared war. The Cabinet's decision was undoubtedly illegal: specie did not figure in the ordained list of contraband goods. Ministers could point rather to some other occasions in the wars of the past century – most strikingly indeed, had they wished, to the advice of the Elder Pitt in 1761, when he was overruled by his colleagues, to do what his son now did with his colleagues' consent.[3] The problem was always sensitive; one of a kind

> to which the conditions of sea warfare are particularly . . . susceptible. The question which statesmen have to answer is no easy one. It is whether, and if so at what precise moment and in what manner, forcible action shall be taken against a Power which, while still neutral, is taking, or being forced to take, steps, and to make dispositions of its

1. Harrowby to Frere [see p. 391, n4 above], no. 1, 29 September 1804 (P.R.O., F.O. 72/53).
2. See Pitt to Harrowby, 18 September 1804 (Harrowby Mss, vol. XII). The Cabinet had consisted of all those in reach. Harrowby himself was at Weymouth with the King, whose consent was sought as soon as 'convenient': a Minute was in fact sent, and submitted, but does not seem to have survived (see *L.C.G. III*, IV, no. 2936n2). According to one account, the Ministers attending the meeting were Pitt, Eldon, Camden, Hawkesbury, Melville and Mulgrave (Holland Rose, II, 514). A copy of the Admiralty's orders, also of 18 September, may be found in Pitt's papers, P.R.O. 30/8/259.
3. See Basil Williams, *The Life of William Pitt Earl of Chatham*, II (1914), 106.

forces, the result of which will place it in a favourable position to open hostilities.[1]

The question of pre-emption in fact. Ministers were clear in this instance that their decision was justified. They were determined to prevent or disrupt naval dispositions by Napoleon which could support or permit an attempt at invasion. Spain had been warned of the consequence of preparations by an unexplained sortie from her ports. Complaints of just such indications had been made without any apparent result; no sustainable 'pretext' had been offered – a possible explanation that the work was undertaken to embark Spanish troops for passage round the coast, or that it related to an ongoing quarrel with the United States centring over the French boundaries of Louisiana which, it was rumoured, might be leading to war.[2] The Spanish Government was having to meet varied demands from France that seriously damaged its pretensions to neutrality. It relied heavily on its American bullion to sustain a war. The circumstances, taken together, led to one deduction in London. As things stood, there was 'certainly' cause to enforce the demand for a reply.[3]

Some points may be noted about an episode that brought such an effect. War would probably have come about in any case. The British Minister left Madrid on 10 November before news of the armed clash arrived, and relations were so poor that some other reason was likely to have sufficed, particularly since the French were now eager to gain Spain as an ally.[4] The dismay in London, however, was not profound when that event came. The transference of a neutral into an enemy was of course a marked blow, falling most immediately on the war at sea. It faced the Royal Navy once more with an arc of hostile forces from the Netherlands to the western Mediterranean, stretching yet farther the responsibilities of 'those distant, storm-tossed ships' – though not in fact most heavily in their exercise of an already full blockade. It increased the naval strength available to France,

---

1. Admiral Sir Herbert Richmond, *Statesmen and Sea Power* (1946), 223, citing further examples, not so closely in parallel as that of the Elder Pitt, and where action *was* taken: from 1740 and 1741, and also from 1807 (the seizure of the Danish fleet) and 1940 (the bombardment of Oran). Addington for his part noted the most recent instance of all, in the course of the subsequent debates on war with Spain which occupied both Houses in the first two months of 1805: that of the detention of Dutch merchant ships before war was declared on Holland in 1795 (for which see II, 548); *P.D.*, III, col. 350, for 11 February 1805.

2. An inquiry indeed was put on this possibility to the United States Minister in London. Cf. p. 692 above.

3. Pitt to Harrowby, 18 September 1804 (Harrowby Mss, vol. XII), and see also loc. cit., same to same, 28 August 1804 for the proviso about passage of troops. The Foreign Secretary's first despatch to Frere in Madrid however was sent only on 29 September (p. 703, n1). See also Harrowby to Frere, no. 3, 21 October 1804 (F.O. 72/54).

Pitt's defence of the Government's conduct in relation to Spain may be followed in *P.D.*, III, cols. 366–85. The most effective attack on it came from Grenville in the Lords (op. cit., cols. 354–64).

4. That indeed was the danger; the Spanish Government itself was by no means eager for war, and feeling in the country had been rising against France.

directly and also indirectly by the provision of Spanish ships for some tasks falling otherwise on the senior ally. It posed a geographical threat to the British Mediterranean fleet, from inside the Straits of Gibraltar, at a time when affairs east of Malta might demand more prominent attention. A Spanish declaration of war in 1796 had forced Jervis and Nelson to withdraw in due course into the Atlantic.[1] To lose a presence in the region now would be a sorry setback, impinging on the rising prospects for a Russian alliance, and on the continued use of the base for whose sake Britain had gone to war. The Russians indeed were not best pleased by the sudden development.[2] Nonetheless British Ministers faced and accepted it coolly enough. War had been on the cards for some months. The Mediterranean fleet's earlier withdrawal had not lasted long,[3] and the Spaniards' competence was not held in high regard. There was the prospect of fresh colonial conquests, perhaps in both hemispheres and particularly in South America where plans for such undertakings had a long history and in fact had already been aired once more.[4] There might even in addition be a possibility of a raid in force on the mainland itself.[5] Nor was Spain's accession likely to be entirely without problems for France: a weaker partner can usually raise frustrating problems for the stronger. If Pitt and his colleagues had risked forcing the pace they had done so deliberately, and did not seem unduly cast down by the result.[6]

In any case they were not in a forbearing mood. The spirit in the country now was one of defiance at large as invasion still loomed, and while that immediate danger in point of fact had perceptibly lessened by the end of the summer, it could not – *pace* the previous winter – be prudentially dismissed.[7] To abandon a prudential course with Spain was a

---

1. II, 611, 630–2, 634–6, 643.
2. See Leveson Gower to Harrowby, no. 8, 28 November 1804 (*Third Coalition*, 71–2).
3. P. 139 above.
4. Cf. I, 385–6. See Mulgrave to Pitt, 7 December 1804: a long reply to a request from Pitt for facts, in detail, about 'Spanish America' (Stanhope Ms U1590, S503/7). Dundas had included the subject in his memorandum on strategy in March 1800, and reverted to it four months later (pp. 354, 368 above); and the indefatigable Miranda (I, 385–6, 562) was now stirring afresh (to Melville, 15 May 1804, shown to Pitt, P.R.O. 30/8/160), possibly with suggestions on which Pitt retained detailed notes which he may have intended to but did not send to the King on 17 September (see P.R.O. 30/8/196, ff. 88–9v).
5. A plan for the occupation of Ferrol – that strategically placed naval base which had attracted military attention in the previous war – was in fact considered seriously by the inner group of Ministers (Pitt, Melville, Camden, Harrowby) at the end of November. It was turned down decisively by General John Moore, summoned for advice from his own coastal command in Kent (p. 543 above), after he had gone out, at his own suggestion, to have a covert look on the spot (see *The Diary of Sir John Moore*, ed. Major-General J. F. Maurice, II (1904), ch. XXI).
6. Eg the tone of the brief matter of fact entry in Canning's diary for 21 November 1804 after talking to Pitt (Canning Ms 29d). As early as May indeed Harrowby had wondered if we should not act before the French forced the Spaniards to do so (*Malmesbury*, IV, 312).
7. Cf. pp. 615–16 above.

firm decision in its own right. It could be taken also as a further sign that an approach for peace with France was not to be expected from Britain. If a serious overture was detected or received from Paris, directly or through others – Russia after all had not dropped its offer to both sides of mediation[1] – it must of course be examined in London with care. But the only hint of that kind which came in 1804 was judged to be distinctly unconvincing; Pitt let it lie pending further evidence, and when that did not follow the incident was closed.[2] Meanwhile his own stance in the conduct of the war itself had been made clear. He had castigated Addington for failing to grasp the potential new scale of this struggle, and the new dimension presented by Napoleon himself – restless, amoral, a military overlord as yet effectively unchecked and correspondingly intent on blocking or removing the only Power that lay across his path.[3] Intense measures were needed for defence, and decisive preparations for offence; and the two could be interrelated as the enemy's plans might mature. In a period when Pitt contemplated active pressure on potential allies – joint leverage with Russia to force a change of Ministers on Austria, and simultaneously to bring Prussia into line[4] – he did not shrink from adding a new enemy in what seemed to be the secondary shape of Spain.

IV

To the watchers from the Channel and the Kentish coast, to British agents and consuls in Europe, to the Admiralty and the Secretaries of State's

1. P. 689 above.

2. The affair is discussed in Stanhope, IV, 199–202, which gives the text of a memorandum by Pitt of 5 June 1804, and in Holland Rose, II, 505–6. A week after the new Minister took office the American envoy in Paris, Robert Livingston, came to London to convey his impression, from talks with Joseph Bonaparte and with Talleyrand, that peace might be reached if 'some arrangement for Malta' (in Pitt's words) could be traded for a French withdrawal from Holland and Switzerland and a restoration of Hanover. The package in itself covered likely, indeed obvious ground – these had been among the most prominent causes of recrimination. But it carried no ascertainable authority – there was no indication above all, however discreet, of Napoleon's own cognisance or approval; it was wholly lacking in substance on what might be proposed for Holland and Switzerland in the future; it required the first avowable overture for talks to emanate from London; and Livingston himself was a particularly unfortunate messenger, who was most unlikely to be welcome, having earlier taken a markedly hostile line in Paris to some repercussions arising from British covert activities. He seems to have tried to approach the Government through his late colleague Whitworth, who however refused to meet him (see Pitt to Whitworth, 28 May 1804; copy in P.R.O. 30/8/102), and managed to do so in the event through Fox, who, quite properly, went with Grey to see the Minister in Downing Street (Fox to Pitt, 4 June 1804; Dacres Adams Mss, formerly P.R.O. 30/58/5. See also *Rose* – who as an archetypal Treasury man had been anxious for some years to avoid further war if that could be secured on reasonable terms – II, 136–8; and for an impression of the episode from Russia, *Third Coalition*, 27).

3. Cf. pp. 626, 688 above.

4. Pp. 697, 701–2 above.

offices sifting rumours and intelligence of invasion, the summer months of 1804 were a more highly powered version of the second half of 1803. The counter preparations were being strengthened in every respect; obstacles to landing improved, troops better trained than the year before. Work on the defences, under way at points since the middle nineties and more seriously since 1802, was now stepped up with the emphasis predictably on the area facing Calais and Boulogne. Pitt of course took a strong personal interest in all that went on there. As the enemy's concentration reached a peak in midsummer, and Napoleon appeared in July in person to review his three corps of troops, the Minister was putting his newly acquired weight behind further means of obstruction. He had earlier inspected the plans for 'driving the country' – for removing transport and stocks; in the late summer he took part in a local meeting to settle final provisional plans for flooding Romney Marsh; he forwarded the construction of a chain of strongpoints – the celebrated Martello towers – which began to rise in the following spring; and ensured the achievement of the novel project that has always been associated with him – the Royal Military Canal, the secondary line of defence running behind the marshes from Hythe to Winchelsea, whose solitary landscape survives in places as his monument today.[1] He was equally involved in the Government's abortive dealings with the American Robert Fulton and the 'experiment' of his submarine-borne torpedoes: a stratagem tried in part against the transports in Boulogne in October and December, and projected indeed on a larger scale for an attack on the enemy's fleets in Cadiz in October 1805.[2] Such instant preoccupations focused his continuous general concern. The familiar weekly states of the forces at home and overseas reappeared among his papers,[3] as he gathered up once more the reins of national defence.

The renewed surge of effort in Kent, preparing earlier, was set on its

1. See eg P.R.O. 30/8/245, ff. 43v, 87–90v; and in general P.A.L. Vines, *The Royal Military Canal* (1972), particularly 32–3, 38–43, 79, 89, and Peter Bloomfield, *Kent and the Napoleonic Wars* (1987), 23–36.

2. 'The Experiment' in October 1804 excited high interest within the close circle in the Admiralty which had been in touch with Fulton in recent months. Witnessed by the First Lord in person, and the results passed by him secretly to the King (who was cautious), it led to negotiations for a contract that failed after Pitt's death, leading to Fulton's withdrawal and leaving the first effective exercise of torpedo warfare to the United States' Civil War. Pitt, who watched one of the tests and indeed set up a small commission to report on the possibilities, kept in his files an undated draft of the proposed arrangements with 'Mr. Francis' [Fulton] 'for attacking the Enemy's Fleet by submarine operations without the submarine Vessel' (P.R.O. 30/8/250, ff. 176–9). See also Melville to George III, 4 October 1804, from Walmer Castle (*L.C.G. III*, IV, no. 2946) and copy of same to Pitt, 14 October 1804 (P.R.O. 30/8/157). The background is conveniently sketched in *The Keith Papers . . .*, ed. Christopher Lloyd, III (1955), 7–9. Pitt's interest in a complementary, or alternative, invention a year later – Congreve's rocket – is demonstrated in 'Congreve's Rockets 1805–1806', ed. Christopher Lloyd and Hardin Craig, Jnr, in *The Naval Miscellany*, IV, ed. Christopher Lloyd (1952), 425, 432–4.

3. P.R.O. 30/8/240. Cf. II, 486.

way in September and October, at a time when in fact the worst fears for
the season were on the wane. Pitt's determination to fire the spirit of alert-
ness was fortified by his enduring belief that the enemy would keep invasion as a high priority. But as Napoleon left the Channel coast and then
toured the Rhine at the end of August, and there was no sign of significant
movement from the Atlantic or Mediterranean ports, the Minister seems
to have come closer to the developing view that an attempt was almost certainly shelved. This indeed was the case. For despite constant or apparent
divagations, Napoleon agreed basically with British naval opinion that a
sizeable crossing carried high risk unless covered by something like a battle
fleet; and disappointed of hopes of a dash from Toulon to open up
manoeuvre in the Atlantic and gain control, however briefly, of the
Channel straits,[1] he was now turning his thoughts largely to other things.
The Admiralty for its part remained convinced, as earlier, that without
such support an embarkation was doomed; so Pellew had argued to the
Commons in 1803, and so Pitt's own First Lord argued now in October, as
he had 'so often' since May. As matters stood, the flotilla in Boulogne could
only rot in harbour, or be burned in the outer road, or destroyed at sea.
The best guarantee of the local lines of defence lay beyond the horizon, in
the squadrons off the Atlantic ports and Toulon with the Channel fleet in
final support. If their dispositions could be held in balance and at
sufficient strength, Melville would clearly agree, for once, with his formidable predecessor – 'I do not say . . . that the French will not come. I only
say they will not come by sea'.[2] The speculations in London in the summer
and autumn of 1804 furnish not only a commentary on the current situation but equally a prologue to the Trafalgar campaign.

Pitt was able the more easily to give personal attention to the defensive
works because the plans matured in the summer recess: Parliament rose at
the end of July. His main business in the part of the session that remained
on his return to office was to introduce and carry a measure for military
manpower. After his attack on his predecessor's Army of Reserve this was
in fact incumbent on him, as he was soon reminded; and on 5 June he
moved his Permanent Additional Force bill.[3] In large part it followed the

1. 'Let us be masters of the Straits for six hours, and we shall be masters of the world':
the famous statement to Vice-Admiral Latouche-Tréville, commanding at Toulon, 2 July
1804.

2. Another famous statement, always attributed to St Vincent in a Lords' debate in
1803; and cf. for Pellew in the Commons p. 632, n1 above. See in general Melville to Pitt, 14
October 1804 (P.R.O. 30/8/157), and the Admiralty's instructions to Admiral Sir William
Cornwallis, commanding the Channel fleet, of 24 August 1804 (*Letters and Papers of Charles,
Lord Barham*, ed. Sir John Knox Laughton, III (1911), 232–9).

3. He had been rebuked for delay by the Irish backbencher Richard Ker on 31 May
(*P.D.*, II, col. 480; for Ker see *H of P*, IV, 333–4). The word 'permanent' emphasised that
the plan was directed not solely at the immediate situation but was meant to provide a
proper means of support for the regular army for the rest of the war. Some Members
chose to regard it as applying 'permanently' to the future, introducing the spectre of a
reinforced standing army.

lines of his speech in April criticising the results of Addington's scheme. The militia, exclusive of the supplementary militia, should be reduced to a figure of 48,000 for England and Scotland, while the quotas for that supplementary force plus the Army of Reserve were merged to supply a total of 79,000, with a first priority to make good the latter's shortfall, which he estimated at 9,000 and was in fact some 12,000.[1] When brought to full strength such a body would provide the key which, in conjunction with the old militia and the improved Volunteers, would 'set the regular army at liberty . . . and render it a disposable force'.[2] But that goal would not be reached unless the methods of recruitment were improved, and the proper lesson was learned from experience. He had formerly accepted the familiar system of the ballot; but, already critical of its failure and also the expense of the recent higher bounties, and also impressed now by its unpopularity in the House, he wished to reject it[3] and instead make the parish officers directly responsible for producing the counties' levies. Bounties were necessary, and would continue to be offered, but at a lower rate so as to reduce the costs and also competition with recruiting for the regular army; and the money would come from the Treasury in this instance rather than from the parish rates. Rewards would apply as usual for numbers raised, and fines for deficient quotas; but to encourage truly voluntary zeal Pitt returned to his favourite idea of forming the recruits (as had not been specifically arranged under Addington's design) into second battalions of designated regular regiments. A bond of loyalties and attachment would thereby be forged, predominantly of a local character, which should surely benefit front-line and reserve formations alike; and while the latter were destined for home duties, following the cardinal principle for auxiliary forces, such connexions might foster the inducements already offered for voluntary general service.[4]

The bill drew criticism throughout its passage towards its enshrinement in a series of Acts.[5] Fresh attacks were launched a year later; and in less than two years altogether its main opponents brought about its repeal. The 'permanent' design indeed had failed by then to meet its object,

1. Cf. pp. 624–8, 633–4, including p. 633, n5 above.

2. *P.D.*, II, col. 485.

3. In acknowledging a recent change of mind here, he attributed it squarely to the Commons' prevailing mood (18 June 1804; op. cit., col. 742). Rose too could perhaps claim some prior success in persuading him to favour abolition (*Rose*, II, 144–5).

4. Cf. II, 486–8 for early, and pp. 124–5, 628 above for later attempts to foster voluntary enlistment from auxiliaries for wider or general service. Pitt's continuing emphasis on local loyalties had been first shown explicitly in 1794 (II, 486) and it was undoubtedly fortified in recent years by his experience as a Volunteer Colonel. Might it also, one wonders, have drawn more distantly on childhood tales of his father's decision to raise Scots Highland regiments in the fifties, helping to expunge the memories of the '45? The well established success of that initiative was cited, not uninterestingly, at one point in the debates on the new bill (by the Scot William Elliot, though himself in opposition, 18 June 1804; *P.D.*, II, col. 700).

5. 44 Geo. III, cs 56, 66, 74 for England, Scotland, Ireland respectively.

supplying in that time fewer than half the numbers produced in six months for the earlier Army of Reserve. Pitt himself was forced to acknowledge the shortfall with a separate bill in March 1805 which turned directly to the supplementary militia to reinforce the regular army.[1] What then had gone wrong? And would it have been likely to continue – for towards the end of the measure's short life recruiting was in fact approaching a more acceptable level?[2] The scheme contained some useful features. The abolition of the ballot was well worth trying, and indeed not widely opposed; the shift of some payments from the local to the central authorities could be welcomed; the specific attachment of reserves to regular regiments strengthened a valuable gain which was already emerging implicitly from Addington's Act.[3] The troubles arose directly from the high degree of reliance placed on the parishes: a panacea urged by Pitt while out of office which in effect imposed on the provisions of the Army of Reserve the pattern of his own Quota Acts of 1795–6. Those measures had certainly played a part in contributing to the level of recruitment in the central years of that war; but in somewhat different circumstances, and with their full share of the shortcomings endemic in local administration.[4] Nor did the parish officers now look kindly on this renewed burden. They found the reduced bounties too low, their own areas of operations too restrictive, and their rewards inadequate; rival inducements – from the Volunteers, and the regular army itself – were hampering their task, and there seemed little point at first in trying too hard. They preferred to pay their fines – the measure became known as the twenty pound Act[5] – and despite repeated adjurations the early rate of success remained dismally low.

In retrospect, one may see Pitt's plan as just another in a lengthy series of attempts to graft onto a system of deliberate limitations of power a solution to the ever growing needs of a conflict for whose scale the system

---

1. The ensuing Act was 45 Geo. III, c31. The passage of the bills of 1804 may be followed in *P.D.*, II, *passim* between cols. 562 and 1055; there were calls in February and March 1805 for repeal of the subsequent Acts (*P.D.*, III (1812), cols. 480–520, 723–85); and this was secured in May 1806. At that point the legislation was said to have produced in all some 13,000 men. See Fortescue, *A History of the British Army*, V (1910), 239–40, 301, Glover, *Peninsular Preparation*, 238. At the beginning of 1805 Pitt was told by his former friend J.C. Villiers (see I, 17, II, 633n4), now saddened and disgruntled, that his 'Army bill' was thought 'a complete disappointment' (20 January 1805; Dacres Adams Mss, formerly P.R.O. 30/58/6), and at the end of the year he had in his files a copy of the Inspector General's instructions on improving recruitment from the 'small Number of Men' obtained under the Act (December 1805; P.R.O. 30/8/241).

2. According to figures produced by Spencer Perceval in April 1806, Pitt himself claimed in March 1805 that this was beginning to happen, and that there should not be too much concentration on the early results (*P.D.*, III, cols. 751–7).

3. P. 635 above.

4. Cf. II, 485, 497, 642–3. Glover, op. cit., 215–16, 238, 252–3 seems to me too harsh.

5. Sheridan in fact professed to regard it as 'a tax bill', which should be called by its proper name (18 June 1804, *P.D.*, II, col. 735; 6 March 1805, *P.D.*, III, col. 734) – a gibe that eventually stung Pitt (op. cit., col. 750).

had not been designed. The result, given short shrift, failed in its turn to surmount the problems of the past. The long list of earlier adaptations and amendments to the pattern – a supplementary militia with extended scope to add to the old militia, a revised organisation of Volunteers, a body of reserves for the regular formations placed uneasily in the nexus of auxiliaries – had thrown up anomalies, complications and contradictions which were proving increasingly hard to digest. In the early, let alone the middle years of the Napoleonic War the task of reading the statute book, confusing enough already despite efforts to recodify it, was becoming a bewildering process. As *The Annual Register* observed later, 'No subject had, of late years, so frequently engaged the attention of parliament . . . Project after project had been proposed. Experiment after experiment had been tried'.[1] They did not end with Pitt, and his immediate successors indeed proved more inept. But his proposals suffered keenly from the fact that they did not shake clear enough of the familiar precedents. The disappointment he caused sprang from the expectations he had excited in his assault on his predecessor's record, and the anticipation of something original, worthy of the talents of 'a giant refreshed'.[2] When the time arrived, the extent of his dependence on parts of the derided plan for the Army of Reserve – a concept to which indeed he felt obliged in the end to pay a passing tribute;[3] the limited nature of his alternative – an appeal to a mode of recruitment already tried with only partial success; the impression of further patching, coming from a Minister once celebrated for his powers of comprehensive review, set the objections to detail in an already critical context. For while there was certainly room for dispassionate administrative reservations, these were not the only factors involved. They were themselves sharpened, indeed largely impelled, by the political legacy of recent months. Pitt in fact was on trial to make good the charges and the claim which had helped him back into office. He was paying a price for the process of Addington's dislodgement and the varied resentments which that finally aroused.

V

This was obvious from the start. There was no real chance for opponents of the new Ministry to show their teeth in Parliament in the first few weeks – though Grenville gave an indication by forcing a division in the Lords, and being rude to Eldon, in a last discussion on the dying stage of the much travelled Volunteer Consolidation bill.[4] The opening came when Pitt introduced his measure for the Additional Force. Genuine objections,

---

1. *The Annual Register . . . for the Year 1806* (1808), 39.
2. The phrase was Stafford's [see p. 652 above], in the Lords on 11 May 1804; *P.D.*, II, col. 409.
3. Speech of 6 March 1805 – see p. 710 above; *P.D.*, III, col. 754.
4. On 28 May; *P.D.*, II, cols. 433–8.

held strongly, influenced the House. But it was clear enough that 'the circumstances under which [he] came into office' accounted for the acrimony of the debates.[1] Grenvillites, Foxites, Addingtonians all joined in the chase; at one moment indeed there was 'a ferment' in the Commons which Addington himself, claiming to have allayed it, thought 'one of the most violent' he had ever seen.[2] At that point in fact the bill looked as if it might be lost;[3] and while the impression proved wrong, the numbers in the divisions – for there was a series of divisions – made uncomfortable reading for the Government. Pitt brought in the measure on 5 June. The vote on the 8th for the second reading was 221 to 181; on the 11th, for going into committee, 219 to 169; on the 15th, it was 214 to 186 on the report stage, after Ministers had been caught out on the way by a snap vote on a particular point and put in a minority of 63 to 69; on the 18th, 265 to 223 on the engrossment. The third reading finally passed the next day without a division;[4] but such figures showed the intensity of the successive occasions – as did those of the second reading in the Lords, 154 to 69, on 25 June. The aggregate vote of 488 on the 18th in the Commons indeed marked the highest division since 1741.[5] The excitement showed likewise in the length of some of the discussions: the debate of the 8th ended at 3 am on the 9th, that of the 18th at 4.30 am on the 19th.

This was not a reassuring start. The Ministry in fact suffered a shock. The opening majority of 40 was certainly less than expected – by 20 or 30 if not more –, it sank at one point to a mere 28, and on the last of the divisions it was 42. That was scarcely higher than the support given to Addington shortly before he resigned.[6] At one stage the bill's opponents

---

1. Eg George Johnstone, a recent and assiduous Foxite recruit, claiming that this was not the ground for an objection of his own (14 June 1804; *P.D.*, II, col. 673). Other allusions to a fact accepted comprehensively may be found op. cit., cols. 691, 713, 725, 745–8 (Pitt himself), 824, 827. After listening to one such passage in the Lords, Mulgrave was reported as saying that 'if anything was wanting to convince him that the opposition to this bill was not given to the principle of the bill, its operation, or its real character, but to the person who brought it in', it was what he had just heard (op. cit., col. 825).

2. To Hiley Addington on 13 June (quoted in *L.C.G. III*, IV, no. 2881n3).

3. Ibid: 'I find it to be the general opinion that Mr. Pitt's bill will not pass'. Addington could count on his personal supporters fully in this particular case, after his own scheme had been so harshly rejected (see *L.C.G. III*, IV, xxi–ii).

4. *P.D.*, II, col. 607; *Colchester*, I, 518; *P.D.*, II, col. 686; *Colchester*, op. cit., 519 (*P.D.*, II, col. 697 being incorrect); *P.D.*, II, col. 753; op. cit., 771. A brief amending Act, 44 Geo. III, c96 had to follow in July on a technicality, and Scotland and Ireland as always in matters of recruitment required their own measures; see p. 709, n5 above.

5. *H of P*, IV, 820. According to one account (see *L.C.G. III*, IV, n3 on p. 198), over 500 Members were present, including perhaps ten pairs. In 1741 the aggregate vote had been 508. The figure in 1804 of course included Irish Members introduced by the Union (*Colchester*, I, 520).

6. As Stanhope (IV, 210) pointed out. The calculation of 20–30 more 'at least' was Nepean's, now Irish Secretary; one Opposition peer, the Marquess of Sligo, went so far as to believe that Rose had expected a majority of almost a hundred (see *L.C.G. III*, IV, no. 2881n2).

appeared 'triumphant', and the King himself, urging 'energy' on the Treasury, showed a momentary doubt.[1]

There was not however any question of Pitt resigning if the bill was defeated. His predecessor did not expect it,[2] and he himself made the position plain.

> If the present bill should be lost, I shall be sorry for it . . . ; but the hon.
> gentlemen opposite will be much mistaken, if they think they will
> thereby be any thing the nearer getting rid of me.

It had 'ever been allowed to be one of the first and most established privileges and prerogatives of the crown' that the monarch had 'a right to choose and nominate' his Ministers, and 'with that conviction' he for his part would continue to serve.[3] As he remarked, he had been 'at issue upon this point in former times',[4] and after what had recently passed it would indeed have been strange if he had urged a wish to retire on the King – without the slightest likelihood that that would have been accepted, with the possibility of a serious royal relapse,[5] and in all probability against the public's wishes when the Ministry had barely settled in. Nor, he could reflect, were the assorted opponents of the measure necessarily well placed to convert a limited into a continuing success. Addington's personal supporters – taking them as a consistent entity[6] – were naturally distinct, in their sentiments and largely their politics, from their partners in this immediate case; they were bred to suspect the Foxites, and they disliked the Grenville clan. The Old and New Oppositions themselves – together in this instance with the leading Carlton House politicians, whose individual ambitions and the focus of their allegiance made them an essentially unreliable group – could not be entirely sure where the path might lead. If there was much now to connect them, there was still a good deal on which to feel mutual reserve. Grenville's own relations with Pitt continued to deteriorate, particularly when his letter of 8 May, declining to take office without Fox, was published in June in the leading Opposition newspaper – a disclosure which his cousin condemned, and for which he

---

1. His close interest during the contest may be seen in his letters to Pitt, in Stanhope, IV, Appendix, xvi–xvii. As so often, he laid his finger on one of the troubles; the whips allowed too many absentees at an important stage. For a glimpse of Opposition's – or at least the Foxites' – feelings see *A.C.*, IV, 199 (nd but probably relating to 8 or, more likely, 15 June), also *Correspondence of Prince of Wales*, V (1968), no. 1887n1, with *L.C.G. III*, IV, no. 2884n1. Fox's own retrospective view in July, *Memorials and Correspondence of Fox*, IV, 57, was unduly buoyant.

2. Addington to Hiley Addington, 13 June 1804 (see *L.C.G. III*, IV, no. 2881n3).

3. Pitt's speech of 18 June (*P.D.*, II, cols. 747–8). Cf. p. 712, n1 above.

4. Op. cit., col. 745.

5. It would presumably have been to such a danger that Addington referred when he commented, on the Ministry's presumed survival if the measure was defeated, 'This I rejoice at under the circumstances' (to Charles Yorke; quoted in *L.C.G. III*, IV, no. 2881n3).

6. See the qualification on p. 666 above.

himself denied responsibility.[1] His resentment of the Crown's policy of 'exclusion' did not weaken, or of its acceptance by the man on whom he had twice pinned his hopes of forming a Government which in effect would be of their own choosing.[2] Active partnership with Fox in the current debates also helped strengthen the links; and his scepticism of the Ministry was reinforced in the later summer by the provocative seizure, as he saw it, of the Spanish treasure ships.[3] Nevertheless he maintained his strong disapproval of 'professed or systematic opposition', and that orthodoxy, agreed by both wings at the start, was upheld by other influential figures, Spencer perhaps most notably, who shared something of Grenville's background and were now accustomed to look largely to him.[4] The profession was not felt so firmly in all parts of the coalition; not equally indeed throughout the Grenville family itself – Thomas was more ambivalent – and within the core of the Foxites scarcely if at all. In 1804 this was an underlying rather than immediate cause for strain, and there were enough reasons for continuing, perhaps growing, co-operation to satisfy both elements of the alliance. Pitt was making a debating point when he declared that the 'troops' of the parties ranged against his bill 'upon no other occasion could ever be made to speak the same language'.[5] But his intentions were not seriously disturbed in any case by an attack which he had foreseen, though not in such degree. He would ride out what remained of the session, the long recess lay ahead, and in those months he relied on attracting enough fresh support.[6]

His greater danger, and Opposition's greatest hope, in point of fact lay elsewhere. The uncomfortable patchiness of George III's recovery, visible in May,[7] persisted for the next three to four months. The frequency of 'incoherence' and 'indiscretions' declined; but 'hurry' and 'agitation' were at times all too visible, mixed with occasions of perfect lucidity and balance and the usual grasp of detail. The doctors, while carefully repeating their belief in the King's capacity to perform his functions, remained equally insistent that he should avoid 'excess of fatigue', and others who saw him in the summer noted how much he seemed to have aged.[8] In

---

1. See Jupp, *Lord Grenville*, 334–5 for mutual reactions conveyed through Bathurst. The letter, for which see p. 662 above, appeared in *The Morning Post* of 18 June – in the midst of the debates on the Additional Force Bill.

2. Cf. pp. 593–4, 615–16 above.

3. Pp. 703–4 and n3 above.

4. See Jupp, op. cit., 334 for the agreement within Opposition in May 1804.

5. 18 June 1804 (*P.D.*, II, col. 745).

6. Cf. p. 667 above.

7. See ibid.

8. Examples of this last impression come from Glenbervie, who was struck in mid August by the King's thinness and 'a glare that one could not look at without uneasiness' (*Glenbervie*, 1, 395), and from an equerry some weeks earlier who found him looking twenty years older (W.H. Fremantle, quoted in *L.C.G. III*, IV, no. 2922n1 on p. 221). See also, for a

these months, too, he began to suffer the growing loss of sight that would end in complete blindness. It was a worrying time for a Minister who came into office relying so heavily on the Crown.

The uncertainty was bound to cast its shadow. If George III were to be afflicted once more, Pitt's future could clearly be in jeopardy, and the fact could not but affect his calculations and those of others at home and perhaps to some extent abroad. The King's prospects were naturally of intense interest in all quarters of the Parliamentary world. They may also have tended to underline doubts in the European Courts being wooed for an alliance: the Russians at any rate, most closely concerned, took note, if briefly, of an added factor in weighing a complex and far-reaching case.[1] This possible dependence on the monarch's durability was nothing new to this particular Minister; nor indeed were the possibilities necessarily as adverse for him as in 1789. At the same time however he had to cope, paradoxically, with a more instant if lesser problem which might prove threatening precisely if George III survived, and particularly in a fluctuating state.

For as he emerged from his latest crisis, the King proved to be in an awkward mood. Unlike the calm in 1789,[2] he was resolved to have his way, and press his rights, in matters affecting himself. His relations with his family, above all with the Queen, were profoundly altered – she was now frightened and disgusted, while he spoke of leading his private life on his own with friends. More seriously for Pitt, he set about making quite sweeping changes at Court, extending from the grooms and pages to the higher appointments including some of the Great Officers of State. As such, these last were of direct and significant import to Government: the choice of the Lord Steward and the Lord Chamberlain was of concern to the King's Ministers as well as to the King. So too was that of the holders of some other Household posts; the Groom of the Stole for instance could

---

bad spell in September, a disturbing account in *Correspondence of Prince of Wales*, V, no. 1958. There is of course a wide range of comment and evidence, good and not so good, on which to draw in such a case. Gossip abounded; and conclusions varied among those in some real position to judge. The doctors themselves were baffled, as earlier, by this strange case: Pitt's copies of their reports until September may be found in P.R.O. 30/8/228. A representative sense may be gathered from successive footnotes in *L.C.G. III*, IV, from May to October, in which Aspinall's great knowledge of collections of private papers bears rewarding fruit. See for comparison McAlpine and Hunter, *George III and the Mad Business*, ch. 7, where the narrative of improvement does not and is not designed to take into account some disturbing actions bearing on politics.

1. See *Memoirs of Czartoryski*, II, 35. The Duke of Northumberland, an ardent Foxite, professed to have had letters to this effect from Petersburg, Vienna, Madrid and Lisbon (to Colonel McMahon (for the Prince of Wales), 5 August 1804 (*Correspondence of Prince of Wales*, V, 66). Cf. p. 690 above for the Russians' inclination over part of the year to await the outcome of a French cross-Channel descent.

2. Cf. I, 663: 'indeed for the rest of my life [I] shall . . . only keep that superintending eye which can be effected without labour or fatigue'. This was applied specifically to 'business' and 'the duties of . . . employments': it did not refer to appointments. But the tone was not that of 1804.

still claim membership of the vestigial 'Grand' Cabinet, the Masters of the Horse and the Buckhounds could be past or future members of the Cabinet itself.[1] All these offices changed hands from May to July 1804, as did others – the Captain of the Yeomen of the Guard, the Comptroller of the Household, the Vice-Chamberlain – with distinct or arguable political connotations. Some of the movements were objectionable to the Ministry or raised complications for it. But there was no sign of consultation in advance from the King.[2]

This, again, raised anxieties for a Minister who perforce depended in working practice to such an extent on the monarch. George III was certainly supporting Pitt to the hilt in Parliament, and on the whole speaking well of him in private.[3] There was no need to suppose that, for the time being, he had any option. But within that framework, decisions on appointments, as always, were overt tests of standing for a Ministry; they were followed keenly as indications of strength; and this opening dismayed observers apprehensive of where it might lead. No doubt it could be taken as a symptom of a still unsteady state of health – not in itself a very reassuring conclusion. It could also however be an indication of the limits of royal favour, which might make the Government's position 'not only unpleasant, but extremely dangerous'.[4] The initial difficulties proved to be the most blatant in the event. But some later minor incidents showed that the King was carrying his exercise of patronage to the limit; and this was a tendency hard to control, given Pitt's situation, his personal attitude now towards the monarch, and his own temperament.[5] The balance on the endless seesaw seemed to have tipped away from him; he shrank from risking too much confrontation and excitement; and if the consequences were of a different order from those of a further, almost certainly crippling relapse, and could be generally endured, they were liable to cause repeated embarrassment for himself and his Administration. In the

---

1. See Aspinall, *The Cabinet Council*, 145–8; also p. 672, n4 above for the possible plan for Camden as Lord Steward with a place in the Cabinet in 1803, and 671, n1 for Westmorland and Montrose respectively as Master of the Horse; I, 181n1 for the Grand Cabinet.

2. List in *L.C.G. III*, IV, l–li, with n1. The new Groom of the Stole succeeded after a death, not a dismissal. Perhaps the most awkward of the changes for the Ministry was that affecting Pelham, removed as Chancellor of the Duchy of Lancaster by Pitt and appointed Captain of the Yeomen of the Guard by the King, against Pelham's expressed wishes to the Minister. For the lack of consultation see eg *Rose*, II, 139–43, 153.

3. Though not always; see the account in *Correspondence of Prince of Wales*, V, no. 1958 (p. 714, n8 above).

4. Rose's diary, 29 May 1804 (*Rose*, II, 143) – though he was proving increasingly something of a pessimist. And cf. the opinion of Mrs Harcourt, who had a long and close knowledge of the Court, that Pitt should talk to the King for the latter's own sake (Malmesbury's diary, 27 May; *Malmesbury*, IV, 319). Cf. also *Life and Letters of . . . Elliot*, III, 337–8.

5. Cf. Bathurst, 'It requires great management to oppose this, and management of this sort is what Pitt's virtues and infirmities peculiarly disqualify him' [for]; quoted in Aspinall, *The Cabinet Council*, 237.

background moreover there might lie the possibility of a greater threat. It was not so long since he had had a 'dear bought experience' to put him on his guard against 'secret management being again practised' at a critical point.[1]

At the end of the Parliamentary session in July there was thus every reason for Pitt to seek to broaden his base. The associated elements of Opposition might not prove cohesive enough to defeat him, provided he could manage to keep his troops in line. But even so they could impose a constant strain, particularly in view of his paucity of debating talent in the Commons.[2] Stern wartime tests lay ahead – alliances to be achieved some of whose conditions might cause dispute, rising pressures to be faced on the assumption of greater activity and expense. As things stood, he was denied the comfort of a more acquiescent House, to help carry the country, reassure Europe, and reduce the wear and tear on himself by allowing a relaxation of the watch on his political flanks. While he retained his old faith in his own capacity, he was too narrowly tied to a source of power whose collapse could further unsettle or remove him but whose survival tended, in its very vulnerability, to strengthen the terms of support. All these considerations prompted the same answer, and after a short pause he embarked on a search for an escape.

He did so against the background of an Administration that was not at ease with itself. Governments in the eighteenth and nineteenth centuries did not expect to be closely knit throughout, and the component parts operated, administratively and politically, often in loose if tenable conjunction. Nonetheless by the end of the previous war the Cabinet itself had become accustomed to rather greater coherence, and a sense of partnership, despite the later strains,[3] that would have now to be established anew. In the event however this did not come about. A body which, if uneven, did not lack ability, and might indeed have been thought capable of settling down on its circumscribed base,[4] soon showed a lack of confidence in its performance and in its members' mutual relations. Camden summed up his own impression after some five months. Melville, who should have been effective, was 'by no means unshaken by the pressure & anxiety of business'; Eldon was 'really of no political use'; he himself did not feel equal to taking 'a very matured & decided line in general Measures'; the effective members of the Ministry were largely in the junior posts. All in all, the Government could only 'scramble thro' the Business of the Country'.[5] Nor was there a want of personal resentments and reservations. Harrowby and Mulgrave appear to have been broadly on satisfactory terms with their

1. Mulgrave to Pitt, 27 December 1804 (Dacres Adams Mss, formerly P.R.O. 30/58/5).
2. Cf. pp. 668–9 above.
3. See pp. 452–7 above.
4. Cf. pp. 672–3 above.
5. To Pitt, Most secret & confidential, 15 October 1804 (Camden Mss, U840 C309).

colleagues. But Westmorland would have been keeping a wary eye open for the feelings at Court, Portland became ill, and Montrose's troubles with Melville's management of Scotland led him in the autumn to announce he had resigned. He was soon talked out of that.[1] But it was not the only such occurrence. In a much more troubling instance for Pitt, Hawkesbury had earlier done the same, as the result of a quarrel with Canning which demanded the Minister's anxious intervention. A good deal lay behind the episode: a light and sometimes wounding patronage by an acknowledged star of a less brilliant but initially more soundly established friend; a suspicion perhaps at one point of rivalry for Pitt's affection; some early jealousy on Canning's part in the pursuit of his political career, culminating in angry disappointment when Hawkesbury was retained in the Cabinet, albeit no longer at the Foreign Office, while he, the favoured son, was relegated to a place outside.[2] In an injudicious passage in a spirited speech on the bill for the Additional Force, he attacked Addington's Ministry, claiming that among his own past censures 'he had objected to the administration of foreign affairs, and that had been achieved'. The remark caused a stir, particularly since Pitt in his subsequent speech said nothing to remove the sting. Addington himself doubted if the two men could remain in office together, as did *The Times*, Ministerialist and formerly Addingtonian, the next day.[3] Hawkesbury was cut to the quick; he sent in his resignation, and there was a further disturbing sign when Castlereagh declared that if that took effect he would go too. Others, in the Cabinet and beyond, might have followed his example. It was clearly very important for Pitt to clear the matter up. He did so with some trouble, not before he had received an offer of resignation in turn from Canning – now alarmed and genuinely upset and intent on persuading 'Jenky' to stay. The affair seemed to be over; but it was to flare up afresh early the next year.[4] Like other indications of tension – Rose too, though silent, was unhappy with his lot[5] – it underlined a general discomfort which the Minister was finding it hard to allay.

1. Montrose to same, 21, 24 November 1804 (Dacres Adam Mss formerly P.R.O. 30/58/5, P.R.O. 30/8/160 respectively; and see p. 670 above). For Westmorland see pp. 607, n1, 615n3, 672n4 above.

2. See pp. 91–3, 671 above. He was not the only ambitious contemporary to harbour such feelings. Mornington had earlier shown a similar jealousy of promotion for 'young Jenky whom I have laughed at ever since I have known him' (to Addington, nd as quoted but before 1798; Butler, *The Eldest Brother*, 79).

3. *P.D.*, II, col. 722 for 18 June 1804; Pellew, op. cit., II, 318; *The Times*, 19 June.

4. Indeed our knowledge of what happened in June 1804 derives largely from the renewal of the row in January 1805. See correspondence between Hawkesbury and Canning, 11 January–2 February 1805 in B.L. Loan Ms 72, vol. 24; Canning's diary, 20, 22 June 1804, 11–17 February 1805 (Canning Ms 29d); paper in Pitt's hand, nd but January 1805, in Stanhope Ms U1590 S5010/16. Hawkesbury's letters to Pitt at the time, of 20 and 22 June 1804, are in Dacres Adams Mss, formerly P.R.O. 30/58/5.

5. He had been appointed Joint Paymaster General, and thought that after so many years of service he deserved something better. His dissatisfaction was compounded by the fact that Pitt, in making the offer, uttered 'not an expression of regret' (to Tomline, 14 or 16 May 1804; Pretyman Ms 435/44). And cf. p. 600, n3 above.

This state of affairs therefore did nothing to dispel a feeling in some parts of the Government, shared by Pitt from his own point of view, that there was a need for greater Parliamentary strength. His first idea was to apply to a quarter which had earlier shown little response and might indeed seem doubtful, but, if gained, could yield a significant return. The Prince of Wales was a figure not to be ignored at this point. The sources of support for the reversionary interest, beyond the familiar quarters within Opposition, might not be mobilised fully while the reversion remained only a prospect; and the politicians in his own circle scarcely provided the focus for a stable connexion.[1] But at least they could be identified as sharing a common concern; and if they, or some, could be recruited it might be presumed that their master did not disapprove, and a signal would be sent out which could have an effect. That however could hardly happen unless he was brought onto a better footing with his father; an aim hitherto obstructed by the Prince's continuing resentment at his failure to gain a military promotion or command, and by a further issue which now came to the boil.

The Prince of Wales's relations, or lack of them, with his wife had for years been a matter of public knowledge, and necessarily a subject of some attention by Government. The Princess had been careful to stay in touch with Pitt, and he with her, and he had done his best to keep her within bounds.[2] The Prince for his part refused to live with someone he detested. But in July he accepted advice from the most sensible of his advisers, Moira, to meet the King's wish to supervise the education of his grandchild, the eight year old Princess Charlotte, who would then be brought up at Windsor. This was something to build on; and Moira had also been working on a possible compromise to meet the problem of the Prince's military hopes. Melville had in fact reported this to Pitt in May, and Moira had also made it clear that in the event of a Regency he favoured the heir to the throne turning to Pitt, with the broad Ministry whose blockage then led him to decline the offer to join the subsequent Government.[3] In the same period, and perhaps profiting from such advice, the Prince did something to mend his fences with his father, or at least did not kick more of them down; and by July, assisted by the wishes of some of his family, he was indeed prepared to seek a reconciliation. As the summer holidays began, therefore, the glimmer of an opportunity

---

1. See pp. 610–11, 713 above.

2. P 527 above; *Rose*, II, 171–2. He did not have much hope by now.

3. *Correspondence of Prince of Wales*, V, 9–10, 54–5; Charles Hope to Melville, 22 May 1804, passed on to Pitt (P.R.O. 30/8/146); Melville to Pitt, 6 April 1804 (Dacres Adams Mss, formerly P.R.O. 30/58/5, and see p. 639, n4 above); p. 669 above.

This last advice had probably had some success before Fox's exclusion, which turned the Prince at once towards Opposition. Early in May he had professed himself friendly to Pitt (*Correspondence of Prince of Wales*, V, 7n1). I suspect indeed that the advice to confirm Pitt in office, given probably in 1801, which the Prince approved (see p. 527 and n7 above), came from Moira. But I have failed to establish that.

seemed to open; and significantly Moira at that time was, briefly, in the south again from his Scottish command.[1] In August it was arranged, through the Lord Chancellor, that the King and the Prince should meet – on 'a visit of civility' only, as the former made clear. But at the last minute the latter pulled out, having learned that his wife and daughter were commanded to see George III in advance. That put a stop to the proceedings. The King was due to go down to Weymouth, where he stayed until late in October, the proposal for Princess Charlotte was dropped, and it was not until mid November that the two men met.[2]

By that time, however, matters had moved on among the politicians. On the basis of his information from Melville, who showed a visible interest at the start in Moira's thoughts – and indeed used them to re-emerge actively on the scene himself[3] –, Pitt seems to have taken a lead, with Eldon necessarily in company, in urging the royal reconciliation and, more likely by himself at first, in political talks. A fresh attempt to accommodate Tierney, this time with the Irish Secretaryship, failed to come to the point in the summer.[4] But the prospect of the King's return from Weymouth, and the closer approach of the new session, set the scene for a comprehensive effort. At the end of October Pitt sought George III's consent to delay the opening of Parliament, already set for November, to January[5] – a postponement that certainly would give him more time to recruit more strength – and within the next fortnight he met Moira. The occasion started a flurry of activity, for the Minister held out the prospect of the Prince's friends co-operating with Government, or possibly joining a broader Administration in the event of a Regency. The exact detail, as reported through the Prince himself, was open to interpretation, and some of 'the high colouring' had to be toned down. But one thing was clear. Moira had been offered a Cabinet post, probably the Lord Lieutenancy of Ireland, and had replied that he must advise his master to consult those who had been more in touch

---

1. Cf. p. 164 above.

2. A précis of events, into which Pitt was drawn in the end, can be found in *Correspondence of Prince of Wales*, V, 10. Correspondence between the King and the Lord Chancellor is in op. cit., nos. 1923, 1929, and there is a retrospective account as reported from the former in Rose's diary for 30 September 1804 (*Rose*, II, 168–9). The suddenness of the breakdown in August may well have arisen from a muddle.

3. P. 638, n2 above; *H.M.C., Hastings*, III (1934), 231–2.

4. For the first see *Correspondence of Prince of Wales*, V, no. 1937 (in which reservations on Eldon's part are mentioned), *Rose*, II, 168; for Tierney, *Glenbervie*, I, 391 (each of the last two accounts being at first hand from conversations with the King), *Correspondence of Prince of Wales*, V, nos. 1913n1, 1937, 1939, *Rose*, II, 173, *Colchester*, I, 528–9. According to this last, by Tierney's own account he declined the offer 'for temporary reasons'; and see also a revealing letter to Pitt on the subject of the royal reconciliation, nd but August 1804, in Stanhope Ms, U1590 S504/5. Cf. p. 673 above for the earlier attempt to recruit him.

5. Unless news from Spain demanded an earlier meeting; to George III, 30 October 1804 (*L.C.G. III*, IV, no. 2961). At the end of July Parliament had been prorogued to September, when the date of reassembly was set at 27 November.

with him in the early summer months.[1] This indeed was done in the next two or three days. In the interval, the meeting between the King and the Prince which should have taken place in August did so on 12 November. It passed off politely, but politics were not discussed, and over the next week all concerned took stock. Pitt, and Melville, nurtured hopes, the more perhaps because the Prince was said now to set less store by his frustrated military command. But Foxites and Grenvillites alike proved reluctant to commit themselves or see Carlton House involved, and within the latter circle Sheridan now fought against Tierney's inclination to come to an understanding with Pitt. The Prince himself likewise hung back; and in any case he would soon not have been in a favourable mood, for the King proceeded after their meeting to follow up his proposal for his granddaughter's future with a paper, drawing in Eldon and Pitt, which only aroused another angry response. By 20 or 21 November all seemed to be over, and Opposition turned to consider its plans for the coming session, only a few weeks away.[2]

Pitt was thus now confronted more starkly by the need to decide if or where he must look to augment his ranks.[3] The failure to recruit a possible semi-detached interest meant a loss of hopes relating to both his current and his potential position. On the one hand, he could not count on immediately weakening the forces grouped against him. At the same time a chance had disappeared of reconciling present alignments with those looking to the future, under a royal rapprochement however constrained, and thereby of facilitating the prospect of a better proportioned common effort.[4] Unless he opted to continue as he was, he could not evade the problem of choosing between a direct approach to the Grenvillites with Fox or one to the Addingtonians. And either would disappoint and might antagonise a section of his own colleagues and supporters; for it would either depart from or confirm his controversial decision in May.

1. The date of their conversation was probably 9 or 10 November. For that and the first report see Thomas Grenville to Lord Grenville, 11 November 1804; an account that had to be modified the next day (*H.M.C., Dropmore*, VII, 237–9). An offer of Ireland, as it happened, would provide a good opportunity to improve matters in Dublin, for the Lord Lieutenant, the Earl of Hardwicke, and the Irish Secretary, Nepean [see p. 712, n6 above], did not get on, and administration was suffering. Nor was Hardwicke's own increasingly benevolent attitude towards Catholic relief very welcome to Pitt.

2. *Memorials and Correspondence of Fox*, IV, 61–4, *Windham Papers*, II, 235–45 and B.L. Add. Ms 37882 f. 119, Buckingham, III, 373–81 and B.L. Add. Ms 41851 ff. 235–8, *H.M.C., Dropmore*, VII, 239–46 and B.L. Add. Ms 41852 ff. 205–9, *Correspondence of Prince of Wales*, V, nos. 1964, 1966–7, 1972, 1975, 1977–86 *et seq.* as the question of Princess Charlotte dragged on, *H.M.C., Hastings*, III, 286–7, Canning Ms 29d for 21 November 1804.

3. It seems likely that he continued indeed for the next few weeks to sound out Moira, and complementarily to try to use him as a mediator between the Prince and the King over the young Princess. But he could make no headway (see Thomas Grenville to Grenville, 5–31 December 1804; Buckingham, III, 383–99).

4. An argument indeed pressed by Melville at the time of Pitt's approach to Moira; to Pitt, 11 November 1804 (Dacres Adams Mss, formerly P.R.O. 30/58/5).

Pitt's associates indeed found themselves in a quandary. Some, Canning most strongly and at least initially, favoured Grenville, though he may not have fairly faced the accompanying question of Fox.[1] Others, Hawkesbury and Chatham for instance, would much prefer Addington.[2] Others again, perhaps most importantly Melville, who at one time had placed weight on 'the large and powerfull Party of great Property and talents' (clearly indicating the whole range of Whiggish Opposition) which might look towards the Prince, moved with the collapse of the recent hopes towards expectations of Addington.[3] Most – like Melville indeed – were moved in the end by practicalities. The former difficulties must persist in any attempt to gain Grenville, the prospects in fact might be more distant now, Addington in one form or another seemed to provide the best answer. According to the latest calculation indeed he could bring a greater addition of numbers in the Commons than Carlton House might have done on its own: in the autumn Long and Rose put the former at about 40 while the latter, reckoned earlier at much the same, might now be reduced by about half.[4] Reckoning therefore purely on such figures, a Ministry including the Addingtonians should be able to carry on in some comfort as long as the King retained his health. And if a broader Government could not be attained, the matter of adequate comfort bulked large. As Long summed it up,

> I have no doubt that as things now stand you would be able to support the Administration through the ensuing Session but I doubt much whether you would be able to carry those strong measures which the situation of the Country appears to require . . .

The signs were pointing in the circumstances to Addington. The question remaining was that of terms.[5]

This however in its turn was a cause for anxious debate. Both Long and

1. Canning's diary, 11–12 December 1804 (Canning Ms 29d; and cf. p. 674 above); Camden to Pitt, 15 October, 21 December 1804 (Camden Ms U840 C30/9, P.R.O. 30/8/119 respectively, and see also Viscount Lowther to Camden, 30 January 1805, Camden Ms C244/3).

2. See Chatham's letter to Pitt of 26 December 1804 (Dacres Adams Mss, formerly P.R.O.30/58/5); pp. 640, 671 above for Hawkesbury.

3. *Colchester*, I, 530; Canning's diary for 25 December 1804 (Canning Ms 29d).

4. Pitt had a detailed estimate of numbers in both Houses, endorsed 'September – 04', in which Addington was given 41 in the Commons and the 'Pr' 23. On the other hand the Prince was given 21 peers and Addington 5 (P.R.O. 30/8/234). Cf. p. 656 above for May; a similar analysis, and comment, on this latter list will be found in *H of P*, I, 172–6.

5. To Pitt, Most Private, 6 December 1804 (Dacres Adams Mss, formerly P.R.O. 30/58/5). And cf. Pitt to Chatham, 25 December 1804 (Stanhope, IV, 238).

Long based his estimate of the Ministry's survival on the suspicion that Opposition would hang together less well than in the past session. Certainly Grenville himself was still averse to systematic opposition (see Jupp, op. cit., 336). He wished, despairingly, that Pitt would tell the King that 'all honest men' would welcome 'an end, (or at least a suspension) of divisions' (to Sir John Newport, 19 November 1804; Bodleian Ms Eng. Lett., d80).

Camden were against the inclusion in Cabinet of Addington himself, the latter at least straight away. Long was scathing about the former Minister: his judgment may have been 'as good as that of some of the members of all Cabinets', but he would want a prominent post and he was not fit for that. Better if possible to reward him liberally in return for support – a peerage and some sinecure for life, with pensions for some of his friends, but '*I should stop there*'. Camden grounded his view on the 'Sarcasms & Observations' that would arise, as well as the feelings that would be 'revolting' to many of Pitt's friends. The same uneasiness affected Mulgrave, who had not forgiven what he saw as Addington's earlier 'Ingratitude and duplicity' and foresaw a loss of credit from his accession, though of course that step would be welcomed by the King.[1] In point of fact, however, Pitt had made up his mind. As early as 22 November, when the talks with Moira had ended, Hawkesbury suspected that some arrangement would be reached with Addington; and on 11 December he himself was given 'the *necessary authority*' to make contact, which he did the next day.[2]

Accommodation nonetheless had still to be reached, and at the start in a frosty atmosphere. Early in December Addington, as much in the dark about Pitt's intentions as every one else, was not pleased to hear rumours that Canning might be chosen to succeed Harrowby at the Foreign Office, and Pitt himself was apparently preserving his distance as coldly as before.[3] But the Minister was now thinking his way to a conclusion. By the 12th he was ready to find places outside the Cabinet for four of Addington's closest supporters: brother Hiley, brother-in-law Bragge-Bathurst, Vansittart, and Nathaniel Bond, all of whom had held office before. Addington himself was offered a Cabinet post with a peerage, on both of which however he expressed doubts; on the former because the suggestion, of the Lord Presidency of the Council, was a second best to a Secretaryship of State, on the latter because he thought himself too poor to sustain the rank. The resolution of his scruples would have to be tackled; and meanwhile three proposals of his own were left to some extent in the air. Pitt was prepared to find a junior place for an old friend of Addington's, Henry Hobhouse; but not to recommend a high honour for St Vincent in view of what had passed, or to see his way, as part of the arrangement, to include Hobart in the

1. Long to Pitt as in p. 722, n5 above; Camden to same, 21 December 1804 (P.R.O. 30/8/119, printed in part in Stanhope, IV, 239); Mulgrave to same, 27 December 1804 (Dacres Adams Mss, formerly P.R.O. 30/58/5).

2. Hawkesbury to Liverpool, 22 November, 11 December 1804 (B.L. Loan Ms 72, vol. 55); same to Pitt, 12 December 1804 (P.R.O. 30/8/143, printed from a copy for the King in *L.C.G. III*, IV, no. 2984).

3. Ziegler, *Addington*, 230, and for Canning see Marshall, op. cit., 277–9; according to Thomas Grenville, retailing the story at second hand, as late as 21 or 22 December Pitt, passing Addington out riding, 'coldly touched his hat', on which Addington observed to his companion that 'even that cold greeting was new to him' (to Grenville, 7 January 1805; *H.M.C., Dropmore*, VII, 249). See also *Colchester*, I, 530.

Cabinet.[1] This last problem indeed proved the most obdurate in the talks that followed through the same channel, for Addington naturally wanted a larger showing in Cabinet than himself alone.[2] He also fought a rearguard action against going to the Lords, and in fact at one point seemed unlikely to accept any post, though he would allow others to do so.[3] But Pitt, having been the one to make the approach, then stood firm on the question of the peerage. He was determined not to have his predecessor as a colleague in the Commons,[4] and the King unconsciously abetted him by his own anxiety, thwarted at the time of Addington's resignation, to recognise that faithful Minister's services. George III's wishes for an arrangement were indeed abundantly evident; when Pitt informed him, on 17 December, that an overture had been made, the immediate delighted response almost took the outcome for granted.[5] Pressures were growing as the start of the session drew near. The time had clearly come for the principals to take up the talks directly themselves.

On 23 December, therefore, they met at Hawkesbury's house at Combe Wood for what proved to be the first of several conversations.[6] The occasion may have come as a personal relief to them both. Certainly it did so for Addington, who two months earlier had confessed that he needed only an expression – as it was described – of 'kindness and sense of justice' to recall a happier past; and Pitt for his part exclaimed on entering the room, 'I rejoice to take you by the hand again'. As he said to Wilberforce, 'we have been friends from our childhood, and our fathers were so before us'; and at that moment of reconciliation the early tone was indeed instinctively reproduced. Other rapprochements are said to have followed: Long

---

1. P. 723, n2 above for 12 December 1804, and see also *Colchester*, I, 532–3. *L.C.G. III*, III, xxx–ii lists the non-Cabinet posts in Addington's Ministry. Hobart, for whom see p. 553 and n2, and cf. 640 above, succeeded his father as Earl of Buckinghamshire in November, and will be so described henceforth. Vansittart had been considered, apparently not very seriously, for the Irish Secretaryship in the summer (see *L.C.G III*, IV, no. 2907 and n1).

2. He tried in fact to have Bragge-Bathurst included as well.

3. See Pellew, op. cit., II, 327–30.

4. There was speculation at the time about Pitt's motives in this. Addington's friends claimed that the Minister was afraid of being outshone – which seems, one might say, unlikely. But he may well have felt uneasy about the awkwardness that would arise: from attacks that would flourish the more readily from the sight of the two recent opponents on the same bench, and from the prospect of Addington's supporters indulging at times in uncomfortable indications of their real loyalty.

5. Pitt to George III, 17 December 1804 (Stanhope, IV, Appendix, xix); George III to Pitt, 18 December 1804 (*L.C.G. III*, IV, no. 2983, printed in part in Stanhope, xx).

6. For the events of the rest of this paragraph see Pellew, op. cit., II, 327–48, Ziegler, *Addington*, 230–5, Stanhope, IV, 236–41, *Colchester*, I, 530, 532–40, *A.C.*, IV, 230–1, *L.C.G. III*, IV, nos. 2986–8, 2990–1, 3004–6 with their notes, B.L. Loan Ms 72, vol. 55, *H. of P*, III–V for the lesser as well as the greater men concerned. Vansittart and two other Addingtonians (one being John Sullivan, the supposed channel for the talk between Addington and Pitt in January 1803; see p. 581, n2 above) were made Privy Councillors on 14 January, at the time of the two greater appointments.

with Addington, Tom Steele – in the shadows since the acrimonious period of 1803 – with Pitt. The remaining difficulties were ironed out over the next fortnight. Addington agreed to take his peerage, as Viscount Sidmouth, and room was found in the Cabinet for Buckinghamshire (Hobart) when Mulgrave succeeded Harrowby from his post at the Duchy of Lancaster, and Portland, still ill and disinclined to carry on, was content to leave as Lord President and did not wish to transfer to the lesser place.[1] Apparently content with that gain as a minimum, Addington did not insist on an immediate distribution of his desired crop of junior places, and only Vansittart was rewarded with the Irish Secretaryship – Bragge-Bathurst having declined it – in due course. On 14 January 1805 Lord Sidmouth took office as Lord President of the Council, and Buckinghamshire as Chancellor of the Duchy.[2] It remained to be seen how the changes would be greeted by the political world.

---

1. See pp. 569, 718 for Steele and Portland above; for Buckinghamshire 723–4.
2. Four days later Pitt dined some of the lesser characters concerned, in a larger party some of whose combinations – Canning for instance and Hiley Addington – would have seemed curious not many months, or even weeks, before (see Abbot's diary for 18 January 1805; P.R.O. 30/9/33).

CHAPTER XX

In Search of Coalitions

I

The year 1805, the last full year of Pitt's life, was the most dramatic for Britain of any in the Napoleonic War until the climax of Waterloo. It was also the most traumatic for himself of any that he endured. It opened with a confirmation of policy. For on 7 January the Foreign Office received a 'very unexpected' communication from Paris, dated on New Year's day, inviting a negotiation for peace. Like the similar message of Christmas 1799 this took the form of a letter from the ruler of France direct to George III, and the content again was general, expressed now from the more confident premiss of established authority and strength. What was England to gain from further war? She was highly prosperous and – an observation that can hardly have gone down well – possessed more territory than she could protect. The world was large enough for both; let all share in the relief that would ensue.[1] The overture was skilful, and one that clearly demanded a reply.

The contents however aroused less discussion than its predecessor had done. In 1799 it had been a matter of balancing the desirability of peace against Bonaparte's dangerous but ambiguous record and an assessment – misleading as it proved – of his prospects within France. Now it was much simpler: after a further five years, not many people, and certainly not Pitt, placed any trust in Napoleon's word.[2] The letter lacked any detail, and its timing was judged to be aimed at confusing the talks with Russia which Novosiltsov's mission was obviously meant to advance. At the same time, a flat rejection was ruled out of court. That would be fully exploited in Paris, and by those in St Petersburg and Vienna and Berlin who opposed or were doubtful of a British alliance. A unilateral decision moreover, whatever its tenor, could suggest to prospective allies that Britain might always be capable at a less comfortable point of acting on its own.[3] And if apprehen-

---

1. The letter is in P.R.O., F.O. 27/71. Pitt forwarded it to the King on 8 January (*L.C.G. III*, IV, no. 3003). For the text see, *inter alia*, *The Annual Register for the Year 1805* (1807), 615.

2. Cf. p. 688 above.

3. This was stressed in fact by Leveson Gower before he knew the contents of London's reply, alluding particularly to the Tsar's suspicion of Addington, as the signatory of the Peace of Amiens, now that he had joined the Cabinet (to Harrowby, 5 February 1805; Harrowby, Mss, vol. X).

sions might be stirred abroad, the threat of criticism must be weighed at home. The tone of the reply five years before, when Grenville's wording was allowed to stand, had caused misgivings even among Government's close supporters, and indeed within Government itself;[1] and public opinion was not to be brushed aside. Pitt was clear about this. As he was earlier reported to have stressed to the Russian Ambassador, he was

> the most hostile man in the world to a peace with France in the state in which she is; but if we continue to fight alone, the nation will grow tired of it, and you are acquainted well enough with this country to know that, when a nation really wants something, one must give in to it, willingly or not;

and again now,

> It is not possible for an English ministry to reject an offer of peace without a motive; the country would not allow it to continue the war at its pleasure. The government must therefore show that it desires an honourable peace that would ensure the safety of Europe.

If the necessary conditions were then rejected, 'the nation would support ... a continuation of the war'.[2]

An answer was accordingly sent on 14 January, by the Foreign Secretary to his counterpart Talleyrand – Napoleon's view of protocol being treated with the same distaste as in the period before he assumed a Crown –, which embraced the prospect of a settlement consistent with Britain's 'permanent safety and interests'. Since, however, these were 'closely connected with the general security of Europe', no talks could be contemplated until the Government had consulted those Continental Powers with which it was 'in confidential intercourse and connection', and especially Russia. This response was made known to Parliament at the opening of the session the next day;[3] and within the following week the Russians were asked to join in a statement of terms necessary for a negotiation, which could in fact be presented most effectively, as a former self-proclaimed mediator, by themselves.[4]

1. See p. 341 above, and at this point Hawkesbury to Liverpool, 8 January 1805 (B.L. Loan Ms. 72, vol. 55).

2. Simon Vorontsov to Czartoryski, 10 October 1804, 21 January 1805; quoted in Fremont, loc. cit., 63, 193. The argument of course served to underline to Czartoryski and the Tsar the need to become more closely involved. That does not make it the less genuine.

3. Mulgrave to Talleyrand, 14 January 1805 (P.R.O., F.O. 27/71); *P.D.*, III, 2–3. The Cabinet's draft, sent to George III on the 8th (p. 726, n11 above), was approved on the 9th (Holland Rose, *Pitt and Napoleon*, 247), so that the date of the communication seems to have been linked with the opening of the session. The purport of the text was despatched to Russia on the 21st (Mulgrave to Leveson Gower, 21 January 1805; P.R.O., F.O. 65/57, printed in *Third Coalition*, 93–6).

4. Ibid. See p. 689 above for the attempt at mediation.

An immediate safe position was thus tactically established; provided of course that the Russians would play. The basic indispensable conditions for talks were clearly set forth: the restoration of the King of Sardinia to his former territories; evacuation of Italy, and specific provision for the future security of Naples; the independence of Switzerland; evacuation of Hanover, measures to prevent sudden irruptions into Germany, and the re-establishment of fortresses on the right bank of the Rhine.[1] These were provisions directed to a particular end. They coincided with and were subsumed in a conspectus of larger scope.

This latter review, building on the required response to the Tsar's ideas, was completed at the same time. By 19 January it was ready to be relayed.[2] In view of its future fame it should be followed in some detail here. The paper opened with an acceptance of the Tsar's own stated aims: to rescue from French 'Dominion' the states subjugated since 1789 and reduce France herself to her former limits; to 'make an arrangement' for the former that would provide for their 'Security and Happiness', and a more effective obstacle against French encroachment; and 'to form at the Restoration of Peace, a general Agreement and Guarantee for the mutual protection and Security of the different Powers, and for reestablishing a general System of Public Law in Europe'. The surrender of conquered territory was 'certainly' the object to which, 'without any Modification or Exception', both British and Russian 'wishes would be preferably directed, and nothing short of it, can *completely* satisfy [their] views'. If the two Powers could be joined by Austria and Prussia, such a combination should suffice to gain all that was proposed. But if, as seemed likely to be the case, it proved impossible to include Prussia, the demands on France might have to be lessened in respect of the Netherlands (the former Austrian Netherlands) and the occupied territories on the left bank of the Rhine. It might then be 'more prudent' to limit the Allies' views to obtaining 'some moderate acquisition' for the United Provinces (Holland) which would form an additional barrier to France for the future. Even in that worst case, however, it remained 'essential' to ensure 'nothing less

---

1. *Third Coalition*, 94.

2. F.O. 65/60. The original document took the form of a communication, officially from the Foreign Secretary, to the Russian Ambassador in London, and a copy accompanied Mulgrave's despatch no. 1 to Leveson Gower, of 21 January 1805 (F.O. 65/57). The procedure, together no doubt with the length and importance of the contents, resulted in a separate volume in the Foreign Office files. Working drafts, largely in Pitt's hand, are in the Dacres Adams Mss, formerly P.R.O. 30/58/8.

The contents have been printed more than once. They were laid before Parliament on 8 May 1815 (*H.C.J.* 80 (nd), 279 and Appendix at 627), following the signing of the treaty of Vienna on 25 March; but with some passages omitted, as no longer applicable, which were restored to a complete text (apart from those proposing forces required at the time) by C.K. Webster in *British Diplomacy 1813–1815* . . . (1921), Appendix I, itself reprinted in *Foundations of British Foreign Policy from Pitt (1792) to Salisbury (1902)*, ed. Harold Temperley and Lillian M. Penson (1928), 10–21.

For the Tsar's ideas see pp. 698–9 above.

than the Evacuation of the North of Germany and of Italy', the 'Re-establishment of the Independence of the United Provinces, and of Switzerland, the Restoration of the Dominions of the King of Sardinia, and Security of Naples'.

French cessions on the Continent, covering the alternatives, were thus defined. That did not in itself address the question of who should benefit from the restorations. As the paper stated, a response involved 'many important Considerations' for two 'pure and disinterested' Powers which, from their particular situations, had 'no separate Objects of Their Own [here] in the Arrangements . . . for the general interest'.[1] Where the former authorities were capable of resuming and protecting their independence that would of course be the most 'congenial' end. But it would not always apply. The 'ancient relations of the Country' might in some instances have been destroyed beyond repair, or independence might be 'purely nominal' and thus inconsistent with security – that 'Security and Happiness' which 'internally' was one of the declared aims, and important likewise for Continental peace. The problems had therefore to be taken one by one within the European frame.

Some could be quite easily answered. The republics of the United Provinces and Switzerland, the kingdoms of Sardinia and Naples, and – in a rather different context – the duchies of Tuscany and Modena should be restored to their earlier forms. But this left Genoa (the Ligurian Republic), the so-called Italian Republic including the Papal Legations, Parma and Placentia,[2] the Austrian Netherlands, and 'the States which have been detached from the German Empire' on the left bank of the Rhine. In Italy, none of the second group of northern states had shown themselves able or some (above all Genoa) by and large willing to resist the French; and it was obvious in fact that 'these Separate Petty Sovereignties would never again have any solid existence in themselves'. 'Force' should accordingly be concentrated as much as possible in the hands of 'the chief Powers of Italy', which in the north should be taken as Sardinia and Austria. Their territories should be brought into direct geographical contact, together with those of the restored Tuscany, which might be considered as virtually Austrian;[3] and on that principle the three Legations might be annexed to Austria, the lands of the Ligurian Republic together with the south-west part of the Milanese[4] and perhaps Parma and Placentia to Sardinian Piedmont, and under such a plan Modena, lying between the enlarged Sardinia and Tuscany, could 'safely' be restored to its Duke.

1. Britain being an island with 'extensive resources' and naval superiority, and Russia enjoying an 'immense power, . . . [an] established Continental Ascendency, and remote distance', which respectively gave security against an attack from France 'even after her acquisitions of Influence, power and Dominion'.
2. See p. 575 above.
3. Referring presumably to the hereditary connexion of Grand Duke and Emperor.
4. See p. 322 above; and cf. II, 307.

The arguments for extending Austria's presence in Italy, however, were not confined to that region alone. They also contained a 'great additional Inducement' for her to accept proposals which the British had in mind for territories nearer home. For of course the most critical question affecting British interests on the Continent was the future of the Low Countries; and that must involve the Emperor's own interests, in the settlement of the Austrian Netherlands and, as a direct consequence, his position within the German Empire vis-à-vis his rival Prussia. The latter issue in its turn was naturally of close concern to Russia, impinging on her policies in an arc from Poland to the Balkans. No one problem in fact bearing on the possible quadrilateral Coalition could easily be divorced from the others; and in London's view, gains for Austria 'on the side of Italy' were highly desirable to balance any gains accruing to Prussia elsewhere.

This was the more so as the latter might fall largely on the Low Countries themselves. Such a prospect could indeed kill several birds with one stone. If Prussia could be tempted thereby into an alliance, an attack by her on the region, after driving the enemy out of northern Germany, would fill an appropriate role within a combined plan. An involvement in the west moreover could help focus Berlin's diplomacy in that direction, rather than on the sensitive quarter in north-east Europe where both Russian and Austrian fears would at once be aroused. And given the exposure of the Austrian Netherlands to France and the need of a stronger barrier for the Dutch, transfers of some territories to a stronger Power could meet a long-felt want.[1] The British therefore suggested that northeast Flanders behind a 'military line' from Antwerp to Maastricht should be annexed to Holland, while Prussia would receive 'the remainder of the Netherlands, together with the Duchies of Luxembourg and Juliers, and the other Territories between the Meuse and the Moselle'.[2] This would be a substantial accession, not least for a nation with no proprietary access to the sea west of the Baltic.[3] But the British proposed more. Prussia's military efforts could be so important, and French counter offers probably so

1. Cf. the effect of Prussia's favourable intervention on Pitt's early crisis with France over Holland eighteen years before; I, 529–38. He and Grenville had moreover contemplated such an accession in 1796 as part of an attempt to lure Prussia back from her recent neutrality (see II, 528, 624).

2. I quote the exact wording because possession of these lands in the cockpit of Europe over the past two centuries constitutes in itself an historical palimpsest. The 'Duchy of Juliers' (Julich) in particular, together with some adjacent territories, had been ruled by Prussia (initially Brandenburg) since the early seventeenth century until they were ceded to France in 1796; and would thus now be returned direct. The rest fell within the Emperor's possessions. Those wishing to follow the bewildering transfers of authority in detail may do so in the *Atlas* to the second edition of the original *Cambridge Modern History* (1924), Introduction, Section IV.

3. Which itself raised the possible objection – as Pitt himself acknowledged in Cabinet (Mulgrave to Pitt, 15 December 1804; Dacres Adams Mss, formerly P.R.O. 30/58/5) – that it would give her extra weight in the maritime Armed Neutrality of which she was a member (cf. pp. 395, 399 above). On the other hand it might draw her into a closer commercial connexion with Britain.

extensive, that it might 'even' be advisable – acknowledging the prospect of Austrian 'jealousy' – to add the territory recovered from France on the left bank of the Rhine east of the Moselle. If the scale of these inducements, taken together, was however thought excessive – and Pitt seems to have been well aware that it might[1] – a larger slice of Flanders might perhaps go to Holland, and other choices (including the retention by France) be considered for the lands between the Moselle and the Rhine, though those between the Meuse and the Moselle should still be consolidated with Prussia's part of the Netherlands. Of course if she failed to enter an Alliance its demands 'on this Side of Europe' might have to be reduced; 'probably' (and presumably initially) to the French evacuation of northern Germany and the re-establishment of an independent Holland with the additional barrier from Antwerp to Maastricht – leaving open, inferentially, the settlement of the rest of the Netherlands, on which the British memorandum had already noted that 'Events have put out of question the Restoration of them to . . . Austria . . . and they . . . evidently can never exist separate and independent'.[2]

Territorial arrangements however would remain imperfect, after the experience of unbridled French aggression and change, unless there was a regulatory system that could offer 'Solidarity and Permanence'. Developing the Tsar's generalised ideas against the background of their own abortive suggestions of seven years before, the British agreed that all the principal Powers should engage by treaty to protect and support one another against any attempt to 'infringe' their respective possessions and rights.[3] A comprehensive system of 'Public Law in Europe' should be 'reestablished' to prevent attempts at disturbance, particularly of the kind inflicted in 'the disastrous era of the French Revolution'; and to give the treaty effect, it should enjoy a 'Special Guarantee' by Britain and Russia which would bind them by a separate engagement to 'take an active Part' in preventing such dangers. Some specific proposals gave detail to the concept. The several Powers of Italy might enter a defensive alliance. The same aim could be considered for 'the Germanic Body', though its unsatisfactory state cast doubt on the prospect of that being achieved. Perhaps the weakness there could be countered by a version of the barrier for the Netherlands – by the provision of fortresses, manned possibly by Austrians and Prussians and maintained at combined German expense, along a stretch from Basle northwards to command the principal approaches from France. The Dutch for their part might be called on to

1. At least according to Vorontsov. On 21 January he reported that the plans for Prussia in the Low Countries and adjacent barrier territories to the south-east were 'not really matters to which importance is attached here'. Pitt had 'often' said that they were put forward because no better ones had been found for the purpose (to Czartoryski; *Memoirs of Czartoryski*, II, 72).

2. This last conclusion, it may be noted, was stated in the paper at a point where the proposals for Prussia herself had still to be introduced.

3. Cf. pp. 134–5, and also 202–3 above.

keep up an army sufficient for defence against 'sudden' attack, while Britain would 'induce' Hanover to maintain a 'considerable' force in support and would act with other Powers to pay for 'German' troops who would garrison a stronger barrier on the future line. Finally, turning to the disturber of the peace herself, the great question remained how far the Allies, now or in the future, should direct their views to the re-establishment of monarchy, and the restoration of the Bourbon line. Like Russia, Britain considered that such a settlement was 'highly desirable' and that it should be promoted on every 'fair occasion'. But it ought to be assessed in the prospective Coalition as 'only a secondary object', and one 'which could in no case justify the prolongation of the War' if peace could otherwise be satisfactorily obtained. In any case, no 'active or decided measures' could be taken until military success allowed and 'a strong and prevailing disposition' was then shown by the French themselves. Meanwhile, and once more in agreement with the Tsar, the greatest care should be taken to give them no cause to apprehend any design to dictate by force, or to 'dismantle the antient Territories of France'.

Such was the frame within which a Project for a treaty had now been prepared and was despatched to St Petersburg a few days later with a copy of the long review.

This deployment of Pitt's ideas for Europe came, quite soon in per-spective, to claim an historical significance that has endured ever since. Within a decade the paper entered the canon of classic statements of British foreign policy. That it was truly Pitt's there need be no serious doubt. The Foreign Secretary of course was involved; he officially signed the document sent to Vorontsov and the despatch to Russia containing the Project. There is also evidence of a personal contribution on his part; even before he succeeded Harrowby, and while he was not yet closely in touch with the progress of Novosiltsov's mission, Mulgrave sent his thoughts on these 'extensive & important subjects' to the Minister.[1] Nor did he do so in response to a request – which might not have been surpris-ing – on the military aspects; for though the Cabinet included one other member, Chatham, who held a military post, Mulgrave was senior to him in rank and had been introduced partly for his military judgment.[2] His observations however were wholly concerned with the matters of policy themselves; and in one respect at any rate they may have been of use. For while Mulgrave made an unsuccessful proposal that Holland should be annexed to Prussia, he argued against doubts of such a transfer of large parts of the Low Countries in case that should unduly increase her

1. 15 December 1804 (Dacres Adams Mss, formerly P.R.O. 30/58/5; published in E. Ingram's 'Lord Mulgrave's Proposals for the Reconstruction of Europe in 1804' (*H.J.*, vol. XIX, no. 2, 511–20)). He referred in his letter to 'the communications' which 'engaged my attention' and 'heard of for the first time at the Cabinet yesterday'.
2. Cf. pp. 672, 670 above.

maritime strength, on lines which could have aided Pitt in reaching his own conclusion.[1] Otherwise there is little to suggest that the advice, submitted in December, seriously affected the subsequent proposals; let alone, as has been claimed, that it contained 'the origin of Pitt's plan for the territorial reconstruction of Europe'.[2] That is not a sequel which follows from the obvious fact that the letter preceded the Minister's paper; and indeed its contents might rather be thought to mark the origin of Mulgrave's own education in foreign affairs. An introductory exposition – as was provided – of basic principles applying to the treatment of territories in a negotiation, with examples taken from beyond the Continental mainland itself, might have been viewed as an otiose product of an intelligent neophyte approaching a subject of which, as he confessed, he had no specific knowledge. His main point – the need for the bulk of Austrian and Prussian gains to be kept apart, in Italy and northern Europe respectively – held nothing new, though the implication for 'petty' states was spelt out perhaps more bluntly than usual. And it may not be fanciful to sense throughout the presentation a certain unawareness of the context of British diplomacy in the recent war.[3] Nor in point of fact is there much sign of Mulgrave's close involvement in the later stage of the talks with Novosiltsov: no particular mention of his name in that capacity occurs in Vorontsov's reports at the critical stage. It was indeed Harrowby's advice that Pitt continued to respect, when the former Foreign Secretary recovered enough to sit in on some Cabinet meetings in the spring.[4] Mulgrave's letter could have bolstered his chances as a replacement, under the Minister's eye: it would have been a remarkable achievement for any one so lacking in direct experience to have immediately moulded a balanced policy deriving from a rich and complex past.[5]

The nature of that balance and derivation – the framework and direction – of Pitt's paper requires some further comment, not least because of the particular occasion of its fame. For the proposals, not published at the time and rendered abortive by the continuing war, came into their own as a basis for the British success at the peace talks in 1814–15. 'They formed', it has been said, 'his legacy to Castlereagh. What the master . . .

---

1. See p. 730 and n3 above.

2. Ingram, loc. cit., 514. His claim, it should be noted, specifically excludes the provisions in the paper of January 1805 for ensuring the longer term future security of the Continent.

3. This suspicion is admittedly conjectural. I can only say that I have the impression of a vacuum – a lack of awareness for instance of the British views expressed in 1798 (see pp. 202–3, allowing for the change in circumstances, above).

4. See *Memoirs of Czartoryski*, II, 69–70, 72–3, 75–6.

5. Even a year later indeed he put the position fairly to Pitt. 'I have so sincere and long-rooted a deference to your opinions that I am not disposed to press any ideas of mine very far, when you make any objection to them in the first instance; nor do I ever recur again to my own suggestions when they are unconnected with the department which you have assigned to me' (6 January 1806; *The Cambridge History of British Foreign Policy*, I, Appendix F, 587–8).

formulated in 1805, the disciple put into practice at the Congress of Vienna.'[1] Castlereagh himself acknowledged the inheritance more than once. Some assessment of its character becomes the more germane.

Changes of emphasis and detail of course occurred within a tumultuous interval; as indeed they had done since the British had last set forth their ideas, in search of a quadrilateral alliance in 1798.[2] To take one prominent example, in that year the Government welcomed any prospect of Prussian operations in the Low Countries, but not necessarily a transfer of territory in preference to the creation of a new single independent state; in 1805 its choice was for Prussia to be given most of the Austrian Netherlands, plus some additions to the south; in 1815 Belgium was included with Holland in a combined kingdom. Such tergiversations, affecting the region of highest consequence of all to this country, might seem to raise the question whether underlying 'principles' can be postulated at all.[3] In reality, however – and bearing in mind Pitt's qualifying doubt about the proposal of 1805[4] –, the search as always to secure the best form of security against France exemplified the strength of the fundamental concept of the balance of power.

For that doctrine, applying strongly and directly to this instance, informed the British approach now as it had done for some two centuries, the means being adapted in furtherance of the ends. It was not seen in London as purely a convenience serving an island state, for it was aimed by definition to embrace the Continental mainland, in practice more often than not enlisting the internal divisions but accepting the classic ideal, deriving from Europe itself, of a comity of nations: 'a kind of republic, the members of which, though independent, unite, through the ties of common interest, for the maintenance of order and liberty'.[5] Thus Burke had cited Vattel's *Law of Nations*; pursuing a line of thought, endemic in Western society, whose current pattern had developed in the century following the Thirty Years War. It was one that supported an ideal of moderation in reaching treaty settlements, which the normal military

1. Temperley and Penson, *The Foundations of British Foreign Policy*, 9. Castlereagh of course was by then the Foreign Secretary.

2. See p. 731, n3 above.

3. As eg in Webster, *British Diplomacy 1813–1815*, xl: 'Castlereagh did not invent, but inherited from Pitt, the principles upon which his actions were based.'

4. P. 730, n3 above.

Some interesting consequences might be envisaged if – but ifs are delusive – that transfer of territory to Prussia had been agreed, and endured: no independent Belgium to be supported if invaded, and a much closer geographical threat from a Power which, as Pitt paused briefly to wonder, might have set out at some point, as eventually it did, to increase its maritime strength.

5. Quoted from Burke's *Thoughts on French Affairs* of 1778 in Stephen R. Groubard, 'Castlereagh and the Peace of Europe' (*The Journal of British Studies*, Volume III, Number I, 86); an article to which I am indebted in general here.

See also F.H. Hinsley, *Power and the Pursuit of Peace* . . . (1963), particularly chs. 8, 9, for developments (not least in Prussia and Russia at this time) in the relationship of the tradition to the specific prospect of a federalist pattern.

constraints of the period did much to impose in any case. Crushing victories were rare, and even then could seldom end a war in the same annual campaign; the defeated or disadvantaged Power was still in existence, with its institutions intact, remaining an entity to be considered within 'the family of nations'. Napoleon had introduced a new dimension in that respect, as he would continue to do. But statesmen's views on the wider considerations had not – all the more emphatically – suffered a basic change. Pitt's own survey, it was true, contained some novel elements in degree, not all of which, it might be argued, were consistent with this fact. The summary elimination of many small sovereignties in Italy and Germany, designed to stabilise Austria's and Prussia's separate interests, was applied to them as a *class*, not merely as specific states.[1] The particular right of two Powers jointly to guarantee a system inclusive of all might in time raise questions for the international order which the claim was designed to protect. Such innovatory aspects attracted the attention of posterity. They do not obscure the conclusion that the review was rooted in assumptions which made the peace whose shape it foreshadowed the last of the great eighteenth-century settlements. The statesmen gathered at Vienna before and after Waterloo – Hardenberg and Metternich, Talleyrand and Wellington no less than Castlereagh – were all thinking, from their different points of vantage, in terms of a doctrine that seemed 'self-evidently true'.[2] It had to be reasserted by necessary adjustments from an upheaval, actual and conceptual, which the 'armed opinions' of revolution in successive French stages had introduced.[3] And the arrangements had of course to be tailored, as in Pitt's own paper, to the situation at the time – as the ample deletions from it showed when it was first published in 1815.[4] For in January 1805 the Minister was writing with a particular object in view. While he looked towards a Grand Coalition, he needed to regain Russia as an immediate partner whether to achieve that end or, in case of its failure, a visible strategic course in default. It was in that frame that he set his picture, in a way designed to satisfy the Tsar's approach: to link Alexander's declaration of principles, unanchored as it stood in specifics, to a conspectus which comprehended both. It was an exercise that came naturally to him. For while he had become cautious of generalities, he had always disliked patching and wherever feasible was impelled to seek a pattern of intellectual control. 'His vision was practical, but it was not the less real for that'.[5] If a combination of qualities once regularly acclaimed as his hallmark had more lately seemed to be uncertain, this occasion produced a reminder that the capacity was not lost.

1. Novosiltsov however had himself been authorised to propose some such treatment for the 'many little States' in the German Confederation (to Czartoryski, nd; *Memoirs of Czartoryski*, II, 65–6). Cf. for Italy p. 729 above.
2. Groubard, loc. cit., 83.
3. Pitt's phrase in 1799; p. 228 above.
4. See p. 728, n2 above.
5. I, 319.

Pitt's views may have made an impact at a remove on the Congress of Vienna, in a period in which British arms were prominent in western Europe. They made less on the Russians now, when there were no British troops on the mainland and at best the prospect of relatively few. The draft of a Provisional Treaty reached St Petersburg on the last day of February. Its immediate reception came as something of a shock.[1] Given the context of the detailed territorial proposals contained in the accompanying review, and the recent declaration of conditions for peace talks to be sent to France, the Project itself concentrated on financial arrangements in relation to the troops to be actively deployed.[2] Russia was to furnish a quota to be agreed towards a force of 400,000 men if Austria too was engaged, or 500,000 including Prussia, in return for a subsidy of £1¼ million a year, payable monthly, for every 100,000 'actually employed'. Austria herself, in view of her poverty, would however be allowed the first few months' payments in her period of preparation.[3] For the rest, no party must make a separate peace; and by a separate article Austria, Sardinia and Prussia (the first and third if combatant) would receive unspecified territory at the peace, the first two in Italy, the third, together with the Dutch, in the 'barrier' country on the left bank of the Rhine. None of this was well received: Czartoryski's answer was dissatisfied and swift. Taking the two British documents together, he objected to both the financial and territorial proposals. Austria had stated her needs as £6 million, including £2 million for her preparations, and the offered sum was quite inadequate; nor did he relish Leveson Gower's hint that, if so, Russia might like to find some of that requirement from the subsidy to herself. The territorial gains for the two prospective partners, on the other hand, were excessive. The proposals for Prussia were 'extravagant': she was already a large military Power, whose strength should not be so greatly augmented; while those for Austria in Italy exceeded Vienna's own aims. Russia could not 'so entirely lose sight of [her] interests' as thus to strengthen the two neighbours on whose borders she had already to keep two armies of observation, while she herself would be devoting 170,000 men, as Czartoryski now disclosed, to the war. He had shown the British ideas to the Austrian envoy in St Petersburg, and the British could expect a Counter Project which he himself would draw up. But this was not a matter to be rushed; it would require 'some little time'.[4]

1. Mulgrave to Leveson Gower, no. 1, 21 January 1805; Leveson Gower to Mulgrave, no. 7, 6 March 1805 (F.O. 65/57).

2. Mulgrave to Leveson Gower, no. 2, 21 January 1805 (F.O. 65/57; printed in *Third Coalition*, 88–92). See pp. 726–8 above for the terms for peace talks.

3. This in total was the £5 million allowed for in Pitt's budget of 18 February; see p. 693 above; and cf. 695.

4. Leveson Gower's expressions throughout (*Third Coalition*, 88–92); and cf. for the last point his private letter to Pitt (7 March 1805; Dacres Adams Mss, formerly P.R.O. 30/58/6).

Faced with such a cold reception, the British Ambassador pinned much faith on Novosiltsov's return. That too, however, proved a disappointment. The Russian had left England with the plaudits of his hosts, carrying 'the highest . . . esteem and regard of every member of His Majesty's Government'.[1] But once back in St Petersburg it seemed clear that either he had misjudged the limits of his brief or that Pitt and his colleagues built too much on the acceptance of points that had still to be confirmed or resolved.[2] The returning envoy's presence helped lighten the atmosphere on his arrival.[3] But while conversations later in March took place in a friendlier spirit, and the Russians remained apparently anxious to reach an agreement as soon as they could, there was no disguising the differences which the recent developments overlaid.

Leveson Gower had now to earn the latitude given him to conclude a Provisional Treaty, a result for which Pitt himself was calling without delay.[4] It was not easy to decide what could be allowed by way of alterations to the Project. The Ambassador recognised that Czartoryski was under serious pressure from opponents at Court, and that the Russians' information from Vienna and Berlin did not point to a wider Alliance soon. The Tsar himself moreover remained displeased with Britain's treatment of Spain and the subsequent rupture, and suspected that the troops intended to act in the Mediterranean would be used against Spanish colonies instead.[5] Such considerations had to be borne in mind when the Counter Project appeared. Meanwhile Czartoryski announced that, in conformity with the British suggestion, the Russians would deliver a joint response to Napoleon's message, and that they would do so by despatching Novosiltsov to Paris, the Austrians and Prussians being informed.[6]

1. Mulgrave to Leveson Gower, 21 January 1805 (*Third Coalition*, 96). And see same to same on 17 April (no. 12; F.O. 65/57), confirming Novosiltsov's 'good disposition & judicious thinking', which gave ground for 'a sanguine expectation' that his arrival would have its effect on Czartoryski.

2. Pitt's own optimism following the talks pervades a private letter to Leveson Gower on the day the British papers were completed for St Petersburg (21 January 1805; P.R.O. 30/29/384). The Ambassador however came to the conclusion that Novosiltsov was responsible for a partly false impression (to Pitt, 12 April 1805; loc. cit.).

3. He arrived on 7 March, and Leveson Gower in the next fortnight thought that he had some effect (to Mulgrave, nos. 10, 11 of 7, 22 March 1805, in F.O. 65/57; same to Pitt, Private, 22 March 1805, in P.R.O. 30/8/152).

4. Cf. pp. 700–1 above; Mulgrave to Leveson Gower, no. 3, 21 January 1805 (*Third Coalition*, 96); Pitt to same, sd (P.R.O. 30/29/384).

5. Leveson Gower to Mulgrave, nos. 6, 9 of 16 February, 7 March 1805 (*Third Coalition*, 107–8, 114); same to Pitt, Private, 22 March 1805 (P.R.O. 30/8/152). See pp. 705, 696, above for Spain and for the British forces on offer for the Mediterranean.

According to the Grenvilles, the Russians were also unhappy about the admittance of Addington – still regarded as incompetent and pacific at heart – to the Cabinet (Buckingham, III).

6. Leveson Gower to Mulgrave, nos. 8, 11 of 7, 22 March 1805 (*Third Coalition*, 113–14, 121).

This was far from satisfactory. The hope in London had clearly been for a firm reply to Napoleon on the lines suggested – his acceptance of conditions *before* talks could take place[1] –, after which matters would be left to him. Now there was a strong possibility that conversations of some kind could not be avoided; and the prospect might be the less welcome depending on what the proposed joint terms might be. The Ambassador soon learned their nature. On 7 April he despatched the synopsis of a Provisional Treaty, in which the Russians' conditions were incorporated and – a disturbing prospect – could be made known selectively in Paris. As his recent discussions had led him to expect, they were not likely all to be to London's taste.

Much of course was perfectly agreeable or tolerable: falling within acceptable limits of negotiation.[2] The objects of the alliance were broadly restated, the independence of Holland, Italy and 'Germany' indeed being added to that of Switzerland, the first with the addition of the former Austrian Netherlands and the fourth with those of Geneva and Savoy. Financial provisions were accepted, with one partial exception on which compromise was soon reached. Some diplomatic provisions were added relating to other Powers: Britain was asked to accept stipulations agreed by Russia with Austria and/or Sweden in return for either of them joining the war in the course of the year, and also her mediation with Spain if the latter secretly agreed to join the Allies within three months of the start of their campaign. And it was confirmed that the form of French government would not be dictated before or at the peace, and – announced slightly later – that the two Allied Powers would make common cause (though the word guarantee was not used)[3] against infractions of the general settlement for which a congress would be duly called. Nor indeed would France be the only country to choose its pattern of government: the same would apply to the Dutch – with a preference expressed for the restoration of the Orange dynasty – and to the Swiss, and a strong hint was included for Sardinia as well. The nostrum of constitutional self-determination, so dear to the Tsar in these years, was thus to be given covenanted form – the need to secure the peace by a concert established on the foundation of justice, equity and human rights ('les droits des gens'). And while this had not so far been a subject arousing comment in London, and was applied more specifically than Leveson Gower approved, he accepted an amended wording rather more likely to allay British fears.[4]

1. P. 727 above.
2. Leveson Gower to Mulgrave, no. 13, 7 April 1805 (*Third Coalition*, 127–30).
3. Cf. pp. 698, 731 above.
4. Leveson Gower's instinctive reaction was instructive: that of a good Whig to a theme reflecting an admiration for British constitutionalism (cf. p. 698 above) but now contaminated by the dreadful example of Continental revolution. For his part, he disliked the Russians' own ideas for northern Italy (see below) as embodying 'the impolicy, as well as injustice of parcelling out countries without regard to any natural tie and relation between the sovereign and the subject' (to Mulgrave, no. 11, 22 March 1805; op. cit., 122).

So far so reasonably good. But the draft contained some less palatable clauses. Prussia was to be granted only the small territories ceded by her to France in 1796, when she had left the war, plus enough land – but no more – to form an efficient barrier line: a deliberately narrow reward, which took no account of Pitt's argument – though one admittedly open to discussion – for an acquisition whose scale would provide a handsome inducement and could also block later calls for territory elsewhere more sensitive to Russia herself.[1] The treatment of Sardinia could likewise have an undesirable consequence. Her old possessions, it was stated, should of course be restored, and enlarged to provide greater security. But if Napoleon needed persuasion to accept the important loss of Piedmont, he might have to be offered, in personal compensation, some other northern Italy territory, which would be reserved for a member of his family as a Bonaparte possession – not one of the French state. This last idea, novel to the British, was the more disagreeable as embodying a general approach which Czartoryski indeed made quite plain. If Novosiltsov was to stand a chance of success – if peace was to be gained without further fighting – Allied firmness must be combined, as an immediate measure, with restraint. France could not be driven too far, let alone accept a British ultimatum which moreover would only encourage the doubts in Austria and Prussia. It was necessary to prove to all – and this, as presented, was a Continental parallel to the position in Britain – that Napoleon had rejected reasonable offers and was bent on war. Unless therefore her line of approach was accepted in London, it was useless to expect Russia to undertake a joint response.[2]

In the light of the truths which past experience had revealed, or underlined, this attitude should perhaps not have caused such surprise. The two previous Coalitions had been replete with examples of deep underlying differences between an island and a continental state. The current hopes of both Powers for a speedy agreement had raised expectations. But the Russians were upset by the apparent lack of concern for their necessary

---

The attitude of Czartoryski, and of the Tsar, to national sentiment and to self-representation has given rise to debate over the years; as indeed, with no very interesting outcome, has Pitt's. Wellington is said to have stated later, to a Spanish general, that in the autumn of 1805 the Minister forecast a popular rising in Spain at some point against the French which would lead to the liberation of Europe, a tale that seems doubtful on several counts (see Holland Rose, II, 524); and certainly with his eyes set on immediate concerns within the context of the balance of power, Pitt made no observation of any kind in reply to this point. His tacit lack of enthusiasm, in fact, disappointed the Russians.

1. See p. 730 and n2 above.

2. The Russians' point of view on Italy was made plain by Leveson Gower to Mulgrave in his no. 11 of 22 March (*Third Coalition*, 121–2); their general view ibid and in his despatch of 7 April (for which see p. 738, n2 above). Cf. p. 727 above for Pitt and opinion at home.

Czartoryski's reasoning on the approach to France, deployed on lines that *inter alia* must satisfy a Tsar who was himself by no means enthusiastic for war and on whom his adviser depended for final support, is well explained in W.H. Zawadzki, *A Man of Honour . . .* (1993), 115–16, 121.

interests, while the British found the argument for restraint with Napoleon – by no means the same in their view as those for a balance with France at the peace[1] – a disturbing reminder of a familiar caution. This applied to Europe. But their disquietude was heightened in its turn by the treatment of their own interests as a maritime nation, on which the Russians proceeded to raise three points. Britain should return her conquests in the present war, and the suggestion was made that as a *bonne bouche* to aid Novosiltsov's talks she might offer something small in addition, say Pondicherry in India, from the previous war. The general proposal in point of fact was unlikely to prove objectionable to London, for certain parts of the world in a general settlement at the peace; but very much less so if it was automatically to include India and the Indian sphere,[2] and meanwhile there was little mileage to be gained in a goodwill offer relating to the past. More serious was a proposal, which would be specifically reported to Napoleon, for a discussion of reform to the British 'Maritime Code', in which Russia would use her good offices in a congress of 'the great Continental Powers'. And thirdly, if the outcome of Novosiltsov's talks was found to turn on a refusal to cede Malta to the British, he should be empowered to promise their evacuation of the island and replacement by a Russian garrison, pending some later arrangement approved by the Maltese.[3]

There was thus a great deal to be done if a treaty was to be signed soon. The pressures for that result however were not to be underrated. Both parties wanted an agreement, the British to pursue a strategy and secure a voice in its direction, the Russians to gain financial support and, if an adequate peace could not be reached, to enjoy the Allied advantages of having been the medium of support for others.[4] Leveson Gower steered an anxious path. He could only go on 'the spirit' of his instructions: 'nothing but the extreme importance of immediately concluding an agreement . . . could possibly have induced me to accede without previous authority' from home..[5] For by the end of the first week in April, after frequent meetings, the Ambassador had decided to go ahead subject to two basic modifications; and, with these secured, a Provisional Treaty was signed on the 11th. Each side – for so the parties might be described by this point – could draw some satisfaction from the document as well as some doubts.[6] All the more open points affecting the territorial arrangements in Europe were left to follow the Russians' preference: on Prussia, on

1. See pp. 729, 734–5 above.
2. Cf. p. 441 above.
3. Cf. pp. 557, and for the last provision 586 above.
4. See p. 697 above.
5. To Mulgrave, no. 13, 7 April 1805 (*Third Coalition*, 131–2).
6. The text may be found op. cit., 265–75. It followed a form, divided into public, 'separate' and 'secret separate' articles, which was altered from the Russians' draft after they had been led to appreciate that the final treaty, containing financial provisions, might have to be presented to Parliament (Leveson Gower to Mulgrave, no. 14, 12 April 1805; op. cit., 133–4). The text of the public articles themselves was not to be made public by either party until after Novosiltsov's return from Paris (and presumably then in case of his failure).

Austria, and on the reservation of land for the Bonapartes – which, Leveson Gower commented, he had agreed because he was virtually sure that it would not be accepted as a quid pro quo. He had also agreed that Novosiltsov might inform the French of Britain's willingness to return its conquests of the current war, though he would not take it on himself to include 'the East Indies'.[1] But on the other two questions affecting the nation's trading and naval interests he stood absolutely firm. He refused, after ten days' pressure, to put his name to any form of words, for any might open a prospect of discussion on the maritime system of law – the recent case of Spain indeed could underline that point[2] – and suggest an indication of possibilities for Malta. He did not budge when threatened with a rupture of the negotiation – a fate which he thought less likely than delay – and in the end both proposals were dropped, from the Provisional Treaty at least. His responsibility had been heavy, and he was understandably nervous of the reception in London: looking 'with a very anxious eye' for approbation of 'arduous and difficult' efforts.[3] Some of those arose no doubt from a not abnormal process of bargaining, and the Russians may also have been playing on the impression that the British would go a long way for an alliance. But there was more to it than that. The two sides had good cause for both their satisfaction and their doubts in each case. The talks had underlined the pressures both favouring and complicating a partnership: in south-east Europe and the Mediterranean, in western Europe, in the concept of Europe after the peace. At this point at any rate there was an agreement on paper, and one achieved quite quickly; some action could ensue pending ratification; whatever obstacles might still be encountered, an instrument was in place on which Russian preparations for their troops, with numbers attached, could be set on foot and the search for a wider Coalition might succeed with greater hope.

A spur indeed would be welcome if this latter goal was to be achieved in time for a combined campaign. The handling of talks with Vienna and Berlin had been entrusted primarily to St Petersburg,[4] and given the new treaty with London matters could perhaps now be brought into focus. The defensive Austro-Russian alliance in November 1804 had committed 235,000 and 115,000 men respectively,[5] and in the warmer atmosphere it

---

1. *Third Coalition*, 135.
2. See pp. 703–4 above.
3. Leveson Gower to Mulgrave, nos. 13, 14 of 7, 12 April 1805 (op. cit., 133, 140). At any rate the Russians were reluctantly impressed; Czartoryski to Vorontsov, 16 April 1805, cited by Fremont, loc. cit., 209.

A letter from Mulgrave to Pitt of 26 April 1805 (Dacres Adams Mss, formerly P.R.O. 30/58/6), wondering from the contents of recent despatches if the envoy was not exceeding his instructions, gives some colour to the latter's fears.
4. P. 697 above.
5. Cf. pp. 701, 736 above.

really seemed possible that a tripartite Coalition might emerge. Even the British Minister in Vienna, a confirmed pessimist, had then detected a partial thaw.[1] But the uncertain glow seemed to fade. No distinct signs of change followed in the first quarter of 1805; Pitt's financial offer produced no reward – the Austrians were looking to a much larger sum; the Russians, themselves finding it hard to gauge the real position, became progressively more doubtful of the prospect; and when they signed the Provisional Treaty with Britain they were indeed wondering if they might not be left to prosecute a land war on their own.[2] The insistence on sending a special envoy to Paris, and the hope of extracting concessions from London, were shaped by the fear that otherwise Austria would not come in.

Nor, it seemed, would Prussia. The French were taking care to conciliate Berlin, and early in the new year the British Minister there was informed that its policy remained one of neutrality. While he, and his Government, remained anxious to move by 'influence [and] attention', the Russians, placed in tactical charge, were convinced indeed that coercion was now required.[3] One more approach was made however, in February 1805, when a special envoy was sent from St Petersburg to propose a bilateral defensive alliance. With its failure – for only a temporising answer could be extracted – their opinion hardened farther over the coming months. They gained Prussia's co-operation in obtaining passports for Novosiltsov's mission to Paris,[4] and Berlin was already trying to use its good offices to avert a chance of war between Russia and France. Those however were at its disposal mainly because Prussian envoys were continuously engaged in talks in Paris, centring on the possibility of garrisoning or obtaining Hanover if the French would withdraw.[5] Hardenberg and his king were still walking a tightrope. But as spring gave way to summer, the balance was increasingly threatened for them by developments elsewhere. A decision was beginning to look unavoidable. French persuasions throughout Europe were inviting. But it seemed that Russia was resolved to resist them; and there were signs moreover that she might be massing forces for the Prussian border itself.

Much of the friction, and Prussian fears of being bullied into an alliance, arose from a prospect of being deprived of the coveted prize of Hanover. And this in turn sprang from the possibility, independent of

1. Paget to Harrowby, no. 62, 16 November 1804 (P.R.O., F.O. 7/72).

2. See eg Leveson Gower to Mulgrave, no. 15, 14 April 1805 (*Third Coalition*, 142).

3. Eg Jackson to Harrowby, no. 128, 27 December 1804 (P.R.O., F.O. 64/66); Leveson Gower to same, no. 14, Secret and Confidential, 24 December 1804 (*Third Coalition*, 80); Mulgrave to Jackson, no. 1, 5 February 1805 (F.O. 64/67). Only four despatches were sent from London to Berlin from that date to mid May.

4. Required because the King of Prussia recognised Napoleon's title while the Tsar did not.

5. Cf. p. 702 above.

French inducements, of a further partner for Britain and Russia who could then itself well assist in freeing the Electorate. An agreement with France was therefore highly attractive. It promised an acquisition, but might also forestall a particularly disagreeable loss. For while the Prussians and Austrians alike were hesitating to commit themselves, an eager candidate for a Coalition had been knocking at the door from the North.

This was an unusual state of affairs for Britain in the perspective of the past three decades. The Northern Powers of Denmark and Sweden had generally been archetypal, and not always passive, neutrals. Of keen interest to London as a source of naval supplies, their mutual quarrels under the shadow of Russia had caused occasional concern even in peacetime; and the deteriorating wartime relations with Denmark had led in the end to Nelson's attack.[1] That however was caused precisely by her involvement in a revived armed Neutral League, for the ebb and flow of sentiment in both northern capitals failed to overturn their legal status of non-belligerency. Not indeed since the later 1780s had either Power actively sought an alliance to include this country.[2] But in August 1804 Sweden proposed talks for such an end.

One says Sweden; and of course a national shorthand often has to do duty for Governments subject in degree to internal differences of view. On this occasion, however, the usage is formally correct. For in this instance and to an extent not paralleled even in Russia – the Foreign Minister Ehrensvärd was no Czartoryski – it was not Ministers or officials who favoured such a move; it was the King, the unpredictable Gustavus IV. Recent events in France – Bonaparte's new title and the fate of d'Enghien above all – had heightened his quixotic legitimism to a state, not infrequent, of paranoia; and the thrust of an autocracy enforced by a dangerously unstable temperament sufficed to carry the policy at least part of the way. A Secret Convention with Britain, pending a full treaty, was signed in Stockholm on 3 December 1804, and ratifications followed early in the new year.[3]

The greatest, indeed the indispensable advantage of such an agreement lay for this country in the prospect of one between Sweden and

---

1. See I, 49–50, II, 275–7, 378, 503–7, 624, pp. 235, 244, 394–5, 555, 612 above for the ups and downs of the consequences of neutrality under wartime neutral trade; I, 543 for British unease over war in the Baltic in 1788, with its implications for peacetime commerce; op. cit., 550n3 for a warning against Denmark's involvement in a European conflict in 1790; II, 9, 13–14, 22 for the Northern Powers' in the Ochakov affair in 1791.

2. Sweden in 1788, for a quintuple alliance building in possible conjunction with Denmark on the so-called Triple Alliance of Britain, Holland and Prussia; I, 541, and see also Ehrman, *Commercial Negotiations with Europe*, 137–40. Cf. p. 244, n2 above.

3. P.R.O., F.O. 73/32 *passim*. The French text is in *Consolidated Treaty Series*, ed. Parry, 58 (1969), 39–40.

A parallel of Gustavus with Paul of Russia, heightened by the fact of eventual removal in each case, springs to mind.

Russia. For talks there were likewise under way, and though they were not yet concluded the result was reached a month later, in mid January 1805. Early in the year, therefore, an Allied front could be envisaged for northern Germany, and one already provided with a base, for Sweden had long held territory in Pomerania on the southern Baltic coast. By the Convention of December Gustavus would provide a force, not yet settled in detail but offered at 25,000 men, in return for a British subsidy, also not yet settled but temporarily set at £60,000. In combination with a larger Russian force, a useful army could thus be poised to strike towards the west; and Britain for its part would be well placed to play a useful and perhaps a profitable role. Hanoverian recruits for the King of England's German Legion could be raised and channelled into Pomerania; and supplies could be stored at its port of Stralsund, perhaps leading to a beneficial reduction of Swedish duties and restrictions on British trade.[1] At the same time there were some problems, which would have to be ironed out. Gustavus was trying to insist that the Russians accept his personal command of their joint forces; and while this did not affect British troops it would obviously be an unwelcome complication for Allied strategy, in the hands of a secondary Power let alone in his own. He was also calling for an 'open avowal' that the object of the 'general' war was the return of the Bourbons to their throne.[2] And, as had been experienced with his father in peacetime, the financial demand was 'exorbitant' for services which, though potentially of value, were not central to British hopes.[3] Such difficulties might be overcome. But in the event the last was compounded by another whose extent had not been clearly foreseen. For within the framework of Gustavus's crusade there lay also a hard-headed territorial concern. Pomerania, gained by Sweden from Brandenburg at the end of the Thirty Years War, had been reduced in the east in 1720 by the successor state of Prussia as a consequence of the Northern War; and the remaining portion might well figure in any prospective arrangement between Paris and Berlin. Rumours to that end indeed were rife, Prussian action was suspected, and while Gustavus had entertained hopes of his neighbour as a fourth member of a Coalition, he was resolved to fortify his province, above all Stralsund, and intended to use British money to that end. In the early months of 1805,[4] as the Government in London pressed for specific Swedish plans, this became increasingly clear while more positive intentions became increasingly vague. There was no doubting the King's persistent devotion to the cause of defeating Bonaparte; nor

1. See Fremont, loc. cit., 172.

2. The phrases were those of the British Minister in Stockholm, Henry Pierrepont, in August 1804 (loc. cit., 165, and see also 244).

3. The phrase here was that of Camden (see p. 700, n4 above) to Pierrepont on 7 December (loc. cit., 172–3). For Gustavus III in 1788 see Ehrman, *Commercial Negotiations with Europe*, 139–40.

4. F.O. 73/33 *passim* for January to early May 1805.

to providing part of an Allied army in Pomerania. But by the spring he was declaring that his troops must be stationed strictly in the province throughout the war; and indeed by May, pleading poverty, was threatening to reduce the strength of the garrison in Stralsund itself. When Britain and Russia signed their own Provisional Treaty, it was not certain that either Sweden or Prussia would pledge a commitment to offensive support.

II

The news of the Anglo-Russian agreement reached London on 9 May.[1] By that time Pitt was in serious, and worsening, political trouble. The introduction of Addington, now Sidmouth, to the Cabinet in January had brought some of the designed Parliamentary comfort.[2] Opposition, as expected, launched a series of attacks on various questions at the start of the new session, in particular on the causes of the war with Spain and, once more, on Pitt's defence legislation. But after some hard-fought debates – the final discussion on Spain took the Commons to an adjournment at 2 am on 12 February and to a division at 6 am on the 13th – the Ministry secured adequate majorities throughout.[3] At the same time however he encountered difficulty, and had to accept some reverses, over his budget;[4] and division figures, as often, told only part of the story. If Sidmouth's connexion lent numbers to the Government lobby, those could hardly be considered reliable;[5] its accession capped the discontents already aroused by the

1. Endorsement on Leveson Gower's despatch no. 14 of 12 April 1805 containing the contents of the treaty (F.O. 65/57).

2. See pp. 722, 725 above.

3. For Pitt's worry of defeat before Addington could be counted in support see *Life of Wilberforce*, III, 208. *P.D.*, II gives the proceedings and papers on these two particular subjects respectively in cols. 155–8, 164–7, 219–22, 256–8, 333–8 (for the Lords), 57–8, 142–4, 149–55, 224–47, 289–306, 365–409, 410–68 (for the Commons); cols. 45–6, 145–6, 219, 480–519 (for the Lords), 54, 55–7, 141–2, 247–56 – on the army and ordnance estimates –, 258–9, 590–626, 634–5, 723–86 (for the Commons). The Ministerial majorities (several motions being unopposed) were, on the first, 114 to 36 in the Lords on 11 February, 313 to 106 in the Commons on 13 February; on the second, 113 to 45 in the Lords on 15 February, 242 to 96 in the Commons on 21 February, 267 to 127 on 6 March. The Government however was foreced to produce papers, particularly on the war with Spain.

A third question, the continuance of suspension of the habeas corpus bill for Ireland (as required annually by law), also gave rise to some lively debates in those two months: see op. cit., cols. 469–70, 541–2, 581–9, 719–22 (for the Lords), 311–36, 473–8, 522–34, 560–2 (for the Commons). Ministerial majorities were 41–13 in the Lords on 21 February, 112 to 33 in the Commons on 8 February and 159 to 54 on the 15th.

4. See p. 686 above.

5. According to Canning (to Granville Leveson Gower, 11 January [1805]; P.R.O. 30/29/8(3)), Pitt said that the Addingtonians' accession would be 'in no way felt or understood but in their votes'. For their possible reliability cf. pp. 666, 724 and n4 above.

arrangements of the previous May; the Ministry gained no noticeable debating strength, and the Cabinet was no more at ease with itself than before.[1]

Nor did the Minister for his part do much to encourage doubters. The recourse of places and grants was certainly not easy at this point: a further batch of recruits had to be accommodated even if the extent proved quite modest,[2] and the process was bound to give renewed offence elsewhere. But Pitt was always bad at paying '*little attentions*' of any kind,[3] as he showed now once more and particularly in one important case. Lord Stafford, at the apex of one of the powerful family connexions, with a stepbrother close to Canning and to Pitt himself and disposing with his wife of six Parliamentary seats, had become increasingly critical over the past half year, inclining towards Grenville in preference to the narrow Administration which had been a disappointment.[4] The admittance of Addington naturally heightened his disapproval. But old ties remained strong, he was not yet committed even to Grenville's own idea of opposition, and might still be won by a personal approach. 'A little *early* attention from you', according to a trusted source, 'would secure him – without that I cannot answer'. But though other friends continued to urge some 'explanations' the Minister did not move, he would not bestow a vacant and widely anticipated blue ribbon, and in the event the Marquess and, at first confusedly, his MPs acted increasingly in company with the Grenvillites.[5] Nor was this the sole instance of this kind, though the outcome was not the same. Lord Lowther had been a friend since Cambridge days and a devoted adherent from the start, was an intimate of Mulgrave's, and now the patron of nine constituencies. But vouchsafed no initial explanation and deeply disturbed by what had occurred, he found himself unable, at least temporarily, to offer his support. While he remained personally as affectionate as ever, and was at last invited to an explanation which he would look forward to hearing 'with every disposition to be satisfied', he

1. See pp. 669–76, 642, 717–18 above. Buckinghamshire, as one of the two accessions, found it necessary to deny early newspaper reports of 'jealousies and differences between the friends recently reconciled' (to Auckland, 4 February 1805; *A.C.*, IV, 231–2), and Canning likewise referred to 'the period' of their 'setting up P & A against each other' (to Leveson Gower, 25 February 1805; P.R.O. 30/29/8(3)). Ministerial journals were also notably quick to issue rebuttals.

2. See pp. 723–5 above.

3. Camden in conversation in May 1804 (*Malmesbury*, IV, 314).

4. Cf. pp. 652, 659, n5. And cf. 674 for Leveson Gower.

5. Harrowby to Pitt, 6 January 1805 (Dacres Adams Mss, formerly P.R.O. 30/58/6); Canning to Granville Leveson Gower, 25 February 1805 (P.R.O. 30/29/8(3)); Viscount Lowther to Camden, 28 February, 31 March 1805 (Camden Mss U 840 C116/3, 244/4). And see Sack, *The Grenvllites*, 81–2. For the Parliamentary seats involved see the Appendix to Sack, 'The Lords and Parliamentary Patronage, 1802–1832', reprinted from an article in *H.J.*, vol. 23 as ch. 17 in *Peers, Politics and Power . . .* , ed. Clyve Jones and David Lewis Jones (1986).

proved not to be entirely so and a few months later was distinctly unsettled at a more critical time.[1]

Such instances of course were not new. They reflected the Minister's familiar indolence and reluctance in these matters, the former if anything increasing, the latter unlikely to diminish when he was told by an agitated Canning that he should not 'apologise' through an intermediary but call on Stafford himself.[2] In any case moreover, he professed in January not to be greatly worried. He expected 'the bustle' to die down quickly;[3] and he probably meant what he said. The recruitment of Addington caused general surprise, a widespread doubt as to their future relations, and among many of Pitt's continuing adherents a deep sense of shock. They had been jolted in May 1804, and many of them badly, though they were prepared to give him the benefit of the doubt. But this was a keener blow. It was perhaps one thing to have turned to earlier associates who had served in Addington's Ministry – originally with his own blessing – when he decided that he could not form the Administration for which he had hoped. But to admit the man himself whose inadequacy had led to the expulsion of that Ministry, and whose conduct to his predecessor some regarded as personally obnoxious, was to go almost to the end of a hateful road. One early friend, feeling sadly 'disregarded', voiced his disagreement with Pitt's recent policies, and his profound disapproval of this step, with a desperate plea.

> You do not know yr present situation. There is a disapprobation of yr conduct, & a preparation for declaring it to an extent & nature of wh I am sure you are not conscious . . . I cannot bear the idea of the mischief wh may happen to you . . .

This came in point of fact from one of Stafford's – or rather his wife's – MPs.[4] Others, more intimately involved, were as much or more

---

1. Lowther to Camden, recalling the early friendship with Pitt (see I, 17) and 'almost invariable' deference to his opinion (Camden Ms U840 C244/3); same to Pitt, 12 March 1805 (Dacres Adams Mss, formerly P.R.O. 30/58/6); copy of Camden to Lowther, 29 June 1805 (Camden Ms U840 C244/2). Pitt's friend Bathurst was clearly nervous about him, probably in February (to Pitt, nd, endorsed February 1805; Dacres Adams Mss, formerly P.R.O. 30/58/6).

Lowther's confidential friendship with Mulgrave is evident from the correspondence in their papers. See p. 746, n5 above for a list of the constituencies involved, inherited from his cousin, Pitt's Parliamentary patron in 1780 (I, 25–6) who four years later was rewarded with a clutch of peerages including the Earldom of Lonsdale (*GEC* VIII, 133–5).

2. Canning's report of conversation to Leveson Gower, 25 February 1805 (P.R.O. 30/29/8(3)). As he acknowledged, 'he [Pitt] has never done anything like it'.

3. Same to same, 11 January [1805]; loc. cit.

4. J.C. Villiers to Pitt, 20 January 1805 (Dacres Adams Mss, formerly P.R.O. 30/58/6). He had been a friend since Cambridge (I, 17), appearing a few years later in *The Rolliad* (see op. cit., 109n1) as 'the "Nereus" of Pitt's forces'. His Scottish seat in this Parliament belonged to Lady Stafford in her capacity as Countess of Sutherland in her own right.

Another, and more important, sorrowful friend was Harrowby, reconciled at first to a balance of advantages but soon disgusted by the names of those on whom posts of distinctions had to be conferred (to Bathurst, 31 January 1805; *H.M.C., Bathurst*, 44).

distressed. Canning, disoriented in 1804, was now virtually distraught: he remained in office, but under the most 'mortifying' and 'intolerable' circumstances. His absentee correspondent Leveson Gower wrote that he for his part would have joined Opposition if he had been in England. Tomline and Rose, those self-appointed guardians of the shrine, lamented 'in Silence', the former restrained by Pitt's evident satisfaction with an accession of strength and, in greater degree, from a more pressing interest of his own,[1] the latter by a conviction that while his 'heart' was 'almost broken' it was *'impossible'* for him to do 'anything *hostile* towards Mr Pitt'.[2] Such feelings in such quarters were not pleasant for the Minister to hear, and they affected him. So likewise did the fresh loss of esteem in other circles to which by nature he remained attached.[3] But he did not allow them – as indeed he could scarcely afford – to deflect him from his course. The condemnation was not universal – Wilberforce for instance was not exceptional in applauding the junction[4] –, the circumstances could be called in defence, and the consequences need not extinguish hope. Pitt could reply to the charge of political tergiversation by pointing out (as he inferred privately) that it was Addington's ineptitude, not differences of constitutional principle, that had caused the initial rift; and the converse line of attack, on the renewed allegation of a servile reliance on the Crown, harked back in essence to earlier occasions – to May 1804 and December 1783.[5] He had no intention now of being forced from office. He always hated to yield on what he might see as a personal challenge, particularly perhaps when he was taking 'a part . . . to which' he was 'not naturally inclined'.[6] And he was sure, predictably and genuinely, that the defence of the country and his 'large and deep schemes'[7] for alliances demanded his presence at a still critical time. He reckoned – as did some others – that he had 'abilities . . . enough' to cope with Addington even on the front from which that Minister had always

1. Discussed on pp. 749–52 below.

2. Canning to Leveson Gower, 11 January [1805] (P.R.O. 30/29/8(3)) – he was rendered the more distraught by the fact that his fracas with Hawkesbury revived, raising added complications for himself and Pitt, at just this time (see p. 718 and n4 above); Leveson Gower to Morpeth in April (Harvey, 'The Grenville Party', 107) – he was of course Stafford's stepbrother (p. 746 above); Tomline to Rose, 11 December 1804 (*Rose*, II, 88), same to Mrs Tomline, two letters nd but endorsed 1804 and 24 December respectively, reporting conversations with Pitt (Pretyman Ms 435/44); and see Holland Rose, II, 517–18.

3. Cf. p. 675 above.

4. *Life of Wilberforce*, III, 210–11.

5. For the first see Tomline's emphasis, after seeing Pitt, on the fact that there had been 'no *difference of principle* between Mr. A and Mr. P' (to Rose, 29 December 1804; *Rose*, II, 100), and Pitt's speech in debate on 6 March 1805 (phrased with greater tact towards his new associates) after he was attacked cogently by Sheridan, as the Minister looked across the floor at the combination of Grenvillites and Foxites (*P.D.*, III, col. 760); for the second, eg p. 645 above.

6. Cf. p. 562 above.

7. P. 700 above.

drawn support.[1] Whatever might be thought or suspected elsewhere, he did not believe that George III would favour, let alone seek, an alternative to himself. He assured Canning that, as the latter put it, 'A has no influence[,] that the K is all his [Pitt's] own'; and, on that expectation, he would 'still' be 'Minister'.[2] In a wider sphere, he had not lost his confidence in his accustomed handling of the Commons; and at the start of the year his hopes for progress with Europe were high.[3]

While this assessment reflected a congenital optimism, it was coolly argued. Grenvillites and Foxites, now more clearly in a 'formed' Opposition, could not hope to overturn Government on their own, or attack enough waverers without Addington's support, unless something unforeseen turned up. Whatever Opposition newspapers might claim – as they did in the early weeks of the union –, Addington himself could hardly mount a challenge[4] or make too much trouble within the Ministry unless, again, some strong and defensible cause occurred. And whatever Pitt's own problems with George III, it seemed rather alarmist to suppose that they would lead to a political break. The Minister may have been uncertainly dependent on the monarch, but the monarch was dependent on the Minister after Addington had been bundled from office and while the spectre of Fox remained. In particular, if Pitt could secure his Continental alliances – and the crucial opening agreement with Russia was looking achievable at that point – his personal authority would be weightily reinforced. There thus seemed reason enough to believe that he had dished his opponents at least for a time; and with foreign affairs standing as they did the matter uppermost in his mind was the immediate future – the current Parliamentary session – before the refuge of the long recess.

Such prognostications nonetheless made the most of the case. In the event it soon proved less comfortable than Pitt had chosen to think. The road towards a third European Coalition had still to negotiate further obstacles; while, at the closer end of the time scale, his relations with George III were badly shaken within the next few weeks. The two men indeed were then brought to perhaps their most violent personal dispute in the whole course of their long association. The trouble once more turned on patronage. On the morning of 18 January the Archbishop of Canterbury died.[5] He had been senile for some months, and the King and Pitt had apparently agreed – or Pitt had acquiesced in the King's wish – that the successor should be Manners Sutton, the Bishop of Norwich.[6] As

---

1. The full phrase, from a hostile source, was in point of fact 'abilities and cunning enough'; Duke of Northumberland to Colonel Macmahon, 3 February 1805 (*Correspondence of Prince of Wales*, V, no. 2010).
2. Canning's diary for 8 January 1805 (Canning Ms 29d).
3. See Wilberforce on pp. 700–1 above.
4. See p. 722 above.
5. The inoffensive Dr John Moore (see II, 65), who had been in place since 1783.
6. So at any rate George III told Rose on 1 November 1804 (*Rose*, II, 194).

the time seemed likely to approach, however, an alternative candidate took timely steps to present his claim. Tomline, as ever aspiring and acquisitive, sounded Pitt through Rose; and in mid December the Minister raised the matter in a letter to the King. As soon as news of the death was received on 18 January he wrote again, seeking an audience; once more on the 22nd; and either by then or on the 23rd the meeting took place.[1] The result was a furious quarrel: many years later Sidmouth told a friend that to the best of his belief such strong language had hardly ever been used 'between a Sovereign and his Minister', and an old friend of the Queen's, passing down the corridor on a visit, was shocked to hear voices loudly and angrily raised.[2]

The passion was roused because much appeared to both men to be at stake. To the King, the see of Canterbury occupied a special place. The Primate of All England, together with himself, was the defender of the Established Church; he was the first subject in the land after the Princes of the blood. George III's devotion to Anglican Protestantism, in its tenets and its constitutional role, arose from the core of his being. He always took a close and informed interest in ecclesiastical preferments, and now that religion and society faced the twin if dissimilar threats of Catholic representation in Parliament and popular revolutionary unrest, he felt all the more keenly the importance of the appointment. It lay within his prerogative, and he was determined to exercise his right. Easily excited, enjoying some successes recently in less august instances, and confronted by a challenge as he saw it to a choice already agreed and mounted now on behalf of a highly personal and inferior nominee – to the Minister's former if unpaid secretary –, he was in no mood to be denied his way.[3]

The situation looked very different to Pitt. As he pointed out, recommendations to this as to other sees came from the First Lord of the

1. It is hard to follow the exact sequence of events. Pitt, having shown Pretyman the draft of his first letter, sent it to the King on 11 December 1804 (*L.C.G. III*, IV, no. 2978; and see Stanhope, IV, 234). He had earlier thought of raising the subject in conversation, but decided against it in George III's 'present state' (op. cit., 233). For the Bishop's previous letters to Rose, who clearly felt reservations at the start – no doubt from having so recently heard the King's wish at first hand (p. 749, n6 above) – see *Rose*, II, 82–7. Pitt's letter of 18 January 1805 was written at 11 am (*L.C.G. III*, IV, no. 3012), only hours after the Archbishop died. I have not traced an acknowledgment arranging an audience; but the tone of his further letter of the 22nd (op. cit., no. 3014) suggests that one might have taken place in the interval. In the same letter, however, he referred to a meeting 'tomorrow', and in acknowledging it on the 23rd the King allowed him to say 'whatever [he] chooses to say' later that day (Ashbourne, *Pitt, His Life and Times*, 354). This last may of course have been only a final reference to a matter already discussed and in George III's view concluded.

2. Stanhope, IV, 252 – Sidmouth was talking to Dean Milman, which would probably assign the date to a period from the 1820s to early '40s. The lady was said to have been Lady Charlotte Finch.

3. Apart from anything else, he was reported as saying that the Archbishopric required a gentleman – a man of family –, which Tomline, though respectably born, was not; see *The Historical and Posthumous Memoirs of Sir Nathaniel William Wraxall . . .* , IV, ed. Henry B. Wheatley (1884), 410, editorial n1.

Treasury, and with a single exception – as it happened, that of the late Archbishop in a brief interval between Administrations – they had been accepted 'for a long course of time'.[1] He had given his reasons to show that Tomline was an appropriate candidate: senior on the Bishops' bench to Manners Sutton, and in charge of the most extensive diocese in the country. This was not a job; others could speak for Tomline's studies and publications, and he would be giving up the Deanery of St Paul's, which he also held and might indeed go to the Bishop of Norwich.[2] So far so arguably valid. But of course the gravamen of the case lay elsewhere. If these qualifications for the appointment were allowed,

> your Majesty's refusal to comply with his [Pitt's] request can hardly be understood by himself, and will certainly not be understood by the public, in any other light than as a decisive mark of your Majesty's not honouring him with that degree of weight and confidence which his predecessors have enjoyed . . .[3]

It must indeed be seen as a further instance of the monarch's readiness to engross his permissible patronage, and, given Tomline's position, as an open rebuff to the Minister himself.

So bitterly in fact did Pitt take this problem that he thought he might have to resign. Without that confidence,

> your Majesty must be sensible how impossible it is, especially under the present circumstances, that he can conduct your Majesty's affairs with advantage.

For clearly the worst aspect of the outcome lay in its timing. The Opposition groups and their newspapers would make the most of the affair; and it would be noted equally by the Addingtonians themselves. 'The public' would be titillated, and support perhaps more ambivalent; the rumours that Sidmouth still enjoyed George III's amity – even carried influence – would be strengthened at a most damaging point.[4] It was only a few weeks since Pitt had proclaimed his assurance that 'the K' was 'all his own'. In an environment in which disposal of places was viewed as of high significance, this one might be taken as a severe reverse.

The show of threat made no difference. The Minister in fact had picked an inappropriate case. Politicians certainly found it unsatisfactory that the monarch seemed determined to be '*de facto* as well as *de jure* the only fount

---

1. 22 January 1805 (p. 750 above). He must have been referring to the weeks between Shelburne's resignation and Portland's appointment as First Lord in 1783 (see p. 749, n5 above, and I, 101, 104).

2. 11 December 1804 (p. 750 above). For the Deanery see I, 13.

3. 22 January 1805 (ibid).

4. One in particular being that it was he who had in fact earlier committed the King to Manners Sutton's nomination.

of honour';[1] but it was unwise to try to carry a point which could scarcely be forced. Pitt was fighting too largely on the King's ground if that was going to be contested, and having done so much to protect the Crown's constitutional position he would have been highly censured if he of all men departed on a question of patronage, and particularly one that would not look undeniably justified. The whole business was 'an evil'; but his feelings do not seem to have been shared by his friends.[2] After giving away too much in recent months, he would do better in fact to strive for a balance by a sterner trading of favours. The episode proved to be a storm in a teacup: Manners Sutton became Archbishop, and Tomline had to rest content with Winchester after a further fifteen years.[3] But it had revealed the force of Pitt's sensitivities at a delicate moment – his resolve to guard what he had suddenly been brought to see as a possibly vulnerable flank.

A much greater danger, however, lay in waiting to upset his forecasts. In the summer of 1803 St Vincent's Commission of Naval Enquiry published its first batch of reports, and a further crop followed in the summer of 1804. The ninth was ordered to be printed, like the rest, by Parliament in January 1805; the tenth on 13 February; and the latter became available on 18 March. Motions on related affairs had been introduced by then – to prolong the Commission's powers under the original Act, and on the state of the navy; and after preliminary skirmishes at the beginning of April, the battle on the Tenth Report began on the 8th.[4]

For the latter had been awaited lately with an eagerness not accorded to its predecessors. The subject was the office of the Treasurer of the Navy, the post held by Melville, in company with his other appointments, through virtually the whole of Pitt's first Administration;[5] and rumours had been growing that he might not emerge unscathed. No one, except Melville himself, was more anxious to read the contents than Pitt; for whether or not, or how far, he had been forewarned, he had not seen

1. The accusation came from Harrowby (see *L.C.G. III*, IV, no. 3014nl on p. 284).

2. See ibid for opinions from Harrowby and Charles Long.

3. And, three years later again, with fishing a dormant Newfoundland baronetcy from the vasty deep. His legacy to his final see was to pull down its ancient metropolitan house at Chelsea.

4. See p. 630 above for the Commission; for the fresh Parliamentary discussions on naval matters, *P.D.*, III, cols. 667–9 for the Commons, and see 336–8, 478–80 for preliminaries in the Lords in February, occasioned probably by the Ministry's intentions for its own new Commission – for which see p. 630 above; op. cit., IV, cols. 18–24, 145–7 for the Lords, and on Melville himself 165–7, 186–90, 225–327 for the Commons. For the date of the order to print the Tenth Report see op. cit., III, col. 1147; for its appearance, *Life of Wilberforce*, III, 218. The Reports, fourteen in all by the end, were published in the *Parliamentary Session Papers* for 1802–3 vol. 4, 1803–4 vol. 3, 1804–5 vol. 2 (Ninth to Eleventh Reports), 1806 vol. 4. The first ten may be consulted more conveniently in *P.D.*, III, Appendix, cols. 865–1211.

5. From January 1784 (see I, 131) to June 1800; he had held it before under Shelburne, from August 1782 to April 1783.

them in advance. When his copy arrived, he was talking to Wilberforce, discussing the slave trade; and his friend was struck by the effect. 'I shall never forget the way in which he seized it, and how eagerly he looked into the leaves without waiting even to cut them open'.[1] What he read made it clear that here was something which would not lightly go away.

1. See *Life of Wilberforce*, III, 217–18. He maintained that Melville himself had not 'mentioned the matter' to Pitt or 'any human being till the Report was printed'; and this could well be so. Melville may have wished to keep off the subject, and with Pitt in particular, for as long as he could. Some years earlier (it would seem in 1797) the then Governor of the Bank of England had mentioned to the Minister the possibility of some irregularities, which Dundas denied and Pitt then thought no more about (see *P.D.*, V (1812), cols. 385–7 and Appendix, cols. viii–x, liv–lxviii; *Life of Wilberforce*, III, 220; *H.M.C., Bathurst*, 46–7). More recently he had accepted his peerage from Addington, in December 1802, a week after the motion for a Commission of Enquiry had been introduced in the Commons; and there was soon talk that he might wish to enter the Cabinet, if possible as First Lord of the Admiralty in order to keep an eye on what might transpire. Early in the following year he agreed with the Paymaster of his former office, Alexander Trotter, to a mutual relief of all financial obligations and the destruction of their papers relating to naval finances, on the ground that he had earlier completed his own account with the public and transferred the remaining balance to his successor (see Cyril Matheson, *Life of Henry Dundas*, 325–7, where however it is conjectured that had he known of the forthcoming motion he might have chosen to stay in the lower House). It is true that he was in Scotland at that time, and had been there since the summer when he had given up his seat at the general election. Even so, he kept in touch; and one might equally conjecture that the House of Lords might have seemed to offer a quieter haven if the wind began to blow.

Melville however was not necessarily the only possible source of information; and whether he had talked to Pitt or not, there is one curious episode that perhaps deserves mention here. On 31 August 1804 Lady Spencer wrote from London to her husband at Althorp with two strange stories (B.L. Add. Ms temp. Althorp G294). She had heard from 'Ross' (almost certainly the Major-General who was the intimate correspondent of Cornwallis, and Surveyor General of the Ordnance) of a most untypical meeting which a 'sensible' and experienced official (pehaps R.H. Crew – see p. 465 above) had had with Pitt the day before. Accustomed 'for many years' to working with him 'tête a tête',

he had seen him under circumstances which would have appal'd the stoutest heart, & Calm, collected & unoccupied did he always find him – but . . . Yesterday, what produced such an effect he could not take upon him to say. He never saw a Man so utterly absorbed in profound thought, & so completely under the influence of anxiety & dejection – so that by no means could he . . . make Mr. Pitt to attend one moment to the subject which had brought them together.

On the same day, one of the Spencer family's dependants (their man of business Thomas Harrison) was walking 'very early' in the morning in St James's Park – presumably from Spencer House – when he saw a man ahead of him

walking by himself with his Arms across, & apparently so taken up in thought & walking so uncommonly slow & unequally that it gave him a curiosity to see who it could be, & on overtaking him he saw that it was Mr. Pitt looking like death with his eyes staring out of his head & steadfastly fixed on the ground . . .

and this was the more odd because, so far as he knew, 'Mr. Pitt never was seen walking up & down the Mall by himself Solus cum Solus . . . before'. He was so amazed that he asked Lady Spencer what she knew of the Minister's health.

What it might produce, however, was by no means so clear. A defence could certainly be raised in mitigation. As the Commissioners of Enquiry themselves pointed out, the Treasurer of the Navy was appointed by patent: 'he does not perform in person any of the official duties of his situation, but nominates and appoints the Paymaster, to whom he delegates the whole charge and conduct of the office by a general power of attorney'.[1] The office in fact was virtually a sinecure, held for an active politician. It was also one that in earlier days had notoriously been of solid personal value, for the Treasurer, like his counterpart the Paymaster General of the Forces, had held the funds officially in his own charge until they were finally distributed for the services allocated under Parliamentary Vote. Even when he died, indeed, his heirs could do the same: a highly useful source of profit in hand, which in practice could continue for years, to augment a quite modest salary from the Crown. This arrangement, as it happened, had been ended under Dundas himself by a statute in 1786 as the result, in those years of partial reform to which he was not unsympathetic, of a report from the newly established Commissioners for Auditing the Public Accounts.[2] Moneys voted for the navy – following the practice recently introduced for those formerly paid

---

The official had wondered if Pitt's deep abstraction and dejection had been caused by news (there were already rumours) that the King was 'downright ill' again. But in point of fact that was not so: George III was on the road to recovery at the time, and Pitt in any case was accustomed to such situations. It is indeed hard to lay one's finger on the source of the trouble – for while the second of the two accounts at least might be exaggerated, neither sounds untrue. Harrison said that he believed the Minister 'to be a diiing man from his appearance'; but the stories taken together suggest 'profound thought' rather than a physical attack. Nothing obvious comes to mind from the flow of affairs abroad or at home at that precise point, nor from Pitt's domestic situation – his finances seem to have been under no more pressure than usual, and in any case it was virtually unknown for him to worry. The treatment of the public finances, on the other hand, was a matter which always concerned him much more; absolutely as a reflection, or emanation, of his own 'character', and, one might perhaps say, at one remove in a case such as that of Melville, a key member of his Administration in the earlier war when the two men were acting so very closely together, as indeed they had done in particular in one instance turning on finance at a difficult point. That occasion will be discussed below (pp. 760–2) as a possible significant addition to a wider cause for anxiety, both on Melville's behalf and on potential implications for Pitt himself. Might it conceivably have been this – the question of honour, in an area of business and conduct lying so near the Minister's heart, and generating possibly dire political effects – that threw him into such a state? He had been down at Walmer on and off in the recess. Might he have now heard something in London from some quarter: perhaps from one of the Commissioners – though only one was a Pittite? For on 26 June they had applied to Melville for certain accounts which they could not explain, and four days later he wrote that those had been destroyed and that in any case he could not have sent them without disclosing 'delicate and confidential transactions of government' (*P.D.*, III, col. 1158). This reply could not but lead to further inquiries.

Speculation – and it can be no more – on such lines may very well be wide of the mark. But it may merit a note.

1. *P.D.*, III, col. 1152.
2. See I, 301–2; and 132 for the whiggish element in Dundas.

to the Paymaster General[1] – were now issued to the Bank of England for the Treasurer of the Navy's account; he had to present drafts specifying the services before he received payment; and on vacating office must transfer the balances to his successor.[2] The Treasury itself had thus been placed more directly in control, and opportunities for fraud reduced. Dundas moreover during his tenure seems to have played within the legal rules: on one occasion, when he was short of capital to invest on his own account in East India stock and his Paymaster, Alexander Trotter, offered to advance it from unused office funds, he refused – according to Trotter's evidence after some sixteen years – 'in the most pointed and decided manner'.[3] The trouble lay in a greyer area: in the earlier, recognised convention, not wholly forgotten in a slowly changing atmosphere; and in Dundas's own long exposure to the usages of an acceptance world, which was evident in his lack of supervision and implicit indulgence of his working subordinates and above all of the Paymaster, who had been his Scottish nominee. For Trotter had been exploiting his personal position to the full, and thus, in the process, indirectly that of Dundas. Carelessness rather than premeditation lay at the root of the Treasurer's culpability.[4] But, as would emerge, it was an inattention that permitted private borrowings whose availability derived in the end from official funds.[5]

The immediate impact of the Report, not surprisingly, produced some strongly differing reactions. Within the Ministry itself, and speaking with all the assurance of the current holder of Melville's post, Canning was certain that Pitt was 'not aware of half the strength of the defence that may be made'; and others in the ranks of Government likewise found no great moral fault – 'all say that he [Melville] has acted like a fool'.[6] Certain members of the Cabinet however, who had to handle the affair, were distinctly cautious. They agreed to stand by their colleague, but from a prepared position. The most disturbing development came from Sidmouth, who was sure that Melville could not be wholly cleared in the public's view

---

1. Op. cit., 90n1.

2. Cf. p. 753, n1 above.

3. Matheson, op. cit., 135. He consented however to a personal loan from Trotter made through a third person, ostensibly on the security of the stock supplied which however was itself guaranteed in essence by the naval funds in the Paymaster's control.

4. Trotter's patron in general was actually Minto; but the appointment of course lay through the Treasurer.

Dundas's attitude towards the senior staff of the office was reflected in his treatment of Trotter's own deputy, one Adam Jellicoe, who had sunk a sizeable sum procured from spare naval moneys in a private investment. The Treasurer on that occasion spotted a discrepancy in the accounts; but he did little on learning the reason and continued Jellicoe in his post pending repayment, until disclosure became unavoidable – and Jellicoe killed himself.

5. One other instance of a loan from Trotter in his private capacity was on the occasion of the Loyalty Loan of 1796, when Dundas had been hard pressed to find the considerable sum deemed proper for a senior Cabinet Minister (see II, 639–40).

6. Canning [for whose appointment as Treasurer of the Navy see p. 674 above] to Pitt, 23 March 1805 (Stanhope, IV, 277); *Life of Wilberforce*, III, 220.

by an uncompromising defence, and called for a Ministerial rejoinder in the form of proposing or accepting a Commons' Select Committee. Speaking to Pitt privately, he seems indeed to have threatened to resign if this was not agreed: Hawkesbury, followed by Castlereagh, was offering the same advice; and Pitt found himself forced to accept it.[1] For the Minister at first was resolved to confront any challenge *à l'outrance*. He did not believe that Melville could be proved guilty of deliberate illegality – he was 'quite sure that there/ was no real pocketing of public money in him'[2] – and would have greatly preferred to try to quash the whole business at a stroke. He was unimpressed when Wilberforce and Bankes called on him together as the keepers of his conscience; there was a case that could and should be defended, and, as he told them, this was a matter that could shake the Government. Nonetheless, on the eve of the day that Opposition moved to the attack, the Cabinet decided to seek the expedient of a Select Committee.[3]

The publication of the Report was meanwhile arousing widespread excitement. By the time the debate came on 8 April, the Foxites, who were making the running, had been able to sense feelings out of doors and were the more encouraged to mount an uninhibited assault. 'The story', it was claimed by a young gentleman of Brooks's, 'has descended to and agitated even the lowest order of people'; and however that may have been, the political public as generally understood was in a state of high expectation.[4] The motion was entrusted, or conceded, to Samuel Whitbread, the rich radical Parliamentary bruiser, who seems to have raised the stakes over the previous weeks. Discarding a less violent alternative considered earlier, he now brought two sets of charges, in groups of resolutions, the first alleging illegal application of public funds, which made Melville guilty of a gross violation of duty, the second connivance at another's

1. Sidmouth's account to the Speaker on 7 April (*Colchester*, I, 546–7). The intention was to forestall a *hostile* motion to such purpose, noted below.

Canning, in his diary for the last week of March, gives a rather different impression, of Ministers and law officers coming in relay to consult him on the possibilities of defence and going away satisfied. And according to him Pitt then 'opened the business' on such a basis to the Cabinet, and found them 'apt' and 'not much reluctance even in Addington' (Canning, Ms 29d). If this was so, however, there was a change in the following week, as news came to hand of the line that opposition was going to take; see the interesting account of the division in Cabinet from Vansittart (doubtless gained from Sidmouth or Hawkesbury) to Lord Hardwicke in Ireland (9 April 1805; B.L. Add. Ms 31229).

2. *Life of Wilberforce*, III, 220, diary for 3 April; and see Canning's diary for 23 March (Canning Ms 29d). For Pitt *à l'outrance* cf. p. 564 above.

3. *Life of Wilberforce*, III, 218, and see I, 230 for the early band of candid friends; for the Cabinet, Stanhope, IV, 279–80.

4. S.H. Romilly, *Letters to 'Ivy' from the First Earl of Dudley* [John William Ward] (1905), 26. Ward may not have been the best of judges: his 'manners' were said to 'smell most strongly of never having been in any other world than that of London' (see *H of P*, V, 478). But see also Creevey's diary for 11 May 1805 (*The Creevey Papers*, ed. John Gore (1963), 33 – the relevant sentence is omitted in the earlier edition by Sir Henry Maxwell). Cf. I, 145 for one definition of the public.

peculation, which amounted to a high crime and misdemeanour – a third possibility, that the former Treasurer had been involved in peculation himself, he reserved ominously, as a 'strong suspicion', until a future day.[1] This line in point of fact went well beyond what some of the combined Oppositions would have wished. The inner ranks of the New Opposition in particular were not united in their response. Grenville was becoming unhappy with the Foxites' tendency to oppose for opposition's sake – the principle of conduct he had always abhorred – and whatever the disputes and incompatibility between himself and Melville in the past he was upset and embarrassed by such violent treatment of his former colleague. Buckingham, Spencer and Windham felt much the same. Thomas Grenville on the other hand did not, and avoided writing to his brothers on the subject. Nor was he the only dissident in important family circles. Buckingham's son Temple, Spencer's son Althorp, differed in sentiment from their fathers; Morpeth, in the contrary direction, was less heated than his father Carlisle. A number of others, less closely attached, were also disposed to be moderate. The outcome of the debate was far from certain; minds were by no means all made up in advance; much might turn, at least in moral weight, on the speeches themselves. Fox for his part, observing the general sense of disapproval and puzzlement, and the open reluctance of some Addingtonians to endorse the defence, was happy to seize so promising a chance and judged that Whitbread's minority would be large.[2]

Melville suffered from some bad disadvantages. He could not necessarily count on personal goodwill: he had been a successful Scot – seldom popular – and he had made enemies, including in Scotland itself, in the course of a long and prominent career. He was, and was thought to be, disliked by the King. And he was the occasion for a heaven-sent opening to assault the latest Ministerial arrangement, with a party spirit which indeed shook some of those who objected both to him and to that event.[3] His case moreover had been somewhat damaged by his evasive reply to the Commission's call for papers.[4] And it was not fully retrieved now by a speech from Pitt which may have been below his normal standard – 'miserable', according to one sympathetic source.[5] Even so, as the

---

1. *P.D.*, IV, cols. 255–79. Whitbread's opening remarks disclosed that he first decided, as precedents favoured in hostile cases when a report to the House was to be considered, to call for a Select Committee – the form in fact which the influential voices in the Cabinet had insisted on seeking or accepting so as to buy time and persuasive effort (p. 756 above). But 'on mature reflection' he had changed his mind. See also Thomas Grenville to Grenville, nd but at some point between 1 and 7 April (*H.M.C., Dropmore*, VII, 255).

2. See Harvey, loc. cit., 113–15; Sack, op. cit., 83. Cf. for Grenville's views on opposition p. 574 above.

3. Eg Minto on 'party rancour' (Matheson, op. cit., 348). Malmesbury, more friendly to Government, thought that this 'exceeded . . . in savage feeling all that I ever recollect in this country' (*Malmesbury*, IV, 338).

4. P. 753, n1 (on 754) above.

5. J.W. Ward, in *Letters to 'Ivy'*, 27.

sitting wore on, matters might have been thought to be going Melville's way, until Wilberforce rose towards the end. Many years later he related how he saw Pitt waiting intently for his opening words, and how it 'required no little effort to avoid the fascination of that penetrating eye'. But those words told their story. He supported Whitbread's motion; and his verdict, on a matter which despite the party virulence was viewed by many as beyond a party question, has always been held to have had a decisive effect – perhaps on as many as 40 votes.[1] When the tellers announced the result it was a tie – 216 to 216. The Speaker had therefore to act. 'White as a sheet', it was said, and after 'some minutes' of 'great anxiety', he departed from the normal rule in such an instance of giving the House time for further reflection and cast his vote in favour of the motion.[2]

An extraordinary scene followed. 'Huzzas and shouts' broke out, and a hunting member from Wales, Sir Thomas Mostyn, gave '*a view hollo*' and cried '*We have killed the Fox*'.[3] According to a celebrated partly if at least, inaccurate story, from Malmesbury's son Lord FitzHarris, who was 'wedged close' on the same bench, Pitt

immediately put on the little cocked hat that he was in the habit of wearing, when dressed for the evening, and jammed it deeply over his forehead, and I distinctly saw the *tears trickling down his cheeks*. We had overheard one or two . . . say, they would see '*how Billy looked after it.*' A few young followers of Pitt, with myself, locked their arms together, and formed a circle, in which he moved, I believe, *unconsciously* out of the House.[4]

1. *Malmesbury*, IV, 347n; Stanhope, IV, 281. It is interesting to note that Wilberforce was sitting at the far end of the Treasury bench, and caught Pitt's eye in turning to address the Chair: an example, at this date, of the continuing flexibility of seating arrangements, on this occasion in a crowded House, for of course he held no Ministerial rank (cf. I, 39–40). Matheson, op. cit., 350 cites the tradition of the effect.

2. See *H of P*, III, 5, quoting a statement by the knowledgeable Sir John Sinclair.

3. *Malmesbury*, IV, 338. Sir Thomas, a member of Brooks's, was better known in the hunting field, on the turf, and in the Four in Hand Club than in the House: a noted and characteristic Welsh border squire of large property.

4. Op. cit., 347n, from FitzHarris's 'Note Book' for 1806. The account, which does not seem to exist elsewhere, must have been written much later, indeed perhaps towards the close of his life, for the words omitted above are 'such as Colonel Wardle (of notorious memory)', and Wardle did not enter the Commons until 1807 and died in 1833. If Pitt left the Chamber he did not leave the House, for the vote was on the first of Whitbread's resolutions (see p. 756 above) and the rest had to be decided, all being carried out before the proceedings came to an end (*P.D.*, IV, cols. 320–2). FitzHarris was a junior Lord of the Treasury.

An account sent on the spot 'from Hse of Commons' by the MP Charles Stewart to his uncle Camden – 'I can hardly describe the Clamor of Opposition this is bad news indeed' – and forwarded by the latter on the 10th to Bathurst, may be found in B.L. Loans Ms 57, vol. 2.

The proceedings then wound on, taking the resolutions one by one, until the House adjourned at 5 am on the 9th, and the Minister and Canning walked up Whitehall to Downing Street in the dawn.[1]

From now on it was a question of trying to handle the retreat. The House was due to meet again on the 10th. Whitbread had ended his triumphant day by calling for an Address to the King to remove Melville from 'his councils', and this formed the subject of the fresh debate. By then there was one development, for Melville resigned from the Admiralty on the 9th. When Pitt announced this he must have hoped that it would help turn the tide; and so to some extent it did. As Whitbread had phrased his demand, it was for the culprit 'to be removed from every office . . . under the crown, and from his majesty's presence and councils for ever'. That however now proved too strong, and he withdrew his motion. Nevertheless it was agreed that the resolutions of the 8th should be laid in person before the monarch,[2] and on the 11th a sizeable body of Members took them to St James's, the Foxite leaders (Fox himself, Grey, Sheridan) together with Windham and Thomas Grenville, and indeed Whitbread himself, absenting themselves. The Easter recess followed, and it was 25 April before the whole subject was resumed, with some petitions from constituencies against Melville's conduct, proceedings against a newspaper's 'libel' alleging disgraceful party rancour permeating the debates, and, finally, a debate on the contents of the Tenth Report itself.[3] The Minister now began to regain some ground. In answer to a demand for Melville's prosecution by the Attorney General he secured the establishment of a Select Committee as earlier put forward, and then, defeating an attempt to name its members on the spot, obtained a ballot according to 'ancient usage'. Government's majorities in both instances were 'easy' – 229 to 151 and 251 to 120; and the next day it gained its own recommended list of names by 124 to 45.[4] Further limited successes followed. On 29 April Pitt proposed the continuation of the naval Commission of Enquiry beyond the completion of its latest Report, as he had agreed to do under pressure on the 8th: but now with a time limit, a proposal which was carried.[5] He followed this by securing agreement to civil rather then criminal proceedings against Melville and Trotter for the recovery of misused naval funds – carrying motions of 223 to 128 and 240 to 98 on the way.[6] And on the 30th the Ministry beat off a belated challenge to the inclusion

1. Canning's diary for 8 April (Canning Ms 29d).

2. *P.D.*, IV, col. 328 for Pitt's announcement, 330 for Whitbread's demand, 370 for its withdrawal and the decision to lay the resolution before the King.

3. Op. cit., cols. 375–427. The newspaper was the Ministerial *Oracle*, and the proceedings continued to occupy the House for the next week, during which the proprietor remained in its custody until he apologised.

4. Op. cit., cols. 426, 427, 433. For the King's 'high delight' at the check to Whitbread's 'asperity' in the first of these votes see Stanhope, IV, Appendix, xxiv.

5. See p. 752 above for this mode, in the circumstances, of replacing St Vincent's instrument by a different successor (see p. 630).

6. *P.D.*, I, cols. 484–97, 497–507.

of Castlereagh's name in the ballot list for the Select Committee, by an overwhelming vote of 219 to 86.[1]

But these remained strictly defensive operations, and the general movement continued to the rear. The main Foxite advance could not be countered, as Pitt found over the next two months. On 6 May he was forced to comply with a renewed demand for Melville's dismissal from the Privy Council.[2] He abstained from speaking, other than moving an adjournment midway, when Whitbread, pursuing to the end, moved for trial by impeachment in two further angry debates on 11 and 12 June. And when that attack seemed to be in trouble and was rescued by an amendment from Fox at the close by amending the motion to one for criminal prosecution, a process which in fact seemed even more objectionable to Melville's friends, the Minister was able a fortnight later to do his former colleague a last service, if such it could be called, by supporting a reversal of that decision in melancholy favour of impeachment once more.[3] The subsequent developments moved beyond his ken. Melville was brought to trial in April 1806, and finally acquitted by his fellow peers in June 1807.

The Tenth Report had done its damage. But it was not the final potential threat arising from the Commission of Naval Enquiry. An Eleventh Report was ordered to be published in its turn, and had appeared indeed by the time that its predecessor was debated. At the end of the stormy discussion on 10 April, when Whitbread succeeded in his demand for the resolutions on Melville to be laid before the King, there was a disconcerting postscript. An Opposition Member, the lawyer William Best,[4] gave notice that after the short Easter recess he would introduce a motion 'founded' on the new Report.

This could spell fresh danger – in a sense greater than that aroused by Melville's own case. For the Eleventh Report's contents arose directly from those of the Tenth, and raised questions which might need answers in this instance from the Chancellor of the Exchequer himself. Pitt's own probity in short was coming under review, and in one respect indeed

1. Op. cit., cols. 529–36. Windham by contrast offered to withdraw his name, as having been a member of the Administration in the period in which Melville's alleged abuses had occurred. His proposal was likewise defeated, by 207 to 80.

2. Gaining only the marginal satisfaction of reducing the length of what could otherwise have been another heated debate by announcing near the start that the King had allowed the dismissal to take place (*P.D.*, IV, col. 601). His letter to George III, of 5 May, is in *L.C.G. III*, IV, no. 3089 (and see for one to Melville ibid n2); the King's reply, lamenting a continued 'virulence . . . unbecoming to the character of Englishmen', in Stanhope, IV, Appendix, xxv.

3. *P.D.*, V, cols. 249–323, 329–77, 567–615. On 12 June, at nearly 6 am, the votes against impeachment were 272 to 195 and for criminal prosecution 238 to 229. On 25 June the vote for impeachment was 166 to 143. Fox swung the decision on the former occasion by an ingenious tactic in the lobby itself (col. 377). See also op. cit., cols. 484–90, 557 for developments between the last two dates.

4. *P.D.*, IV, col. 371. Best, always accorded his legal title of serjeant in reports of the debates, was a somewhat unpredictable politician who in these years was counted usually with Opposition.

might seem particularly vulnerable. Three main queries were raised: on transactions related to the issuing of Navy bills without Parliamentary sanction, which, as a form of loan on the analogy of Exchequer bills,[1] they were said to require; on their allocation to a purpose – the payment of debt – which was not for current naval use; and on the use of naval funds by the Treasury rather than a naval authority, for secret services – which themselves were supposed to fall generically on the civil list. These, then, were illegal actions. Why had they been necessary, and what above all were the secret services that were fed from such a source?

Best brought forward his motion on 23 May.[2] By that time more was known about the matters at issue, which had caught the attention of the Commissioners earlier as they examined Melville for the Tenth Report, and then led to preliminary detailed inquiries following its presentation. These last included five examinations of Pitt, from 6 to 10 May and again on the 17th, the first two concentrating on what soon emerged as the most serious of the problems.[3] The rest indeed were quite easily disposed of, as Pitt made clear in his answer to Best in the debate. The advocate had ignored or overlooked the fact that Navy bills could be issued by custom between the Commons' sessions, in circumstances that would otherwise be detrimental to credit – such occasions, Pitt took care to remind the House, having been reduced by regulations of his own for the short-term debt, which bore also on the application of new loans to make timely repayments of past indebtedness. At worst the infringement had been simply a matter of accounting procedures which, given the real inflationary difficulties of the relevant year, 1800–1, might hardly have been expected to attract the Commons' 'microscopic eye'.[4] The explanation, whose technicalities in any case might well have clouded that vision, was accepted with little trouble. The gravamen of any charge really lay in the identity and treatment of the payments for secret services, on which Melville had refused to enlarge.[5]

Such a stance could not be maintained now and Pitt did not attempt it when he attended the Commissioners in his turn. He was able to satisfy them on most of the episodes, relating to several occasions. But one remained that prompted searching questions, to himself and others, in the weeks preceding the debate.[6] It went back almost ten years, to a transaction in 1796 whose own origins had begun to cause him embarrassment the year before.[7] The imbroglio then had arisen from his reliance on the banker Walter Boyd to manage the Loans for that year, domestic and to Austria, at

1. See I, 258.
2. *P.D.*, V, cols. 59–63.
3. Op. cit., Appendix, cols. xlviii–lxiii.
4. Op. cit., cols. 63–7 for a detailed account.
5. See p. 753, n1 above.
6. *P.D.*, IV, cols. 67–8 for his speech on 23 May; op. cit. as in ns 3, 4 above together with cols. xxxii–xlviii, lxvi–lxxv for the investigations during that month.
7. For the rest of this paragraph see II, 519–20, 522, 524–7, 617–21.

a point when fears in the Bank of England of the effect of rising liabilities on reserves of specie were threatening to damage its essential support of Treasury and Exchequer bills. The need had led him to some curious shifts, at first by way of reward which attracted critical Parliamentary debate, and later, as the banker showed signs of failing – which he eventually did –, to an effort at support through a device which came to light only at this point. In the latter instance, and with Dundas's connivance, cash worth £40,000 had been transferred to the Treasury from 'idle' naval funds and thenceforth in Boyd's direction, through Charles Long as joint Secretary, in acceptance of a nominal equivalent in East India Company and Government bills. Pitt had undoubtedly felt under an obligation: the scale of the war was continually outstripping Parliamentary appropriations, the main traditional channel of business was threatening to dry up, and he was desperate to keep Austria in the field. But this last transaction was clearly improper. It had escaped notice before. The threat it might pose at this juncture was hard to foretell.

In the event, and despite Opposition's initial hopes,[1] the Minister emerged unscathed. He proposed a Secret Committee to look into all relevant allegations on the payments for secret services, which would sit separately from the Select Committee into Melville's conduct in general which was already extant. As Fox commented, this put the matter 'on a good footing', and he seemed ready for that to be so. One of Pitt's friends had forecast that on this occasion any attack would either die away or be unlikely to give ground for alarm; and he proved correct.[2] The Minister himself called for little delay in holding a debate if that was wished; there was support among his backbenchers for taking the question to the enemy; and when discussions came, on 14 June, he put up a spirited performance.[3] No further detail, if any still existed, was vouchsafed in this public hearing; but it was soon clear that it was unnecessary. The members of the Select Committee themselves were said by the start largely to have excused the wrongdoing, and Fox for his part was anxious to let the affair die. '. . . there was much to complain of and even to deplore'; but there was a distinction to be drawn between 'a crime of high enormity' and 'a light delinquency', he did not wish to act from 'party feelings', and he proposed a bill of indemnity which could contain a censure. The House agreed after debate, the censure was mildly worded, a bill was brought in and became law on 2 July.[4]

---

1. Eg in particular Thomas Grenville to Grenville, 22 April 1805 (*H.M.C., Dropmore*, VII, 260).

2. *P.D.*, V. cols. 69–70; Bathurst to Camden, 11 April [listed ?1802, but clearly 1805] (Camden Ms U840 C226/5).

3. . . . 'an uncommonly fine speech', according to Hawkesbury (to Liverpool, 15 June 1805; B.L. Loan Ms 72, vol. 55). See *P.D.*, V, cols. 149–50 for Pitt on 30 May; 161–2 for Henry Lascelles the next day.

4. 45 Geo. III, c78. See *P.D.*, V, cols. 385–424 for the debate; 161–2 for Lascelles on feelings within the Select Committee.

Pitt was thus able to put behind him the last element in the dealings with Boyd that had led him into conduct he would normally have rejected. An attempt at that time to bring him to book before a committee had been defeated by his large majorities. But those had been reduced now, and what remained was no longer fully under his control; and it was not in fact due to them alone that he was spared a contest here. It was thanks also to the sense of the House, already beginning to draw back from extremes after the traumatic first vote on Melville, and now clearly much more strongly in his own case. When it came to this point indeed, Members appear to have felt they must pause. While the evidence of wrongdoing was not disputed, the circumstances were unusual; the motives were accepted, and there seems to have been widespread reluctance to bring him sternly to book. Considering the acerbity pervading his treatment in the previous summer[1] and the Ministry's tempting disarray now, such obvious disinclination was a notable mark of restraint, and respect. The assault had stopped short, thanks to his candid and persuasive account, at Pitt's person. It was at least in part a tribute to the recognition that his misconduct was an exception to a remarkable rule.

The effects of Melville's case on Pitt's future were both immediate and lasting. The most troubling feature was the obvious lack of willing support among the Addingtonians: if one takes as a basis the Treasury ascriptions near the time, 15 to 17 of Sidmouth's definite adherents and 17 to 15 of the more 'doubtful' voted with the majority of 8 April – a total, broadly, of 32. That was a worrying figure, particularly when earlier estimates of his overall numbers are borne in mind.[2] It was not necessarily dangerous in itself: Melville's case was quite out of the ordinary, cutting into the whole range of the Government's normal support – Pitt suffered losses from among his own constant as well as less regular adherents, and the force of the initial widespread challenge was soon reduced to some extent. Nor indeed was Opposition in a good state to sustain a broader consistent threat. The two main wings were not wholly at one in general on their attitude to the immediate chase. Grenville could not agree with Fox, but neither could he fully control his followers, particularly at the start – some 20, it has been reckoned, including his brother Thomas and less enthusiastically Windham, supported Whitbread on 8 April; he was further dismayed by

---

1. See p. 711 above.

2. I have done my sums from the biographies of Members in *H of P*, III–V. The ascriptions cannot of course be precise: many considerations have as always to be taken into account – personal as well as more strictly political backgrounds, and strongly varying degrees of independence. The kaleidoscope of the House could sometimes be a nightmare even to the expert makers of lists, and in addition I have tentatively ventured in a few cases to transfer 'doubtful Pitt' to 'doubtful Sidmouth' and thereby perhaps introduced further uncertainty or error. See p. 722 above for a fairly recent calculation of the Addingtonians' strength.

the attack on Pitt; and beyond those related issues lay others on which he, and Spencer, differed increasingly from the Foxites and indeed from many in his own party, a term which he had, increasingly again, to recognise and deplore.[1] He much disliked 'the greatest part of what is now going on', particularly in a period when 'the very foundations' of the country's safety were being 'shaken'.[2] At the same time, however, he himself disturbed his associates' opinion in both Houses, and likewise the feelings of some useful allies, by pressing one particular policy in close company with Fox. The question of Parliamentary relief for the Irish Roman Catholics had been the single most positive link between the two men in the partnership formed to topple Addington.[3] It had lain in the wings since, deferred by qualms within the Old Opposition. But at the start of the session in 1805 both leaders were prepared to try their hand. After querying the annual renewal of suspension of habeas corpus in Ireland in February, they presented a petition from the Irish Catholics in both chambers in March; and this was debated in both in May, at very great length.[4] Motions for a review in committee were heavily dismissed,[5] and the attempt did its champions no immediate good. It disturbed many Grenvillites and Foxites, it lost some influential sympathetic interests – the Duke of Northumberland for instance, and most notably the Prince of Wales, who at this point gave clear indications of dynastic recall –, damaging the impression of strength at the very time of Ministerial weakness and detracting from a unity already more ostensible than real. The situation facing Pitt was confused. But so long as Sidmouth could be kept in line there was no need to panic; the Government might well endure.

That qualification however was paramount. As the joint Secretary of the Treasury told Grenville's nephew, 'in plain English, there are four parties in the country; and if your two parties expect to govern without a third, you will fail'.[6] The same still applied in converse, allowing for two parties, to the Ministry; but in the aftermath of Melville's resignation it was far from certain that Sidmouth would stay. Trouble arose almost at once. A new First Lord of the Admiralty was needed as soon as possible,

1. Sack, op. cit., 83. His figure is based on the division list as given in Joshua Wilson, *A Biographical Index to the Present House of Commons* (1806), 612–14. And see pp. 619–20 above for the fragmentation, characteristic of all quarters of the House in the course of the debates.

2. To Buckingham, 22, 27 May 1805 (Buckingham, III, 418–19, 421–3). He was referring in part to motions in the Lords in March and May on the state of the navy under Melville which included references to a time when he, Melville and Spencer in particular had been in office, and which he would not attend.

3. Pp. 618–19 above.

4. See p. 745, n3 above for habeas corpus; for the petition, *P.D.*, IV, cols. 97–105, 651–729, 742–843 in the Lords, where the House adjourned at 4 am in the first debate on the 10th–11th and ended at 6 am in the second on the 13th–14th; 834*–950, 951–1059 in the Commons, where there was an adjournment at 3 am in the first debate on the 13th–14th and the second, of the 14th–15th, ended at 5 am.

5. In the Lords by 178 to 49, in the Commons by 336 to 124.

6. William Sturges Bourne as reported in conversation with Earl Temple on 27 June 1805 (Buckingham to Grenville, sd; *H.M.C., Dropmore*, VII, 282).

for the situation at sea would brook no delay. Pitt turned first to Hawkesbury. But the Home Secretary was reluctant. 'It is certainly the Office next to that of Prime Minister of the most Importance and of the Greatest Power and Responsibility' – a testimony not only to the current shape of the war and fears of invasion, but also to the impact of the past twenty years. For that very reason however, the post should be filled by 'some Person who enjoys a due Portion of Public Esteem'.[1] He preferred to concentrate on his existing task of leading the House of Lords, of which indeed he had made a distinct success. No better candidate appeared to offer. Among the politicians, two members of Addington's own Ministry came to mind; but Buckinghamshire, the former Secretary for War and now once more in the Cabinet, did not impress at that level, and the competent former Secretary at War, Charles Yorke, had then shown signs of nerves and irritability which had 'startled Pitt' –though others reckoned that 'he would be a different Man with him [Pitt] from what he was with Addington'. Among the sailors, etiquette as well as polit-ical attitudes posed problems: of the most likely active prospects, Lord Gardner's abilities were thought to be confined to his quarterdeck, and Lord Keith was politically doubtful and, more important, too junior to Gardner and also to Admiral Cornwallis, both wearing their flags afloat, for either to continue to serve if he was First Lord. So, 'at last', the Minister's finger pointed to the unemployed '*old* Sir Ch Middleton'.[2] The decision was taken by the last week in April, he took over on the 30th and was created Lord Barham on 1 May. The choice, which seemed to some close to the centre 'the best out of the very indifferent candidates'[3] and greatly surprised the political world – Middleton had never commanded a squadron or fleet at sea –, could nonetheless be defended, for he had recently been brought back from obscurity after his contacts with Pitt in the 1780s and a brief, finally unhappy spell as a Sea Lord in 1794–5, to be consulted during Melville's brief tenure of the office.[4] In the event all turned out well. Aged seventy-eight, the veteran proved to be a master of his craft, alert and sternly forceful, in his short but auspicious reappear-ance; 'the brain behind every movement of the fleets'.[5] But in Sidmouth's

---

1. Hawkesbury to Liverpool, 17 April 1805 (B.L. Loan Ms 72, vol. 55). He continued – a commentary on St Vincent's legacy followed by that of Melville himself – 'and also will be able to keep down that Party Spirit which has of late been spreading itself very widely in the ... Navy'. See also for Hawkesbury's subsequent refusal Camden to Bathurst, 22 April 1805 (*H.M.C., Dropmore*, 47).

2. See Harrowby's account, to Bathurst, on 21 April 1805 (op. cit., 45–6).

3. Camden to Bathurst, as in n1 above. And cf. Pitt to Sidmouth, 21 April (Pellew, op. cit., II, 358).

4. See I, 314–17,II, 379, 498, 613; *Letters and Papers of Charles, Lord Barham ... , 1758–1813*, III, 273.

Middleton, for all his great administrative qualities, had been an awkward subordinate and colleague; but this does not seem to have entered into the question now. He owed his appointment to the professional sensitivities of other senior Admirals.

5. Oliver Warner, *Trafalgar* (1959), 156–7.

eyes he was the last man to be given the place. He was a relation of Melville, an opponent of St Vincent's reforms, and had been preferred to Buckinghamshire, the only other Addingtonian to be accepted for Cabinet rank. The appointment was received as an insult. The Doctor in fact found it 'a decisive proof' that he himself could not continue in office. He would withdraw, maintaining a personal friendship with Pitt and – edged words – a 'fixed adherence to the King'; and if he went, Buckinghamshire pledged that he would go too.[1]

A break indeed seemed inevitable. It was avoided at the cost of compromise: Middleton's appointment would be temporary, Melville must not be consulted again on public affairs, the Minister must keep his restive colleague properly informed of what was going on and if the latter wished to become a Secretary of State that would be arranged. Thought also would be given to some more places – hitherto scarcely forthcoming – for Sidmouth's friends. Such terms underlined the fragility of relations, revealed all too starkly by Melville's affair. Both sides in fact were thoroughly suspicious of one another. The Addingtonians had felt that Pitt was cold, 'not . . . cordial and sincere':[2] Pitt's circle never looked on the junction as providing more than a statistical need. The truce did not stand the strain for long. In the continuing debates over the form of Melville's treatment – impeachment or criminal proceedings – Sidmouth's brother Hiley and his prominent associate Bond went into the lobbies against Pitt. They were free to do so; but they accompanied their votes with provocative speeches, and the Minister, disgusted and affronted, told the Doctor that he would do nothing for them by way of posts. He was out to show that his disapproval was '*marked*', and his response brought matters to a head. On 24 June he saw or was summoned by the King. The King then saw Sidmouth to advise the two men to talk things over. They did so on the 30th and again on 4 July. And after the second conversation Sidmouth resigned. There had been no personal animosity, he told his family, and Pitt took him by the hand at the end.[3] But this time it was the end, and though the Minister visited him once in September, when his favourite son was dangerously ill, political relations were never resumed.

This, then, was the close of a chapter, which was bound to have its consequences. Melville's case furthermore made a lasting impression on Pitt himself, in the time that remained. Although he had escaped serious personal censure, the whole affair cast a shadow, and he took it, as he could not but take it, to heart. The lofty disdainful statesman had been seen plainly to

---

1. Sidmouth to Pitt, 22 April; Buckinghamshire to Sidmouth, 23 April (Pellew, op. cit., II, 358–9 and see also 360). See p. 630 above for Middleton's opinion of St Vincent's programme; pp. 723–5 for Buckinghamshire's inclusion in the Cabinet.

2. Pellew, op. cit., II, 362–4. Cf. pp. 723–5 above for the question of posts.

3. Pellew, op. cit., II, 368–75, 385n, 389–93; *Colchester*, II, 12–15; *L.C.G. III*, IV, no. 3105n5; and see Hawkesbury to Liverpool, Private and Confidential, 7 July 1805 (B.L. Loan MS 72, vol. 55) for a view sympathetic to Pitt.

be emotionally affected; and his conduct, his very 'character' as he knew, was under fire. Had he not shrunk, it could be asked, from his natural wish to dismiss the attack on Melville out of hand? Should he not, conversely, have paid attention years earlier when advised of what might be afoot; and, again, refrained from allowing the possible effect on the Ministry's survival to influence a behaviour which his old admirers could sadly contrast with the heyday in his youth? Could he really say that he had acted like a juror in this case?[1] The experience was later surmised – perhaps with exaggeration – to have affected his health.[2] It certainly made an impression on the public that was not shortly effaced. In the last weeks of his life, when the war on the Continent had suddenly taken a disastrous turn, he was said to have told Huskisson that 'such' was 'the nature of Englishmen', the Government could get over such a setback, but 'never . . . the Tenth Report'.[3]

Sidmouth's departure of course was accompanied by that of Buckinghamshire, whose fortunes were now inseparable from his own.[4] The consequent adjustments brought some greater strength to the Cabinet, for Harrowby's health had improved enough for him to take the Duchy of Lancaster, and Castlereagh, remaining at the Board of Control for India, became in addition Secretary of State for War and the Colonies in place of Camden, who moved into Sidmouth's non-Departmental post.[5] But this limited though not unimportant reshuffle – giving Castlereagh his first major chance – was not regarded as necessarily destined to last long. For a greater prospective opportunity was rising above the horizon once more: to see indeed if the earlier panacea of a broad Government might not be revived. As soon as Sidmouth became awkward, indeed, some of Pitt's circle took the occasion to sound out the possibility of looking farther afield. At the very start, in mid April, Bathurst, dismissing any idea of Pitt's own possibly enforced

1. Cf. I, 448n3 for his behaviour in Warren Hastings's case; but also op. cit., 445–6 for different political circumstances. For the first of the possible charges now, see Liverpool to Auckland, nd but 27 June 1805 (*A.C.*, IV, 236–7); p. 753, n1 above for the second.

It was not only in response to the traumatic vote in Whitbread's first attack that Pitt showed his distress. His voice shook and he seemed to be briefly on the verge of tears when he had to announce Melville's resignation from the Privy Council (for which see p. 760 above); Stanhope, IV, 295, relaying a conversation with Macaulay.

2. Eg by FitzHarris, for whom see p. 758 above (*Malmesbury*, IV, 346–7n), and, partly following him, Rosebery (*Pitt*, 251) who was himself versed in the old traditions.

3. This was Lord Holland's later account, in his *Memoirs of the Whig Party*, II (1854), 48. For Huskisson see p. 595 and n4 above.

4. And, outside the Cabinet, Vansittart followed suit in September in Ireland, where he was at odds with the Lord Lieutenant, Hardwicke, himself something of a thorn in Pitt's side. The reliable Charles Long was then persuaded to go reluctantly to Dublin, under (or alongside) a new and in practice equally reluctant Lord Lieutenant, the affable cypher the Earl of Powis.

5. As Lord President of the Council; see for the posts in January p. 725 above. Camden, who had never liked being a Secretary of State (p. 669 above), had been wanting to leave his Department for some months (draft to Bathurst, 13 February 1805; Camden Ms U 840 C17).

resignation – a prospect held seriously within the Treasury itself –, thought that the Minister must cast his net wider in due course, ridding himself of the Addingtonians and enlisting 'a Union of all parties' which could strengthen the Cabinet with desired 'talents'.[1] The animus increased over the following weeks. 'Many of the Friends of Govt.', reported Hawkesbury in mid June, '. . . are in a Rage with Lord Sidmouth and his Adherents'; and a week later Camden, who had once counselled caution on Pitt in the days when Addington was Minister and guardedly favoured their junction when that came, was now outspoken in his condemnation. 'The Administration with Lord Sidmouth a part of it [,] is from his past conduct less able to govern the Country well than if he had quitted it'. Pitt should tell his erring colleagues outright that he 'look[ed] forward to make a more comprehensive Administration if after the Parliament is up, it can be formed', or, if he preferred not to do so, Camden would like to be assured that 'the Idea' was 'really' in his mind.[2]

By the end of June in point of fact something was stirring. Camden himself appears to have taken an earlier uncharacteristic initiative, calling on Grenville, perhaps early in the month, to broach the possibility of an 'extended' Government. He claimed that he did so 'perfectly *unauthorized*'; and he stressed the caveat a few weeks later, when he repeated his visit on the 23rd or 24th.[3] However that might be – no doubt it was scrupulously true – two events by then had contributed to the prospect. Pitt's personal position under the Eleventh Report had been settled, in a manner highly 'honourable on the part of Opposition'; and Fox had let slip a remark at which politicians pricked up their ears. On 20 June, in a debate brought by Grey on the state of the nation, he observed that if the present Ministry were to be replaced by one containing 'all that is respectable for rank, talents, character and influence in the country', no one could suppose that any individual would allow personal ambition – and thus by implication disappointment – to stand in the way.[4] In the subsequent stir, particularly among his own supporters, he affirmed that this had been uttered without consultation, and should not be taken to mean anything more than he had

---

1. Bathurst to Camden, 11 April listed '?1802', but 1805 (Camden Ms U840 C226/5); *L.C.G. III*, IV, no. 3068n1 for opinion in, and indeed beyond, the Treasury.

2. Hawkesbury to Liverpool, 19 June 1805 (B.L. Loans Ms 72, vol. 55); Camden to Pitt, 27 June 1805 (Dacres Adams Mss, formerly P.R.O. 30/58/6), and see also same to Bathurst, sd (B.L. Loan Ms 57, vol. 2).

In July, furthermore, Treasury experts set to work on a fresh estimate of the Addingtonians themselves, and their possible future relationship with Government or Opposition. Their numbers were put at 33 plus 10 doubtful (*H of P*, I, 177). Cf. p. 720 above.

3. Grenville to Thomas Grenville, 24 June 1805 (*H.M.C., Dropmore*, VII, 278–9), and see Thomas Grenville to Spencer, 6 [but perhaps from the context 26] June 1805 (B.L. Add. Ms temp. Althorp G59).

4. *P.D.*, V, col. 526. If the quoted words were correctly reported, the combination of attributes formed a perfect expression of accepted constitutional thought.

been saying for the past year.[1] Grenville for his part, under Camden's questioning, took no responsibility for the statement. He confirmed his own position; that in such a case he would not be detached from others within the 'party'. But he did vouchsafe that, if Pitt was in earnest, he should see the King very soon and then get in touch with Opposition '*direct*'.

Pitt did not follow such a course. Indeed it would have scarcely been either possible or wise. In the first place, George III was about to disappear from London and Windsor for some months. He had indeed announced his intention of making a progress through the western Midlands starting early in July, before carrying on to Weymouth where he was now used to spending a sizeable part of the summer. Denied the first part of the plan at the last minute by a marked worsening of his sight, which in fact was entering its final phase, he nonetheless set off for his favourite watering place despite his Ministers' hopes of postponement on both medical and, privately, political grounds.[2] The crucial figure was therefore absent at a time when his presence might be needed for ready consultation. But in any case Pitt would not wish to beard the King on such a subject without an indication of the prospects from others; and that could well be affected by the turn of wartime developments in a period of fine balance from which the outcome might impinge on political tactics. Despite rumours, matters accordingly hung fire in July and into August. Bathurst was sent to see Grenville before the summer dispersal – never a good time in which to bring manoeuvres of this kind to a point; and following their conversation, Pitt gave permission for his cousin to let Fox know very privately what might yet be in the air. Fox for his part in point of fact was uncertain and torn: genuinely prepared if necessary to accept a broad Government from which he was excluded, but as always distrustful of Pitt and now hoping to bring Sidmouth into Opposition, and thus in due course see the Minister displaced outright by the House.[3] That would at last be the proper answer to the events of 1804 and 1783. And Grenville himself had not abandoned the central plank of a more burdened position: he remained resolved not to sanction a further royal exclusion of Fox, and it seemed clear that only Fox could induce him, if

---

1. To Dennis O'Brien, 23 June 1805; to Robert Adair, July 1805 (*Memorials and Correspondence of Fox*, IV, 79–81, 85–6).

2. Cf. p. 715 above for the King's sight. He already had a cataract in one eye, and was now told that one was forming in the other. He was indeed obliged for the first time to take a private secretary, Colonel Herbert Taylor, to help him with his correspondence, and in the next few months relied on him increasingly to read and write the letters. By the end of the year he was virtually blind.

For Pitt's anxiety to keep the monarch closer at hand see eg Countess Spencer to Spencer, 10 June 1805 (B.L. Add. Ms temp. Althorp G294).

3. See Pellew, op. cit., II, 370 for a message from Fox to Sidmouth before the latter had left office, disclaiming hostility to his inclusion in a broad arrangement; otherwise, Fox to O'Brien, Adair, and Grey in July (*Memorials and Correspondence of Fox*, IV, 87–102), Thomas Grenville to Grenville, 18 July 1805 (*H.M.C., Dropmore*, VII, 296–7).

need be, to change his mind.[1] So matters stood at the end of August, while Pitt still awaited a turn of events which by then he was daily expecting from Europe,[2] He wished 'the line of foreign politics settled' before he approached Grenville direct; the more so as he was sure that it was one with which the former Foreign Secretary would agree. The news however was still not to hand. He did not want to move without it. And as the summer recess wore on and time began to shrink before Parliament might meet, it seemed far from certain that a new, expeditious political arrangement could be formed.[3]

III

Parliament rose on 12 July, a few days, as it happened, after Sidmouth resigned. If Pitt looked back then on the fourteen months of his second Ministry, he could not have found much cause for cheer. He had in his possession a Preliminary Treaty with Russia for an offensive alliance; but one that, in its specifics, favoured Russia rather than British preferences including some that could be seriously damaging, prompting further review before agreement could be reached. He had indeed been travelling down that path over the past two months, only to learn within the past fortnight that Novosiltsov was nonetheless leaving for Paris, on the mission of which the Government in London had always disapproved. The prospect in Austria remained elusive, in Prussia it was scarcely visible, in Sweden dependent on Russia for effect and then subject to doubt.[4] All was still uneasily poised in Europe. And the year at home had been one of increasing Ministerial and personal strain. In May 1804 Pitt had returned with widespread expectation to the place which was his, it seemed, almost by right. Since then his command of the Commons, still potent, had been shaken at important points;[5] his opening Cabinet had failed to settle down; and its enforced reshapement, to accommodate safer

1. Bathurst to Pitt, 12 July [nd and listed 1804, but 1805], 29 July [nd and listed 1805], P.R.O. 30/8/112; same to Camden, nd but possibly 15 July (Camden Ms U840 C95/3); Pitt to Bathurst, 15 July 1805 (*H.M.C., Bathurst*, 48–9). Grenville had in fact, and naturally, informed Fox of Camden's earlier approach (*H.M.C., Dropmore*, VII, 279–80). See further Jupp, *Lord Grenville*, 340n122.

2. This is discussed in section IV below.

3. See Camden to Bathurst, 30 August 1805 (*H.M.C., Bathurst*, 49). Parliament had been prorogued to November, after the session had ended in July.

4. Cf. pp. 738–45 above for the state of affairs in Europe three months before. As summarised here, the current position applies to the date to which it refers – 12 July. A sudden event in point of fact, for which see pp. 783–4 below, had just changed everything. But the transformation was not yet known in London; the latest, depressing news was that Novosiltsov was on the eve of setting out for Paris, without the British difficulties having been resolved (see Leveson Gower to Mulgrave, no. 25, 10 June 1805 (*Third Coalition*, 174–8), which was received on 3 July (endorsement in P.R.O., F.O. 65/58)). The despatch from St Petersburg heralding the reversal of fortune, dated 29 June, reached the Foreign Office on 29 July (endorsement loc. cit.).

5. See pp. 708–12 above for 1804.

Parliamentary majorities, produced an outcome worse in some respects perhaps than if the experiment had never been made. He himself was carrying a larger share of the burden than he had known since his first decade in office, and the burden itself was much heavier than in those days. How effective in such circumstances was his own conduct of affairs?

As such facts showed, the conditions were adverse. We have followed the arguments which persuaded – in his own view drove – Pitt to act at different stages as he did: a history traceable step by step from his resignation in 1801. He was operating throughout in the shadow of that event, and later of George III's instability: a context which, for constitutional and strictly political reasons, he felt unable to ignore. But of course circumstances and performance react intimately upon one another. How far may the latter in these years have subscribed to the former's effect?

At an immediately visible level, Pitt's handling of routine business certainly grew worse. Always distinctly individual, it was now increasingly erratic. As earlier, he put on one side whenever possible applications for places and appeals for influence, and his reluctance to write letters was if anything more marked than before. His final private secretary, William Dacres Adams, admitted that his master 'got into many scrapes' thereby. The mass of papers found at Walmer at his death included correspondence, some up to twenty years old but mostly of the past few years, in no sort of order and much of it left unattended. George III himself claimed later, by then 'with the utmost good humour' – and in point of fact some exaggeration –, that the Minister 'used not to answer' his letters. 'I have frequently said to Mr. Pitt the next time I saw him after I had written to him "Mr Pitt I did not receive an answer to that letter I wrote to you the other day" – and the King then described Mr Pitt's embarrassment & *hums* & *Sirs* etc: etc'.[1] The inattention in this case, when it occurred, could have arisen sometimes from a hope of evasion. But the hours that Pitt was now keeping likewise suggested a growing disorder. According to Adams, a good witness, he seldom stirred before noon, and unless absolutely necessary disliked being disturbed with business after dinner – a meal, it may be recalled, taken generally in the late afternoon or very early evening.[2] He

1. William Dacres Adams's account of a conversation with George III at Windsor, 30 January 1810 (copy in Stanhope Ms U1590 C404/15). The secretary informed Pitt's biographer Stanhope half a century later that the papers at Walmer were 'scattered about in various places' (25 May 1861; ibid). When they were deposited in the Public Record Office after a further century, I was told that on some letters the seals were unbroken. For Pitt's abiding epistolary habits see I, 323–4.

2. Stanhope, Ms U1590 C404/15, 30 January 1810. Cf., by way of contrast, his habits in the 1780s as described in I, 578; and see op. cit., 577 for the time of dinner – though in some high advanced Whig circles, for instance at Devonshire House, that could now sometimes be as late as eight o'clock.

On one occasion in 1805 the Speaker called on Pitt and waited for him to come down to breakfast at 2 pm (Abbot's diary for 12 June 1805, P.R.O. 30/9/33); but that was hardly surprising after the Minister had had to wind up the debate on Melville's impeachment which had ended at 6 am (see p. 760, n3 above).

may of course have spent the morning in bed with papers in Churchillian fashion; he would not have been the only Prime Minister to like his evenings free; and the House, with its foetid atmosphere, naturally would claim him sometimes late into the night. The secretary's picture may be set alongside that, often quoted, painted dramatically by Hester Stanhope.[1]

> Up at eight in the morning, with people enough to see for a week, obliged to talk all the time he was at breakfast, and receiving first one, then another, until four o'clock; then eating a mutton-chop, hurrying off to the House, and there badgered and compelled to speak and waste his lungs until two or three in the morning! – who could stand it! After this, heated as he was, and having eaten nothing, in a manner of speaking all day, he would sup with Dundas, Huskisson, Rose, Mr Long, and such persons, and then go to bed to get three or four hours' sleep, and to renew the same thing the next day, and the next, and the next.

> ... during the sitting of Parliament, what a life was his! Roused from his sleep (for he was a good sleeper) with a despatch from Lord Melville; – then down to Windsor; then, if he had half an hour to spare, trying to swallow something: – Mr. Adams with a paper, Mr. Long with another; then Mr. Rose; then, with a little bottle of cordial confection in his pocket, off to the House until three or four in the morning; then home to a hot supper for two or three hours more, to talk over what was to be done next day: – and wine, and wine! – Scarcely up next morning, when tat-tat-tat twenty or thirty people one after another, and the horses walking before the door from two until sunset, waiting for him. It was enough to kill a man – it was murder.

One should not labour inaccuracies in a brilliant sketch; though one must remember that Hester first found refuge with her uncle in his period out of office and had not been used to the life of a powerful Minister in critical years. Nor for that matter should one apply without exceptions Adams's replies to specific queries: there is evidence of Pitt at work at all kinds of times in the day. But together the accounts set the scene in one compelling respect. Both convey an unmistakable impression of a man whose reserves were running down.

For the apprehensions of Pitt's health, shared by himself without illusion, were being borne out all too well.[2] His stamina was not eclipsed, and his powers of recovery were still marked. The signs of exhaustion seem to have been continual; but he did not suffer a prolonged physical collapse, or a return of the psychological near breakdown that he showed in 1800.[3] Those who worked with, and particularly for, him were struck by his

1. *Memoirs of the Lady Hester Stanhope* . . . , II, 63–4, 65–6 respectively.
2. Pp. 575, 669 above.
3. Cf. 82, 547–50, 604 above.

composure and cheerfulness almost to the end. His private secretary echoed a retrospective appreciation by Rose applying to the circumstances of the final few years.

> During his last Administration, forsaken by old friends, which he bitterly felt with declining health – and almost the whole weight of the Government on his own Shoulders – so delightful was his temper, that . . . no hard word or look ever escaped him, but all towards me was kindness and indulgence.[1]

But there was a cost. 'Every public event of importance' now had 'a corresponding effect upon the body', and a growing enfeeblement could be seen at moments of emotion in a growing tendency to weep. The traumatic occasion of the first debate on Melville was not in fact unique; he wept at least twice when talking to the King, and a certain lessening of control over a temperament that had always been far from phlegmatic seems to have been remarked by his friends.[2] He was keeping going on his hopes and his willpower, assisted by medicines some of which were ineffectual and stimulants some of which sound fierce. Even before he took office for instance, Mulgrave on one occasion – 'As I am persuaded that you will not take proper precautions for yourself' – sent 'a Vinegar Box for the debate tonight' whose contents were 'very corrosive';[3] and laudanum, and drink once more, were playing their part. We do not know the quantities in these last years; but whatever the levels of consumption, the effects – and less port now would doubtless have gone farther – are unlikely to have been innocuous when, by 1805 at least, his constitution was wearing out.

The deepening fatigue tended to confine him, particularly as anxieties rose, to what he saw as the vital issues, above all of the war itself. He did not have much energy to spare otherwise for colleagues who, apart to some extent from Melville, stood on a different footing from that of his major associates in the 1790s. The only other candidate for such a

1. Dacres Adams to Stanhope, 26 April 1861 (Stanhope Ms U 1590 C405/15). Rose's encomium is in *Rose*, II, 234. And cf. a similar account from a clerk in the Bank of England cited in Mark Boyd's *Recollections of Fifty Years* (1871), 1.

2. See Farquhar's retrospective account (*The Monthly Review*, No. 1, Dec. 1900, 50) for the quotation; p 515 above and *Glenbervie*, I, 390 for weeping while with the King. In an age, and with a heredity (cf. op. cit., n2 above) not necessarily given to concealing emotion, he had always put on a brave face, and these episodes aroused interest and sometimes concern. Hester Stanhope however said later that she had seen him shed tears 'but twice' (*Memoirs*, II, 73). Lady Bessborough was pleased to observe him doing so when watching the boy actor Master Betty, 'the young Roscius', at Drury Lane – a prodigy whom, he greatly admired, together with much of London, and for whose performance of Hamlet he is supposed to have adjourned a sitting of the House of Commons (see *Correspondence of Leveson Gower*, I, 495).

3. 'The Vinegar must' in fact 'be kept from fingers' (Mulgrave to Pitt, 25 April 1804; P.R.O. 30/8/162).

relationship, Harrowby, was distanced, though he could be consulted, by the ill health which kept him from the Foreign Office; Mulgrave could not fill the gap; and of the other Secretaries of State – 'the connecting links of an Administration'[1] – Camden was highly inadequate, Hawkesbury's record did not inspire, and he and Castlereagh were too junior, not so much because of age as from lack of hard earned experience at Pitt's side. The rest of the Cabinet were in an outer circle; among the lesser posts Charles Long and Bathurst, carrying personal confidence, were subordinate instruments in domestic politics; and if Canning, the over zealous disciple, could still claim a kindly reception it was no longer so readily obtained. Pitt had never been good at exerting himself to bind people together. He found no great difficulty in accepting what fate brought him in the form of associates, and friends,[2] and commanded loyalties in other ways – to those admitted to his privacy by his quality and charm, allied to the public talents and character that impressed the rest. He made no great effort now to stamp an identity on the Government, and it in turn could show no clear record of success to secure such a result. In default there was a sense of malaise. 'Invisible', 'too late for everything', 'deciding nothing between two contending parties' – between Hawkesbury and Canning, or in Ireland between the Lord Lieutenant and his Chancellor of the Exchequer[3] –, the Minister was not providing the focus for business that he alone could supply, particularly when the Ministry was uneasily placed, deprived of a broader choice of talents which many of its own members increasingly missed. They found themselves – as colleagues on occasions have done since in their leaders' second Ministries, and indeed had done with Chatham in extreme degree – dominated by a figure of unrivalled prestige who was no longer coping with the day to day affairs.

For in the midst of these shortcomings the dominance persisted nonetheless. Pitt's scope was narrowing; but as a figure he himself did not dwindle. We have a glimpse of him at an awkward, and as it turned out an important meeting, with a deputation from the Irish Roman Catholics' Committee that was seeking his agreement to introduce a petition for Parliamentary relief. One of those present recorded his impressions. Pitt, wearing 'dirty boots, and old-fashioned lank leather breeches', was 'otherwise well dressed & cleanly, his hair powdered etc.' His manner was 'very direct & distinct. He speaks rather in a measured articulation', but 'his eyes (tho' bad & ill coloured) are very busy and speaking', and he looked about him at his hearers, seeming after a time to see where weight lay. There was plenty of civility; but what he had to say was certainly direct. The measure would be a very salutary one when the proper time arrived. But it was 'not at all a question of right or justice . . .

1. II, 531.
2. See I, 586–7.
3. See R.G. Thorne's biographical article on Pitt in *H of P*, IV, 822.

he considered it as always, & solely, in a view of its policy & expediency' and 'the *time*' had accordingly to be considered. After some fifty minutes, in which he made it clear that he would not act as they wished but would have to speak against a petition, and particularly strongly if it was introduced by the Opposition, he accompanied his deputies to the hall, 'bowing and smiling all the way'.[1]

The decision – foreseeable, though not to them, after his promise to George III[2] – had an immediate consequence: the Irishmen at once turned to Fox and Grenville. The Minister's conduct of the meeting itself suggests that he had not lost his poise or his earlier grasp of how to size up his audience. On a larger stage, the familiar Parliamentary skills remained evident; and if there were fewer occasions for eloquent set pieces on the state of the nation, he was still capable for instance of limiting the damage in the fall-out from Melville's affair. The 'deep, *bell-like* tone'[3] deploying a case had not lost its magic to convince and impress. And within the circles of government, as he exercised his highest function in the formulation and control of war policy, he was now supreme. The Cabinet unanimously endorsed his objectives and the means to achieve them; he no longer had to reconcile or choose between increasingly competing strategies – Napoleon was doing him that service – or define and defend his war aims, as in the earlier conflict. It was in that central area in fact that Pitt gave his second Ministry a character essential to its survival and synonymous with himself. It was there, in that crucial respect, that he seemed wholly indispensable; no one among his colleagues could pretend to take his place. There was little to show as yet by way of firm results at the time of his political discomfiture in the spring and early summer months of 1805. 'Nothing ever', it could then be said, 'was more disastrous' than his '*second* career'.[4] But to those with the requisite knowledge there was no indication that grasp or persistence were diminished in his handling of the European theme.

Pitt's style of authority had not changed basically in this later phase: an alteration of that kind in any case is unlikely at such a stage. The elements were familiar; it was their balance that shifted, largely as a result of his physical decline. None was more marked than the enveloping acceptance

---

1. *The Irish Catholic Petition of 1805, The Diary of Denys Scully*, ed. Brian MacDermot (1992), 81–6 for 12 March 1805. The italic, like Pitt's words as given throughout, was the diarist's. For the resultant effort in Parliament see p. 764 above.

The political nature of the response was echoed some days later, after the deputies had approached Fox, by the joint Secretary of the Treasury Huskisson, who told them that Pitt *could* 'co-operate' over the 'mode' of approach but wished they would not put that in the hands of those in 'systematic' opposition (op. cit., 98).

2. P. 528 above.

3. The description was that of the artist Henry Edridge, who had sketched him in 1801 (*Diary of Farington*, VI, 2405 for 8 September 1804).

4. Countess of Bessborough to Granville Leveson Gower, 10 April 1805 (*Correspondence of Leveson Gower*, II, 54).

of his personal fame, to an extent that in point of fact was of quite recent date. He had naturally been an object of high attention throughout his long ascendancy; but not invested, as he was now in his troubles, with a deference amounting to awe. A deepening respect of course was not at all surprising. The atmosphere surrounding a great national figure is not easily dispersed if fortunes change. Fame clings; he or she becomes a part of history and is treated as such. What was very rare, by any standard of comparison, was the degree of such recognition, within Parliament and society and diffused in the country at large. The flavour may perhaps be captured against two dissimilar backgrounds, showing the two sides of the coin. Pitt had always liked very simple games when he was in the right company: blindman's buff for instance in a friend's house, playing with a companion's children,[1] romping with his own young relations when they were around. One day in 1804 Hester Stanhope and her halfbrothers, with their friend the future historian William Napier, had succeeded in blacking his face with burnt cork, when it was announced that Hawkesbury and Castlereagh had arrived on business. They were shown into a room while the battle went on, until Pitt decided that he must be cleaned up; and when the two Ministers entered – so Napier noted – 'a new phase of Mr. Pitt's manner appeared'. 'What was my surprise to see [them] both . . . bending like spaniels on approaching'; but it was Pitt himself who riveted the young man's attention.

> His tall, ungainly, bony figure seemed to grow to the ceiling, his head was thrown back, his eyes fixed immoveably in one position, as if reading the heavens, and totally regardless of the bending figures near him. For some time they spoke; he made now and then some short observation, and finally, with an abrupt stiff inclination of the body, but without casting his eyes down, dismissed them. Then, turning to us with a laugh, caught up his cushions and renewed our fight.[2]

Another glimpse of the prevailing atmosphere was furnished on a quite different occasion, by the painter Thomas Lawrence, invited to a small gathering by one of his patrons to observe the Minister for a possible portrait. He 'noticed how high above the rest Mr. Pitt appeared to be in the consideration of the whole party. It did not prevent social conversation, but all seemed to be impressed with an awe of him. At times it appeared like Boys with their Master'. The party contained four men in office – Hawkesbury and Castlereagh once more and the Attorney and the Solicitor General –, two peers and their wives, and the host the Earl of Abercorn, a friend of Pitt since Cambridge days. The Minister does not

---

1. Eg Edward Hamilton to fifth Earl Stanhope, II November 1862; Sir Archibald Edmonstone to same, 21 July 1860 (Stanhope Ms U1590 C405/2).
2. H.A. Bruce, MP, *Life of General Sir William Napier*, . . . , I (1864), 31–2; he was nineteen at the time. And cf. 32 for another if less vivid example, applying to himself.

seem on this occasion to have been in a good mood: the company may not all have been to his taste, or certainly of the kind in which he liked to relax, and he did not apparently say much, but made 'rather pithy remarks & frequently sarcastic observations', in which Abercorn himself was not spared.[1] This was the face much more familiar to the world than that known to a close circle; 'the chill' that kept men at their distance, could put them down regardless of rank – he rebuked the Bourbon Prince, d'Artois, for presuming as a Frenchman to denigrate Tierney's principles in Opposition – and, as for instance with Erskine, could 'awe' them, in Wellington's description, 'like a school-boy at school'.[2] It was not attractive; but it was formidable. Even more so was an aura now of remoteness that discouraged too close an approach.

Something of this image emerges from his last portrait, completed in October 1805. It was not by Lawrence, though Pitt agreed to sit; but that did not come about, and his eventual picture (or rather pictures, for he made a copy) was executed in 1808, after the Minister's death.[3] The artist rather was Hoppner, working from the life on a commission from Mulgrave. To a fellow painter, who had himself produced a portrait from sittings some six years before, it revealed 'the Hauteur and something of a disdainful severity' which were 'so predominant'.[4] To Wilberforce, studying it many years

1. See *Diary of Farington*, VI, 2436 for 7 November 1804. Lawrence also observed that while Pitt would take someone by the arm and walk with him, 'the same was not continued to Him, if accidentally done even by the highest in company'.

The peers were Charlemont and Darnley: the first a prominent opponent of the Union and with a man whose son voted regularly in the Commons Opposition, the second another Irish grandee, who had been an associate of the Prince of Wales and, despite an admiration for Pitt's talents (see p. 643, n1 above), voted in the Lords in Opposition and was a leading supporter there of St Vincent's naval reforms. The Law Officers were Spencer Perceval, of whom Pitt thought well, and Thomas Manners Sutton, the latter inherited from Addington and a younger brother of the Archbishop of Canterbury who had been preferred to Tomline.

Abercorn, whom Pitt made a Marquess, had a notorious 'attachment to Ancestry' – he was said to have worn his Garter (secured through Pitt in January 1805) out shooting. On this occasion he remarked on the impressive physical appearance of the nobility as a body in the Lords, on which Pitt commented that that might be 'owing to the new *Nobility*'.

2. See *The Journal of Elizabeth Lady Holland* . . . , ed. the Earl of Ilchester, II (1908), 50, for the incident with d'Artois, relayed by Tierney in 1799 – 'a reproof to a very ill-judged question'; Stanhope, IV, 347 for a conversation with Wellington in 1838 relating to December 1805, and cf. I, 611 and n7.

3. *Diary of Farington*, VI, 2436. The painting would have been for Abercorn. Of the two executed, one is the splendid study that hangs at Windsor.

The Princess of Wales was also thinking of commissioning Lawrence.

4. Op. cit., 2693. The opinion was William Owen's; his picture a half length, in Windsor uniform.

See for the history of Hoppner's portrait pp. 836–7 below. The frontispiece in this volume may be compared with that, by Gainsborough in 1787, in I.

Pitt was probably a difficult subject to catch. By all accounts he looked uninspiring until he was interested and began to speak, when his face lit up. Opie, who never painted him, was so struck on meeting him in 1804 by the expression of fire and power during a conversation that he sat down to try to seize it on returning home (*Diary of Farington*, VI, 2328).

later, it was 'a vile picture – his face anxious, diseased, reddened with wine, and soured and irritated by disappointments. Poor fellow,' he concluded, 'how unlike my youthful Pitt!'[1] The years had certainly taken their toll. The high and passionately felt expectations, never lost, had been buffeted by experience.[2] And that customary process was now intensified

1. Diary for 28 July 1820 (*Life of Wilberforce*, V, 73).
2. I should note here an intriguing but I regret to say unsolved small mystery. In May 1892 the journal *The National Review* (no. 111) published some verses sent by 'a granddaughter of the 1st Earl of Harrowby' (as he eventually became), affirmed by her to have been written by Pitt and given by him to her grandfather, and to have been the only declared example of verse by him apart from the juvenile drama which caught Macaulay's attention (see I, 7n1). They apparently carried no date, and the original manuscript has not surfaced. If they were what she claimed, however, the concluding four stanzas (of fifteen) are so apt that they should be quoted. The poem was entitled 'On the rebuilding of Coombe Neville, nr. Kingston, Surrey, near the seat of the great King-making Earl of Warwick, and late in the possession of the Harveys'.

> Each smiling joy was there that springs
> In life's delicious prime:
> There young Ambition plum'd his wings
> And mock'd the flight of time;
>
> There patriot passions fir'd my breast
> With Freedom's glowing themes;
> And Virtue's image rose confest
> In bright platonic dreams.
>
> Ah me! my dreams of harmless youth
> No more thy walks invade:
> The charm is broke by sober Truth,
> Thy fairy visions fade.
>
> No more, unstain'd with fear or guilt,
> Such hours of rapture smile:
> Each airy fabrick fancy built
> Is vanish'd as thy pyle.

Combe Wood (or House), said to have been rebuilt in the decade 1754–1764, was acquired in 1801 by Hawkesbury (cf. p. 724 above), who then altered and enlarged it by stages to plans by Soane and lived there until his death in 1828. The property had been owned for the past half century by the Spencer family, being inherited as part of the estate of Sara Duchess of Malborough, grandmother of the first Earl, and purchased in 1753 by her trustees. For a century before it had been in the possession of the Harveys, and then known as Coombe Nevill. From 1765 it was let for a succession of short periods, mostly to peers and MPs, presumably as a convenient base for Westminster; and there the difficulties start. None of those tenants can be shown to have been at all closely connected with Pitt's youth; the only link, even faintly, is Rockingham, who was there in 1771–2 and thus briefly during a time of association with Chatham. The area certainly housed a number of politicians, and perhaps the child or young man could have known the woods ('Along thy Woods

by the separation from old colleagues and supporters whom shared memories had turned into friends. His sadness had been glimpsed before the end of 1801.[1] It had had cause to grow since, and the wound was acute. Pitt could muster defences, more robust than Wilberforce ever believed. If it was late in the day to be given new companions, familiar faces were still around; and his own character held its tougher elements. It was quite untrue to say, as some hostile to him did, that he 'had no feeling or attachment to anybody';[2] but the terms had long been in his favour, and if the strong strain of innocence in his nature made disappointment the deeper, he had equally strong inner reserves. His essence, if bruised, remained intact. His spirit was not sunk in gloom, and neither did he surrender to cynicism, that refuge of the inadequate. Questioned one day at this time by Eldon whether, from his 'station in life', he concluded that 'Men . . . were governed by reasonably honorable Principles, or by corrupt motives', he replied

> that he had a favorable Opinion of Mankind upon the whole, and that he believed the Majority was really actuated by fair Meaning and Intention.[3]

But above all, if his private burden increased the weight of external pressures it was they that drew from his innermost forces the most profound response. The final portrait shows the pride, the severity and the disappointment. It is also a study, and more deeply, in resistance and

---

I stray'd'), as well as ridden or hunted in the hills ('the chace I led'), and have written the verses a good deal later, perhaps again on or after a visit to Hawkesbury (we know that he paid at least several there) in the early years of the new century. In view of the date of rebuilding a house 'late in the possession of the Harveys', it is of course possible that the lines were composed by the elder rather than the younger Pitt. But then why should the latter have given them to Harrowby (or Ryder as he was until 1803), and why should the family tradition have arisen that they were the only acknowledged adult example from his hand (see pp. 111–12 and n1 above for some unacknowledged)?

It is all problematic. In trying to clear up the matter, I am much indebted to Dr D.B. Robinson, the County Archivist of Surrey, for information from the rate books of Kingston upon Thames and from a monograph on the manor of Coombe by L.E. Gent published as an occasional paper by the borough's Archaeological Society in 1979; to Professor Norman Gash for information on Hawkesbury's time at Coombe and Pitt's visits there; to Mrs Jane Waley for searching the Earl of Harrowby's archives at Sandon; and to Viscount Sandon for an inquiry into family history. Even so I have failed to pin down any attribution of authorship, to identify the granddaughter concerned, or to find the original manuscript.

1. P. 566 above.

2. Cf. p. 96 above. The remark quoted came from Hatsell, the veteran retired Clerk of the Commons [see I, 28] who had come to dislike Pitt, on the day after the Minister's death (*Diary of Farington*, VII, 2674).

3. *Lord Eldon's Anecdote Book*, ed. Anthony L.J. Lincoln and Robert Lindley McEwen (1960), 73. I have followed the original style here rather than that printed in Twiss, *Life of Eldon*, I, 498–9. The conversation, in Eldon's recollection, took place 'not long' before Pitt's death.

concentration. The resulting statement is both personal and public. For as Pitt moved about his business, now in a year of rising threat, it was amid a sense that he personified a national resolve in the struggle on which his powers were fixed.

IV

This recognition was heightened in a summer of suspense. For as Parliament and Ministers were plunged in continuing disputes by the Melville affair, the war was seen to be entering on a phase which might witness a crisis. The invasion season was opening; the Army of Boulogne was poised once more; and on 25 April news was received that this time, in contrast to the past two years, a French squadron in Toulon had escaped from port and was past the Straits somewhere at sea. Its destination was unknown, and it had in fact linked up with a Spanish squadron. There was no First Lord of the Admiralty in London; that indeed was a reason for hastening Middleton's appointment,[1] and a few days later he was making his first dispositions. Napoleon, it seemed, might at last have been given the key to unlock the plans for his landings. Meanwhile British efforts for a Continental Coalition were still at an uncertain stage.[2]

Unlike Barham's appearance in office, these were not hastened by the political confusion. It was not until early June that Pitt found proper time, 'the Business of Parliament' having been so pressing, to decide with his colleagues on 'Points so critical' in the preliminary agreement with Russia.[3] The Government had reserved its position after inspecting the contents in May, meanwhile asking Novosiltsov not to carry on to Paris pending its considered response. That was now produced in a lengthy letter to Vorontsov and despatches to St Petersburg which the Minister accompanied with his own letter.[4]

The main source of the trouble still was Malta. There were other

---

1. See pp. 764–5 above. Camden mentioned this reason for speed in his letters, where something of the pressure can be seen. Pitt himself was meanwhile taking a hand; eg a note at 2.30 am on 30 April, at the end of a tiring night in the House in the course of the Melville affair: 'I will go to Bed for a few hours but will be ready to see you as soon as you please, as I think We must not lose a Moment in taking Measures to set afloat every Ship that by any species of Extraordinary Exertion We can find Means to man' (Coppet Sale, Sothebys, 14 November 1955; present owner unknown).

2. Pp. 737–45 above. For the role of the French fleet in Napoleon's plans see p. 708 above.

3. Pitt to Novosiltsov via Vorontsov, 7 June 1805 (copy in Dacres Adams Mss, formerly P.R.O. 30/58/6).

4. Mulgrave to Novosiltsov via Vorontsov, 18 May; same to Vorontsov, 5 June and to Leveson Gower, nos. 15, 16 of 7 June 1805 (*Third Coalition*, 152, 155–64, 165–74, which omits despatch no. 15, drafted and initially dated 5 June in F.O. 65/8, repeating the letter to Vorontsov. The two despatches in total occupy 93 ff. in the file). Leveson Gower's despatch with the contents of the Provisional treaty had been received on 9 May.

unwelcome issues, affecting both southern and northern Europe: the Russians' design would leave French influence, in the form of the Bonapartes, in a critical region of Italy – a stark contrast to one of the demands to be made on Napoleon at the start[1] –, and it was inadequate for Holland and northern Germany, of such close concern to this country. Nonetheless, given the circumstances, Ministers were reluctantly prepared to consent. Again, protesting their generosity, and noting that Continental allies had no claim to interfere in a settlement which here affected Britain and France alone,[2] they confirmed their intention to return all overseas conquests from the war, and now including any in India. They seemed to have calculated that the Tsar might be willing to drop or at least postpone action on the proposal to refer the 'Maritime Code' to a European conference; at any rate they avoided the subject as far as they could – it occupied a modest part of a lengthy communication. But the case for Malta was fought hard, with real anxiety and strength.[3] The Mediterranean was a theatre vital to the conduct of this war – to the protection of Egypt, on which the French were known still to cast their eye, and of Turkey and Greece and Italy – and the island formed an ideal base for the exercise of power in the Mediterranean. That could not be provided by Russia, if she entered hostilities, against a strong French naval presence; and if she remained neutral she should not count on us to protect joint concerns in the region – at least, as was left unsaid, without challenging her own asserted status with the Knights.[4] British occupation was the best guarantee of communications between the Mediterranean and the Black Sea, as Russia's naval power in the Baltic was for communications in northern Europe. We certainly had an interest of our own – access to regions of Asia whose safety was significant for our concerns in India – but that was now to Russia's interest as well;[5] and the stability offered to southern Europe by our presence was purely defensive – as the Tsar knew, we had no territorial ambitions on the Continent.[6] Britain had shown its zeal for an alliance by agreeing to return conquests elsewhere: it should be the more favoured in this one, important exception. And if Russia were to argue, as an obstacle, that Napoleon was pledged to enforce our withdrawal from the island, what would she say to his other pledges relating to other aims? As Pitt himself summed up to Novosiltsov, 'The Possession of Malta appears to be one of the most essential

---

1. Cf. pp. 739–40 above. For the Russians' proposals referred to in this paragraph see pp. 738–9 above.

2. Cf. II, 598, 626, pp. 736, 740–1 above.

3. It was indeed one, according to the Russian Ambassador, that was supported not only within the Ministry but also by the most 'respectable' members of Opposition and beyond them by all ('unanime') those 'estimable' and 'independent' figures who influenced public opinion (Vorontsov to Czartoryski, 6/18 May 1805; *Archw Knyazya . . . Vorontsova*, ed. P.I. Bartenev, XV (1880), 303).

4. See p. 395 above.

5. Though cf. here p. 446 above.

6. P. 729 and n1 above.

Importance to great and valuable Interests of our own, and to our means of Connection and Cooperation with other Powers'.[1]

Having said so much, however, he did not close the door. Such was his anxiety for a Definitive treaty that he also sketched a less attractive alternative. If an outcome could be reached with really effective barriers for Italy and Holland, we would be ready to 'overcome our difficulties' by accepting 'the only Substitute for Malta which We think could at all answer the purpose (namely Minorca).' The implications of this phrase were spelt out in a despatch to Leveson Gower.[2] Malta could be garrisoned, after a 'limited' time, by Russian troops; and conditions for any settlement with France should include the 'absolute re-establishment' of Savoy in Piedmont with a line of defence in the Alps, and properly substantial protection for Holland on the ground and with assistance from 'some great military Power' (ie Prussia). On such a foundation Britain would, reluctantly, settle for Minorca, to be yielded by Spain, compensation to that Power being found somewhere in Italy for the 'King of Etruria'.[3] This sacrifice, the 'last' in the prospective list, would however depend on a satisfactory outcome to talks for peace with France; and if they should not take place, or were not successful, it could not be raised in the future as matter for negotiation.

Conditions were thus inserted, which it might be hoped could avoid an unwelcome choice. Talks with France might yet drag on and there was always a distinct possibility of failure. Given Napoleon's record, much might happen on the way.[4] But such an unforeseeable development could not disguise the fact that in the last resort Malta would have to be abandoned for the sake of a general agreement. The language on this subject, in the despatch and in Pitt's letter, was one of appeal; invoking a reasoned response of goodwill from a potential ally. He felt himself driven into a corner by the need, as he saw it, for haste; and in fact the completed form of British ratification of the Preliminary treaty was sent with the communications, for Leveson Gower to exchange as soon as the Russians would comply. Whatever might befall Novosiltsov's mission, it should not

1. 7 June 1805 (p. 780, n3 above); and see throughout, Mulgrave to Leveson Gower, sd (loc. cit., n4). The word 'possession' raises questions. Pitt took the occasion in his letter to clear up what he thought had been a misunderstanding stemming from his talks with Novosiltsov, following a report from Leveson Gower in March (to Pitt, Private, 22 March 1805; P.R.O. 30/8/152). The Minister had apparently then referred to the British aim of gaining 'a real and secure' *independence* for Malta under the treaty of Amiens, and the Russian Government seemed to assume that this still held good. But with French infraction of that treaty by their conduct, and the advent of a fresh war, the treaty's terms were no longer binding and in his view had been overtaken by the arguments he was now obliged to employ.

2. Mulgrave to Leveson Gower, no. 15, 7 June 1805 (p. 780, n4 above). Cf. p. 152 above for Minorca's significance in the past.

3. See p. 586 above for this Napoleonically established puppet of Spanish origin. A further 'condition' for the Continent was once more repeated – the independence of Switzerland.

4. In point of fact, as became known in due course, he did not intend at this point to listen to a Russian approach.

start to negotiate without the prior signing of a Definitive Anglo-Russian instrument; we could ill afford to be excluded from a process designed to be on behalf of both states.[1] And there may have been a further source of pressure. For while the anxiety lay of course in the state of the delicate international balance, and increasingly for the prospects of a strong and, for Britain diversionary, force in the field,[2] it may also have included as an offshoot the political balance at home. A diplomatic success was highly desirable with which to face Parliament as soon as possible, or at the least after the summer recess. It might furthermore become necessary if certain indications proved to be of substance; for no one could count now on Sidmouth's long continuance in Cabinet, and his going would virtually demand and perhaps ease that Ministerial approach to Opposition of which the first signs were soon duly to be seen.[3] In such an attempt a new European Coalition could provide an important inducement, achieving an object that would presumably please Grenville and a good many of his associates as well as a range of less committed elements in many parts of the House. There were thus significant reasons for persuading Russia to conclude, as the key, it must be hoped, to a timely wider Alliance; and it was against such a background, in Europe and in London, that judgment on the possible future of Malta had to be cast.

The dilemma turned out to be immaterial. It was indeed removed in essence before the British letters and despatches reached St Petersburg, or for that matter were sent on their way. On 4 June a deputation from the Ligurian republic, waiting on Napoleon, conveniently asked him to annex the territory, which he consented to do, granting a principality around Lucca to one of his sisters and adding the valuable resources of Genoa to his naval strength. The news was learned in Russia by the 22nd, and Novosiltsov, en route for Berlin where his passports now awaited him, was at once ordered not to proceed to Paris. Two days later the mails arrived from England, and Leveson Gower had to endure more reproaches from Czartoryski on Malta and the Maritime Code. But the immediate heat had gone out of those questions; the production of the British ratification went down well; and while the Russian Minister would not commit himself, the British envoy hoped to send the Tsar's counterpart with the next messenger home.[4] It was not all over yet. The British explanation of their case did not remove Czartoryski's qualms; indeed, if anything the logic of the argument increased them.[5] Much of what was stated with

1. P. 737 above.

2. Cf. p. 702 above.

3. *Third Coalition*, 174–5, 182. And see pp. 768–70 above.

4. Leveson Gower to Mulgrave, no. 27, 29 June 1805 (*Third Coalition*, 182–5), received 29 July (F.O. 65/58); he was nonetheless far from certain in a private letter the same day (to Mulgrave, sd; copy in P.R.O. 30/29/384).

5. Not least perhaps by introducing the shadow of possession now, as distinct from occupation. Pitt's own use of the word (p. 782 and n1 above) could be taken in context as referring to either; but it had been used.

such emphasis could be antipathetic to Russia's long-term interests, and he was not at all disposed to drop the subject. He had moreover, quite properly, informed the Austrians of the difficulty, and they in return supported his stand and suggested a modified clause.[1] He now proposed that this should be considered, so that an agreement was not held up further which could have a bearing on the timing of operations if an offensive was to be launched. There were other problems, too, which needed to be settled with Prussia and with Sweden, the former particularly in the light of the cancellation of Novosiltsov's mission. By the third week in July Leveson Gower was becoming worried. But in point of fact the Russians were now as anxious to sign as the British. The Tsar had recently been watching Napoleon's attitude to Italy with growing concern. The annexation of Genoa was the last straw; he was outraged and alarmed; and if, as was now almost certain, he decided on war, further troop movements should be set on foot very soon. Provisional plans for a campaign had already been concerted with London, and were currently being brought to a point. And on 28 July the ratifications of the treaty were exchanged, an earlier article on Prussia and the controversial questions of Malta and maritime rights being excluded. The documents were forwarded to London on the last day of the month, arriving at the Foreign Office on 23 August.[2]

The final stage of the Anglo-Russian talks witnessed similar hopes and uncertainties in the complementary exchanges with Austria. There were grounds for hope, for the centre of gravity in London's dealings with Vienna lay so firmly now in St Petersburg that their outcome turned very largely on Russia's influence. Such a situation was gratifying for the Tsar; Czartoryski could seek to exploit it;[3] and by the end of June Leveson Gower was optimistic, anticipating an alliance within two months. He recognised however that obstacles could still lie ahead; and in the upshot the balance of his judgment proved correct. The Austrians were in fact preparing for the contingency of war; but as they recalled past experience they were far from eager to embark, and they hoped to delay active operations to the spring of 1806. They seemed indeed to be 'like children who put off minute to minute taking their physick though they know that the dose must be taken at last';[4] and in the interval they could raise fresh points. As it was, they insisted that the independence of Piedmont must be

1. Vorontsov in London had indeed warned Pitt of the European implications of a British determination not to leave Malta, in this instance referring to Russia's support of the presentation of The Two Sicilies [for which cf. p. 568 above] (to Pitt, Private, 13 May 1805; P.R.O. 30/8/191).
2. Leveson Gower to Mulgrave, nos. 29–32, of 21, 22, 31 July 1805 (*Third Coalition*, 188–97; endorsement of receipt on no. 32 in F.O. 65/68).
3. Cf. pp. 689, 697 above.
4. Leveson Gower to Harrowby, Private, 29 June 1805 (Harrowby Mss, vol. X).

Bishop Pretyman (Tomline), *by James Green*

Charles Long, *by Henry Edridge*

Lord Harrowby, by *Thomas Phillips*

Lord Mulgrave. *Attributed to Richard Cosway*

added to the list of absolute requirements in any talks with France that might yet take place. The British subsidy must be extended to cover a longer period of military preparation, though at the same time Austria could not move to a full war establishment until such possible talks were either rejected or had failed. And if she entered the war – and the reluctance was obvious – Britain must agree to send 5,000 troops for a joint campaign in northern Italy.[1] Leveson Gower found such demands, particularly the last, exasperating. But in point of fact it disclosed the Austrians' absence of choice. Their interests indeed were too closely involved in the southern approaches to the Alps for them to evade the consequences of Napoleon's annexation of Liguria. That, as in the Russians' case, was the determinant. The Russians themselves pressed the British hard by refusing to sanction the march of their own troops before an agreement was reached with Austria, or to help argue against her demand for the extended subsidy; and faced by such seeming intransigence the Ambassador committed his Government to payments covering preparations over five months.[2] He also consented to add Piedmont's independence to the list of irreducible demands on France;[3] and in return for these concessions Austria undertook to enter into an offensive alliance. Exchanges between the two Ambassadors and Czartoryski were concluded on 9 August, and Leveson Gower forwarded the 'Declarations', trusting once more that in his 'eagerness to seal' a further 'bond of the confederacy' he had not yielded too much, and in particular been 'too lavish in the pecuniary resources of Great Britain'.[4]

This last apprehension must have seemed the more pertinent in view of what was happening in Sweden, the other most likely if problematical immediate adherent to a plan of campaign. For money in that case had become the governor. All now hung on its provision, and Gustavus IV was running true to his father's form before the previous war. The British had earlier refused to consider his 'exorbitant . . . demand'.[5] The deadlock persisted into the summer, and by July the British envoy, Henry

---

1. Leveson Gower's despatches *passim* June–July (F.O. 65/68). The discrepancy, indeed the contrast, in weight between these and Paget's from Vienna in the same period (F.O. 7/73–4) reveals where the centre of information and action lay for the British throughout. A succinct account of developments can be found in Fremont, loc. cit., 232–42.

2. As compared with three agreed earlier; cf. p. 740 above. The increased demand now had been for six.

3. A return in point of fact to the British position at the outset (p. 729 above) which had since been overtaken in the talks with Russia, but might now be accepted in the expectation that Napoleon would reject any terms that might yet be put (Leveson Gower to Mulgrave, no. 33, 14 August 1805; *Third Coalition*, 201).

4. Same to same, op. cit., 197–203, with the Declarations at 277–82. The form of the agreement was adopted at Czartoryski's behest - a further indication of the balance of influence – in order to forestall the delay that the procedure for a tripartite treaty would entail.

5. Mulgrave to Leveson Gower, 15 March 1805 (P.R.O., F.O. 65/57). See p. 744 above, and cf. II, 17 for Gustavus III's demands during the Ochakov affair in 1791.

Pierrepont, had almost given up. Possibly, he reckoned, the powerful peace party was once more in the ascendant; possibly the King, still finally in charge, was too obsessively greedy to drop his demand. The matter by then had become critical, for the terms of the Russo-Swedish agreement had taken for granted those of the earlier arrangement between Sweden and Britain, and Russian troops could not land at Stralsund in Pomerania until the latter were concluded.[1] That difficulty was overcome in principle. But as operational plans were still not put into active effect, the uneasiness in St Petersburg grew. A special envoy was sent towards the end of August to press for the programme to be speeded up; Czartoryski was urging the British to reach some understanding if they could; and indeed at the end of the month, before he could receive instructions from London, the unfortunate Pierrepont signed a further Convention by which Britain paid £2,700 a month to maintain a Swedish force of 8,000 men at the port.[2] A further treaty, of subsidy and alliance, followed early in October, whereby 12,000 Swedish troops would be committed to offensive operations for a rate of £12 10s a man. That was the rate which Pitt had stipulated at the outset. But, as he knew all too well, the resulting £150,000 a year was an outrageous bargain in favour of Gustavus.[3] The full extent of the money would be forthcoming even if only 10,000 men were found; those could include the garrison at Stralsund – which the King had earlier indicated might be purely defensive; and a special grant of £50,000 was added for its maintenance. Sweden had blackmailed Britain, at a total of almost £250,000, to a tune effectively of double the rate offered to the various prospective partners at the start.

The financial surrender to Gustavus was proportionately the most expensive instance of the lengths to which Pitt would go for a Continental campaign in the current season. As a result there was now in being a Coalition of three major and one minor Powers. Russia indeed was hard at work from August to enlist others as well. Rather like the British in 1793, their hope was now to 'bring down every power on earth to assist them', and within the next month they were approaching Denmark, a range of German states, The Two Sicilies, and Turkey for closer links. Only The Two Sicilies responded with a defensive treaty which by then in any case

1. Fremont, loc. cit., 255. See pp. 744–5 above for the Russo-Swedish Convention of January 1805 and the Secret Anglo-Swedish Convention of December 1804.

2. Leveson Gower to Mulgrave, no. 31, 31 July 1805 (*Third Coalition*, 195–6; received 23 August); Pierrepont to same, nos. 51, 51, 1 September 1805 (F.O. 73/34). He had signed the previous day, and two days later in point of fact instructions for some easement of the earlier British terms were sent from London (Mulgrave to Pierrepont, no. 5, 3 September 1805; loc. cit.).

3. See Sherwig, *Guineas and Gunpowder*, 163–4 and Fremont, loc. cit., 256–7 for the settlement; p. 745 above for the garrison of Stralsund. The despatches are contained in P.R.O., F.O. 73/33–4. Raymond Carr, in 'Gustavus IV and and the British Government 1804–5' (*E.H.R.*, LX, no. CCXXXVI, 46), has reckoned that the true rate per man amounted to £21. For the French texts of the Convention and the treaty see *Consolidated Treaty Series*, 58, 195–200, 227–9.

was on the verge of completion;[1] but such endeavours were not in any case of central military importance – Naples indeed would require rather than supply an offensive consignment of troops. The great question remained that of Prussia; and sentiment in Berlin in August was inclining more distinctly again towards France.[2] A further offer of Hanover, definite this time, was received from Paris on 8 August, and the case for a Franco-Prussian alliance was accompanied by the argument that this could in fact promote the cause of peace by convincing St Petersburg and Vienna of the folly of challenging two formidable Powers. The pretext was gratifying, the bait alluring, and by the end of the month the Prussians seemed ready to take the plunge. Only an ultimatum to France from Russia and Austria, following their alliance, counselled a fresh bout of caution; but in mid September the Tsar, to Czartoryski's dismay, suddenly suspended marching orders which would have taken his troops en route through Prussian territory in order to force compliance with the Allies, and instead made an overture for a meeting with King Frederick William.[3] The immediate outcome thus hung in suspense; the Prussians could rest tantalisingly neutral while they weighed their options yet once more; and as the autumn of 1805 approached the British had perforce to contain their impatience while the curtain began to rise with the last leading player still offstage.

1. Zawadzki, op. cit., 122–3. The quotation of 1793 comes from a report of Dundas's speech in the Commons five days after France was known to have declared war – see I, 272 & n3; and pp. 695–6 above for Russian and British intentions for southern Italy.

2. Cf. pp. 742–3 above.

3. Two recent summaries of this short complicated period, in which Alexander gave the first significant indication of departing from Czatoryski's advice, may be found in Zawadzki, op. cit., 128–31 and Fremont, loc. cit., 273–4.

CHAPTER XXI

Hope Destroyed

I

In the opening days of September 1805, when the documents confirming the Third Coalition had just been received, several meetings took place in Downing Street and around the corner at the Admiralty on an issue of more pressing and, to the nation at large, more vivid importance.[1] The escape of a French squadron from the Mediterranean in March and its subsequent junction with a Spanish force had set off an alarming uncertainty which was only now removed.[2] The Admiralty had modified its dispositions throughout the North Atlantic while Nelson embarked on 'the long chase' which took him, after some doubt, to the Caribbean and – memories of the Nile – a frustrating miss of his quarry. No one in London could tell for some five months where the enemy might be, or where they might reappear. In July however they had in fact been sighted returning to Europe, and engaged inconclusively by a British squadron to the west of Finisterre. Escaping from a running action in mist, they slipped into Vigo on the 20th, two days later they were in Ferrol, and after picking up a Spanish reinforcement the Combined Squadron made port in Cadiz on 21 August.

This last news reached London on 2 September, and Captain Blackwood of Euryalus, carrying the despatches, paused briefly on his way to tell Nelson, now in his house at Merton by the Portsmouth road. For Nelson too was back. Judging that the enemy, of whom he had had intelligence in the West Indies, would not stay there long, but after doing some damage would head for home – though whether with a northerly or southerly intention he could not tell –, he himself headed for Gibraltar, where he set foot on land for the first time in almost two years. Learning that no French or Spanish ships were known to have re-entered the Straits, and detaching some of his own for Malta, he at once turned north, and after detaching others to reinforce the Channel squadron watching Brest, made for Portsmouth where he landed on 19 August, two days

1. Leveson Gower's despatch no. 33 with the Declarations for an Alliance with Austria was endorsed in the Foreign Office on 1 September (F.O. 65/58), following the receipt of the copy of the Definitive treaty with Russia on 23 August (p. 784, n2 above). See I, 575 for the departmental geography of Downing Street.
2. See p. 780 and n1 above for an early reaction.

before his opponents put into Cadiz. He feared a reprimand. But though Barham sent for his journal, it was then to approve it; he met with a hero's welcome in the streets of London; and his future was soon made plain. For the Combined Squadron, now joined with the Spanish strength in the latter's main Atlantic base, had become the Combined Fleets; and there was plenty of scope for them to do widespread or perhaps supreme damage. Large British convoys from both East and West Indies were expected in the Western Approaches in August, though in the event these entered the Channel somewhat ahead of time; and an expedition from Ireland to capture the Cape of Good Hope was putting to sea.[1] The disruptive effect of the French escape had indeed been felt throughout the spring and summer, severely interrupting the passage of a fleet of transports with some 4,000 troops to the Mediterranean. And beyond all that, invasion itself was now on the cards once more if the fleets from Cadiz were to rendezvous with the French from Brest. As Barham studied his charts and gave his fresh orders, he faced an interesting choice of French options. But one conclusion was sure; Cadiz held a key to their resolution. A battle hinging on that prospect must be sought, if the enemy did not stay inert in port; and the victor of the Nile and Copenhagen, having acted correctly, was providentially at hand.

Nelson was therefore brought into the higher counsels. Over the next ten days he saw the First Lord and others – certainly Castlereagh and also Canning, the latter perhaps as Treasurer of the Navy – as well of course as Pitt. According to his own evidence indeed he attended at Downing Street on 1 September, the day before the latest news arrived and while it was thus still possible to debate the enemy's course. The Minister, by this account after much discussion, accepted the Admiral's view that the Combined Squadron would return to Europe, and told him that he would be sent out to command a reinforced fleet. That in any case was Barham's decision as soon as the situation cleared, and on the 4th he drew up a memorandum on 'what is so obvious to be done'. The instructions covered the immediate future of Nelson's Mediterranean command: extending its limits to cover Gibraltar, Cape St Vincent and Cadiz so that his deputy Collingwood's squadron, currently on the spot, could sustain a reinforced blockade, 'after' which Nelson himself could carry on to Gibraltar and then visit 'the other parts' of his area of operations.[2] In point of fact however, every one was looking to the same outcome: that a battle would be brought on while he in person remained at full strength off Cadiz.

1. Pp. 557–8 above for the return of the Cape to the Dutch at the peace. Strategic plans are followed on pp. 793–6 below.

2. There is a variety of accounts of what took place in these days. Carola Oman in *Nelson* draws on correspondence in Nicolas's *Dispatches and Letters*, VII (1846) and in James Pettigrew's biography, II (1849), and on the diary of the Admiral's nephew George Matcham who was staying at Merton at the time. Barham's letter to Pitt of 4 September with his memorandum sd for Nelson is in *The Barham Papers*, III (1911), 312–14.

This expectation indeed was evident from Pitt's behaviour at the close of a further meeting on the 5th at which the Admiral heard his orders and explained his understanding, as he recorded afterwards, that it was, 'as Mr Pitt knows, . . . annihilation that the Country wants, and not merely a splendid victory' over a possibly numerically stronger foe. The two men had not enjoyed close personal relations: although Nelson had long admired Pitt they had in fact scarcely known each other, the Minister had never used his influence on behalf of Nelson or his connexions, and the Admiral's politics, in so far as he was a politician, had leant rather towards Addington.[1] But when he now took his leave, Pitt rose to escort him out of the house to his carriage; a compliment which, the recipient told his hearers on return to Merton, he did not think would have been paid to 'a Prince of the Blood'.[2] Ten days later, in company with such ships as had been found and manned in the time and with a promise of some others to follow, he sailed from Portsmouth on the passage that took him to the squadron off Cadiz and final triumph at Trafalgar. And when the tale was told – when the first reports of the battle and Nelson's death reached the Admiralty, on 6 November at 1 am – the effect on the Minister, informed at once, was confessedly profound. A young friend, happening to dine with him that evening, would '*never forget* the eloquent manner in which he described his conflicting feelings, when roused in the middle of the night to read Collingwood's despatches'.

> Pitt observed, that he had been called up at various hours in his eventful life by the arrival of news of various hues; but that whether good or bad he could always lay his head on his pillow and sink into sound sleep again. On *this occasion*, however, the great event announced brought with it so much to weep over, as well as to rejoice at, that he could not calm his thoughts, but at length got up, though it was three in the morning.[3]

The 'splendid victory' of 21 October had consequences indeed which could not all be foreseen immediately, amounting in sum as they did to those of an 'annihilation'.[4] It bore the mark of that exceptional event, one that makes its impress on the long term. The instant recognition, continuing ever since, of a supreme national hero entered into folk memory and

---

1. Who, however, had also not 'done anything for me or my friends'. At one time Nelson had also been attracted to Moira; but in the upshot he now told Pitt that he was no longer concerned with politics. For a meeting in 1801 see p. 544 above.

2. This account was sent to Pitt's biographer Stanhope by Nelson's great-nephew, who had it from his father (see p. 789, n2 above) who heard it at first hand (Nelson Matcham to Stanhope, 13 November 1861; Stanhope Ms U1590 S5 C60/15), a week after a report appeared in *The Times*.

3. Lord FitzHarris's 'Note Book', in *Malmesbury*, IV, 341n. Cf. I, 131 and pp. 29–30 above for some rare contrasting occasions.

4. Cf. above.

helped in turn to mould the nation's image of itself. The tactics marked the highest professional achievement in a major confrontation in the age of sail. The outcome clinched in undeniable form the supremacy in battle of the British fleet, putting paid to any likely hypothesis of invasion in the foreseeable future, imposing its limits on the enemy's conduct of the war at sea for the rest of the conflict, and crowning a pattern of confidence sustained for a further century. It set a culminating standard for the victors in the period of their greatest international influence, during which it embodied a strategic assumption and, eventually in part for ill, of assured success. Such a legacy is unique in the history of Britain at war. To contemporaries themselves, Trafalgar was a supreme exemplification of the fact that 'Spectacular battles lighten for brief moments the darkness which by its nature shrouds naval strategy'.[1] And in this instance, when the obscurity had covered the anxious months of 'the long chase', the illumination fell on the prelude to the battle as well. For this had been no ordinary period, when the war at sea pursued its course largely unobserved. The significance of the campaign that ended in Nelson's reappearance and apotheosis was heightened immeasurably in the popular mind by its role in the prospect of invasion.

In point of fact the battle itself did not decide that matter. Napoleon started to break up the camp at Boulogne on 23 August, two days after the Combined Squadron entered Cadiz and at a point when he was faced with the alternative choice of swift action in Europe, almost two months before Trafalgar was fought. It was then that he abandoned the plan, adopted and brought to detail some six months earlier, to concentrate his naval strength following the Caribbean diversion so as to force an entry into the Channel and give the landings the necessary cover.[2] For him, the maritime strategy of the year had settled finally on that aim. To the British however the issue seemed by no means so clear. Nelson himself, as Commander-in-Chief, was absorbed by the threat to the Mediterranean; that had been his first thought, governing his actions when the French slipped out of Toulon, and it endured until the eve of their emergence seven months later from Cadiz. But he was not alone in his judgment: it figured, as one of several choices – the Caribbean, India, invasion – in the Government's mind,[3] and when the Combined Squadron returned it was quite widely expected in London to make its way back through the Straits.

There were persuasive reasons for this last point of view. Throughout the past few years, and aided recently by the absence of a hostile Coalition, the French had pursued a continuously energetic policy beyond the Alps. It was in fact their activities in Italy and south-east Europe that opened the most likely prospect for Britain of partnership with Russia, bringing its

1. Gerald S. Graham, *The Politics of Naval Supremacy* . . . (1965), 1.
2. Cf. p. 708 and n1 above.
3. Pitt himself, according to Nelson (Oman, op. cit., 591–2, citing Matcham's account), may have been inclined as late as August to favour the first as a continuing object. And cf. p. 217 above for the not dissimilar conundrum in the late spring of 1799.

rewards and demands to amplify and deepen an attention to the region already aroused. The Mediterranean had indeed been of focal interest in London since war had been renewed. Its geography served strategic interests of high importance which a maritime Power was well fitted to sustain. It afforded a choice of access to the Continent and to the coasts of the Ottoman Empire, the former of course particularly under circumstances of alliance, the latter in the light of the rising emphasis which the Revolutionary War had witnessed on establishing extended links in the diverse chains of approach to India.[1] And now a new scene was opening up. Contacts with Russia, emerging from common apprehensions in the eastern basin, seemed perhaps about to be sealed by a fresh comprehensive treaty. And these might also embrace co-operation, in whatever degree, for defence of common interests in southern Italy; a possibility adumbrated by Pitt and Grenville in 1798,[2] then largely from an assessment of Austria's role in a wider Coalition, and carried a step farther, this time under Russian pressure, when Pitt was back in office. The Mediterranean did not displace attractions elsewhere when those seemed to be in sight: that was made quite clear in the course of 1805. But a pattern was developing in which the theatre's affairs were brought prominently to the fore within the requirements of a revived alliance whose own necessity was accepted in London as the paramount aim.

This indeed was shown in the spring of that year. The Russians' earlier dissatisfaction with the scale of the British responses to their appeals for the Adriatic and Naples[3] did not directly modify London's subsequent plans. It was already certain that Malta would receive a reinforcement or replacement which would help make up the numbers destined for Corfu; and an additional force was under consideration to act in the central basin as a strategic reserve. This last however was not designed in answer to the request for participation on the mainland of Italy: if the troops could be found, it would be to secure the safety of the island of Sicily should a French attack appear likely and thus, with naval protection, to serve the essential purposes of the fleet. In January 1805 it seemed that some 4,000 men could be released to make an available force of 7,000 in the region; the battalions were preparing in March; and on 19 April the convoy set sail from Portsmouth, early in the course of what ended as the Trafalgar campaign. The orders for the commander, General James Craig, were explained to the King on 26 March without mention of the mainland.[4] But the claims of diplomacy, coming as it happened at this juncture, at once made their weight felt. Information reached London from the envoy in

---

1. See pp. 443–6 above.
2. Pp. 137–40 above.
3. See pp. 695–6 above.
4. For what follows see Mackesy, op. cit., 59–63. The Minister to The Two Sicilies was Hugh Elliot (for one episode in whose career see I, 543–4). The instructions to Craig are in P.R.O., W.O. 6/56; the explanations to the King by Camden from 25 to 29 March in *L.C.G. III*, IV, nos. 3054, 3058.

Naples that the Russians, inherently distrustful of Britain's intentions in the area, were saying that the real reason for denying larger forces capable of action in Italy was the determination to gain possession of Sicily at The Two Sicilies' expense after Naples was deliberately manoeuvred into a war without proper support. 'So incredible a want of confidence appears almost incredible,' commented the Foreign Secretary. But Ministers were shaken, and a separate instruction was added to those already approved, empowering Craig to co-operate with the 'Allies' (as the Russians were prematurely termed) to protect Naples against a French attack or in operations to exploit a withdrawal. In doing so he could place himself under a foreign commander if the latter was senior in rank; but he must weigh his responsibilities for the theatre before taking a decision – his strategic reserve might be needed in defence of Sardinia or Alexandria – and must always bear in mind the importance of preserving 'a communication with the sea'. He was instructed furthermore to provide shipping if requested by the Russians for transporting the force designed from Corfu, even if he had not been informed that an alliance had been signed.

This was a remarkable reaction to an indirect, unchecked report, conveyed from a Court whose reliability and judgment could scarcely command respect.[1] The episode demonstrated the supreme value put on an alliance with Russia. The British troop convoy made its way to Malta while the last bargaining for that event took place, while Austria continued to hang back, and an enemy squadron was loose in the Atlantic. The passage was prolonged by this last development, as the force took shelter in the Tagus in May[2] and was then held in Gibraltar as a possible reinforcement in any quarter from which news might emerge. Towards the end of June it was allowed to sail on, and in mid July it reached its base. With its arrival a further chapter opened on the southern European flank.

While the Trafalgar campaign was in its last phase another British expedition set sail, this time from Ireland and destined for the Cape of Good Hope. At a strength of over 6,000 men it further reduced the numbers in the United Kingdom, and again at a time when the exact whereabouts of the Combined Squadron were still unknown.[3]

The expedition nonetheless had its origin in the reaction to the maritime events. The Government had warned the West Indies as soon as it learned of the enemy's westward escape, and in mid May, at a critical period for possible invasion but requisitioning a force from the Irish

---

1. Paradoxically indeed Leveson Gower in St Petersburg reported at the same moment that the 'momentary dissatisfaction' (it proved not to be momentary) over British intentions for the Mediterranean had 'entirely subsided' (to Mulgrave, no. 12, 22 March 1805; *Third Coalition*, 125). But that despatch was not received until 18 April (endorsement in F.O. 65/57).

2. Cf. pp. 792, 789 above.

3. See pp. 140, 789 above.

command, a reinforcement was ordered for the colonies amounting to some 7,000 men. This was held awaiting further intelligence, and in mid June, following reports of measures of defence in the islands, was reduced to one of 2,000, an order itself cancelled early in July when news was received that the hostile squadron had come and gone. By the end of the month the troops were assigned to a different operation. The armament for southern Africa was provided from that designed for the Caribbean.[1]

But the decision to attack the Cape, at such a time, was itself influenced by the threat from the Atlantic. This may perhaps seem surprising, for the importance attached to the former base had been fluctuating in recent years. Experience since its seizure in 1795[2] suggested that it was a convenient rendezvous rather than a commanding strategic point – Nelson for instance went so far as to call it a 'tavern on the passage' to India and the Indies; it had proved a rather expensive commitment; and, of equal significance, the attention now paid to Egypt tended to dilute the concentration on the southern ocean route. The very weight, indeed, placed on Britain's maritime superiority made the return of the Cape to the Dutch at the peace distinctly easier to accept.[3] The scare in 1805 however went far to revise ideas once more. The new Secretary for War, Castlereagh, now echoed the earlier assumptions: the Cape should be 'treated at all times as an outpost subservient to the protection and security of our Indian possessions'; and apprehensions of a descent, fed by false reports from France, had in fact played their part.[4] There was moreover a timely opportunity to act at this particular stage, for some 2,000 troops were earmarked in any case to take passage for the subcontinent, and they would lend strength to an operation, expected to be brief, before continuing on their way. Even so, the decision cannot have been an easy one to take.

The expedition accordingly set out, after the familiar delays, in the last days of August. On 4 January 1806 it came to anchor off Table Bay. On the 6th and 7th the troops landed unopposed; on the 8th they routed the small Dutch garrison; two days later Capetown surrendered; on the 18th a capitulation was signed.

The object was therefore achieved, and the possession was not abandoned again. The defence of Cape Colony, and from 1910 of the Union of

---

1. Fortescue, *A History of the British Army*, V, 255–6, 258–9, where the initial strength is calculated; *L.C.G. III*, IV, nos. 3083 – where 'at least' 5,000 men is stipulated –, 3093 including a Cabinet Minute of 10 May, 3104, 3117.

2. See II, 561–2.

3. See p. 566 above. Nelson was speaking in the Lords in November 1801 in favour of the Preliminary peace treaty.

4. Castlereagh to Admiral Sir William Cornwallis, 10 September 1805 (quoted in Graham, op. cit., 40); for intelligence reports of French intentions see L.C.F. Turner, 'The Cape of Good Hope and the Anglo-French Conflict, 1797–1808' (*Historical Studies Australia and New Zealand*, Volume Nine, Number 36), 375. In the event, a small French squadron which escaped from Brest in December 1805 in order to harass shipping did approach the Cape before heading west early in 1806.

South Africa, remained a British obligation in one form or another until 1921. More immediately however the easy occupation was not the end of the story; for just as it arose from the precautionary protection of an Eastern empire, so it led from its 'intermediary position'[1] to a further venture in the Western hemisphere, itself deriving from an old interest in the region concerned.

The episode appeared at first to be of slight significance. It was indeed unauthorised from London. The commander of the escort to the troop convoy, and now of the naval station at the Cape, was Commodore Home Popham, that enterprising man of ideas; a specialist in combined landings, and of materiel and questions of transport, and on one occasion in consequence involved in a semi-diplomatic role.[2] A persuasive advocate, a name familiar to Ministers, successful at his level, but also somewhat suspect for engagement in commercial transactions one of which had led to an investigation, he was a sailor rather of the type of Sidney Smith and Lord Cochrane than of the more regular denizens of the battle line. Among the varied subjects of which he had some knowledge was the coastal geography of Latin America, and as far back as in 1790, in the peacetime crisis of Nootka Sound, he had been concerned with the plans for a possible assault on the Gulf of Mexico.[3] Removed now conveniently far from home, within striking distance of the main Spanish colonies, and alert to continuing reports of disaffection there and incipient revolt, he conceived a design for an attack with his squadron and a battalion of troops on Monte Video. The attractions of some such exploit were clear: disruption of the import of specie to Europe, exploitation of volatile circumstances, the successful anticipation of any French movement into the same theatre. And beyond the event itself there beckoned far-reaching prospects. For while Popham acted on his own, he was drawing on a known and at times serious interest in a strike at Spain's transatlantic possessions, severely damaging her capacity for war but also yielding a future influence for Britain on a prospectively independent area with potential commercial expansion in a region of great primary wealth.[4]

The Commodore spoke from some recent personal experience. For the long series of plans, harboured intermittently for over half a century,[5] had in fact received a recent addition. The revival of such ideas in 1796, following Spain's entry into the war, had proved abortive. But Popham himself returned to them in the new war as early as the winter of 1803; other proposals were in the air; the unwearying Miranda was at work again in London in the summer of 1804; and in October, when relations with Spain had come to a crisis, he and Popham submitted plans to Melville for an assault from Trinidad on Caracas which appear to have

1. Castlereagh again, as in p. 794, n4 above.
2. For which see pp. 218, 235–7 above.
3. See I, 386.
4. Cf. Dundas's views on p. 354 above.
5. I, 385.

been seen by Pitt, as were others from a Mr Jacob for more ambitious operations mounted from the West Indies and the Pacific against Panama and Guinea, Valparaiso and Buenos Aires.[1] It is possible that Popham had talked to the Minister at that time or afterwards, and gained an impression of unwritten support which he carried, rashly, to the Cape. It would have been one that suited his familiar keen concern for his personal finances – prize money would bulk large – and he may have reckoned that, once successful, he could get away with the gamble and that the achievement, authorised or not, would have to be followed up. He proved right, thought not exactly as he had reckoned. In the spring of 1806 he gained the consent of the commander of the troops in the Cape, and in June, altering his tactical intention, he landed with some 1,600 men at Buenos Aires, which surrendered at once. As he had forecast, the audacious stroke pointed the way, initially reluctant, to a growing commitment, though the victor in the event found himself recalled. The operation and the outcome by then however were not matters for Pitt.

The unexpected descent on Brazil obscured a generally contradictory trend. For in point of fact the reoccupation of the southern tip of Africa stands out the more distinctly because, in a reversal from the early operations by Addington's Ministry, no other effort was made from London in succeeding years to support overseas offensives in the West. Normal replenishments and minor reinforcements were supplied to garrisons. But in marked contrast to the early stages of the Revolutionary War, and its predecessors through much of the century, no fresh expedition was sent from Britain in the course of Pitt's second Ministry, and in two instances local proposals for assaults were turned down. In so far indeed as further Caribbean gains were made throughout the rest of the Napoleonic War, it was by forces already in those parts.[2] The reluctance to become deeply involved in the familiar Atlantic strategic policy, on the part of a Minister who had once taken a different view, underlined his resolve at this stage to husband all available strength for a potential contribution to a decisive result in Europe.

It is not the least of the legacies from the first of Britain's three 'Great Wars' in the past two hundred years that it brought into a novel prominence, for an island Power within an Alliance contemplating Europe as a whole, the problem of allocation of resources between different Continental fronts. The constraint in manpower and so in shipping

---

1. See II, 364 for 1796; NLS Ms 67a, Popham to Melville, 26 November 1803, 12 July 1806; loc. cit. Ms 1075, ff. 125–30 for some anon. ideas; P.R.O. 30/8/190, 395 for Miranda from 1799 to 1804; loc. cit., 395 also for some other, anon., papers, and 196 for 'Walter' Jacob (who was in fact 'William', according to John Lynch in *Journal of Latin American Studies*, Volume I, no. 1).

2. C.D. Hall, op. cit., 95, 124. The specific refusals referred to Curaçao and Martinique respectively, both in the summer of 1804. See pp. 793–4 above for the action approved but then found unnecessary during the Trafalgar campaign.

placed on Craig's force for the Mediterranean marked a prelude to strategic discrepancies of ends and means over the next decade, and, on its minor scale, to the vastly greater complications in the two twentieth-century wars. It arose in part from the need to keep enough troops of quality in the United Kingdom. But even at a point when home defence claimed high priority that was not the only cause, as was made plain. There was also 'the intention', as the Russians were told, 'to collect and keep in readiness a large active force . . . to operate as a diversion on the coasts either of France or Holland'.[1] Later in the year both the room for manoeuvre and the call for precision grew, and Pitt indeed had probably had a definite object in mind for some time. One of his quarrels with Addington's Ministry had been the lack in his eyes of offensive spirit,[2] and once in office he formed his own preparatory design for action north of the Alps. To an initial hope of 15,000 British troops for '*South of Italy*' he added 'a diversion from England' in the '*North of Germany*', to be provided in concert with 40,000 Russians, 'a body' of Hanoverians, and 'a Swedish army', the whole 'To advance towards the Low Countries'. The diversion itself, he noted, should not involve 'any descent . . . in the beginning', but rather 'after some decided success'; at first we would 'continue to menace [the] coasts'. This may have been a sketch made some months after he returned to office.[3] But the pattern remained the same thereafter; the enemy was to be 'attacked in all Quarters from Italy to the Elbe',[4] and the negotiation with Russia included a discussion of their own plans in the context of the related talks with Sweden for a British subsidy. When a financial Convention was signed in Stockholm at the end of July 1805 and a treaty followed early in October,[5] there was an apparently firmer basis for a Russo-Swedish offensive to which the Government in London could offer a military contribution as well.

By the autumn indeed there was the promise of enough initial strength, from an appropriate quarter, to do so. Since the French had occupied Hanover in 1803, men had been arriving in England in the hope of being taken into service, and a King's German regiment was formed which soon expanded into a Legion which by this time mustered some 14,000 men. Arrangements were included in the Anglo-Swedish Convention of December 1804 covering further recruitment and the provision of depots on Pomeranian soil;[6] and with the accession of troops so largely of good

---

1. Mulgrave to Vorontsov, 19 January 1805 (Mackesy, op. cit., 400). The claims of home defence had been explained already (Leveson Gower to Mulgrave, no. 10, 28 November 1804; *Third Coalition*, 73).

2. See p. 610 above for the early growth of the feeling.

3. Undated notes on the war, printed in Stanhope, IV, 223–5. Since Sweden did not make her approach for an alliance until August 1804 (p. 743 above), they seem likely to date at their earliest from the late summer of that year.

4. Notes, nd in 1805, by Pitt on Allied forces prospectively available for operations in southern Italy and northern Germany; Dacres Adams Mss, formerly P.R.O. 30/58/8.

5. Cf. pp. 785–6 above.

6. P. 744 above.

quality, trained and patriotic, a design could be advanced which would fit well into the Allied operations. The immediate specific object would be the liberation of Hanover itself, lying beyond the Elbe from Swedish Pomerania; and beyond the western border of Hanover across the Weser and the Ems lay the Dutch United Provinces. On 4 October Vorontsov in London was informed that the German Legion would be sent to Stralsund.[1] On the 5th Russian troops, waiting offshore there, were finally allowed by the Swedes to land; and on the 10th a force of 6,000 Hanoverians under a British General received orders to embark for foreign service. Six days later the commander was told that it would be increased to one of 11,000, including some British, with a further 5,000 in all held in readiness.[2] But the recent letter to Vorontsov was now out of date in one respect. The troops were to sail, as soon as possible, to the Elbe.

In notifying the Russian envoy, the Foreign Secretary had stressed that the precise British plan must depend largely on circumstances.[3] The change of destination almost certainly followed advice from a senior Hanoverian officer, and the urgency of the orders reflected the hopes of a rapid complementary Allied advance. The first echelon of the troops from England, however, held up by contrary winds, were able to disembark at Cuxhaven only on 17 November; and on arrival they found a scene of some disarray.[4] The march from Stralsund had got off to a poor start – the King of Sweden was in a state of pique – and operations, particularly by his troops, thereafter had not gained much pace. The British were directed to take up a line along the lower Weser around Bremen and there prepare with their allies on their left for a combined attack on Holland aided, it was hoped as in the past, by a Dutch insurrection.[5] But transport for artillery was lacking and could not be found quickly, planning was subject to the all too familiar delays and indecision of a mixed army, while the Government in London, increasingly impatient, was urging an immediate advance. Late in the month a further 12,000 men were allocated to the expedition and a more senior General, Lord Cathcart, was appointed to command what would now be a considerable force. The aim however proved impracticable. The Russian commander was reluctant to move farther west without blockading a fortress on his southern flank; this would demand a reduction of his numbers which must impose delay; and it was therefore agreed to wait until the lagging Swedish contingent caught up, and, as it was hoped, Prussia would have decided to join. By then the coming frosts should have eased the passage across the remaining rivers, and the operations against

1. Mulgrave to Vorontsov (F.O. 65/59). The proposal had been made officially to Pitt by 'His Majesty's German Government'.

2. Fortescue, *History of the British Army*, V, 285–6; Mulgrave to Leveson Gower, no. 33, 15 October 1805 (F.O. 65/59).

3. Cf. p. 797 above.

4. See Fortescue, op. cit., 287–90 for the rest of the paragraph.

5. Cf. pp. 201, 215, 220, 244–5, 256–7 above.

Holland could be set on foot. So matters stood in Hanover at the start of December 1805.

The Prussian factor was not introduced at random by that time. For the initial succession of orders for Germany may have owed its pace not only to expectations of the Russians and Swedes. It would also have been spurred by hopes of converting the neutral into an ally who could help clear the Low Countries, but at a point at which a British presence was simultaneously introduced to a territory whose future could concern both Powers.[1]

In the first half of October, moreover, the hopes seemed unusually bright. As so often, this was due more to Napoleon than to Allied efforts. The position in September had been confused. The Tsar's meeting with Frederick William awaited the Russian army's march, and this had been postponed;[2] meanwhile he was privately considering a scheme from Czartoryski to reopen the Polish Question, in concert with Austria, at Prussia's expense. The Prussians for their part were expressing their willingness to join the Coalition, though probably in 1806, if 'treated with consideration';[3] but also threatening to side with France if Russian troops crossed the border. This uncertainty was worrying Austria now that she herself was engaged. Her signature to the Declarations in St Petersburg[4] had been followed by an offer to mediate between Britain and France, and this was accepted in London at the beginning of September. But that gesture was essentially a pretext for delay while she pursued her military preparations, and sought prompter payment from London of advances due – and, it soon transpired, a fresh argument for a higher subsidy.[5] The French response in any case was hostile. Vienna's offer was refused, with a demand for the removal of Austrian troops from the border of Italy; and an ultimatum to that effect indeed followed on 30 August. It was rejected on 3 September; on the 8th an Austrian force crossed the Inn; and on the 11th – after Paget had made a payment – the alliance with Britain was ratified. Events now began to move as swiftly as past negotiations had been hesitant and slow. The Emperor called on his neighbour Bavaria to unite their forces. But unknown to him Bavaria had in fact been forced out

---

1. See for the element of apprehension Mulgrave to Pitt, 13 October 1805 (P.R.O. 30/8/162).

2. P. 787 above.

3. Zawadzki, op. cit., 129; and see 126–32 for Czartoryski's policy for his Polish homeland.

The rest of this paragraph relies very largely on Zawadzki's account op. cit., and on Fremont's loc. cit. which dwells particularly on Austria at this point.

4. P. 785 above.

5. Payments had been held up by a Russian erorr in failing to confirm for some months the tripartite financial arrangement reached in St Petersburg, which caused the British authorities to withhold any advance. Leveson Gower, and later Paget in Vienna, made themselves responsible meanwhile when they judged they must. But it was an embarrassing business (Sherwig, *Guineas and Gunpowder*, 167; Fremont, loc. cit., 269–71, which discusses the request for an enlarged subsidy as well).

of neutrality, signing a treaty with France on 24 August; and in mid September the Austrians learned that the army for the invasion of England had struck camp at Boulogne and was on the move. In these circumstances they had no wish for trouble on their northern flank. They counselled caution on the Tsar, and after some hesitation he agreed. Early in October Czartoryski was obliged to draft a proposal abandoning the armed demand for passage across Prussia's territory, and offering a provisional indication of support for her acquisition of Holland at the peace in return for joining the Coalition and agreeing to support some appropriate Russian gains.[1] This might have been considered a not unhopeful proposition, though one needing careful scrutiny by other partners concerned. But in the event it proved unnecessary for the immediate purpose. For on 3 October French troops, intent on a junction with the Bavarians, entered Prussian territory in the German province of Anspach without seeking consent. Frederick William at once acceded to the transit of Russian troops farther east and invited Alexander, visiting Poland on his way to headquarters, to a meeting in Berlin.

The reports of these various developments reached London with varying degrees of delay: their contents in fact were not known to the Government sometimes for two or even three weeks. But after the frustrations of recent months[2] Ministers were now becoming progressively more hopeful; by the end of September Pitt himself was on the threshold of expectation; and his congenial optimism had in fact much on which to build. Russian forces were gathered, and those in the north awaiting the start of their operations. Austria was finally at war, and opening a campaign. Sweden was engaged; even Denmark was preparing forces to defend Holstein from all comers, and while remaining strictly neutral had been showing signs of watching favourably to see how the Allies might fare.[3] And Prussia herself was now widely expected, despite continuing French inducements, to incline towards Austria and Russia and perhaps even enter the war. The Minister was buoyed up, not least by the credit accruing from the emergence of a fresh Coalition – 'Never was any measure (as far as human foresight can go) better combined, nor better negotiated'; and he was 'very justly sanguine' at this point 'as to the result'.[4] This was certainly so: he was 'extremely sanguine'. Austria was acting 'beyond our expectations', while Prussia's 'decision', which would probably be taken very soon, would 'I think . . . not be hostile'. There was indeed 'some room to hope that it will be favourable'; and his mood remained the same in the next few weeks. On

---

1. Cf. pp. 702, 742, 787 above.

2. See pp. 736–45, 784–7 above.

3. Eg Benjamin Garlicke [Minister in Copenhagen] to Mulgrave, no. 13, 1 July 1805; Francis Hill [chargé d'affaires] to same while Garlicke was in London, nos. 4, 5 of 24, 25 September 1805 (P.R.O., F.O. 22/47).

4. Malmesbury, in retrospective judgment on a conversation of 26 September (IV, 339).

24 October he was reported to be 'in great spirits' after receiving some 'good news' from Berlin.[1]

The sense of promise buoyed up a decision which was made on a sense of immediacy. As soon as Pitt learned that French troops were in Anspach and the Russians allowed to cross Prussian territory, he decided to take a step which would have seemed ill advised until then.[2] As recently as 8 October Jackson in Berlin had been told that he was not to 'take the lead in anything like menace' to Prussia.[3] An Austrian special envoy was in fact already there, to persuade or warn. But now there would presumably be no harm, and perhaps much good, in a mission from London, which could hasten a bilateral treaty that could be followed by military plans to complement any agreed by Frederick William and the Tsar.[4] Pitt had been down at Walmer, returning to London on the 14th. The next day he asked Harrowby to come up for a talk on 'many things'. On the 17th however he sent a messenger who might be expected to meet him on the road, to show him the latest news before he arrived. There was a real opportunity with Prussia at last, and

> The whole Fortune of the War, and the Destiny of Europe may turn upon having a Person on the Spot at Berlin in whom unlimited Confidence can be placed, and who may turn the favorable Disposition at Berlin to the best Advantage, and communicate expeditiously from there with both Emperors. I need not tell you who that Person is.

Harrowby should think about this 'in your Post-Chaise'.[5]

It was a good move. The emissary would be a recent Foreign Secretary who was still a member of the Cabinet;[6] and the presence of a figure of that calibre would be highly desirable, to judge developments on the spot and help mould the terms of a partnership which in every aspect – military, financial, and not least diplomatic – must be carefully assessed. Speed was important – probably necessary – if an arrangement was to be

---

1. *Rose*, II, 198 after a conversation on 17 September; Pitt to Harrowby 27 September (Harrowby Mss, vol. XII); same to Bathurst, sd (*H.M.C., Bathurst*, 50); George Jackson to his brother in Berlin after talking to the Minister on a visit to London, 24 October 1805 (*The Diaries and Letters of Sir George Jackson . . .* , ed. by Lady Jackson, I (1872), 345–7).

2. The successive despatches from Berlin with those important pieces of information, nos. 105, 107 of 7, 10 October 1805, were endorsed in the Foreign Office as received on the 17th and 18th respectively (F.O. 64/69). But Pitt had the news on the 16th – perhaps it was the cause of his seeking an audience of the King that day (George III to Pitt, 16 October 1805; Holland Rose, *Pitt and Napoleon*, 248) – and acted on that (to Harrowby, 17 October 1805; Harrowby Mss, vol. XII).

3. Mulgrave to Jackson, 8 October 1805 (F.O. 64/69).

4. See. p. 800 above.

5. As in n2 above.

6. See p. 767 above. And the importance attached to his mission was underlined in due course by the inclusion of George Hammond, the veteran of other such undertakings (see II, 625, pp. 54–6 above) and senior Under Secretary in the Foreign Office.

reached; care was necessary in reaching it. Pitt had always had great confidence in Harrowby; Harrowby was free of Departmental duties; and, though never well or disposed to underrate the fact, he proved ready to perform a duty whose significance he appreciated as fully as Pitt himself. The preparations went ahead as fast as the work to be completed, and the requirements of a mission abroad, allowed. The instructions would be complex, for guidance in Berlin and, prospectively, beyond. They were ready on 27 October; Harrowby and his suite left London that day; and on 4 November, after a delay from contrary winds, they set sail.

II

Almost a month before he decided to send a special envoy to the Continent, Pitt had paid a visit to Weymouth bent on putting his wish for a broad Ministry to the King.[1] His mind had been made up – he had been 'in earnest' – since at least the end of August. The delay thereafter was still caused by the great advantage, as he saw it, of being able to talk to Grenville first: to 'State to him directly' the Government's expectations for Europe, a course on which he placed the more emphasis since the policy was one on which 'Lord G cannot fail to agree'.[2] That would pave the way for the former Foreign Secretary to recall his antecedents while the Minister proceeded to tackle George III. But the approach would come much more satisfactorily if 'the line of foreign politics' had already been 'settled',[3] and as September wore on he waited for the despatches to take a solidly favourable turn. He could not do so for too long, however, if Parliament was to reassemble in November as earlier announced. Time would be needed to negotiate with Opposition if the King consented, and for the consequential 'bilious' arrangements to emerge.[4] A promise to Harrowby to go down to Weymouth early in the month was not followed up; but by the 15th Pitt was ready to set off without having talked to Grenville, staying on the way in the New Forest with Rose, who was himself due shortly to join the King. On the 21st the Minister spoke to George III.[5]

Pitt's preferred tactic, which had been denied him, was sensible as far as it went. If Grenville could have seen a way to carry Fox or persuade him effectually to abstain on foreign policy, Opposition would be subscribing in practice to the Government's Continental aims. And if he

1. See pp. 767–70 above.
2. Camden to Bathurst, 30 August 1805 (*H.M.C., Bathurst*, 49).
3. Ibid.
4. Cf. p. 665, n1 above.
5. Camden to Bathurst, as in n2 above; *Rose*, II, 108–9 for 17, 21 September. Some social details of Pitt's visit of five days – sailing with the King and his family in the royal yacht, and riding with him and others – can be found in *The Times* and other newspapers from 18 to 25 September.

could not, this was a moment at which, if challenged, he might feel driven to make a hard choice. Grenville was far from happy with the Foxites' – and many of his own party's – behaviour, above all in the Melville affair;[1] and as suspicions of a coming approach from the Minister increased, the inner family circle was beginning to ask where it really stood on European affairs. One fly indeed had recently disturbed the water; for Leveson Gower in St Petersburg was now wanting to come home, and Mulgrave had asked the Grenvillite Minto, who was well qualified, if he would like the post. The bait was declined, after consultation and explicitly on Minto's 'line in Parliament'.[2] But the whole situation gave food for uneasy thought, when the New and Old Oppositions might not respond from the same starting point as things were *'just drawing to a crisis* in which this country must take a decided part'.[3] Grenville in fact, as Pitt judged, could once more hold the key; the trouble, again in his judgment, was that there was no time to wait for it to turn. He had therefore to act on the unfavourable assumption that his cousin and Fox – 'the two parties' – would remain together.

Nevertheless, as he prepared for the King, the Minister was ready to suggest some changes of posts.[4] And he may perhaps have nourished some hope that this time detailed talks could take place between the leaders. Rose at any rate suspected, from the tone of conversations twelve months before, that George III would accept any nominations for Cabinet except Fox, though that proscribed figure could be offered a diplomatic post or perhaps a place at home which did not entail readmission to the Privy Council.[5] This cast back to earlier failure would not have sounded very propitious, were it not for the Continental prospects which might make Grenville more amenable now; and in any case Rose's impressions may no longer have carried much weight.[6] Whether that was so or not, they would shortly be tested; and the outcome left no room for doubt.

For George III had not changed in essence. Indeed, at least temporarily, he had hardened farther. In May 1804 he had sanctioned recommendations, apart from Fox, not all of which he liked. But now he appeared all too clearly to have taken a deep dislike to Grenville as well – or revived an old suspicion of Grenvilles in general – and was determined to veto any one at all from Opposition: 'he could not trust them, and they could have

1. P. 757 above.

2. Minto to Lady Minto, 2 September [1805] (*Life and Letters of Elliot*, III, 368); Thomas Grenville to Grenville, 14 September 1805 (*H.M.C., Dropmore*, VII, 300–1). Minto had of course been Viceroy of Corsica and later Minister in Vienna (II, 346–7; p. 239 above).

3. Thomas Grenville to Grenville (using the phrase 'the old Opposition'), 20, 26 September 1805 (*H.M.C., Dropmore*, VII, 302–5).

4. See *Rose*, II, 198. Referring to Opposition, op. cit. 200, he used the phrase 'the two parties'.

5. Ibid; and cf. p. 659 above. A Privy Councillorship moreover carried with it the right to claim an audience (see eg p. 44 and n4 above).

6. Cf. pp. 600 and n3, 718 and n5 above.

no confidence in him'.[1] He could not be moved from this attitude in two conversations on successive days, and on 23 September the Minister left without result.[2]

Pitt had tried hard. Particularly at the second meeting 'I urged every Topic that I thought could produce an Impression': his potential weakness in numbers in the coming session, the advantages of a broad-based Government to face the coming Continental campaign, even, according to one report, his own state of health.[3] It was to no avail. George III had perhaps been listening to talk that tended to sustain his prejudices – Rose himself, after his stay in Weymouth, went so far as to suspect Eldon, Hawkesbury and possibly Mulgrave.[4] Probably more important, however, was the conclusion on which the monarch took his ground. For in his view 'there was no necessity' for any adjustment.[5] 'I am convinced', Pitt concluded, 'the Resolution is fixed of running all Chances, and never agreeing to take the Step proposed but in case of absolute Necessity'.[6] That provision in fact, as would be proved within months, could be quickly decisive. But short of such an event there seemed nothing more to be said. Perhaps 'the Scene opening on the Continent' might yet overcome Grenville's feelings of loyalty to Fox. But there was too much doubt now, after a fresh proscription, to count on any such thing.

In the upshot, the fact was that Pitt had misread George III's mind. Where he himself had seen a successful foreign policy as an inducement to a domestic Coalition, the King saw it at once in a precisely opposite light. To him, the formation of a Coalition in Europe made one unnecessary at home. Pitt's position – his popularity and authority – would be strengthened. Why then truckle with Opposition? Rather than seek a

1. *Rose*, II, 200. The King made this remark, to which Rose gave the double quotation remarks indicating *oratio directa*, '*in a manner that precluded any reply*'.
Pitt himself thought that the monarch's dislike of Grenville had been occasioned by a much publicised fête at Stowe in August, attended by the three brothers, which had revolved around the presence of the Prince of Wales (to Bathurst, 27 September 1805; B.L. Loan Ms 57, vol. 2).

2. Same to Harrowby, 27 September 1805 (Harrowby Mss, vol. XII).

3. Same to Henry Bankes, 24 September 1805 (Bankes Mss from Kingston Lacy, Dorset). Charles Long was still at hand in Weymouth (see p. 767, n4 above) for Parliamentary calculations.

4. *Rose*, II, 201–2. Ministers' individual places would of course be at stake in the last resort, and Eldon, it is true, would scarcely have plumped for a change. Hawkesbury – for whom George III had earlier had little use (p. 693 above) – resented Grenville's public contempt of his performance as Foreign Secretary; while Mulgrave, as a devoted friend of Pitt, might have foreseen tiring problems from the same quarter (there was indeed a report among the Grenvilles that some months earlier Pitt had discounted a juncture with his cousin, recalling the troubles he had had with his obstinacy; see *H.M.C., Dropmore*, VII 308). But Rose's suspicion seems far-fetched, at least in emphasis; Mulgrave after all had approached Minto (p. 803 above).

5. As he put it to Rose in conversation on the 22nd (*Rose*, II, 200).

6. To Harrowby, 27 September 1805 (Harrowby Mss, vol. XII). Writing in the same strain to Bathurst (sd; B.L. Loan Ms 57, vol. 2), he used the words 'before the Moment of actual Necessity'.

junction the Minister could face a challenge, fortified by an achievement widely seen as his own, and the more so if the politicians gathered that the Crown was wholeheartedly involved in his fate. The prognosis was thus accepted; its conclusion was completely denied. The King in effect had trumped the Minister's hand.

But should Pitt have continued his efforts, whether for a Government in which Fox could be included or for one in which he could not? George III had spoken of being prepared to risk a civil war rather than accept the former result.[1] That was characteristic; but it was not really on the cards. Pitt for his own part suspected that the feeling against Grenville might moderate if that statesman showed signs of 'taking a different Line'. But he was not ready to depend on that,[2] particularly against the monarch's medical record. And of course it was in that context that he felt he could not go farther. For if the King was talking wildly about a civil war, it *was* on the cards that under further pressure he might be plunged back into his malady. All the familiar arguments indeed applied, in this latest revival of a familiar drama: the King's suspect state, the Minister's refusal to storm the closet. The degree of difference this time lay in the current chances of his own Parliamentary survival;[3] and on that question he felt bound to accept what might emerge.

One thing at any rate could be done. Pitt at once considered postponing the opening of the new session until after Christmas, and by mid October this was agreed.[4] The delay would give time for the news of the Continental arrangements to sink in, on Opposition and waverers and the Crown's Parliamentary forces alike. On that expectation there was accordingly 'Nothing' for it 'but to prepare to fight the Battle as well as We can'.[5] Meanwhile he asked Bathurst, as a previous channel, to inform Grenville in writing that the communication mentioned earlier was unlikely to be made. The trend of the past two months was now perforce reversed. 'We must . . . prepare to fight the best Battle We can with our own Strength'.[6]

III

In October it thus seemed almost certain that Pitt's Parliamentary fate would turn directly, and perhaps very early in the session, on the response to European events. In principle, the plans for the Allies' campaign would

---

1. So Rose told Tomline, from his own hearing (Holland Rose, II, 530). Whether the King had also said that to Pitt himself we do not know.

2. To Bathurst, 27 September 1805 (B.L. Loan Ms 57, vol. 2).

3. Cf. p. 722 with p. 763 above for estimates of numbers; pp. 616, 716 for Pitt's reasoning and feelings, which he was unlikely to jettison now.

4. Sidmouth to Hiley Addington, 29 September 1805, after a visit from Pitt – for which see p. 766 above (Stanhope, IV, 337); Hawkesbury to Liverpool, 19 October 1805 (B.L. Loan Ms 72, vol. 55). Cf. p. 770 and n3.

5. Pitt to Harrowby, 27 September 1805 (Harrowby Mss, vol. XII).

6. Sd (B.L. Loan Ms 57, vol. 2). Cf. pp. 769–70 and n1.

involve operations from the Mediterranean to the North Sea. South of the Alps the Russians and the British would guard the Adriatic and provide a force to defend The Two Sicilies and, in Russian eyes at least, drive the French from southern Italy with Neapolitan help. In northern Italy the Austrians – as the British had hoped – would take the offensive, with some 90,000 men.[1] On the extreme northern flank the Russians and Swedes, now with a Hanoverian and British force, would free the Electorate and advance on Holland and perhaps Flanders. And on the central, German front the Austrians would act with the Russians, the former deploying a main army of some 60,000 men under the Emperor's command, with a further 30,000 in the provinces covering the approaches to the Alps, the latter supplying a first contingent of over 50,000 to be reinforced shortly by two further corps, all under the command of the Tsar. The numbers were large. Including a strategic reserve of some 50,000, Austria had a broad strength of 230,000 men under arms, while the Russians on the central front alone planned to have over 100,000. Musters in reality, as always, were well short. But these were considerable forces to be brought to bear, for whose maintenance, allowing as well for German mercenaries and some inducement to Prussia, Britain stood by the autumn to pay in all nearly £7 million with perhaps £1 million more if Prussia came in.[2]

Operations did not start well. The Austrian army in northern Italy was commanded by the Archduke Charles, skilled but cautious and in any case sceptical of the wisdom of renewing war. It did very little at the outset while he waited to be reinforced. In northern Germany the Swedes and the Russians fell behind their programme, at a time of year and in a latitude which boded ill for success before winter closed in. And in the vital central sector, by contrast, a movement that kept up to schedule found itself quite suddenly courting an unsuspected fate.

For while the Tsar was deliberating in September over his treatment of Prussia, through whose lands his troops would pass, the Austrian advance guard, effectively under the direction of General Mack – earlier held in respect by the British –, marched unsupported across Bavaria from the Inn to the line of the river Iller, along which it would await the first Russian corps.[3] It was a reasonable enough plan as originally formed when the main French concentration was held on the Channel, and it was confirmed at the last minute after Mack's own advice to the Emperor that he could forestall the effects of any change. He underestimated his opponent. Moving at an entirely different pace from the Allies, after his disappointment of invasion, Napoleon was heading in September with a redeployed Grand Army of some 190,000 men in an extended arc

---

1. See p. 785 above.

2. See Sherwig, op. cit., 158–69. Cf. p. 693 above for Pitt's initial allocation of £5 million, not called on in practice in the first half of 1805.

3. For Mack in the campaign of 1794 see II, 335, 338n3, 339–40; for 1798 in Italy p. 204 above; for Bavarian support, pp. 799–800 above. The advance corps was nominally under the command of an Archduke.

towards the central and upper Rhine. It strength confounded expectation – even Hanover had been stripped of troops – and its speed outdistanced intelligence. Four weeks after breaking camp at Boulogne the French forces crossed the river at successive points from Strasbourg to Mannheim, and within the next few days they were poised to strike south-east. The Danube in turn was reached on 6 October, and in a few more days a wing of the enemy was in Munich and the main bulk in and around Augsburg with a corps grouped on the line of the river itself to the north-east. The troops had covered the last two hundred miles in a fortnight in broken weather, while their numbers had been brought with fresh drafts and formations to a strength of over 200,000.

Still waiting for the Russians, and unaware of what was going on, Mack was thus caught exposed – to Napoleon's surprise indeed as well as his own. In the manoeuvres that followed he failed to adjust to a confused scene. By 17 October he was surrounded at Ulm, at the junction of the Danube and the Iller, and though some elements of his corps escaped he was forced to surrender on the 19th with 25,000 men.

The news reached Vienna on the 24th. It caused something like a panic, particularly since there were strong rumours at first that larger numbers were involved. The British Minister indeed talked even a week later of a loss which was double that sustained.[1] But while the disarray was strikingly apparent the prospects were not necessarily dire. There was a great deal still in fact for Napoleon to do. The main Austrian forces remained in being, the first Russians had reached the border east of Munich, their successors were due in a few weeks, the Archduke Charles in the last resort could come north to threaten the French flank. The high command and the Government were in turmoil, the public was largely dazed; but the Emperor and his Ministers at any rate were not talking of peace – rather, on the contrary, of carrying on the war. Efforts were redoubled to persuade Prussia to join, now that the Russians would form a common front; Britain was urged to stage a diversion against Holland.[2] Meanwhile it had to be seen if the line of the Danube could be defended as the two Imperial armies assembled and regrouped.

Rumours of the defeat began to reach London at the end of the month. Pitt refused to accept them – 'Don't believe a word of it,' he exclaimed on one occasion in a loud voice – and he and Mulgrave continued to write encouragingly while the picture was still obscure.[3] On 3 November however a full account was received from a Dutch newspaper, which the two men took to Malmesbury to translate in his house at the top of

1. Paget to Mulgrave, no. 104, 1 November 1805 (F.O. 7/75).
2. Same to same, Private, 24 October 1805 (loc. cit.).
3. *Malmesbury*, IV, 339–40; Pitt to Harrowby, Private, 30 October 1805 (Harrowby Mss, vol. XII); Mulgrave to same, Private, 31 October 1805 (loc. cit., vol. XI).

Whitehall. The effect on Pitt was 'all too clearly' visible, though the Minister did his best to conceal it: 'his manner and look were not *his own*'.[1] As usual he rallied, and the news of Trafalgar, arriving three nights later, was a stimulus – one that should operate 'even on the Continent' to balance 'the impression of *Ulm*'.[2] But the already urgent sense of hope and concern which was sending Harrowby to Prussia now intensified in an ever mounting anxiety for intelligence from Europe.

It was against this background - with the news of Ulm followed by Trafalgar within the past week – that Pitt gave the most memorable speech, for posterity at least, of his life. On 9 November he attended the Lord Mayor's banquet in Guildhall. The pendulum had swung his way, the more strongly in the emotion of the great sea battle, and he was acclaimed in the streets, the horses were removed and his carriage pulled through the City by the people as it had been on a notable occasion over a quarter of a century before.[3] When his turn came early among the toasts, his health was proposed as 'the Saviour of Europe'. The reply in the traditional version has itself passed into history.[4]

> I return you many thanks for the honour you have done me: but Europe is not to be saved by any single man. England has saved herself by her exertions and will, as I trust, save Europe by her example.[5]

'Nothing could be more perfect'.[6] The few words, encapsulating a lifetime of oratory and experience, struck home with high authority at a momentous point.

1. *Malmesbury*, IV, 340. Pitt took the journal to him because he had been Ambassador at The Hague in the 1780s and 'actually knew Dutch' (I, 521–2), and it was a Sunday and the Government offices could not provide. *The Times* in point of fact published an 'Extraordinary' edition that day with a translation; but it would not have been on sale until the 4th.

2. To Harrowby, Private, 6 November 1805 (Harrowby Mss, vol. XII). Shades of the Nile (p. 150 above). A few weeks afterwards he took some pains, as a relaxation, to vet a poem by Canning on the two recent contrasting battles.

3. Cf. I, 665; and for that matter 140–1.

4. Those words of this man Pitt
 . . . that ring tonight
 In their first mintage to the feasters here,
 Will spread with ageing, lodge, and crystallize,
 And stand embedded in the English tongue
 Till it grow thin, outworn, and cease to be. –
('Spirit of the Years' speaks; Hardy, *The Dynasts, Part the First* (1904), 173).

5. Stanhope, IV, 346. There is no ms evidence – naturally, in the circumstances – in Pitt's hand, and versions varied at the time in newspapers and elsewhere. Stanhope himself kept one among his papers (Stanhope Ms U1590 S5 09/64) which differs somewhat from that which he published. But he looked carefully into the matter; he limited himself to claiming that Pitt 'spoke nearly as follows'; and we may take his received conclusion on that basis.

6. Sir Arthur Wellesley's (Wellington's) phrase (Stanhope, IV, 347). It was there also that he heard Pitt warn Erskine, about to reply to a toast to his own health, to 'remember' that he would be speaking as 'a distinguished Colonel of Volunteers' rather than as a politician: an example in Wellesley's view of how the one man governed the other by 'the ascendancy of terror' (see I, 611).

They would not have lost anything in the speaker's own mind from the consciousness that the potentially decisive special mission was on its way to Berlin. Harrowby's instructions covered almost every eventuality – so much so in fact that he asked, successfully, to be allowed a virtually unlimited discretion.[1] Prussia should be added if possible to the Anglo-Russian treaty of alliance.[2] Or a fresh arrangement, conditional of course on the consent of the other signatories, might be made for her in common with Britain, Russia, Sweden and Austria. Or if neither suited, she should commit herself to immediate hostilities against the French, to force them back across the Rhine in Germany and to drive them out of Holland. Or again, if the first of these goals was not favoured she might mount diversionary operations in Germany while placing the main effort on clearing the northern region and subsequently Holland. In either of these last two military options she must not make unilateral peace without consent, and must uphold the independence of the states of northern Germany and of the Low Countries until the form of their security was generally agreed at the end of the war.

Finance of course would be all-important. Steps were already being taken in Berlin to engage Russia's support – as Britain had proposed in the case of Austria – in settling the size of a British subsidy; and this was achieved when the Tsar, in his reconciliatory halt on the way to the front, agreed to seek one for 180,000 troops.[3] In point of fact the detail had already been overtaken, though the Prussians did not yet know it, by a decision in London to offer £2½ million for 'an active force' of 200,000 on which talks there were under way; and Pitt had authorised payments of up to £50,000 in all if requisite in the next three months, and in the event of a treaty without waiting for ratification – a recognition of recent experience elsewhere and the importance of the case.[4] Equally of course there must be some indication of territorial gain. Harrowby would have to discover, and where necessary discourage, his hosts' ideas; our own interests would be best served by some version of the now familiar concept of directing Prussia's ambition towards the west rather than towards Austrian or Russian possessions. An expanded frontier with Holland and a continuing guarantee of Dutch independence would probably provide the wisest form of deterrence to

1. To Mulgrave, Private, 30 October 1805 (copy in Harrowby Mss, vol. XIII).

2. Mulgrave to Harrowby, no. 1, 27 October 1805 (*Third Coalition*, 207–15).

3. See p. 800 above for the meeting in Berlin; Fremont, loc. cit., 291 for this part of its outcome, and cf. pp. 736, 799 and n5 above for the procedure with Austria.

4. Mulgrave to Harrowby, no. 1, as in n1 above. Talks on finance were held with the Prussian Minister in London, Baron Jacobi – a name familiar from the Revolutionary War, when he was considered an Anglophobe (II, 295n2). A figure amounting to £1¼ million had been offered in September for 100,000 men (Mulgrave to Jackson, no. 8, 10 September 1805; F.O. 64/88). For Pitt's authorisation of early payments see his Private letter to Harrowby of 29 October in Harrowby Mss, vol. XIII. Cf. for the case of Russia herself p. 736 above.

France and relief from anxiety for our two main Allies.[1] The envoy was therefore given a sketch of our ideas of compensations for them, lying from Poland to Bavaria and Italy and the Adriatic.

But none of these circumstances might emerge; and if at the worst Prussia could not be drawn into an alliance, she must be discouraged from perceiving advantage in allying herself with France. Part of Harrowby's instructions related to an offer of armed mediation or a state of continuing neutrality.[2] The first would not be much welcomed, by us let alone the other Allies; if it were to be accepted, it must be only on the basis of the Anglo-Russian conditions of April and with the British exclusions to the Anglo-Russian treaty. The second might still require a financial douceur to prevent something worse, but would also engender British efforts to acquire further troops from lesser Powers.[3] Possibly between some 50,000 and 70,000 men could be found by such means, which would have to be brought into play as Harrowby thought fit to propose.

This elaborate combination of hypotheses required a highly favourable climate. The fragility of the base for Anglo-Prussian relations at any time, and particularly at this moment, was exposed on the envoy's arrival on the German coast. On 10 November he sent his first, unhopeful despatch.[4] In his talks in Hamburg he had learned the latest developments, not yet known at home, springing from the talks between the King of Prussia and the Tsar. These had resulted in a treaty signed at Potsdam, on the 3rd, whereby the former was to offer an armed mediation which if not productive by 15 December would be followed by a declaration of war. The overt terms were not all satisfactory, though many of them were: independence for The Two Sicilies, Switzerland, Holland, and the states of the Germanic Empire; a sovereign independent 'kingdom' in Lombardy; territorial indemnity for Sardinia; and the extension of the Austrian frontier to include the strategic point of Mantua. The future security of Piedmont on the other hand was hard to ascertain, as was the programme for French withdrawals; and Britain in any case was being moved towards the circumference of events. Such potential problems were not of course insuperable; they were part and parcel of the diplomatic process. Far more serious, however, was a disagreeable secret article: Russia would undertake, with Austria, to negotiate for the cession of Hanover to Prussia at the peace.[5] Nor was the sequel to the meeting encouraging: the veteran Prussian Minister Haugwitz, the leading proponent of neutrality, was sent to the French headquarters at

---

1. Cf. pp. 730–1, 739–40 above. Hardenberg claimed much later in his memoirs that, at some undisclosed point in the talks, Harrowby offered Prussia the whole of Holland (see Fremont, loc. cit., 329). In view of the envoy's instructions it seems unlikely, though given his knowledge of the spread of ideas in London at the beginning of 1805 (p. 809 above) a suggestion is not impossible.

2. Mulgrave to Harrowby, no. 2, 27 October 1805 (*Third Coalition*, 216–20).

3. Ibid.

4. P.R.O., F.O. 64/70.

5. See *Consolidated Treaty Series*, 58, 269–87.

once to seek Napoleon's acceptance, while a Russian official, Count Oubril, was despatched to London to inform Vorontsov and the British Government. Travelling via Hamburg, he spoke to Harrowby on his way.

The British envoy was badly shaken. The treaty and Haugwitz's 'actual departure' seemed to him to have transformed the situation, to the point where his instructions could no longer apply. He would probably be obliged to wait passively in Berlin pending further guidance. The Russians were saying that only by such means could their new ally be drawn into the war: Napoleon was most unlikely to accept the main terms, and the Prussians were unimpressed by earlier British proposals for their involvement in Holland.[1] Their eyes indeed were set firmly on Hanover, the bait already offered in the summer by France.[2] Since such an accession formed no part of his brief, wide-ranging though it was, Harrowby was at a loss to know how to proceed if the subject arose.

It was certainly a most awkward one. The complication of the Electorate, once a powerful factor affecting British foreign policy and still normally a latent – and occasionally indeed an active – influence,[3] was the last thing that Pitt and his colleagues could have wished to confront now. They were looking forward on the contrary to an occupation including British troops which would secure the territory for the future. Of one fact the Minister was sure. He could not tell George III: 'such a proposal might either kill the King or drive him mad' – and that, he told the Russians, would stop any more subsidies 'for Continental wars'.[4] He did not therefore say anything, and Harrowby was informed that Ministers had thought it inexpedient 'even to convey the communication of the proposal'. Pitt told Vorontsov and Oubril categorically that the article in the treaty was inadmissible, and official silence on it was enjoined in due course on Harrowby himself in Berlin.[5]

The injunction, as it happened, came too late. The Cabinet met, for what would seem to have been a long discussion, on 23 November. That same day the British envoy brought up the subject with the Prussian Minister Hardenberg, who showed no reaction.[6] The fact however can

---

1. To Mulgrave, copies of two Private letters of 10 November 1805 (Harrowby Mss, vol. XIII). Jackson (see p. 701 above) heard the same from the Tsar and Czartoryski themselves while they were at Potsdam (to Mulgrave, nos. 126, 127 of 2 November 1805; F.O. 64/69). The Russians' uneasinesss was shown also by the fact that they did not reveal the territorial terms of the treaty to him, or to Leveson Gower.

2. P. 787 above. The most recent confirmation of this fact was known to the British Government at some point from a French memorandum of 25 October (date of acquisition unknown; F.O. 64/69).

3. Cf. I, 473–6 for the effect of the Fürstenbund in 1785.

4. Vorontsov reporting a conversation to Czartoryski, 29 November (misdated September) 1805 (*Memoirs of . . . Czartoryski*, II, 81).

5. Mulgrave to Harrowby, no. 4, 23 November 1805 (F.O. 64/70). And cf. Pitt to same, Private, 19 November 1805: 'Hanover is clearly out of the Question' (Harrowby Mss, vol. XII).

6. For the Cabinet meeting see Camden to Pitt, 24 November 1805 (Dacres Adams Mss, formerly P.R.O. 30/58/6); for Harrowby's with Hardenberg, Harrowby to same, Private, sd (P.R.O. 30/8/142).

have made no difference: announced or unannounced, the question of Hanover was bound to throw its shadow over the talks. 'This horrible secret article', as Harrowby called it, did much to set the scene in November. It also went far, as he forecast, to 'finish' and 'devour' Harrowby himself.[1] He had already found Hardenberg, known as an Anglophile, confined to 'vague and indefinite expressions'.[2] By the end of the month, apprehension had given way to despair. A difficult task was not made easier by the condition of his health: always a victim of his nervous system, he soon fell into an alarmingly unhelpful state. 'A succession of severe headaches have embarrassed my brain'; 'I have been . . . wretchedly ill for some days past with nervous headaches and sickness'; he felt 'unequal to anything', 'literally unfit' even 'to give an account of what I have done'. By the end of the first week in December – 'I hardly keep my senses' – he was asking leave to come home.[3]

This was a bad blow. There had been some speculation in London society about Harrowby's health when he was appointed; but neither he nor others can have expected a breakdown of this kind. Pitt did not – could not afford to – lose heart. His letters were kind and designed to reassure; and in point of fact he remained genuinely sanguine. He stressed the '*essential*' need for action, which Prussia alone could now provide: for harassment 'in the rear of the French army in Germany', though that should not rule out preparations for a timely attack on Holland. The British force for the north was being augmented to swell an Allied army in that quarter which could 'scarce be resisted'. Taking it with the Russians (and not counting the Swedes) available for a continuing advance, the numbers could amount to 40,000; surely the Prussians could supply some 30,000 for that front also, if the subsidies were increased?[4] The talks on finance were in fact going quite well at this point, and there was a distinct optimism in London, despite Harrowby's early reports, that Prussia would come in.[5] He was told to stay in Berlin until agreement was

1. To Pitt as in p. 811, n6 above; extract printed in Holland Rose, II, 545.

2. To Mulgrave, no. 2, 17 November 1805 (F.O. 64/70).

3. To Pitt, Private, 24 November, 8 December 1805 (respectively P.R.O. 30/8/142, copy in Harrowby Mss, vol. XIII), and see also same to same, Most Secret, 12 December 1805 (Holland Rose, II, 545–6), Most Secret, 17 December 1805 (P.R.O. 30/70/4). Jackson, who was not best pleased to have a Cabinet Minister wished on him, commented privately that the special envoy was 'insensible for hours together' (see *Diaries and Letters of Sir George Jackson*, I, 377). Cf. p. 670 above for his congenitally suspect health.

4. To Harrowby, 5 December 1805 (Holland Rose, II, 543–4; first printed in Stanhope's *Miscellanies*, I (1863), 25–8).

5. From the endorsements in the Foreign Office (F.O. 64/69, 70), despatches from Hamburg and Berlin were taking between one and two weeks to arrive at this time, and private letters presumably the same. For the optimism in London early in December see also *Malmesbury*, IV, 342–3. Harrowby presented a Project of a subsidy treaty for Hardenberg's inspection on the 6th (to Mulgrave, no. 15, 7 December 1805, and see also his no. 14 of the 1st; F.O. 69/70. Fremont, loc. cit., 316n1 however ascribes this last to the 10th, by which time circumstances had altered for the worse (p. 814 below) as reflected in the tone. The argument is persuasive, but the problem of the number on the despatch remains).

reached.[1] But by the time that order was sent, the situation had drastically changed.

The weeks following Mack's surrender at Ulm were anxious for Napoleon as well as for the British. Unexpectedly advantaged by his early victory, his position was nonetheless exposed. The command of the now combining Austro-Russian forces had passed for the time being to the latter's Marshal Kutusov; and while he could not halt the French advance he managed in the course of a rearguard action to inflict some significant damage. Meawhile he was due to be reinforced by the larger formations under the Tsar; and the Archduke Charles, on hearing the news of Ulm, hastened a withdrawal from Italy with the bulk of his troops.[2] The French themselves were suffering from the effects of their achievement in the march into Germany: from wastage and the problems of ever lengthening communications. Napoleon's haste indeed had already brought one dangerous complication, in antagonising the King of Prussia with the incursion through Anspach.[3] He must therefore continue to move fast if he was to neutralise a potential gathering of powerful forces: Austrians and Russians in the centre linked possibly with Austrians from the south and assisted perhaps by diversionary Prussian operations to the north. The balance might tilt either way, and his own speed could be critical at the head of a force under his personal command. As Pitt made his approach to Berlin, Napoleon was intent on reaching Vienna, from which point of vantage he might make a favourable peace.

The capital indeed, now undefended, soon fell as he had hoped. The French entered on 13 November and Napoleon took up his quarters at Schönbrunn, from where, in conjunction with Talleyrand, he heightened his diplomatic attack. Its emphasis now was directed at Russia; particularly since the news of Trafalgar had recently come to hand, suggesting a role for the Baltic Powers in a heightened system of pressure on Britain by economic blockade. While a proposal for a meeting with the Tsar was unsuccessful, Alexander sent his aide-de-camp for a talk at the French outposts, to be offered the suggestion of annexing the Turkish province of Moldavia with forces withdrawn from the west. Austria was treated more distantly. She had already been refused an armistice, offered in the hope of gaining time, and a fresh attempt to open talks was held off towards the end of the month while Haugwitz arrived for his interview with Napoleon.[4] Brief though this turned out to be, the tone was amicable, the subject of Hanover was not overlooked, and the Prussian stayed conveniently at

1. Mulgrave to Harrowby, no. 8, 22 December (F.O. 64/70). '. . . a good treaty', Pitt wrote at the same time 'will send you back to us in better health than you went' (21 December 1805; Harrowby Mss, vol. XII).

2. See pp. 806–7 above.

3. P. 800 above.

4. See pp. 810–11 above.

hand. But everything still hung in the balance, and the prospect for the French was clouded, for the Allied armies, of some 90,000 men with the Tsar and the Emperor at their head, were more fully joined by this time and closing on Vienna. Napoleon, with typical boldness, accordingly planned an early battle which would be fought at a point of his choice. The main French body was by now disposed in its corps in an arc northwards from Vienna. A force, some 53,000 strong, was ordered to the east to occupy the town of Brunn and its small neighbour Austerlitz, near which it would take up and prepare a defensive position. This should attract the attention of the Russian and Austrian armies. As soon as that was evident, the troops around Vienna would withdraw and further corps would move from the north-west, to reinforce with some 22,000 men. Carefully reconnoitred tactical plans brought the strategic concept into play. When the sun rose through a foggy dawn on the field of Austerlitz on 2 December, Napoleon could see from the Russians' movements that the day was likely to be his. That duly followed. By late afternoon the Allies, with their sovereigns, were in total retreat.

The completeness of the victory ended the campaign and the diplomatic alignments at a stroke. If Napoleon had brought the Third Coalition into being, he had successfully broken his creation. The Emperor was granted an armistice on 4 December, the Russians pulled out of Austria, and the dejected Tsar advised the King of Prussia to come to an arrangement with France. That was soon done. On the 15th Haugwitz signed a treaty at Schönbrunn, exchanging Prussia's detached possessions of Anspach and Neuchatel for Hanover. Austria followed suit at the French headquarters at Pressburg on the 26th, recognising Napoleon's arrangements in northern Italy, ceding Venetia (including Istria and Dalmatia though not Trieste) to France,[1] the Tyrol and Vorarlberg to Bavaria and some other territories and rights in southern Germany; losing in all three million subjects and significant resources and wealth. The repercussions of the battle were felt farther afield. Bodies of Prussian troops had in fact already moved into Hanover when the French were withdrawn to join the march to the south,[2] and the tardiness of Allied operations, Russia's loss of heart, and the change of fortune as now seen in Berlin grounded the British force on the Weser until it was embarked for home in February 1806. The Russians and the Swedes themselves retired to Stralsund whence they had come,[3] and Prussia was left in sole occupation of her promised reward. Pitt's diplomacy had been overthrown, and George III had lost a hereditary possession in the failure of a military effort which ended, as others had done, in the evacuation of a British force.

An equally dramatic reversal took place at the other end of the

1. Cf. p. 131 above for terms after the previous surrender in 1797.
2. See pp. 806–7 above.
3. As late as 8 December a Russian representative had taken part in a conference to arrange the dispositions of Allied forces in Hanover (Harrowby to Mulgrave, no. 16; *Third Coalition*, 259). Cf. pp. 798–9 above.

spectrum, in the central Mediterranean. Craig's force at Malta had been available since July for an operational role, with a strong possibility, under Russian pressure, of action on the mainland of southern Italy.[1] This last demand seemed the more likely to be received from September, when Russia's persuasion of The Two Sicilies into a treaty of alliance[2] encouraged her allocation of a larger force, to be shipped from the Black Sea to augment that destined for Corfu. In such case there would be an Allied army of almost 30,000 men, including the British contribution of 6–7,000. The object of the exercise, however, became confused almost as soon as its prospect had improved. For Napoleon had countermanded his strategy for the area under the circumstances raised by his decision to strike in strength at the two Imperial Powers. Rather than secure southern Italy with a detached force in the face of possible Allied attack, he was now anxious to remove the region from his list of commitments for the present by diplomatic means. The troops could be used to greater purpose farther north. No sooner accordingly had The Two Sicilies become an ally of Russia – though the precise timing was coincidental – than a French envoy arrived in Naples with a treaty of neutrality, to be signed forthwith under pain of French occupation of the city if that was refused. The tactic, as might have been expected, was successful; signature followed on 21 September, and the French at once began to withdraw, to engage the Austrians in November in northern Italy. There was therefore no military call to protect Naples, and an Allied landing could indeed now be called in question under international law. Nevertheless it was undertaken, as the Russians wished.[3] The prospects of a British presence in the central basin, and a linkage with the Austrians, continued to attract, and Craig, conforming to his instructions, prepared from mid October for an operation of which, within the context of his initial orders, he strongly disapproved. The expedition landed on 20 November; by then an awkward time. The news of Ulm had been digested, the host Government, despite Trafalgar, was frightened and in fact asked to be left alone; and when the tidings of Austerlitz followed, the heart went out of the venture. The Neapolitans feared French vengeance; the British command discounted a serious defence of the mainland and was correspondingly anxious to ensure that of Sicily; and at the turn of the year the Russian commander was brought to agree. The matter was clinched on 7 January 1806 when orders were received from the Tsar to return his force to Corfu. By the 19th all the Allies

1. Pp. 792–3, 797 above.
2. P. 786–7 above.
3. The Government of Naples in point of fact secretly repudiated the treaty of neutrality as soon as it was signed, so that the situation was debatable. The terms included the prohibition of British shipping and resistance to incursion of mainland territory (*Consolidated Treaty Series*, 58, 213), the first of which might also have been taken in London as a warrant for action. But while the resident British Minister, Hugh Elliot, almost certainly knew and initially liked the idea of a military answer, the decision was taken in the event before any higher sanction could be considered at a distance, let alone conveyed.

had left, and headed their separate ways. Their presence had not been without effect. It caused the French in northern Italy to keep an eye over their shoulder, helping the Archduke Charles to pull out in better order than he might otherwise have done;[1] and the intervention set the scene for a British role whose next phase followed in 1807, one which would affect grand strategy in the longer term beyond the shores of the Mediterranean itself.[2] None of that was to the point now. All that could be seen in the aftermath of Austerlitz was the futile collapse of yet another plan in which British troops had been involved.

In December, despatches from the Continent were received intermittently, taking between two and four weeks across wintry country and as vessels were able to sail.[3] Continuing exchanges with the Allies became increasingly out of phase as first rumour and then conflicting evidence came in from a range of sources. Instructions from London on arrangements for the subsidies, guidance on the latest thinking, sent with a new special envoy to Vienna via Berlin,[4] advice of the reinforcement of British troops in the north, crossed with intelligence received of the Russians' withdrawal to Hungary, the French dictation to Austria of terms of peace, Haugwitz's agreement with Napoleon – slower to come to light –, the first signs of Allied disengagement from northern Germany. By the end of the year the full extent of the disaster had become clear to the respective British envoys, and Harrowby himself announced his intention of coming home. Any lingering doubts in Berlin had vanished with Haugwitz's return; there was nothing more to be done 'and in fact . . . they wish me away'.[5] Seen in retrospect, against this renewed example of the time lags of information, the final phase in the British efforts to gain Prussia as an ally, or at least to keep her suitably neutral, appear as a sad illusion.

It was not quite like that at the time, even to Harrowby himself. Highly optimistic as he found Pitt's earlier messages, and now grossly so,[6] his native staunchness, almost smothered by exhaustion, struggled into life towards the end. He did his best to work through Hardenberg on the King

1. P. 815 above.
2. See Mackesy, *The War in the Mediterranean*, 89–91, 371, 373, 375, 377.
3. P.R.O., F.O. 7/75, 64/70, 65/59 for the three Courts principally concerned. Cf. p. 800 above.
4. He was the Earl of Harrington, provided with credentials including Prussia as well, and furnished with authority to advance £300,000 to Austria if urgently required. Recently chosen to become Commander-in-Chief in Ireland, he was recommended for his 'professional science' and 'general character' (see *L.C.G III*, IV, no. 3156).
5. To Pitt, 23 December 1805 (P.R.O. 30/8/142), Private, 5 January 1806. He quit Berlin shortly afterwards, leaving behind him a combination, or confusion, of Harrington, Hammond (p. 801, n6 above) and Jackson, each with his own credentials or powers, while Leveson Gower was given authority to transfer to Russia the day to day handling of any future talks with Prussia on behalf of both Powers.
6. Eg Harrowby to Paget, 27 December 1805 (Fremont, loc. cit., 333).

Pulteney Street and Laura Place, Bath

Bowling Green House, Putney Heath. Sketch by Eliza Holland Ross

of Prussia when the news of Austerlitz was received; nor did the prospects seem immediately hopeless, for Frederick William's first reaction was to inform the Tsar that he was prepared to join Russia and Austria if they decided to continue the campaign, and he repeated the offer after a week's reflection.[1] Events overcame this belated sign of vigour, as the King contemplated his future need for security. But the fact that it had surfaced at such a moment bore witness to the truth that policy in Berlin had been subject to divisions and was far from settled throughout. Harrowby indeed concluded, despite his prognostications, that the issue had been a close-run thing.

This Court (he told his colleague in Austria)[2] was so far engaged that, had not the unfortunate battle of Austerlitz taken place, even if the scattered armies maintained their position in Hungary after it, the Prussian Army would, I believe, have advanced rapidly and all might have been saved.

Pitt himself could have gone no farther; and the verdict may perhaps be borne in mind when assessing British policy towards Prussia in the course of two critical months.

As it was, the Ministry persisted in hopes which it refused to believe were doomed. The first reports from the British envoys concerned did not reach London until 2 January 1806 – not that the hasty initial information could be conclusive as to the effects.[3] Meanwhile a spate of rumours and professed accounts were hard to assess; some of the earliest indeed bore news of a victory, which was duly carried to George III.[4] Contradictory reports of developments in November had in fact been so rife that no one in England could be sure for some weeks about subsequent events. But by the end of the year the evidence pointed to the worst: a 'formal and particular . . . statement' of an Austrian armistice was received on 29 December.[5] Pitt had declined characteristically to credit unproven depressing news, particularly in the French newspapers, and the maddeningly optimistic messages from London continued to arrive in Berlin.[6]

---

1. See loc. cit., 317.

2. To Paget, 27 December 1805 (loc. cit., 319). One may place an 'or' in the second line.

3. The despatches, which came all together in one batch, were Paget's nos. 113, 114 of 3, 9 December 1805 (F.O. 7/75); Leveson Gower's no. 52 (misnumbered for 53, in a confusion of numbering lasting for the next ten days) of 5 December (F.O. 65/59); Harrowby's no. 17 – an indication only – of the 8th (F.O. 64/70). Paget's account and subsequent assessments were found particularly inadequate (above all his no. 117 of 25 December, in which he thought Napoleon's situation could yet be 'desperate' if the Archduke Charles appeared).

4. Stanhope, IV, 361 and Appendix xxvii–xxviii.

5. See Canning to Pitt, 31 December 1805 (op. cit., 364–5); and for earlier glimpses of some of those better qualified than most to form an opinion, *H.M.C., Dropmore*, VII, 319–25, *A.C.*, IV, 257–60.

6. As Harrowby complained; p. 807 above, and Harrowby to Pitt, Private, 5 January 1806 (copy in Harrowby Mss, vol. XIII).

Now however there seemed no room for doubt, and this was confirmed in the next few days. On 3 January Castlereagh brought him the contents of the official mails just arrived from Germany. He tried to appear measured and steady, as he had done in adversity over so many years – 'it is the more provoking, because subsequent to the action the allied army is stated to have been still 85,000 strong' – and turned at once to the future of the British forces in the north and the south. Maybe all was not lost: the Russians might still be operational, Prussia still held in play.[1] But this was an instinctive response; no real expectation survived; the blow, as was at once observed, struck to the core.[2] The great design was overturned. It would not soon be revived. Patience and marginal action alone could be envisaged for Britain in Europe. If the war continued elsewhere, that could be a lengthy business and the finances would remain under pressure. Meanwhile the immediate political future of the Government was bleak. Wherever one looked, hopes were crushed or, once more, delayed. And for him there was no relief, for hope itself was destroyed.

---

1. To Melville, 3 January; to Bathurst, sd (*H.M.C., Bathurst*, 51); to Castlereagh, 6 January (Stanhope, IV, 366–8); and see also Mulgrave to Leveson Gower, no. 1, 11 January 1806 (F.O. 65/62). For Castlereagh as the messenger with the despatches see the evidence of W.D. Adams, to 5th Earl Stanhope, 26 April 1861 (Stanhope Ms U1590 C405/15).
2. Pp. 822–3 below.

CHAPTER XXII

Death

I

When Pitt received the confirmed news of Austerlitz he was staying for a spell at Bath. He had indeed been there for almost a month, since December.[1] His health had again been giving cause for concern, and some of his friends would have liked him to have taken the waters earlier.[2] But he had not wanted to be too far from London when much needed or might need to be done. The sudden change of attitude in Prussia in particular held him in the second half of October; and he was also engaged in the early autumn in seeing, so far as he could, to his preparations for the coming session. He was anxious to reinforce the Cabinet with greater debating ability in the Commons, where his burden would be heavy, and the limited arrangements had been settled in his mind before he left. He intended to add two new members if he could: Canning and Charles Yorke. The latter, if willing, could take over the Board of Control for India from Castlereagh, who still combined the post with his recent appointment as Secretary of State for War; for despite his contests with Pitt during Addington's Ministry, as Secretary at War and then Home Secretary, he remained basically a political friend. Encouraged by the outgoing Minister in 1801 to serve from 'the *imperious necessity of the times*', he had become anxious since early in 1804 for the former leader to return. There were disadvantages: Yorke, like Windham, could be impetuous and 'wrong-headed'; he was moreover a brother of Hardwicke, the Lord Lieutenant in Ireland who had been increasingly dissatisfied with Pitt over the past year. But he was capable and well disposed and, though he would have to be 'courted', might agree to act in a situation for which men of experience might be hard to find.[3] Canning of course was a different matter, despite his earlier indiscretions, and he longed for Cabinet rank.

---

1. Pitt to Bathurst, 9 December [1805] (B.L. Loan Ms 57, vol. 2).

2. Eg Canning to Pitt, 27 November 1805 (P.R.O. 30/8/120); Bathurst to same, 6 December [1805] (P.R.O. 30/8/112).

3. See *H of P*, V, 667–9. Pitt was supposed to have said of him and Windham in 1800 'I never see either of them get up but I clap my face between my two hands frightened to death lest their natural violence, impetuosity and wrong-headedness should start some subject absolutely indefensible'; and cf. p. 765 above. But he had since been impressed by Yorke's ability at the War Office, as also had the King.

There remained only one difficulty; to persuade him to accept without a change of place. It was not in fact unknown for the Treasurer of the Navy to be included: the post, being regarded normally as a sinecure, was available if political circumstances suggested, and a few years earlier Pitt himself had called it as fit 'from Practice' as was the Secretaryship at War 'to be had with a Seat in the Cabinet'.[1] It ranked indeed with, if slightly below the Mint, itself a usefully flexible borderline case.[2] But Canning had been chafing for almost eighteen months at his lack of advancement – 'one continued series of mortifications' – and he was not pleased now, the more so since arrangements would be announced only shortly before Parliament met. There could yet be a slip. In the end however, as on most occasions, he agreed that he would act as Pitt might require.[3]

Meanwhile domestic arrangements went ahead to cover the coming weeks. A house was found in Bath – 2 Johnson Street, off Laura Place, across Pultney Bridge from the centre of the town[4] – and there Pitt settled in for a stay probably into the new year. The anxiety of business had been producing the stomach pains and loss of appetite that were always particularly worrying, and now 'flying pains in the feet and limbs' announced a fresh onset of gout. The waters were accordingly prescribed, and they soon produced the 'perfectly regular' effect in the ball of the foot. Desirable as this was thought to be, however, it proved excessive, confining the patient to the house for a spell and interrupting the regime for about a fortnight.[5] Over much of this time he seems to have been in good spirits – Pitt always bore pain with fortitude and could still, if briefly, 'throw off [his] load' of business with remarkable speed –, the gout eased, and the early false reports of an Allied victory doubtless played their part.[6] He had kept out of sight from the start as much as he could – as *The Bath Herald* commented in poetic flow on his visits to the Pump Room,

> He comes by stealth
> . . . With thoughts uplifted but retiring mien

1. To Windham, suggesting an exchange, 24 April 1800 (*The Windham Papers*, II, 152).

2. See Aspinall, 'The Cabinet Council', 155n3.

3. Cf. p. 452 above. Pitt had in fact said, on 24 October, that Canning could go to Ireland as Chief Secretary initially, or take the Board of Control if he insisted; but, not surprisingly in the face of his disciple's anguish, he stressed that it was membership of the Cabinet that mattered (see Marshall, op. cit., 287–95). That offer, settled as it seemed by 21 November, was not indeed made easier, at a time when the Minister could not afford to offend other colleagues by redisposing 'effective' posts to suit a fairly unpopular entrant, by Canning's openly critical view of the current German expedition; or, conversely, by his last minute qualms about accepting in case it heightened the Minister's difficulties.

4. Pitt to Bathurst from that address, 9 December (p. 819, n2 above). It seems to have been secured by Harrowby's brother Richard Ryder (to Pitt, 17 November 1805; P.R.O. 30/8/174); not far from his lodging on a comparable visit for his health in the autumn of 1802 (see p. 548 above).

5. Farquhar's account, relying on reports from Mr Crook, Pitt's local 'medical attendant' (*The Monthly Review*, I, December 1900, 51).

6. P. 817 above. See I, 589 for the load.

– and his days were relieved by a succession of visitors, among them Bathurst, Hawkesbury, Canning, Mulgrave, Mulgrave's brother General Edmund Phipps, and Melville (the last an occurrence which was said to have greatly shocked Addington). They formed indeed a 'mess' in their comings and goings, providing the familiar company he always enjoyed. When possible he took an airing in his carriage; otherwise he read, from state papers to novels – one such, *The Novice of St Dominic*, apparently engaged him so much that he could not put it down –, touched up Mulgrave's and Canning's verses on Trafalgar, and wrote such letters as he felt obliged.[1]

But at the turn of the year things began to take a turn for the worse. A return of gout stopped Pitt again from taking the waters, and on 1 January 1806 he began to wonder if he would be well enough to attend Parliament when it opened in three weeks' time.[2] The next day he wrote to ask Farquhar, who had offered at the start to accompany him, to come down;[3] and when the doctor arrived on the 4th he was shaken, according to his later account, by what he saw. Pitt was 'much emaciated, very weak, feeble, & low'. He found it hard to take his place at the dinner table, and ate very little, drinking a glass of madeira and water. The old mysterious enemy in the stomach and bowels had to be relieved once more, and in consultation with a well known local physician, Dr John Haygarth, drops of 'Paragoric Elixir', soon replaced by 'cascarilla' and subsequently rhubarb, were added to the usual 'absorbent Draught', with asses' milk (helpful on former occasions) supplied for nutrition on the 6th.[4] By this point he was scarcely taking anything – an egg beaten with a spoonful of brandy two or three times a day seemed the best hope – and agreed with the doctors (a third opinion being sought from a Dr William Falconer) that he had best leave for London. A visit to Badminton, already postponed, was cancelled, and the journey was planned, to take five days, offers of accommodation coming at once from Hawkesbury and Camden and Canning.[5] And so he

1. Holland Rose, II, 548, 550; Stanhope, IV, 353–4; Edmund Phipps to Mulgrave, 7 January 1806 (Normanby Mss, bundle 31). Cf. p. 111 above. For the novel see a note by Stanhope (Ms U1590 C404/14) based partly (though confirmed elsewhere) on the *Memoirs of Lady Morgan* published in 1863. She commented 'So now every one reads the 'Novice of St Dominic.'

Pitt appears to have exercised a function of poetic criticism and encouragement among his circle, at any rate when verses were to be published on public affairs. In 1797 he called on Mornington for some Latin lines for *The Jacobin* on the victory at Camperdown.

2. Pitt to Farquhar, 1 January 1806 (Stanhope, *Miscellanies*, I, 33). Cf. p. 805 above. Parliament was due to meet on the 21st.

3. Op. cit., 35.

4. Farquhar's account (published from the Pretyman papers by Rosebery in *The Monthly Review*, I, no. 3, December 1900, 52). Paregoric elixir was a camphor tincture of opium (cf. pp. 550–1 above), flavoured with aniseed and benzolic acid; cascarilla, known more commonly as bark, a bitter tonic from the bark of the plant *croton eleuteria*.

5. *The Monthly Review*, loc. cit., 52–3; Pitt to Castlereagh, 6 January 1806 (see Stanhope, IV, 366n8, 367–8); op. cit., 370–2 for offers of accommodation; Phipps to Mulgrave, 7, 8 January 1806 (Normanby Mss, bundle 31). For the visit to Badminton see Duke of Beaufort to Pitt, 25, 28 December 1805 (P.R.O. 30/8/112), Pitt to Bathurst, 1 January (*H.M.C., Bathurst*, 50).

set out on 9 January, leaning on the arms of his nephew Charles Stanhope, who had arrived some days before, and General Phipps.[1] They made their way to the travelling carriage through a crowd which parted silently as he emerged.

The marked deterioration took place against the growing probability and final confirmation of the disaster at Austerlitz; ushered in by the detailed newspaper report of 29 December and made certain by the despatches received on 3 January.[2] Until that point indeed Pitt's companions were not unduly worried by his state; Phipps for instance, who described him on the 8th in much the same terms as Farquhar did on arrival, had still been surprised that the doctor found him more ill 'than we were aware of'.[3] He suspected exaggeration in fact; and it is true that Farquhar may have been on the defensive, as he remained in some degree in his final account. Even so his reaction and alarm were clearly genuine. A collapse had taken place. And the conclusion in general was soon drawn, as it has remained, that this stemmed from the news. Some embroidery was not lacking. It was not the case for instance, as one story had it, that the Minister read the fatal despatch during a visit to the picture gallery of a country house – Shockerwick House. And while at some point he may well have spoken on the lines of the famous remark, 'Roll up the map of Europe. It will not be wanted these ten years', no proof can be found as to when or where or in fact if he did so.[4] Wilberforce coined the telling phrase, according to Macaulay, of Pitt's 'Austerlitz look'. But he did not see Pitt at or after Bath, and applied it retrospectively to his friend's closing months.[5] Such evidence as exists points indeed rather to an instant attempt to remain calm and balanced. The official news had been heralded in some sort, and it was still possible at first to see the outcome of the battle as not necessarily fatal to the alliance. The private secretary Dacres Adams, arriving 'that very day' from some leave, recalled many years later that

> depressed as Mr. Pitt was by his severe and mortal illness, and the overthrow of all his hopes and Labours for the rescue of Europe, I was

1. Phipps to Mulgrave, 9 January 1806 (Normanby Mss, bundle 31). Like his brother, the General had come closer to Pitt in recent years. For some reason, they were accustomed to refer to him in their correspondence as 'the Modern'; could this have referred to his sudden interest in military theory arising from his service with his Volunteers in Kent (see p. 000 above) – the very model of a modern Colonel?

2. Pp. 817–18, above.

3. To Mulgrave, 8 January 1806 (loc. cit.).

4. The first, local tradition received lustre in due course from its appearance in Hardy's *The Dynasts*. The second – given licence there to the same occasion – has been ascribed alternatively to the moment of Pitt's return home, on seeing a map in the hall. The remark however was not apparently heard by Hester Stanhope, who was watching from the stairs and might have been expected not to forget so strikingly prescient a comment; and in any case the hall seems a rather unlikely place in which to hang a political map.

5. Essay on Pitt, in *The Miscellaneous Writings of Lord Macaulay*, II (1860), 367.

struck by the wonderful fortitude with which he bore such a mental and bodily pull upon his nearly exhausted resources.[1]

The instinctive effort might have been expected, and the language of Pitt's letters in immediate response was practical and provisional.[2] But the blow was nonetheless mortal: 'his appearance at this time [4 to 9 January] was that of a man much worn out'. His eyes were 'almost lifeless', his voice was 'hollow', his pulse highly erratic and 'remarkably weak'; and 'After the arrival of Dispatches these Symptoms were always considerably encreased'. Bath, it was clear, could no longer serve a purpose. He himself indeed was now intent on getting home.[3]

The journey, in Stanhope and Farquhar's company, went better and thus faster than expected. Pitt was furnished with a feather bed on which to lie, and took some reading matter from a circulating library – Schiller's *Thirty Years War*, and the *Secret History of the Court of Petersburgh*. After an unsatisfactory halt at Chippenham, intended for the night, he pressed on to Marlborough – where Sidney Smith, happening to lodge at the same inn, predictably pressed for an interview. After stopping for succeeding nights at Reading and Salt Hill near Windsor, he reached his destination on the evening of the 11th.[4]

He was heading for Putney. Since regaining office he had had no house within convenient near distance of London: Holwood was sold and Walmer of course farther away. Dundas was no longer available at Wimbledon to provide a bed and an opportunity to discuss business; and others – Long, Canning, Hawkesbury for example – did not stand on quite the same ground. The Minister needed something of his own, accessible and cheap. At one point in 1804 the idea had been mooted of renting Walpole House in Chelsea village – later incorporated, by Soane, in the infirmary of the Royal Hospital – with its garden running down to the river. But that was not taken up, and he ended by renting a modest building, ready furnished: Bowling Green House on Putney Heath by the Portsmouth road, which had been enlarged at some time from an old inn presiding over bowls and cockfighting.[5] Although he had survived a tiring experience fairly well and was claimed to be in 'tolerable spirits', Hester

1. The secretary recalled that he dined with Pitt, Charles Stanhope and Farquhar; and, he thought, Castlereagh, come down with the despatches to discuss the implications (see p. 818 above). His account is printed in part in Stanhope, *Miscellanies*, I, 30–1.

2. Cf. pp. 817–18 above.

3. Farquhar's account (*The Monthly Review*, I, no. 3, 53); Pitt to Castlereagh, 6 January 1806 (Stanhope, IV, 368).

4. *The Monthly Review*, loc. cit., 53–4; Edmund Phipps to Mulgrave, 9 January 1806 (Normanby Mss, bundle 31); John Upham [the proprietor of a circulating library] to Chatham, 10 March 1806, asking for the return of his volumes (Stanhope Ms U840 C404/15).

5. Mulgrave to Pitt, nd (endorsed with a query November 1804) for 'Lord Yarborough's House' [Walpole House], and see *The* [LCC] *Survey of London, Parish of Chelsea (Part 1)* (nd but 1909), 6–7 and Plate 6; Charles Lennox to same, nd, for a possibility at Wimbledon, and John Eamer or Eames to same for one at Putney, 9 June 1804 (both Dacres Adams Mss,

Stanhope was deeply shocked by the changed tone of his voice and his struggle for breath as he climbed the stairs.[1]

Nonetheless, Pitt was able to summon the joint Secretary to the Treasury, Sturges Bourne, to Putney the next morning, and later to take his 'airing' by carriage; and a plan of treatment was settled that day at a consultation of Farquhar with two other doctors – Henry Reynolds, one of the group of leading practitioners called in during the King's three major attacks, and the more impressively equipped Matthew Baillie, nephew and pupil of William Hunter and, appropriately, the first anatomist to define exactly the condition of cirrhosis of the liver.[2] The next day, 13 January, the Minister again appeared 'favourable', enough so in fact for Farquhar, who had been staying in the house, to feel able to leave his patient until the morrow. When he returned, the picture was different. Pitt had agreed on reaching Putney that he would not open letters or attend to business, and that Tomline, on hand at the Deanery at St Paul's, should come for the time being to act as personal secretary. The Bishop accordingly moved in, with mournful alacrity. But the second part of the 'pledge' was ignored, as the summons to the Treasury showed, and despite renewed assurances Pitt saw callers as soon as the doctor's back was turned. He talked to Sturges Bourne again, with the latter's colleague Huskisson, and after they left to Castlereagh who was later joined by Hawkesbury. There was certainly much to discuss: Parliament was due to be opened in eight days' time, and there was a King's speech to be written; and the Minister would wish to consider the latest reports from the Continent, particularly on the stranded British northern expedition.[3] His colleagues doubtless tried to be as brief as possible. But the result was a collapse. That evening Pitt confessed to Tomline and Charles Stanhope that he was feeling 'very shabby indeed'.[4]

---

formerly P.R.O. 30/58/7). The house chosen in the end, however, belonged probably to a Mr Pigou (retrospective note by W (or N) Ward relating to the gardener's wages, nd but August 1820 (Pretyman Ms 562:1820)). See also Holland Rose, II, 554 and illustration. The building has been demolished, and the ground is occupied by houses some bearing names connected with Pitt – Chatham, Pitt, Holwood; rather as some features in Hayes still recall the site of his birthplace in Chatham's beloved Hayes Place (see I, 3).

1. *The Monthly Review*, loc. cit., 54; Sturges Bourne [see p. 764 and n6 above] to Rose, 12 January 1806 [date misprinted] (*Rose*, II, 206); *Memoirs of the Lady Hester Stanhope*, II, 79.

2. Sturges Bourne to Rose, as in n1 above; *The Monthly Review*, loc. cit., 55. The most detailed account of this period from the afternoon of the 12th is however by Tomline, who arrived at the house that afternoon (to Mrs Tomline, 15 January 1806; Pretyman Ms 435/26).

Reynolds had been called in by Farquhar on at least one previous occasion, at Walmer – probably in 1802 – when he was staying nearby (Rose to Pretyman, nd; Pretyman Ms 435/44).

3. See pp. 821, 818 above.

4. This paragraph is based on Tomline's account and Farquhar's in *The Monthly Review*, both as in n2 above. According to one report which Sturges Bourne seems to have given to Malmesbury on 23 January, Pitt told Tomline after seeing Castlereagh and

To Farquhar himself he went farther – 'Sir Walter', he announced in the doctor's recollection, 'I have been compelled to disobey your injunctions – I have done too much. When in conversation with persons upon important business, I felt suddenly as if I had been cut in two'.

That 'abominable' conversation, as Dacres Adams called it, was indeed the turning point, if such was still available. The resilience which Pitt had shown since leaving Bath proved to be a final effort; from the 14th his symptoms became 'truly & immediately alarming'.[1] One may pause at this point, therefore, to see if any further light can be cast at the end, beyond such as has already been glimpsed, on the cause or causes of his death.[2] One thing is virtually certain. As the attacks continued in his last twenty months in office, the remedies which gave some relief were pre-scribed increasingly or taken with decreasing caution. Farquhar's 'con-stant drugging' was suspected at the time of doing harm. In so far as it did so, that perhaps quite largely because it was misused. Some at least of the stimulants were supposed to be taken to prop up the Minister on par-ticular occasions, not '*habitually* or frequently' as they probably were.[3] Draughts of opium too, in one form or another, may well have had a debilitating effect towards the close. Nevertheless, whatever its impact, the treatment does not cause the initial disease. Nothing in the final stage of Pitt's life seems to have introduced a significant new factor; perhaps the most striking single observation – his own – was his sudden sensation of being 'cut in two'. Had a gastro-intestinal lesion, an inherent weakness, produced a last and now decisive result?[4] His stomach and bowels were felt, by different physicians, on two occasions in January, and no 'organic mischief' was found.[5] Given the resources of the day, however, that was by no means conclusive, and at the close there are plenty of hypotheses to choose from or to combine. Some of the symptoms over the later years – the vomiting, the sallowness, the anaemia, the rapid pulse particularly at the last – could have come in varying permutations from a variety of sources, with hyperuricaemia suggestively to the fore. Pitt possessed a vul-nerable but a tough constitution; he suffered and recovered from a long series of violent attacks, growing in frequency from the later nineties, which interacted increasingly with independent pressures in a life of

---

Hawkesbury that he felt something in his stomach 'not cold, but a general giving way' (*Malmesbury*, IV, 345–6). Canning sensed on the 14th that 'he knew his own situation but too well!' (diary, Canning Ms 29d).

1. *The Monthly Review*, loc. cit., 55. 'Abominable' was the word of the absent Adams in Downing Street (to his brother-in-law P. Courtenay, Most Private, 16 January 1806, copy in Stanhope Ms U1590 C66/7); Hester Stanhope's – purposing perhaps to quote Farquhar – was 'infernal' (to W.D. Adams, sd (loc. cit., C419/9)).

2. Pp. 549–51 above.

3. See quotations in Reilly, *Pitt the Younger*, 338.

4. Cf. p. 551 above. In his account of Pitt's conversation, Farquhar here used inverted commas.

5. At Bath or, again, at Putney (*The Monthly Review*, loc. cit., 54).

rising strain. At the end there may have been a 'cascade type' effect from failure of a number of vital organs; not least among them, if one may so put it, that of confidence and will.

The alarm now felt by Farquhar, and soon shared by his colleagues, could not stop the Minister seeing some more people on the 14th. He managed some belated light breakfast and drove out with Hester for about an hour. But on return he did not at first feel up to talking to his brother, who eventually came in 'rather abruptly' bringing a message from the King. Others also called – Canning, for what turned out to be a short last meeting, Sturges Bourne who was also seen briefly, Mulgrave and the Duke of Montrose who were not allowed in.[1] Another visitor, this time expected, spent a little longer. Wellesley, returning from India, reached Spithead on 7 January after a five months' voyage. He wrote at once, receiving a reply from Pitt on reaching Putney some days later which asked him to come as soon as he was free. They talked, not at length and keeping off business, though the Minister took time to commend Arthur Wellesley, of whom he had been seeing something, as a soldier who 'states every difficulty before he undertakes any service, but none after he has undertaken it'. His spirits seemed to rise on seeing an old friend after an absence of over eight years, and according to one witness he 'did not suffer' ill effects, though by another story he fainted before Wellesley left the room.[2]

Thereafter Pitt saw scarcely any one beyond those based on the house.[3] Rose was allowed a few minutes on the 15th, and experienced the consternation of all those who had not lately been in touch. Chatham may have been admitted two days later. Otherwise the patient lay quietly in his 'small and closed' room, hardly speaking though conscious and rational. Occasionally he tried to take a small cup of broth, with little success, and he could be heard coughing and sometimes retching at night. On the 19th James Stanhope joined his brother Charles and Hester. He found George Rose near the house in tears, for Pitt had just fainted away;[4] but the next

---

1. Tomline to Mrs Tomline, 15 January 1806, as in p. 824, n2 above; and see op. cit. n4 above for Canning's impression.

2. The Marquess published Pitt's letter to him, of the 12th, and an account of their meeting, thirty years later in *The Quarterly Review*, no. cxiv. For his departure from India see p. 000 above. Tomline's testimony to his wife on 15 January of the physical effect of the conversation must be set against Sturges Bourne's to Malmesbury on the 23rd (*Malmesbury*, IV, 346).

3. For this paragraph see *Rose*, II, 222–30, and James Stanhope's account from 19 January (see below) printed in Stanhope, IV, 378–88. According to Tomline (to Mrs Tomline, nd but endorsed either 18 or 20 January; Pretyman Ms 435/110), Sidmouth and also Buckinghamshire called at this time; so too did Joe Smith (to Margaret Smith, 20 January 1806; Saumarez Smith Mss), and perhaps Camden (to Pitt, 15 January 1806 (P.R.O. 30/8/119).

4. This may have been the occasion of which Tomline wrote to his wife in an undated letter (Pretyman Ms 435/26) that Pitt, in 'extreme debility' had been 'fainting away & only supported by Madeira'.

day went better, with signs even of a slight appetite. On the 21st the doctors, Reynolds and Baillie, came again from London; and once more not the doctors only. Chatham returned, but could not see his brother, and the house was busy with more callers – the royal Dukes of Cambridge and Cumberland, Canning, Sturges Bourne, Steele, Rose '&c'. On the 22nd Farquhar finally gave up all hope: Pitt's pulse at times was 130, he was entirely exhausted and could hold nothing down. The time had arrived to consider offering the last rites of the Church.

Tomline accordingly proposed to administer the sacrament. He had not ventured so far to broach such a subject, the doctors having warned of the risk of 'agitating' Pitt's state. But as the Bishop watched the silent figure he was sure that it was in thought. What might not those thoughts concern? He knew, on Farquhar's verdict now, that he must provide for the end.[1] He could probably not expect more than a kindly considerate response; and that he received. Pitt had never shown a notable interest in the arguments for belief – very few volumes of devotion or apologetics were to be found on his shelves – or a noticeable capacity in fact for religious feeling. Tomline himself later claimed for his friend an early imbibement of Christian truth which remained 'throughout life' as 'an habitual principle'. The theme occupied eight lines in an appreciation of over three times as many pages.[2] No one indeed pretended to detect the pursuit of a lively personal faith. Hester Stanhope put the position plainly, though with limited experience and probable exaggeration: her uncle did not go to church at Walmer – a curious example perhaps from the Lord Warden – and he 'never even talked about religion, and never even brought it upon the carpet'.[3] Wilberforce, a more important guide, more than once lamented this sad deficiency in the midst of so many fine human qualities – 'His regard for truth was greater than I ever saw in any man who was not strongly under the influence of a powerful principle of religion'; as too did Tomline's wife – 'O that your friend would learn the *only* wisdom he is in want of!' His virtues indeed seemed not to spring from a transcendental source: 'he appeared' for example 'to adhere to it [the regard for truth] out of respect for himself, from a certain moral purity which appeared to

1. *Rose*, I, 230; Tomline's account, introducing ch. XXVII of the unpublished final volume of his *Life* of Pitt (see I, xi). Some of the latter, in an abbreviated form, was published in Gifford's *Political Life of Pitt* in 1809 (for which see p. 111, n2 above), and the ch. itself, under the title of 'Tomline's Estimate of Pitt', by Rosebery in *The Monthly Review*, XII, no. 35 for August 1903.

2. 'Estimate of Pitt' (*The Monthly Review*, loc. cit., 34); as printed there, the ch. fills some 28 pages. The Bishop's claim however later received support from Wellesley, in his article on Pitt in *The Quarterly Review* of 1836 (see p. 826, n2 above), where he drew attention to the regularity of his friend's early instruction (partly, presumably, from Pretyman himself, at Cambridge) and his 'accurate and extensive' knowledge. See Pretyman Ms 562: 21 and Maggs's ms catalogue of 1911 (I, 670) for the library.

3. Quoted by Sack, op. cit., 85; who however draws attention (op. cit., 255–7) to the dawning change in attitude to church-going and religiosity among public men between the later decades of the eighteenth century and the early period of the nineteenth century.

be a part of his nature'.[1] His approach to doctrine could be distinctly heterodox – he warmed to an idea, as he conceived it, that God 'never interposes for the preservation of men or nations without their own Exertions';[2] and it was indeed in national terms that he thought most instinctively on the subject. In his war speeches, he spoke explicitly on occasions as a Christian statesman, proclaiming the cause of 'the laws, liberties and religion of our country'.[3] Similarly, as a constitutional Minister particularly in a period of dangerous instability, he maintained the place and subscribed to the tenets of the Anglican creed. The humanism of his temperament, the inherited background of secular sympathy with Dissenting interests, the genuine anxiety to recognise the secular aspirations of Irish Roman Catholics and in fact in part of Catholics at large, had all to accommodate to the superior demands of Church and State when circumstances pressed.[4] His reading of the combination was not strictly traditional – his favoured author Paley brought a 'distinctive interfusion of utilitarian calculus and Christian morality' to an influence in the longer term 'within Christian political discourse'[5] – and it was not always comfortable to the Anglican ranks themselves. But he strained their loyalties to the limits only once, and then in any case he resigned. He acted when required as a buttress to the Establishment, and he saw it as a buttress in turn. His personal emotion, however, was not engaged by his religious allegiance or experience. Its focus lay elsewhere.

The sacrament was not administered; Pitt replied that he had not the strength.[6] But, announcing that 'like many other men' he had neglected prayer too much for it to be 'efficacious' now, he affirmed that he threw himself *'entirely* on the mercy of God through the merits of Jesus Christ' and joined in quietly with his friend. The Bishop moved on at the close to ascertain any wishes for a will, apparently not made before and in which he himself was now named as executor together with Chatham. Its provisions were dictated, and signed with difficulty in the presence of Farquhar and a servant, Pitt's 'own and faithful footman, Parslow'.[7] All this was

1. 'Sketch of Pitt' in *Private Papers of Wilberforce*, 69, and see also op. cit., 72, 77 and cf. *Life of Wilberforce*, II, 269, and p. 31, n3 above; Mrs Pretyman to Pretyman, nd but endorsed 8 February 1801 (Pretyman Ms 435/45).

2. Cf. p. 110 above, with Mrs Pretyman's comment.

3. Speech of 10 November 1797, after the collapse of the peace talks at Lille, as one eg (*P.R., 3rd ser.*, IV, 180); and cf. to Grenville, writing 'as an English Minister and a Christian' (Rosebery, *Pitt*, 137). See II, 148–9 for the concept of 'liberties'.

4. Cf. II, 161; and cf. eg pp. 177–8 above. For another example see a conversation with Pretyman and Mrs Pretyman in December 1801 (Pretyman Ms 435/29).

5. David Easton, review (*E.H.R.*, vol. CVIII, no. 429, 1040) of Robert Hole, *Pulpits, Politics and Public Order in England, 1760–1832* (1989). But Paley too in Pitt's later years was not so much in favour as he had been (conversation in 1801; see n4 above).

6. Rose, whose account came from Tomline (*Rose*, II, 230). The statement is not in Tomline's own account for ch. XXVII of his biography (*The Monthly Review*, loc. cit., 14–15).

7. Or 'Purssler' as he appears in a list of Pitt's servants (Pretyman Ms 562:1820) where he is named as valet.

exhausting, and he then slept. Hester, forbidden the room by Farquhar, managed to look in while the doctor ate his dinner; otherwise James Stanhope remained, out of sight in a corner, as others came and went.[1] Pitt was now slipping into the disorientation of the death-bed. He asked frequently for the direction of the wind, and on hearing it was in the east, said it would bring a messenger faster from Harrowby. Sometimes he cried hear! hear! to a debate in the Commons. He moaned a good deal. But in the night he fell quiet, and in the early hours of the morning a chill was detected in his head and feet. Suddenly, in a tone which James Stanhope would never forget, he called out 'Oh, my country! how I leave my country!' He did not speak again, and at half past four on the morning of 23 January he died.[2]

He was in his forty-seventh year – aged forty-six years and almost eight months – and had first taken his seat in the House of Commons twenty-five years before to the day.

1. The rest of this para. draws on his account as printed – with one exception below – in Stanhope, IV, 380–2.

2. The last words, as is well known, became the subject of debate. Stanhope in fact first published the sentence 'how I love my country' (IV, 382), and changed it to 'leave' (letter to *The Times* of 24 April 1862, announcing that it would so stand in future editions) after rereading the ms by James Stanhope – in a very bad hand – which he possessed (it is Stanhope Ms U1590 S5 C60/4). A perusal leads one to agree. 'Love' however continued to be given circulation. Rose (on Pursley's evidence; *Rose*, II, 233) recorded 'My country! oh, my country!' Canning, who thought such expressions unlike Pitt's 'simplicity of charac-ter', preferred, on Tomline's authority, the latter's ineffably typical 'I am sorry to leave the country in such a situation' (*Private Correspondence of Leveson Gower*, II, 169). Farquhar's memory, according to Lady Malmesbury who saw him a few days after Pitt's death, was 'Oh, what times! Oh, my country!' (*Malmesbury*, IV, 346). The doctor, Tomline, the Stanhope brothers and the servant had been in the room.

Some other renderings are diverting. Sydney Smith pronounced in the 1840s that Rose (who he seems to have assumed was there) 'made it out to be "Save my country, Heaven"', but 'the nurse' said that Pitt asked for barley-water (*The Letters of Sydney Smith*, ed. Nowell C. Smith, II (1953), 778). Disraeli preferred his own version, taken allegedly from an old doorkeeper at the House of Commons, 'I think I could eat one of Bellamy's pork pies'.

CHAPTER XXIII

The Legacy

I

The news of Pitt's death came for most people as a shock. Whatever his own suspicion in the final week, and the impressions of the few – or most of the few – who saw him after the return to Putney, the political world and public, while fed with rumour, was by and large stunned by the event. Those not abreast of the latest developments may well not have appreciated how things stood – Pitt's ill health and recoveries were familiar, and Charles Grey in the distant north, told of reports that the sick man would resign, could reply that he would 'not be surprised to see him making a speech of two hours on the first day of the Session'.[1] Even among those more in the know, hopes could survive to the end – Canning, who could not bring himself to despair, was unprepared and aghast.[2] The most prominent feeling when the moment came was a sudden recognition of a great gap: one that affected political opponents as well as friends. When the Speaker, announcing a motion in the Commons that a memorial be erected, 'came to the *name* . . . The silence was death-like, and several of the hardiest oppositionists said it was like an electrical shock upon the House, and that they could hardly breathe'. The Whig Duchess of Devonshire confessed, 'It is awful to the mind to reflect on a death of such magnitude, . . . of a man who had so long filled an immense space in the universe'; and Fox himself was reported as turning pale and finding 'something missing in the world – a chasm or blank that cannot be supplied'.[3]

Beyond the wide instantaneous reaction, responses of course varied. Some – the two elder Grenville brothers by one account – professed

1. Grey to Thomas Creevey, 13 January 1806 (*The Creevey Papers*, ed. Maxwell, I, 74).

There was a rather unattractive parallel at the start in Chatham; he thought his brother's trouble was 'mere weakness from Gout', and according to Tomline 'accosted him in a manner & tone as if he had been sitting in Downing Street!' (to Mrs Tomline, 15 January 1806; Pretyman Ms 435/26). For some background see II, 463 and pp. 666, 671 above.

2. Countess of Bessborough to Granville Leveson Gower, citing Charles Ellis, 23 January 1806 (*Correspondence of Leveson Gower*, II, 162).

3. *H of P*, III, 5; Duchess of Devonshire to Marquess of Hartington, 23 January 1806 (Earl of Bessborough, *Georgiana, Duchess of Devonshire* (1955), 276–7); *Correspondence of Leveson Gower*, II, 162–3.

indifference; old hostilities and grievances surfaced; cooler assessments – a dawning balance – began to be drawn up.[1] In general however there was consternation, above all at such a point, and this was often mixed with a personal grief perhaps surprising in its range. Many of the 'Noblemen and Gentlemen' at the funeral service were 'afflicted to shedding tears'; so, earlier, had been a steadfast if mild member of the Old Opposition.[2] The impact, on Parliamentarians and the public 'out of doors', was indeed a combination of the personal and the public. It was naturally felt with special depth by those who had special private memories – Wellesley for instance could not at once 'estimate the public misfortune . . . in the recollection of . . . private virtues'[3] – but the sense of deprivation was far spread, for Pitt's death had about it a heroic tragic quality. He had sacrificed his life to his country, 'as much', Rose wrote, 'as Lord Nelson did';[4] and the occasion was at least as poignant, for Nelson had fallen in the moment of victory while Pitt succumbed in apparent defeat. The note was caught in a lament which appeared after an interval.

> Now is the stately column broke
> The beacon-light is quench'd in smoke
> The trumpet's silver sound is still
> The warden silent on the hill.[5]

Among those who could claim intimacy, at their own levels, the grief was vivid, often intense. Past and present secretaries recalled, even years later, a nature which 'it was impossible to know, without loving'; Mulgrave, overcome at the funeral, spoke of the 'affection of a brother'; Canning 'could not cry or speak'.[6] Many letters passed between the inheritors of a common bereavement. Possibly the strongest evidence however came from some of those who, after long friendship, had more lately felt cause in varying degrees for resentment. Rose, deeply upset by signs of neglect when his master returned to office, mourned in 'agony of mind'

1. For Buckingham and Thomas Grenville see *Diary of Farington*, VII, ed. K. Cave (1982), 2697; for eg Windham p. 833 below; for eg Glenbervie, his letter to his son Frederick, 23 January 1806, in Bodleian Library English Letters Ms C552: 'Pitt's character will now be more justly appreciated – Many will abate in their rancours . . . Some in their admiration'.

2. *Diary of Farington*, VII, 2697 on the funeral, 2677 on the Earl of Essex (a Northite adherent to the Coalition with Fox).

3. Quoted in Reilly, *Pitt the Younger*, 347.

4. *Rose*, II, 234.

5. Walter Scott in *Marmion*; composed in 1806–7, published in 1808.

6. W.D. Adams to Earl Stanhope, 26 April 1861 (Stanhope Ms U1590 C405/15), and see his anguished letters to his brother-in-law Thomas Courtenay at the time, in Dacres Adams Mss, formerly P.R.O. 30/58/11. To Joseph Smith, 'in private and domestic life it was like living with an Angel' (biographical notice in Saumarez Smith Mss) – a word also used in after years, unsparingly, by Hester Stanhope. For Mulgrave see *GEC* IX, 394nb; for Canning, p. 830, n2 above, and to Leveson Gower, 29 January 1806 (P.R.O., 30/29/8).

an 'incalculable' loss. Sidmouth, with ample reason for complaint and despite his reservations, could write of an 'affection that has never been extinguished'. Grenville learned of his cousin's impending death with 'an agony of tears', repeated, in possible contrast to his brothers, when the news came.[1] Perhaps the hardest struck of all was Melville, whose almost paternal loyalty had survived the disagreements and latterly the shifting relationship of testing years. His affliction, Wellesley wrote, was not to be described; he could not speak for his tears on meeting Aberdeen – once the ward of Pitt and himself – on the morrow of hearing the news; Hester Stanhope recalled his 'eyebrows turned grey, and his changed face' several weeks later. Of course he had suffered a bad time in the past year and knew that his best shield was now removed; but his language bore unaffected witness to his state. 'I am certainly very miserable, and as there is not an hour of my life for these twenty four years past, that does not at this moment and for ever continue to bring his image to my Mind, I cannot summon up or suggest to myself any Recourse from which I can collect a Ray of consolation'. 'I must wait patiently', he went on, 'for that Species of Apathy which buries every thing past in one indiscriminate Oblivion'.[2] But that did not happen, with some of those most devoted to Pitt, for many years.

The funeral took place on 22 February, in Westminster Abbey. The Dean and Chapter prepared for the interment in what was becoming the family vault, and since in answer to an Address from the Commons to the King the ceremony was to be a 'public' one, much of its conduct passed to the Lord Chamberlain and the College of Arms.[3] The pattern repeated that followed for the Elder Pitt. The coffin lay in state for two days in the Painted Chamber of the House of Lords, where 'a vast concourse of people' viewed it at a rate of over a hundred ('110 to 120') every two minutes for six hours a day. When the time for the ceremony came, the surviving derivatives of feudal forms were observed. The penniless younger son went to his grave with a retinue based on that of a medieval lord. The procession which moved on foot on its short way to the west door of the Abbey included forty-seven poor men, for the years of his life, with his crest emblazoned on their arms, the Heralds, 'the Bearers of the Standard, the Guidon, the Banner . . ., the Great Banner, the Helm and Crest, the Sword and Target, the Surcoat, etc.'. The pall was preceded by his elder brother with the

---

1. *Rose*, II, 233; Ziegler, *Addington*, 248; Stanhope, IV, 375; *Diary of Farington*, VII, 2697 (cf. p. 830 above).

2. *The Wellesley Papers . . .*, ed. Lewis Melville, I (1914), 190; Lady Frances Balfour, *The Life of George, fourth Earl of Aberdeen*, I (1923), 42, 45; *Memoirs of the Lady Hester Stanhope*, II, 79; Melville to Huskisson, 28 January 1806 (B.L. Add. Ms 38759).

3. For what follows see *The London Gazette*, 11–15, 15–18 February 1806 and *The Times*, 24, 28 January, 3, 17, 20, 21, 22, 24 February 1806. The vault contained Pitt's father and mother and his favourite sister Harriot (for whom see I, 582); cf. p. 588, n1 above.

The Commons' address was moved by the backbencher Henry Lascelles (*P.D.*, VI (1812), cols. 41–2).

'assistant mourners', among them Wellesley and Grenville, and the train ended in a detachment of the Cinque Ports Volunteers. Music played, and the Foot Guards lined a route along which the crowd, like that which had passed through the Painted Chamber, was 'well ordered and quiet'.[1] In the service the music was much the same as that for Nelson's funeral in St Paul's six weeks before. At the close Pitt's 'Comptroller, Treasurer, and Steward of the Household' – figures from the present and the past in unfamiliar guise – broke their staves, which Garter King of Arms threw into the vault. In one notable respect the occasion differed from its model. 'The Court', Pitt had written as a young man at his father's funeral in 1778, 'did not honour us with their countenance, nor did they suffer the procession to be as magnificent as it ought'.[2] George III indeed had then accepted the Commons' Address with marked reluctance. Thirty-eight years on, three royal Dukes, with York 'much affected', were present.

The Address itself, moved in the House of Commons on 27 January, could hardly expect from its wording to pass *nem. con.* It repeated in all particulars the form agreed when Chatham had died. The obsequies were to be at the public charge; and a monument was to be placed in the Abbey, at an expense made good by the House, likewise 'to the memory of that excellent statesman, with an inscription expressive of the public sense of so great and irreparable a loss'. Some members of the Old Opposition at least were almost bound to demur. Fox himself, as he remarked afterwards, was in great difficulties. Genuinely affected as he had been by Pitt's death, he could not accept such phrases after all that had passed, and speaking, as Castlereagh acknowledged, 'by no means in the spirit of an adversary', he felt obliged to vote against. There were a few other adverse contributions, heralding the minority in the lobby, one of which however caused much surprise and some disquiet. For Windham could not forgive the rejection of his policy for France – of a concentration of support for a Bourbon restoration – by the Ministry in which he had long served, and his speech now culminated, from a stance very different from the Foxites', in a hostile vote. The motion passed, after quite a short debate, by 258 to 89.[3]

There was no such disagreement however when a further motion was brought a week later. On 3 February another backbencher, William Cartwright, proposed that Pitt's debts should be paid by the public, and in this case there was unanimity, Fox and Windham expressly concurring.[4] It

1. So Tomline (to Mrs Tomline, Saturday, endorsed 22 February 1806; Pretyman Ms 435/26). He observed a large crowd; *The Times* thought it only moderate.
2. I, 65n2.
3. *P.D.*, VI, cols. 41–72; *H of P*, IV, 377–8. Lascelles gave notice on the 24th, unexpectedly to Pitt's friends, and the decision to follow the precedent of Chatham was taken on Rose's suggestion. Fox commented on his difficulty afterwards to the Speaker, particularly since Grenville had hoped he would desist (*Colchester*, II, 31).
4. *P.D.*, VI, cols, 128–40. Cartwright seems to have stepped in when Wilberforce refused, to Rose's 'deep regret', to propose such a motion, which he thought would not meet with a good enough reception (Rose to Tomline, nd but endorsed 25 January 1806; copy of letter from Wilberforce enclosed (Pretyman Ms 435/26)).

gave both of them in fact the chance to acknowledge pleasure in doing so, and the House could feel that once more, and this time to the letter, it was following the course it had taken with Chatham. Meanwhile an annuity of £1,200 a year was granted to Hester Stanhope and one of £600 to each of her two surviving sisters, and the same for that matter to her two half-brothers.[1]

The debts indeed loomed as a problem, the more formidable from its unknown extent. One thing was certain: until they were met, they must extinguish the financial provisions of Pitt's will. He had put on record there that he owed a thousand guineas to Farquhar for professional services, and £12,000 plus interest since October 1801 to those who (in his recollection) had then subscribed to his support – Long, Steele, Carrington, Tomline, Camden and Joseph Smith. He wished his executors, 'if means can be found for it', to pay double wages to his servants at the time of his death. And – rather confusingly ascribed by Tomline to a separate clause in a 'copy' of the signed document – he hoped that pensions of £1,000 or £1,500 a year might be settled on Hester Stanhope and each of her two sisters and of £1,000 on each of their two half-brothers, if his public services were thought to have earned it.[2] But as he recognised, 'I owe more than I can leave behind me'; and the search began at once to establish the facts.

The Commons' vote allowed for a sum of £40,000 to be paid 'towards' the debts. The executors were virtually certain that a larger total would come to light;[3] but the promise of Parliamentary support at any rate relieved potential embarrassment and difficulty which might have arisen if the likely alternative of a public subscription had had to be tried.[4] More private awkwardness however obtruded at the start, with those concerned

---

1. For their detail see Stanhope, IV, 395.
2. The detail, not surprisingly in the circumstances, is not wholly clear. Stanhope (IV, 384–5) prints the will, of three clauses, but in addition gives the sum for the pensions to the three nieces as £1,000 or £1,200, which from Tomline's account in *The Monthly Review* for August 1903 and Rose's version of subsequent discussions (on p. 835 below), was incorrect. Tomline however should not have added the hope of the pensions as an unsigned fourth clause in a separate 'copy', since this was not proved in the will as submitted, and from Pitt's own words such a grant would obviously have to be placed in so far as might be possible on the public purse. The debt for Farquhar's services is phrased in the will as 'from October, 1805'; in current terms this seems a remarkably high sum for a period of at most four months – probably it included a debt already standing at that date.

Stanhope examined the document and the circumstances carefully (see his letter to William Tomline enclosing a facsimile taken at his request in April 1873; Pretyman Ms 435/45).
3. See Tomline to Mrs Tomline, nd but before 3 February 1806 (Pretyman Ms 435/27) and 30 January for the prospective inadequacy of the figure; before Pitt died, it looked as if he might have run up bills in the past year alone of at least £24,000 (same to same, 15 January 1806; Pretyman Ms 435/26).
4. On which Pitt's friends were divided; see eg Rose to Tomline, endorsed 25 January, *Rose*, II, 238; Tomline to Mrs Tomline, nd but endorsed 31 January 1806 (Pretyman Ms 435/26), and cf. p. 833, n4 above.

in the loan to the retiring Minister in 1801. His memory of the names had been inadequate on his deathbed – Rose, who should have been one of them and had done so much, was greatly upset at the omission of himself – and others as well, from a 'second batch' of contributors, had to be asked if they wished to be repaid from the estate, the provision on which Pitt had insisted at the time. In the end, only two of the latter group did so.[1] But the matter, coming on top of arrangements for the funeral, gave Tomline a lot of trouble; and he too, alone among the first group, in fact put in his own claim. Not unnaturally that caused some resentment, which was not removed by his argument that he had never asked for payment while acting as Pitt's secretary – one might indeed have thought that a Bishopric and Deanery would have sufficed – and that the Minister had insisted on his recoupment of the loan when the time came.[2] Nor did the arrangements and indeed the personalities combine effectively in a protracted business: Joe Smith, recruited to try to sort things out, had to report to executors who after a time did not work closely together or indeed get on together particularly well.[3] Their increasingly intermittent attention had to be applied over the next fifteen years. In July 1821 probate was at last obtained; in August, the twenty servants in Pitt's employment at his death – or the survivors – were paid from his will with interest; and in September Coutts's bank was able to close its books and Chatham and Tomline to clear their account.[4]

They ended, surprisingly, with a surplus of some £7,600, which was divided in thirds between Chatham and the daughter of Pitt's dead sister Harriot and (again divided equally) the two surviving daughters of his dead sister Hester.[5] Despite Tomline's fear that the grant of £40,000 would not suffice, the generosity of friends in declining for the most part to reimburse themselves for their loans, the grant itself, and sales of various assets, combined over a period to meet the demands. Some lists survive of

1. See pp. 536–7 and ns2, 3 above; and for Rose now, *Rose*, II, 232. The 'second batch' of contributors were probably nine in number.

2. Tomline to Mrs Tomline, 30 January (Pretyman Ms 435/27); Steele to Chatham, 27 June 1806 (Saumarez Smith Mss); Mrs Tomline's memorandum, nd but 1828 (Pretyman Ms 562:1828). The Bishop had indeed wished these loans to be included in the application to Parliament for a grant to cover the debts; according to Stanhope (IV, 394) he was dissuaded from such a course by all the others affected and above all by Wilberforce.

3. Scattered material in Pretyman and Saumarez Smith, from which I have drawn an impression.

4. Documents in Pretyman Mss 562:1820, 1821; Coutts's Bank ledger for 1821 (Coutts & Co. archives). Pitt's nieces received their portions in July 1822 (Ward to Chatham, 28 July 1822; Pretyman Ms 435/39).

5. Pretyman Mss 562:1821, 435/39; Coutts's ledger for the year. See I, 68 for Pitt's sisters, pp. 544–6 above for the nieces. Canning was under the mistaken impression that the King had agreed to provide for 'Lady Hester Stanhope and her Brothers' (to Leveson Gower, 29 January 1806; P.R.O. 30/29/8). For the technical arrangements in 1806–7 to meet Pitt's request in part – £1,200 as an annual pension to Hester, £600 to each of her sisters – see Stanhope, IV, 395.

the sales and valuations taken after Pitt's death. Wines from Downing Street and Walmer fetched some £2,633 – a sum to be compared with his only freehold property, the cottage at Walmer, estimated at £500. Furniture at Downing Street and Walmer was valued in all at some £4,943.[1] And beyond these there were 'trinkets' and silver, carriages and books, on both of which last items the Bishop cast an eye.[2] Given Pitt's life-long attitude to his private finances, it was a measure of his public impact that his executors were able in the end to make some modest bequests.

Another legacy, not stipulated in his will, was not directly financial or regarded as such. The bulk of Pitt's papers went to his brother Chatham. He in turn died without issue, and they were then divided between his two executors; one the husband of his niece through his sister Harriot, the other the eldest son of another niece, the youngest daughter – the spirited Lucy –[3] of his sister Hester. Both portions passed, separately in due course, to the Public Record Office.[4] But they were not in fact complete. Tomline had moved quickly in 1806 to gather up all the papers in Downing Street; but not quickly enough in the case of Walmer, for Pitt's secretary Adams, acting in compliance with advice from Hester Stanhope, to whom the Bishop 'was no favourite', removed all that he and James Stanhope found 'scattered' about the Castle, and the executors received only enough from there to put in a box. This group of documents, substantial and particularly important for the final years, surfaced only after the Second World War to be placed for some years in the Public Record Office, on deposit in this case and since reverting to family possession.[5]

Relations and friends naturally wanted memorabilia, and these remain, some in their first homes. Locks of his hair, fine and still brown with a suggestion of auburn, were distributed, and pieces of furniture, and silver and some personal objects – a mourning ring for Harriot, a watch, at least one desk, a port glass for example – are still preserved.[6] The most concerted demand however was for a likeness, and this could be met in a number of

1. Saumarez Smith Mss for the wines; Pretyman Mss 562:22, 562: 1 for the furniture at Downing Street and Walmer respectively and the Walmer cottage (for which see p. 541 above). The fruit trees on his rented land beyond the Castle's bounds (ibid) were also valued. The Bishop had expected a lower sum for furniture and wine (to Mrs Tomline, nd but in January (Pretyman Ms 435/27)).

2. Most of Pitt's library passed into the possession of Tomline's descendants. For the two carriages, a landau and landaulette, see Tomline to ?Mrs Tomline, nd but endorsed 25 February 1806; and indeed for the 'trinkets (such as they are)' same to same, 'Saturday' [22 February], both in Pretyman Ms 435/26.

3. See p. 546 above.

4. The series P.R.O. 30/8.

5. W.D. Adams to Earl Stanhope, 25 May 1861 (Stanhope Ms U1590 C405/15); Tomline to Mrs Tomline, nd but endorsed 25 February 1806 (Pretyman Ms 435/26). For the contents of the Dacres Adams Mss as the series P.R.O. 30/58 see the List and Index Society's volume 12 (1966) of Gifts and Deposits [to the Office], Part 3.

See also for the question of Pitt's papers, I, 667–8, where 'Downing Street' in line 2 of p. 668 should read 'Walmer'.

6. Cf. for Pitt's hair I, 105n3.

instances, for Hoppner's portrait had recently been completed but had not yet left his studio, and he was willing to make some copies. Mulgrave, who had commissioned the painting, gave individual permissions, and others – 'many others' according to his son – were taken later.[1] One other virtually contemporary representation was produced, in a marble bust by Nollekens modelled from the death-mask and the loan of Hoppner's picture. Interestingly, Hoppner himself acknowledged on seeing the cast that he had not done justice to the shape of Pitt's nose, which 'from the circumstance of the Nostrils being drawn down . . . had appeared to *turn up* at the end'. The mask however revealed 'a fine form'; one may still be seen at Chevening, which viewed in profile shows a distinct if less obtrusive likeness in bone structure to the Elder Pitt's striking beak.[2]

Posthumous creations then took over. Far the finest by common consent – often indeed thought the finest of all – was that by Lawrence, who had studied Pitt closely when invited to meet him by Abercorn in 1804.[3] A long series of busts and statues, engravings and medallions followed. The country houses of England were soon adorned with busts in particular, of either Pitt or Fox – occasionally of both. The public monuments began to rise: Nollekens in Cambridge, the statue by Westmacott over the west door of Westminster Abbey, the representation with allegorical figures and Canning's inscription in London's Guildhall, the large bronze statue by Chantry in Hanover Square, repeated in Edinburgh. But the most numerous representations, profiles in medals hung on the coat or as a collar, had a more active continuing purpose, for they were worn at the dinners dedicated to 'the immortal memory' in the Pitt Clubs that now spread over a generation through the land.

In almost all known instances, these had not existed during Pitt's life. An exception was the London club, which met on the King's and Queen's birthdays from 1793. In 1802, however, it emerged in more convivial form from the celebration inspired by Canning of the Minister's birthday, and as a dining society it has continued, one of three such survivors – the others being the Cambridge University and the Mid-Cheshire clubs.[4]

---

1. Marquess of Normanby to Stanhope, 2 May 1862 (Stanhope, 2nd edn., IV, 398, correcting 1st edn.). See for some of the copies, and for what follows, the Appendix by Sir George Scharf to Ashbourne, *Pitt*, 369–92, itself an abridgement of a catalogue in the Stanhopes' possession in 1886 of all known representations of Pitt from 1779 to 1862. Of the 162 items recorded, 96 were executed before 1807.

2. But cf. for a more general impression with the portrait of Pitt's mother in I, 16. For Nollekens's remark, relayed by the portraitist Owen, see *Diary of Farington*, VII, 2693.

3. Pp. 776–9 above. Of the two similar paintings he produced in 1808, one is on view at Windsor.

4. This paragraph relies on the privately printed *The Pitt Clubs, A short historical guide* (nd), by Mr J.B. Lewis, the archivist of the Mid-Cheshire club. See pp. 571–2 above for Canning and the celebrated occasion in 1802.

One other possible survivor is extant as the Holbeck Conservative Club in Leeds.

The toast of 'The Immortal Memory' was not confined to Pitt. The Fox Club drank to it after their hero died in 1807; and Nelson is remembered by the navy likewise to this day.

After the metropolitan foundation – itself two years after that of the Fox Club –[1] the earliest may have come in the provinces in the year of Pitt's death, and his birthday was toasted in Scotland – whether formally in a club or not – certainly by 1809. One of the annual dinners may have had a connexion with earlier Jacobite gatherings; some may have overlapped with those of True Blue Clubs.[2] But the movement seems really to have gathered pace in the second and third decades of the century – 53 Pitt Clubs in all have been traced from the start –, rallying points for a Toryism by then firmly linked with the name of a revered statesman who early in the 1790s had poured scorn on the term and never thought of himself as other than generically a Whig on 'the principles of liberty settled at the [Glorious] Revolution'.[3]

II

When it became clear that the Minister would not be able to attend the start of the new session, his colleagues thought how best to cope. That indeed was among the subjects of the tiring conversation with him which set the seal on his final collapse.[4] Whether or not to cheer his spirits, Hawkesbury and Castlereagh said that Government could survive an intended attack on the conduct of the war and that, as Pitt cheerfully phrased it, they could 'get on . . . three weeks without me very well'.[5] It was only towards the very end that the Cabinet had to face the near certainty of his death. The usual dinner in Downing Street had been fixed for 18 January, and he was specific that it should take place, as it did in a spirit of gloom. The next day a meeting of Ministers together with some Privy Councillors in office met at Castlereagh's to consider the terms of the King's Speech – to be as unexceptionable as possible in the hope of heading off trouble on the Address. On the 20th there was a second dinner at Number 10, when Castlereagh read the document to the guests.[6] On the 21st Parliament reassembled, two days before Pitt died.

The Cabinet had of course to consider what they would do if, or latterly when, Pitt died. Hawkesbury, the senior Secretary of State who was emerging as a locum tenens, was opposed to any formal discussion meanwhile. But he and Castlereagh, Chatham and Camden were privately in favour of some arrangement that would enable the Government to carry on with as little alteration of membership as possible. Mulgrave and Montrose on the other hand were thought to incline towards a Ministry headed by Grenville and Fox, which they would be prepared to support in the best interests of

1. II, 78.
2. Cf. p. 675 above.
3. II, 389; and for an earlier stage see I, 58.
4. Pp. 824–5 above.
5. Canning to Leveson Gower, 29 January 1806 (P.R.O. 30/29/8).
6. Stanhope, IV, 386–8.

the country.[1] The moment of decision came on the 24th, for on the previous day the King had sent for Hawkesbury and asked that Cabinet Ministers should give him their individual advice. By this time, when the shock of the event had taken hold, Hawkesbury himself did not believe that there would be 'any material difference of opinion'; and that was confirmed in a Minute which was submitted collectively, Harrowby still being en route from Berlin and Portland and Chatham absent but informed and concurring. They rejected the 'practicability' of continuing in office as they were, or of finding enough additional strength 'within reach'.[2] The King was therefore faced with the agitating prospect of looking at any rate in part elsewhere. He made a vigorous effort to retain at least a First Minister of his opening choice; so vigorous indeed that in a second conversation he seemed for a while to have induced Hawkesbury to take the post. In the upshot however he failed; Hawkesbury ended by counselling him to drop his veto on Fox, and left with the impression that this would be so, and the comforting personal prize of Pitt's Wardenship of the Cinque Ports. Portland too gave what came to similar advice, for an approach to 'some *at least*' of Opposition;[3] and on 27 January George III summoned Grenville and invited him to submit names for a Ministry 'without exclusion'. On 4 February, after a slight hiccup over intentions on army reforms – a matter as always close to the Hanoverian heart, and to the interests of the Duke of York – he approved the proposed Cabinet appointments.[4] By the time that Pitt was laid to rest in Westminster Abbey, Grenville was First Lord of the Treasury and Fox a Secretary of State.

So it had come to the 'case of absolute Necessity' which Pitt had mentioned in passing some four months before.[5] It seemed that it had taken his death to bring such a thing about. But while the King talked predictably of the late Cabinet's 'running away', there was no more mention of a civil war rather than Fox; he took the bitter medicine quite quietly when he saw no immediate alternative. Tired, and perhaps apprehensive of another of his terrifying attacks, he accepted a situation which Grenville and Fox himself for their part made as easy as they could. Once the deed was done, in fact, a cloud seemed to lift from his spirits.[6] The tale must go on; he was relieved by the opening signs of courtesy; and it remained to be seen how matters might turn out.

1. Gash, *Lord Liverpool*, 65.
2. Cabinet Minute, 24 January 1806 (*L.C.G. III*, IV, no. 3171 and ns 1, 2).
3. Gash, op. cit., 66; Portland to George III, 24 January 1806 (*L.C.G. III*, IV, no. 3172).
4. Op. cit., nos 3175 & n1, 3177 & n1, 3180n5; and see Jupp, *Lord Grenville*, 346–52. The King sent for Hawkesbury again for consultation at the beginning of February, after he had tried to probe Grenville on intentions for policy, particularly for the army. It was his final flicker of hope.
5. P. 804 above.
6. His daughter Princess Augusta's account, cited in John Brooke, *King George III*, 381. He was hardly in any case taken by surprise; Grenville was in his mind even on the day before Pitt died – and he must have appreciated that that could well mean the admittance of Fox (see Jupp, op. cit., 346).

How in particular might Pitt's colleagues and followers behave? Not all the late Ministers themselves were happy with the agreement to resign. Eldon would have hoped to fight on, relying on the current majority and above all the King's Friends to save the monarch the potential disturbance of having to accept his old foe. Canning and Spencer Perceval too, excluded from consultation as not belonging to the Cabinet, would have been prepared to test the temperature in the House. Such a prospect however did not look rosy. Perhaps if Pitt had lived and shown signs of recovery sufficiently marked for a return to his post, the Ministry might have survived a series of opening attacks; his biographer Stanhope – who was brought up in the world of politics and sampled them himself – thought that it would.[1] But even then, given the state of the parties concerned, one may wonder for how long;[2] and his largely demoralised colleagues would have stood little chance on their own. Once the choice was made, moreover, the removal of a focus left them uncertain where to look. To some the new scene was entirely open. Allegiance, as Canning put it, was buried in Pitt's grave; 'all bond of union', in Carrington's words, 'was dissolved; no obligation remained with anyone to abide with a party which had lost its leader, *and with its leader everything*'.[3] Others nonetheless were less precipitate. There was a common recognition that they must consult and try to act together: so thought Hawkesbury and Camden and Castlereagh, Mulgrave and Portland, Bathurst and Long, and Canning himself in his own way. As 'the Ministry of All the Talents' settled in, with the addition of Sidmouth and his legal ally Lord Ellenborough and the exclusion from Cabinet of 'Pitt's friends',[4] the latter made the best of their position for the time being by following the traditional line of conduct which Pitt himself had adopted increasingly in the uncertainties of 1802–4. They would support the new Ministers except

> upon any measure brought forward by them either in derogation from Mr Pitt's system, or in discredit of his memory, and upon any measure originating with them in itself really objectionable and felt to be so by the country and still more by the K[ing] to feel no difficulty in stating our opinions broadly and plainly, and (if the matter should be of moment enough) to take the sense of Parliament upon them.[5]

1. IV, 359–61.
2. Cf. pp. 764, 766–70, 802–5 above for the position.
3. See *L.C.G. III*, IV, xxix.
4. Charles Long, the Chief Secretary for Ireland, and Lord Charles Spencer, one of the Postmasters General, were however invited to join the Ministry, the former in his late post. He refused; Spencer accepted, becoming Master of the Mint.
Ellenborough's inclusion in Cabinet, in his existing office of Lord Chief Justice, drew much critical comment. It has proved indeed to be unique of its kind.
5. Canning to Lord Titchfield [his wife's brother-in-law, and Portland's heir], 20 [26?] April 1806 (Portland Ms PwH 414), quoted in Harvey, *Britain in the Early Nineteenth Century*, 181. Cf. pp. 575–6, 617 above – and also for Grenville in his own perplexities.

This left a good deal of scope to a connexion which soon saw itself in fact as the Opposition: Mr Pitt's Friends or the Pittites, as they soon came to be known. They remained indeed under that title over the next six years or so: through the Grenville Ministry, as it endured after Fox died in September 1806 until its dislodgment in the following March over the revived Roman Catholic question; returning to form the Cabinet and the material part of the Portland Ministry until September 1809, and of its Spencer Perceval successor until May 1812.[1] The collective title in point of fact suggested a more harmonious leadership than was really the case. Canning pursued an active early policy of opposition, with the declared aim of detaching Grenville from Fox; but while he had the broad support still of Portland and Camden and Bathurst, others, who did not like his pretensions, were also less in favour of the man who had stymied Pitt's own attempt at a broad-based Ministry in 1804. The party was thus in a state of tactical indecision, unable to suggest an alternative unless or until the monarch himself should give a sign; and its cohesion indeed was secured as much by its failure to dent the Talents' Parliamentary strength – which was destroyed in the end by their own hand – as by any positive achievement. Nor was the atmosphere unclouded given the prospect of a struggle for primacy in the event of success, as Canning made it clear that he would not serve under Hawkesbury or Castlereagh. It was in fact that fissure, masked by the elderly Portland's reincarnation as First Lord of the Treasury after a gap of twenty-four years, that erupted amid the military confusions – the early problems in the Peninsula, the farcical expedition to Walcheren – which led to the duel between Castlereagh and Canning and the Duke's own subsequent resignation. When the compromise Spencer Perceval faced the task of forming a Government in the autumn of 1809, the disarray was such that the Speaker thought 'it would break up, if not destroy, the remains of the Pitt party', and the new incumbent himself confessed that 'We are no longer the sole representatives of Mr Pitt. The magic of that name is in a great degree dissolved' and the main binding element was now 'the public sentiment and attachment to the King'.[2]

That was not a very comforting forecast for the continuing influence of a Minister of such exceptional renown. The personal legacy appeared to be crumbling in the heirs' own hands. The short-term outcome however proved misleading in many essentials as a guide. The disappearance of a dominant figure is almost bound to cause dissensions among the followers: rivalries tend to emerge, and diverging interpretations of the message. With some passage of time it is also apt to see an influence settle, and not always in the most obvious places, beyond the ranks of 'the representatives' themselves. Certainly however it was among the latter that the

1. In fact the only member of Portland's Cabinet who could scarcely claim the true title of Pittite was Leveson Gower, and he was introduced late in the day; for his balancing act from 1806 see *H of P*, III.

2. See for both quotations Harvey, op. cit., 263.

political future lay for a lengthy spell. The somewhat unexpected Perceval, as it happened, brought together a happier Ministry in which the Pittite element was once more prominent, but now more firmly controlled; and after his untimely assassination in 1812, it fell to Hawkesbury after all, as second Earl of Liverpool since 1808, to take up an authority which he managed to sustain, with unassuming skill, over some fifteen challenging years. It was indeed in that long period, when

> Nought's permanent among the human race,
> Except the Whigs *not* getting into place,[1]

that the last part of Pitt's life, the part beyond the grave, took its more enduring form.

The process thus began in years of continuing national pressures, which in the 1820s moved to a crisis on issues of fundamental change. Those decades saw bitter political controversy, and judgments and claims on Pitt himself were continually called in aid. They brought with them much distortion, indeed much caricature. The 'expedient' statesman[2] emotionally unmoved by religious sentiment was zealously portrayed as spiritually devout, and hailed further as a convinced opponent of Catholic Emancipation. The upholder of balance in the Constitution, whose attitude to the exercise of the royal prerogative was as watchful and indirectly reductive as it was supportive in the appropriate sphere, became the toast at dinners dedicated to his memory which both Castlereagh and Canning refused at times to attend.[3] The politician who had been viewed with reservations by such figures as Jenkinson throughout and Eldon near the beginning of the century acquired a party label he had never worn and would not have recognised. His sanction was blazoned on behalf of attitudes he would often have disliked by men to whom he would have given some nasty surprises; 'who clubbed him with them, and prided themselves on a travesty of his principles'.[4]

The reasons are not inexplicable. Such developments were produced readily enough by the current demands, to help meet current needs; and within a broader reading of Pitt's career as a whole they were given a particular impetus by the sequence of events, largely adventitious, precipitated by his own resignation in 1801 and yielding the Parliamentary uncertainties that followed – four Administrations in just over six years.

1. *Don Juan*, Canto the Eleventh, stanza LXXXII.
2. See p. 775 above.
3. See J.J. Sack, 'The Memory of Burke and the Memory of Pitt: English Conservatism Confronts Its Past' (*H.J.*, XXX, no. 3, particularly 630–9). As Croker wrote in 1830, 'I will only . . . sum up what I have to say to those Tory gentlemen who belong to what are called Pitt Clubs, that the two most formidable objects of their apprehensions, Parliamentary Reform and Catholic Emancipation, were the measures of Mr Pitt' (quoted in J.C.D. Clark, *English Society 1688–1832* . . . (1985), 359).
4. R.G. Thorne, in *H of P*, IV, 823.
See I, 635–43 for the quietly reductive aspect of the treatment of the prerogative.

The consequences contributed to the place assigned him posthumously in party history; an assessment completed in the first quarter of the nineteenth century and lodged in public consciousness since.[1] Nonetheless, important though that was, it represented one strand of a fuller inheritance. For over much the same period a different set of issues was providing matter of longer term significance for attitudes and approaches to the substance of business with which parties are formed to deal.

As in Pitt's last full decade in fact, the defence of an order against unrest was not the sole story. Liverpool himself was a not uncharacteristic 'improver' by nature and training, and while the Ministry contrived to postpone the constitutional changes, above all Catholic relief, which would clamour increasingly at the door, it was engaged on a range of financial, economic and administrative reforms. The conditions led it along paths pointing in directions which Pitt had not pursued.[2] His strict devotion to the Sinking Fund was relaxed by stages as part of a redirected financial policy – cautiously from its association with the great man's name – and the early stage of the bullionist controversy posed an opening challenge to the prolonged suspension of a convertible pound. Taxes and duties were reduced, whereas he had raised them in his later years. Moves were made towards a wider freedom of trade, in Europe and at the expense of the shipping interest in a neo-mercantilist colonial policy. Nonetheless his example was present, and consciously felt: by men who had scarcely worked under or even known him in office – by Vansittart and Frederick Robinson and Peel – as well as by the survivors who in their differing degrees maintained a personal link. Some debts were direct and strong: in the persistent wartime commitment to a Continental strategy, in the pattern of approach to peacemaking as the war approached its end. And if policies diverged on finance, they returned in point of fact to some of Pitt's early intentions and practice – in the insistence on cheap government, in the reductions of duties and a measured liberalisation of commerce – which he had had largely to forgo in his wartime decades. Even so, that last experience was still brought directly to bear. The Far East was still reserved from the broader easing of colonial protection; and indeed a freer system of trade, presented later as a palladium of international peace, was seen rather as an alternative to excessive cuts in the size of the armed forces by producing a higher revenue from a boost to consumption.[3] On the question of law and order itself in England, so starkly to the fore in the postwar years, there were echoes of his stance on repressive legislation: a cost to personal liberty was to be accepted, but one which would retain the core of constitutional liberties. Even in the affairs of Ireland, where gloom revived in London, the despondency reflected Pitt's own.

1. Cf. pp. 675–6 above.

2. Much can be learned in what follows here from the matured reflections of Norman Gash, in his *Lord Liverpool* of 1984 and several of the essays collected in *Pillars of Government* ... in 1986, particularly no. 3.

3. See Boyd Hilton, *Corn, Cash, Commerce* ... (1977), 233 and also ch. VI.

Such lines of inheritance can easily be drawn too sharply, and in any case precedents give way to patterns with time. But the transmission of 'Mr Pitt's system',[1] in so far as it was a factor of influence in the middle term, was arguably clearer and had a more significant impact in the great areas of governmental policy than in those of political controversy which had absorbed so much of his attention, not least in his last years. He had of course been virtually born to Parliamentary politics; coached in them as a child by his father, immersed from his youth, living them to the end. His treatment of them however was singular, as his father's had been; the very course of his involvement in the party manoeuvres after 1801 pointed an abiding sense of distance as applied to himself. He seems indeed to have stood always at an angle even to the question of the royal prerogative, central as that was to Parliamentary concerns and providing a frame for his Ministerial life. It was the part of the Constitution, he observed at the start, that would be the 'first' to 'perish', along with the authority of the House of Lords:[2] a comment which seemed more of a truism a hundred years later than when it was made. This was in fact an example of the 'patience' he was said to find so important in the contemplation of events.[3] It was also a glimpse of a rather different emphasis from that of most other prominent politicians, allowing him to pursue his own objects of concern within a body of current assumptions which he was content to accept and exploit.

For Pitt's view and treatment of politics were affected, in a degree exceptional in his day, by his relationship to the system as a vehicle for business. With whatever inconsistencies and diversions, he undertook his improvements and reforms for their own sakes, and in particular without immediate reference to the political position of the Crown. This was a perceptible shift of attitude from the earlier period of Economical Reform;[4] and, deployed over a lengthy and largely uninterrupted span, it made an unmistakable contribution to a development of far-reaching importance. It applied what one may genuinely call a more professional, dispassionate appreciation to problems of government whose range was still capable of being brought within an individual's grasp but which demanded such an approach increasingly over an era of accumulating change. Pitt helped enlarge the equipment which a Minister needed to bring to his work, and with qualities, as described in a famous eulogy, unusually apposite to an enlarging scale:

> a clear and comprehensive view of the most complicated subject in all its relations; . . . fairness of mind which disposes a man to follow out, and when overtaken to recognise the truth; magnanimity, which made

1. P. 840 above.
2. I, 136. The remark was made, on Wilberforce's authority, in 1783. Cf. pp. 491–2 above for the House of Lords.
3. I, 88 and n2.
4. Cf. op. cit., 66.

him ready to change his measures when he thought the good of his country required it, though he knew he should be charged with inconsistency on account of the change; willingness to give a fair hearing to all that could be urged against his own opinions . . . personal purity, disinterestedness, integrity

– in short a probity which remained an abiding standard. But it was also the unaccustomed weight that he placed on 'topics' traditionally considered 'of a low and vulgarising' nature for a statesman, 'almost incapable of an association . . . with wit and grace', that in the long run was of fundamental significance.[1] Systematic information and measurement were becoming recognisable tools of administration. He encouraged the development, and its practitioners, in a spirit that gave it a firmer lodgment. His habits of work could be spasmodic, as his attention was engaged or dropped: to the experts themselves he could seem something of an amateur on occasions – to an agriculturalist and statistician like Sir John Sinclair, or a Parliamentary technician like Charles Abbot, or a naval reformer like Middleton let alone the impatient – and fallible – St Vincent. But he was himself at least the equal to any one in financial management. He understood the language the experts spoke, and the circumstances in which the active economic forces of the country moved; as they in turn, with whatever sectional disagreements or more general disappointments, recognised that they had a knowledgeable Minister in Downing Street. His emphasis on the role and status of the Treasury sought to impose a sharper focus on the machinery of administration. He gave a modernising tone to the practice of government – unevenly and early in a protracted process – that was well suited to current needs, and in more developed form became a part of the mental furniture of political generations in which the Blue Book came to replace the pamphlet of his own youth.

This was a bequest that, with some of the policies themselves, was not confined to the initial Pittites. As Spencer Perceval admitted, they were soon not their model's 'sole representatives', and a broader recognition of his aims and concepts could be acknowledged across old divisions when at last, in 1822, 'the Grenville part of Mr Pitt's original connection' was 'reunited' with Liverpool's Ministry.[2] The prominence accorded to his name in a compound of influences descending from a complex period – the range and frequency of the appeals – stemmed not least from the decisive significance of the period itself. For in the longer retrospect Pitt was fortunate – and earned his fortune – in his time. His life spanned years that saw foundations laid for the transformation of Britain from a leading European Power to one of global primacy, introducing the century of its

1. Both quotations, in their dissimilar directions, from Wilberforce (*Life*, III, 249–50; *Private Papers*, 79). He instanced the subject of excise duties specifically as being typically vulgar. Cf. I, 280.

2. Liverpool's wording (Gash, *Lord Liverpool*, 182); for Perceval see p. 841 above.

greatest domestic wealth and highest international stature. His own primacy at a critical and formative stage gave him a symbolic place, as the pilot who weathered the storm and also the source from whom so many strands of development flowed. A watershed was found to lie, to later view, on the farther side of which stretched the different world of the eighteenth century; and so much of the change, in specifics and outlook, might from such a view be traceable to him. That was of general application in a lengthening perspective. And within the conception of party itself a line of continuity was drawn, running through the post-war battles of Tory and Whig and the parcel of 'liberal–conservative' developments in a period when those last designations were still unknown in organised form, down to the reaches of Peel's more fully fledged Conservatism and indeed the mixed Peelite Ministry of Pitt's own ward Aberdeen. Legacies were still being claimed, from diverse or conflicting sources. Meanwhile the man himself was passing into history, to use a favoured term of the age – into the hands of its interpreters, the historians.

That debate continues, and doubtless will for so long as interest survives. As happens with pre-eminent figures, the controversy in Pitt's own lifetime set patterns from which subsequent judgments took their forms. The disagreements have been deep, and followed varied paths: from veneration of 'the greatest Statesman this, or any other Country ever produced' to dismissal of the 'eloquent Blunderer' or condemnation of 'the great fiend'.[1] He was 'as good, and as honest as a public man could be': he was the 'patron' of 'hypocrisy, folly, fraud and anything else which contributed to his power'.[2] For, it was claimed on either side, there was an exceptionally strong personal element which gave shape and meaning to his career. We have seen some of the verdicts proclaiming its virtues. The most hostile of all versions was articulated from the start by Fox.

For to Fox a basic flaw lay at the root of Pitt's nature. The love of office would always decide in the end. Whatever his rival's abilities – indeed the more significantly because of them, for Fox was more perceptive here than many Foxites[3] – he was the great persistent traitor of his time. 'If Mr Pitt could be persuaded (but I despair of it)', he had written even before the young man took the highest post, 'I am convinced if he could, he would do more real service to the country than any man ever did'.[4] The betrayal, as he saw it, of December 1783 confirmed his worst suspicions,

---

1. The confident praise came from the country gentleman Sir John Legard, one of Wilberforce's constituents, to Wilberforce; rebuking him in point of fact for his possibly decisive intervention, so distressing to Pitt himself, in the debate on Melville in April 1805 (for which see p. 758 above); quoted in Furneaux, *Wilberforce*, 235. For Sydney Smith's opinion in 1806 see pp. 847–8 below; for Creevey's in 1803 p. 605 above.

2. Legard and Sydney Smith again as examples.

3. See II, 41; p. 39 above.

4. A comment of September 1783 (I, 134).

and from then on he judged every development in the same light. Given that premiss, a dossier could certainly be compiled. Pitt, it could run, had seized the reins by a brazen exercise of unprincipled opportunism, which his actions thereafter under any form of pressure did nothing to redeem. He deserted the Dissenters, who had counted on him, and his own cause of Parliamentary reform as soon as he saw them losing credit even before the French Revolution aroused real alarm. He talked of resigning under the reverse of Ochakov, but nothing came of that. He failed at a final stage to avert a war with France which he professed he did not want. He abandoned the liberal sympathies, for which he had been well known, as early as 1792 under unnecessary alarmist influences of which he made full use. He dropped his support for the abolition of the slave trade, at first discreetly, finally altogether. When he did resign in 1801 it was not for the reason he gave, which in any case he very soon promised secretly he would not raise again while the King lived. His conduct in 1804, in January and in May, was explicable only on the same old basis: it even disgusted Grenville, that hitherto most unlikely opponent. And the explanation was obvious: Pitt was content to surround himself with mediocrities, and as always gratify his ambition, by focusing his hopes once more on that reservoir of power 'the Court! the Court!'[1]

This was a monocular vision, in which all evidence was pointed one way – and neglected great areas of government which did not interest its author. The suspicion was never far below the surface even at the rare moments when it looked as if Fox and Pitt might end by joining forces. It was held with a force that did not lessen as it was transmitted for at least a century – the historian G.M. Trevelyan for instance was brought up in a tradition he proudly acknowledged as flowing uninterruptedly from the source.[2] It was a starkly alternative view, emotionally as well as intellectually, and while it would be absurd as a full critique it concentrated on a side to the subject – for instance blunting the sharp distinction between Pitt in peace and in war – which the stream of adulation left largely out of account.

That distinction however was itself advanced at and near the time, on both sides of the argument: by Pitt's advocates as sufficient explanation of his change of course, by his detractors as augmenting Fox's reading. For what good, the latter could hold, did the Minister's ambition do him? It ended by leading him into an impasse that lowered his reputation, politically in the last stage and meanwhile as a figure for whom victory was beyond his grasp. Rhetoric and reality diverged progressively as the persuasive speeches were followed by a British reverse or an Allied collapse.

> . . . he was one of the most luminous eloquent blunderers with which any people was ever afflicted . . . At the close of every brilliant display an expedition failed or a Kingdom fell, and by the time that his Style

1. See p. 645 above.
2. See eg Mary Moorman, *George Macaulay Trevelyan, A Memoir* (1980), 123.

had gained the summit of perfection Europe was degraded to the lowest abyss of Misery.[1]

Such a verdict achieved its most influential and enduring form, in typically trenchant language and as a product of a 'more recent and scientific school', by Macaulay's celebrated essay of 1859.[2]

All these judgments, contemporary or retrospective, laudatory or otherwise, took for granted the importance of Pitt's personal impact on events. In more recent and scientific schools again, this has not necessarily been the case. The perspective itself in point of fact is once more not entirely new. Coleridge in 1800 pondered the relationship between Pitt's individual contribution and 'the accident of his fortune, the circumstances that enabled such a mind' – which Coleridge did not rate highly – 'to acquire and retain such a power'.[3] He wrote while faced by the living presence of authority, and how to account for it: historians in this century have been approaching the question from developing insights into the circumstances themselves, placing prominent personages more firmly within the complex structures and movements of their times. The light has shifted accordingly to a large extent from the statesman alone on his plinth; and in such a context some have seen Pitt as a figure of reduced interest. They have not rated his talents so highly, and, partly in consequence, have found his achievements of secondary note on an historical scale. A commanding Parliamentarian, a renowned Chancellor of the Exchequer; but had he sufficient abilities, and success, beyond that? He did not originate or then carry through any measure of lasting significance lying beyond the strict confines of Governmental responsibility. In that last sphere itself he showed his limitations in great issues of extensive consequence: his prescription for British rule, as it became, in India was an instant political compromise, in the case of Ireland he failed to provide the necessary commercial relationship and settled for Union without achieving Catholic Parliamentary relief. In war he pursued an ambitious strategy without a proper understanding of the means; and his ideas for peace, drawing in essence on past concepts, were imprecise in crucial respects – on the future of the Low Countries and the small states of Germany – when brought up to date. The larger policies themselves owed much in practice to colleagues and advisers, between whose choices he was apt to hesitate. Did he in short do much more than respond to events and pressures, or to trends of thought already in motion whose

---

1. Sydney Smith on 30 January 1806 (*Letters of Sydney Smith*, I, 112).

2. The effect is visible, in the 'severe division' of Pitt's career into two parts, and a forceful contrast for good measure between him and his father (cf. the quotation from Macaulay's essay in II, 537), in Rosebery's *Pitt* (see 279, 284–5), written some thirty years later and itself carrying an influence beyond the turn of the century.

3. 'The Character of Mr. Pitt', in *The Morning Post*, 19 March 1800. This, he concluded characteristically, 'would form a subject of a philosophical history, and that too of no scanty size'.

aims he appreciated but to which his managerial contribution was too often acutely aware of the odds? The impression was unmistakably imposing; but in reality he was carried largely by his 'fortune'. When all was said and done he was not an inherently creative force, of the type or dimensions – as some contemporaries indeed had proclaimed – of Napoleon.

There was, it might be said, a distinct asymmetry in such a contrast. Napoleon for his part did not command his circumstances as freely as the assertion implied. But in any case the comparison would not have been one to trouble Pitt. It would in fact have seemed to him wholly irrelevant. For his conception of his task, his own historical view, was entirely otherwise. He had the enviable fortune to work within a Constitution which in essence was a model of its kind – 'sufficient' indeed, he had been taught from childhood, 'to pervade the whole World'.[1] His aim was to bring it, by accepted methods, into line with requirements and aspirations, which meant practical improvement and reform where required and defence when necessary against a basic threat. Revolution in such a context was the enemy of true advance; sweeping dictatorial visions in France were founded on destruction; there was no need here for new constitutions, and every reason to prevent violent change. Attempting to wipe the slate clean, in this country, would indeed not only cause demolition and disruption; it might also, he seems to have held, prove pointless in the end. When he talked in his later years of Tom Paine, with surprising mildness according to one – unfortunately questionable – source, and set his face against 'a bloody revolution', he was said to have added 'and, after all, matters would return pretty much as they were'.[2] There was a form of wisdom in this, of a different order from the prevalent reaction of mere fright and repression; though he certainly had his frights. There was also a reminder, through all his experiences, of a confidence strengthened by a restricted imagination. 'Never fear . . . depend on it we shall go on as we are . . .'. His vision, capacious in its own territory, was set here at the other end of the spectrum from that of Burke, to whom these earlier words were spoken.[3] It was rooted in the tradition he knew and whose modes of operation governed his assumptions. Parliamentary majorities, not imperial decrees, were the prime instrument to his ends. It was through those more circumscribed means in a system whose structure he respected that he looked for more firmly founded attainable measures of success.

The questions accordingly return to a less messianic level. It must be the hope of these volumes to have supplied evidence which the reader can balance in the scales.[4] Much of it does not point towards specific successes

1. Shelburne's expression, as a disciple of Chatham; see I, 99.
2. The source is Hester Stanhope; see II, 80 and n4. Her memories would have been drawn at their earliest from the later 1790s, and very likely after 1800; but while she was unlikely to have misunderstood what she heard, her emphasis was of course always at the mercy of a congenital exaggeration.
3. I, 188.
4. Cf. op. cit., xiv.

or failures in categorical terms: those concepts have to be defined within a web of contingent issues. The pursuit of one object may demand compromise with another, perhaps at the expense of a third; the aims may be discrete, but they remain linked by the needs of attainment, and the goods achieved are thereby likely to be partial.[1] Pitt brought high aims, public and personal, to the practice of government, and qualities that were not commonplace. And these formed prime ingredients in a process hinging on temperament and will. For if full weight is given to his circumstances in order to explain him, it remains the case that they should not be allowed to explain him away.[2]

This applies in both public and private terms. Pitt's *course* – his policies – lay firmly in his country's inheritance: one that he helped readjust after the disturbance, political and material, of the American War, advanced and sought to guard under pressure, and was seen increasingly to embody on a world scale. So aimed and directed, his *instincts* were genuinely creative. At the same time, if often less visibly, his endeavours were served by a singular nature. For except to those standing confidently at the extremes of praise or blame, the essence of his personality has proved hard to isolate; and perhaps, after all, that is not the right approach. He has been said to take his place in the public recognition as 'a statue rather than a man':[3] the great orator, the senatorial statesman, an imposing monument. In so far as this may be so, he could well have approved of the impression – have thought it indeed highly fitting, taken from the classical figures he knew so well – and indeed it contained much that was real. He looked on himself, one might say, as the living representative of his work, and there was a weight and gravitas about him from the start which the years of office confirmed. Nevertheless such a picture would be far from complete: it would not in itself convey the personality through which the end was reached; the fuller sensibility of the man as he was. Such a picture suggests for instance a well regulated, impersonal statesman, of steady temperament and calm preparation. But Pitt was not like that. On the contrary he was highly mercurial, intensely buoyed up or intensely cast down: seizing on a piece of business, often belatedly, and confidently divining a way through the obstacles, as suddenly perhaps losing interest, delaying or turning to something else. The 'Eager Mr William' of his childhood and youth was never entirely transformed by the years. '*I cannot allow myself to doubt*'; 'I am half mad with a project which will give our supplies the effect almost of magic in the reduction of debt'; he 'contended that the Service in Flanders would not interfere with any of His other Plans & talked eagerly about them'; in matters of peace or war he was 'always in a garret or a cellar'.[4] He had an instinctive tendency, which he

1. A paraphrase of Richard Pares in 'Human Nature in Politics' (*A Historian's Business and Other Essays* (1961), 37).
2. See I, xii.
3. Pares, 'The Younger Pitt' (op. cit., 124).
4. I, 5, 215, 261; II, 268; p. 561, n1 above.

never lost, to feel that once a measured conclusion was reached it would argue for itself; in the way that he could argue it successfully so often in debate. He could invest a great deal of emotional capital in a case, particularly one where he had reconciled the arguments and was intellectually satisfied. When opposition or circumstances spoiled the pattern, his enthusiasm and attention could wane sometimes as much from that loss as from the strength of the circumstances themselves.

Pitt's creative instincts in fact had to be brought to a point in a sphere where creativity has meaning only in relation to external pressures and demands. The arena indeed is an intractable one for the exercise, requiring the incessant persuasion and manipulation of others, individually and in their collective interests and institutions. The setting is arduous above all for a First or Prime Minister, whose preoccupations and ambitions must be widely spread. They cannot be devoted to a single cause and rest on a single achievement: survival in Downing Street on that basis would not be prolonged.[1] Pitt had no intention of exposing himself to such a fate; and he was well equipped. He had his share of the toughness, the exploitative skills, the lack of remorse in dismissing a setback, the preserving sense of caution, which public life exacts at its higher levels. He was also able to find genuine means of relief from tension: the ability to 'throw off all' his 'Load' in private,[2] in simple pleasures where complexities did not intrude, and the equally revealing capacity for unbroken sleep. But tension of course could not be removed, and he needed resources to face as well as to avoid it. Drink played its part, though the scale of consumption and the effects lost nothing in the telling;[3] and so did the image he built to impose on others and on himself. In its degree this last was partly an artefact: the defence of a penniless young man projected astonishingly into a central role on a crowded stage, and of an awkward, reserved personality – 'the shyest man alive'[4] – in a world with which in some ways he never felt at ease. He needed to be bold and assertive, and he claimed his position as of right. Nonetheless his answers were not simply dictated, though they were conditioned, by the pressures: one can hardly live indeed with a wholly unreal personality for so long a time. They took their form in fact from a picture that he found perfectly real. He had for many years a virtually complete, and to the end a high confidence in his powers; they might prove fallible against an absolute standard, but he did not underrate them as compared with the norm. Pitt behaved as he did in public not only for protection but also because that was how he saw himself: an entirely natural leader, from his own point of vantage and in his own distinctive way. The picture served him well, alike when things were going well and when they were not. It was a source of confidence

---

1. Cf. I, 322.
2. Op. cit., 589.
3. See op. cit., 585–6; II, 461; pp. 548–9 above.
4. His own words (Furneaux, op. cit., 13).

and a spur in the days of early acclaim, and also in the middle and later years when the country was faced by alarming challenges calling for a reassuring presence: for a sense of resilient and experienced pilotage through the storm. In that lengthy trial it sustained his native toughness and his willpower: like his father, he gave heart to those who served him, and to much of the nation at large. These were natural strengths of character; but they needed, as they displayed, an inspiration. The image was the ultimate support in easing the tensions of which it was itself a part.

For throughout his life in politics and government Pitt cherished an inviolate ideal; something that could animate him through the daily round. He was a hard-headed if volatile practitioner, skilled in manoeuvre and resource; there was nothing high-flown in his attitudes to the business before him; his eloquence suited, while it might elevate, the matter of fact tastes of the House of Commons. It was his expectations that were extravagant; of his position and himself. He sought and claimed power. Equally he pursued and claimed personal virtue. And the two were not separated in his own mind. Both were declared unequivocally, in action and in speech. He had been in Parliament barely a year when he announced that 'he never would accept of a subordinate situation', outside the Cabinet; some twenty years later, when out of office and offered a post in Addington's Ministry, he remarked that he really had not bothered to ask what it might be.[1] Similarly his early refusal of a sinecure that fell within his gift, and could have eased his finances, was a public avowal of how he saw his role; 'the act of a man, who feels that he stands upon a high eminence, in the eyes of that country, which he is destined to govern'.[2] He proclaimed his identification with 'the noblest and most disinterested modes of serving the public';[3] and his repeated treatment of unbecoming conduct, in applications for places or in the places themselves, underlined the demands he made of himself over the years. 'Pure' was a word constantly attached to his own conduct and person – in curiosity or often derision when it came to matters of sex; and his friends were always conscious indeed of something unworldly that gave even his young supporters a protective regard.[4] It shone out to the end in his persistent refusal to enrich himself; and politically it was not a mere sham, a label adopted only for public consumption. The 'romantic' pledge of support to Addington, apparently under any circumstances, the pursuit of 'character' that ensued,[5] the struggles of conscience and ambition, may serve to illustrate his claim.

High pretensions give a hostage to fortune, and in Pitt's case they had their underside. Threats to his status or reflections on it drew an immediate vigorous reaction. If he considered differing arguments carefully, and

1. I, 80; p. 584 above.
2. I, 152.
3. See Stanhope, I, 100; and 101 & n5.
4. Eg p. 96 above.
5. Pp. 564–5 above.

could be swayed by his associates, sometimes unduly, in making up his mind, he did not take a personal challenge lightly, as his colleagues found. Nor did he look kindly on 'any little rub'; and he could go to an extreme in public defence of a position he had taken up.[1] Of greater consequence, his intense feeling for his personal purity could lead to a contradiction when it encountered the demands of an impure world. There was a great deal that he would and believed he must accept; well rooted practices which he expected to be whittled away in time. But the external conditions, again, were not the sole force at work. 'If he could not satisfy himself, he was content to satisfy others';[2] in the haphazard creation of peers for instance, where he did not feel his attention centrally engaged. Operating amid an unusual amalgam of pressures and impulses from without and within, no one could be sure how he would respond.

For Pitt's nature, obviously, was unusual. As with some other occupants of the political pantheon – that small number whose enduring names are recognised as somehow to be distinguished from the rest – it cannot be described as well adjusted on ordinary lines. His performance in his long peak may have been rounded;[3] his personality was not. Its facets were assorted rather than visibly complementary: they did not fit neatly into a pattern which explained them all. It would be rash to trace too confidently the psychological springs, in a man long dead and, one would think, not susceptible of easy analysis. Something can be ascribed to heredity – the infusion perhaps of Grenville practicality and staying power into the Pitt strain of brilliance and extravagance; something again to upbringing – the exposure of a precocious boy to Chatham's demands on the world.[4] Beyond that we are in unknown and probably unknowable territory amid surmises: among them the predictable suggestions of a fundamental sense of inadequacy, showing itself alike in an overcompensating pride and a retention of innocence induced by envy of his father and/or a homosexuality practised or repressed, or a virtual absence of sexual drive. This is a search, sensitive always, that can carry particular risk when possible clues cannot perforce be closely followed up. Less hazardous, and perhaps less misleading, to stand on mappable ground from which to trace a mix of disparate elements, some contrasting, under conditions of rising stress.

Such signs can point towards breakdown, and Pitt came near to it at one point. He was saved from Chatham's fate by a less fissile temperament and an innate hopefulness and resolve. And those qualities could find a focus in an object to which his whole nature could subscribe, one that could contain if it could not reconcile the diverse competing strands. There was indeed no other to be shared: he had no feeling for revealed

1. Pp. 456, 562 above.
2. See I, 322.
3. Pp. 455–6 above.
4. Cf. I, 3–9.

religion, and no family of his own. His energies and ambitions were subsumed in a fierce love of country which was no mere abstract concept; a fact starkly visible by the end, and stamped on the nation's memory in return. When his last words were reported, Canning thought them so unlike his normal plain manner that they were not to be believed.[1] But they were recorded by a good witness, startled at the sudden strength of an exhausted voice. In their very passion indeed they welled up from the depths of Pitt's being. At the nadir of his fortunes he found his apotheosis in the moment of release.

1. P. 829, n2 above.

Notes on Sources

For Volume III and Volume IV

The researches of Stanhope and then Holland Rose (see Abbreviations) set a framework for all later studies of Pitt. Even where not mentioned specifically in these Notes, it is axiomatic that their works should be consulted. One recent compilation may also be cited here: A.D. Harvey's *William Pitt The Younger 1759–1806 A Bibliography* (1989).

CHAPTER I

The French landing in Wales, which precipitated the financial crisis of February 1797, is the subject of E.H. Stuart Jones, *The Last Invasion of England* (1950), and David Salmon, 'The French Invasion of Pembrokeshire in 1797' (*West Wales Historical Records*, 14). Edouard Desbrière, *Projets et Tentatives de Debarquement aux Iles Britanniques, 1793–1805* (4 vols., 1900–2) remains a classic. For the Bank of England see Sir John Clapham, *The Bank of England, A History 1694–1914* (2 vols., 1944), W.M. Acres, *The Bank of England from Within, 1694–1900*, I (1931), I.P.H. Duffy, 'The discount policy of the Bank of England during the suspension of cash payments, 1797–1821' in *Ec.H.R.* (see Abbreviations), *2nd ser.*, XXXV, no. 1; for provincial banking, L.S. Pressnell, *Country Banking in the Industrial Revolution* (1956). N.J. Silberling, 'British Financial Experience, 1790–1830' (*Review of Economics and Statistics*, I), E. Victor Morgan, *The Theory and Practice of Central Banking 1797–1913* (1943), Frank Whitson Fetter, *Development of British Monetary Orthodoxy, 1797–1875* (1965), and the first two chapters, by J.K. Horsefield, in *Papers in English Monetary History*, ed. T.S. Ashton and R.S. Sayers (1953), provide general surveys. A.E. Feaveryear treats of *The Pound Sterling, A History of English Money* (2nd edn., 1963), and Peter Mathias discusses copper coin in ch. 10 of his *The Transformation of England, Essays in the Economic and Social History of England in the Eighteenth Century* (1979). Sir John Craig is the historian of *The Mint, A History of the London Mint from A.D. 287 to 1948* (1953). P.K. O'Brien, 'Government Revenue 1793–1815, A Study in Fiscal and Financial Policy in the Wars against France' (D.Phil. thesis, University of Oxford, 1967) is of fundamental importance in its comprehensive treatment. A further notable unpublished study is Richard A. Cooper, 'British Government Finance, 1793–1807' (Ph.D. thesis, University of North Carolina, 1976).

Two significant contemporary publications on the crisis are Francis Baring's *Observations on the Establishment of the Bank of England* (1797), and Henry Thornton's *An Enquiry into the Nature and Effects of the Paper Credit of Great Britain* (1802) which was edited in 1939 by F.A. von Hayck. The reports of the Committee of Secrecy of the Lords and Commons contain the main elements of Pitt's correspondence and meetings with the Bank of England and his evidence before the Committee itself; they may be found in *H.L.J.* (see Abbreviations), XLI, pp. 186–262 (and in *P.H.* (Abbreviations), XXXIII (1818), cols. 294–324), and *Reports from Committees of the House of Commons*, XI (1803). These last, XII–XIII (1803) contain the report of the Commons' Select Committee on Finance of 1797.

Pitt's papers hold scattered material. P.R.O. (see Abbreviations) 30/8/101, 276 include some of his correspondence with the Bank of England; 107, a letter from Charles Abbot as chairman of the Commons' Finance Committee; 110, 115, 178 proposals from Auckland, Walter Boyd, Sir John Sinclair respectively; 152, letters from Lord Liverpool; 183, one from Samuel Thornton; 196, ff. 209–12v, Pitt's own notes on causes of the crisis, and ff. 237–40v on the current situation in Ireland; 197, f. 189v, some on copper coin; 276, ff. 129–37, notes in another hand relating to his evidence before the Commons' Committee of Secrecy; 326, letters from Camden in Ireland which include much on its finances. Liverpool's papers on coin and the Mint are principally in B.L. (see Abbreviations) Add. Ms 38423, and there are a few on the crisis in 38354. B.L. Loan Ms 72, vols. 54, 55 contain correspondence on coin from his son Hawkesbury. The Dacres Adams Mss for 1797, formerly P.R.O. 30/58/2, include one letter from him to Pitt. For guidance to the proceedings of the Privy Council's Committee on Coin see M.S. Giuseppi's *Guide to the Contents of the Public Record Office* (revised edn. 1963), II, and the List & Index Society's vol. 35.

There are two good accounts of the main naval mutinies, from rather different points of view, in Conrad Gill, *The Naval Mutinies of 1797* (1913), and G.E. Manwaring and B. Dobrée, *The Floating Republic* (1935). Both contain some primary material in appendices. They may be supplemented by James Dugan, *The Great Mutiny* (1966). Selections from Spencer's papers are published in *Private Papers of George, Second Earl Spencer, First Lord of the Admiralty 1794–1801*, II, ed. Julian S. Corbett (1914). For the background of naval life see above all N.A.M. Rodgers's *The Wooden Walls, An Anatomy of the Georgian Navy* (1986). The position in the army is discussed in the Hon. J.W. Fortescue's *A History of the British Army*, IV-Part II (1906), and Alfred H. Burne, *The Noble Duke of York, The Military Life of Frederick Duke of York and Albany* (1949). Roger Wells, *Insurrection, The British Experience 1795–1803* (1983) argues the political dimension, and Marianne Elliott, *Partners in Revolution, The United Irishmen and France* (1982) the Irish.

The Windham Papers . . ., II, ed. Lewis Melville (1913) and *The Diary of the Rt. Hon. William Windham*, ed. Mrs Henry Baring (1866), *H.M.C.* (Abbreviations), *Dropmore*, III for William Grenville, *The Life of William Wilberforce, by his Sons Robert Isaac Wilberforce . . . and Samuel Wilberforce*, II (1838), *Correspondence of Charles, First Marquis Cornwallis*, ed. Charles Ross, II (1859), *L.C.G. III* (see Abbreviations), II (1963), give scattered published indications of reactions from Ministers and others less fully engaged than Spencer. Among ms sources for those most centrally concerned, Pitt's papers are patchy for the mutinies: P.R.O. 30/8/102, 146, 173, 259 have items from Bridport, Howe, and George Rose, and the Dacres Adams Mss formerly P.R.O. 30/8/2, from Bridport and from Spencer. Spencer's own papers in B.L. temporary Althorp Ms G197 add something to the published *Private Papers* above. For Dundas, the Melville Castle papers in S.R.O. (see Abbreviations), GD 51/2 are relevant. B.L. Add. Mss 37844–6 give glimpses of Windham's alarm.

Parliamentary debates for the year are published in *P.R.* (see Abbreviations), *3rd ser.*, I–IV (1797–8), *The Senator*, XVII–XIX (nd), *P.H.*, XXXII–III (1818).

CHAPTER II

Politics in the first half of 1797 attracted much comment scattered through private diaries and correspondence and in the London newspapers, particularly *The Morning Chronicle* and *The Morning Post* in opposition and *The True Briton* and *The Times* (the latter rather uncertainly) in support, not least for the petitioning movement and for Cabinet and other Ministerial meetings. *H of P* (see Abbreviations), I–V are indispensable. The episode of the 'armed neutrality' is examined by Arthur Aspinall in *L.C.G. III*, II, xxi–xxix, and see also his edition of *The Correspondence of George Prince of Wales 1770–1812*, III (1965). Sinclair's role is discussed in Rosalind Mitchison, *Agricultural Sir John, The Life of Sir John Sinclair of Ulbster 1754–1825* (1962). Albert Goodwin, *The Friends of Liberty: The English Democratic Movement in the age of the French Revolution* (1979), J.E. Cookson, *The Friends of Peace, Anti-War Liberalism in England 1793–1815* (1982) examine the background of the uneasiness that produced the wave of petitions. See Note on Sources to Ch. I above for the Parliamentary debates. Pitt's papers, in P.R.O. 30/8, P.R.O. 30/70, and the Dacres Adams Mss, are rather disappointing, though 30/8/170 suggests something of his attitude in letters concerning John Reeves.

The Minister's thought of resigning to be succeeded by Addington is mentioned in the Hon. George Pellew, *The Life and Correspondence of the Right Honble Henry Addington, First Viscount Sidmouth*, I (1847), and in Bishop Tomline [Pretyman's] 'Estimate of Pitt together with Chapter XXVII from the Unpublished Fourth Volume of the Life', ed. by Lord Rosebery in *The Monthly Review*, XII, no. 3 for August 1903 and republished privately in the same year. The episode is recounted in greater detail by Mrs Pretyman in Stanhope Ms U1590 S5 C41, in the Stanhope Mss on deposit at the Centre for Kentish Studies, Maidstone. Versions of drafts for the Bishop's chapter are in B.L. Add. Mss 45107 (H) and 45108 (F) and Tomline Ms 35.1–13 at Pembroke College, Cambridge.

British interests and diplomacy in Europe, excluding the process of the negotiation at Lille for which see below, may be followed in the Foreign Office papers in P.R.O., F.O. 7/48–50 (Austria), 9/14, 31/9, 33/13, 68/11 (states in Germany), 22/27–8, 97/117 (Denmark), 28/17, 42/2, 67/24–5, 70/10, 79/15, 81/2 (states in Italy), 29/12–14 (Army in Germany), 43/2 (Thomas Graham in Italy), 63/24–6 (Portugal), 64/43–6, 95/6 (Prussia), 65/36–8 (Russia), 73/25, 97/399 (Sweden), 74/20–1 (Switzerland), 78/18 (Turkey). For the enemy states F.O. 37/59, 38/2 cover Holland, 72/45, 95/7 Spain, 27/51–2 intelligence on France. Grenville's own papers in B.L. Add. Mss listed by countries (and see A.D. Harvey, *Lord Grenville 1759–1834 A Bibliography* (1989), 24) contain much of the same material. Michael Duffy, 'British Diplomacy and the French Wars 1789–1815' in *Britain and the French Revolution, 1789–1815*, ed. H.T. Dickinson (1989) is an excellent introduction; his 'Pitt, Grenville and the Control of British Foreign Policy in the 1790s' in *Knights Errant and True Englishmen, British Foreign Policy, 1660–1800*, ed. Jeremy Black (1989), an interesting study; his D.Phil. thesis Oxford (1971) 'British War Policy, The Austrian Alliance 1793–1801' an authoritative account of relations for which *The Cambridge History of British Foreign Policy*, ed. Sir A.W. Ward and G.P. Gooch, I (1922), Appendix, contains a précis of selected documents. Some light is shed on intelligence and subversion in *The Correspondence of the Rt. Hon. William Wickham from 1794, ed . . . by His Grandson William Wickham* (2 vols., 1870), from material now largely in the Hampshire R.O. (Abbreviations); the study by Harvey Mitchell, *The Underground War against Revolutionary France, The Missions of William Wickham*

1794–1800 (1965) has been superseded in part by Maurice Hutt, *Chouannerie and Counter-Revolution* . . . (2 vols., 1983) and also by articles with important fresh material by Elizabeth Sparrow, 'The Alien Office, 1792–1806' and 'The Swiss and Swabian Agencies, 1795–1801' in *H.J.* (see Abbreviations), 33, no. 2, 35, no. 4 respectively.

Pitt's moves for peace from April to June 1797 are documented in Stanhope (Abbreviations), III, Appendix, J. Holland Rose, *Pitt and Napoleon*, Part II (1912), *H.M.C., Dropmore*, III, *L.C.G. III*, II. Canning's diary in Canning Ms 29d in the Harewood deposit at the City of Leeds Archives Office, and Windham's *Diary* (see Ch. I above) are also useful. So too is Peter Jupp's *Lord Grenville 1759–1834* (1985) for that subject and the subsequent negotiation at Lille, and for the latter one should also note Ephraim Douglas Adams, *The Influence of Grenville on Pitt's Foreign Policy 1787–1798* (1904). I have drawn very largely for the talks themselves on a detailed unpublished survey by Dr Anthony Smith, to which I am greatly obliged. The despatches are in P.R.O., F.O. 27/49–50. Malmesbury's private correspondence is published, quite extensively here, in *Diaries and Correspondence of James Harris First Earl of Malmesbury* . . ., ed. by *His Grandson* . . ., III (1844), and see also op. cit., IV, 128; and *The Private Correspondence of Lord Granville Leveson Gower (first Earl of Granville) 1781 to 1821*, ed. Castalia, Countess Granville, I (1916) augments that of his principal. The Grenville papers in B.L. (see above) add little here to *H.M.C., Dropmore*, III and the F.O. papers. Canning Mss 29d, 30, 58, 63 and the less central 34a, 62, 69; Leveson Gower's papers in P.R.O. 30/29/6, 384; Pitt's in P.R.O. 30/8/120 (Canning), 140 (Grenville), 155 (Malmesbury), 195 (notes of October), and in the Dacres Adams Mss formerly P.R.O. 30/58/2 for Canning, Grenville, and Malmesbury, provide some added information. So do letters from him in the Camden [Pratt] Mss in the Centre for Kentish Studies, U840 C102, C106, and some to him in the Stanhope Mss loc. cit., U1590 S5 03, 06. Windham's correspondence in B.L. Add. Mss 37844, 37846, 37876–7 shows the Secretary at War's unvarying views. Dundas's early support for a negotiation appears in draft in S.R.O., Melville Castle Muniments, GD 51/1/526. P.R.O. 30/8/147 (for Huskisson), more substantially 115 for Walter Boyd – not supplemented materially in this instance by S.R. Cope, *Walter Boyd, A Merchant Banker in the Age of Napoleon* (1983) –, 364 (for Chatham), throw some further flickering light on the French approach for a douceur to reach a settlement, as does *L.C.G. III*, II.

CHAPTER III

Letters relating to 'Pitt's One Love Story' were published, under that title, in *Pitt: Some Chapters of his Life and Times. By the Right Hon. Edward Gibson, Lord Ashbourne* (1898). The whole correspondence was gathered together by Lord Rosebery in *Letters Relating to the Love Episode of William Pitt* . . ., in *The Monthly Review*, I, no. 3 of December 1900, and reprinted privately at the same time. The contents may be followed in B.L. Add. Mss 46491, 59704, which reached the Library in 1948 and 1976 respectively. Letters between Auckland and Pitt in P.R.O. 30/8/110 and a later note in Stanhope Ms U1590 S5 C60/19, B.L. Add. Ms 46519, *A.C.* (see Abbreviations), III, shed light on the two men's relations over the rest of the year.

Personal finances are as hard to construe for 1797 as for any other time. Pointers in a confused situation can be gained from Thomas Coutts's letters to

Pitt in P.R.O. 30/8/126 and, more fully, in the Bank's Ledgers and Private Ledgers, and from investigations by others rather than by Pitt himself. There is important material in *The Diaries and Correspondence of the Right Hon. George Rose . . .*, ed. the Rev. Lewis Vernon Harcourt, I (1860) and B.L. Add. Mss 42772–3, in the papers of Pitt's private secretary Joseph Smith, lately in the possession of Mr W.H. Saumarez Smith, and some in Pretyman's deposited at the Suffolk R.O. at Ipswich (Pretyman Mss) and in the Stanhope collection at Maidstone. Pitt's own papers contain references to expenditure and borrowing, particularly in P.R.O. 30/8/196–7, 201–3, 213–14, 219 Part 6. They, and Joseph Smith's, include purchases of books. A list of his library at Walmer, strewn about the rooms on his death, is in Pretyman Ms 562:21.

Information on health to 1801 is widespread, suggestive and in the last resort baffling. It will be discussed again for Chs. XVI and XXII below. I have been much indebted throughout this volume to an article by R. Guest Gornall MRCP, 'The Prime Minister's Health, William Pitt the Younger', in *The Practitioner*, 179 (1957), and to expert assistance in correspondence with Mr T.G.J. Brightmore FRCS. Pitt's doctor Farquhar wrote an account after his patient's death, which was published by Rosebery to accompany his article on *the Love Episode* in *The Monthly Review* which was then reprinted (see above); the full title in fact was *Letters Relating to the Love Episode of William Pitt together with an Account of his Health by his Physician Sir Walter Farquhar*. Some letters from Farquhar to Pitt are contained in P.R.O. 30/8/134, and there is much scattered material elsewhere among which one may mention in particular P.R.O. 30/8/203 for consumption of wine, the Saumarez Smith Mss for lists of medicines, B.L. Add. Ms 41852, B.L. Loan Ms 72 vol. 54, Pretyman Mss 435/42, 44 at Ipswich, Camden Ms U840 226/4, and references of varying significance in Stanhope, III and Appendix, *A.C.*, III, IV, *Life of Wilberforce*, II, *Diaries and Correspondence of Rose*, I, *P.R.*, *3rd ser.*, VI (for the summer of 1798), *The Diary of Joseph Farington*, ed. Kenneth Garlick and Angus Macintyre, III–IV (1979).

Pitt's interest in architecture – illustrated by a sketch of the library for Henry Thornton's house in Clapham, with which he is credited, in E.M. Forster's *Marianne Thornton . . .* (1956), but focusing on his patronage of Soane for alterations, actual and envisaged, to Holwood – is noticed in Dorothy Stroud's *Sir John Soane Architect* (1984) and in Howard Colvin's *A Biographical Dictionary of English Architects 1660–1840* (2nd edn., 1978). There are two letters from Soane to Pitt in P.R.O. 30/8/179; more interesting material is to be found at the Sir John Soane Museum in Lincoln's Inn Fields in London, in plans, designs and views for Holwood in drawer 2, sets 9 and 9A and 14/1, journals nos. 1 and 3, Ledgers B, C, D, and one document of 1807 in Private Correspondence. For the complementary area of landscape gardening, Humphrey Repton's memoirs in B.L. Add. Ms 62112 are useful (as they are for Pitt at home); and there is a financial 'memorandum' in the Saumarez Smith Mss. Holwood is mentioned in Repton's *Observations on the Theory and Practice of Landscape Gardening*, and there is a brief account of the house and grounds in Sidney Gammon, *The Story of Keston, in Kent* (1934). Pitt's occupations at Walmer, which were more extensive later, are covered more fully in Ch. XVI below; but one may note here some mentions in his correspondence – eg to Rose in B.L. Add. Ms 42772 and from Dundas in the Dacres Adams Mss formerly P.R.O. 30/58/2. The London and Kentish newspapers are helpful for his movements, which they followed assiduously in these years.

Material on the Minister's circle in the later nineties is, again, widely scattered.

But there is plenty to be found on Canning, very largely emanating from himself in his own papers and those of his friends as well as in the correspondence and diaries of others. Letters from him to Pitt fill P.R.O. 30/8/120; the Canning Mss in the Leeds City Archives Office holds his diary (Ms 29d), and relevant correspondence and papers include Mss 30–1 (for Pitt), 34a, 58, 62–7, 69, 76–7. Selections are printed in Josceline Bagot, *George Canning and his Friends*, I (1909). Dorothy Marshall, *The Rise of George Canning* (1938) is excellent, as is Wendy Hinde, *George Canning* (1973). Both cast light on Hawkesbury also, for whose youth see C.D. Yonge, *The Life and Administration of Robert Banks, Second Earl of Liverpool . . .*, I (1868) and Norman Gash, *Lord Liverpool* (1984). Gabrielle Festing, *John Hookham Frere and his Friends* (1889) conveys something of the atmosphere of the younger men in their regard for Pitt.

CHAPTER IV

Pitt's proposals for the Triple Assessment and his handling of the issue are treated at length in the unpublished theses of O'Brien and Cooper (Ch. I above), and more briefly in Cooper, 'William Pitt, Taxation, and the Needs of War' (*The Journal of British Studies*, XXI, no. 1). Stephen Dowell, *A History of Taxation and Taxes in England from the Earliest Times to the Present*, II (1884), William Kennedy, *English Taxation 1640–1799, An Essay on Policy and Opinion* (1913), with Arthur Hope-Jones, *Income Tax in the Napoleonic Wars* (1939) for an introduction to a sequel, are useful. The question of the real impact of taxation in this country, particularly as compared with France, falls more easily to Ch. IX below. The Parliamentary debates for the year, extensive on finance, are covered in *P.R., 3rd ser.*, IV–VII (1798–9), *The Senator*, XIX–XXI (nd), *P.H.*, XXXIII. *L.C.G. III*, III, Stanhope, III, Appendix, Buckingham (see Abbreviations), II, *H.M.C., Dropmore*, III, Camden Ms U840 O190 A, show Pitt in action with the King and Ministers over the Voluntary Contribution. W.R. Ward, *The English Land Tax in the Eighteenth Century* (1953) gives the background for its sale, and P.R.O. 30/8/282 and the Dacres Adams Mss formerly P.R.O. 30/58/2 contain some of Pitt's papers on that subject. His approach to the Triple Assessment itself may be seen in P.R.O. 30/8/197, 273 (or 302), 282. *H.M.C., Dropmore*, III, 382–4 contains his forecast of yields. Some letters from Rose to Pretyman in Pretyman Ms 435/44 are concerned with the problems of persuading the Commons and the public.

Jeremy Black, *The English Press in the Eighteenth Century* (1987) is a helpful survey of a wide period, and the same author writes on 'The Challenge of the Revolution and the British Press' in *The Press in the French Revolution: Studies on Voltaire and the Eighteenth Century*, ed. Harvey Chisick (1991). Other useful sources for a subject which attracts much attention for the wartime years are A. Aspinall, *Politics and the Press c. 1780–1850* (1949), *A History of The Times . . .*, I (1935), Ivon Asquith, 'Advertising and the Press in the Late Eighteenth and Early Nineteenth Century' (*The Review of English Studies*, XXII, no. 85), Ian R. Christie, 'British Newspapers in the Later Georgian Age, James Perry and The Morning Chronicle' and 'James Perry of the Morning Chronicle', in his *Myth and Reality in Late-Eighteenth Century British Politics and Other Papers* (1970). Donald Read, *Press and People 1790–1850, Opinion in Three English Cities* (1961) is one example of a concern with the provinces which is a fruitful field of study. Notices of some editors may be found in *The Annual Register, The Gentleman's Magazine, DNB*.

Light is thrown on Pitt's relationship with *The Anti-Jacobin* in his letters to Canning in Canning Ms 30 at Leeds; extracts from the journal are printed in *Poetry of the Anti-Jacobin*, ed. L. Rice-Oxley (1924), and there is material in Emily Lorraine de Monthuzin, *The Anti-Jacobins, 1798–1800, The Early Contributors to the Anti-Jacobin Review* (1989), which is concerned more largely with a successor to the original.

An extensive literature has been building up in the past thirty years on the nature and dimensions of loyalism and discontent. It will be followed more conveniently in the Note on Sources to Ch. X below, but one should mention here some publications on measures against disaffection, and their reception in the law courts. The management of Government's intelligence is discussed in Kenneth Ellis, *The Post Office in the Eighteenth Century* (1958), R.R. Nelson, *The Home Office, 1782–1801* (1969), Clive Emsley, 'The Home Office and its sources of information and investigation 1791–1801' (*E.H.R.* (Abbreviations), no. CCCLXII), Roger Wells, *Insurrection* (Chapter I above), Elizabeth Sparrow, 'The Alien Office, 1792–1806' (Ch. II above), with the Irish dimension in Marianne Elliott, *Partners in Revolution* (Ch. I) and Stanley H. Palmer, *Police and Protest in England and Ireland, 1780–1850* (1988), and sidelights in W.J. Fitzpatrick, *Secret Service under Pitt* (2nd edn., 1892). J.R. Western, 'The Volunteer Movement as an Anti-Revolutionary Force, 1793–1801' (*E.H.R.*, LXXI, no. 4) is no less useful for the later than for the earlier years. Leon Radzinowicz, *A History of English Criminal Law and its Administration from 1750* (4 vols., 1948–68) is the prime general account. F.K. Prochaska looks into 'English State Trials in the 1790s: A Case Study' (*The Journal of British Studies*, XIII, no. 1); Clive Emsley works on a wide canvas in 'Repression, 'terror', and the rule of law in England during the decade of the French Revolution' (*E.H.R.*, C, no. 397) and 'An Aspect of Pitt's 'Terror': prosecutions for sedition during the 1790s' (*Social History*, 6, no. 2); Douglas Hay brings a different emphasis to bear in 'Prosecution and power: malicious prosecution in the English courts, 1750–1850' (*Policing and Prosecution in Britain, 1750–1850*, ed. Douglas Hay and Francis Snyder (1989)). State trials are published in *A Complete Collection . . .*, compiled by T.B. Howell and T.J. Howell . . ., XV–XVII (1819–20).

Plans against invasion may be found in P.R.O., W.O. 56–62, 64–71, particularly in 64 and 70. Pitt's interest in them emerges from P.R.O. 30/8/245. An account of the land forces, regular and auxiliary, is given in Fortescue, IV-Part II (Ch. I above), which is corrected and supplemented in Piers Mackesy, *Statesmen at War: The Strategy of Overthrow 1798–1799* (1974), J.R. Western, 'The Recruitment of the Land Forces in Great Britain, 1793–99' (Ph.D. thesis, University of Edinburgh, 1953) and *The English Militia in the Eighteenth Century, The Story of a Political Issue 1660–1832* (1965). Linda Colley, in *Britons, Forging the Nation 1707–1837* (1992), ch. 7 and Appendix 3, examines the social contexts and regional responses, as does J.E. Cookson in 'The English Volunteer Movements of the French Wars, 1793–1815' (*H.J.* (Abbreviations), 32, no. 4) and some separate studies of local corps. Christopher Oprey is valuable on 'Schemes for the Reform of Naval Recruitment, 1793–1815' (M.A. thesis, University of Liverpool, 1961). *Correspondence of Cornwallis*, II (Ch. I above) and *Private Papers of Spencer*, II (ibid) throw light on measures of defence, the latter not least for his colleague Dundas's views, which also emerge vigorously in letters to Pitt in P.R.O. 30/8/157 and B.L. Add. Ms 40102, and to Windham in B.L. Add. Ms 37877. Difficulties over the militia and volunteers may be followed in B.L. Add. Mss 40101–2, *H.M.C.*, *Dropmore*, IV, Buckingham, II.

P.H., XXXIII is the best single source for Tierney's speech which led to Pitt's challenge and the duel on Putney Heath. Sir George Clark, *War and Society in the Seventeenth Century* (1958) and J.C.D. Clark, *English Society 1688–1832* . . . (1985) are among the many who have considered the institution of duelling itself.

CHAPTER V

The search for a Quadruple Alliance or a substitute is followed in *The Cambridge History of British Foreign Policy*, I (Ch. II above), John M. Sherwig, 'Lord Grenville's Plan for a Concert of Europe, 1797–1799' (*The Journal of Modern History*, XXXIV, no. 3), E.D. Adams, *The Influence of William Grenville on Pitt's Foreign Policy*, Michael Duffy, 'Pitt, Grenville, and the Control of British Foreign Policy', Jupp, *Lord Grenville* (all Ch. II). Karl F. Helleiner, *The Imperial Loans, A Study in Financial and Diplomatic History* (1965) and John M. Sherwig, *Guineas and Gunpowder, British Foreign Aid in the Wars with France* (1969), examine the question of the Austrian Loan, which is related in further detail to its diplomatic setting in Duffy's admirable 'British War Policy, The Austrian Alliance' (Ch. II above). See also Karl A. Roider, *Baron Thugut and Austria's Response to the French Revolution* (1987). Andrei Lobanov-Rostovsky, *Russia and Europe, 1789–1825* (1947), T. Naff, 'Ottoman Diplomacy and the Great European Powers 1797–1802' (Ph.D. thesis, University of London, 1960) are helpful for their subjects which are linked in one aspect in Norman E. Saul, *Russia in the Mediterranean 1797–1807* (1970).

The link is further important for the revival of a British naval presence on the southern flank of Europe, discussed by Piers Mackesy in *Statesmen at War* (Ch. IV above) and, from its own point of coverage, Edward Ingram's *Commitment to Empire: Prophecies of the Great Game in Asia 1797–1800* (1981). Ingram has also assembled some relevant articles in *In Defence of India, Great Britain in the Middle East 1775–1842* (1984). Other sources on that extensive theme will be found for Chs. XI & XII, XIII below. Nelson's fortunes in the summer of 1798, discussed to exhaustion in naval histories and biographies, are placed in a context by A.B. Rodger in *The War of the Second Coalition 1798–1801, A Strategic Commentary* (1964). Fortescue's treatment of operations in the Caribbean, in his *History of the British Army*, IV-Part I (1906), is superseded by Michael Duffy, *Soldiers, Sugar, and Seapower, The British Expeditions to the West Indies and the War against Revolutionary France* (1987). The secular issue for British strategy of the balance, or choice, between seapower and a direct contribution to Continental warfare, treated in the classic works of Mahan, *The Influence of Sea Power upon the French Revolution and Empire* (2 vols., 1892) and Admiral Sir Herbert Richmond, *Statesmen and Sea Power* (1946), has been given new approaches in recent years in such studies as Paul M. Kennedy's *The Rise and Fall of British Naval Mastery* (1976) and Nicholas A.M. Rodger, 'The Continental Commitment in the Eighteenth Century' in *War, Strategy and International Politics, Essays in honour of Sir Michael Howard*, ed. Lawrence Freedman . . . (1992). Some elements of seapower itself are underlined in Michael Duffy, 'The Establishment of the Western Squadron as the Linchpin of British Naval Strategy' in his edition of *Parameters of British Naval Power* (1992) and Daniel A. Baugh, 'Maritime Strength and Atlantic Commerce' in *An Imperial State at War, Britain from 1689 to 1815*, ed. Lawrence Stone (1994). We await the forthcoming volumes of a new comprehensive naval history of Britain by Rodger; meanwhile G.J. Marcus, *A Naval History of England*, 2 (1971) is a serviceable account. Some older narratives are listed in my II, 661.

There are useful publications of European documents in A. von Vivenot and H.R. Zeissberg, *Quellen zur Geschichte der deutschen Kaiserpolitik Österreichs während der französischen Revolutions-Kriege* (5 vols., 1873–90), *Arkhiv Kniazia Vorontsova . . .*, ed. P.I. Bartenev (40 vols., 1870–95), *Correspondance de Napoléon Ier: publiée par Ordre de l'empereur Napoléon III* (32 vols., 1858–70). For the texts of treaties see *The Consolidated Treaty Series*, 54, ed. Clive Parry (1969). Sources for Britain include *L.C.G. III*, III, *H.M.C., Dropmore*, IV, *Private Papers of Spencer*, II (Ch. I above) and IV, ed. Rear Admiral H.W. Richmond (1924), *Diary of Windham* (Ch. I above), and for the scene as watched by Mornington in India *The Despatches, Minutes, and Correspondence of the Marquess Wellesley, K.G., during his Administration in India*, ed. M. Martin, I (1836).

Relevant Foreign Office papers are P.R.O., F.O. 5, series II/22 (United States), 7/51–3 (Austria), 14/1 (Brunswick), 63/27–9 (Portugal), 64/47–51 (Prussia), 65/39–41 (Russia), 70/11 (The Two Sicilies), 78/19–20 (Turkey), 81/13 (Venice). There is intelligence on French plans and naval movements in F.O. 28/18 (Genoa), 42/3 (Ionian Islands), 79/16 (Tuscany). P.R.O., W.O. 1/219–20 contain despatches from the British force in Portugal. Papers for Holland and Switzerland are listed for Chs. VII–VIII below. Pitt's papers in P.R.O. 30/8 are disappointing; the Dacres Adams Mss formerly P.R.O. 30/58/2 have letters from Portland and from Canning in October 1798. Dundas's voluminous correspondence for the period is covered expertly in Ingram's *Commitment to Empire* (above); his letters to his Under Secretary William Huskisson in B.L. Add. Ms 38735 also reveal his state of mind. Grenville's unpublished papers add marginally to *H.M.C., Dropmore* and the F.O. files: in B.L. Add. Mss 59023, 59048, 59057 (for Portugal), 59031, 59038–9 (Naples), 59044, 59076–7 (Russia), 59049 (United States), 59081 (Turkey). 59306 has his surviving list of Cabinet Minutes and associated memoranda. His subordinate Canning's mss at Leeds are occasionally helpful (29d, 30, 67). There is a letter from Pitt to Windham in September 1798 in B.L. Add. Ms 37844; two to Rose indicating the Minister's state of mind in August and early September, in B.L. Add. Ms 42772, and others from Rose to Pretyman at that time in Pretyman Ms 435/44. The Bishop's account of Downing Street on receipt of the news from Nelson at the Nile is also to be found loc. cit. Stanhope Ms U1590 S5 048 has a letter to Pitt from Mornington on the victory's possible effect.

CHAPTER VI

Lecky's great *History of Ireland in the Eighteenth Century*, III–V (1892 edn.) for long towered over the scene for Ireland. Much work has been done since, for which David Dixon, *New Foundations: Ireland, 1660–1800* (1987) is a good introduction. In the multi-volume *New History of Ireland* the relevant volume is IV, ed. T.W. Moody and W.E. Vaughan (1986), in which L.M. Cullen contributes to the economic treatment and R.B. McDowell to the political. Both have published valuable studies: the former *An Economic History of Ireland since 1660* (1972), the latter *Irish Public Opinion 1750–1800* (1944) and *Ireland in the Age of Imperialism and Reform 1760–1801* (1979). See also, more recently, *Nationalism and Popular Protest in Ireland*, ed. C.H.E. Philpin (1987), and *Cultures et pratiques politiques en France et en Irelande, XVII–XVIII siècle . . .*, ed. Louis M. Cullen and Louis Bergeron (1991). E.M. Johnston, *Great Britain and Ireland 1760–1800* (1963) is helpful on the administrative and political structure. Marianne Elliott, Stanley H. Palmer and also Roger Wells (Chs. I, IV above) are required reading for the final years of the century; Thomas Pakenham, *The Year of Liberty, The Story of the Great Irish Rebellion of 1798* (1969) tells the story of their centrepiece, and Desbrière (Ch. I above) covers the scene from France. G.C. Bolton examines *The Passing of the Irish Act of Union* (1966).

Among biographies, A.W. Malcolmson provides an important study of the influential *John Foster, The Politics of the Anglo–Irish Ascendancy* (1978). Jupp's life of *Lord Grenville* (Ch. II above) is very useful, and so is H.M. Hyde's *The Rise of Castlereagh* (1933). Primary published sources include Cornwallis' *Correspondence* (Ch. I above), *The Correspondence of the Right Hon. John Beresford, . . .ed. the Right Hon. William Beresford*, II (1854), *Memoirs and Correspondence of Viscount Castlereagh, Second Marquess of Londonderry, edited by his Brother, Charles Vane, Third Marquess of Londonderry*, I–IV (1848–9), *L.C.G. III*, III, *H.M.C., Dropmore*, IV–V, Buckingham, II, *A.C.*, II, *Life and Letters of Sir Gilbert Elliot, First Earl of Minto, from 1751 to 1806*, ed. by the Countess of Minto, II (1874). Stanhope, II, Appendix, Ashbourne (Ch. III above), J. Holland Rose, *Pitt and Napoleon* (Ch. II above), contain significant letters and papers; *Correspondence of the Prince of Wales* (Ch. II above), IV (1967), those on the offer of himself for Lord Lieutenant.

The debates in Dublin are covered in *Reports of Debates in the House of Commons in Ireland* [1796–1800] (1797–1800); those at Westminster in *P.R., 3rd ser.*, VII–IX, XI (1799–1801), *The Senator*, XXI–XXIV (nd), *P.H.*, XXXIV–XXXV (1819). Maurice Hastings, *Parliament House . . .* (1950) alludes to the physical alterations introduced to the British House of Commons by the Union, described more fully in Orlo Cyprian Williams, 'The Topography of the Old House of Commons' (unpublished; a copy is held by the Department of the Environment).

Unpublished material abounds, on either side of the Irish Sea: on this side in the Home Office files in P.R.O., H.O. 100/66–100, 123/4–5, 19–21, augmented by Pitt's papers in P.R.O. 30/8/320–30 and the Dacres Adams Mss formerly P.R.O. 30/58/2–3, and by Camden's in Camden Mss U840 C98, 102, 106, 112, 0107–0110, 0153–0209. Of interest also are B.L. Add. Mss 59254–5 (Grenville), 33103–6, 119 (Thomas Pelham), 34455 (Auckland), 37844–5, 37847 (Windham), Canning Ms 29d, Pretyman Ms 435/44.

CHAPTERS VII & VIII

The material on negotiations for a new Coalition is covered largely in the Notes on Sources for Ch. V above, to which may be added for background to the later phase T.C.W. Blanning, *The Origins of the French Revolutionary Wars* (1986), ch. 6, and Norman Frank Richards, 'British Policy and the Problem of Monarchy in France, 1789–1802' (Ph.D. thesis, University of London, 1954). Texts of treaties are taken from *The Consolidated Treaty Series*, 54 (Ch. V above). D.C. Elliot, 'The Grenville Mission to Berlin, 1799' (*The Huntington Library Quarterly*, XVIII) is helpful for a critical year, and of the works cited earlier Duffy's thesis on the Austrian alliance and Mackesy's *Statesmen at War* are essential reading for policy in these Chs. A useful balance for Mackesy is provided by Paul W. Schroeder in 'The Collapse of the Second Coalition' (*The Journal of Modern History*, 59, no. 2). Maurice Hutt, 2 (Ch. II above), Wynne Lewis, *The Second Vendée, The Continuity of the Counter-Revolution in the Department of the Gard, 1789–1815* (1978), Jacques Godechot, *The Counter-Revolution, Doctrine and Action 1789–1804* (transl. 1972), are authorities for France; Simon Schama, *Patriots and Liberators, Revolution in the Netherlands 1780–1873* (1977) sets the scene in the other region from which much was expected in 1799. Fortescue, IV-Part II (Ch. I above) disparages the British Government's handling of the Dutch expedition; Alfred H. Burne, *The Noble Duke of York* (ibid), and *Lieutenant-General Sir Ralph Abercromby, 1793–1801, A Memoir by his Son, James, Lord Dunfermline* (1861) argue the case for the British commanders. Richard Saxby, 'The Blockade of Brest in the Revolutionary War' (*The Mariner's Mirror*, 78, no. 1) supplements works cited in Ch. V above. Parliamentary debates are covered in Ch. VI above, with the addition of *P.R., 3rd ser.*, X.

Primary published sources for the Continent include von Vivenot and Zeissberg, and *Arkhiv Vorontsova* (both Ch. V above), and Hermann Hüffer, *Quellen zur Geschichte der Zeitalters der französischen Revolution*, I (1900). See also *The Paget Papers: Diplomatic and Other Correspondence of . . . Sir Arthur Paget, 1794–1807*, ed. Sir Augustus B. Paget, I (1896), for Bavaria, and *The Life and Letters of Sir Gilbert Elliot*, III (Ch. VI above) for Austria. Wickham's *Correspondence*, II (Ch. II above) sheds light on his overt as well as his covert diplomatic activities. *H.M.C., Dropmore*, IV–V – supplemented by Holland Rose, *Pitt and Napoleon* (Ch. II above) – contain material of central interest; *Diary of Windham*, *Private Papers of Spencer*, II (Ch. I above), III, ed. Rear Admiral H.W. Richmond (1923), *L.C.G. III*, III, may also be consulted.

Manuscript material is voluminous. P.R.O., W.O. 1/179–82, 6/20,25 are concerned with the Dutch expedition, 1/408 with the missions of Malcolm and of Maitland to Flanders, 1/411 with Home Popham's to Russia. Foreign Office files are in P.R.O., F.O. 5, Series II/22, 25A (United States of America), 7/53–7 (Austria), 9/17–18 (Bavaria), 14/1 (Brunswick), 33/17–19 (Hamburg), 37/59, 38/4 (Holland and Flanders, Frontiers of Holland), 64/52–5 (Prussia), 65/40–5 (Russia), 70/11–12 (The Two Sicilies), 73/27 (Sweden), 74/22–8 (Switzerland), 82/2 (Württemberg).

The most useful volumes in Pitt's papers are P.R.O. 30/8/12 (Hester Countess of Chatham), 101 (Countess of Chatham), 102 (Sir Charles Grey), 106 (York), 119 (Camden), 122 (Chatham), 140 (Grenville), 147 (Huskisson), 160 (Admiral Mitchell), 191 (Vorontsov), 197 (memoranda), 240, 243a (army), 335 (France), 336 (Holland), 339 (Empire and Austria); and the Dacres Adams Mss formerly P.R.O. 30/58/2 contain letters of interest from Windham, Chatham, and particularly Grenville. Stanhope Ms U1590 S5 09/53 in the Centre for Kentish Studies has a memorandum in Pitt's hand on a landing at Brest. Of other collections, Spencer's papers contain a series of letters from Thomas Grenville in Berlin (B.L. Add. Ms temporary Althorp G33), and G208–13 supplement his published private Admiralty correspondence. There is some material in Dundas's papers in B.L. Add. Mss 40101–2 and S.R.O., Melville Castle Mss GD 51/1/529, 548; in Huskisson's, B.L. Add. Mss 38735, 38759, 38764; and Windham's, B.L. Add. Mss 37844, 37846, 37877–8. Canning Ms 63 has Grenville's interesting letter on the question of the Foreign Secretary's going in person to Holland. Grenville's own private correspondence is published extensively in *H.M.C., Dropmore*, IV; but further material from his voluminous papers (many duplicating the F.O. volumes) may be found particularly in B.L. Add. Mss 59028–9, 59033, 59045, 59052, 59061, 59076–7, 59306 (Cabinet Minutes). There is more in his correspondence with his brother Thomas in the Stowe Mss at the Huntington Library in California; but this has been combed and noted so fully by Mackesy (Ch. I above) that it would be otiose to particularise here. Little of importance for the period can be gleaned from Thomas's papers in B.L.; but see Add. Mss 41852, 41854–5.

CHAPTERS IX & X

The theses of Patrick O'Brien and Richard Cooper (Ch. I above) are prime sources for Ch. IX. See also O'Brien, 'The Political Economy of British Taxation, 1660–1815' (*Ec.H.R.* (Abbreviations), XLI, no. 1), O'Brien and Peter Mathias, 'Taxation in Britain and France, 1715–1810 . . .' (*The Journal of Economic History*, 5, no. 3), and Cooper, 'William Pitt, Taxation, and the Needs of War' (Ch. IV above); also Dowell, Kennedy, and for the Land Tax W.R. Ward (Ch. IV), and for the background of central management J.E.D. Binney, *British Public Finance and Administration 1774–1792* (1958). Arthur Hope-Jones, *Income Tax in the Napoleonic Wars* (Ch. IV above) greatly advanced knowledge of the subject, and A. Farnsworth, *Addington, Author of the Modern Income Tax* (1951) – a claim discussed in Ch. XIX below – is useful here on Pitt's abortive second bill of April 1800. Henry Beeke, *Observations on the Produce of the Income Tax* (1799, enlarged edn. 1800) supplies an interesting contemporary view of early yields, whose figures may be obtained from B.R. Mitchell and Phyllis Deane, *Abstract of British Historical Statistics* (1962; enlarged edn. 1988) with comment on them in Phyllis Deane and W.A. Cole, *British Economic Growth 1688–1959, Trends and Structure* (1962), Appendix II. Parliamentary debates are important, in particular *P.R., 3rd ser.*, VII, X, XII, XV (1799–1801), *P.H.*, XXXIV. Pitt's papers in P.R.O. 30/8 contain much material: in 136 (Fordyce), 170 (Mitford), 183 (Samuel Thornton), 196–7, 235, and, within the series of files on finance 272–305, particularly 273–4, 278–82, 304. P.R.O. 30/8/341 includes a misdated memorandum; Dacres Adams Mss formerly P.R.O. 30/58/8, one undated on the redemption of the Land Tax. The Treasury Board Minutes for the period occupy P.R.O., T 29/73–7. Some remarks of interest occur in Pretyman Mss 435/44, 45, B.L. Add. Ms 42772 (Rose), B.L. Loan Ms 72 vol. 54 (Hawkesbury), the published diaries of Rose, I (Ch. III above), and of Charles Abbot, *The Diary and Correspondence of Charles Abbot, Lord Colchester, ed. by his Son, Charles, Lord Colchester* (1861), I.

Selected publications on loans and credit and monetary policy are mentioned in the Note on Sources for Ch. I. The rest of Pitt's files P.R.O. 30/8/272–305 are necessary to gauge his knowledge of the state of duties and stamps, and 275 contains papers on the National Debt. E.L. Hargreaves, *The National Debt* (1930) remains useful on that subject, as indeed does J.J. Grellier, *The History of the National Debt, from the Revolution of 1688 to the Beginning of the Year 1800* . . . (1810). The same author's *The Terms of All the Loans which have been Raised for the Public Service during the Last Fifty Years* (1799), and William Newmarch, *On the Loans Raised by Mr. Pitt during the First French War, 1793–1801* . . . (1855) are valuable.

Dearth, disaffection, and the connexions between them attract much attention. The complexities of the problems are observed in R.B. Outhwaite, *Dearth, Public Policy and Social Disturbance in England, 1550–1800* (1991). Bearing them in mind, and while I cannot agree with the balance of Roger Wells's political conclusions in his study of *Insurrection* (Ch. I above), his *Wretched Faces, Famine in Wartime England 1793–1801* (1988) has furnished a basis on which to discuss the dimensions of shortage and of the discontent in the years around the turn of the century. Some earlier works on agricultural matters are noticed in my II, Notes for Ch. XII, to which should be added the Cambridge *Agrarian History of England and Wales*, vol. 6, *1750–1850*, ed. G.E. Mingay (1989). Much has been written on the question of unrest since E.P. Thompson published the first edition of *The Making of the English Working Class* in 1963. Some of it may be found in the Notes on Sources for my II, Chs. IV & V; and I would repeat or add here, highly selectively from a substantial literature, John Stevenson, *Popular Disturbances in England, 1700–1870* (1979) and, more specifically, in ch. 3 of *Britain and the French Revolution, 1789–1815* (Ch. II above), John Bohstedt, *Riots and Community Politics in England and Wales 1790–1810* (1983), Ian Gilmour, *Riot, Risings and Revolution, Governance and Violence in Eighteenth-Century England* (1992). Local and regional attitudes and responses are of course of central importance, and have been increasingly investigated – examples can be found through bibliographies; a wide introductory survey is available in A. Charlesworth, *An Atlas of Rural Protest in Britain, 1548–1900* (1982); and three urban studies may serve as illustrations, J. Ann Hone, *For the Cause of Truth, Radicalism in London 1796–1821* (1982), John Money, *Experience and Identity, Birmingham and the West Midlands 1760–1800* (1977), C.B. Jewson, *The Jacobin City, A Portrait of Norwich in its Relation to the French Revolution 1788–1802* (1978). All three embrace broad fronts in the debate between the respective cases for the strengths and influences of loyalism and radicalism; the latter ranging from hostility to the Government, through movements for political and social reform, to revolutionary feelings and activities. Clear opposing conclusions are reached by Roger Wells in *Insurrection* (above) and Ian R. Christie in *Stress and Stability in Late Eighteenth-Century Britain, Reflections on the British Avoidance of Revolution* (1984); and see also studies of policing and of the Courts cited in Ch. IV above. But the debate moves on. Books and articles by Emsley and by Cookson (Ch. IV above), Linda Colley, *Britons, Forging the Nation 1707–1837* (ibid), take their place with eg R.R. Dozier, *For King, Country and Constitution: The English Loyalists and the French Revolution* (1983), Robert Hole (as one example of the denominational factor), *Pulpits, Politics and Public Order in England, 1760–1832* (1989), and chronologically more narrowly in ch. 1 of *The French Revolution and British Popular Politics*, ed. Mark Philp (1991), H.T. Dickinson, 'Popular Conservatism and Militant Loyalism, 1789–1815' in his edited *Britain and the French Revolution* (above), David Eastwood in 'Patriotism and the English State in the 1790s' (*The French Revolution and British Popular Politics*, above). J.C.D. Clark, *English Society, 1688–1832, Ideology, Social Structure and Political Practice during the Ancien Regime* (1985) is a central document in the rediscovery of the confessional state. Mark Philp, 'The Fragmented Ideology of Reform', together with Eastwood and with John Dinwiddy, 'Interpretations of Anti-Jacobinism' (all in Philp's edited volume, above) bring a note of scepticism to balance the more enthusiastic advocates for the effects of traditionalist teachings. In a different framework, C.R. Dobson, *Masters and Journeymen, a prehistory of industrial relations, 1717–1800* (1980), John Rule, *The Experience of Labour in Eighteenth-Century History* (1981), John V. Orth, *Combination and Conspiracy: A Legal History of Trade Unionism, 1721–1906* (1991) are important. David Eastwood, *Governing Rural England, Tradition and Transformation in Local Government 1780–1840* (1994) demonstrates from the point of vantage of the main instruments of social order the role of applying poor and price laws and conventions; themes treated in works, cited in the context of the dearth of 1795 but for the most part equally applicable here, in my II, Note on Sources to Ch. XII. The ever continuing discussion among economic historians, economists and econometrists over the standard of living of the population is best followed in the latest current articles and reviews in the appropriate journals.

Parliamentary proceedings are highly important for policies in Ch. X. *P.R., 3rd ser.*, VIII–XV may be compared with *The Senator*, XXIII–XXVI (nd), the last particularly for the Combination Acts which *P.H.*, XXXIV–XXXV ignore. *H.C.J.*,

54–6 and *H.L.J.*, XLII (Abbreviations) are useful for the passage of legislation, and *Sessional Papers of the House of Commons in the Eighteenth Century*, ed. Sheila Lambert, vols. 131, 121 (1975) are of great interest.

Correspondence and diaries for this Ch. include the *Life* of Wilberforce (Ch. I above), III, his *Private Papers*, ed. A.M. Wilberforce (1897), *A.C.*, IV, *H.M.C.*, *Dropmore*, VI, *H.M.C.*, *Kenyon*, *Diary and Correspondence of Colchester*, I (above). Manuscript material is plentiful. In Pitt's papers, P.R.O. 30/8/291 (corn), 308 (relief of the poor) are particularly helpful, and 148 (journeymen), 152 (Lord Liverpool), 177 (Lord Sheffield), 178 (Sir John Sinclair), 193 (Arthur Young) convey specimens of opinions and advice, as do the Dacres Adams Mss formerly P.R.O. 30/58/3 for Grenville. This last also has a letter from Hawkesbury on the London Bread Company, on which see also Liverpool's thoughts on economic principles in B.L. Add. Ms 38311. Further sources are B.L. Add. Ms 42772, Pretyman Ms 435/44 (Rose and Pretyman), Harrowby Mss vol. XXXIV at Sandon Hall in Staffordshire (Pitt on importation of corn), P.R.O., P.C. 2/153, B.T. 5/11–12, H.O. 42/48–56.

CHAPTERS XI & XII

The locus classicus for the study of British strategy after the failure of the expedition to Holland in 1799 is Piers Mackesy's *War Without Victory, The Downfall of Pitt 1799–1802* (1984); taking over chronologically from its predecessor (Ch. I above), overtaking A.B. Rodger (Ch. V above) for the same years, and superseding Fortescue's comments in his IV-Part I (ibid), though this last remains important for detail. Biographical studies for commanders include Lord Dunfermline's of his father Abercromby (Chs. VII & VIII above) and Walter Frewin Lord, *Sir Thomas Maitland* (1897); Home Popham's contribution in Russia is followed in Hugh Popham, *A Damned Cunning Fellow* . . . (1991); Mahan (Ch. V above), I, ch. X remains well worth reading on Sidney Smith in the Mediterranean. For works on the navy see the Notes to Chs. V, VII & VIII, to which may be added R.C. Anderson, *Naval Wars in the Baltic During the Sailing-Ship Epoch, 1522–1850* (1910) and *Naval Wars in the Levant, 1559–1833* (1952). Duffy's *Soldiers, Sugar, and Seapower* (Ch. V) deals succinctly with the war's closing phase in Central American waters; C. Northcote Parkinson considers the *War in the Eastern Seas, 1793–1815* (1954).

Parliamentary debates on Bonaparte's peace message of December 1799 may be followed in *P.R., 3rd ser.*, X, *The Senator*, XXIV, *P.H.*, XXXIV, the last being the most comprehensive. Coverage for the period is as in the Note to Chs. IX & X.

For the place of counter-revolution in France see Chs. VII & VIII above. For policy in general, add to *The Cambridge History of British Foreign Policy*, I (Ch. II), Jupp, *Lord Grenville* (ibid), Sherwig, *Guineas and Gunpowder*, Duffy, 'British War Policy', Roidier, *Baron Thugut* (all Ch. V); H.M. Bowman, *Preliminary Stages of the Peace of Amiens . . . November 1799–March 1801* (1899); D. Gregory, *Minorca, The Illusory Prize: A History of the British Occupancy . . . between 1708 and 1802* (1990); Guy Stanton Ford, *Hanover and Prussia 1795–1803, A Study in Neutrality* (1903); Hugh Ragsdale, *Detente in the Napoleonic Era, Bonaparte and the Russians* (1980), Lobanov-Rostovsky, *Russia and Europe* (Ch. V), Ole Feldbaeck, *Denmark and the Armed Neutrality, 1800–1* (1980), the same author on 'The Foreign Policy of Paul I: An Interpretation' (*Jarbücher für Geschichte Osteuropas*, IV, pt. 2), Roderick E. McGrew, *Paul I of Russia, 1754–1801* (1992), Saul, *Russia in the Mediterranean* (Ch. V), M.S.

Anderson, *The Eastern Question 1774–1923, A Study in International Relations* (1966), Naff, 'Ottoman Diplomacy and the Great European Powers, 1797–1802' (Ch. V), T. Stanford Shaw, *Between New and Old, The Ottoman Empire under Selim III* (1971), Schroeder, 'The Collapse of the Second Coalition' (Ch. VIII above).

The question of Egypt has attracted increasing attention. Its ramifications for British policy in Asia will be noticed in that for Ch. XIII below. But one should mention here François Charles-Roux, *L'Angleterre et l'expédition française en Egypte* (2 vols., 1925), as an introduction to Ingram's important study *Commitment to Empire* (Ch. V). The biographies of Dundas by Cyril Matheson, *The Life of Henry Dundas, First Viscount Melville, 1742–1811* (1933) and Holden Furber, *Henry Dundas, First Viscount Melville, 1742–1811* (1931) are naturally relevant; and see further J. Holland Rose, 'The Political Reactions to Bonaparte's Eastern Expedition' (*E.H.R.*, XLIV, no. 1), Edward B. Jones, 'Henry Dundas, India, and British Reactions to Bonaparte's Invasion of Egypt, 1798–1801' (*Proceedings of the South Carolina Historical Association*, 1973).

Documents bearing on strategy are published in *Private Papers of Spencer*, IV (Ch. V above), *The Keith Papers, Selected from the Letters and Papers of Admiral the Viscount Keith*, II, ed. Christopher Lloyd (1950), *The Dispatches and Letters of Vice-Admiral Lord Nelson*, III, ed. Sir Nicholas Harris Nicolas (1846), Sir John Barrow, *Life and Correspondence of Sir William Sidney Smith*, II (1848), *The Diary of Sir John Moore*, I, ed. J.F. Maurice (1904). *L.C.G. III*, III, and two additional letters published by W.B. Hamilton in 'Some Letters of George III' (*The South Atlantic Quarterly*, LXVIII, no. 3), illustrate the King's fast-growing unease; and see also *The Diaries of Sylvester Douglas Lord Glenbervie*, I, ed. F. Bickley (1928). For diplomacy see the Note to Chs. VII & VIII above. Sir Francis Piggott and W.T. Omond, *Documentary History of the Armed Neutralities of 1780 and 1800* (1919) is helpful.

Despatches are contained in P.R.O., F.O. 7/57–62 (Austria), 9/18–21 (Bavaria), 22/35–9, 97/118 (Denmark), 27/54–6 (France, 55 being for Otto), 31/10–11 (German States), 33/19–21, 97/241–2 (Hamburg), 38/5 (Frontiers of Holland), 42/3–4 (Ionian Islands), 43/3–4 (Italian States and Rome), 49/2 (Malta), 63/31–5 (Portugal), 64/55–60 (Prussia), 65/44–7 (Russia), 67/28–9 (Sardinia), 68/13–14 (Saxony), 70/12–15 (The Two Sicilies), 72/46 (Spain), 73/27–8, 97/399 (Sweden), 74/25–35 (Switzerland), 78/21–30 (Turkey), 79/17–18 (Tuscany), 81/13 (Venice), 82/2 (Württemberg). P.R.O., W.O. 6/21 includes instructions for expeditions, and 6/55 orders to Minorca. P.R.O., Adm. 2/139–40 are equally relevant, and the Board's Minutes are in Adm. 3/123–5. Pitt's files hold correspondence and papers in P.R.O. 30/8/101 (Chatham), 119 (Camden), 120 (Canning), 140 (Grenville), 157 (Dundas), 195–7, 243 (memorandum by Dundas), 339; and there is further material in the Dacres Adams Mss formerly P.R.O. 30/58/3 and 8. Within a range of scattered sources, Grenville's unpublished papers in B.L. under countries and correspondents, and in Add. Ms 59306 for Cabinet Minutes, again complement *H.M.C.*, *Dropmore*, VI; there are papers for Dundas in B.L. Add. Mss 40101–2, John Rylands Library Manchester Eng. Ms 907, S.R.O., Melville Castle Mss GD 51/1/725/1 (as well as duplicated papers widely spread among the recipients' collections); for Spencer in B.L. Add. Mss temporary Althorp G38–40; for Huskisson in B.L. Add. Mss 38736, 38759; for Canning in Canning Mss 29d, 30; for Rose in Pretyman Ms 435/44; for Windham in B.L. Add. Ms 37924, and in 37844–6, 37878–9.

CHAPTER XIII

Ministers' retrospectives on the Government's wartime achievement are given in Ch. XVII below. George Rose's defence of its economic and financial performance, *A Brief Examination into the Increase of the Revenue, Commerce, and Manufactures of Great Britain from 1792 to 1799*, was published in the latter year, to run quickly into succeeding edns. I have found the following of particular help amid a range of publications in past decades: E.R. Wrigley and R.S. Schofield, *The Population History of England 1541–1871* . . . (1981), M.W. Flinn, *Scottish Population History from the 17th Century to the 1930s* (1977), *Land, Labour and Population in the Industrial Revolution*, ed. E.L. Jones and G.E. Mingay (1967), particularly for A.H. John's ch. on 'Farming in Wartime: 1793–1815'; Judith Blow Williams, *British Commercial Policy and Trade Expansion, 1750–1850* (1972), Ralph Davis, *The Industrial Revolution and British Overseas Trade* (1979); N.F.R. Crafts, *British Economic Growth during the Industrial Revolution* (1985) – including some significant corrections to Mitchell and Deane's tables (see Ch. IX above) and following a series of articles –, Phyllis Deane, 'War and Industrialisation' in *War and Economic Development, Essays in Memory of David Joslin*, ed. J.M. Winter (1975), W.A. Cole, 'Economic Growth Revisited' (*Explorations in Economic History*, 10, no. 4); A.D. Gayer, W.W. Rostow and A.J. Schwartz, *The Growth and Fluctuation of the British Economy, 1790–1850* (2 vols., 1953), T.S. Ashton, *Economic Fluctuations in England 1700–1800* (1959), Julian Hoppit, 'Financial Crises in Eighteenth-Century England' (*Ec.H.R., Second Series*, XXXIX, no. 1) and *Risk and Failure in English Business 1700–1800* (1987), P.H. Duffy, *Bankruptcy and Insolvency in London during the Industrial Revolution* (1985); J.L. Anderson, 'Aspects of the Effect on the British Economy of the Wars against France, 1793–1815' (*Australian Economic History Review*, XII, no. 1), Glenn Hueckel, 'War and the British Economy, 1793–1815: A General Equilibrium Analysis' (*Explorations in Economic History*, 10, no. 4), François Crouzet, 'The Impact of the French Wars on the British Economy' in *Britain and the French Revolution*, ed. Dickinson (Ch. II above) and *Britain Ascendant: Comparative Studies in Franco–British Economic History* (1990), Patrick Karl O'Brien, 'The Impact of the Revolutionary and Napoleonic Wars, 1793–1815, on the Long-Run Growth of the British Economy' (the Braudel Center *Review*, XII, no. 3).

The British concept of empire in its initial stages is illustrated in Daniel Szechi and David Hayton, 'John Bull's Other Kingdoms, the English government of Scotland and Ireland' (*Britain in the First Age of Party 1680–1750, Essays Presented to Geoffrey Holmes*, ed. Clyve Jones, 1987), and in more familiar guise in Richard Koebner's *Empire* (1961). A stimulating survey of a crucial period is to be found in C.A. Bayley, *Imperial Meridian, The British Empire and the World, 1780–1830* (1989); an economic analysis of fundamental importance in P.J. Cairn and A.G. Hopkins, *British Imperialism and Expansion, 1688–1814* (1993). For the themes followed in this Ch. there is material in John Manning Ward, *Colonial Self-Government, The British Experience 1759–1856* (1976), *Imperial Reconstruction 1763–1840, Select Documents on the Constitutional History of the British Empire and Commonwealth*, II, ed. F.W. Madden with D.K. Fieldhouse (1987), A.F. McFadden, 'The Imperial Machinery of the Younger Pitt' in *Essays in British History Presented to Sir Keith Feiling*, ed. H.R. Trevor-Roper (1964), D. Mackey, 'Direction and Purpose in British Imperial Policy, 1783–1801' (*H.J.*, 17, no. 4).

The question of the slave trade has of course long received continuing attention, some of which is cited in the Note on Sources to my I, Ch. XIII. Eric Williams's *Capitalism and Slavery* (1944) has given rise to 'A Critique' by Roger T. Anstey (*Ec.H.R.*, 2nd ser., XXI, no. 3) and *British Capitalism and Caribbean Slavery: The Legacy of Eric Williams*, ed. Barbara L. Solow and Stanley L. Engerman (1987). Other contributions have been J.R. Ward, *British West Indian Slavery, 1750–1834, The Process of Amelioration* (1988), Seymour Drescher, *Econocide, British Slavery in the Era of Abolition 1760–1810* (1977), and further on figures David Richardson, 'Slave Exports from West and West-Central Africa, 1710–1810 . . .' (*The Journal of African History*, 30, no. 1). The process of the abolition of the trade itself is followed closely in Anstey's *The Atlantic Slave Trade and British Abolition 1760–1810* (1975), and see Alan M. Rose, 'Pitt and the Achievement of Abolition' (*The Journal of Negro History*, XXXIX, no. 3), P.C. Lipscomb, 'William Pitt and the Abolition Question: A Review of an Historical Controversy' (*Proceedings of the Leeds Philosophical and Literary Society*, XII, Pt. IV). David Turley, *The Culture of English Antislavery 1780–1860* (1991), and Seymour Drescher, 'Whose Abolition? Popular Pressure and the Ending of the Bristol Slave Trade' (*Past & Present*, no. 143) investigate the influences, some of them changing, within the country. Pitt's own papers on the Caribbean, which are not particularly revealing, are in P.R.O. 30/8/148–52: he talked, with Wilberforce (but see loc. cit. 189, Dacres Adams Mss formerly P.R.O. 30/58/4) and others, more than he discussed his ideas on paper; and see the biographies of Wilberforce, by his sons (Ch. I above), by Robin Furneaux (1974), and John Pollock (1977). Papers for the other main British possession in the Western hemisphere, Canada, are in P.R.O. 30/8/346–7.

In addition to Ingram, *Commitment to Empire*, and to Naff and Stanton and Shaw on the Ottoman Empire (all Chs. XI & XII above), I have drawn for the East on John Marlowe, *Perfidious Albion: The Origins of Anglo-French Rivalry in the Levant* (1971), J.B. Kelly, *Britain and the Persian Gulf, 1795–1880* (1968), M.E. Yapp, *Strategies of British India, Britain, Iran and Afghanistan 1798–1850* (1980), Ingram, *Britain's Persian Connection 1798–1828 . . .* (1992). Lobanov-Rostovsky (Ch. V above), Feldbaeck, McGrew (Chs. XI & XII) discuss Russia's aims, as do J. Lee Schniedman, 'The Proposed Invasion of India by Russia and France in 1801' (*The Journal of Indian History*, XXXV) and John W. Strong, 'Russia's Plans for an Invasion of India in 1801' (*Canadian Slavonic Papers*, VII). P.J. Marshall, the pre-eminent authority for India itself within the British context in the 18th century, provides an introductory survey in *Problems of Empire, Britain and India 1757–1813* (1968). Sir Penderel Moon, *The British Conquest and Dominion of India* (1989) is a fine account. Iris Butler, *The Eldest Brother, The Marquess Wellesley, The Duke of Wellington's Eldest Brother* (1973) portrays the principal British figure in the subcontinent in these fateful years. His policies are displayed in *The Despatches, Minutes, and Correspondence of the Marquis Wellesley* (Ch. V above); his relations with London more confidentially in *Two Views of British India, The Private Correspondence of Mr. Dundas and Lord Wellesley, 1790–1801*, ed. Edward Ingram (1970). The treatment in Furber's biography of Dundas (Chs. XI & XII above) is strong on Indian affairs; and the bulk of that statesman's ms sources – in S.R.O. and N.L.S. (Abbreviations), the John Rylands Library at Manchester, the former India Office Library (now B.L.) in London – compared with Pitt's in Dacres Adams Mss formerly P.R.O. 30/58/4–5 reflects a balance that neither man abused.

CHAPTER XIV

Arthur Aspinall, *The Cabinet Council 1783–1835* (1952) and Richard Pares, *King George III and the Politicians* (1953) are basic studies for the Cabinet to which may be added I.R. Christie, 'The Cabinet in the Reign of George III' in his *Myth and Reality in Late-Eighteenth Century Politics* (Ch. IV above) and, focused more directly on the period of this Chapter, E. Willis, 'Cabinet Politics and Executive Policy-Making Procedures, 1794–1801' in *Albion*, VII, no. 1. There are useful documents, from Parliamentary debates, correspondence, diaries and memoirs, in *English Historical Documents 1783–1832*, ed. A. Aspinall and E. Anthony Smith (1959), Part I, B, and, above all, in *L.C.G. III*, II–IV. Pitt's papers in the P.R.O. 30/8 series contain no file comparable with Grenville's of (selected) Cabinet Minutes in B.L. Add. Ms 59306, and impressions of his dealings with his colleagues and position as First Minister derive from the proceedings and statements and allusions in the range of sources used for other Chapters. Evidence of Cabinet meetings and attendance from London newspapers in these years is interesting, though far from conclusive.

The administration of the armed forces has naturally attracted much attention. C.M. Clode, *The Military Forces of the Crown, Their Administration and Government* (2 vols., 1869), and Fortescue's *History of the British Army*, IV-Part II (Ch. I above) should not be neglected. Richard Glover, *Peninsular Preparation, The Reform of the British Army 1795–1809* (1963), J.R. Western, *The English Militia in the Eighteenth Century*, J.E. Cookson, 'The English Volunteer Movements of the French wars' (both Ch. IV above) – together with some stimulating articles on specific corps –, throw valuable lights on the land forces, regular and auxiliary, and Glover extends the examination by Arthur Forbes of *A History of the Army Ordnance Service* (1929). David Gates investigates a significant specific question in *The British Light Infantry Arm, c 1790–1815: its Creation, Training and Operational Role* (1987).

Michael Lewis gave a pioneering rigour to *A Social History of the Navy 1783–1815* (1960), and some other, administrative studies are cited in my II – Christopher Oprey, 'Schemes for the Reform of Naval Recruitment, 1793–1815' (Ch. IV above), Clive Emsley, 'The Recruitment of Petty Offenders during the French Wars' (*The Mariner's Mirror*, 66, no. 3), N.A.M. Rodger, *The Admiralty* (1979), articles by P.K. Crimmin on its staff and on relations with the Treasury in *The Mariner's Mirror*, 55, nos. 1 & 3, Bernard Pool, *Navy Board Contracts, 1660–1832 . . .* (1966), Christopher Lloyd and Jack S. Coulter, *Medicine and the Navy, 1200–1900*, III (1961). Paul Webb follows the 'Construction, Repair and Maintenance in the Battle Fleet of the Royal Navy, 1793–1815' in *The British Navy and the Use of Naval Power in the Eighteenth Century*, ed. Jeremy M. Black and Philip Woodfine (1988). R.A. Morriss, *The Royal Dockyards during the Revolutionary and Napoleonic Wars* (1981) is an authoritative study to which Jonathan Coad, *Historic Architecture of the Royal Navy . . .* (1983) is an architectural complement. Michael Steer, 'The Blockade of Brest and the Victualling of the Western Squadron, 1793–1805' (*The Mariner's Mirror*, 76, no. 4), examines a specific problem.

One contemporary published source of primary material joins the Departmental unpublished files to underpin secondary accounts of central administration in general: the important 36 reports of the House of Commons Select Committee on Finance of 1797, which were printed in series from 1798, collectively in vols. XII and XIII of the *First Series of Reports* in 1803, and may now be found in *Sessional Papers of the House of Commons in the Eighteenth Century*, ed.

Sheila Lambert (Chs. IX & X above), vols. 107–114. They were particularly searching on the navy, particularly the dockyards. But they covered almost the whole of the Government's financial responsibilities, for which some secondary authorities are noted below, providing on the way many of the figures which George Rose used in his *Brief Examination* of 1799 (Ch. XIII above). One office however which escaped survey was the Alien Office, annexed to the Home Office: an institution whose secrets, of British, Irish and European intelligence and British subversion on the Continent, have recently been under investigation, by Roger Wells, by Marianne Elliott (both Ch. I above), and most interestingly for Europe by Elizabeth Sparrow, whose searches continue but have already yielded two articles as given in Ch. II above; and see also, in this grey area, J.J. Kenny, 'Lord Whitworth and the Conspiracy against Tsar Paul I: The New Evidence of the Kent Archives' in *Slavic Review*, xxxvi. On the more regular main civil Departments, Henry Roseveare examines *The Treasury* . . . (1970), R.R. Nelson *The Home Office 1782–1801* (Ch. IV above), Charles Ronald Middleton *The Administration of British Foreign Policy 1782–1846* (1977). The lists of *Office-Holders in Modern Britain*, I, III–VIII, compiled by J.C. Sainty (I–VI) and by J.M. Collinge (VII–VIII) (1972–9) are of very real value. Pitt's surviving papers in P.R.O. 30/8/255–6 are of interest for the development of the Port of London.

The practice and procedure of the House of Commons in the greater part of the century are covered in P.G.D. Thomas, *The House of Commons in the Eighteenth Century* (1971), while O.C. Williams examines *The Clerical Organization of the House of Commons 1661–1850* (1954) and Sheila Lambert the legislative procedure of both Houses in *Bills and Acts* . . . (1971). The five volumes of *H of P* for 1790–1820 (Abbreviations), ed. R.G. Thorne, are of course essential reading, and among the notices of the Members themselves the editor's own contribution on Pitt is a masterpiece in miniature. Two recent complementary studies may be mentioned, the latter too recent for me to use properly: the more general by Peter J. Jupp, 'The Landed Elite and Political Authority in Britain c 1760–1850' (*The Journal of British Studies*, 29, no. 1), and Ian R. Christie, *British 'non-élite' MPs 1715–1820* (1995). Philip Laundy, *The Office of Speaker* (1964) is a general account; Charles Abbot's *Diary and Correspondence of Lord Colchester* (Chs. IX–X above) of some use for that indefatigable holder of the Chair, and the ms of the diary starting for our purposes in P.R.O. 30/39/32, together with 39/12 (2), 25 are more so. See also his entry in *H of P*, III (again by Thorne). Patrick Howarth, *Questions in the House, The History of an Unique British Institution* (1956) is of interest. Peter Fraser, 'The Growth of Ministerial Control in the Nineteenth-Century House of Commons' (*E.H.R.*, LXXV, no. CCXCVI) has observations relevant to the immediately preceding period. Wilberforce noted some particulars of Pitt's oratory, to be found in Bodleian Library Ms C254.

The House of Lords has attracted fresh attention in the years since A.S. Turberville's *The House of Lords in the Age of Reform 1784–1837* . . . (1958): in Michael W. McCahill, *Order and Equipoise, The Peerage and the House of Lords, 1783–1806* (1978), and in articles by himself, by David Large, by G.M. Ditchfield, and by James J. Sack – on the Scottish peers, the 'party of the Crown', Parliamentary reform, Parliamentary patronage, creations in the peerage – assembled in *Peers, Politics and Power: The House of Lords, 1603–1911*, ed. Clyve Jones and David Lewis Jones (1986). Maurice F. Bond has produced the authoritative *Guide to the Records of Parliament* (1971). The topography of the old Palace of Westminster before its destruction is described in Maurice Hastings, *Parliament House*, and in greater detail with the stated emphasis in an unpublished account by Orlo Cyprian Williams, 'The Topography of the Old House of Commons' (both Ch. VI above). Pitt's files in the P.R.O. 30/8 series contain miscellaneous papers and lists in 234–5, 238. Correspondence on the proposed Order of Merit appears in 143 (Hawkesbury), 144 (Sir Isaac Heard).

CHAPTER XV

Pitt's correspondence with the King on his resignation was published in 1827 as the second part – his first bearing on the question in 1795 of membership of Parliament for Irish Roman Catholics – of a volume (assembled by Henry Phillpotts, Bishop of Exeter) entitled *Letters from His Late Majesty to the Late Lord Kenyon on the Coronation Oath, with His Lordship's Answers: and Letters of the Rt. Hon. William Pitt to His Late Majesty, with His Majesty's Answers, Previous to the Dissolution of the Ministry in 1801*. Stanhope republished the latter in his III, Appendix, xxiii–xxxii. The ms material, some original, some transcribed, had been in the possession of the 1st Lord Kenyon, Lord Chief Justice, and remains in that of his descendant at Gredington in Shropshire. Pitt's copies of his own letters are in P.R.O. 30/8/101; the originals of the King's answers may be found loc. cit., 104.

Pretyman's draft account on the events centring on 3–4 February 1801, for the unpublished volume of his Life of Pitt, is in B.L. Add. Ms 45107, and again with some variations in 45108; and notes and memoranda on the whole affair are scattered in his papers. The most useful single account of earlier proceedings in Cabinet is that of Camden, in Camden Ms U840 O197 at Maidstone. This has been printed with a commentary by Richard Willis in *Bulletin of the Institute of Historical Research*, XLIV, no. 110, itself discussed with a different conclusion by Charles John Fedorak in 'Catholic Emancipation and the Resignation of William Pitt in 1801' in *Albion*, 24, no. 1. Other members of the Cabinet have left us less on the various stages of the business affair: among those who likewise resigned, Grenville noticeably so, though there is an interesting undated letter to Pitt in the Dacres Adams Mss formerly P.R.O. 30/58/4; Dundas's attitude and exertions may be seen from a few scattered documents, among them letters to Pitt loc. cit. and in P.R.O. 30/8/157, and a hopeful list for a new Cabinet under Pitt in B.L. Add. Ms 40102; Spencer's papers in B.L. yield nothing notable of his own; for Windham see his diary in B.L. Add. Ms 37924. For those who did not resign with Pitt, there are letters to his brother Chatham from the King in P.R.O. 30/8/364, from Addington loc. cit. 369 and P.R.O. 30/70/4, and Pitt himself in Ashbourne, *Pitt: some Chapters of his Life and Times* (Ch. III above); for Portland see Malmesbury's diary (Ch. II above), for Liverpool and Loughborough Glenbervie's (Chs. XI & XII), for Loughborough again that of Rose (Ch. III above), I. Addington's position emerges to some extent from that of Charles Abbot [Colchester], I (Chs. IX & X), and is discussed in Pellew's *Life of Sidmouth* (Ch. II above); his papers in the Devon R.O. at Exeter are of course essential from his own point of view. The King's illness is treated in ch. 6 of Ida MacAlpine & Richard Hunter, *George III and the Mad-Business* (1969). His views emerge clearly above, and in *L.C.G. III*, III, with Aspinall's notes. The position of his heir has been well summarised by Aspinall in *Correspondence of the Prince of Wales*, IV (Ch. VI above); a problematical surmise of his attitude to Pitt's future in the event of a Regency is raised by a document now in the Royal Archives as RA 3/77.

Reactions from men less closely involved – Canning, Pretyman, Auckland, Thomas Pelham – emerge likewise in the diaries of Malmesbury, Rose, Glenbervie. They show how normally well-informed figures were living on a mixed diet of fact, rumour and speculation. Canning's sentiments as distinct from knowledge – his diary in Canning Ms 29d is empty for this period – may be gauged in a letter to Pitt of March (Stanhope Ms U1590 S5 02/1). Pretyman corresponded with his wife and received letters from Rose (Pretyman Mss 435/45, 44). Auckland's own exertions in self-justification may be seen in *A.C.*, IV. Published diaries and correspondence within the political and social world, and the London newspapers, convey the atmosphere in the course of the baffling drama.

CHAPTER XVI

Pitt's finances, for which sources for earlier years are given in Ch. III above, began to yield depressing information shortly before and immediately after he resigned. Correspondence and papers between Rose and Pretyman in the latter's Ms 435/44 and the former's B.L. Add. Ms 42772–3, Rose's published diary (Ch. III), some accounts in Stanhope Ms U1590 S5 C44, lists of income and expenditure in the Saumarez Smith papers, illustrate the process of examination which led to the loan subscribed by a circle of the Minister's friends, for which see Stanhope, III, 348 and Pretyman Ms 108/45. Further evidence survives in Pitt's own papers, P.R.O. 30/8/202–3, 218–19.

The Saumarez Smith Mss continue to be valuable for the next three years, as do Coutts's ledgers (Ch. III above) over the whole period. The sale of Holwood, as one measure of economy, is covered in Stanhope Mss U1590 S5 C44, 60/6. The Saumarez Smith papers provide some information on purchases of books; Pretyman Ms 561:21 contains the list of those at Walmer at Pitt's death. Walmer itself begins to figure more prominently in the financial records at this time. A good account of life there is given in ch. V of The Marquess Curzon of Kedleston, *The Personal History of Walmer Castle and Its Lords Warden* (1927); but some details can also be gained, at a period when memories could still be tapped, from Stephen Pritchard, *The History of Deal and Its Neighbourhood* (1864), itself corrected in places by John Laker, *History of Deal* (1917). Other accounts occur in John Lyon, *The History of the Town and Port of Dover* (2 vols., 1813), R.S. Elvin, *The History of Walmer and Walmer Castle* (privately printed, 1894), Ernest Law, *Walmer Castle Illustrated – with a Catalogue of the Pictures, Prints and Furniture* (1906); and there is a good official *Guide* (first published in 1952). Pitt's biographer Stanhope printed for private circulation in 1866 *Notes and Extracts of Letters referring to Mr. Pitt and Walmer Castle 1801–1806*, and this was published in *Miscellanies. Collected and Edited by Earl Stanhope. Second Series* (1872). Reminiscences of life at the Castle were published in *Memoirs of the Lady Hester Stanhope . . .* (3 vols., 1845). They must be treated with the caution required for this source throughout; but her contemporary descriptions may be found in letters to Francis Jackson in Stanhope Ms U1590 C240, published in the Duchess of Cleveland's *The Life and Letters of Lady Hester Stanhope* (1914), and thereafter to William Dacres Adams in Dacres Adams Mss formerly P.R.O. 30/58/9. The best account of her, and her half-brothers', relations with Pitt is in Aubrey Newman's *The Stanhopes of Chevening* (1969); a sidelight on him as for once a disapproving uncle to a member of the family, in Stanhope Ms U1590

S5 C30. The retired Minister's enthusiasm for his military duties as a Colonel of Volunteers is shown in Curzon and in Cleveland above and can be glimpsed in *The Diary of Sir John Moore*, II, ed. J.F. Maurice (1904) and the General's *Life* by John Carrick Moore, II (1813). Some letters to Pitt's subordinate officer Carrington, in Bodleian Library Mss Film 121, convey the flavour. Peter Bloomfield, *Kent and the Napoleonic Wars* (1987) and P.A.L. Vine, *The Royal Military Canal* (1972) discuss his involvement in the wider regional issues of defence, glimpsed also in letters to the Secretary of State for War and the Secretary at War in B.L. Add. Mss 40862, 45040. Other, social, aspects of life at Walmer may be found in Moore's diary, in Cannng's for 1802–3 (Canning Ms 29d), and in Kentish newspapers. A highly coloured impression of Pitt's (sole) visit to the Pretymans at the Bishop's palace emerges from his hostess's account in Pretyman Ms 435/29.

By this time Walter Farquhar was well installed as Pitt's physician, and his retrospective diagnosis was published in *The Monthly Review* of December 1900 by Rosebery and given private circulation (Ch. III above). Some of the doctor's correspondence is printed in Stanhope's *Miscellanies. Second Series* (see above), and there are a few further letters in P.R.O. 30/8/134, which can be supplemented from Stanhope Ms U1590 C419/8. There are lists of medical supplies in the Saumarez Smith papers. Canning's diary (Canning Ms 29d) for September 1802 shows the position on a visit after Pitt's severest attack, and reports on a reduced consumption of wine in the autumn appear in Pretyman Ms 435/44. There have been various diagnoses of the causes of Pitt's apparently congenital constitutional weaknesses. Pretyman's own thoughts are given in drafts for the unpublished part of his biography (Ch. XV above). I have learned much from Dr R. Guest Gornall's article in *The Practitioner*, and in correspondence with Mr T.G.J. Brightmore FRCS (both Ch. III above).

The young Lord Haddo's letter to Pitt announcing his choice of him and Dundas as guardians under Scots law is in P.R.O. 30/8/107. Later letters from Pitt are in Aberdeen's papers in B.L. Add. Ms 43227, and see also Muriel E. Chamberlain, *Lord Aberdeen: A Political Biography* (1983).

CHAPTERS XVII & XVIII

Pellew's biography published in the 1840s (Ch. II above) did not carry enough guns to counter the widely received tradition that Pitt's successor was a nullity as First Minister: one deriving largely from the fact that he was not Pitt, crystallised by Canning's sarcastic attacks, enshrined in Whig historiography after the war, and not disturbed by subsequent studies – Stanhope (III–IV), Rosebery, Holland Rose (II) – of Pitt himself. Certainly Addington was not a great Minister; he could not emerge from his predecessor's shadow; but more recent examination suggests that the verdict may have been exaggerated, and without favouring excessive revisionism one should take into account Philip Ziegler's biography, *Addington* . . . (1965), the entry on Addington (by R.G. Thorne) in *H of P*, III, C.D. Hall, 'Addington at war: unspectacular but not unsuccessful' (*Historical Research*, LXI, no. 3) and *British Strategy in the Napoleonic War 1803–15* (1992), and above all Charles John Fedorak, 'The Addington Ministry and the Interaction of Foreign Policy and Domestic Politics 1800–1804' (Ph.D. thesis, University of London, 1990). Family background is provided in E.M.G. Belfield . . ., *The Annals of the Addington Family* (1959).

In a period in which Pitt's intentions while out of office were a lively subject of rumour, and were indeed hard to forecast, the reliability of different sources poses particular problems. Some recent studies of the political scene are most helpful. A.D. Harvey, *Britain in the Early Nineteenth Century* (1978) draws on his own Ph.D. thesis for Cambridge (1972) 'The Grenville Party, 1801–1826', and there are other studies of Addington's opponents in J.J. Sack, *The Grenvillites 1801–1829: party politics and factionalism in the age of Pitt and Liverpool* (1979), Richard E. Willis, 'Fox, Grenville and the Recovery of Opposition, 1801–1804' (*The Journal of British Studies*, XI, no. 1), Peter Jupp, *Lord Grenville* (Ch. II above).

Private diaries and correspondence, bearing on a retired but increasingly central figure whose own correspondence as often was uneven, provide the evidence for his developing attitudes over the three years. The reactions to Pitt's defence of the Preliminary peace treaty from former colleagues who had resigned with him emerge from letters in *H.M.C., Dropmore*, VII (and marginally in B.L. Add. Mss 60487A, 69067), in B.L. Add. Ms 37877 and *The Windham Papers*, (Ch. I above), II, the Dacres Adams Mss formerly P.R.O. 30/58/4, B.L. Add. Mss temp Althorp G42, 48, 221–2 – with 293 for Lady Spencer – for Spencer's papers. The texts of the peace treaties are in *Consolidated Treaty Series* (Ch. V above), 56 (1969). Signs of Pitt's rising uneasiness in the first half of 1802 are to be seen in the Grenville brothers' correspondence – *H.M.C., Dropmore*, VII and the political letters in B.L. Add. Mss (see A.D. Harvey's bibliography in Ch. II above, 24), Buckingham (Abbreviations), III and the Stowe Ms at the Huntington Library, California, Thomas Grenville's papers in B.L. Add. Mss 41851–2, 41856; in the Dacres Adams Mss as above; Canning Mss 29d, 30 and his letters to a favourite correspondent, Granville Leveson Gower, in P.R.O. 30/29/8; Addington's papers in the Sidmouth Mss at the Devon R.O., 152M C1802; Pretyman Ms 435/44 and B.L. Add. Ms 42772, for the hopeful watch kept by the Bishop and George Rose. Canning's activities may be followed in Marshall's biography and Wendy Hinde, *George Canning* (both Ch. III above), and P.C. Lipscomb, 'Party Politics 1801–1802: George Canning and the Trinidad Question' (*H.J*, XII, no. 3).

The same primary sources, published and unpublished and adjusted for date, apply through the rest of the year and 1803. To them may be added in rising proportion a number of publications: the *Diaries and Correspondence of Malmesbury* (Ch. II), IV, Rose (Ch. III), I–II, Abbot, I (Colchester – Chs. IX & X above), Glenbervie, I (Chs. XI & XII above), *L.C.G. III*, IV (1968), *H.M.C., Bathurst, Life of Wilberforce* (Ch. I), III, *Life and Letters of Sir Gilbert Elliot* (Ch. VI above), III. Of the further ms sources one may mention Hawkesbury's reports to Liverpool (B.L. Loan Ms 72, vol. 55), Bathurst's unpublished papers (B.L. Loan Ms 57, vol. 2), Dundas's – Melville's – (P.R.O. 30/8/157, B.L. Add. Ms 40102, John Rylands Library Eng. Ms 907 as well as those in S.R.O. and N.L.S.), Huskisson's (B.L. Add. Ms 38737), Mulgrave's (the Normanby Mss at Mulgrave Castle, Yorkshire). Canning Ms 31 holds copies, presumably from Pitt, of the latter's correspondence with Addington in the spring of 1803, for which see also Sidmouth Ms 152M C1803. For details of publications in the pamphlet war starting later in that year see p. 622, n1 above.

The growing rift, culminating from the turn of 1803–4 in Pitt's attacks on the Ministry and ending in his return to office in May, brings Fox's position to the fore; see *Memorials and Correspondence of Fox*, ed. Lord John Russell, III–IV (1857) and ch. 10 of L.G. Mitchell's *Charles James Fox* (1992), together with E.A. Smith,

Lord Grey, 1764–1845 (1990) and the studies of Grenville and the Grenvillites above. For the Prince of Wales see Ch. XV above and for Moira also *H.M.C., Hastings*, while *The Letters of Richard Brinsley Sheridan*, ed. Cecil Price, II (1966) contains some interesting material. The specific causes of Pitt's onslaught on Addington, the manning of the land forces and reforms to the civil administration of the navy, are set in context for the former in Glover, *Peninsular Preparation* (Ch. XIV above), Fortescue's *History of the British Army* (Ch. I above), and the latter's *The County Lieutenancies and the Army, 1803–14* (1909) and Western for the militia (Ch. XIV above), and for the latter in Roger Morriss, 'St Vincent and Reform, 1801–04' (*The Mariner's Mirror*, 69, no. 3) as well as his work on the dockyards (Ch. XIV above), *Letters of Admiral of the Fleet Earl St Vincent, while First Lord of the Admiralty, 1801–4*, ed. David Bonner Smith (2 vols., 1922–7), Jedediah S. Tucker, *Memoirs of Admiral the Right Honᵉ. The Earl of St Vincent*, II (1844), *Letters and Papers of Charles, Lord Barham . . . 1758–1813*, ed. Sir John Knox Laughton, III (1911). Pitt's papers in P.R.O. 30/8/240, 243–5 include some material for the land forces and in 257 for the navy. The prelude to the return itself yields some evidence in *Secret Correspondence connected with Mr. Pitt's Return to Office in 1804 . . .*, which was privately printed by Lord Mahon (Stanhope) in 1852. As the subtitle made clear, the compilation drew chiefly on the mss in Melville Castle. These are now in the S.R.O., and their account of events can be supplemented from the diary and letters of Alexander Hope in the Hope of Luffness papers, S.R.O., GD 364, which are also useful for his earlier contacts with Pitt. The Dacres Adams Mss formerly P.R.O. 30/58/5 are interesting, and there is some material in the Normanby Mss boxes J, VII bundle 13, 37. Michael W. McCahill, 'The House of Lords and the Collapse of Henry Addington's Administration' (*Parliamentary History*, VI, Part I) brings out the importance of the Upper House in the spring of 1804. The introduction to *H.M.C., Dropmore*, VII by the editor, Walter Fitzpatrick, is a well argued energetic case for Grenville over a controversial period.

Further information on the final stage is to be found in *H.M.C., Bathurst*, almost certainly from Pitt's conversation. Horace Twiss, *The Public and Private Life of Lord Chancellor Eldon . . .*, I (1844) is useful, as are the sources already cited on the Grenvillites and Foxites. Stanhope, IV, prints in the text and Appendix letters between Pitt and the King from the Dacres Adams Mss. Macalpine & Hunter (Ch. XV above) give an account of the recurrence of George III's illness.

Parliamentary debates are of high importance particularly from the late autumn of 1803–4. *P.R., 3rd ser.*, XIV–XVIII (1800–2), *4th ser.*, I–III (1803–4) cover the period March 1801–August 1803. The publication then ceased, and Cobbett's *Parliamentary Debates* (*P.D.*, see Abbreviations) began their life, opening the famous series 'Under the Superintendence' of T.C. Hansard as the edition of 1812 stated, with I–II (1804) covering November 1803–July 1804. *The Senator, 2nd ser.* had meanwhile ceased publication after covering January 1801–June 1802 in I–V (nd). Cobbett's later *P.H.*, XXXV–XXXVI (1819–20) cover March 1800–August 1803.

CHAPTER XIX

Sources for Ch. XVIII supply much of the political information here. For the formation of the new Ministry and attitudes to it one may cite in particular Stanhope IV, the diaries of Rose (Ch. III), Colchester, I (Chs. IX & X), *Glenbervie*,

I (Chs. XI & XII), *Malmesbury* (Ch. II), IV, Twiss, I for Eldon (Chs. XVII & XVIII), *H.M.C., Bathurst, L.C.G. III*, IV, *Correspondence of Prince of Wales*, V (1968) with Aspinal's notes, to which one may add *Correspondence of Leveson Gower*, I (Ch. II above), *Letters to 'Ivy' from the First Earl of Dudley*, ed. Samuel Henry Romilly (1905). Among unpublished ms material (and much is published) the Dacres Adams Mss formerly P.R.O. 30/58/5 – and marginally 8 – are of interest, as are P.R.O. 30/8, eg 112 for Bathurst, 119 for Camden, 120 for Canning, 133 for Euston, 146 (Hope, on Moira), 160 Duke of Montrose, B.L. Loan Ms 57, vol. 2 (Bathurst), Canning Mss 29d, 30, Camden Ms U840 C209/3, Normanby Mss box 37, Pretyman Ms T435/44.

Most of the sources for financial affairs repeat publications cited for Ch. IX above. O'Brien and Cooper are fundamental, and Farnsworth's claim for Addington's contribution to Pitt's income tax calls for attention. Mitchell & Deane, Hope-Jones, Newmarch are of value; the diaries of Rose, II and Colchester, I shed light on Pitt's opinion of his predecessor as Chancellor of the Exchequer. The Parliamentary debates (below) are important, but need supplementing by *The Times* of 14 July 1803 for Pitt's speech of the day before. P.R.O. 30/8/173, 197, 275, 303–4, Sidmouth Mss 152M C1802 OT 14, C1803 OT 29 are relevant, as is B.L. Add. Ms 31229 for Vansittart.

The study of foreign affairs, like that of finance, benefits from two unpublished theses: by Fedorak (Chs. XVII & XVIII above) and by G.B. Fremont, 'Britain's Role in the Formation of the Third Coalition against France' (D.Phil., Oxford, 1991), both providing necessary background and bibliographies from Addington's period, for which Norman Gash, *Lord Liverpool* (Ch. III above) gives a further well balanced judgment on Hawkesbury as Foreign Secretary. The older account of policy by Holland Rose in *The Cambridge History of British Foreign Policy*, I (Ch. II above) retains its value, and he also edited *Select Despatches from the British Foreign Archives, relating to the formation of the Third Coalition against France 1804–5* (1904). Russia, the other party most actively involved, is well served by published documentation; in Simon Vorontsov's correspondence in London, *Arkhiv Kniazia Vorontsova* (Ch. V above), X, XV, and, for those qualified, more comprehensively in *Sbornik Imperatorskago Russkago Istoriceskago Obscestva*, LXVII for relations with France and *Vneshniaia Politika Rossi XIX i nachala XX veka. Dokumenty rossiiskogo Ministerstva del Ministerstvo Inostrannykh del SSSR*, I, II (1960) for policy in general. Patricia M. Grimsted reproduces 'Czartoryski's System for Russian Foreign Policy, 1803: A Memorandum' (*California Slavic Studies*, V, no. 1), the *Memoirs of Prince Adam Czartoryski and his Correspondence with Alexander I* are edited by Adam Gielgud (II, 1888), and M. Kukiel, *Czartoryski and European Unity, 1770–1861* (1955), Grimsted, *The Foreign Ministers of Alexander I . . . 1801–1825* (1969), and – particularly – W.H. Zawadzki, *A Man of Honour . . .* (1993), are most useful. See also M.S. Anderson, *The Eastern Question* (Chs. XI & XII above), Lobanov-Rostovsky, *Russia and Europe, 1789–1925*, Saul, *Russia and the Mediterranean, 1797–1807* (both Ch. V above). Sources for Prussia are contained in *Briefwechsel König Friedrich Wilhelm's III . . . mit Kaiser Alexander I*, ed. Paul Bailleu (1900), and *Preussen under Frankreich von 1795 bis 1807 . . .*, ed. Bailleu (1887). For Austria see *Österreich und Russland in dem Jahren 1804–5*, ed. Adolf Beer (1875), August Fournier, *Gentz und Cobenzl: Geschichte der österreichischen Diplomatic in dem Jahre, 1801–1805* (1880). For France herself see the *Correspondance de Napoléon I* (Ch. V above), and also *Lettres inédités de Talleyrand à Napoléon, 1800–1809* (1889). Harold C. Deutsch, *The Genesis of Napoleonic Imperialism* (1938) is a good study. Some light is thrown on Francis Jackson in Berlin in letters to his brother (*Diaries and Letters of Sir George Jackson, from the Peace of Amiens to the Battle of Talavera*, ed. Lady Jackson, I (1872)), and on Arthur Paget in Vienna in *The Paget Papers* (Chs. XI & XII above). The former's relevant papers are in P.R.O., F.O. 353, the latter's in B.L. Add. Mss 48389–414; Granville Leveson Gower's for Russia in P.R.O. 30/29. Harrowby's papers as Foreign Secretary are in the possession of the Earl of Harrowby. Pitt's files containing correspondence on Europe and the United States are P.R.O. 30/8/332–45. There are letters from Vorontsov loc. cit. 191 and from Novosiltsov 163. Foreign Office papers are in P.R.O., F.O. 5/33, 36, 39, 41–3 (United States), 7/63–72 (Austria), 9/22–9 (Bavaria), 22/41–5, 118 (Denmark), 27/57–70 (France), 28/18 (Genoa), 31/11–13 (German States), 33/21–6 (Hamburg), 37/60–1, 38/6–7 (Holland and Netherlands, and Frontiers), 42/4–5 (Ionian Islands), 49/3 (Malta), 63/35–45 (Portugal), 64/60–6 (Prussia), 65/48–56 (Russia), 67/30–3 (Sardinia), 68/15 (Saxony), 70/16–23 (The Two Sicilies), 72/46–54 (Spain), 73/29–32 (Sweden), 74/36–8 (Switzerland), 78/31–45 (Turkey).

Pitt's activity in plans for defence has been noted while he was out of office (Chs. XVII & XVIII above). One may add for his return P.R.O. 30/8/157 (for Melville), 240, 245, 250, with background for Fulton's 'experiment' in *The Keith Papers* . . ., ed. Christopher Lloyd (Chs. XI & XII above), III (1955) and 'Congreve's Rockets, 1805–1806', ed. Christopher Lloyd and Hardin Craig, Jnr (*The Naval Miscellany*, IV, ed. Christopher Lloyd, 1952). His political difficulties, shown at once in his proposals for the land forces, are illustrated clearly in the Parliamentary debates, *P.D.*, II (see Chs. XVII & XVIII above). Relations with Grenville, deteriorating further after a newspaper leak, are followed in Jupp, *Lord Grenville* (Ch. II) and the other sources cited for Chs. XVII and XVIII above, and see also B.L. Add. Mss 37846, 37882, 37884 for Windham; those with the King and with his heir in *L.C.G. III*, IV and *Correspondence of Prince of Wales*, V – and see Stanhope Ms U1590 S5 04/5 for Tierney –, the diaries of Rose, II (Ch. III above), Malmesbury, IV (Ch. II), Glenbervie, I (Chs. XI & XII), the Dacres Adams Mss formerly P.R.O. 30/58/5; those within the Ministry similarly and in Camden Ms U840 C309, P.R.O. 30/8/146 (Alexander Hope), 160 (Montrose), 120 and Canning Ms 29d, B.L. Loan Ms 72, vol. 24 (Hawkesbury) with Stanhope Ms U1590 S5 010/16, P.R.O. 30/70/4 for a letter from George Villiers, Pretyman Ms 435/44. For the Minister's efforts to improve his situation one may cite in addition *Memoirs and Correspondence of Fox*, IV, *H.M.C., Dropmore*, VII, Buckingham, III, *H.M.C., Hastings*, Pellew (Ch. II above), II, the published diaries of Colchester and P.R.O. 30/9/33, P.R.O. 30/8/143 (Hawkesbury), B.L. Add. Ms 31229 (Vansittart). The studies by Harvey and Sack (Chs. XVII & XVIII) continue to be of great use.

CHAPTER XX

The authorities cited in Ch. XIX for foreign affairs apply again here, particularly for Russia on which the main weight of British policy was concentrated in the first eight months of 1805. I therefore confine references for this Ch. to some specific items. Bonaparte's letter to George III at the start of the year with a suggestion of peace, and the British reply, are in P.R.O., F.O. 27/71, the King's response to Pitt is printed in Holland Rose, *Pitt and Napoleon* (Ch. II above), Part II, drafts of the British reply are in the Dacres Adams Mss formerly P.R.O. 30/58/6. Pitt's survey, in answer to the Tsar, of a European peace and its maintenance is in F.O. 65/60, and there are working drafts, mostly in his hand, in the Dacres Adams Mss formerly P.R.O. 30/58/8. The text was made available after a decade in *H.C.J.*, 70, and the bulk was published in C.K. Webster, *British Diplomacy 1813–1815; select documents dealing with the reconstruction of Europe* (1921). E. Ingram, 'Lord Mulgrave's Prospects for the Reconstruction of Europe' (*H.J*, XIX, no. 2) claims credit for the Foreign Secretary. Stephen R. Graubard, 'Castlereagh and the Peace of Europe' (*The Journal of British Studies*, III, no. 1), F.H. Hinsley, *Power & the Pursuit of Peace* (1963), chs. 8, 9, are among those who trace the legacy of ideas. Foreign Office papers for 1805 in the P.R.O. follow numerically on those given for the period of Ch. XIX; to the private papers cited loc. cit. may be added Leveson Gower's letters to Pitt in P.R.O. 30/8/152 and letters to him from the Minister in P.R.O. 30/29/384, Pitt's corresponcence with Novosiltsov in Dacres Adams Mss formerly P.R.O. 30/58/6 and letters to Harrowby in Harrowby Mss vol. X, some letters from Harrowby to Pitt in P.R.O. 30/8/142, Mulgrave's papers as Foreign Secretary in the Normanby Mss. Figures for financial provisions of the treaties of alliance with Russia, Austria, and Sweden are examined in Sherwig, *Guineas and Gunpowder* (Ch. V above). For the terms of the agreements themselves see *Consolidated Treaty Series* (ibid), 58 (1969), and *Select Despatches . . . relating to the Third Coalition* (Ch. XIX above) for the Provisional treaty with Russia. The engagements with Sweden are followed in Raymond Carr, 'Gustavus IV and the British Government' (*E.H.R.*, LX, no. CCXXXVI) as well as by Fremont (Ch. XIX above) who gives the most detailed account of British diplomacy in these months throughout.

For the Parliamentary events of the period see *P.D.*, III–V, *P.H.*, XXXVII. As in foreign affairs, and for the same reason, I concentrate on particular sources for domestic politics. Dissatisfaction with Pitt is reflected in correspondence in P.R.O. 30/29/8, The Dacres Adams Mss formerly P.R.O. 30/58/6, Camden Mss U840 C116, 244, *H.M.C., Bathurst*. His quarrel with George III over the choice of a new Archbishop of Canterbury can be followed in Stanhope, IV, *L.C.G. III*, IV, Rose's *Diaries* (Ch. III), II, Ashbourne, *Pitt, His Life and Times* (ibid). The great upset of the investigation into Melville's conduct takes up much space in *P.D.*, III and IV; the text of the Tenth Report of the Commission of Naval Inquiry is printed there, as also in the Commons' *Parliamentary Sessional Papers* for 1804–5 (Chs. IX & X). See also Stanhope, IV, Matheson, *Life of Henry Dundas* (Chs. XI & XII above), P.R.O. 30/8/157, *Life of Wilberforce* (Ch. I), III, *H.M.C., Bathurst* and B.L. Loan Ms 57, vol. 2, *Diaries of Colchester* (Chs. IX & X), I, Canning Ms 29d, B.L. Add. Ms temp Althorp G294 – Lady Spencer's curious tale in the preceding August –, B.L. Add. Ms 31229 (Vansittart to Lord Hardwicke); *H.M.C., Dropmore*, VII, Harvey and Sack (both Chs. XVII & XVIII above) for the Grenvillites; *The Creevey Papers*, ed. John Gore (1963), *Diaries of Malmesbury* (Ch. II above), IV, *Letters to 'Ivy'* (Ch. XIX above), *H of P*, IV (Whitbread). The Commission's Eleventh Report and Pitt's response are covered in *P.D.*, V; and see a letter from Bathurst to Camden, 11 April misendorsed 1802 but 1805 (Camden Ms U 840 C226/5). The subsequent problems precipitated by the appointment of Middleton (Barham) to the Admiralty – see *Letters and Papers of Charles of Barham*, III (Chs. XVII & XVIII above) – and Addington's (Sidmouth's) resignation provoked a flurry of correspondence and ideas for rearrangements: one may draw attention to Pellew (Ch. II above), II,

Diaries of Colchester, II, B.L. Loan Ms 72, vol. 55, Dacres Adams Mss formerly P.R.O. 30/58/6, *Memorials and Correspondence of Fox*, IV (Chs. XVII & XVIII), Jupp, *Lord Grenville* (Ch. II), Camden Ms U840 C95/3, *H.M.C., Bathurst* and B.L. Loan Ms, vol. 2, *H of P*, I.

When writing his biography, Stanhope collected information from survivors on Pitt in his later days. Most of it was published, but one interesting account was not, of a conversation in 1810 between Dacres Adams and the King, and this may be found in Stanhope Ms U1590 C405/15. Hester Stanhope often spoke of her uncle and her remarks were reported in the *Memoirs*, II (Ch. XVI above). Stanhope, IV gives glimpses of some carefree relations with children and the young; *The Diary of Joseph Farington*, VI, ed. Kenneth Garlick and Angus Macintyre (1979) contains the painter Thomas Lawrence's report of one less unbuttoned social occasion, and also has some interesting comments from portrait artists on him as a subject. We catch a sight of the Minister in action towards the end with an embarrassing deputation, in *The Irish Catholic Petition of 1805, The Diary of Denys Scully*, ed. Brian MacDermot (1992).

CHAPTER XXI

The Trafalgar campaign is a tale oft told. Nelson's return to England after the long chase, and the consultations in London, are covered in Carola Oman's *Nelson* (1947) and in *The Barham Papers*, III (Chs. XVII & XVIII above) which are also of course of value throughout. Both, together with P.R.O. 30/8/111 and Dacres Adams Mss formerly P.R.O. 30/58/6 for Barham, indicate Pitt's involvement. Stanhope Ms U1590 S5 C60/15 contains an account of the Minister's farewell of the Admiral in Downing Street, and see *Diaries of Malmesbury*, IV (Ch. II above) for his reception of the news of the battle and Nelson's death.

The balanced study of *British Strategy in the Napoleonic War* by Christopher D. Hall (Chs. XVII & XVIII above) deals briefly with plans in 1805 for the southern flank of Europe which receive definitive treatment in Piers Mackesy's *The War in the Mediterranean 1803–10* (1957). P.R.O., F.O. 70/22–7, W.O. 6/56 bear on the local scene; F.O. 65/57–9, with 42/7 for the Ionian Islands, together with Saul (Ch. V) and sources for Ch. XX above, on the all-important exchanges with Russia.

For the expedition to the Cape of Good Hope see the documents edited by W.G. Perrin in 'The Second Capture of the Cape of Good Hope 1806' (*The Naval Miscellany*, III, ed. W.G. Perrin, 1928), L.C.F. Turner, 'The Cape of Good Hope and the Anglo-French Conflict, 1797–1808' (*Historical Studies Australia and New Zealand*, 9, no. 36). Fortescue's *History of the British Army* (Ch. I above), V (1910) examines – as for other operations – the provision of the force and the outcome, and *Memoirs and Correspondence of Castlereagh* (Ch. VI above), VI (1851) apply to his period as Secretary of State for War and the Colonies. The capture of Buenos Aires by Home Popham is set in context by John Lynch, 'British Policy and South America, 1782–1808' (*The Journal of Latin American Studies*, I, no. 1); his past efforts of persuasion in that direction can be seen *inter alia* in N.L.S. Ms 67a (for Melville) – and see Hugh Popham's biography (Chs. XI & XII above) –, those of Miranda in P.R.O. 30/8/190, 395, and other, anon examples loc. cit., 395, N.L.S. Ms 1075, S.R.O., Melville Castle Mss GD 51 series. A letter to Pitt from Mulgrave in December 1804, in Stanhope Ms U1590 S5 03/7, gives an impression of the official interest.

The heightening pace of the search for an Allied Coalition embracing Prussia yields a complicated story, followed carefully by Fremont (Ch. XX above). Stanhope, IV and Holland Rose, II are also useful, as is the latter's edition of selected documents in *Third Coalition* (ibid). The relevant Foreign Office papers are F.O. 7/74–9 (Austria), 97/74 (Bavaria), 22/46–7 (Denmark), 64/68–71 (Prussia), 65/58–9, 62 (Russia), 73/34–5 (Sweden). A crucial complement lies in the private correspondence between Pitt and Harrowby in Harrowby Mss vols. XII–XIII, P.R.O. 30/8/142, Dacres Adams Mss formerly P.R.O. 30/58/6, P.R.O. 30/70/4, and between Harrowby and Mulgrave in Harrowby Mss vol. XI. For other private ms material (Leveson Gower, Paget, Jackson) see, as for published, Ch. XX above. The diaries of Rose, II and Malmesbury, IV, and *H.M.C., Bathurst* in particular, give further glimpses of Pitt's hopes and expectations; some notes by him in the Dacres Adams Mss formerly P.R.O. 30/58/8 relate to the expedition designed for Hanover, for which see also Fortescue, op. cit., V.

The Minister's hopes of a coalition in domestic politics, frustrated by the King in September 1805 but not entirely abandoned, can be followed in *Rose*, II, *H.M.C., Bathurst* with P.R.O. 30/8/112 and B.L. Loan Ms 57, vol. 2, the Dacres Adams Mss formerly P.R.O. 30/58/6, Harrowby Mss vol. XII, B.L. Loan Ms 72 vol. 55, the Bankes Mss at Kingston Lacy, Dorset in the possession of the National Trust.

CHAPTER XXII

Some of Pitt's thoughts at the end of 1805 on political appointments – to Ireland and to the Cabinet – appear in P.R.O. 30/8/112 (Bathurst), 119 (Camden), 120 (Canning) for whom see Marshall, *The Rise of Canning* (Ch. III above), the diaries of Rose, II, Malmesbury, IV (Chs. III, II above).

For the Minister's time at Bath see accounts in *The Bath Herald*. B.L. Loan Ms 57, vol. 2 and P.R.O. 30/8/174 (Richard Ryder) show friends at work to find him rooms. Reports and memories were gathered by Stanhope for his IV and also in his *Miscellanies. First Series* (2nd edn., 1863); see eg Stanhope Mss U1590 C404/14, 405/15. There is a particularly interesting contemporary series to Mulgrave from his brother Major-General Edmund Phipps in the Normanby Mss, bundle 31. P.R.O. 30/8/112 (Duke of Beaufort) and *H.M.C., Bathurst* contain some correspondence on Pitt's projected visit to Badminton. There are letters from Farquhar to his patient in P.R.O. 30/8/134, and his retrospective account of his visit was first published by Rosebery in *The Monthly Review*, I, no. 3 in December 1900 (Ch. III above).

The final period, at Bowling Green House in Putney (of which Stanhope made descriptive notes in 1872; Stanhope Ms U1590 S5 C60/23), of course produced much correspondence from those closely involved, let alone from those on the margins. Hester Stanhope was frequently in touch with Adams (Dacres Adams Mss formerly P.R.O. 30/58/9, and see also Stanhope Ms U1590 C419/9), and Adams sent news to his brother-in-law Courtney of his own visits (Dacres Adams Mss formerly P.R.O. 30/58/11, and see also Stanhope Ms U1590 C66/7). Tomline (Pretyman), reappearing on the scene, reported continually to his wife (Pretyman Mss 435/26–7, 44, 110), Rose (Ch. III above) II, noted the Bishop's information at the time, Ashbourne, *Pitt* (ibid) published an extract of his subsequent memorandum, and his full account for the unpublished part of his Life of

Pitt first appeared in *The Monthly Review*, XII, no. 3 in August 1903. Canning resumed his diary after a lapse of three months (Canning Ms 29d). For Wellesley's visit see Iris Butler, *The Eldest Brother* (Ch. XIII above). Stanhope published in IV James Stanhope's account, the ms of which is in Stanhope Ms U1590 C60/4, and amended for future editions his own first reading of Pitt's last words (letter to *The Times*, 24 April 1862). For other, less impressive versions see p. 829, n2 above.

CHAPTER XXIII

For the proceedings in Parliament on Pitt's death see *P.D.*, V–VI; also *H of P*, I (for Abbot), V (Windham). For his lying in state and funeral, *The London Gazette*, London newspapers, Pretyman Mss 435/15, 123, P.R.O. 30/8/364 (Chatham).

The lengthy process of clearing up the finances may be followed principally in the Pretyman Mss (435/26–7, 39, 45, 123, 503:3, 10, 562:1, 21, 22, 1820–3, 1826, 1828), P.R.O. 30/8/369 (Chatham), together with the Saumarez Smith Mss, Coutts's Bank ledgers, Stanhope Mss U1590 S5 C42 (for Coutts), 06/54 (Thomas Steele), Rose (Ch. III above) II. Adams's capture of Pitt's books from Walmer is recalled in Stanhope Ms U1590 C405/15; as are the circumstances of the distribution of Hoppner's portrait of Pitt in Stanhope, IV, 2nd edn. (1862–3), with results listed in Ashbourne, *Pitt* (Ch. III above), Appendix. *The Pitt Clubs, A short historical guide* (nd) by J.B. Lewis enumerates and traces authoritatively those constituent if almost entirely posthumous elements in a legacy whose longer-term context is discussed in J.J. Sack, *From Jacobite to Conservative, Reaction and orthodoxy in Britain, c. 1760–1832* (1993).

Index

For Volume III and Volume IV

Names and ranks of persons are given as far as possible in the style by which they were generally known in the period of this volume.

www.ingramcontent.com/pod-product-compliance
Ingram Content Group UK Ltd.
Pitfield, Milton Keynes, MK11 3LW, UK
UKHW021822270225
455667UK00006B/16